INDIGENOUS AFRICAN INSTITUTIONS

George B. N. Ayittey

 Transnational Publishers, Inc.
Ardsley-on-Hudson, New York

Library of Congress Cataloging-in-Publication Data

Ayittey, George B.N., 1945-
    Indigenous African institutions / George B.N. Ayittey
        p.   cm.
    Includes bibliographical references and index.
    ISBN 0-941320-65-0 : $55.00 (est.)
    1. Indigenous peoples--Africa. 2. Africa--Politics and
government. 3. Africa--History. 4. Customary law--Africa--History.
5. Chiefdoms--Africa--History. 6. Africa--Social life and customs.
I. Title.
GN645.A95 1991
960--dc20   91-19161
                                                                   CIP

**Dedicated to African Leaders and Elites —
For their re-education**

Forthcoming books by the same author:

Africa Betrayed
The African Economic Crisis: The Indigenous Solution
Developing Africa Using Africa's Own Indigenous Institutions
Makola, Makolamatics

(For other publications by the same author, see Appendix A at the end of the
bibliography in this book).

TABLE OF CONTENTS

CHAPTER 5: GOVERNMENT IN NATIVE AFRICAN EMPIRES

CHAPTER 6: THE NATIVE SYSTEM OF GOVERNMENT: A SUMMARY AND AN ASSESSMENT

ACKNOWLEDGMENT

My debt of gratitude, on a project such as this, is enormous. Several individuals, both Africans and non-Africans, foundations, and institutes have actively or indirectly supported my research into indigenous African institutions. This support has been indispensable, especially when my spirits were faltering.

As most researchers of African issues would testify, the obstacles that stand in the way of scholarly enquiries can be daunting. They range from absence of reliable data, difficulties in conducting field work in Africa and the attendant problems with transportation, communications, logistics to the uncooperative attitude of suspicious African government officials and even personal safety. In November, 1989, for example, Kenyan security agents raided my Intercontinental Hotel room in Nairobi and seized copies of my articles. Support at such times was invaluable.

Deserving of foremost mention is Earhart Foundation, Ann Arbor, Michigan, which provided me with funding grants for two summers (1987 and 1988) to help cover the cost of research and field trips to Africa. The Hoover Institution, Stanford University, where I spent a year (1988-1989) as a National Fellow, equally deserves my gratitude. Hoover provided me with such facilities — archives, office space, outstanding computer facilities and excellent secretarial support — that I was able to complete three book manuscripts: *Indigenous African Institutions*, *Africa Betrayed* and *The African Economic Crisis: The Indigenous Solution*. My special thanks go to Professors Thomas Henricksen, Larry Diamond, Lewis Gann, Thomas Sowell, Wendy Minkin, Silvia Sandoval, and many more.

From the Hoover Institution, I went to the Heritage Foundation in Washington, D.C, which also provided me with office space, research facilities, outstanding support staff and valuable critical reviews to make this work possible. Charles Heatherly, Teri Ruddy, Michael Johns, Ed Hudgins and many others at the Heritage Foundation were very helpful with comments. I am deeply grateful to the Heritage Foundation and its staff.

Other institutions are equally deserving of mention. Bloomsburg University was where my work originally picked up steam. Professors John Baird, Peter Bohling, Robert MacMurray, Robert Obutelewicz, Elis Majd, Mehdi Haririyan, W. B. Lee, Tamrat Mereba, Walter and Rose Brasch, Oliver and Ann Larmie and many others must be thanked for their support and encouragement. From University of Manitoba, must be mentioned Professors Henry Rempel, John Rogge, John Loxley, Richard Lobdell, and from Canada generally Randolph Gorvie, Percy Christian Quao, Sandy and Margaret Matheson.

I also drew particular inspiration from Professor James Buchanan, Nobel Laureate, when I was a Visiting Scholar at the Center of Study of Public Choice in 1988. John Palmer and the staff at the Institute of Humane Studies; David Boaz, Ted Carpenter and Ed Crane at the Cato Institute; Dr. Isaac Amuah and Larry Afesi of the Foundation for Democracy and Development in Africa; as well as Thomas Ahart of the Crispus Attucks Society have always been supportive.

During my tenure at The American University, I have been fortunate to receive critical reviews and encouragement from Professors Robert Lerman, Alan Isaac, Barbara Bergmann, Jim Weaver, Jon Wisman and excellent secretarial support from Jane Dolingo, Peggy Blank, Sheila Budnyj, Sharon Childs-Patrick and many others in the Economics Department.

There are many others that I still owe a debt of gratitude: Professor Walter Williams, John Fund, Grace Ortiz, Lynne Criner, Melanie Tammen, Dianne Hicks, Margaret Calhoun, Roberto Santiago, Gregory Simpsons, and others.

Last but not the least have been the numerous Africans who have shown unflinching support for my work and writings. Among them must be mentioned Rev. G.B.K. Owusu, Silva Upusunju, Kobina Annan, Stanley Ansong, Joseph Clegg, Lily Danso, Marjorie Winfred, Dr. Emmanuel Ablo, Dr. Kofi Apraku, Ablorh Odidjah, Kwaku Danso, Augustine Edusei, Dr. Derek Gondwe, Charles Mensah, Okezie Patrick Okezie, Dr. Victor Teye, Rev. Ndabiningi Sithole, Peter Abbam, Sekoe Sengare, Moses Tesi, Dominic Ntube, Manfred Tumban, John Okoh, Michael Atadika, Edward Nyarko, Walusako Mwalilino, Professor Edem Kodjo (former secretary general of the Organization of African Unity), Paati Ofosu-Armah, Maina Kaia, Nii Akuetteh, Dr. Kojo Yelpaala, Banda Ngenge, Emeka Chukunjindo, Charles Ayensu, and many, many others.

Although my debt of gratitude is enormous, the views expressed in this book are solely my own. Any errors, omissions and misstatements are entirely my responsibility.

George B.N. Ayittey, Ph.D.
The American University,
Washington, D.C.

March, 1991.

INTRODUCTION: THE RAPE OF AFRICA

Intelligent Retrogression is the only Progression that will save our beloved country (continent). This may sound a perfect paradox, but it is, nevertheless, the truth; and if all educated West Africans could be forced by moral suasion and personal conviction to realize that "Back to the Land" signifies a step forward, that "Back to the Simple Life" of our progenitors expresses a burning wish to advance, that the desire to rid ourselves of foreign accretions and excrescences is an indispensable condition of National Resurrection and National Prosperity, we should feel ourselves amply rewarded.

- S.R.B. Attoh Ahuma in 1911.

For any reform to be permanent and enduring, it must be based on and rooted in the principles of the aboriginal institutions.

- John Mensah Sarbah (1864-1910), a Ghanaian philosopher.

Africa's Deepening Crisis

The 1980s have been described as a "Lost Decade" for Africa. Once a region with rich natural resources as well as bountiful stores of optimism and hope, the African continent now teeters perilously on the brink of economic disintegration, political chaos, institutional and social decay. The continent's unrelentless slide into economic doldrums is now common knowledge.

Africa's share of world trade in 1990 was half what it was a decade ago and its share of world exports has fallen by one-third since then. The drop in trade was marked with its main trading partner, Western Europe, declining by 25 percent between 1980 and 1987. And despite receiving $100 billion in cash and various forms of aid, the continent's economy fell by more than a fifth.[1] Agricultural growth has been dismal, with output growing at less

---

[1] See, David Ewing Duncan's article, "The Long Good-Bye," *The Atlantic*, July 1990.

than 1.5 percent since 1970. Industrial output across Africa has also been declining with some regions experiencing *deindustrialization*.

To maintain income and investment, African governments borrowed heavily in the 1970s. Total African foreign debt has risen 19-fold since 1970 to a staggering $257 billion which is equal to its Gross National Product (GNP), making the region the most heavily indebted of all (Latin America's debt amounts to around 60 percent of GNP). Debt service obligations absorbed 47 percent of export revenue in 1988, but only half were actually paid with the arrears constantly being rescheduled.

With scarce foreign exchange increasingly being devoted to service debt obligations, less became available for imports of spare parts, drugs, textbooks and other essential supplies. Infrastructure began to crumble for lack of maintenance. Roads started to deteriorate and telephones refused to work. Even hospitals in many African countries had no running water. At the Akomfo Anokye Hospital in Ghana, patients were asked to bring their own bandages, blankets and food.

In sub-Saharan or black Africa, the crisis was particularly trenchant. Black Africa with a population of 450 million generated a Gross Domestic Product (GDP) of $135 billion in 1989 which was about the same as that of Belgium with a population of only 10 million.[2] Worse, black Africa's income per capita fell consistently from $621 in 1981 to $352 in 1987. The decline has been calamitous in Nigeria, which could not translate its oil bonanza into sustainable economic prosperity.

According to the World Bank,

> Sharply rising oil prices boosted exports from $4 billion in 1975 to $26 billion in 1980, while GNP per capita rose from $360 to more than $1,000. Rising public expenditures fueled by oil revenues shifted production from agriculture to services. When the price of oil collapsed, so did Nigeria's export receipts. By 1986, they were down to $6 billion, while external debt rose from $5 billion in 1980 to $25 billion in 1986. Real imports contracted at an average annual rate of 20 percent. Growth rates turned sharply negative, and GNP per capita fell to $370 (*Sub-Saharan Africa: From Crisis to Sustainable Growth*, Washington, DC: Nov. 1989; p.48).

In addition, black Africa was burdened with a mountain of foreign debt — $143.2 billion in 1989, up from $139.6 billion in 1988. It had nothing to show for this debt except a multitude of "black elephants", decaying infrastructure, economic destitution and social disintegration. With a debt exceeding its GDP, black Africa had the highest debt burden in the

---

[2] Africa's total external debt reached $256.9 billion in 1989, according to the Economic Commission for Africa - a UN agency.

developing world. Twenty-four of the world's 26 severely indebted low-income countries were in Africa.

On per capita basis, the debt statistics were horrifying in some African countries. For example, in 1988, Guinea Bissau's debt per head stood at $450 with a GNP per capita of only $160 and a debt-service ratio of 91 percent. Ivory Coast's debt per capita of $1,219 far exceeded its GNP per capita of $740, while the two were similar for Nigeria: $279 against $290. Both Nigeria and Ivory Coast, however, had debt-service ratios of over 70 percent.

Economic performance of this region, measured crudely by the rate of growth of income per capita, has been dismal. The overall picture is even more depressing when compared to the performance of other regions of the Third World. Social and economic indicators of development, such as output growth, health and literacy, have shown persistently weak performance in black Africa. For example, black Africa's rate of growth of GDP per capita for the two periods, 1965-1987 and 1980-1988, were 0.6 and -2.5. For Asia, these were 4.0 and 5.5, while those for Latin America and the Caribbean were 2.1 and -0.6. While all other regions of the Third World advanced, black Africa retrogressed.

The exceptions to the general economic atrophy in black Africa have been few. Botswana continues to serve as a shining black success story, followed by Mauritius and Cameroon, while Senegal struggles to keep its head above water. In the early 1980s, Ivory Coast and Kenya used to be members of this select club but by 1990 were suffering from serious economic crises.

The worst performers have been Ethiopia, Ghana, Liberia, Mozambique, Niger, Nigeria, Sao Tome and Principe, Sudan, Uganda, Zaire and Zambia, all of which are characterized by civilian/military dictatorships. These economic statistics paint a grim picture, even without taking into account ecological degradation, institutional decay, a growing refugee problem and appalling human suffering. About one in four children dies before the age of five in Burkina-Faso, Ethiopia and Mali. Malnourishment accounts for 40 percent of infant mortality in Zambia.

What Went Wrong?

Responsibility for Africa's economic crisis is shared.

— The World Bank.

A diagnosis of Africa's ills always generates heated and emotional debates. The fundamental reason is the deep-seated and pervasive belief that *all* black problems owe their origins to racism, slavery, colonialism, Western imperialism or a "white conspiracy." This has often been the position of those on the left, while right-wingers make no such attribution or apologies. Either position, however, is extreme. Thus, the real intellectual challenge is how to exorcise these extreme positions and replace them with a more mainstream, more balanced and more realistic view. This holds that, however abominable the iniquities of colonialism and slavery, they alone are not sufficient to explain *all* black or African problems.

Blacks or Africans as a people *will* always have problems whether the white race or the West existed or not. Certainly, pre-colonial Africans had their problems. But when these problems persisted, they blamed not whites or foreigners but their kings for failure to resolve them and removed those kings. Even they had some *institutionalized* process of resolving their problems.

But for years and even decades, almost everything that went wrong in Africa was always the fault of Western colonialism, American imperialism, a hostile international economic environment, some natural calamity such as drought. Even a water shortage was on occasion attributed to "an imperialist plot" and price rise to a "neo-colonialist conspiracy." By 1980, even illiterate peasants were fed up with the "colonialist and imperialist" claptrap. In fact, in 1981, some Ghanaian peasants called upon Britain to recolonize the country. In Nigeria, a former governor in the Second Republic Sam Mbakwe, publicly "advocated for the return of the colonists who, he stressed, would lead the country back to political sanity" (*West Africa*, March 18-24, 1991; p.409). Not that colonialism was preferable, but that call represented an unequivocal indictment of African heads of state and kleptocrats who had failed their people.

In recent years, more and more Africans have been echoing these sentiments. For example, Osa Kingsley wrote:

> It has become trendy for enlightened writers on Africa to put all the blame for Africa's backwardness on the West. I think the West should not be blamed anymore for Africa's predicament. . .

> I may ask, what is our goal as Africans? It sounds funny that a country like Nigeria cannot boast of any significant supply of good drinking water even after 30 years of independence.

> One is tempted to think that the goal for Africans is to drive a flashy car, and own a house in Britain, US or France. This is very common among our leaders, some of whom think it is a mistake not to have a Swiss bank account or a castle in France.

> It is not a shame to admit our failures, set our priorities right and

forget about blaming the West always for our woes. In fact it is a
lazy society which puts all the blame for its troubles on its neighbors.

Let our leaders set clear-cut goals for our countries, and not Swiss
bank accounts. I don't think George Bush would set himself a goal
of owning a bank account in Ghana or Nigeria (*New African*, August,
1990; p.45).

Nigerian head of state, General Ibrahim Babangida almost said as much at
the July 9-11, 1990 Organization of African Unity (OAU) Summit in Addis
Ababa at which Nelson Mandela and Sam Nujoma were special guests of
honor. General Babangida remarked that African leaders have failed their
people – a dramatic admission coming from a black African head of state.
"In a widely reported speech President Babangida of Nigeria told the
summit it was time Africa stopped behaving as if its survival depended on
the charity of the developed countries" (*West Africa*, July 23-29, 1990;
p.2147).[3]
Back in May 1986, African leaders collectively made a similar admission
before the United Nation's Special Session on Africa: that past government
policies were misguided and had contributed in no small measure to Africa's
economic crisis. This admission was all the more stunning, coming from
leaders with a mordant predisposition to lay the causes of Africa's economic
woes at Western doorsteps. Finally came the refreshing concession from
these leaders that they themselves played a role in Africa's precipitous
economic decline. But African leaders were not alone. They were "aided,"
intellectually and financially, in the destruction of Africa and the pursuance
of misguided policies by various international aid agencies, financial
institutions and all sorts of people, even including African Americans. The
World Bank (1989) admitted:

Responsibility for Africa's economic crisis is shared. Donor agencies
and foreign advisers have been heavily involved in past development efforts along with African governments themselves. Governments and donors must be prepared to change their thinking
fundamentally in order to revive Africa's fortunes. However,
Africa's future can only be decided by Africans. External agencies
can play at most a supportive role (p.2).

[3] At the same summit, the newly elected Chairman of the OAU, President Yoweri
Museveni of Uganda declared: "We should not practise dictatorship under the guise of
independence, because independence does not mean dictatorship. . .Leaders must be elected
periodically; they must be accountable. There must be a free press and there must be no
restriction on who participates in the democratic process" (*West Africa*, July 23-29, 1990;
p.2147). Ironically, President Museveni did not see it fit to submit himself to a "periodic
election."

However, a mere admission of culpability is not enough. A careful examination of the contributory factors in *both* the West and Africa is required to prevent a repetition of this economic disaster in the future. Of particular significance are the practices, attitudes and the general understanding of African problems by the donor agencies and foreign advisers. Among these agencies and advisers, there is appalling ignorance about basic facets of African society. This impairment is further compounded by an ideological and a general intellectual reluctance to be candid about the fundamental causes of the African crisis.

The West was so fearful of communist expansionism that it was willing to support any African despot who professed himself to be "pro-capitalist" and "anti-communist," regardless of his appalling human rights record *and* neo-communist (state-interventionist) practices. In the words of Margaret Thatcher, former Prime Minister of Britain: "In the battle of ideas, we had all but ceased to aim at furthering freedom and had settled for containing communism" (*The Washington Times*, March 11, 1991; p.D1). This provided shrewd African dictators with a rich opportunity to dupe the West or play off one super-power against another for maximum advantage. As we shall see shortly, ideology was irrelevant in Africa as *both* "pro-West" and "pro-East" regimes failed their people.

Further, a peculiar intellectual environment prevails in the West which has aided and abetted Africa's ruination by its deafening silence over the atrocious policies pursued by African leaders. First, collective guilt over the turpitudes of colonialism and slavery have prevented Westerners from scrutinizing African political regimes and condemning tyranny and economic mismanagement on the continent. The typical Western resignation was: "Who are we to criticize them when our own past record of dealing with Africa has been opprobrious?" Consequently, most Westerners shied away from criticisms of African leaders, preferring to send loads of money perhaps to soothe their collective conscience. But the money seldom reached the needy, ending up instead in Swiss banks.

The second has been the prevailing racialist mentality — a hybrid of what is now called "political correctness" — which maintains that blacks, oppressed and enslaved in the past, can do no wrong. Thus, a white person criticizing a black person or leader (say, Rev. Jesse Jackson or Nelson Mandela) is accused of being "insensitive" and denounced as a "racist." A black person offering the same criticism is condemned as an "Uncle Tom" or a traitor.

The result is a maddening silence that compounds black problems and exacerbates the plight of blacks. When Idi Amin, for example, was butchering Ugandans at the rate of 150 a day, the West said and did nothing, shamefully nothing. But had that many African giraffes been slaughtered, Western outrage would have been ear-shattering.

Some African Americans, as well Africans, are troubled by public exposure of the misdeeds of African leaders, arguing that "washing our dirty linen in public" only perpetuates the myth and the offensive notion that "nothing good comes out of black Africa." "Negative" stories and statistics on black Africa only serve to feed the colonialist and racist mentality; for example, providing the racists in South Africa with ammunition to sustain apartheid. "Politically correct" (PC) statements require emphasizing the "positive" to uplift black dignity and pride.

While these concerns are understandable, the harsh reality is that an attempt to conceal the truth only impedes the search for their solutions. Problems are not solved by sweeping them under the rug. Poverty can be found in all societies and grinding poverty in Africa is no proof of the alleged innate inferiority of blacks. The causes of Africa's economic woes lie not in genes but in the pursuance of misguided *policies* by African leaders with substantial help from Western governments and aid agencies.

Africans are angry at their leaders and are demanding change. But Westerners, burdened with self-doubt and excess colonial baggage, seem helpless in offering effective assistance. While Africans are being butchered by their heads of state and national treasuries being looted, Americans fumble for "politically correct" forms of speech on Africa. Talk about being "sensitive" to grieving Africans. "Political correctness" which eschews criticisms of African dictators aggravates the plight of the victims of oppression in Africa. PC ideology operates from a rather naive and absurd premise that *all* blacks are the same and that they see no difference between *themselves* and their leaders. Therefore, a criticism of one means an attack on the whole race. This is unbridled nonsense. Criticizing black leaders does not necessarily mean one is a racist or a traitor.

Black Africans themselves criticize their leaders all the time. Censorship prevents their criticisms from being heard in the media. In Africa, the news is managed by state-owned and state-controlled media. In the West, criticisms are blocked or diluted by self-imposed censorship to assure "political correctness" or to avoid being "negative" about Africa. This censorship, real or voluntary, gives the illusion that blacks speak with one voice and are always united behind their leaders. This is an arrant myth. There is as much diversity of opinion among blacks as among whites.

By nature, Africans may be considered republican, fiercely independent — a nature that explains why there are still over 2,000 tribes in Africa today. Black Africans generally "united" in the face of adversity or threats to their survival. Many of their social and political structures were geared toward survival in a hostile physical environment. The individual by himself was not powerful enough to battle extrinsic forces and found an association with "a group" more expedient. Consequently, when there was no external threat, the passion for independence tended to predominate. For example in the struggle to drive out the "colonial infidels," all black Africans were united. But as soon as independence was achieved and the "external threat" removed, each group drifted along its separate ways.

Historically and *culturally*, blacks have never been united. Cultural diversity, not uniformity, was the hallmark of traditional Africa. This lack of unity is evident even among ethnically homogeneous Somali today:

> Everyone in Somalia is a Somali. But the lack of tribal conflict is more than made up for by rivalries between clans, of which there are 26 major ones and countless minor families. They all hate each other, and this is the root of Mr. Barre's interminable presidency. None of the factions, including rebels in the south, is prepared to ally with any other clan to throw the former British policeman out. And by baronial patronage, he has kept his own clan happy and himself on the throne (*The Washington Times*, Nov. 26, 1990; p.A7).

The constant harp on "unity" by current African heads of state is indicative of what was culturally absent. For if it existed, there would hardly be any need to preach unity. There have always been ideological, philosophical and religious differences among blacks, just as in any other group or race. But black Africans achieved unity of purpose through *a process of consensus-building*; not by the chief demanding blind and obtuse allegiance to his decrees by banning criticisms — a fact which needs telling to modern black leaders.

Third, black Americans often create especial problems for Africans with their unquestioning solidarity with African leaders. It is important to note that black Americans and black Africans have different agendas. While black Americans seek the eradication of racism and the achievement of true equality, black Africans today seek *freedom*, something they are supposed to have attained after gaining their independence from colonial rule in the sixties. In appropriating African issues to suit or promote their agenda, black Americans unwittingly place obstacles in the path of black Africans and hamper the latter's struggle for true freedom.

In the 1950s and 1960s, black Americans helped Africans in their struggle against Western colonialism. They have also been instrumental in the campaign against apartheid in South Africa. For all this, Africans have been grateful. But tyranny and *de facto* apartheid regimes also exist in the rest of Africa. In the struggle against these, black Americans have offered little or no help. Black Americans only see oppression when it wears a white face and have been all too willing to defend and embrace African dictators as "brothers." But who are the "brothers": the tyrants or the victims of tyranny? And who stands for the true people of Africa?

This miscalculation on the part of African Americans is understandable. For one thing, most are misinformed and miseducated about *contemporary* Africa. Most would have extreme difficulty identifying Uganda on the map of Africa. African Americans can vote and were proud when Rev. Jesse Jackson, a commoner, ran for the Democratic presidential nomination in a white country in 1988. But few African Americans know that their black "brothers and sisters" cannot vote in their own black African countries. Nor could Rev. Jackson run for president in many African countries.

For another, the black American historical experience is different from the black African and there is a problem of "relating." Throughout their history, black Americans have seen their oppressors as white while black Africans have seen *both* white and black oppressors. Black oppression is something which African Americans have never experienced and probably would never be able to relate to or understand.

It is painful to admit that most of Africa's heads of state today are tyrants, kleptocrats, "Swiss bank" socialists, and brutal military dictators who, while loudly denouncing the lack of political freedom for blacks in South Africa and calling for one-man one-vote, deny their own African people the very same rights and freedom. In fact, most of those ruling Africa today are not *true* Africans, despite their skin pigmentation. The "modern and educated" leadership is a far cry from the supposedly "backward and primitive" leadership under African chiefs and kings. Wherever possible, the contrast between the indigenous and the modern leadership will be highlighted in this book.

The exposure of the misdeeds of African tyrants is excruciatingly embarassing and it is understandable why African Americans would want to cover them up. But black Americans complain *publicly* about problems buffeting them. Why would they want to prevent Africans from holding their disgraceful leaders to public account? Doing so only helps to sentence millions of their "brothers and sisters" in Africa to the slaughterhouse.

To be fair, black Americans have occasionally taken African dictators to task. But too often in the past, they criticized only those African leaders who professed themselves to be "pro-West" (for example, Mobutu of Zaire and Moi of Kenya) while shielding, at least seemingly, the socialist and Marxist tyrants in Angola, Ethiopia, Ghana, and many other African countries. Oppression *is* oppression irrespective of the skin color and ideology of the oppressor.

The fact of the matter is that ideology is not particularly relevant to the resolution of Africa's problems. Most of Africa's modern leaders, despite their ideological predilections, have been a failure, by Africa's own *indigenous standards*. Therefore, the East-West dichotomy or resurgent Cold War rhetoric is truculently irrelevant to Africa's needs. Moreover, Africa had its own *indigenous* ideology before the Europeans arrived in Africa.

But Africa is a tragedy in more ways than one. So many people, organizations, foreign aid agencies, and even African leaders and in some cases charlatans, sought — some with magnanimity, others with "we-know-best" arrogance — to help the African people lift themselves out of poverty.

Enormous resources were expended on various development projects. But with beguiling staccato, most of them came to a crashing grief. How could so many "experts" be so wrong?

The fundamental cause of the monumental development failure was probably ignorance. Few really understood the very people they set out to help. Few, if any, of the "experts" understood what motivates African peasants, how they conduct their economic activities, how they secure farmland to raise their crops or even how they obtain funds to purchase a dug-out canoe. Ecology, culture, politics, law and development are inextricably intertwined. Development must be custom-tailored to fit the recipient's topography: culture, politics and institutions. In practice, however, it was often the other way round. Various "canned" and "ready-made" development strategies were prescribed for Africa and its people were expected to "change" to fit them or make them work.

Obviously, the process should start with a study and understanding of the African people and their ways of life. Since most development experts and even African leaders tragically lacked this knowledge, it was often a case of the blind leading the blind. To add more confusion, the benefactors hardly agreed among themselves. While the World Bank and the United Nations Economic Commission on Africa (ECA) were quarrelling, the European Economic Community (EEC), the Lome Convention, and the Organization of African Unity (OAU) were waging their own guerrilla warfare on the type of remedies needed to cure Africa's ills.

Unsurprisingly, many of these efforts, noble as some might have been, floundered, resulting in scandalous waste of resources and a grievous deterioration of living conditions. Most African countries in 1990 were worse off in terms of income per capita than they were at independence in the sixties.

One cannot blame the aid agencies for not understanding the African people. But then few bothered to ask them directly what type of aid was best suited for them. To help American farmers, one asks them the type of aid they require, not what some technocrat in Washington decrees. But unbelievably, this was not the case with the African people. Perhaps, they were too "backward" to know what was good for them. As Wayne Ellwood complained:

> Time and time again local communities are ignored. Misconceived, harmful development projects are dropped in their laps without consultation and the people of the industrialized countries, who bankroll most of the Bank's activities, are asked to pay the bill.

> 'The Bank needs its own *glasnost* so that informed public debate can take place,' says Probe International's Pat Adams. 'Decision-making,' she adds, 'should be returned to the people who have to live with the

physical consequences of the decision; they're the people with the best judgment about what risks to take with their environment' (*New Internationalist*, Dec. 1990; p.6).

Myths and Misconceptions about Africa

The main obstacle that has bedevilled foreign efforts to help Africans has been the difficulty of penetrating the layers of mythology, ignorance and prejudice enshrouding Africa and its people. For many centuries, Africa remained a mystery. It attracted the curiosity of explorers while fascinating and captivating empire-builders by its vast wealth. The length and breadth of Africa were explored, discovered, conquered and colonized. Its people were denigrated as "backward and inferior":

Harris (1987) wrote:

> The image of Africans as inferior was reinforced further by arguments of several Christian missionaries, ministers, and others who explained that an African was better off a slave in a Christian society than free in "African savagery". . .Hugh Murray, a popular geographer of the early 19th century, described the continent as an area of mystery with wild and strange aspects of man and nature. Africa was a strange place, inhabited by strange men, where monsters dwelt and strange things happened.

> African or black inferiority as a concept reached its high point when it became intellectualized by philosophers of the Enlightenment. In a footnote to his essay entitled 'Of National Character,' which appeared in his *Essay and Treatises* (1768), the influential Scot philosopher, David Hume wrote:

> I am apt to suspect the negroes. . .to be naturally inferior to the white. There never was a civilized nation of any other complexion than white, nor even any individual eminent either in action or speculation. No ingenious manufacturers amongst them, no arts, no sciences..

> Given that position, it was natural for Europeans to conclude that Africans had no history and no written language, two other great myths. But a society which justified its expansion overseas, and into Africa in particular, in terms of the 'civilizing mission to uplift the heathens and savages of Africa,' could not regard the history or language of the latter group as being worthy of serious study (p.21).

The ignorance and mythology continue to dominate impressions of the continent even to this present day, albeit for different reasons. One is the widespread but erroneous belief that Africans had no culture. Their traditional cultural structures were destroyed by colonialism (Coquery-Vidrovitch, 1976; Gutkind and Waterman, 1977). It was argued, for example, that the structure of rural life was no longer respected, and this loss of respect accelerated the destruction by instigating a movement away from "exploitation of (foreign) neighbors to the exploitation of individuals within their own communities" (Gutkind and Wallerstein, 1976).

While it is true that the colonialists reordered African society to suit their purposes with brutal force, it is inaccurate to assert that Africa lost its cultural identity totally. Most of the indigenous cultures and institutions underwent some transformations and adaptations to survive the onslaught of colonialism. This view is also shared by Bell (1987), who argued: "the traditional structures were profoundly altered by external influence, but they were hardly overthrown" (p.64).

The view that the traditional structures underwent processes of transformation and adapted themselves to the "invading" cultures in order to survive was also advanced by Wrigley (1960):

> The idea of Negro Africa as savagery modified by the influence of European or quasi-European intruders is clearly no more than an extrapolation from the situation that has existed in recent times; and sufficient knowledge has been accumulated to make it no longer legitimate to theorize *in vacuo* about 'waves' of invasion. Although tropical Africa has certainly received major cultural imports from time to time, the archaeological record suggests, on the whole, continuous indigenous development rather than a succession of external impacts.

Another reason for the pervasive mythology was the fact that much of what was known about Africa was compiled by foreign researchers and writers. Africa saw itself through "foreign eyes." There was little written scripture about African heritage by native Africans — largely due to the cultural practice of handing down historical information from one generation to the next through the oral tradition. Most people therefore accepted what foreign writers told them about Africa.

While some of these writers did credible and painstaking service to Africa, the works of others were profusely tainted with various ethnocentric and scholastic biases. In the heyday of colonialism, for example, there was a notable proclivity on the part of European writers to deprecate African civilizations and portray Africans as "savages." Yelpaala (1983) observed that: "It might be said that the anthropologist created the savage, the barbarian, and the primitive and his state of statelessness, lawlessness, and self-help to provide a rational basis for colonialist subjugation and exploitation of the savage. All these categories of (anthropological) studies had various problems; derived from Eurocentric, ethnocentric, and possibly racist perspectives, they could hardly reflect the people studied" (p.350).

African chiefs and kings were routinely depicted as "despots." Naturally, Africans "yearned" to be freed from their own "autocratic" rulers. What could be more godsend to the Africans themselves than the arrival and imposition of colonial rule — to "cilivize" and "liberate" them from tyrannical rule by their own "terrible" leaders. Colonial archives and documents are full of references to such "horrible" rulers.

Clearly, such "terrible" African rulers must have been generally those who gave the colonialists the most "trouble"; that is, offered the stiffest resistance to European domination and conquest. Of course, to their people, such chiefs were not "terrible" or "despotic" at all but rather heroes who fought to resist the colonial subjugation.

Besides ethnocentricism and self-serving colonial propaganda, there were unavoidable, or more appropriately, honest biases in the description and documentation of African culture. These arose primarily out of errors in translations and difficulties in interpretations of African languages. Williams (1987:169) put it best:

> Africans generally prefer to dwell on the constitutional theories and not on the constitutional practices. They proudly speak of the freedom and absolute powers of the chief or king. Some will even tell you that the king 'owned all the land' in the country. They are not trying to deceive. Words of another language often fail to translate the people's concepts or meaning. When they say the king is supreme or has absolute power they mean that he has absolute power to carry out the will of the people. It was so well understood that supreme power rested in the people that it was never thought necessary to state such a fact. Likewise, they would say, and say proudly, the king 'owns all the land in the country' since everybody but a fool knew that he didn't, that nobody owned the land (in the Western sense), and that the king's role was that of custodian and overseer, his principal duty being to see that the land was fairly distributed among all families.

Nevertheless, some anthropological studies were objective and some Westerners are now taking a second look at the so-called "primitive cultures." We are also now being told by Western scholars that the so-called primitive cultures of the cave men may after all have attributes worth aping today. Consider the following story which appeared in *The Wall Street Journal* (Oct. 21, 1986; p.35) which is paraphrased below.

"Dr. S. Boyd Eaton is one of a group of scientists studying the diet and lifestyle of early humans to determine what is 'natural' for the human body.

Our bodies haven't evolved much since prehistoric times, they reason, so the diet and activity patterns of that era may still suit us best.

'Natural' isn't what we did when great-grandmother was around,' says Dr. Eaton, a physician and professor at Emory University School of Medicine. Irven DeVore, a Harvard University anthropologist, adds:'We were vaulted into the 20th century with the heart, mind and body of a hunter-gatherer.'

"Duplicating primitive diet and exertion, these scientists suggest, may yield more energy, better health and greater chance of beating modern 'diseases of civilization,' such as osteoporosis, obesity, cancer, hypertension, hiatal hernias and heart disease. They cite skeletal evidence that humans living 30,000 years ago were taller and more muscular than modern Americans and had better teeth — all indications, the scientists say, of a healthier diet. . .

"Not that prehistoric life was a bed of roses. Melvin Konner, a physician and head of the anthropology department at Emory, says child mortality was 50 percent and few people lived to be 60. But most early humans died from falling off cliffs, infectious disease or battles, not poor health, Prof DeVore says. Anthropologists' studies of the remaining hunter-gatherers in Africa, whose diets are similar to our ancestors', show little heart disease, lung cancer or hypertension, he says. . .

"Humans in paleolithic times, before the development of agriculture, had no dairy foods, for instance – yet osteoporosis was unknown, Dr. Kratz notes. Apparently, milk wasn't nature's way of preventing bone disease, he says. And pre-agricultural people didn't eat wheat, either, he says. . .

"Cave men ate more meat than modern humans. The meat was lean, but it had plenty of cholesterol. That leads Dr. Eaton to suggest that fat, not cholesterol, poses the dietary danger."

Until recently, the field of African culture had been neglected and much of what was written by Westerners was biased and incomplete. While Westerners should be excoriated for their biases and distortions, one should not overlook the perpetration of the *same* myths and distortions by black scholars and African leaders. For example, European writers denigrated the African chief as a "despot." But how many modern African leaders redeemed this image? Instead, they used "African tradition" to justify the imposition of all sorts of despotic regimes on their people.

The Problem with Afrocentricism

If the denigration of Africa by Westerners and their white injustices were reprehensible, so too are those by African leaders and elites. There have been biases among black writers as well. Foremost is the general tendency among black authors to glorify, romanticize and exaggerate "great" African achievements and civilizations. It is absurd to condemn these excesses in Western writers and commit the same transgressions. Now, some black writers even claim that African culture is "superior" to Western culture. In fact, Molemi Asante, regarded as the founder of Afrocentrism, demands that "all Western curricula should be replaced with African teachings" (*The Washington Post,* March 10, 1991). Other black scholars assert that Africa contributed more to Western civilization than vice versa. For example, "the West has contributed far less to the industrialization of Africa than Africa has contributed to the industrial civilization of the West" (Mazrui, 1986; p.164). Further, Western civilization is doomed to "grind to a standstill in Africa" (Mazrui, 1986; p.19).

The debate over "superiority" of African culture is rather sterile and of little utility when the continent is inexorably enmeshed in the throes of a deep economic crisis. But these are some of the tenets of what has now been labelled "Afrocentricism." As reported by *The Washington Times* (Nov. 13, 1990):

> An army of angry black scholars is determined to reclaim what it says is a glorious African past that was stolen or trashed by racist historians. . .
>
> The black scholars leading the charge for African-centered education, and the teachers and educators who are the foot soldiers, see it as salvation for hundreds of thousands of black children who are doing poorly in the nation's public schools. They reason that giving black children a past anchored in the spectacular achicvements of Egypt will boost their self-esteem and their desire to learn. . .
>
> African-centered curriculums are based on the belief that Africa was the cradle of civilization and Egypt was a black African society.

Molefi Asante, a Temple University professor who is regarded as the father of Afrocentricism, demands that "All things African must replace all things European" (*Washington Post,* March 10, 1991; B2). The irony is that black African culture was *never* all-exclusive. On the contrary, black culture was always *open*. In fact back in the 17th century, the Asante king (*asantehene*) retained the services of Dutch advisors. It is a shame that black intellectuals must now preach the gospel of the "closed mind." How does that differ from the closed or narrow mind of the white racist?

We blacks have every reason to be proud of our cultural heritage. But many of those black scholars and leaders championing this crusade are disgracefully ignorant of their own black culture and distort African heritage. It is true African achievements and contributions to Western civilizations have been belittled in "racist" literature. However, there is a movement among even Westerners themselves to take a second look, as noted in the cave men story recounted above. Further, some displays of African cultural achievements in the arts can be found in the Smithsonian (Washington, D.C.) and other Western museums.

It is also true that black children perform poorly in America's public schools. Few would question the need and the objective to raise their performance. But there are several ways of attaining any objective and "Afrocentricism" may not be the most efficient and appropriate. And criticizing the *means* of achieving an *objective* does not mean one is opposed to that objective. Many black leaders and scholars fail to grasp the significance of this crucial distinction. Perhaps further amplification is necessary.

If the objective is get to Chicago (or black economic emancipation), several means exist: walking, "marching," running, riding a bike, driving, taking the train or a bus, flying or even taking the space shuttle. Each modality has its own inherent advantages and demerits in terms of speed, cost, safety, convenience and comfortability. Criticizing one modality as "inefficient" or "inexpedient" does not mean one is against the objective of getting to Chicago. But for the criticism to be *constructive*, a more efficient and expedient alternative *must* be offered.

Even then, what constitutes an efficient modality does not remain invariant under *all* circumstances and conditions. For example, if driving is deemed the most cost-effective, an imminent blizzard may rule out this possibility. But sadly, many black leaders, rigidly wedded to obsolete strategies, show themselves incapable of adapting modalities to suit changing circumstances. For 24 years, Julius Nyerere of Tanzania stuck doggedly to a 1950s "socialist path," even though world conditions had dramatically changed and things in Tanzania were going glaringly wrong. Meanwhile in the U.S., some black leaders cannot divorce themselves from the 1960s civil rights strategy of activism and confrontation, believing that marching to Washington, D.C., for example, would solve *every* black problem.

Too often, many black leaders fail to distinguish between a criticism of the *means* to achieving an objective and the *objective* itself. In Africa, constructive criticism of a government plan to eradicate poverty is misinterpreted as subversion, while in America a criticism of a particular means to achieve black economic emancipation is often misinterpreted as treachery. But the critics too deserve censure. Often, they offer no alternatives, preferring to attack the character of the person proposing an idea rather than the idea itself, which explains the persistent tendency of debates among African elites and African Americans to degenerate into name-calling and shouting matches.

Let us now return to "Afrocentricism" as *means* to achieve better educational performance among black children. As a means, Afrocentricism is fraught with several flaws and pointing these out does not mean one is a "racist" or a "traitor." First, exaggerated claims about Africa falsify history and introduce further distortions that compound the problem. Even most Africans would affirm that ancient Egypt was *not* a black African civilization. Egyptian society was Arabic but mixed. Further, Islam was *never* part of indigenous African cultural tradition. Even Mazrui (1986) agreed: "In the seventh century AD, Islam was brought to Egypt by Arab conquerors" (p.46). Technically, then, there was no difference between the Arabs and the Europeans. *Both* were invaders, conquerors and colonizers except that the Arab invasion preceded that of the European.

Second, the accent on Egypt or Arab North Africa is rather Arab-centered. "Where Islam is already established (in Africa), the decay of Western civilization is good for Islam since it helps neutralize a major threat" (Mazrui, 1986; p.19). Many black Africans are likely to be rankled by this statement for its gross insensitivity to those suffering under Arab racism.

Arab-black African relations have deteriorated rapidly in recent history, largely due to the expansionist ambitions of Colonel Khaddafi of Libya. His destabilization campaigns against Burkina Faso, Chad, The Gambia, Niger, Mali, Sudan, Ghana, Somalia, Togoland, and Zaire in the late 1970s and 1980s were thinly disguised. Frustrated in his megalomaniac designs, he referred to his African neighbors as "monkeys and slaves who understand nothing but the whips of France" (*Insight*, Dec. 10, 1990; p.31).

Despite the existence of a slave market in the Fezzan, Colonel Khaddafi insisted slavery was never part of Libyan society. In fact, the official Libyan line coincided with that of the Arab world:

> The Arab countries are a natural extension to the African continent. The African Arabs, or those who carried the indulgent message of Islam, were the first to effectively oppose slavery as inhumane and unnatural. The claim that Arabs were involved in the trade at all is a mischievous invention of the West, made in order to divide the Arabs from their brothers and sisters who live in the African continent (*New African*, Nov. 1984).

This absurd official line confutes historical evidence and reality. The brutal forms of slave trade that was conducted by Arabs on the East African coast in the 19th century cannot be erased from history books. And far from acting as "brothers and sisters," Arabs in Africa still lord over their black counterparts. Arab *apartheid* reigns supreme in Mauritania and Sudan. In Mauritania, blacks have no political power and cannot vote. Like their counterparts in South Africa, they are persecuted and discriminated against by Arab masters. The enslavement of blacks by Arabs was only abolished by Mauritania in 1980. But according to Africa Watch, a New York-based human rights group: "The (1980) abolition was essentially a public-relations exercise prompted by external considerations. It was never intended as a well thought-out policy aimed at eradicating the age-old practice of slavery." In fact, the group charged that:

> Policies maintaining slavery continue to be widely enforced. In fact, ten years after being legally abolished for the third time, slavery is still thriving in Mauritania. Today, there are between 100,000 total slaves and 300,000 part slaves and former black slaves in the service of Arab masters, who constitute only 25-30 percent out of a total population of 2 million. Slaves work without pay, cannot marry freely or associate with other blacks, do not have access to education, and are often subjected to exceptional cruelty and brutal torture (*Africa Report*, Sept.-Oct., 1990; p.7).

Arabs dominate the government and the economy. In 1986 when black Mauritanians agitated against the predominant positions held by the Moors of Arab-Berber stock, brutal reprisals and mass purges were inflicted upon them. More than 500 non-commissioned officers of Negro stock were expelled from the armed forces, according to *Forces de Liberation Africaine de Mauritania (FLAM)*, a movement of black intellectuals based in Dakar, Senegal. Three black army officers were executed in December 1986 on trumped-up charges of plotting a coup. In October 1987, 54 black officers were arrested and three executed following an abortive coup attempt by members of the Peul community. Shortly after, a group of 36 black political prisoners were hastily tried and sentenced to long-term imprisonment for distributing a document entitled *Le Manisfeste du Negro-Mauritanien Opprime* (The Manifesto of the Oppressed Black Mauritanians). This document criticized the ruling Arab-Berber government for systematic discrimination and injustices against the country's black population.

Of that 1987 group of black political prisoners in Mauritania, Tene Youssouf Gueye (60) died in detention in September 1988. Subsequently, Lt. Abdoul Ghoudouss Ba; Ibrahim Sarr, a radio and TV journalist; Amadou Moctar Sow, an engineer; and Ly Mamadou Bocar, a former government official, all died in prison. Their deaths brought this angry reaction from Kwaku O. Sarpong:

> Abuse of black people by Arabs, especially Syrians and Lebanese, has been ignored for too long. The painful fact is that this abuse occurs under our noses in African towns and cities where they have come to enjoy our hospitality. It is high time Arabs were made officially aware of this and reminded of the black solidarity they have enjoyed for years in their conflict with Israel.
>
> In the late 1970s, it was an open secret in New York that Arab diplomats never invited their black counterparts to their receptions. The ex-President of Senegal, Leopold Senghor, was hesitant in

giving recognition to the Polisario Front of SADR because whenever the Front took Moroccan prisoners the blacks amongst them were segregated and shot because the little food they had was not meant to feed black people.

Recently at a pre-football match ceremony in Kumasi, Ghana, the Egyptian players after shaking the hands of Justice Annan, went to wash their hands. Talk to any black soldier who has served with UNIFIL in South Lebanon and ask how they were treated by the two sides in the conflict (Arabs and Israelis); they always have praise for Israelis while wondering why the Arabs hate black people (*West Africa* (March 7, 1988).

In Sudan, the forcible imposition of Islamic law (the *sharia*) by the Arab north on the blacks in the south sparked an 8-year civil war that has devastated the economy, exacted an enormous human toll and produced starvation. Incredulously, Arabs still enslave blacks in this day and age. As *The Economist* (Jan. 6, 1990) charged:

Arab tribal militias formed and armed by the northern-dominated government are trafficking in slaves from the southern Dinka tribe. Dinka children and women seized in raids are either kept by the militias or sold north. In February, 1988 a Dinka child could be bought for $90; so many slaves are available that the price has now fallen to $15 (p.42).

Lt.-Gen. Omar Bashir, Sudan's head of state, himself was reputed to have "a number of Dinka and Nuer slaves in his own home, from the time he was military commander in Muglad, south-west Sudan" (*New African*, July, 1990; p.9).

Africa has always welcomed foreigners: Arabs, Europeans, Afrikaners, Asians and others. But it will withdraw its hospitality and welcome mat if foreigners insist on enslaving its people and imposing the *sharia*, apartheid, Marxism and other alien "isms" on its people. Black Americans are of course free to adopt and glorify Islam or Christianity if they so wish. But they should of course realize that neither is *indigenous* to Africa.

The third difficulty with Afrocentrism lies with the false "sense of pride" it seeks to instil in black children. This pride is unlikely to improve educational test scores. By way of constructive criticism, performance may be better enhanced by inculcating achievement motivation, discipline, strong family and morality values. The role played by the family in a child's education is vital, as demonstrated repeatedly by Asian high-achievers in American schools. In some universities in California, the admission of Asian students into graduate programs has been severely curtailed under some rather strange "quota" system:

Five years ago (in 1986), Asian-American activists began to complain about straight-A students being denied admission to the University of California (Berkeley), a favorite spot for students from the large Chinese community in the San Fransisco Bay Area. Federal investigators since have looked at admissions procedures there and at the University of California at Los Angeles (*Washington Post*, March 5, 1991; p.A3).

Asian Americans increased from 5.3 percent of California's population in 1980 to 9.6 percent in 1990. But at UCLA, the percentage of ethnic Asians in the freshman class increased from 28.8 percent in 1989 to 39.6 percent in 1990. By contrast, black freshmen dropped from 8.5 percent to 6.5 percent over the same one-year period. As the *Washington Post* (March 5, 1991) reported:

At a recent speech to the Chinese Consolidated Benevolent Association in San Fransisco, Sen. John Seymour of California praised Asian Americans for their commitment to family values and education and said that, when he spoke at high school graduations as a state senator in Orange County, 'hardly ever was the valedictorian not an Asian American' (p.A3).

A study Harold W. Stevenson, a University of Michigan professor of psychology, found that:

American mothers are very attentive to their children's learning before kindergarten, taking them on outings, buying them books, playing games with them, reading to them. Asian mothers pay more attention to their children's physical wellbeing, making sure they get enough sleep and proper nutrition.

But once American children start first grade, American mothers tend to believe that it's now the school's job to educate their children. They don't follow through. Asian parents, on the other hand, start taking their children's academic lives seriously at grade one. They see that as the time for them and their children to get down to work on the long process of education (*Washington Times*, March 5, 1991; p.A6).

That Asian-American parents provide strong family support and show avid interest in their children's education is now well documented. But this is not new to Africans. In fact, in the African cultural tradition, the family played a pivotal role in a child's education.

Because of the absence of written literature, education of Africans was by the oral tradition, which literally meant passing down knowledge and information by mouth from generation to generation; that is, from father, mother and relatives to children through stories, proverbs and rituals. The role of the parents or the family and their interest in the "proper" education of the African child cannot be overemphasized. That was the essence of the oral tradition. Black Africans did not rely on "schools" or someone else to teach their children. Nor was it necessary for someone to instil a "great sense of pride" in them before they learned.

Further, there was a strong sense of morality in indigenous African society. For example, rape was abhorred and punishable. In fact, among the Asante of Ghana, having sex with a woman in the bush was a *capital* offense! True, it was an extreme form of punishment but it indicated how seriously the offense was viewed. Laziness was also frowned upon in traditional Africa. These are what may be termed "proper" cultural values that must be instilled in black youth if their educational achievement is to improve. But how many black American fathers read to their children or tell them stories *in the oral tradition*?

In Atlanta, parental shirking of responsibility became so serious that the city imposed a youth curfew to keep those under 17 off the streets from late at night to 6.00 a.m. with emphasis on "known drug locations" and "places of ill repute." City Council member, Davetta Johnson, a black American, said: "What we have asked is for parents to ultimately have responsibility for their children" (cited in *The Wall Street Journal*, Nov. 20, 1990; p.A20).

Parental responsibility is also not new to black Africans. In fact, black Africans took this one step further. In descending order, the family, the lineage (extended family) and the clan were *answerable* in a native court of law to the actions of its individual members. In cases of theft, the family was liable to make restitution.

This indigenous African practice provided an important form of *social control* and helped deter crime. Black Africans know that criminal activities and other reprehensible behavior bring shame not only to themselves but also to their families and clans.[4] How about making black American families liable for the criminal activities of their children in the *true* African tradition?

Of course, firebrands would always argue that it is not only black youth who "cause trouble." To think otherwise is "racist." White kids too steal, mug, go to jail and perform poorly in school. These are all true. But who gets hurt the most? It is this "whites-too-do-it" mentality which paralyzes

---

[4] Perhaps a personal experience may be illustrative. In 1973 while teaching at the University of Ghana, Legon, a servant helped himself to some of my personal effects and absconded to his village in northern Ghana. The Ghana Police, as usual in cases such as this, was hopeless (unless bribed) in bringing him to justice. But help came from his own brother, who sacrificed four days of work and led me on a 2-day journey over 500 miles to his village in northern Ghana to ferret out his brother. I met the parents who expressed deep regret over the case and offered to make restitution which I politely declined. They all did this because of the dishonor the servant had caused the family to suffer. To most Africans, this story is not unusual.

the search for solutions to black problems and causes its abandonment. As observed earlier, blacks, as a people, will have problems whether the white race or the West exists or not. It is absurd to believe that blacks have no cultural values or systems by which to evaluate their own actions. Morality, diligence, industriousness, accountability and altruism, for example, are not Western cultural inventions but exist in indigenous African systems as well.

The obsession with racism among black leaders too often blinds them to their own biases, ignorance and inadequacies. Some are no better than the racists they so loudly condemn. Many of the black leaders who preach "diversity" and "pluralism" are themselves shamefully intolerant of diversity of opinion and cannot understand that even within a nuclear family there are disagreements. This despicable behavior is worst in academia, especially in departments dealing with African American, Afro-American, African or Black Studies programs. Only those who have a particular viewpoint or think in a certain way are allowed in these departments. Those who have alternative viewpoints or philosophy are discriminated at and even hounded off campus. Intellectual discrimination, racial discrimination; what the heck is the difference? Both have the same effects on the victim — rejection and withdrawal of recognition. This black-against-black discrimination ought to be exposed by the media and condemned. During the immoral days of slavery, it was whites who told blacks what to think. Today, it is black academic plantation masters who dictate how a black person should think.

Intellectual discrimination was *never* part of indigenous African tradition. Members of the African chief's council of elders were not all of the same viewpoint. The council allowed all shades of opinion to be aired for a *consensus* to be reached. It is a disgrace that alternative viewpoints are not allowed in most black studies programs on campuses.

In Africa too, the elites were not any better than the colonialists they loudly denounced. Consider this: "While Eurafricans and Western-educated African 'auxilliary' elites sought political and social equality for themselves, they often regarded the indigenous African masses as backward and not ready for full political and civil rights until they acquired a modicum of Western education and values" (Gellar, 1986; p.128). So what is the difference between the attitudes of the European colonialists and African elites toward the peasants?

It has now become clear that the *real* enemies of black people today are invariably the *self-appointed* black leaders and spokespersons who quite often perform the *wrong* analysis of black problems, prescribe the *wrong* solutions and are generally intolerant of constructive criticism. Worse, some of these black leaders are incapable of analyzing the root causes of black problems outside a racism/colonialism model. They insist upon injecting racism/colonialism in all analysis, even where this may not be appropriate, to insure their own self-importance.

Many blacks are angry and resent vehemently the misguided placement of *every* black problem in a racism/colonialism context. For one thing, it creates a debilitating sense of helplessness and resignation, which amount to a surrender of power. It tells blacks that progress is impossible unless racism is totally annihilated *by somebody else.* Complete eradication of all vestiges of racism is a worthy social goal but practically unattainable. To believe otherwise is an exercise in self-delusion. There was racism in the 15th century and there will be racism in the 27th century. Must we blacks wait for the 31st century before we take steps to improve our lot? This is no defense of racism but realism is the operative command.

For another, the obsession with racism portrays blacks as of monolithic "one-issue" mentality. The insulting implication is that blacks are incapable of comprehending or analyzing any of the myriad of problems afflicting the world today, *unless* they specifically deal with race. Many angry blacks want to liberate themselves from this intellectual slavery or break out of these intellectual chains they have been shackled with by their leaders. There is more to life than race and a mind obsessed with one issue has no room to develop along other lines. And this is how a mind is truly wasted.

Other black leaders, immensely steeped in black pride, are hopelessly at a loss whether to prescribe "black" or "white" solutions to essentially black problems. The indictment of Williams (1987:315), himself a black American, is even more scathing:

> The black people of the world have come at last to destiny's crossroads. They must make some fundamental decisions as a single people. . .But there is a terrible crisis of leadership at the cross-roads. There is no united leadership group or any real effort to create one. The great difficulty is that black leaders, unlike the Jews, do not know their own heritage. They are almost wholly ignorant of their own cultural source from which independent, original thinking springs and progress is inspired. The 'Negro' leaders who spearhead and carry on the campaigns for integration, not only do not know the great heritage of the Blacks, they do not want to know it. They wish to draw on the Caucasian heritage and matter; they keep on trying, because the white 'liberals' do encourage them to hope by mixing with them from time to time. Other leaders, equally ignorant of their heritage, simply do not know which way to lead. They, too, feel compelled to adopt and follow Caucasian ideologies because they do not feel free, equal and competent enough to develop an ideology of their own, an African oriented ideology.

Shamefully ignorant of their own cultural heritage, many African leaders used "African tradition" to justify the imposition of all sorts of despicable systems on their people: Marxism, one-party states, and military rule. It is true the African chief ruled for life. But he was appointed; he did not appoint himself. There was a fundamental difference. Nor did the African chief declare his village to be one-party, impose alien ideologies on his people and suppress dissent. At village meetings, people could express their views *freely* without fear of arrest or detention. Furthermore, in traditional Africa, no jackass waving a bazooka just got up and declared himself president. *Rule of law* (or custom) was the imperative in most indigenous African societies. And no traditional African king or chief could by himself issue a decree and impose it on his people. These chiefs and kings were surrounded by councils, without whose consent a law could not be passed. In addition, laws had to be ratified by a village assembly composed of commoners.

It is also true that some African political structures and kingdoms were extirpated through colonial conquest. However, after independence, the onslaught against the indigenous cultures and institutions was relentlessly intensified by black neo-colonialists, who by force of arms, forcibly installed alien regimes on their people to the detriment of their indigenous cultural heritage. After independence in the sixties, many African leaders hauled down the statutes of European monarchs, erected and saluted those of Marx, Engels and Lenin — not even those of Dr. Martin Luther King, Jr. or Tunkamenin, but another set of white aliens — and ludicrously called themselves "free and independent under black rule."

To be ruled by European colonialists was invidious enough. But to be told by black African leaders that, within Africa's own culture and history, there were no black revolutionaries and philosophers for its people to salute and that they must therefore submit themselves to the indignities of worshiping another set of aliens was the ultimate insult to black people. Even a moron can see clearly that Marx, Engels and Lenin were not black Africans. Amazingly, this cultural incongruity escaped the notice of many intellectuals. How does Afrocentrism square with Marxism?

Even after the collapse of Marxist dictatorships in Eastern Europe where they copied their political systems, some African leaders and intellectuals continued to insist that democracy was alien to Africa in the teeth of centuries of true African tradition of *participatory democracy* and consensual government. Nor were these leaders willing to give their African people the economic freedom they enjoyed in their indigenous system by removing the plethora of government controls and regulations that were strangulating their economies.

Free village markets and free trade were always part of indigenous African economic heritage. African chiefs seldom fixed prices on village markets. The natives *bargained* over prices which fluctuated freely in accordance with market forces of demand and supply. When fish was scarce, its price rose. African natives did not blame foreigners for an "imperialist conspiracy."

Nor did the natives queue in front of the chief's hut for permission to trade. Trade was open to all willing to engage in it.

But African leaders are not alone in this cultural sabotage. Some African Americans also propagate and defend all sorts of vulgarity, profanity and uncouth behavior as "black culture." Indigenous African society may be "primitive and backward" but it upheld some tenets of decency, respect and good manners. Rituals and taboos were examples of mechanisms by which such behaviorial attributes were sustained.

Black leaders and scholars ought to know their own heritage. It is difficult to communicate the deep sense of outrage, frustration and palpable sense of betrayal seething in most Africans. They have every reason to be angry at the rape of Africa. First came the Arabs and the Europeans to enslave its people and take away its gold and other minerals without leaving much behind. Then came the black neo-colonialists after independence to rape and plunder its wealth for deposit in Swiss banks. Now come Afrocentrists to snatch and bask in its glory and heritage without doing much to help its suffering people. Africans are angry.

The Common Sense Approach to Africa's Ills

What has been missing in all these efforts to help or liberate the African people has been ordinary plain *common sense*. To break out of this paradox, reverse Africa's economic decline, save the continent, its environment, develop the region and above all provide the African people with some food security and some measure of freedom, certain common sense maxims must be recognized and accepted as matters of fact.

First, the solutions to African problems must be African. Foreigners can only help, but they cannot supplant efforts that must be made by the African people themselves. Obviously, those Westerners who entertain "we-know-best" proclivities or believe in "throwing money at a problem to soothe their conscience" do more harm than good. Similarly with African leaders who expect every solution to an African problem to drop like manna from heaven or the West. Back in 1959, Alioune Diop, the publisher of the newspaper, *Presence Africaine*, was quite succinct: "Experience has shown that we have always solved our problems without difficulty, when we have approached them from an authentically African point of view" (cited in Italiaander 1961; p.287). Further back still in 1901, John Mensah Sarbah, a Ghanaian philosopher, observed rather tersely that, "For any reform to be permanent and enduring, it must be based on and rooted in the principles of the aboriginal institutions" (cited in Langley, 1979:98).

Unfortunately, this has not often been the case. By 1989, the total number of expatriate consultants and experts employed by the World Bank alone to work to solve Africa's economic problems had reached a staggering 80,000, costing cash-strapped African governments between $1 to $4 billion annually in fees and compensation. This was probably a case of "too many cooks spoil the broth." Less than one-half of one percent of these management consultants were native Africans. Describing this as "the great consultancy rip-off," *South* magazine (Feb. 1990) wrote:

> There is increasing concern that the advice is often over-priced, poorly researched and irrelevant. Although some management consultants give value for money, many simply recycle standard off-the-shelf reports, regardless of whether they are appropriate, say critics. Frequently, management firms send rookie staffers with little experience of Africa (or knowledge of African ways of life) to advise on sensitive political issues there, critics charge. Or they provide theoretical studies, full of high school economics, but with no practical application (p.43).

Second, the solutions to the African crisis lie in Africa itself; in its own backyard, so to speak. They do not lie in the corridors of the World Bank or the IMF; nor in the inner sanctum of the Soviet presidium. These solutions entail returning to Africa's own *roots* and building or improving upon them. The Ga of Ghana have this proverb: "The needle you are looking for in the haystack may be right there at your feet." The main obstacle is African elite mentality. Preoccupied with Swiss bank accounts, Mercedes Benzes and copying alien systems, the elites of Africa are incapable of looking inside Africa for *internal* solutions.

Senseless and endless civil wars rage on in many African countries, as useless idiots armed with a few bazookas blow up their countries in behalf of foreign ideologies. "If you think my brand of Marxism is bad, wait till you see theirs," declared a confident Comrade Mengistu of Ethiopia. The civil war in Ethiopia raged for more than 15 years.

More generally, these civil wars in Africa have exacted a devastating human toll and diverted enormous resources from development. Chaos, carnage and political strife now grip many African countries. Peasants, the majority of the population and the producers of Africa's real wealth and foodstuffs, now see their lives recklessly disrupted by crocodile liberators who leave wanton destruction in their wake. More than 10 million Africans have fled their villages to escape the generalized state of terror and violence, and countless others are trapped in their own countries. The United Nations estimates that Africa has more than half of the world refugee total. Never in the history of Africa, even during those abominable colonial years have its people been subjected to such traumatic dislocation.[5]

---

[5] These issues are further explored and discussed more forcefully in my forthcoming book, *Africa Betrayed* (1991).

These peasants have no voice. Through various legislative devices, African elites have monopolized political power and the media, refusing to share political power or tolerate alternative viewpoints. A "culture of silence" prevails over many African countries. As if the political subjugation was not enough, the same elite class instituted a multitude of administrative controls to assure the economic exploitation of the peasant majority. How are they different from the colonialists?

Over the decades, the peasants were milked through exorbitant taxes and levies to provide funds for development. But the elites developed only the urban areas for themselves, their Mercedes Benzes and their own Swiss bank accounts as well. Peasants have no such accounts. Quite aptly, East African peasants named them the *wabenzi* — "men of Mercedes Benz."

Each year an estimated $15 billion leaves Africa in capital flight. In 1990, What Nigerian *bazongas* (raiders of the public treasury) had stashed abroad was more than enough to pay off their entire foreign debt of $32 billion. A Nigerian army general, Brigadier Ishola Williams, claimed that "a recent report of Morgan Trust Guarantee Bank of New York had estimated Nigerians' private holdings in foreign banks at $33 billion, with accounts in almost every country of the world" (*National Concord*, August 16, 1990).

Much of this capital flight is booty, illegally acquired wealth siphoned out of Africa by elites who have no faith in their own economies to invest it there. Yet, they are often the same ones who berate "colonial exploitation" and also the same ones who feverishly beseech foreigners for investment in Africa. In addition, African leaders annually spend about $12 billion on the importation of arms and the maintenance of the military. These two "leakages," alone add up to $27 billion, which is far more than the $11 billion Africa receives in aid from all sources.

A bucket full of holes can hold only so much water. Pouring in more water makes little sense, as it will all drain away. To the extent that there are "leakages" in Africa (capital flight, senseless and endless civil wars, corruption, wasteful military expenditures), no amount of aid will rescue Africa. As a matter of topmost priority, the leakages must be plugged so that the little water (aid) that comes in stays. Instead of doing so, African elites furiously argue over the role of colonial and imperial forces in causing Africa's woes.

Third, there have been *both* external and internal causes of the African crisis. Unforbidding pragmatism dictates an unerring scrutiny of *both* causes. The average intelligent person looks *both* ways *before* crossing a street or risks being hit by a truck. Africa is in bandages because most of its leaders looked only one way — at the external. They never saw the hideous tyranny, appalling corruption, flagrant violations of human rights, inane civil wars and the rampant looting in their own countries. They only saw the abominations of apartheid, the iniquities of colonialism and imperialism.

Fourth, to control or influence the course of a natural phenomenon requires prior intensive study of its behavioral patterns. For example, to save beluga whales from extinction and improve their welfare, it would require a careful study of their habitat, feeding as well as their migratory behavior. This maxim may seem too elementary to even state here. The Igbo clan, Efik, recognized this in a proverb: *"Enyene Idem ofiok oto nte Mfat edebede enye"* meaning, only an organism knows best its own needs and can best serve them.

Yet, this maxim was hardly applied in efforts, noble as they might have been, to help the people of Africa. Proposals and programs were drawn up to help or save them with perfunctory understanding of their culture or "way of life". It should come as no surprise that so many international aid-funded agricultural projects withered in Africa. Consider the following examples:

- In Egypt, 5,000 U.S.-made stoves were useless because they were designed for pipeline use rather than tanked gas used in Egypt. . .Twenty-six irrigation pumping stations established as part of a $19 million U.S. AID project were not working, in part due to lack of electrical power at the sites; at the same time AID sponsored a separate $32 million renewable-energy project involving water pumping without linking it to the irrigation project. . .A $108 million AID-financed grain-silo complex completed in 1987 was unable to operate for several years due to insufficient power (Melanie Tammen in *The Wall Street Journal*, Jan. 23, 1989; p.A19).

- In Senegal, the United States built 50 crop-storage depots but placed them in locations the peasants never visited. The depots, which cost about $2 million, now stand empty. . .In Uganda, a railroad expert discovered to his amazement that a repair shop built with foreign funds was 7 times as large as the one he ran in Germany. . .A fifth of Ivory Coast's foreign borrowing went to build two sugar mills that started production just 4 years ago and now are closed. . .In Sudan, the Soviets built a milk bottling plant at Babanusa. Babanusa's Baggara tribesmen drink their milk straight from the cow and there aren't any facilities to ship milk out of Babanusa. The 20-year old plant hasn't produced a single bottle of milk (*The Wall Street Journal*, July 29, 1985; p.18).

- In Sudan, a plant for making tomato paste was placed in an area where the farmers cultivate date palms, not tomatoes. A milk dehydration plant was built in an area where there are no dairy cows. . .In northern Kenya, Norwegian aid officials built a fish-freezing plant near a lake for the Turkana tribesmen. But the Turkana are pastoral people who survive by raising cattle, goats and camels. Worse, after the plant was built, it was discovered that freezing fish in the daily 100-degrees temperatures would take more electricity than was available in the entire Turkana district (Whitaker, 1988; p.74).

It is now generally accepted that foreign aid programs have been a disastrous failure. In February 1989, U.S. AID administrator Alan Woods even admitted this in a report that "no country receiving U.S. aid in the past 20 years has 'graduated' from less-developed to developed status" (*Development and the National Interest*: A Report by the Administrator, Agency for International Development, Feb. 17, 1989). The report further noted that U.S. aid, all too often, promotes dependence on yet more aid.

One reason for the dismal failure was that the administration of many aid programs was cocooned in a maze of bureaucratic red tape. In an editorial, *The Wall Street Journal* (March 2, 1989) lamented:

> Over the past four decades, the U.S. has provided the developing world with some $400 billion in aid. Yet through this period the American people have heard from various pulpits only that poverty somehow persists in these lands, and they are obliged to send more money. Before sending in their checks, they logically might ask: What happened to the previous $400 billion?..

> A bi-partisan task force of the House Foreign Affairs Committee said current aid programs are so encrusted with red tape that they no longer either advance U.S. interests abroad or promote economic development. The task force skewered Congress and past administrations for piling 33 differing and often conflicting foreign-assistance objectives on top of each other. It noted that current programs are caught in a maze of 75 different statutory priorities and 288 separate congressionally mandated reports. Changes in any of 700 programs must be reported to Congress (p.A16).

But African leaders were equally culpable, if not more so. In many cases, they themselves , in a fit of megalomania, drew up the grandiose projects that emphasized prestige rather than economy. Donor countries simply could not "unload" useless projects in Africa *without* the consent, acquiescence or connivance of African leaders — a perspective (the complicity of African leaders) which is often neglected in scholarly discussions; perhaps for the sake of "political correctness." It stretches the bounds of incredulity to portray "educated" African leaders as hapless victims of crooked foreign merchants who sell them useless products. Why would anyone living on the 20th floor of an apartment complex buy a lawn-mower and claim fraud?

Many African leaders and officials did exactly that because of the "commissions" they were reaping on foreign loans and aid projects. According to Lamb (1983), "Of every dollar coming into Zaire, whether in the form of a foreign aid grant or a business contract, Zairian officials took twenty cents off the top for their personal cut" (p.45). In March 1990, *Le Monde*, a Paris newspaper reported that "Every franc we give impoverished Africa comes back to France, or is smuggled into Switzerland and even Japan."

The fifth maxim is a corollary of the second; that is, one can improve the efficiency and performance of an automobile, if and only if, one understands how it operates. In Africa, many leaders and elites lacked an understanding of how the indigenous system operated. Consequently, they could not improve its performance and productivity. When the peasants' agricultural machinery needed ordinary firewood to continue running, some of Africa's leaders and elites were pouring in rocket-jet fuel. After all, the fuel was "modern and scientific." Naturally, the peasants' machinery sputtered and groaned to a halt, producing an agricultural crisis that claimed over 3 million lives in 1985.

Sixth, everyone, including even the illiterate peasant, knows that what grows well in one part of the world may wither in another part because soil conditions, topography, drainage systems, temperatures and rainfall may be different. Just because California grows apples does not mean they must grow everywhere else. Of course, it is technologically possible to grow apples anywhere, even on the moon, using the latest advances in technology. But the costs would be astronomical, no pun intended.

Economic efficiency, or common sense, dictates planting what is suited to one's own *environment*. In the field of agriculture, this environment consists of the type of soil, the amount of rainfall, and the type of pests and diseases a plant will face, and so on. These must be known *before* the seeds are planted since if the *environment* is not suitable, the seeds will fail to germinate.

The same idea is conveyed by the statement that before a building is erected, it must be determined if there is secure enough foundation, well rooted in the surrounding ground culture. A building without such rooting will collapse in no time.

An application of this reasoning to the field of development requires ensuring that a development project, scheme, seed or idea is well rooted in the host environment if the project is to succeed. This maxim was scarcely applied to African development. A horrendous array of models was "imported" only to prove unsuitable for Africa's socio-economic topography. It is now widely acknowledged the old "hand-me-down," big project approach has been a miserable fiasco and that a "bottoms-up" approach is now deemed to be far superior. But what is there at the bottom save the peasants and their institutions?

Development deals with people. In Africa, the people are the *peasants* — the majority in *every* African nation. Yet, they have no political power, representation or say in the decision of matters affecting them in most African countries. Since these peasants constitute the majority, the *environ-*

ment in the field of development is their socio-economic and political set-up; that is, the whole gamut of their social, economic, cultural and political institutions, at the grass-roots level. Like a seed, if a development project does not fit into this socio-economic milieu or set-up, it will fail. Few development "experts" understood this milieu or the peasants' way of life. But faulting the experts alone is only half the story.

Elite Development Approach

After independence from colonial rule, African nationalists and elites set themselves the task of developing the continent. But the development that took place can succinctly be characterized as development by imitation. Huge sums were borrowed abroad to import shiny pieces of modern, sophisticated and scientific equipment and prestigious projects, planting all these in Africa. Big dams and grandiose agricultural schemes were built to impress. Foreign systems were copied and imposed upon Africa.

California grows apples; so too must Africa. American farmers use tractors; so too must we in Africa. If copying is all that African elites are capable of, then they might as well bring back the foreigners to rule Africa. Quite frankly, the phrenetic propensity to imitate rather betrays feelings of insecurity and inferiority. They induce some African leaders to acquire symbols of modernity (skyscrapers, grandiose projects) and some blacks to straighten their hair, bleach their skin, drive pink Cadillacs in the misguided and vain hope that they might "gain acceptance" from whites or Westerners.

Unfortunately, these imitations are often counter-productive. In fact, in some instances, a conscious effort to prove that you are *not* inferior proves precisely the opposite. Why drive a pink Cadillac when you have no place to sleep? Or why import Mercedes Benzes when you have no roads to drive them on? And how can you expect others to accept you when you have rejected yourself? The fact of the matter is, nobody, *absolutely nobody* can call you inferior *without* your own consent and acquiescence.

This point is important because the obsession of many African leaders and intellectuals with gaining Western or white acceptance meant that they had rejected themselves and their heritage. Indeed, there were many who, despite their pronouncements, believed African culture was too primitive and backward and must therefore copy Western or foreign systems in order to develop Africa.

The tragedy here was that the rejection by African elites and leaders of their own native institutions was not only perfidious but unwarranted. Botswana's economic success amply demonstrates that Africa does not have to renounce its culture in order to develop. Back in 1911, S.R.B. Attoh Ahuma, a Ghanaian, issued pertinent advice that was little heeded:

Intelligent Retrogression is the only Progression that will save our beloved country (continent). This may sound a perfect paradox, but it is, nevertheless, the truth; and if all educated West Africans could be forced by moral suasion and personal conviction to realize that "Back to the Land" signifies a step forward, that "Back to the Simple Life" of our progenitors expresses a burning wish to advance, that the desire to rid ourselves of foreign accretions and excrescences is an indispensable condition of National Resurrection and National Prosperity, we should feel ourselves amply rewarded (Cited in Langley, 1979:162).

Aim and Purpose of Book

This book about indigenous African institutions is intended not only for scholarly consumption but also to provide useful information to various groups concerned with African issues. The first are foreign aid officials who sincerely wish to help Africa overcome its difficulties. Sincerity and magnanimity, however, are not enough. To help African peasants, one clearly needs to understand them and their way of life.

The second are black Americans. It is hoped that this book will provide them with the missing cultural link to the "Motherland." One of the cultural traits of black Africans is their strong family tradition and ties. This tradition was crucial in holding blacks together to enable them to survive the ravages of slavery and racial injustices in America. Sadly today, however, this family tradition has rapidly vanished, leaving the black American family in disintegration. There is no excuse for this.

The third group this book is intended for are African leaders, elites, and development practitioners. Africa can only be developed by building upon its existing institutions. Merely copying foreign systems to impose them on Africa is, to say the least, absurd. In fact, it is a debauchery of the concept of development. The true challenge for development practitioners is how to coax large surpluses from the peasants, *using their existing institutions*, regardless of how "primitive and backward." But one cannot do so without an operational knowledge of these institutions. Though tattered and embattled, these structures still govern and condition the peasants' response to changes in their social, economic and political environment. Moreover, these institutions constitute an integral part of their culture.

There are about 2,000 tribes in Africa, with not less than 200 in Zaire alone. This makes political structures and other indigenous institutions necessarily diverse and any thought of their study daunting. But what is amazing are the remarkable similarities between them. The basic African beliefs, political, legal and economic institutions are strikingly and structurally the same across much of Africa. Their specific forms and names, of course, vary from place to place.[6] Maps have been provided at the end of the book to facilitate the location of the major language and ethnic groups discussed in the text.

Chapter 1 examines the social structure and organization of African societies. Included in this chapter is a discussion of African beliefs and philosophical tenets. Chapter 2 is an examination of the indigenous legal institutions. Native courts of law were in existence in Africa before the Europeans arrived. This chapter looks at procedures for court cases and how conflicts pertaining to property rights were resolved by the native courts.

There have been four main categories of political organizations in Africa. Chapter 3 discusses government in the stateless societies and chiefdoms. Of particular note are the discussions of the the African traditions of *participatory democracy*, government by *consensus*, the role of headmen and chiefs and how they were selected and removed. They serve as reference points for the evaluation of modern African leaders and the lugubrious one-party state systems they imposed on Africa. The glaring contrast between the indigenous and the modern leadership will become apparent in the course of this chapter.

Chapter 4 provides a discussion of African kingdoms. Several examples of African kingdoms are presented, and the role of the African king in the political arena as well as his selection and deposition are discussed.

In Chapter 5 is a discussion of government in African empires. This chapter is of especial interest for two reasons. First, it demonstrates that imperialism was not invented by the West, so to speak. There were empires in which different tribes came under the rule of dominant tribes. But of particular importance is how these empires were governed, since an African nation today is similarly composed of several tribes. As will be seen in this chapter, confederation and federation were the most common forms of government in the native African empires. This fact would seem to suggest that the unitary form of government, characterized by a strong, centralized authority is not suitable for Africa. Chapter 6 is an assessment of the native system of government, noting its weaknesses and strengths.

In Chapter 7 can be found an account of the indigenous economic system: ownership of the means of production and how production was organized. Chapter 8 provides a discussion of the distributive system and the role of the government in the tribal economy. Is the indigenous African economic system characterized by pervasive state interventionism? Is the system "capitalist" or fundamentally "socialist'? These issues are addressed in Chapter 8.

Chapter 9 assesses how African indigenous institutions fared under

---

[6]An additional problem is introduced by spelling, which has not always been consistent in the scholarly literature. For example, Asante is variously spelt as "Ashanti" and "Ashantee." Similarly, *"alaafin"* and *"alatin"* or *"ooni"* and *"oni."* Such inconsistencies should be overlooked.

colonialism. Contrary to popular misconceptions, the indigenous systems, through various processes of adaptation, survived the onslaught of colonialism. A few were annihilated, but most survived, attested to by the fact that there are still traditional chiefs in Africa and peasant farmers go about their economic activities according to centuries-old customs and traditions.

If these institutions survived colonialism, to what extent did African elites and nationalists build upon them after independence? Chapter 10 examines this question. As is common knowledge, what African elites, with all their "education" have to show for 30 years of self-rule are telling: destruction, economic ruination and looting of Africa. So who ruined Africa: the colonialists or benighted vampire elites and black neo-colonialists?

The final chapter, 11, attempts to draw some conclusions and implications for developing an African economy. Botswana's success story is analyzed and an actual example of how to return to the indigenous roots is sketched, using Benin as a test case.

Before proceeding, a few precautionary statements would be in order. It would be useful to keep in mind that the indigenous institutions have been undergoing a slow but perceptible transformation — a process which began centuries ago. Consequently, much of the textual material has been gleaned from history books and, where possible, has been supplemented with recent material. As a result, grammatical switches from the past to the present frequently occur in this book. For example, "The Zande King was chosen" and "Each village has a market." Admittedly, these switches can be vexingly confusing. But the complete usage of the past tense would suggest extinct or archaic institutions, which would be incorrect. There are still chiefs in Africa today: "Among Ghana's 32,000 chiefs, there are 200 paramount chiefs, 2,000 divisional chiefs and about 30,000 'Odikros' (village chiefs) and headmen" (*West Africa*, February 8, 1988; p.232). At the same time, however, it would also be inaccurate to suggest, with the use of the present tense, that all the indigenous political institutions still exist. Of course, certain political practices and structures have ceased to exist.

In addition, studies of various aspects of African institutions are scattered in the literature. This book attempts to collect and synthesize these various strands systematically. There is no attempt to "rewrite" African history. Rather, the approach taken in this is institutional. That is, it describes how the natives of Africa governed themselves, how they produced wealth and how they established law and order. There is little or no account of the arts: religion, dancing, music and African art. Nor is there any attempt to give a chronology of events as in pure history books.

Because of pervasive ignorance in this area, great efforts have been made to cite authors, both African and non-African, who have made noteworthy statements about the native institutions. Such statements have been liberally used in this book to preserve their original content and texture. For example, various writers have commented that, the Igbo political system is "the most democratic and egalitarian in the world" and that "southern Africa is the home of the world's finest legal system." Needless to say, this approach unduly lengthens the book. But it is better to erase doubts than to create them. We now proceed with these caveats in mind.

CHAPTER 1

THE INDIGENOUS SOCIAL SYSTEMS

African culture, art and science, whatever the diversity of their expression, are in no way essentially different from each other. They are but the specific expression of a single universality.

- The Pan-African Cultural Manifesto adopted by the Organization of African Unity (OAU) at Algiers in July, 1969.

A. THE PEASANTS' SOCIAL STRUCTURE AND ORGANIZATION: A COMPARATIVE OVERVIEW

In the West, the individual is the focal point of social organization, attitudinal behavior and motivational achievement. In Africa, many studies have shown that kinship is the articulating principle of social organization as a whole, and the basis of social integration (Hill 1977; Schapera, 1953).[1] According to Bell (1987:52),

Kinship relations were the main relation of production. They were also the juro-political and ritual relations. In addition, they governed the way in which societies organized and used the resources of the environment, notably the land, and the spatial interaction between members.

In traditional Africa, the lowest social unit within the lineage system is the nuclear family.[2] This normally consists of a man, his wife (or wives) and

---

[1] In some quotes and historical accounts, kinship is referred to in the past tense as though it no longer existed. This however is not to be taken to imply that it has disappeared completely. Kinship and tribal ties are still strong in rural Africa.

[2] Traditional and indigenous Africa are used interchangeably in this volume, to distinguish this sector, where the peasants live, from the modern sector or modern Africa where the elites

1

children. In the past, such a family would include the man's domestic slaves or *Ohu, Osu* and *ume* as they were called by the Igbo of Nigeria (Olaniyan, 1985: 24). A number of nuclear families tracing their descent from a single ancestral line (unilineal descent) would make up a family group which consisted of men, their wives, children, son's wives and their children. A collection of family groups would then become the lineage, kinship or the extended family.

Vaughan (1986) determined that:

> Approximately 88 percent of African societies reckon descent unilineally with a marked preference (74 percent) for patrilineal descent, as among the Nuer. Matrilineal descent occurs in only about 14 percent, most of which are concentrated in a belt running across South-Central Africa. The Suku, the Tonga, and the Bemba have matrilineal descent and are located in this area. Of the remaining societies approximately 7 percent reckon their descent *bilaterally,* and 5 percent combine both forms of unilineal descent into a form called *double unilineal descent.* . .such as the San, the Pygmies and the Kanuri (p.170).

Each person was attached to several latent groups of solidarity which provided mutual support for its members (Kopytoff, 1989; p.24). The clan provided vital services and protection to the individual members comprising it. The clan was the individual's ultimate reference model. It was the source of a person's identity, reputation and pride. This often served as a form of behavioral control as a person would desist from acts likely to bring shame to the clan as a whole. Lineages also afforded economic security by providing "essential insurance to individual householders" (Curtin, *et al.,* 1978:159).

In times of famine or economic hardship or ceremonial need, the lineage, as a larger group, could share its resources with less fortunate members. Members also relied upon one another in times of political uncertainty or individual crisis. In times of general insecurity, the lineage was often the key to the individual's survival. The lineage was the most important unit in the African social, political and legal scheme of things. The lineage was answerable, in most cases, to a court of law in respect of the actions of its individual members. This is akin to the statutes governing the activities of a modern corporation, leading some scholars to characterize the African lineage as a "corporate body." In fact, Vaughan (1986) asserts: "(Clans)

live. In between these is the informal sector, which has more in common with the indigenous than the modern sector.

The informal sector consists of a heterogenous mix of people engaged primarily in distribution (import merchandise); transportation (taxis, "mammy" lorries, *mutatis*); light secondary manufacture (bakeries, dress-making); and repair works (bicycle, tire repair) and so on.

often are corporate groups in that they have a legal identity, land being ultimately owned by these bodies rather than by individuals. Although individuals have full use of land, they are restricted in their right to transfer it to any person not a member of the clan" (p.170).[3]

The lineage could also provide armed men for protection. In times of conflict, support was mobilized from contextually relevant groups. "Since traditional African societies were largely structured in terms of corporate groups, individual survival was possible only by being under the protective umbrella of one or another such group, and the larger the group and the more powerful it was, the safer one was" (Kopytoff, 1989; p.24).

The most immediate and most secure groups of support were those based upon kinship. The lineage was one such primary group. "When a member was taken captive in a raid, a fund of common lineage wealth was sometimes used to pay the ransom" (Curtin et al., 1978:159). As discussed later, common lineage funds (the "family pot," for example) were also used for other purposes, such as education and funerals.

A group of extended families cohabitating in a place but in different huts would form the village or maximal lineage. The next unit up would be the town, a collection of related villages. The hierarchical structure might then extend to the tribe, the province and ultimately to the kingdom in the case of monarchies or the empire.

It must be emphasized that although traditional African societies laid a great deal of emphasis on social harmony and cooperation, an individual was not "forced to live" with an extended family group against his will. This crucial distinction is often overlooked by scholars and modern African leaders.

Tensions within the family group, or even the village, inevitably arose. Residential separation or migration was an "exit" option that could ultimately be exercised to relieve such tensions. In other words, social harmony did not preclude *freedom of choice*. As Jackson (1982) noted of the Kuranko of Sierra Leone:

> The considerable variability of Kuranko residence patterns reflects the extent to which Kuranko men can choose where and with whom they wish to live. This *freedom of choice* can be related to several factors (apart from the emphasis placed on amity among the family members): land is not owned by the kinship group and, since land is nonheredita-

---

[3] This suggests that the Western economic development models, based upon individual actors or individualism (incentives to individuals and individual initiative), may not be appropriate to traditional Africa. The appropriate agents of development may be clans as corporate entities as in the Japanese model. A modern-day Japanese corporation is one large extended family. For example, in rural Africa, it would probably make more sense to give agricultural loans to clan heads than to individuals as default would "bring shame" on the whole clan.

ble, property and inheritance considerations do not make a man beholden to his senior agnates; land for farming is readily available if a man does not mind cutting himself off from his community in order to establish a hamlet in the bush (p.13).

Even when land was owned by the lineage, it did not act as a constraint on freedom of choice. Land has always been plentiful in Africa and millions of Africans, seeking their independence, have broken away from family groups and migrated to establish their own hamlets, villages and towns. But such undertakings (isolated existence in the wilderness) entailed considerable risks which could be reduced the larger the migrating party ("safety in numbers").

Consequently, indigenous African social and political cultures are characterized by remarkable enterpreneurship in acquiring followers and making alliances to achieve independence or favorable terms of dependence. In fact, "the drive to acquire relatives, adherrents, dependents, retainers, and subjects, and to keep them attached to oneself as a kind of social and political 'capital' has often been remarked upon as characteristic of African societies and of African political processes" (Kopytoff, 1989; p.40).

Since there was an ever-present need to expand the kinship group, there was always intense competition for people. This competition was seldom noticed *within* the group but *inter-group* competition was keen. Kopytoff (1989) observed:

> Traditionally, African kin groups had an almost insatiable demand for people and jealously guarded those they already had. Socially, this meant the existence of corporate groups of kinsmen, collectively holding resources, carefully enforcing their rights in membership. Thus, a very high proportion (usually over half) of customary court cases in Africa have to do with disputes over marriage, divorce, and bridewealth — matters that above all involve the social appropriation of progeny. . .Every new born was legally spoken for and and eagerly appropriated at birth by one or another autonomous kin group; and the various rights over the child by the respective kin groups of each of its parents had to be clearly, often tortuously, defined. Similarly, the reproductive capacity of every woman was a resource to be appropriated at birth. . .Culturally, all this had produced a variety of elaborations of systems of rights in persons, so that these appropriations could be accomplished unambiguously, flexibly, and with minimum of conflict (p.43).

Kopytoff's use of the term "rights" however is misleading. To Westerners, it may suggest "ownership" or treatment of people, especially women, as "commodities" that could be "owned." This was not the case in most traditional African systems. Even land, an inanimate object, was not "owned" by the African king, much less women. What is often not mentioned were the reciprocal obligations contraposed against these "rights." For example, the various kin groups which "claim" a child were also tangentially obligated for its welfare: nourishment and education, for example. Far from "servitude," this situation was rather advantageous to the child. Competing kin groups provided for his education and other needs as one group tried to outperform the other to secure the child's loyalty. In this situation, the child could play one kin group against another to obtain maximum benefits. For example, a child attending school may extract "pocket money" from the father's kin group *as well as* the mother's.

African women traditionally found themselves in a similar position with competition over their reproductive capacity. Women could similarly play off one kin group against another. Women traders, for instance, can claim trade capital from the husband's kin or from a suitor's.

Nevertheless, the tendency across much of Africa was to establish claims ("rights") to people and what they could offer and keep these claims "flexible, separate, and divisible into subsidiary rights, and to transact in them in a great number of different ways" (Kopytoff, 1989; p.44). The basic objective was to enhance the survivability of the kinship group and the settlement.[4]

Regardless of the political status, however, five basic social units could be observed in African village societies. For example, among the Igbo of Nigeria, the largest political unit was the *village group*, (*mba* or *obodo*), formed by a number of contiguous villages which believed themselves to be related by common ancestry, common custom and by a common shrine of *Ala*, the earth deity. Each village (*mbam* or *ogde*) was composed of a number of family groups or extended families. Each family group had a family head called the *okpara*. The *okpara* was usually the head of the senior branch of the family and he was the holder of the family *ofo* — a staff symbolizing the ancestors. The various classifications are presented below:

IGBO	English Equivalent
Mba (Obodo)	Village Group
Mbam (Ogbe)Village	

[4] This may also explain the tendency, noted by Kopytoff (1989), of investing certain social and political positions held by individuals — chiefships, titles, administrative posts, councillorships, ritual offices, etc. —in the kin group of the first incumbent to remain so vested, becoming part of the corporate estate of the kin group. Similarly, rights and wealth acquired by persons in their individual capacities can become integrated into the corporate kin's group. But such private property could only be transmuted into corporate property with the consent of the individual. Most often when this occurred, the corporation consisted of the individual's descendants.

Onumara	Lineage (Extended Family)
Umunna	Family group
Umunne	Nuclear Family

Among the Tswana,

> The smallest of these (units) was the family household, consisting of a man, his wife or wives, dependent children and other dependents. Several different households, linked patrilineally through a common male ancestor and situated close together in the same village, made up a family group. An elder, the senior male descendant of the common ancestor, exercised some authority over this group. A number of family groups together made up a ward, which came under the control of a hereditary headman. Each ward was a distinct administrative unit, occupying its own separate part of the village or town, or forming a separate village itself. But a ward was generally not a geographical unit, as its residential, agricultural and grazing areas tended not to adjoin each other. Within a ward the headman's authority was considerable; and collectively the headmen represented a kind of nobility, the *dikgosana*. Ultimately, however, power lay with the chief (Maylam, 1986:47).

Some village societies have fewer than five social units. The Mbeere of Kenya, for example, have the nuclear family (*nymba*) and a collection of extended families which form the village (*mucii*). Each social unit, nonetheless, has a head, who is usually a male. The criteria used in his selection are very much uniform in many parts of Africa. In the nuclear family, the father or the oldest male is the head, politically, socially, economically and religiously.

In the selection of a family head, the rule of primogeniture is applied, subject to the proviso that the head must descend from a family whose ancestors were responsible for the founding of the settlement or the unit. Certain duties are expected of the family head. Among the Igbo, for example,

> As the custodian of the family traditions and ancestral cults, the head acted as the intermediary between the family's ancestors and the living members. Normally, his old age kept him free from the influence of the older members of the village, of sexual desires, of jealousy and greed and he was expected to be a man of wisdom acquired from long experience in the religious, political and social life of the people (Olaniyan, 1985: 25).

Among the Asante, it was the work of the family head to instruct his wards in the ways of loyalty and obedience. He was held responsible for the freaks of recalcitrant members of his family, and he was expected as well to keep them within bounds, to insist upon conforming to the customs, laws, and traditional observances of the community (Casely Hayford, 1911).

Above the family heads are clan heads (among the pastoral Somali) or ward heads (among the Igbo). The Somali clan head, *suldaan*, mediates in internal clan affairs. The office is not tied to any particular lineage but the "appointment must be subject to popular approval" (Gibbs, 1965;p.346). Within each social unit, there are further stratifications along the lines of gender and age. Among the Annang of Nigeria, for example, the village is stratified along sexual lines and was further divided into age grades as follows:

MALE	*FEMALE*	*ENGLISH EQUIVALENT*
Ndem Isong	Akani Iban	Elders
Nka Ikpo Owo	Nka Ikpo Iban	Middle-Aged
Nka Mkparawa	Nka Nkaiferi	Youth
Ndito Owon	Ndito Owon	Children

Each age or sexual classification performs certain political, economic and social functions. The youth are in general responsible for keeping their wards or compounds clean and for other chores such as weeding. Other age grades have more specific functions. For example, the men's age grades of the Afikpo Igbo of Nigeria are responsible for the following.

AGE GRADE	*AFIKPO IGBO NAME*	*APPROX. AGE OF MEMBERS*	*FUNCTIONS*
Young Men	Uke ekpe	30 - 50 years	Village Police Force
Junior	Ekpe uke eto	55 - 64 years	Executive arm of government
Middle	Ekpe uke esa	65 - 83 years	Legislation and adjudication
Senior	Oni ekara	84 years and over	Advisory functions

Women also have certain responsibilities according to their age grades. The Afikpo women's age grades make and enforce rulings on the farming and harvesting of crops. In Botswana, female members of the Tswana society are responsible for the cultivation of crops while the grazing of cattle is the responsibility of the men. In fact, across Africa, there is pronounced sexual division of labor in occupation. Of the Kuranko of Sierra Leone, Jackson (1982) noted:

A strict sexual division of labor is maintained within the household,

and a strict division exists between 'male' and 'female' areas of the
house. . .

Paternal and maternal roles in child-rearing are different and
complementary: the paternal role connotes jural authority, discipline, provision of food, and social identification; the maternal role
connotes emotional attachment, personal care, and nurturance
(p.12).

In most African societies, fishing, hunting, waging war, craftmanship and
wood-working are almost exclusively a male preserve. Sculpturing and
building huts are also male occupations. The female, on the other hand, is
responsible for gathering wood, fetching water, raising children, and
harvesting crops. Food preparation and trading are also female occupations,
which explains the fact that, "The African woman produces 70 percent of
the food grown on the continent, according to the United Nations" (Lamb,
1985:38).[5]

In most indigenous societies, four main socio-political groupings can be
distinguished. The first is the "founder group", that is, all those members of
the tribe who are related by blood to and descended from the original
forefather who is reputed to be the origin and founder of the tribe. The term
"royal" or "governing" is also used to refer to this lineage since it is usually
from this lineage that the "ruler" of the tribe is drawn.

The second group is made up the "commoners", the "common" members
of the tribe who are not genealogically related to the governing class and
who usually form the majority of tribal members. The third are the
"strangers", who have come to reside in the territory of the tribe after
having asked and been given the required permission. They may live as
individuals, single families, family groups or tribal sub-groups which may be
break-aways from other tribes or remnants of other tribes. Among the
Bantu, it is explained:

Most of these (strangers), in the course of time become completely
integrated in the administrative and cultural pattern and social life
of the tribe; if, however, they are allowed to settle in the form of
groups, they usually retain a large measure of their own culture,
way of life, customs, etc., but obviously owing unqualified (political)
allegiance to the tribe in whose territory they have come to live.
This is very often also the way members of tribes who have been
conquered are treated (Olivier, 1969).

---

[5] This sex composition of Africa's farmers clearly suggests that an agricultural development
strategy, which places undue emphasis on male-driven tractors or machinery, would be
woefully misguided.

The fourth group are the "servants" or the servile class. In many West African ethnic societies, this class would include slaves attached to dignitaries or other prominent people of the tribe.

Socially, therefore, a tribe would consist of a varying number of clans, sibs, or extended family groupings having, as an outstanding characteristic, a common family name which denotes genealogical descent from a common forefather. The clans, or groups are hierarchically classified according to their genealogical relationship to the ruling (royal) family. In many systems, these differences may determine succession to office and protocol. In addition, there is further stratification within each group along age and sex lines.

Notwithstanding the differentiation, common ancestry is the glue that holds virtually each autonomous ethnic community together. For example:

> All Tswana ruling lineages are traced to one of three founding ancestors, named Morolong, Masilo and Mokgatla. Morolong appears to have lived in the western Witwatersrand area around the 13th-14th centuries; Masilo appears to have lived in the northern Witwatersrand area around the 14th-15th centuries; Mokgatla appears to have lived in the north-eastern Witwatersrand area around the 15th-16th centuries (cited by Maylam, 1987; p.45).

The history of each of these lineages was marked by processes of fission, giving rise to the numerous chiefdoms that appear in later Tswana history. The same can be said of the Yoruba of Nigeria, the Fanti of Ghana and the Shona of Zimbabwe.

African societal organization based upon kinship or group attachment and solidarity however had a downside. Conflicts in Africa, even if of individual origin, always carried the risk of escalating to pit one group against another. "Conflicts between individuals have been known to expand in a flash and involve all market sellers, or all women, or all youth, or all soldiers (warriors)" (Kopytoff, 1989; p.24). Great care, therefore, was exercised in traditional African societies to contain individual conflicts and prevent them from becoming an all-out group confrontation. This practice was much evident in legal jurisprudence where heavy emphasis was laid on restoring harmonious social relationships rather than the pursuit of abstract notions of justice.

Less formally, the same motive underscored actions or intervention by group leaders and elders in personal disputes, even if they were not directly concerned, since "someone else's business" could become their business if the conflict escalated. In such cases, group leaders and elders employed various informal ways of reconciling the parties. The moot was one such custom.

B. AFRICAN BELIEFS, RELIGION AND CUSTOMS

Society is not a fabric composed of resolvable parts, but an organism
of which the parts are necessarily interrelated and indivisible.

- Kobina Sekyi (1892 - 1956). Cited in Langely (1969;p.243).

Philosophical Tenets

Africans have always believed that their universe was composed of three
elements: the sky, the earth and the world. The sky and the earth made up
the world, which was the place where all people, ethnic and non-ethnic,
lived. Each component, however, could not exist independently of the
others, but the sky was recognized in many ethnic societies as supreme.

The sky was the domain of the spirits of the living and the unborn as well
as thunder, lightning, rain, drought and other natural phenomena. The earth
was the burial place of dead ancestors and other tribesmen as well as being
the dwelling place of the people and their activities: agriculture, hunting,
fishing, government, etc. The world was the domain of all people, both
ethnic and non-ethnic, and as such embraced inter-ethnic relationships: war,
peace, trade, etc.

Each component was represented as either a force or a god. The names of
each god, of course, differed from one ethnic society to another. For
example, among the Yoruba, the sky god was the *Olorun Oldumare*, the
supreme god. He was the source of power of his subjects, the *orisa* or gods,
who influenced relations between the sky and the world. The earth goddess
was *Onile* and the *Ogboni* was the earth cult. The principal organ of the
Ogboni was the *Oyo Mesi* or council of state. Among the Asante, the supreme
god was *Onyame*, and he could be referred to as the sky-god although he had
terrestrial functions in providing protection to the people. With the Nandi
of Kenya, the supreme god was *Asis*, whose being was identified in the sun,
asista. He regulated the balance between man and nature.

> The Zulu called the Lord-of-the-Sky *iNkosi yaphezulu* and *iNkosi
> yezulu*. Zulu belief systems considered the sky to be a rock, blue in
> color, which stretches from one end of the flat surface of the earth to
> the other. The great vault of rock rests on the edges of the earth, while
> the earth itself, being a flat surface, is held up by four bulls, 'carrying
> the earth on their horns. When one of them shakes its head, the earth
> also shakes.' This is how earthquakes are accounted for.
>
> The sky is above the sun and the moon. Both the sun and the moon
> move 'along their paths underneath the floor of the sky. They do

not reach up to the sky because they must shine on the earth only'
(Berglund, 1989; p.32).

Most traditional African societies believed the universe, composed of the
three elements (the sky, the earth and the world) was ordered like one giant
equation. Each being had a specific place in this universe. Human animation
corresponded to the animation of nature and each gesture correlates with
some aspect of the universe. African art, dance, music and other human
activities were a reflection of the rhythms of the universe. Hence, the
metaphysical sphere was not abstractly divorced from concrete experience,
especially since the physical and the metaphysical were aspects of reality, and
the transition from the one to the other was natural (Onwaunibe, 1984).[6]
This led some observers to derogate Africans as having no speculative
inclinations. But Onwaunibe further argued that the misrepresentation
stemmed from ignorance of the true nature of African philosophical
thinking. African expressions appeared complicated or chaotic, but they had
simple internal logic (Diop, 1987; p.60).
   According to Yelpaala (1983:374):

> Endowed with lethal powers, all the supernatural and cosmic forces
> exhibit and maintain an intricate, delicate, and mysterious balance
> with their normative and functional inter-relationships harmonized
> into a set of coherent and non-contradictory higher norms, prohibi-
> tions, and prescriptions to human beings. Therefore all other
> norms, legal or social, subordinate to and originating from ances-
> tors or humans cannot contradict these higher norms of supernatu-
> ral origins. The Dagaaba ideal picture of their world is therefore a
> system exhibiting congruency, symmetry, consistency, and constant
> cooperation among all the component parts and humans are
> enjoined to maintain the symmetry by observing these higher
> norms. In this type of setting, the supernatural enters the legal
> system so directly that the lawmaking functions of the entire society
> are effectively preempted and controlled by the supernatural. In
> fact, a formal legislative body is unnecessary.

Thus, metaphysically, the cosmos ran in a strictly orderly manner. It was
essential for the components to be in perfect harmony and order, called *kiet*
by the Nandi of Kenya. If an element was out of balance, there would be
chaos, disease and death. For example, if the sky was out of equilibrium,

---

[6] The connection between the physical and the metaphysical in African philosophy has also
been emphasized by Mbiti (1970) with the observation that, "the spiritual universe is a unit
with the physical, and that these two intermingle and dovetail into each other so much that it is
not easy, or even necessary, at times, to draw the distinction or separate them" (p.97).

thunder or floods would result. Similarly, if the earth was "angry", there would be disease, poor harvests, famine and barren women.

An individual was not a mere spectator in this potentially turbulent cosmos. Among the Igbo "a man was perceived to be the union of the three elements" (Carlston, 1968:190). Another group with such a belief was the Arusha of Tanzania. An individual's personality was the outcome of the interplay of natural forces. A "good" child resulted from the concurrence of agreeable forces whereas a "bad" child signified the wrath of some "displeased" force. Sickness and death were similarily interpreted.

Most indigenous African societies recognized a hierarchical ordering of supernatural and cosmic forces. Among the Dagaaba of northern Ghana, for example, at the top of the hierarchy was the omnipotent god *Naamwini* (literally "chief" of all supernatural beings) - the equivalent of the Asante *Onyame*. Subordinate to this were a plethora of other supernatural beings (*mwime*) whose existence was manifested in or through certain natural phenomena such as hills (*nakotang*), rivers (*gyel*) and lightning (*saa*). Lower down was the *tengan*, "owner of the land", and lastly were ancestral spirits (*kpiime*).

All these supernatural forces were believed to have emotional intelligence and certain rules of prohibited human behavior. Compliance with these rules was blessed in the form of longevity, freedom from sickness and individual prosperity. Violations elicited punishment which often came in the form of sudden death, affliction by a terrible disease, or financial ruin on an individual basis and collectively by poor harvests and barren women. The ancestral spirits, for example, supervised and maintained the social norms that had been handed down from time immemorial.

There was the need to communicate with these gods and spirits, to placate them in order not to incur their displeasure or wrath and to make atonements in cases of wrongdoing to prevent vengeful acts. Above all, however, it was essential to maintain order and a state of harmony between the sky, the earth and the world. To agricultural societies, the harmony between the sky and the earth was particularly important. The set of beliefs associated with this harmony is known as the earth cult. An aspect of this cult was the attribution to the earth of the power to bring good or bad fortune to the people in such matters as fertility of the land in crops and fertility of wives. The Asante, for example, honored the earth goddess in the annual *Adae* ceremony held on Thursdays. Thursday was the natal day of the earth goddess and work on that day was prohibited, otherwise misfortune would result. The Ga fishermen also banned fishing on Tuesdays.

The function of maintaining harmony and order among the three components of the universe or what Rappaport (1968) called "cognized environment," was reserved to ritual leaders or priests. The precise forms and methods, of course, varied from tribe to tribe. Among the Bashu of Zaire, for example,

The world is divided between opposing spheres of existence. On the one hand is the world of the homestead, in which the Bashu live, grow their crops, and keep domesticated animals. Surrounding this world, and impinging upon it, is the world of the bush, inhabited by the untamed and chaotic elements of nature, including powerful medicines and spirits. While these worlds are ideally separate, the continuity and productivity of the homestead depends on the performance of certain ritual actions that mediate between these two worlds and bring them into contact with one another on specific occasions. This mediation permits the domestication and incorporation into the homestead of certain spirits, medicines, and elements of nature, which are essential to the productivity of the homestead but are associated in their natural state with the chaotic world of the bush. Ritual mediation also serves to purge the homestead of untamed forces of the bush that have penetrated the homestead, causing misfortune, sickness, and famine. In other words, ritual mediation temporarily resolves major contradictions within the Bashu view of the natural environment in which they live and in which rain, spirits, and medicines are at once necessities of their existence and potential sources of misfortune (Packard, 1981; p.4).

Accordingly, there was also a hierarchical ordering of intercessors. At the lowest level were such posts as priests, diviners, witches, sorcerers, witch doctors, priests, medicine men, who together with shrines, fetishes or other objects embodying supernatural powers were the agents that were believed to be capable of communicating with the supernatural world and able to influence the impact of supernatural power on human affairs or to influence its aid in attaining desired goals. Such goals included the averting of misfortune or inflicting injury on adversaries.

This mediation was the primary function of local or family priests in stateless societies; the chief in states and kings in kingdoms. Among the Ga people of Ghana, each family had a priest whose function it was to ensure that the family tradition was followed and if not, to propitiate the ancestral spirits. The Bashu chief, *mwami* "is ultimately responsible for mediating between the opposing spheres of Bashu existence and for resolving the antinomies of Bashu experience. It follows that the death or weakness of the *mwami* results in misfortune or famine" (Packard, 1981; p.4).

Thus, in African states, the chief or the king had a precise function, a definite role, and that was to "maintain harmony between society and its natural environment by means of ritual action" (Davidson, 1970; p.192). To accomplish this, the king somehow needed to possess some force to deal with the three elements. Clearly, his power had to be greater than that of the witch doctor, priest or even a witch. Further, his force had to be supernatural and as such, he had to be the one only with the greatest vital force in the whole kingdom. Only in this way could he serve as mediator with the superior universe, without throwing any of the three elements out of equilibrium. In most ethnic societies, the king's throne, or stool, was the repository of ancestral powers as well as the confluence of all residual powers in the kingdom. In sitting on the stool, the king was expected to have his own powers enhanced sufficiently by all other ancestral powers to enable him to perform this mediating role.

If African religious beliefs are compared with the orthodox Western Christianity, it becomes apparent that there are little essential differences between them. The book of Genesis starts with: "In the beginning God created the Heaven and the Earth.." God, the supernatural being, omnipotent and omniscient, was incarnated in Jesus Christ, his son born of Virgin Mary. Christ died for our sins to make atonement for the human race and deliver us unto God. Though dead, his Holy Spirit is ever present. Between an individual and God were two important intercessors: the pastor and Christ. In Islam, the supreme power is *Allah* and the intercessors are the Prophet Mohammed and the living Ayatollahs and *mullahs*.

Each religion has a supernatural being or power who created the universe. Each also has some figure who intercedes between human beings and the supernatural power. These intermediaries are deified, worshipped, and propitiated. Each also has rigidly laid down rules of conduct or commandments that must be followed for "deliverance." For example, polygamy is not acceptable to the Judao-Christian faith and Islam forbids stealing, the charging of interest and the consumption of pork.

Indigenous African religion and philosophy also have similar beliefs as we have seen. There are various gods, supreme and lesser gods. The gods take human, inanimate and spiritual forms. Indigenous African religions also have several intercessors, both dead and living. Ancestors generally comprise the first category, and witch doctors, priests, chiefs and kings the second. But rather strangely, Christianity is called a religion. So too is Islam. But that of the natives of Africa is called paganism.

The Individual Versus The Society

In traditional African societies, as in other, non-African cultures, there is acute awareness of the effects of the environment on people. Karp (1986) argued that,

> A careful comparison of African and Western cultures shows that they share in common spheres of concern with the limits on the controls people can hold over their social and natural environment and with how they can reassert control or influence their worlds. In

both Western and African cultures this set of questions and problems includes technology, morality, and belief. . .

The great conclusion of E.E. Evans-Pritchard's pioneering study of the Azande systems of thought was that differences between the Azande and Westerners were not differences in logic or thinking capacity. The Azande and other Africans reason much as people everywhere do. They also govern their lives with a mixture of skepticism and belief, and they have the same ambivalent and helplessly dependent faith in their specialists and doctors (p.202).

Normally, an individual's power was not considered adequate to overcome or to mediate between the society and the natural environment. Auxiliary power was required, which could come from several sources: from his own intelligence, capabilities, ingenuity; from the ancestors; or from magic or even witchcraft. The Tiv of Nigeria, for example, believed that, "individuals who rose above the general level of the group could not have achieved power without an ability to call upon magical forces to promote their advance" (Carlston, 1968:212).

The vital forces required to deal with the supernatural were considered to be additive. In walking in the shoes of a powerful person, an individual may somehow assume some of his powers to add to his own. Or if one cooperated with another, the sum total of two forces would be greater than each individual force. Consequently, the accent was on promoting cooperation. Accordingly, indigenous African societies developed various mechanisms to achieve these. For instance,

The Kuranko say that one of the functions of the *kere* (working bee) system is to create a network of mutual obligation and interdependence. . .If labor recruitment for farming were based solely on lineage ties then there would be fewer bonds among neighbors. Bonds of amity are created among villagers by less formal means: visiting and sharing food, eating kola or drinking palm wine together, giving sympathy gifts to the bereaved, attending and participating in village festivals and rituals, greeting and talking to people during the business of day-to-day life, assisting friends and neighbors with labor, money or food (Jackson, 1982; p.19).

Cooperation was also necessary for the survival of the group. By himself, the (Kuranko) individual could not deal with *rival* (the world). "The fortunes of the (Kuranko) individual are inextricably bound up with relations with kinsmen, friends, mentors, neighbors, strangers, ancestors, God, and other beings. *Sabu* refers to the dynamic interactions within this field of relations" (Jackson, 1982; p.19).

Group effort or cooperation was vital. This underscored the general cultural practice among Africans to extend the terms "brother" and "sister" to other kinspersons and non-kinspersons as well. "Naive Europeans or Americans have sometimes thought that Africans could not understand such terms as sister, mother, or son because they seemingly used the terms so loosely, when in fact it was the non-Africans who failed to understand the African system" (Vaughan, 1986; p.171).[7]

At any rate, the African emphasis on cooperation did not rule out the existence of the individual as a person capable of making an effort on his own initiative. This issue of the individual versus the community has been the source of much confusion. In the West, individuals would say, " I am because I am and I want what I want when I want it." In Africa, the peasant would say, "I am because we are." This is well expressed by a Vais (Sierra Leone) proverb: "What belongs to me is destroyable by water or fire; what belongs to us is destroyable neither by water or fire." Again: "What is mine goes; what is ours abides." The we or us connotes kinship. The community plays a crucial role in the individual's acquisition of full personhood. But the individual alone defines the self, or person, he is to become.

> Western writers have generally interpreted the term 'community' in such a way that it signifies nothing more than a mere collection of self-interested persons, each with his private set of preferences, but all of whom get together nonetheless because they realize, each to each, that in association they can accomplish things which they are not able to accomplish otherwise. In this primarily additive approach, whenever the term 'community' or 'society' is used, we are meant to think of the aggregated sum of individuals comprising it. And this is argued, not just as an ontological claim, but, also as a methodological recommendation to the various social or humanistic disciplines interested in the investigation of the phenomenon of individuals in groups; hence the term 'methodological individualism' so much bandied around in the literature (Menkiti, 1984).

Survival is the primary objective of the leader of every African tribe. Within the tribe, individuals are free and independent, but their rights and interests are subordinate to those of the community as an entity. As the Ga of Ghana say, "Individuals don't live to be a hundred years old; the tribe does."

In Africa, primary duty is owed to the community. Persons exist only in relation to one another; individual rights are secondary. "The essence of moral responsibility among the Kuranko (of Sierra Leone) springs from the view that a person's actions affect and implicate all those who are related to

---

[7] The naivete however was even more astonishing among African elites when they called themselves "comrades" and not "brothers." There is an ocean of difference between a comrade and a brother as the latter implies a greater degree of intimacy.

him" (Jackson, 1982; p.18). This is expressed by the Kuranko proverb: "*Soron i la ko yolke*", meaning "one's birth is like a chain." Individual self-sufficiency is as absurd to the Kuranko as the notion that the individual is essentially the proprietor of his own person or capacities, owing nothing to society for them (Jackson, 1982; p.17). "One's head is in the hands of others," say the Kuranko.

The teleological perception is from the society to the individuals making up the community whereas in the West it is from the individuals to the society. Accordingly,

> In the west, we find a construal of things in which certain specified rights of individuals are seen as antecedents to the organization or society; with the function of government, viewed, consequently, as being the protection and defense of these individual rights (Menkiti, 1984).

Similarly, Oguah (1984) argued:

> The Fanti system of ethics is essentially anti-egoistic. Egoism, the theory that each individual should seek his own good and not the good of his neighbor or his community, is frowned upon by the Fanti moralist. For the Fanti, the good of the individual cannot prosper unless the society prospers. A great emphasis is placed on social ethics as opposed to the ethics of self, the kind of ethics which the west, with its maxim of 'Each one for himself and God for us all,' practices. Here the West may learn something from Africa.

However, it must be pointed out that many Africans also misinterpreted the indigenous system of ethics. Recall the dictum: "I am because we are." Many African leaders emphasized the "I" component and ignored the "we." For example, President Houphouet-Boigny of Ivory Coast once declared:

> Here in Ivory Coast, there is no number two, three or four. There is only a number one; that's me. It is I who decide and I don't share my decisions (*West Africa*, August 8, 1988; p.1428).

Two years later, a similar line was echoed by Charles Taylor, the rebel leader who set out to overthrow the late President Samuel Doe of Liberia, accused of corruption, incompetence and dictatorship. Said Taylor: "I want to make Liberia the Hong Kong of West Africa" (*West Africa*, August 6-12, 1990; p.2231. The statements by both Houphouet-Boigny and Charles Taylor were *un-African*. The emphasis on the "I" alone by both leaders was indicative of dictatorial tendencies.

But then other African leaders and writers laid exclusive emphasis on the "we" to the neglect of the "I" part of the statement. The emphasis on the "we" implied "unity" and "cooperation," which was half correct. However, the presence of the "I" indicated "individualism" and "independence." Consequently, it would be incorrect to emphasize either one to the total exclusion of the other. Williams (1987) described it best: "Individual freedom was unlimited until it clashed with the interests or welfare of the community."

The boundaries within which the individual could exercise "unlimited freedom" were prescribed by the cultural norms and practices of the community. These norms were in turn influenced by the need to maintain harmony among the cosmic forces and to comply with behavioral rules required by ancestors as well as the supernatural forces. In other words, the philosophical beliefs, social mores, obligations and value systems merely set the parameters within which the individual could operate freely.

The limits were in general not imposed by the chief or king — an important distinction. The imposition of rigid boundaries is the hallmark of dictatorship whereas the prescription of limits by the community, or the people themselves, is not. Thus, a reluctance on the part of an African to do something does not necessarily signify an obedience of an order from a chief.

The limits set by the community, of course, varied from one tribe to another. Further, the degree of individuality or independence also varied from tribe to tribe. But the preeminence of the societal interests prevailed in all systems. Accordingly, it would be more useful to consider the ontological schema as a continuum along which various African ethnic societies may be placed, depending upon the degree to which the "I" or the "we" is emphasized. For example, the Igbo, the Somali, the Nuer (Sudan) and the Arusha (Tanzania) are known to be highly individualistic and independent. In fact, according to Carlston (1968): "The Arusha were a people who placed a cultural premium on individualism and showed a strong attachment to egalitarianism" (p.310).

In many other African societies, proverbs uphold individual responsibility. No able-bodied African native could expect to receive hand-outs from the group to which he was attached. Nor could he demand provision for his daily welfare from the tribal government. Support was mutual, not unilateral and a great deal of emphasis was placed on reciprocity. In fact, it was *never* the function of the group or the tribal government to supplant individual effort and initiative. As the Fanti of Ghana say: *Ibu dzea idua* - You reap what you sow. Individuals are responsible for their own actions. Another Fanti proverb says: *Obra nyi woara abo* - Life is as you make it.

These beliefs also governed the life of the Mogopas of South Africa. Prior to 1912 when blacks owned their land, the Mogopas settled on the fertile plains west of Johannesburg:

> They built a community with two schools, four churches, a clinic and several hundred stone houses. They nurtured peach and

apricot trees, harvested wheat and corn and tended hundreds of cattle. They fed themselves, and usually had a surplus to sell in the nearby white town of Ventersdrop.

'We never asked the *government* for anything,' says Matthew Kgatitsoe, his 68-year old body swelling with *pride*. 'We built our own schools and churches. We didn't need any police. We took care of ourselves' (*The Wall Street Journal*, Nov. 20, 1990; p.A16).

At the other end of the spectrum may be placed such societies as the Ewe of Ghana, the Kikuyu of Kenya, and the Kuranko of Sierra Leone, which show a greater disposition toward cooperation. Recall that the Kuranko created a network of mutual obligations and interdependence. Bonds of amity were forged through participation in village festivals, visiting and sharing food.

Generally, African philosophical beliefs did not preclude individual or private ownership, as many African Marxists have assumed. Recall the Vais proverb: "What is mine goes; what is ours abides." The "mine" clearly connoted personal or individual property. There was nothing in that statement that debarred the individual from owning property or decreed that ownership always had to reside in the "we" or the community or the state. The inference from that statement was clear: the individual's single property may not endure but the community's as a whole would. If the individual could make his property last, it was his business, so long as the pursuit of wealth or prosperity did not conflict with the greater interests of society. Under those circumstances, his property might be in danger.

The Ga of Ghana have a unique way of inculcating this value system.

An unmarried Ga boy has no property of his own. All his earnings belong to his father, and his father provides him with all his needs. The boy goes to work every day on his father's farm or with his father's canoe or nets. When he reaches the age of about fifteen his father gives him one day a week on which to 'make a farm' of his own. At harvest time he 'shows his profits' to his father, who 'takes a little for tobacco' and gives the boy the rest. . .He is expected to save it (Field, 1940; p.54).

The same practice could also be observed among the Tallensi of northern Ghana. According to Carlston (1968): "The (Tallensi) son could have fowls and livestock of his own or even his own private plot of land given him by his father or the head of the household. He was considered to be entitled to the fruits of such property. A father who interfered with his son doing as he wished with his 'things' was considered to deprive him of a right. For example, a father could not rightfully forbid his son to use the proceeds of the sale of fowls raised by his son to buy desired clothing, though he had the naked power to do so" (p.102).

It is necessary to distinguish between cooperation and collectivity as the two are often mistaken as synonymous. Collectivism precludes individualism or independence whereas cooperation permits some degree of independence and volition. To characterize the traditional African society as "collectivist" would be inaccurate. As we have shown above, there is the "I" or individualism present, although somewhat subdued in some tribes but accented in the Igbo and the Nuer, for example. But its existence is indisputable even among the Kuranko of Sierra Leone. *Miran* is their term for any personal property. "One's protective charms and ointments, one's clothing and personal belongings are all *mirannu* (Jackson, 1982; p.22).

Similarly, Carlston (1968:365) observed:

> Nuer society was marked by recognition of the independence and dignity of the individual. This was linked with a high degree of preference for individual freedom action and for life within the circle of the family and the homestead. . .

> The Nuer were highly egalitarian and democratic. No one recognized superiority in another, although respect to elders was shown. Desired action by others was not elicited when it was communicated in the form of a command. . .There was no duty to obey any authority if the result was against one's interests.

> Other people were held in contempt. The submissiveness of other peoples to chiefly authority was a matter of astonishment. Strangers were treated with indifference. Yet, the Nuer were kind and gentle to one another in misfortune and sickness. They accepted friendship if it was offered on the basis of equality of status.

Nevertheless, independence and community awareness coexisted at the same time, prompting Field (1940) to suggest "togetherness" as a better term since this implies some weak element of individual volition. This spirit is often reflected in what many Africans call "communal labor" activities, as occurred when villagers gathered to build schools. But communalism or cooperation is not the same as communism. Nor is being socialistic (as in "man is a social animal") the same as being a socialist. Imprecise definitions and poor understanding have given rise to much confusion about African philosophy and spurned various bastard ideologies that bear little relation to indigenous African value systems.

Much of the difficulty originated, as we have seen, from lack of understanding of indigenous African philosophy and therefore African personality. In the West, the individual is answerable to himself and God, if he is religious. In the communist countries, the individual owes primary allegiance to the state. In Muslim countries, he is answerable only to Allah. The average African, on the other hand, is subject to four levels of authority or sources of control. In ascending order, Yelpaala (1983:375) states:

> First, there is the authority of the living exercised by such personalities as the king, the chief, and the lineage heads. Second, there is the authority of the ancestral spirits over the living. The authority of the living, particularly that of the lineage heads, is monitored and subordinate to that of the ancestors. Third, there is the authority of other supernatural forces whose cosmic norms and authority take precedence over those of the ancestors and the living. Finally, there is the authority of the supreme omnipotent being, who rewards or punishes the dead according to the quality of their lives on earth.

The average African must consult four standards before initiating any action on his own and resolve any resultant conflicts and contradictions. Obviously, it is far more complex and taxing than answering to one or two lines of authority. This is not to suggest that the average African is far more intelligent than other species. The main point is that, foreigners who consult only themselves or Allah may not understand the African who consults, not only himself but also four other authority reference points as well.

Parallel to the strong sense of community is the universal set of beliefs and practices centering upon ancestors - the original founders of the community and settlement. The peasant is made to believe he owes his existence to his ancestors and therefore owes them a duty to carry out their commands and uphold their name and dignity. Although they are dead physically, they are spiritually ever-present, influencing the course of daily life and mediating between the earthly and the supernatural. "Among the Yoruba and the Edo (of Nigeria), festivals in honor of ancestors have become definitely religious festivals. The cults of *Oro* and *Egungun* and what in Benin is known as *Agwe* are illustrations of this fact" (Olaniyan, 1985:240).

The supreme satifaction in life is the knowledge that one will become an ancestor, a satisfaction achieved through children, even though becoming an ancestor ultimately means death (Wilson, 1967). Accordingly,

> It becomes a duty to produce children, and sexual intercourse between a man and his wives is looked upon as an act of production and not merely as the gratification of bodily desire. The Gikuyu tribal custom requires that a married couple should have at least four children, two male and two female. The first male is regarded as perpetuating the existence of the man's father, the second as perpetuating that of the woman's father. The first and second females fulfill the same ritual duty to the souls of their grandmoth-

ers on both sides. The children are given names of the persons (ancestors) whose souls they represent. The desire to have children is deep-rooted in the hearts of both man and woman, and on entering into matrimonial union they regard the procreation of children as their first and most sacred duty. A childless marriage in Gikuyu community is practically a failure, for children bring joy not only to their parents, but to the *mbari* (clan) as a whole (Kenyatta, 1938).

The Fundamental Rights Of The African People

Though the rights of the community predominate over those of the individual, the notion that individuals are free-born is universal. In fact, many tribes do not permit the enslavement of their own tribesmen, since that would not help the tribe survive.[8] According to Yoruba tradition, "an *Oni* (a Yoruba king) named Akinmoyero (also known as Odunle, the fourth *Oni* before Abeweila) was dragged from his palace by the *Oro* and beheaded because he was selling Ife people into slavery, permitting them to be captured by Oyo refugees living in the outlying towns in the Kingdom" (Bascom, 1984; p.31).[9]

Each African enjoyed certain basic human rights which were established by customary law and tradition. Since these were not written, it gave the appearance that no such rights existed for Africans. However, Williams (1987) compiled such a list, which is presented below:

"Every member of the community had -

1. The right to equal protection of the law.
2. The right to a home.
3. The right to land sufficient for earning livelihood for oneself and family.
4. The right to aid in times of trouble.
5. The right to petition for redress of grievances.
6. The right to criticize and condemn any acts by the authorities or proposed new laws. (Opposition groups, in some areas called 'The Youngmen', were recognized by law).
7. The right to reject the community's final decision on any matter and to withdraw from the community unmolested - the right of rebellion and withdrawal.

---

[8] Slaves generally were other tribesmen who were prisoners of war or captured in raids.

[9] Relations with other tribesmen, however, are completely different. Other tribesmen are "strangers" or outsiders who could be potential enemies. Consequently, many tribal groups go to the extraordinary lengths to wear distinctive "tribal marks." The Pygmies, for example, chip their teeth to distinguish themselves from others.

8. The right to a fair trial. There must be no punishment greater than the offense, or fines beyond the ability to pay. This latter is determined by income and status of the individual and his family.

9. The right to indemnity for injuries or loss caused by others.

10. The right to family or community care in cases of sickness or accidents.

11. The right to special aid from the Chief in circumstances beyond a family's ability.

12. The right to a general education covering the morals and good manners, family rights and responsibilities, kinship groups and social organization, neighborhoods and boundaries, farming and marketing, rapid mental calculation, and family, clan, tribal and state histories.

13. The right to apprentice training for a useful vocation.

14. The right to an inheritance as defined by custom.

15. The right to develop one's ability and exercise any developed skills.

16. The right to protect one's family and kinsmen, even by violent means if such becomes necessary and can be justified.

17. The right to the protection of moral law in respect to wife and children - a right which not even the king can violate.

18. The right of a man, even a slave, to rise to occupy the highest positions in the state if he has the requisite ability and character.

19. The right to protection and treatment as a guest in enemy territory once one is within the gates of the enemy's village, town or city.

20. And the right to an equal share in all benefits from common community undertakings if one has contributed to the fullest extent of his ability, no matter who or how many were able to contribute more.

> These constitutional principles and practices were held on to and carried by the migrating Blacks to every part of the African continent. This fact is one of the most remarkable parts of the black man's story - most remarkable because even those societies that sank to barbarism held on to the fundamentals age after age as though they were clutching the last threads of life itself. (p.175).

Sadly, most of these rights have disappeared in modern Africa. As Mongo Beti lamented: "Respect for human beings was once part of African tradition. We must now, however, recognize that we have lost this tradition. When? How? Why?" (*Index on Censorship*, October, 1987; p.42).

The Concept Of Wealth

Most lineages in traditional Africa have a "family pot," a general welfare fund managed by the head of the extended family. Income-earning members are *obligated* to make contributions to this fund. Obligations vary from family to family and tribe to tribe. A minimum regular payment may be made by the contributor in some cases. In other cases, the contribution may be irregular and based upon financial ability. In some families, contributions may be entirely voluntary for those who no longer live in the village. However, failure to contribute is often interpreted as an abandonment of one's family, which is considered a serious transgression. The offender may be ostracized or caused to forfeit his inheritance rights. However, an atonement can often be made with one "large" contribution to cover past arrears.

Across Africa, the family pot, called the *agbadoho* among the Ewe seine fishermen of Ghana, is used for a variety of purposes: to provide the initial start-up capital for a business or trade; to finance the education, hospitalization and the foreign trip of a member of the extended family; to cover funeral expenses; to finance improvement costs to the family land; or to construct new dwellings. The Ewe seine fishermen, for example, borrow from this pot to buy their canoes and nets and pay back the loans.

The African family pot, not well understood, has also been the source of much confusion and myth. To earlier visitors and writers, it conjured up notions of "forced sharing," "primitive communism" or "to each according to his/her needs." The erroneous corollary was the assumption that there were neither poverty nor rich peasants in pre-colonial Africa. This myth was "widely held by colonial officials, and anthropologists and transmitted to nationalist intellectuals and international agencies" (Iliffe, 1987; p.3). Even the United Nations Regional Department on Social Welfare Policy and Training of the Economic Commission for Africa, succumbed to this myth in 1972:

> In rural Africa, the extended family and the clan assume the responsibility for all services for their members, whether social or economic. People live in closely organized groups and willingly accept communal obligations for mutual support. Individuals satisfy their need for social and economic security merely by being attached to one of these groups. The sick, the aged and children are all cared for by the extended family. In this type of community, nobody can be labelled poor because the group usually shares what they have. There is no competition, no insecurity, no big ambitions, no unemployment and thus people are mentally healthy. Deviation or abnormal behaviour is almost absent. (Cited by Iliffe, 1988; p.3).

The society described in the aforementioned quotation is not an accurate characterization of traditional African society. There were competition (among kin groups) and even deviant behavior. Forced sharing was generally not the rule in many African ethnic societies. There were rich merchants, traders and poor peasants. Inequalities of wealth were very much a feature of indigenous Africa. For example,

> Among the Igbo (of Nigeria) inequality was recognized in age, status, wealth, religion, birth and descent. Royalty was in name and not in fact, as the Igbo recognized achievement rather than hereditary-bestowed greatness (Olaniyan, 1985:24).

There was a general recognition in indigenous Africa of the inevitability of inequities in wealth distribution. Not all members of the lineage are engaged in the same occupation. Some might be farmers or pastoralists. Others might be traders, artisans, fishermen or hunters. Since each occupation offered different fortunes and opportunities, differences in wealth were bound to occur. Changes in perceived opportunities or prospects induced occupational shifts; from say carpentry to gold mining. A man might well have a dozen occupations before the age of 35 (Iliffe, 1987). Some succeeded in their occupations; others failed and switched. Successes were often attributed to a combination of luck, ancestral blessing and hard work.

Africans accumulated wealth just as any other people, and differences in wealth were recognized. In the view of Schneider (1986),

> The Hausa (of West Africa) are not equal in wealth. Wealth differences are indexed by the fact that some *gandu*, a productive unit composed of a father and his married sons, are much larger than and contain many more subunits than do others. Furthermore, these large *gandu* have more manured land in crops, more bushfields (unmanured fields) and more marshland. In this society, a good deal of effort is expended by people to increase the size of their holdings and the scale of their production in order to increase their wealth — and obviously some people are more successful at this than are others (p.186).

African beliefs in inequalities of wealth were expressed in many proverbs. According to the Masai (Kenya) proverb: *Merisio ilkibunyeta le tunyanak*, "the fingers of people are not all the same length." The Fanti of southern Ghana, known for their proverbs, had this one: "All mushrooms grow in the same place but some are eaten and others are not." Other Fanti proverbs regarding wealth were: "The wealthy man is senior" and "A good name cannot be eaten but it is money that counts."

Most people tend to conceive of wealth as money, oversized bank accounts, fancy mansions, a collection of rare paintings and so on. Economists, however, define wealth as the possession of an asset that generates income. For example, a plot of agricultural land, a coal mine, a steel mill and stocks and bonds all produce income. This definition creates problems when applied to indigenous Africa since the use of money was not well advanced. A better and more general definition of wealth would be the possession of a property that produces in return "something of value." This expansion at once embraces what may be regarded as social, organic and even psychic wealth since "something of value" is determined by cultural as well as economic factors. For example, in the West, the possession of a good name or title (Lord or Baron) may bring an individual respect and status, even though such titles may have no pecuniary emoluments attached. Thus, what may be of social value to a Westerner may be worthless to the peasant and vice versa.

Much of the wealth in indigenous Africa was of the social type; that is, of the non-pecuniary or psychic variety, some of which was valueless to Westerners. The Masai in Kenya and the Zulus of South Africa counted their wealth in cattle. Among the Gikuyu, "cows give the owner a prestige in the community. . .The owner of a large number of cattle was sentimentally satisfied by praise names conferred upon him by the community in their songs and dances (Kenyatta, 1938:62). "All the Tsimihety of Madagascar aspire to keep large numbers of cattle" (Wilson, 1967). Cattle performed a social, not economic, function of yielding prestige and respect to their owner. That was one reason why they were rarely slaughtered by the owner for consumption. In Nigeria, "the economic goal of the Bororo is not to raise their material standards but to accumulate livestock. The rich man's satisfactions reach far beyond those of the less affluent when he silently contemplates the evening, his flocks back within the kraal, having assumed one of those meditative poses that express the pleasure of possession" (Dupire, 1962).

The Somali for wealth is *hoolo*, which means primarily wealth in livestock. Camels were the most prized possession. To the Sonjo of Kenya, goats and beehives constituted wealth while the Lele considered rights in women and children as the highest form of wealth or security. In his old age, the Lele man could count on his wives, children and grandchildren to look after him.

Evidently, Africans accumulate wealth just as Westerners do. The only difference, however, is the form of accumulation. Due to the absence of capital markets, wealth took the form of acquiring physical possessions. Wealth could not be "hidden" in paper currencies, credit and debt instruments such as stocks and bonds. Wealth in indigenous Africa had a physical presence. The wealthy in the village could be identified easily by the number of heads of cattle, the number of wives and children. Upon this basis, it immediately becomes apparent that, since not all the peasants had the same number of cattle, there were inequalities in the distribution of wealth in indigenous Africa.

Clearly, the general absence of economic or pecuniary wealth did not mean the people of Africa had no conception of wealth and were uninterested in its accumulation. There was no African native law that forbade Africans to help themselves to prosper and be wealthy. In fact, each king or chief desired prosperity for his people. Ritual incantations, religious sacrifices, and invocation of ancestral spirits were generally performed to seek the assistance of the gods and dead ancestors to protect the tribe and *help it prosper.*

The pursuit of wealth was a cultural occupation! Prestige, status, honor and influence were all attached to wealth in indigenous systems. The wealthy were "important people" with influence in governmental affairs. It was no accident that political figures in traditional African societies were also wealthy. The Fulani headman, *ardo*, for example, was the one who had the greatest number of cattle. Among the Gusii of Kenya, "the social status of a homestead head and his influence in community affairs were largely dependent on his wealth. A rich man (*omanda*) was respected and listened to, while a poor man (*omoraka*) was despised, at least covertly, and ignored" (LeVine, 1962).

"Sidamo men (of Ethiopia) aspire to positions of wealth" (Hammer, 1970). In Kuba society of Zaire, "wealth is a powerful means of acquiring prestige, and prestige is the basic value of society. Wealth is displayed in order to give prestige; it has to be shown in rich clothing, furniture and hospitality" (Vansina, 1962). Among the Igbo, "the attainment of wealth meant the attainment of prestige and influence, through respect, clientage, assumption of titles, and achievement of political influence" (Carlston, 1968:191). Among the Hausa, "customary exchange (of gifts) marks wealth and its pursuit as legitimate at the same time that it demonstrates status and affirms prestige. The generosity of wealthy men evokes admiration for wealth and emulation in its pursuit. It also leads the Hausa to set high value on the freedom to pursue wealth limits set by Islam on the one hand and by customary norms on the other" (Smith, 1962).

It is important to stress, for the benefit of modern African elites, that political power or office in traditional Africa was not used as the basis to accumulate wealth. As we shall see in Chapter 3, the African chief was forbidden to accumulate personal wealth. Any such accumulation or gift to the Akan chief was regarded as "stool property." The rich in traditional Africa did not owe their wealth to political office or connections. Nor did those in office use their position to enrich themselves. The successful Igbo man owed his prosperity to his own *individual ability*:

> (In Igbo society), strong emphasis was placed on achievement, and ways to achievement and leadership were open. Achievement was encouraged by many social groups, who aided their members as they sought to move upwards in status and influence. Achievement and initiative were permitted within many of the social groups and were facilitated by the number of contacts with social groups which were possible. . .An individual could turn to many different

groups for land, political support, and other purposes. His initiative and shrewdness in doing so, together with his industry and judgement, determined his success. (Carlston,1968;p.192).

For the Bushoong of Congo, "work is the means to wealth, and wealth the means to status. They strongly emphasize the value of individual effort and achievement, and they are also prepared to collaborate in numbers over a sustained period when this is necessary to raise output" (Douglas, 1962).

In most other ethnic societies, however, success was due to "help" from ever-present ancestral spirits. Such spirits could be tapped by following certain customs, rituals and family tradition as well as obligations. One of these was helping the family, being kind, being truthful and cooperating with members of the lineage. For example, among the Ga people of Ghana, "life, health and prosperity are the reward of goodness" (Field, 1940:216). These value systems are noteworthy as they are often mislabelled as "Western values." Goodness means two things. First, it is what keeps the peace in the family, or between the families, and enables the members to hold together against misfortune. "It is therefore truth-telling, honesty, generosity, industry, and obedience to authority" (Field, 1940:215). Second, goodness is keeping with family tradition and custom.

Since these beliefs are still held today, the perception of the wealthy in traditional Africa is far different from what is imputed to the peasants by foreigners. The rich are admired and praised for their success in overcoming numerous odds in their occupations. They are often regarded as having vital forces greater than the average person's. Part of their success is attributed to the "blessing or help" they received from the ever-present but invisible ancestral spirits for being of good character. Accordingly, in many ethnic societies, the elders set the wealthy up as role models for the younger generation to emulate although among the Nuer, "wealth did not create deference by others, only envy" (Carlston, 1968:364).

Contrary to foreign misconceptions, the wealthy, in most tribal systems, are not required to share their wealth *equally* with all members of the extended family. Ga men of Ghana would wish this was the case. "The food that his wife grows on her own farm is her own, even when her husband has kindly helped her to hoe her land, and when she markets it the money is hers and no one can touch it" (Field, 1940:60). Furthermore, "a Ga man has no control over his wife's money, but any extra money she can extract from him for herself can never be reclaimed" (Field, 1940:56). Ga men typically lament that: "The women do not respect us; they have more money than we have. Money always spoils respect."[10]

---

[10] Cited by Field (1940:218). The author of this present book, incidentally, is a Ga. It must be pointed out, however, that not all African women are in this enviable position. Nyakyusa women of Tanzania occupied a very subordinant position. "They were not expected to assert

Wealth may be divided up when someone dies and the estate is being distributed according to either custom or a will. But even so, in some tribes, "so far as possible property is not divided" (Field, 1940:45). For example, among the Ga of Ghana, a number of coconut, mango trees, and a cocoa farm remain as one unit. In this way, individual wealth or property may be transformed into corporate wealth (or lineage property) for a person's descendants.

In sum, there was no indigenous Africa law which prohibited individuals from accumulation or acquiring valuable possessions. And there was no law which mandated that wealth, individually acquired, must be shared equally with all kinsmen. There were, however, two important caveats which were operative in many ethnic societies. First, the pursuit of wealth was to occur within certain boundaries prescribed either by religion (Islam) or social norms. For example, it was wrong for an individual to pursue prosperity at the expense or injury of his kinsmen. In other words, a tribesman could not exploit a fellow tribesman for his own advancement. Exploitation of kinsmen, in most indigenous African systems, was a taboo but there were no such prohibitions against the exploitation of other tribesmen.

The Somali, for example, were well aware of the potential conflict between the desire for personal gain and the responsibilities of clanship. They upheld loyalty to one's kin to be more important than the possession of wealth. The fact that wealth was "less important" did not mean the Somali could not accumulate it. They could do so as far as they wished only to the extent that it did not conflict with clan loyalty. The Somali believe that, "although riches, if wisely spent, bring renown and influence, pride, dignity and 'name' are in the end more important" (Lewis, 1962). The Konso of Ethiopia have a similar attitude toward wealth:

> Accumulation of wealth was highly regarded, but wealth must not be 'misused' against co-members of one's village or other social group. . . *The Konso system allows for individual industry and material development, but provides checks and balances to ensure that the less favored individual has reasonable opportunity for competition with those who are better off*. There is opportunity for material increase, but only within the framework of the social controls and values of the society as a whole. . . Members may go as far toward the accumulation of wealth or personal comforts, provided that in so doing they do not come into conflict with the community (Kluckhohn, 1962). (Italics mine).

Thus, one would generally not see tribesmen competing against one another, except in a few systems such as the Igbo and the Nuer. That

themselves but instead to show obedience and respect and to display a submissive manner. They were meekly to comply with the demands of their husbands" (Carlston, 1968:338).

however did not mean competition was totally absent in indigenous Africa. Only the arena of competition shifted. Competition among various kinship groups and societies was very keen, evidenced by tribal rivalries, feuds and wars, whereas intra-tribal competition was generally absent.[11]

Second, in most tribal systems, the rich were generally free to keep their wealth. It was not expropriated by their chief for equal distribution to all tribesmen. The rich were, however, expected to contribute to the family pot and help their less fortunate kinsmen, which is still true today. Most successful Africans abroad and at home are expected to help. Some do so by sending remittances.[12] But the exact amount of help and to whom was left to their discretion. It is true that the rich were harassed by a large contingent of kinsmen. But they were also at liberty to manufacture as many excuses as they could. Most Africans today know of tight-fisted rich relatives.

Education

Without any written literature, the natives of Africa relied upon oracles, proverbs, storytelling and music to educate and inculcate in their children a strong sense of community and other values. Around the ages of six and seven, primary education included storytelling, mental arithmetic, community songs and dances, learning the names of various birds and animals, the identification of poisonous snakes, local plants and trees, and how to run and climb swiftly when pursued by dangerous animals. Child training also included knowing and associating with members of one's age group.

There was much reliance on proverbs to inculcate various beliefs. For example, the Fanti proverb: *"Se amma wo nyenko centwa akron a wo so irrentwa du,"* meaning, "If you do not allow your neighbor to have nine you will not have ten." This was to instill the spirit of cooperation. Kenyatta (1938) summed it best,

> Before the advent of the white man the institution of serfdom and wage workers were unknown to the Gikuyu people. The tribal

---

[11] This has important implications for a modern African government. To the extent that the tribes perceive differences between themselves and have traditionally competed against one another for military supremacy, a program of "forced collectivism" that is envisaged under "socialism" is most likely to fail. Far from being a liability, inter-tribal competition is in fact an asset. All it takes is channelling the rivalries from the destructive, military arena to the productive economic sphere. Let the tribe which claims to be superior prove its mettle by the number of hospitals, markets, roads, schools, bridges and agricultural fairs that it has and not by the number of soldiers or spears it possesses.

[12] Note however that this obligation does not require them to steal. In the indigenous system of values, stealing from the "other tribe" was considered a patriotic duty. Of course, today, the government can scarcely be regarded as the "other tribe." Unfortunately, today's corrupt elites cannot make this distinction.

customary law recognized the freedom and independence of every member of the tribe. At the same time, all were bound up socially, politically, economically, and religiously by a system of collective activities and mutual help, extending from the family group to the tribe. The Weltanshauung of the Gikuyu people is: "*Kanya gatuune ne mwamoka-nera*" ("Give and take"). For economic and political reasons, every family was expected to be able to protect its own interests and at the same time help to protect the common interests of the tribe from outside attack.

Proverbs also serve to communicate indigenous beliefs and values. Accordingly, African proverbs provide a rich source of information on indigenous value systems. Articles of morality, ethics, thrift, and industry are often hidden in these proverbs. These may have been missed by many foreign researchers because of language barriers, leading to much distortion of the native system of values.

Laziness, in most parts of traditional Africa, is frowned upon. In fact, the lazy are shunned and chastised by the elders. The reason is simple: a tribe composed of lazy people would become extinct or fall prey to a warrior tribe. Valor and diligence are qualities most stressed by the elders for survival. The Fanti of Ghana have many proverbs that abjure laziness. One says, "If you depend on someone else for breakfast, you go without food." In modern parlance: "If you depend upon someone for foreign aid or a welfare check, you will go without food." Another Fanti proverb says: *Obi nhuhu na obi nkeka* - No one prepares the food for another to eat. According to the Vais of Sierra Leone, "the lazy man is always left behind" (Ellis, 1914:153).

The Ga of Ghana have a way of punishing the lazy ones to instill industry. Boys share meals with their fathers, but they may not touch the meat or fish until an elder hands them a piece. "A rude, lazy boy can expect little or no meat; a helpful, pleasant, popular boy receives plenty. Girls are similarly treated by their mothers and aunts. Any child's protein intake is in direct proportion to his popularity (obedience and industriousness)" (Field, 1940:61).

Clearly, industry, the work ethic and other social values are not uniquely "Western inventions." Jackson (1982) noted:

> *Morgoye* denotes altruism and magnanimity, virtues which the Kuranko set at the foundation of the social order. Of a generous person, mindful of others, who gives without ulterior motive, it is said *ke morgo* ('this is a person'). If a person behaves in some exemplary way, people may comment *morgo le kela* ('this is true person') and a magnanimous person will receive the remark *ke l morgoye ti fo* ('this one's personhood is beyond the telling'). A true person thus does more than merely conform to social rules; he realizes or exemplifies social ideals (p.15).

The Kuranko also emphasize respect (*lembe* and *obiliye*). Besides regard for convention, *lembe* also means consideration or being mindful of others. Sociability is also stressed through giving and sharing:

> One who enjoys the company of others is a 'sweet person' (*morgo di keye*). An unsociable person is considered to be 'not a person' (*morgo ma kela*), or is called a 'bush person' (*fira morgo*). A mean person is known as a 'broken down person' (*morgo kore*). . .Sometimes the phrase *morgo kende ma* ('a sick person') is used to describe someone who set himself apart from others (Jackson, 1982; p.16).

The following proverbs of the Vais of Sierra Leone, taken from Ellis (1914), give some indication of some aspects of indigenous value systems:

> "A little rain everyday will make the rivers swell." This is used not only to encourage people to save but also to persevere little by little to accomplish great deeds.

> "A snake cannot outrun its head." It suggests that some final authority or judge exists. This is used when dealing with pretentious, boastful and incorrigible braggarts.

> "Your food is close to your stomach but you must put it in your mouth first." This is told to individuals too impatient to follow native procedures and are constantly looking for shortcuts.

The Yoruba of Nigeria have this one: "However small the needle, a chicken cannot swallow it." It conveys the message that an apparently weaker individual can prove difficult to vanquish. (Bascom, 1984; p.98).[13]

Story-telling is another means by which Africans inculcate values. Animals feature prominently in African children stories. For example in Ashanti stories, the spider (*anansi*) plays various roles: the star, the villain and the bungling idiot. In some stories, he is clever and cunning; in others, he falls victim to his own mischief ("hoist with his own petard"). Among the Kuranko of Sierra Leone, the hare is also associated with cleverness, ingenuity and adroitness (*hankili*) and cunning (*kio*). The hyena is stupid (*hankili ma*), clumsy, inflexible and lacking in foresight (Jackson, 1982; p.91).

Ordinarily, the stories are long but the children are supposed to listen attentively to extract any morals. If they fail to absorb any lessons, the stories

---

[13] Since proverbs are important in African cultural systems perhaps one should be coined for modern African leaders: "A goat that butts its tail hurts its own tail." An African dictator who oppresses his people oppresses himself.

are repeated. Upon absorption, they are subsequently instructed to pass them on to their brethren. Consider the following, taken from Ellis (1914):

> Two men lived in a neighborhood and each of them heard that the other was a big story-teller. One day they met at a big dinner (and challenged one another). 'Things are small now, but when God created the world everything was big. I myself saw a big bird passing and the bird was so big that it took seven days before just its neck had passed.' The other man braced up, saying: 'I think you are right, because I saw one tree, and it was so large that God gave all the angels an ax and told them to go down and cut it, and they cut on it for six months and did not cut it down.' 'Oh! it is not so,' said the first man; 'one angel is able to take this whole world, and what kind of a tree could it be that all the angels could cut on it for six months and not cut it down?' The second man answered: 'Well, if God did not make this tree, where would your bird have to sit down. This is the very tree God made for your bird' (p.202).

> Two story-tellers met one day and began to tell stories. Each of them thought that he could excel the other. The first man said, 'I will tell you the story of what I saw. One day I went into the field and saw two birds fighting. One bird swallowed the other, and then in turn was swallowed by the other bird, so that the two birds swallowed each other.' 'Oh! that's nothing,' said the second man. 'One day I was going out to the field and I saw a man on the road who had cut off his own head and had it in his mouth eating it.'

The Ashanti of Ghana tell this story to their children which may be of value to modern African elites and leaders. It is culled from Appiah (1967:37):

> There was once a country which had many small kingdoms including the kingdoms of Yaw, Kwasi, Kwaku, Kwadwo and Kwabena.

> King Kwadwo heard innumerable tales about the prosperity of King Kwabena and his kingdom and how wonderful everything was in his kingdom and how happy his people were.

> After a time King Kwadwo called his councillors together and asked them why it was that everyone brought tales of King Kwabena's kingdom and what it was that made it better than all the other kingdoms. The councillors shook their heads and pleaded ignorance. So King Kwadwo decided to visit Kwabena's kingdom and find out for himself.

When King Kwadwo reached the Kingdom of Kwabena he was greeted with great pomp and ceremony. The people all came to cheer him and there was much drumming and dancing. He saw how happy and prosperous the kingdom looked.

King Kwadwo asked questions about how the kingdom was ruled. But try as he could, King Kwadwo could not see how the governance differed from his own. At last, when King Kwadwo was having a banquet with King Kwabena, he noticed that the King ate with his left hand — his right arm being covered with his cloth. As time went on he came to the conclusion that it must be this eating with the left hand which had been responsible for the good rule and happiness in the kingdom. He returned home determined to imitate this habit so that he too might be famous.

When King Kwadwo arrived, he was welcomed by his councillors. At once, he beat the gong-gong and called all the people together. He ordered that from then on, all the people in his realm must eat with their left hands.

But an old, old man was not pleased with the order. Slowly the old man hobbled up the the King. 'I cannot agree, O King!' he said — and the people gasped at his audacity.

The King was angry but considering the old man's age only demanded an explanation. The old man replied: 'When you visited the Kingdom of Kwabena, Your Majesty, did you not enquire why he used his left hand? Did you not ask him for the reason? Surely you did not come to this serious decision without asking the question?'

The King was now very angry: 'Why do I need to ask? Is not the prosperity of his kingdom proof enough? Since this was the only difference I could see between our kingdoms I knew that it must be the reason.'

'Alas,' said the old man, 'that you should not copy things without asking for the reason and knowing the circumstances. King Kwabena's right arm was bitten by a lion when he was young. Over time, his arm withered and he lost his hand. That is why King Kwadwo eats with his left hand. He has no right hand!'

The councillors who had heard the tale turned to the King. 'King Kwadwo,' they said, 'you have wronged us. You have ordered your people to do a difficult thing without knowing the reason why. You have copied blindly the acts of another man. You are not fit to be King.'

King Kwadwo knew not what to say. With the people behind them his councillors dethroned him and asked the old man to act as regent until they could find a wiser and more suitable ruler.

There are many modern African heads of state who are not fit to be presidents "for copying blindly." Rome has a basilica; so too must Ivory Coast. Eastern Europe had one-party state systems; so too must Burundi, Kenya, Mozambique, Somalia, Tanzania, Zaire and numerous African countries. The Soviet Union has statues of Marx and Lenin; so too must Angola, Benin, Ethiopia and other African countries. Cuba has People's Defense Committees; so too must Ghana. The list is endless.

Yoruba children's education stresses economic and psychological independence, but not social independence (Bascom, 1984; p.58). The child learns to respect the bonds of kinship, to perform economic activities, to watch out for his own interests, to make decisions for himself. From the beginning of imitative play there is a gradual transition to the adult activities which the child will perform throughout the rest of his life.

What the natives teach their children can be quite substantial. A recent full-page advertisement placed by the Chevron Corporation in *Newsweek* magazine was quite instructive:

CAN SOMEONE WHO HAS NEVER SEEN A SCHOOL TEACH AMERICANS ABOUT EDUCATION?

THEY CANNOT READ. They cannot write. Yet, the Baka Pygmies of Cameroon can teach us volumes about their rain forest home.

In fact, the average Baka's knowledge would rival a university degree. But perhaps the most fascinating thing we're learning is about learning itself. About a heritage of teaching. And passing on of knowledge. Because while it may seem an unlikely source, the Baka people and their ways could prove helpful in American search for more effective ways to educate young people.

APPEARANCE OF PARADISE

As many as 120 inches of rain per year can fall down through the towering canopy of a tropical forest. But while botanical riches abound, the animals are elusive. The vegetation is often poisonous.

And both plants and animals are constantly evolving new defenses to survive. An evolutionary battleground. It is here the Baka live. And their children must grow and learn. This is their classroom.

COURSES IN BIOLOGY, BOTANY, AND CHEMISTRY

Enlisting the chemical defenses of the forest is the genius of the Baka. Children quickly learn how to locate and prepare certain poisons to paralyse fish. How to crush certain seeds, making lethal paste to tip their wooden arrows. How to extract substances from the forest for a variety of medicines. And how to indentify by name hundreds of species of trees and plants.

HANDED DOWN FROM THE MINDS OF THEIR PARENTS

A Baka father carefully explains how a chimp hunts termites. 'A chimp gets the termite out with a leaf stem, like this. The termite hangs onto the stem and the chimp eats it.' And a Baka mother reminds her young of the correct way to contribute. From food preparation to looking after siblings. Baka children are, in a sense, constantly in school.

Traditional knowledge. Understanding nature and respecting the environment. Ideals that are precious to the Baka and strongly supported by the people of Chevron (*Newsweek*, Jan 16, 1989; p.l4).

Modern Africans could also use this sort of education. Modern education in Africa equips students with "foreign tastes" and an inimitable propensity to imitate. Many a traditional ruler and elder have lamented the disrespectful modern students with no morals. In fact, the Vais of Sierra Leone coined a proverb for precisely this situation. If, after scrounging resources for his education, a child returns to the village a hopeless disaster, disappointed Vais elders would look at him, shake their heads and say: "The moon shines so brightly but it is still dark in some places."

Take one look at modern African elites. Three decades of independence, after enormous resources spent on "education," modern Africa is a disaster, economically and politically. As one irate Nigerian, Peter Senam Anyomi of Lagos, wrote:

In almost three decades of independence, Africa can hardly boast of an instance where the incumbent government or leader has been removed peacefully via the ballot box. Hence the 'bullet' rather than the 'ballot' has become the only effective means of removing many an inept and undesirable ruler. But as we march toward the 21st century, Africa's youth are saying enough is enough. The old rulers should give way to more dynamic and progressive younger men. After all the throne is not the personal property of any ruler (*New African*, August 1989; p.40).

Summary

The discussion above was intended to offer some glimpses of the social and psychological make-up of the African peasant. Though by no means complete, the general picture that emerges is one of an individual imbued with a strong sense of kinship, community identity and responsibility. Within the community he enjoys personal freedom, independence and respect for his property rights. Native courts uphold and enforce these rights. However, his individual rights are subservient to those of the community as a whole. The degree of independence or subservience of individual rights varies from one tribe to another. For example, though infused with strong kinship ties, the Igbo are also known to be very individualistic. If may sound like an oxymoron but the following popular joke exaggerates the differences Nigerians see among themselves:

One day, a Hausaman, Yorubaman and an Igbo man set off on a jaunt. Soon they came to a wild mango tree laden with well-ripened fruits.

'Allah be praised,' exclaimed the Hausaman. 'How nice it will be for me to share these fruits with my kith and kin. The Yorubaman felt the same. 'I will take these to my wives and children,' he said. But the Igbo said nothing, he was busy working out how much money he could make if he picked the whole tree and took the crop to market.

But Igbos, of course, see things differently. 'The real story is like this,' said one who heard it. 'One day an Hausaman, Yorubaman and an Igbo set off on a trip and came across a wild mango tree laden with fruit. The Hausaman said, 'These fruits look lovely, let us pray that Allah makes them fall for us.' 'And the Yorubaman said, 'I will go home and seek the help of my kinsmen to help me climb up and pick some. The Igboman simply rolled up his sleeves, climbed the tree and after much sweat and toil picked the lot, but when he climbed back onto the ground he found his two friends were already arguing and politicking about sharing the harvest.' (Told in *New African*, August, 1988; p.34).

The indigenous philosophy is not one of complete individualism. Nor is it total communism or socialism. The modern definition of socialism - as state ownership of the means of production and control over distribution of goods

- does not exist in traditional Africa. The means of production, except possibly land, is privately owned. The chief or the tribal government certainly does not supervise equitable distribution of goods to each according to his/her needs. Within the confines of religion and social norms, the individual is at complete liberty to pursue his/her own interests and economic activities. Some succeed; others fail. Consequently, there are inequalities of wealth in traditional African society.

The rich enjoy high status and are expected to help their unlucky kinsmen, but the chief does not impose heavy taxes on the rich for transfer to the poor. This does not mean the poor are abandoned. There are voluntary and self-help organizations which help the poor. One such organization was the *compin* of Sierra Leone (Iliffe, 1987; p.107).

It is easier to describe what the indigenous system is not than what it is. There is certainly some degree of both individualism and communalism.[14] Perhaps, the term INDINALISM may be suggested.

---

[14] Oguah (1984) suggested "Libertarian Basicalism."

CHAPTER 2

THE INDIGENOUS LEGAL INSTITUTIONS

Indeed, Africa is one of the homes of advanced legal institutions.
Perhaps the most famous of these institutions are the courts still
found among the Bantu states of the southern third of the
continent.

- Bohannan, 1968:199.

The previous chapter dealt with the social organization and units of
traditional African society (the family, kinship groups, the village, the town
and the larger polity). In addition, the belief systems of the African, the
realation of the individual to society and the educational process were
examined. This chapter is devoted to conflict resolution, legal systems and
jurisprudence in traditional Africa.

A. NATIVE COURTS AND CUSTOMARY LAWS

Disputes arise in any family or society with regards to property, and
African societies were no exception. To resolve these disputes, various
mechanisms and institutions were created. However within the traditional
African *modus operandi*, there was an additional unique dimension. Individual
attachment to lineages and latent groups of solidarity always carried the
potential risk of transforming personal disputes into broader group conflicts
as was often the case among the Nuer and the Ganda. Consequently, great
emphasis was placed on peaceful resolution of disputes and the promotion of
social harmony while upholding the principles of fairness, custom and
tradition.

Among the Arusha of Tanzania, "there was a very strongly held value that
disputes should be settled peacefully by persuasion and by resort to the
established procedures for settlement" (Carlston, 1968:310). Similarily, the

Tallensi of Ghana abhorred killings and violent resolutions of conflicts. For precisely this reason, they celebrated the *Golib* festival, during which all feuds and hostilities between clans were prohibited. This festival emphasized "the themes of food, harmony, fecundity, and the common interests of the people as a whole" (Carlston, 1968:109).

Cosmological factors provided additional reason for the general emphasis on peaceful resolution of conflicts. It may be recalled that Africans stressed the maintenance of order and harmony in the universe which consisted of the sky, the earth and the world. Order and harmony in the universe required the maintenance of corresponding conditions within the various kinship groups in the ethnic society as well. Gikuyu elders considered as their primary duty the prevention of strife between members of a lineage or between lineages and the prevention of both from resorting to supernatural powers and open hostilities.

The maintenance of peace within most African communities followed four principles. The first was settlement of disputes by deliberation and discussion, rather than by force. The second was the correction of wrongdoing by compensation except in serious offenses such as murder. The third was adjudication and assessment by elders who were considered to be impartial. The fourth was fairness. These principles were upheld by the use of courts, their constitution and the right to appeal.

Conflicts or nefarious activities were generally classifed into "private" and "public" matters. For the Ashanti, "private" offenses (*efisem*) concerned the living only, and were deemed to affect only the social relations of persons or groups living in the community. "Public" offenses (*oman akyiwade*) affected the relationships between the community on the one hand and the chief or the ancestors on the other (religious offenses).

Private disputes arising within the family were settled by its head. If the case was unresolvable or if the aggrieved party failed to obtain satisfactory resolution, the case could be appealed to the lineage head, called *mutongoria wa kithaka* among the Mbeere of Kenya (Glazier, 1985).

The lineage head would assess the substance of the case and, if it merited further deliberation, would empanel a group of elders as a family court to adjudicate. Such family courts usually deliberated on disputes involving a father and his son or between a man and his wife.

In the family court,

> The matter was, in effect, settled by arbitration. A pacification or conciliation (*mpata*) was claimed from the offender for the injured man, who was expected to accept it, not only as proof that the injury has been annulled but also as a sign that friendly relations had been restored between the parties. The pacification was small: a fowl or a few eggs for the injured man to 'wash his soul' (*adware ne kra*) so that his feelings might be assuaged. In more serious offenses gold-dust to the value of 7

shillings or at most 10 shillings was paid as pacification (Busia, 1968; p.51).

Carlston (1968) found that the decisions of the Asante lineage head "in such disputes were not arbitrary commands of patriarchal authority but were reached after consultations with his household and were supported by religious sanctions" (p.125). This was also observed among the Mbeere of Kenya. Consider the following 1970 family court case that is paraphrased from Glazier (1985; p.146):

A man called Ireri physically assaulted his father, Njiru, and smashed his gourd of beer. Thereupon, Njiru cursed his son, not only wishing him physical death, but also his social death with the saying that Ireri would produce no sons.[1] Both men had been drinking and on a number of occasions engaged in vexatious verbal exchange and fired arrows at each other before the case came to the family court. The elders realized that *both* men were at fault and ruled that the son, Ireri, should be fined one goat. The father, upon receiving it, should swear an oath to the effect that he would not curse his son again. Njenga, one of the elders explained the decision thus:

> We have decided this because you beat the old man, although we know that Njiru made a mistake in throwing soil (issuing verbal insults). Even if you appeal anywhere else you will be told to provide a goat because you beat your father. Even if you go to London, you'll be told to bring a goat. With the goat, Njiru will take the oath, 'may this oath kill me if I throw soil and curse my son' (Glazier, 1985: 146).

The right of appeal was widely respected in traditional Africa. Ordinarily to keep peace in the family, Ireri might decline to exercise this right. Had he wanted to, however, he could have appealed the verdict to the village or the chief's court.

When a dispute arose between persons of *different* lineages, however, a slightly different procedure was adopted. The aggrieved person could, in Ashanti, submit the matter for arbitration by any respected member of the community, say the head of his lineage who would call upon the head of the offender's lineage to settle the matter. They might call in other elders to help ensure impartial arbitration, as kinsmen of the offender were expected to help put the matter right. Similarly, members of the injured person's lineage were expected to see that the injury was repaired. The elders decided who was in the wrong and settled how much compensation was to be paid

---

[1] This is deemed a serious curse since in many other African tribes such as the Mossi of Ghana, a man without sons is considered to have been a failure (Skinner, 1961).

to the injured person. A second course of action was open by which the matter could be submitted to the chief's court for arbitration.

Each state (an ethnic group with an organized bureaucracy and a central authority) possessed a system of courts. Stateless societies resolved cases in a treaty-making process, akin to the moots of 13th century England whereby Anglo-Saxon communities settled their disputes by meeting outside, under the shade of a tree. Similarly in most stateless African societies, disputes were settled informally rather than by a specifically constituted body.

Jurisprudence In Stateless Societies

The Kpelle of Liberia had an informal dispute-settlement forum known as a *berei mu meni saa* (a "house of palaver" or moot). It was an ad hoc council of kinsmen and neighbors of two complainants who gathered to solve disputes involving marital matters and other domestic problems.

The moot was held not in a courthouse but in someone's home. There was open and full participation by all those attending. The person found at fault at the end of the deliberations, rendered an apology and presented the aggrieved person with small gifts. At the end of the moot, all shared a drink. Similar moots were used by the Somali and the San of the Kalahari.[2]

The legal system of the Arusha of Tanzania has been described as "Africa's finest and worthy of emulation" (Carlston, 1968). The absence of centralized authority in Arusha society, its highly individualistic nature, its egalitarianism, the absence of coercive measures against norm violations, the absence of even the typical African belief that the ancestral spirits would punish wrongdoing, created an unusual problem in tension management in the society. "The resulting system for the control of conflict by the peaceful settlement of disputes was an extraordinary achievement. It was a complex system of interdependent parts of much ingenuity and sophistication" (Carlston, 1968:323).

The whole Arusha people were divided into two moieties or divisions, each of which was composed of two clans. Each clan was divided into a pair of clan-sections, which were in turn divided into a pair of sub-clans. The sub-clans were divided into two *ilwasheta* (singular, *olwashe*), composed of the various maximal lineages.

Each maximal lineage was composed of a number of inner lineages, each

---

[2] Gibbs (1965) argued moots are better able to deal with marital disputes and bring reconciliation between spouses than courts. "The court, by its formal nature, tends to drive the husband and wife farther apart. But the moot's procedures have many features of group psychotherapy, such as catharsis, and commonly result in a consensual solution that is agreed to by the couple, who can start off on a new footing with the insights gained in the group session" (p.226).

of which was divided into two *ilwasheta*. Each of such two divisions of the inner lineage was not divided into two parts but simply consisted of a number of families. Each family, however, was divided into two *ilwashuta*

The pairing process appeared in substantially all the important groupings of the Arusha and provided a frame of reference for perceiving the character of disputes in regards to their relevance to the social structure. When a dispute could not be settled at the lineage level, which was often the case, an Arusha would try to reach an *olwashe* or the division which had the closest ties of kinship and geographical proximity. He would request the assistance of spokesmen, or notables, who had the best success in moots. The other disputant would do the same. If the dispute was between residents of a parish, the case was taken to the parish assembly for adjudication but a moot was used for those between members of different lineages.

At the parish assembly, the plaintiff would present his case, the defendant would follow and each would be questioned by anyone who so wished. A party's supporters gathered around him, giving verbal approval or disapproval of varying degrees of loudness on his behalf to points made in the proceedings. "The vigorousness of such support was an important factor in reaching a favorable settlement" (Carlston, 1968:320). In reaching a settlement, the supporting group played a crucial role. The leader of the group sought the settlement itself and the rest of the group exerted pressure on the litigant to accept a reasonable settlement acceptable to the opposing side.

The settlement process was partly an informal consensus in that discussion took place until an agreement was reached. It was partly a bargaining process in that offers and counter-offers were made until agreed terms were reached. It was also a negotiating process partly because persuasion, artifice, and stratagem were employed to reach an agreement. At the same time, however, it constituted an adversary process as each disputant was represented by spokesmen or counsellors. "There is no process in western society closely comparable to the dispute-settlement procedures utilized by the Arusha. . .One is struck with the comparability of the Arusha settlement procedure with international law and the diplomatic settlement of disputes in the international society today" (Carlston, 1968:322).[3]

---

[3] Carlston argued further that,

The experience of the Arusha points to a possible new model of an international society of peace. One of the currently held models of a world order of peace is a monolithic world government which would possess sufficient power of forceful coercion to prevent any one state or group of states from resorting to war. The other is universal disarmament. The new model suggested by the Arusha would be a pluralistic world order, in which states would have overlapping memberships in a wide variety of international organizations and forms of international cooperation so

Carlston identified several attributes which accounted for the effica-
ciousness of the Arusha system in arriving at peaceful settlement of disputes.
Among them were:

1.   The Arusha society was so organized that its members belonged to a
number of overlapping and complementary groups. This lessened the
tendency to perceive disputes in rigid terms and to diminish the likelihood
of inter-group conflict developing in situations of interpersonal conflict.
Stability is thereby promoted.

2.   Parties to a dispute in Arusha had less power at their disposal than the
other actors engaged in the mediation process. This made the disputants
more willing to accept compromises or settlements.

3.   In an Arusha litigation, there were elements of fairness and adequacy
of hearing, presentation of pertinent evidence, and search for fact consensus.

4.   There were people skilled in the performance in leading the
mediation process, negotiating, and arriving at a settlement acceptable to
both sides.

Jurisprudence In States

In African societies with central authority (states), however, there were
formally constituted courts to settle disputes. Ellis (1914) observed the
existence of such courts among the Vais of Sierra Leone at the turn of the
century.

In every Vais town or village, there was a court, of which the chief was
the judge. Murder, treason, and witchcraft were punishable by death,
according to Ellis (1914). Crimes such as rape, abduction, seduction,
adultery, arson, and theft were punishable by fines or imprisonment. The
tendency was to compel offenders to pay costs and a certain amount in goods
to the injured party as in civil cases. In criminal matters appeals could be
taken up as in civil matters.

> A person desiring to enter a suit calls upon the chief and presents
> him with a 'dash' called 'cold water'. This 'dash' may consist of rum,
> gin, tobacco and so on. After the 'dash' the chief hears the
> statement of the case. When it is finished, he sends his messenger
> with his cane or whip and summons his assistant and the elders of
> the town. He summons the defendant, and next the medicine man
> to administer the oaths to the witnesses in the case. After the taking
> of the oaths, the testimony begins. During the hearing of the
> testimony, the members of the court ask such questions as they

that they would value peace more than war - at least to the extent of cutting down
very markedly and in an increasing degree their resort to war (p.336).

desire. When the testimony is finished, every member of the court, except the chief, votes and a majority rules. When the case is a tie, each side pays half of the cost. . .If the plaintiff wins the case, the judgment is that the defendant shall pay all costs, pay the amount adjudged to be due the plaintiff and in addition give him one gown (Ellis, 1914:84).

Similar procedures were observed in other West African societies; for example, among the Fanti, the Asante, the Igbo and the Yoruba. Casely Hayford (1911) reported that:

At a 'palaver,' which is the word for a suit before the Court, the King sits with his Councillors; and the Court is an open one, which any member of the community may attend. There is no secrecy about the proceedings. The complainant states his case as fully as he can, and he is given a patient hearing. In the course of his statement questions are freely asked him by the Councillors, and doubtful points elucidated. The same process is gone through with the defendant, and with the witnesses called by either party. The Council then retires to deliberate upon the facts, and its verdict is given by the King's Linguist.

For the Fanti, Christensen (1958) noted:

From before control by Europeans down to the present, the Fanti (of Ghana) have had a rather complex system of courts and hearings. Presiding at any dispute or trial may be a group of elders, a chief and elders, or a panel of chiefs, depending on the nature of the case. A dispute, after submission to a group of elders for arbitration, may be further referred to a higher authority, such as a sub-chief or the paramount chief of a state. The latter, known as the *omanhene*, was the ultimate authority. The plaintiff and defendant generally present their own case to the court, call witnesses and cross-examine those who give testimony for the opposition. During a hearing, proverbs are quoted by the litigants. Proverbs may be regarded as the verbalization of social norms or 'laws' which govern interpersonal relations.

Many proverbs may be regarded as legal maxims since they are utilized most frequently in disputes. For example, a request for the postponement of a case may be supported by the statement, 'it takes time to make a dress for the hunchback.' Another proverb often quoted to indicate prior ownership in a land dispute is, 'The bathroom was wet before the rain fell.'

The hierarchy of Akan courts was studied by Arhin (1985). The first was the extended family court known as *badwa*, and the members known as *badwafo*, which consisted of heads of the households of the family groups, the heads of other family groups with whom certain relationships from intermarriage or occupying the same *brono* or ward; and respected heads of other family groups. The *badwa*, an arbitration gathering, settled internal disputes between members of the family groups. These included, for example, theft; certain kinds of abuse, such as slander and tale bearing; cases regarding property and pawning; loans, surety, and recovery of debt; rights to land, inheritance to property, quarrels between married couples, adultery, and petty squabbles that did not affect the village as a whole. These disputes were referred to as *afisem*.

> The settlement of a household case aimed at *reconciling the parties and ensuring good relations within and between the family groups*. *Mpata*, a reconciliation fee, normally in the form of a drink, accompanied by an apology, was given to the offended. Both parties then swore by the elders present that they would thereafter live at peace with each other (Arhin, 1985; p.25) (Italics mine).

The *badwafor* relied upon the respect due to the family elders and other elders and the force of public opinion for compliance of any judgment reached. Those who refused to comply with their decisions would be disowned by their close relatives.

Disputes between members of the different family groups which could not be settled by a joint *badwa* of the family groups concerned, were referred to the *Odikro's nhyiamu* (village chief's court). The *odikro's* court also settled cases that involved rules made by the council. There were village *afisem*, which concerned such issues as clearing paths leading to the main farming areas and the performance of ceremonies in connection with village shrines.

> The settlement of disputes at the *odikro's* court differed from that at the family group level in that the former was supported by the physical force at the disposal of the village as a whole. Offenders found at fault could be compelled to comply with the decisions of the court. In cases of refusal to comply, or if a party was dissatisfied with the court's decision, the oath of the *ohene* (king) was sworn, and the case transferred to the divisional court. The case then ceased to be an *afisem* of the village and became a matter for the division (Arhin, 1985; p.22).

The divisional court, or *ohene's* court, was a court of "original jurisdiction" as well as an appeal court. It could hear cases which originated in the division and appeal cases brought up from the *odikro's* court. At the apex of the hierarchy was the *omanhene's* court, the final court of appeal.

Public offenses, some of which carried the death penalty, were tried at any level of jurisdiction and decisions could be appealed. Such offenses, called *akyiwadee* (taboos) by the Akan, included: murder, (*awudie*), homicide, suicide; certain sexual offenses, such as incest, sexual intercourse with a woman in her menstrual period; with a half-sister by one father, and with a woman in the bush; assaults on the ruler; theft of royal regalia or material symbols of the state and the property of the state shrine, such as sword, a stool, a quantity of gold dust or nugget; and treason, which included breaking the oath of allegiance to a ruler or the cowardice of a warleader in battle.

The trial of public offenders in Akan courts proceeded as follows. The similarity between the Akan and the Shona described below should be noted.

> The parties made preliminary payments, *dwomtadie*, a kind of earnest money. Witnesses were named and *sent into concealment*, and, after the parties had made full statements in court and been questioned by the court, were brought to testify under oath. They were then questioned by the parties to the dispute and the court panel, after which the court retired to consider its verdict which was delivered by an *okyeame*, a spokesman of the ruler, who acted as interpreter. The court was concerned with reconciling the men to one another but above all with pacifying the spirits disturbed when a breach of the taboos was committed through the offense under adjudication, or through the swearing of an oath, and doing justice to the wronged party. The hearing and resolution of public offenses entailed repairing the damage done to society as a result of the alienation of the spirits due to the offense (Arhin, 1985; p.26).

In the Igbo judicial system, the nuclear family was the first court over which the head presided, settling minor cases between members. According to Olaniyan (1985),

> The lineage heads settled cases involving fighting, assault, petty theft, family disputes, adultery and even divorce. The village court handled inter-lineage cases over which the lineages involved could not reach agreement. Both plaintiff and defendant paid settlement fees in kind although the plaintiff paid the summons fees. The innocent party had a part of its settlement fees refunded while the guilty party forfeited its fees and was subject to further fines in line with the gravity of the offence. . . The right of appeal was always upheld (p.28).

The Yoruba legal system was similarly structured. Disputes which could not be settled within the clan and those involving different clans were referred to the ward chief. If the judgment of the ward chief was not acceptable to one of the parties, the case was referred to the palace chiefs who met daily outside the palace gate and jointly with the town chiefs every fourth day (*ojo Oja Ife*). If the matter was serious and involved members of Ife clans, the town chiefs were summoned, regardless of what day it was. Their decision was referred to the *Oni* (king) for his approval and if no decision could be reached, the case was referred to the *Ogboni* House. Beyond this, the last court of appeal, which rarely met, was held at the palace and included the town and palace chiefs, other *Ogboni* members and the *Oni* himself (Bascom, 1984; p.38).[4]

Bascom (1984:44) continued that:

> The Bale serves as the principal judge of the compound, presiding when disputes are brought before him, but cases are heard by all the elders and by any other members of the compound who may be present. If a titled chief lives in the compound, he is also responsible for settling disputes. A husband is responsible for settling quarrels within his own family; but if he is unsuccessful or if an argument involves members of two different families within the compound, it is referred to the Bale. Any cases which he cannot settle may be referred to the town chiefs, but every effort is made to reach a peaceful settlement within the compound.

Generally, the elders and chiefs would make decisions based on a knowledge of the traditional way of life, circumspection, and adherence to the truth. Because of the more inclusive rights and obligations resulting from these principles, the Sidamo tribe of Ethiopia even allow "strangers" (those outside the lineage or clan) to participate in court cases and in general decision-making processes involving property (Hammer, 1970). Gibbs (1965) noted that, "During the entire court proceedings among the Bantu Tiriki of western Kenya, all adult men and elderly women present may ask the judicial elders for permission to express their opinions on the case, or add further evidence, and the elders may themselves call on anyone, including women and children, to present testimony" (p.49).

With the Ganda of Uganda, the following is pertinent:

> In each court case, a fee of twenty cowry-shells was paid by the plaintiff when stating his case, and a further fee of a goat and a barkcloth, before the accused was summoned to appear in court; the accused also paid a goat and barkcloth before the case was tried. These sums were called the *bitebi*. When sentence was given, the judge fined the offender two goats and one barkcloth, which were given to the plaintiff in addition to the whole amount which he

---

[4] It is important to note the difference between the elaborate system of appeals in many indigenous legal systems with the public tribunals established by some "modern and educated" African revolutionary leaders and which allow no rights of appeal.

claimed from the defendant. When an appeal was made from one court to another, ending in the *Katikiro*'s (the highest court of appeal), the plaintiff paid the fee of twenty cowry-shells, a goat, and barkcloth to each of the lower courts, but to the *Katikiro*'s court he paid ten goats and five barkcloths (Carlston, 1968:254).

Among the Tutsi of Rwanda, court hearings were held in the open air. The complainant aired his grievance first, followed by the defendant. Their respective witnesses and supporters spoke in the same sequence. At the end, the judge or his associates repeated the main arguments and tried to find inconsistencies. Judgment would then be rendered. If unacceptable, the case might be heard several times or appealed to a higher (town) court. The Somali, however, allowed only a maximum of three hearings after which the case was declared insoluble (Gibbs, 1965).

Moving down to southern Africa, one finds what Bohannan (1968) considers to be Africa's finest:

Indeed, Africa is one of the homes of advanced legal institutions. Perhaps the most famous of these institutions are the courts still found among the Bantu states of the southern third of the continent (p. 199).

In these states, the local or provincial chief was one of a number of judges on a large and inclusive bench. The bench included representatives of all important social groups of the community. The judges formed a regular and pronounced hierarchy, and were seated in a row or an arc. The provincial chief sat in the middle; at his immediate right was the second most senior person and at his left the third most senior, and so on until the whole court was deployed in a row.

Litigants stood or sat in certain areas. There were assigned places for witnesses and for the community as an audience. The court sessions were held out of doors, but there was a building to be repaired to in case of inclement weather.

There was, in all cases a known and demanded decorum and order of proceedings. The plaintiff first made his case. The defendant would then respond. Witnesses would be called. After the testimony had been heard, the most junior member of the bench would pronounce judgment. His sentence would be followed by his immediate senior, who might disagree and add new perspectives. The third most junior man followed until they arrived at the middle where the head chief sat. After weighing all the evidence, and the sentences and opinions of his junior judges, he would pronounce his final judgment.

Among the Bantu societies of southern Africa, if a man was killed or badly injured by another, his relatives would inform their headman, who would then inquire into the origin of the crime. When he had obtained all the relevant information, he would go with them to the chief and report the case. If the culprit or suspect was known, the chief would send emissaries to bring him to the *kgotla* (the chief's court). If the suspect was not known, a regiment would be sent for detective work. When the suspect was apprehended, the chief would inform the headman to hold an inquiry and report the findings. Olivier (1969) found that:

> All these Bantu societies therefore seem to have a well-developed system of law and a system of courts which have judicial authority to pronounce in legal matters and to enforce their judgments; provision is made for appeals to higher courts, the highest being the court of the chief (or tribal court), which is often the court of first instance in serious criminal matters.

The Tswana in Botswana are also one of these Bantu states. They are divided into "tribes", each occupying its own territory and managing its own affairs. Each tribe has its own chief who performs executive, judicial, and legislative functions. Within each ethnic grouping, the major administrative unit is the "ward", a body of people living in their own village or part of a village under the leadership and authority of a "headman" who, in addition to other duties, judges cases between members of his ward or involving them as defendants or accused. Xhosa litigants, however, generally make every effort to resolve the matter informally before appealing to the headman.

> A Bantu person conceiving himself to have a just claim against another, proceeds to the kraal of the defendant, accompanied by a party of such advisers, witnesses and adherents, as he considers necessary. His appointed spokesmen, as a rule, will state his case to the defendant. On this occasion the defendant is considered justified in supposing himself at a disadvantage, inasmuch as he may not be prepared to make his defense; nevertheless he is in a position to elicit from the plaintiff's party sufficient information to enable him to realize the nature and strength of the claim. Having done this, he may inform the plaintiff that there are only "children" at his kraal, incompetent to take part in a matter of importance; the plaintiff and his party then withdraw on the understanding that they will return at an appointed time.

> In the meantime, the defendant will have consulted his advisers, witnesses and adherents, and for their benefit the plaintiff causes his case to be stated again on the appointed day, and witnesses are called for both sides. The whole matter is disputed from every possible angle.

Although there is no referee present, nevertheless the procedure partakes of a semi-judicial character and is known by Bantu as 'taking action,' and is the customary initial step in a legal action. This 'taking action' at the kraal of the defendant is not merely a waste of time and energy; the matter is thoroughly ventilated, and if the defendant perceives that he has no defense or that the plaintiff has the odds in his favor, he may well capitulate. If the defendant presents a good defense to the plaintiff, the latter may well conclude that it is not worth while taking the matter further. In fact, in a disputed claim the 'taking action' seems to constitute the *litis contestatio*. Certainly the issues are made clear.

If the defendant admits liability, the plaintiff's claim is thereby established and only the matter of payment has to be considered; for one or another, payment may be deferred for some time, even years. Where the defendant categorically denies the plaintiff's claims, or refuses to acknowledge defeat, the plaintiff has no option but to withdraw his party, but is able to take the matter on 'appeal' to the headman of the defendant's ward or district (Seymour, 1970; p 17).

If the plaintiff does not obtain satisfaction at the headman's court, he has the right to take the matter up to the chief's court. Schapera (1957) provided this account of the procedure at the chief's court:

People involved in a dispute or accused of an offense always appear and speak for themselves, i.e.., they plead in person. . . In reaching his decision on questions involving customary law, the judge (the chief) has no written records to refer to (nor does he bother to consult the records of his own). He continues to rely upon his personal knowledge of the law and upon the guidance of others present in court. All cases are heard in public, and any tribesman is free to attend and take part in the proceedings. But in every court there are usually one or more men who, because of constant attendance and long experience in such matters, have become well-informed about details of law and procedure. Such men, sometimes referred to as *bagakolodi* (remembrancers) or *banna ba lekgotla* (men of the court, not only play an important part in the questioning of litigants and witnesses; in the second stage of each trial, when the matter is thrown open for public discussion, they also review the evidence, state the law as they know it, and if possible cite precedents. In this way, they help the judge to arrive at a verdict. He is not bound by their advice, but unless he himself has had a good deal of experience it is seldom that he will decide otherwise than as they suggest.

However, "the chief, in consultation with his counselors, uses his common sense in deciding how to deal with it and comes to a finding" (Bekker, 1989:30). He then renders a judgment, depending upon the claim. He may then extract a small fee for himself for hearing the case. A party feeling aggrieved by the judgment of the chief has the right of appeal to the Paramount Chief of the tribe, who has the power to override the judgment of the lower chief, request payment for the judgment rendered and deduct his fee from it in the same manner as the lower chief.

Similar legal practices exist among the Shona of Zimbabwe. Family disputes are resolved within the family. However a serious quarrel within a family may be resolved at an informal gathering of the senior men of the family with the family head or a senior *muzukuru* ("sister's son") presiding.

Any Shona village headman may hold an informal court (or *dare*) to try and solve conflicts within the community for which he is responsible. He may do so even for people outside the village community. If the village headman cannot solve a case, the dispute may be taken to the higher court of a ward headman or minor chief. The highest court in the Shona traditional system is the chief's court. "It operates in practice as a court of appeal from the more informal lower courts and many difficult cases are taken straight to the chief's court" (Bourdillon, 1976; p.147).

Most Shona chiefs set aside one or two days a week on which they preside over their courts, but in smaller chiefdoms the courts do not always have business to deal with on the appointed days. When the court meets, the chief presides and usually sits in a conspicuous position apart from the gathering of attendants. These include the chief's appointed advisers, his messengers, the disputing parties with their supporters and any men who have an interest in the case or who wish simply to be present.

> The plaintiff opens the proceedings by placing before the court a token with which he expresses his submission to the court's jurisdiction and where he obtains a hearing. When the defendant has heard the complaint, he too must submit a token by which he accepts the jurisdiction of the court. These tokens are often the court fees (in the order of $1.50 for the plaintiff and 50¢ for the defendant) which are placed for all to see during the case; after the case they are divided between the chief (who takes the greatest share), his messengers and the appointed advisers (Bourdillon, 1976; p.148).

As in the Ashanti and Yoruba legal systems, material tokens were frequently required for other purposes in Shona court procedures. Besides their use to open court proceedings, a token was required as an admission of guilt and had to be physically given to the other party as such an admission. A material sign of reconciliation between the disputants was often required as well. A verbal statement alone was not considered enough by the Shona since one of the customs of social conversation is to be polite and pleasing. The Shona have a tendency to "suppress" the truth if it might offend. Thus, "when a Shona man endorses a statement by giving a visible token, it is his personal and irrevocable commitment to what has been said in words. The token shows that the man is serious in the matter" (Bourdillon, 1976; p.151).

After each party made a formal statement of its case, the discussion was thrown open to the public. Here too among the Shona, one notices the practice of "open" public court hearings. But at no stage in the proceedings would the disputants argue directly with one another. Normally before a settlement was reached, one of the parties would give a token to show that he admitted his guilt and would ask what compensation was required.

> Punishment may include compensation to the other party in the dispute, a small fine to the chief, and the guilty party may have to pay *the full costs of the case*, refunding his adversary the court fees paid at the beginning. The party who wins the case may be asked to give the chief a portion of the compensation he receives as a token of his gratitude to the chief for giving him a fair hearing (Bourdillon, 1976; p.153).

Olivier (1969), who studied the legal system of the Bantu extensively, concluded that the administration of justice found among the Bantu people could be summarized as follows:

1. The chief, as the principal organ of the tribe, is the chief executive, chief prosecutor, chief justice.

2. The administration of justice is a public affair; a trial 'in camera' is generally unknown.

3. The public (i.e., all adult men of the tribe) freely participates in all court sessions. The men present have the right to cross-question the parties before the court and to express an opinion as to what the decision or verdict should be.

4. Judgment by default is usually unknown in Bantu law; both parties must be present when the case is heard, and the chief (or court) has the power to compel a man to be present.

5. There is absence of legal representation. In other words, advocates, attorneys, etc. are unknown in Bantu law.

6. The judge is judge-in-council. The presiding judge formally pronounces the verdict of the court, but in doing so he merely reflects the consensus of opinion expressed by the tribal members present.

7. No record is kept, all evidence etc. being done orally.

8. The proceedings are usually conducted in an atmosphere of complete informality, and in this respect differ greatly from the position in Western

courts of law. As long as they don't make too much noise, the men present are allowed to come and go as they please, busy themselves with handicrafts such as the (dressing) of skins, etc. (p.147).

B. CONTRACTS AND PROPERTY RIGHTS

Native African courts did not only resolve interpersonal disputes but also protected and enforced contracts as well as property rights, even including those pertaining to land. A contract is an agreement or understanding to perform a service either to discharge a debt or in return for some compensation.

Since rights under contracts arise by agreement, rather than in law, the question of which system of law governs a contract is unrelated to the status of the contracting parties. When an agreement has been concluded, it is governed by the system of law which the parties had in mind when entering into the contract. If this system is the customary law, then a breach of contract may be taken to the chief's court for adjudication.

There were various contracts in indigenous Africa. None was written; they were merely understandings, verbally reached in the presence of one or two witnesses. In some cases, witnesses might be absent, depending upon the nature of the contract or the level of trust that existed between the parties. The contracts were either commercial or social. Perhaps a few examples would be useful.

The Xhosa have several social contracts, though some do have economic consequences. These contracts are expressed as the "customs": *ukufakwa*, *ukwenzelela*, and *ukongoma*.

Ikazi in Xhosa is bride money which usually takes the form of livestock a young man pays to his wife's father on occasion of marriage. A man with unmarried or yet to be married daughters may borrow cattle against the livestock (*ikazi*) he expects to receive from the grooms when his daughters marry. For example, upon borrowing a cow, Thandwefika would say, "I will refund you with a beast out of the *ikazi* of my daughter." Under the custom of *ukwenzelela*, cattle are given to a man to enable him to pay *ikazi* for his wife because has a few of his own or his father's and needs to be supplemented.

> *Ukungoma* is a loan of livestock whereby the receiver is entitled to the benefit of the use of the stock for the general purpose for which stock is used, for example, ploughing, drawing water from the river and carting mealies from the lands during the reaping season. The cows are milked, likewise, by the receiver and it is only the wool of sheep and the progeny of all kinds of stock, whether it be cattle, sheep or goats, which is the property of the giver. The giver places his earmark on the stock so

lent and carries out an inspection from time to time. Whenever he should so decide he can retrieve his stock with all increases and often a reward is given to the *nqomee* who has acquitted himself well of his responsibilities (Koyana, 1980:73).

This customary contract is not unique to the Xhosa alone but is also common among the Zulu (called *ukusia*), the Sotho (*mafisa*) and the Shangana (*fuyisa*).

Returning to the Xhosa, the *ukothula* custom, similar to *ukwenzelela*, is bride money paid by a household or its head on behalf of a son or inmate when he marries. The expectation is that the provider will recoup himself from the bride money (*ikazi*) paid for the eldest daughter born out of the marriage in question.

There are other social contracts among the other ethnic divisions in southern Africa. Koyana (1980) provides the following examples:

Ukuhlama is a custom known among the largest subdivisions of the Transkeian populace, the Pondos and the Thembus. It is an extraordinary contract of gift or loan whereby the giver expects to receive something from the donee but under which no action lies in the event of the donee not paying back the gift. And there is never any stipulation as to the time within which the said gift is to be repaid, nor how it is to be repaid. The contract could be made with a stranger, thus illustrating the kindly disposition of the people in general (p.77).

Ukubusa is a unilateral contract of donation known among the Pondos. The donor signifies his intention to be bound as such by permitting the donee to kiss his hand at the time of the handing over of the gift, usually a beast. If the donee in return refuses to have his hand kissed, this is an indication that the "gift" is made without prejudice to the giver's right to claim the beast and its progeny later (p.78).

Isondlo. It is a feature of African society that a child born away from its home is left to grow at its place of birth. At a later stage, however, the parent or guardian will turn up and claim custody. It is the right of the person who brought up the child to claim a maintenance fee which is called *isondlo*, derived from *ukondla* (to maintain). The maintenance fee is a beast for each child and it is known as *isondlo* beast. It is immaterial whether the child is a boy or girl. . .

Isondlo is not claimable in the following cases:
1. A child who has not been weaned.
2. A man who had lived as a son at a home from infancy to manhood and for whom *ikazi* had been provided.

3. An adult, unless he joined the household of the claimant as a child and grew up there.
4. Persons who are dead at the time of the claim.

Some of these "social" contracts may not be valid in terms of Roman-Dutch law. However the force of custom generally makes them binding and breaches can be adjudicated in family courts or the headman's court if members of different lineages are involved.

A commercial contract may take the form of an understanding between, for example, a palm-wine seller and a tapper. She would agree to sell the produce and return, say, two-thirds of the proceeds to the tapper at the end of the day or week. Another common example was the agreements reached between market women and long-distance traders or European commercial house operators and importers. The women would accept to market the merchandise and render an accounting after a certain period of time. This was in effect a trade credit system and required a great amount of trust for it to work. As we shall in chapter 8, it did work for the most part.

There were also indigenous agricultural credit schemes and contracts. The typical and most common in West Africa was the pledging of farms, especially cash crops such as cocoa and peanuts. A farmer, strapped for cash to meet unforeseen exigencies (say funeral expenses), may pledge a certain proportion of the produce of his farm. This was possible because produce was privately owned although the land on which it is grown might not be. (Chapter 7 discusses systems of land tenure in much greater detail).

Failure to deliver on any of these agreements (breach of contract) could result in legal action. Often the parties would try to resolve the matter privately or informally. Unsuccessful resolution would bring the case before a chief. Chiefs usually held court at the marketplace. The chief would try to determine the intentions of the parties, the nature or terms of the contract, the environment of the parties and rely on circumspection to reach a decision after hearing from the witnesses. The verdict may be the chief's own decision or in consultation with advisers.

Property Claims

Native property rights were perhaps one area least understood and enshrouded in mythology. This might have been the result of the application of the erroneous concept of "communal ownership" of land to every other piece of property. Land in traditional Africa was nobody's property until someone settled on it. As we shall see in a subsequent chapter, although the African chief exercised enormous powers over the distribution of land, much land was lineage-owned. Further, the chief could not recklessly exercise his powers of appropriation and confiscation without the full consent of the council of elders.

In much the same vein, the ocean, lakes, and rivers did not belong to anyone. This was the meaning conveyed by Africans when they said "these items belong to us all" just as one would today assert that the air or the environment belongs to us all (the human race). In the African scheme of things, the ocean belonged to all members of the tribe and therefore any individual tribesperson was at liberty to fish in it. Europeans might have misinterpreted the phrase "belongs to us all" as indicative of "communal ownership." But once an African applied his or her labor to something, the resulting product became personal property.

A dam across the river was private property but the river was not. Similarly, wild game and fish in the ocean and the rivers were "communal property" but became private property as soon as they were caught or killed. As Koyana (1980) observed:

> Apart from the division of things into movable and immovable, the main emphasis being on cattle and land, Xhosa law, like Roman law, takes the concept of kinds of things much further. Thus the attitude to air is consistent with the Roman and modern idea of its being *res extra commercium*. Next to livestock, *res communes omnium* are, in contrast to modern society, largely relied upon in daily life and are the main source of occupation. By a simple act of appropriation, a family head or household becomes the owner of the *res* in which he has an interest. Thus stones are collected from commonage by men and boys at will and are used for building stock-kraals and, in some areas, dwelling-huts. Thatch-grass for roofing huts, river water and spring water for domestic use and firewood are obtained from the commonage and bushes and forests by women and girls and are used as if they were own property (p.67).

Similar property rights have been observed among the Luvale who fish in Lake Bwangelu, which lies west of the Zambezi River in Zambia, using two traditional methods: weirs and fish poisoning.[5] According to Skinner (1964),

> Rights in weirs and pools suitable for poisoning are owned by individuals. These rights are acquired in the first instance simply by

---

[5] Fish poison, called *usungu*, was of several varieties produced from different plants. One amazing aspect of the different varieties was their selectivity. Certain types of fish were susceptible to only certain kinds of poison. The poison, however, had no effect on humans. Fish poisoning is now illegal but this practice ought to be the object of scientific enquiry to identify its active ingredients. The Luvale also proscribed certain types of fish for pregnant women. They could not consume *musuta*, *pungu* (tiger fish) and *kundu* (a Tilapia) lest involuntary abortion or miscarriage might be induced.

finding a suitable site and setting up a weir or finding a suitable pool and fishing it with a poison.

In most indigenous African societies, all the means of production were privately owned, with the possible exception of land. Fishing canoes, goats, cattle, hunting gear, huts, farms, hoes and fishing nets were all private property. The fact that there were thieves in traditional Africa should dispel myths about communal ownership of all property. Myburgh (1980) noted:

Theft (*bogodu*) is the intentional appropriation of a movable thing or of movable things owned by others or forming part of public resources. Among the Tswana theft of private property is a delict. . .Unauthorized borrowing constitutes theft among the Hurutshe, unless relations between the persons are such that one can safely assume permission. Among the Kwena and Hurutshe each of the following is theft: taking a thing from owners who think it belongs or is owing to the recipients, preventing the return of a thing borrowed by one's groups, and appropriating lost property. . .

Among the Tswana theft of public resources is a crime, not a delict by reason of the fact that these resources are not held in ownership but are controlled in public law. . .In the old days theft of public resources was punished by death. It seems to occur that where theft of private property is a crime as well as a delict, foreigners are more severely dealt with than countrymen and that stock-theft is viewed in a particularly serious light, for we are told that stock-theft on the part of a foreigner carried the death penalty. Today punishment takes the form of a fine. . .

Courts would seem inclined to dispense with punishment if the things stolen are not of great value (such as fowls, utensils, and small stock) and the thief can make restitution (p.92).

For the Xhosa, Koyana (1980) stated:

In Xhosa law, as in other African legal systems, livestock in general and cattle in particular, are the main objects of private ownership. The field of law of things is like a huge dam to which several rivers flow continuously and thus maintain a regular supply of water, the rivers here being the other branches of the law. Via the law of persons, a man will become owner of cattle because of *amakhazi* paid for his daughters or wards or because of cattle contract a man will become the owner of cattle he has bought, or earned as *isondlo*, or as reward for having looked well after *nqoma* cattle or as reimbursement for *faka* or *ukwenzelela* cattle. Via the law of delict some men have

become rich overnight because of damages earned for seduction of their
daughters and/or adultery committed with their wives. And via the law
of succession a man or even a boy becomes the owner of many cattle
because he is the heir to his deceased father and sole person entitled to
succeed to his whole estate in terms of our law (p.63).

For the Bantu generally,

> With regard to the kinds and nature of things, Bantu law originally
> knew only land, dwellings and cattle kraals, livestock, grain,
> primitive clothing and domestic utensils, elementary instruments of
> agriculture and war, and things of the like nature. And with regards
> to rights therein, it knew ownership and possession of movables,
> and occupation and use, but not ownership of land.
>
> But just as the law of the land is automatically extended to any new
> invention, so Bantu law and custom are automatically extended by
> the Bantu to any kind of movable thing which they have introduced
> into their lives by contact with European civilization, for example,
> money, furniture, glassware, cutlery, modern clothing, modern
> farming implements, and a myriad of other things.
>
> Generally speaking, Bantu law cannot be adapted to ownership of
> immovable property (for example, rivers, mountains, etc.) for there
> is no such Bantu law. Thus while matters of ownership, mortgage,
> servitude, sale or lease of immovable property must normally be
> dealt with under the law of the land, rights of possession, occupation
> or use of land are often intended by their grantor or possessor to be
> governed by Bantu law, and may be dealt with under that system
> (Seymour, 1970:45).

Even among the !Kung and the San (derogatively referred to as the
Kalahari Bushmen), there were property rights. The !Kung organize
themselves into hunting parties. Members of such a party may spread out
and, in a crouched position, stalk their prey for miles. They hunt with
poisoned arrows. For small preys such as antelope, the poison may work
quickly, but for a large animal like a wilderbeest, it may take a day.
Endurance and the ability to track stricken animals are the !Kung's attributes.
When a game is killed,

> The meat belongs to the owner of the first arrow that penetrates the
> animal so that it stays in. He has the responsibility of making the
> first distribution. Anyone in the band may be the owner of the
> arrow. A hunter carries arrows he acquires in three different ways.
> Each man has his own that he makes himself, shaping the points

with some little distinction so that he will know them from the arrows of other men. In addition, he carries arrows that have been given or lent to him. When an arrow is given to him, he is the owner as much as if he had made it himself, but if he uses that arrow he must make a special gift of meat to the donor. When he uses an arrow that is loaned to him, he merely shoots for the person who lent it and who remains the owner (Gibbs, 1965; p.253).

Settlement Of Disputes And Court Cases

Disputes, of course, arise over property claims; for example, when two arrows penetrate and stay in. Such disputes are resolved by arbitration or moot. In more organized societies, property claims and rights are settled and upheld in native courts. Schapera (1957) reported the following cases among the Tswana:

- Among the Tswana, a man who had forcibly attacked another's household goods to secure payment of a debt was fined two head of cattle, because, said the chief, 'the law (native law) is that a person should not seize from another but must bring him to the chief' (Segment v. Makgala Kopo, 86/1938).

- Among the Khurutse, a man killed an ox that was eating corn in his garden. He was ordered to give the animal's owner a heifer as compensation: 'according to our law' said the chief, 'you are not entitled to seize payment for yourself, you have behaved like a thief' (Kombane Chepele v. Maboiwa Mpambi, 9.5/1941).

- Among the Kwena, a man who had removed the rafters from his step-mother's hut and used them for himself was ordered to replace them and look after the woman's property, 'because according to our law and custom she is your mother' (Mmano Kebohula v. Kenalekgosi Kebohula, 33/1936); a man who had assaulted another in the latter's compound was fined an ox, 'because it is against native law and custom to go and fight a person at his home' (Thebeng v. Gaorekwe, 3/1936); a man who after publicly divorcing his wife went one night to her parent's home and induced her to come away with him was fined 'for doing what is contrary to native law and custom' (Botshabelo v. Lelamma, 10/37).

- Among the Ngwaketse, a man who claimed compensation from another whose donkey stallion had injured his mare was told that, 'according to our custom a man cannot be held responsible if his bull injures a cow in copulation' (Dibeela v. Tlhobolo, 15/1912).

Evidently in traditional Africa, one could not arbitrarily seize someone else's property. Even the chief could not do so. Theoretically, he could dispossess someone of his land but

Only in cases of, for example, the commission of a grave offense against the community, abandonment of the land. There could therefore be 'despotic acts' giving evidence of unbridled exercise of power, but there was always the safeguard that the powers were not exercised recklessly. There was always the councillors whose advice was as a rule taken into account by the chief. In practice, therefore, the rights of the individual were never nullified (Koyana, 1980:69).

Because of the traditional emphasis on kinship, indigenous courts have venerated parenthood and upheld respect for one's parents as a cultural command. Acts of disobedience against parents were generally not condoned. Disapprobation was particularly severe in cases of insubordination against mothers. The mother in most ethnic societies, enjoyed a much greater esteem and respect than the father. The reverence for the mother perhaps sprang from the natural bond between her and her offsprings. Together with the father, they were regarded as the source of procreation and nurturing and therefore vital for the longevity of the tribe. Accordingly, verdicts rendered in the native system of law tended to favor parents as the following cases from Schapera (1957) illustrated:

- Among the Nawaketse, a man who pushed his father away during a quarrel was sentenced to a thrashing, 'because it is Ngwaketse law that a child should not raise his hand against his father, or become incensed when he is scolded, that is a great offense'(Motlohelwa Moitoi v. Medupe Motlohelwa, 18/1939).

- Another man who violently assaulted his step-mother and in other ways ill-treated her was both thrashed and sent to gaol, 'because custom forbids a child, no matter how old, ever to quarrel with his parents, let alone assault them' (Kgosidikae v. Keitumetse, 22/1940).

- Among the Khurutshe, a man who slapped his senior in the face was told, 'It is against native law and custom to strike his senior,' and was reprimanded and warned not to repeat the offence (Modie v. George, 30.8/1939); and among the Kgatla, a man was punished in an assault case, 'because it is an offence to swear at a person older than yourself' (Leshome Mabeko v. Moremi Moatshe, 4/1938).

Though the chief was the judge and arbiter at the village court, he had to take public opinion into account when rendering a judgment. He was not infallible and could be overruled by those present in court, as the following cases demonstrate:

Among the Kwena, as among most other Tswana tribes, it is the traditional rule that a man who abducts another's wife should forfeit all of his property to the injured husband. In 1902, a man named Kgotodue abducted the wife of Ome Lesokwame. Chief Sebele I, who tried the case, ordered Kgotodue to pay Lesokwame ten head of cattle as compensation, but added that he could take the woman to wife. Thereupon, says the official report of the District Officer, 'The majority of the headmen objected to this, on the ground that it would be creating a bad precedent, which might lead wealthy men into breaking up others' homes for ten head of cattle.' Sebele was accordingly forced by the pressure of public opinion to alter his judgment and ordered Kgotodue to have nothing more to do with the woman, lest he be deprived of all his property (Schapera, 1957).

Bourdillon (1976) also found a similar situation with the Shona chief:

> According to traditional ideals, a chief could never force his people to do what they did not want to do; *he was a leader rather than a ruler*, relying for his position on influence rather than force. This ideal comes into the traditional courts where ideally the chief was a chairman rather than a judge (p.165).

In the olden days, most chiefs conducted their courts according to this ideal, overseeing the conduct of the case, helping parties who appeared before them and allowing his elders and people to speak their minds before giving his own summing up which depended largely on expressed public opinion.[6]

In traditional Africa, ignorance of the customary law in general was no excuse in many court cases. But extenuating circumstances were often considered. This was due to the fact that the judge's decision was partly shaped by the opinions of those present in court. There was thus a tendency for judgments to be based more upon recognized general principles than upon specific decisions of the past. "This in turn means that the law is not rigid but flexible, and can be readily adapted to meet new situations or, if need be, to reject customary norms that are now considered obsolete" (Schapera, 1957). Similarly among the Shona,

> One of the aims of traditional Shona courts was to reconcile disputing parties within a community and to restore social harmony: to this end the courts delved into the root cause of disputes that came before them. Occasionally courts even go against accepted custom in order to appease the disputants; the Shona do not generally make the law more important than the people it is supposed to serve. . .Apart from court decision against accepted custom, customs are frequently bent to suit particular occasions, as

---

[6] Part of this ideal was lost during the colonial period when the opinion of the colonial government counted more than public opinion to the government-appointed chiefs. It virtually vanished in post-colonial Africa when the opinions of dictatorial governments became the rule.

rules of inheritance and succession are altered in consideration of the characters of, and the actual relations between, the persons concerned. Shona customary law is flexible, and the traditional courts make use of this flexibility. . .

Traditional Shona courts attempt to persuade disputants to come to a reasonable agreement in a spirit of give and take. In this process, customary law provides no more than a broad and flexible basis for discussion. It can be argued that the purpose of Shona courts is to solve conflicts rather than rationally and impartially apply abstract rules of law (Bourdillon, 1976; pp.157-158).

Generally in indigenous Africa, the application of precedents was not important. A kind of "situation" ethic was applied with the aim to resolve conflicts in accordance with general social values rather than predetermined codes of law. Certain acts were recognized as crimes: theft, rape, extortion, murder, assault, etc. and were punished accordingly. But punishment alone, which of course varied from one society to another, was not enough to heal the social wounds.

Most native Africans believed wrong-doing strained social relationships and displeased the ever-present spirits of the ancestors. Thus, while the concept of justice was clearly known, it was pursued within certain parameters or with additional objectives: repairing frayed social relationships and pacifying the ancestral spirits.

Thus unlike the Western legal system, the indigenous African arbitration process laid a great deal of emphasis on reconciling the disputing parties *to promote social harmony* rather on the punishment or the settlement. Justice was pursued with broader societal and spiritual objectives. It may be recalled from the previous chapter that the pursuit of wealth similarly occurred within social and religious demarcations.

In this way, the peasants were able to adjust legal arbitration decisions to changing values, standards and circumstances of the community. "Such a flexible legal system readily adapts itself when this is necessary to maintain some social unity, and unity was a condition for survival in the small closely-knit communities of the Shona past" (Bourdillon, 1976:160).

Traditional African custom required that the elders, the "old men" instruct the youth in native law and custom. As instructors, the elders were expected to be of good behavior and comport themselves well to serve as role models for the youth. Consequently, contraventions of the law by elders were viewed more seriously and punished more severely because the elders were expected "to know the law." Consider the following cases from Schapera (1957):

- Among the Kwena, a man who hit another on the head with a stick was fined an ox, 'because as an elderly man he should have been aware that he was doing wrong' (Gasebatho v. Philip, 21/1936).

- Among the Kgatla, a man who had refused on demand to give up cattle that he was looking after for someone else was not only ordered to do so, but was also fined, 'because he is an old man and ought to know the law' (Kgamanyane Pilane v. Ntwai Moeng, 22/1938).

- In a matrimonial dispute among the Ngwato, the husband's conduct was found especially reprehensible , 'because he is an old man, from whom younger people should learn how to behave' (Dikeledi v. Makgoeng, 153/1938).

- And in another Ngwato case, a village headman who had abducted another's wife was fined more heavily than usual because in his position he was expected to set a good example to others (Monyanda v. Radipitse, 151/1938).

In a more recent case, a head fishermen was deposed for the commission of what might be considered a trivial crime:

> Fishermen at Kromantse Number One in the Central Region have destooled their chief fisherman for diverting about half of their allocation of fishing gear and selling it to others outside the town at *kalabule* (black market) prices.

> The ex-chief fisherman, Opanyin Kow Mensah, also allegedly sold 0.9 meters of the net at C200 *(cedis)* to some of them, while he had enough to build for himself a complete fishing net. Announcing this at a meeting of the local branch of the National Canoe Fishermen Council, the branch secretary, Mr. John Kwame Ennusin, said Opanyin Mensah was found guilty at an arbitration presided over by the Odikro of the town, Nana Kwansa Panyin II (*West Africa*, January 10, 1983; p. 113).

There was unity between African law and African philosophy. Yelpaala (1983) expressed this well:

> Among the Dagaaba, there was no separation between law, morality, ethics, religion, and the social and political organization. In particular, law and morality were constantly and continuously in an organic elemental embrace. Thus one could not talk about law without simultaneously talking about its moral or utilitarian quality. The system was constantly being evaluated by the living individually and collectively, by the dead, and by the cosmic forces for conformity with moral and religious norms. Every new social norm had to be justified in the face of the ancestral and supernatural norms. If there was doubt about the quality of a norm, the elders would solve that by referring the issue to diviners or sooth-sayers or

even by a sacrificial offering that yielded a 'yes' or 'no' result. The burden of social change was great and the elders did not toy with it. The social and political organization was hardly anarchic (p.377).[7]

It may be recalled that African peasant's maxim was: "I am because we are." The teleological emphasis on the community overshadowed the interests of the individual. Consequently, in African law, the fundamental principle was embedded in a contractual liability to maintain what Davidson (1970) called the "ideal equilibrium."

This equilibrium or principle, expressed in every aspect of the social fabric, upheld that any action tending to harm others was a threat to the whole society, and must be purged by appropriate counteraction. Right behavior was accordingly seen in terms of debt: of a negative liability on the individual not to do what was wrong, but also a positive liability to do what was right. Purging and punishment were frequently a matter of compensation. Gluckman (1965) noted that the law of the Barotse of Central Africa could be written largely in terms of debt, whether one was dealing with transactions, obligations of status, injuries or offences and believed this could be true of the general structure of all African law.[8]

It may also be recalled that the supernatural entered the legal system directly and thereby produced a union between law and philosophy. Yelpaala (1983) noted that, among the Dagaaba:

> The supernatural influences the legal systems in two ways: the substance and the procedure. . .Given the set of higher supernatural norms demanding conformity from lower human norms, the supernatural directly influenced the continuity of existing substantive law and the nature and direction of new substantive laws. It is common among the Dagaaba to have consultations with ancestral spirits through various divinations to ensure conformity with these higher norms, particularly when the new substantive law involved a major shift in custom (p.375).

In law procedures, the influence of the supernatural is most dramatic and visible. The importance of the supernatural can be seen in dispute

---

[7] Yelpaala went on to observe that,
   The disorder came with the introduction of British colonial rule, the positivist legal system, and chiefs when the Dagaaba were suddenly confronted with the problem of institutionalized power and authority backed by physical force and corporal punishment or threat of it.

[8] Davidson (1970) noted that much of European law was not much different:
   The contract of vassalage was essentially a matter of obligations, and it was not sufficient for right behavior to abstain from doing wrong: it was just as necessary to do right. Ideally, at least, the contract was expressed in a duality of debt. Africa might be far away; it was evidently not so far as we have often thought (p.203).

settlement. Because they are omniscient and all powerful, cosmic forces are called upon to judge the probity of a witness if the veracity of a testimony is in doubt. Among the northern tribes of Ghana, the most powerful supernatural force that can be called upon in trials is lightning (*saa* among the Dagaaba). Disputants and witnesses are often required to swear under oath to be struck by lightning if they perjure themselves. So immediate and dramatic is this punishment that litigants are not prone to lying under oath. If someone nevertheless perjured himself, "he must act swifly to pacify this highly temperamental supernatural power by telling the truth and providing some sacrificial offerings to the custodian of that power (*saasob* or *saadaana*) for pacification" (Yelpaala, 1983:375).[9]

Though the above discussion placed emphasis on settlement of inter-personal disputes, African customary law also dealt with such issues as divorce, succession, land tenure, and criminal acts as robbery, fraud, extortion and even bribery as have been discussed by Bekker (1989), Koyana (1980), Nakec (1988), Myburgh (1980), and Seymour (1970).

C. INTER-ETHNIC CONFLICTS AND DISPUTES

The history of Africa is replete with inter-tribal wars, rivalries and feuds. Many of these were due to the general absence of an institution for resolving disputes between tribes. Within many tribes, there were courts of course but there were no inter-tribal court systems except a few sparing efforts at diplomacy and the adoption of ad hoc measures. These were, however, generally inadequate. But after the abolition of the slave trade in the 1820s, they became increasingly important in lessening tension between African societies.

In the main, five pressure points could be identified. The first was trade. It was generally recognized by trading communities that a peaceful atmosphere was required for commerce to prosper. To promote peace and facilitate trade, many traders intermarried or took wives in the towns they went to trade. It was exactly for this reason why a trade group known as the *Aro* arose along the Niger Delta to provide protection for trade and resolve inter-tribal trade disputes. The second practice was the use of intermediaries who were generally European traders and missionaries. They often intervened to restore peace among feuding tribes. The third was the use of diplomacy. Often emissaries were sent to settle disputes with neighboring tribes as well as with Europeans. For example, Adjaye (1984) observed that:

The art, skills and techniques of diplomacy were known to, and

[9] These divinations are also common among many African tribes. The Yoruba are also known for their consultations with shrines in judicial trials.

practised by the Asante themselves in the 19th century. Diplomacy
a l'Asante is neither an invention of the 20th century mind nor a
conceptualization of the 19th century Western observer; diplomacy
was indigenous to Asante. . .

The use of envoys in diplomatic communication and the resolution
of differences by peaceful negotiation and other diplomatic instruments constituted the cornerstones upon which Asante's foreign
policy was built. . .In 1820, the British officer, Joseph Dupuis, had
the opportunity of observing the workings of the Asante bureaucratic system in Kumasi. Through the diverse discussions that
Dupuis had with the Asante government over the readjustment of
its relations with the British and the southern provinces, the British
consul concluded that Asantehene Osei Tutu Kwame 'took particular pains to ingraft an impression upon my mind that it was a maxim
associated with the religion he professed, never to appeal to the
sword while a path lay open for negotiation' (p.2).

Fourth, there was "lobbying" by internal pressure groups that advocated
for peace with neighbors. It was generally realized that without peace, trade
and other relations could sour. Distant kinsmen often lived in neighboring
tribes. Within the Asante kingdom itself, a pressure group was formed that
stood "for peace, trade and open roads and opposed the continuation of
warfare by the Asante military elite as it threatened these objectives" (Bates,
1987:32). A similar lobby existed in the Oyo Empire.

Among the Mende and Temne of Sierra Leone and Vai of Liberia, secret
societies could mediate between two feuding chiefdoms. For example, the
Poro, a male secret society, "could also act as an arbitrator in disputes
between chiefdoms by sending a band of its officials masked as 'devils' to
pressure the group which ignored its ruling (Stride and Ifeka, 1971:229).

Fifth, after colonialization, mechanisms were provided for the resolution
of conflicts of disputes between different ethnic societies, albeit under the
threat of use of force.

D. SUMMARY

In summary, the indigenous court system stressed reconciliation and the
promotion of social harmony to resolve disputes and conflicts while
pursuing a fair degree of justice. Court hearings were open and the
administration of justice was flexible. Indigenous courts were not conducted
according to a rigid and abstract code of law. This flexibility was necessary
to permit the court system to achieve its twin objectives of justice and social
harmony. Perhaps, this was the primary reason why the proceedings were

open to the public or any interested person. Those present could "speak their minds" freely and contribute to the administration of social justice. Thus, a fair trial could be assured and, moreover, court decisions could be appealed.

Though the legal system worked reasonably well in intra-tribal affairs, the indigenous institutions for resolving inter-tribal conflicts were not as elaborate and well developed. The use of diplomacy in averting hostilities between tribes was limited.

Nevertheless, one of the most interesting features of the indigenous African court system was the use of "tokens," even before the start of court proceedings. Even more interesting was the rule that the party which lost a case not only forfeited his token and paid a small fine (usually two goats) but also reimbursed the winner for all court expenses. Not surprisingly, frivolous lawsuits, common occurrences in the West, were not a regular feature of indigenous African court systems.

However, it is African governments and elites, if anything, who should have drawn pointers from and built upon the indigenous African system of law. Tragically, they failed to strengthen the indigenous institutions for resolving inter-tribal disputes and conflicts during the post-colonial period. This explains the proliferation of ethnic rivalries and hostilities which have taken the lives of countless Africans. Since independence in the sixties, more than 5 million Africans have perished from various inter-ethnic feuds. In the Biafran War, 1967-70, for example, more than one million Nigerians perished.

Urgently needed in modern Africa, are courts or institutions that can resolve disputes, peacefully, fairly and impartially; first between groups within a country, and, second, between African countries. Incessant wars still rage in Angola, Ethiopia, Mozambique, Somalia, Sudan, Uganda, and many other African countries.

Perhaps an "international" African court should be established, say in Dar-es-Salaam, along the Arusha principle to adjudicate matters of conflict between African nations. The Organization of African Unity (OAU) is supposed to be responsible for the attainment of this objective. It has however proved itself hopelessly ineffective in this regard.

To assure impartiality, perhaps a special court should be established in each African country and staffed by Africans from other countries to adjudicate conflicts between different ethnic groups. For example, such a court in Ghana would be manned by Nigerians. While it is true there are courts in Africa today, they are often biased and rendered useless by capricious government interference. In addition, African leaders have seldom shown themselves to be impartial observers in inter-tribal rivalries. In fact, in many cases they themselves actually instigated the feuds by using the state machinery to oppress rival tribes. Post-colonial African history is rife with numerous documented cases in Burundi, Ethiopia, Liberia, Kenya, Malawi,

Rwanda, Somalia, Uganda, Zaire, Zimbabwe and many other African countries.

The native system of justice was not perfect. However, regardless of its imperfections and defects, the "primitive" legal system was far superior to the kangaroo courts and tribunals that are ubiquitous in modern Africa. In most tribal systems, there was no such thing as a "kangaroo court." At least, the peasants understood and safeguarded private property rights unlike many modern African governments which arbitrarily seize property without due process of law:

> One warm day in August, 1990, Somalia's Special Military Police went out on the streets of Mogadishu, the capital, calmly set up roadblocks and stole every single four-wheel-drive car that went by. They took 25 cars from international organizations alone. They then went down to the port, where the haze comes in off the Red Sea in the blistering heat, and helped themselves to 15 more brand-new cars off a ship.

> The Special Military Police are the sole guardians of law and order in Mogadishu. When off duty they pass the time committing armed robberies, and the streets routinely echo to the sound of automatic gunfire by night. When they're not shooting, they sell arms on the street instead (*The Washington Post*, Nov. 26, 1990; p.A7).

> Nairobi, Kenya. In an usually broad attack on corruption, a prominent church leader charged that misuse of power for economic gain had become the norm among Government officials. . .

> The Archbishop of the Church Province of Kenya, the Rev. Manasses Kuria, told an Anglican congregation that the situation had become so bad that *the 'organs of the state machinery'were seizing property from ordinary people.*

> 'Unless God rescues Kenya, we shall sink,' said the Archbishop (*The New York Times*, Aug. 13, 1990; p.A6).

CHAPTER 3

INDIGENOUS POLITICAL INSTITUTIONS

Then our people lived peacefully, under the democratic rule of their kings. . .Then the country was ours, in our name and right. The land belonged to the whole tribe. There were no classes, no rich or poor and no exploitation of man by man. All men were free and equal and this was the foundation of government. Recognition of this general principle found expression in the constitution of the council, variously called *Imbizo*, or *Pitso* or *Kgotla*, which governs the affairs of the tribe. The council (of elders) was so completely democratic that all members of the tribe could participate in its deliberations. Chief and subject, warrior and medicine man, all took part and endeavoured to influence its decisions. There was much in such a society that was primitive and insecure, and certainly could never measure up to the demands of the present epoch. *But in such a society are contained the seeds of revolutionary democracy* (Mandela, 1984; p.53). (Italics mine).

A. INTRODUCTION

The organizational structure and objective of indigenous political systems were generally based upon kinship, ancestry and survival in much the same way as social organizations were. Each ethnic group devised its own system of government. There were no written constitutions and the procedures for government were established by custom and tradition. This lack of written literature and laws gave rise to much mythology about Africa.

The potential for diversity was extant in indigenous political systems. Surprisingly, however, there were many commonalities. Vaughan (1986) asserted:

There is so much diversity in the structures and complexities of African political systems that a fundamental underlying principle may be overlooked. Virtually all of these diverse political organiza-

71

tions are based upon the validity of public means of resolving disputes and conflicts, that is, upon the *rule of law*. This is not to say that societies have statutes which in and of themselves regulate behavior. Rarely is there anything so conscious or formal; rather, members of societies accept that there is a moral basis to public order and that publicly sanctioned resolutions of disputes and conflicts are necessary for the continuance of social life beyond the family or clan (p.175).

The emphasis on *rule of law* should be noted. In indigenous African systems, this may be interpreted as respect for and adherrence to institutionalized or customary ways of resolving disputes and upholding the traditions governing political behavior. More importantly, traditional African "laws" were not mischievously decreed by the chief or king in collusion with a platoon of soldiers. Customary laws were subject to full public debate and in fact as we shall see, chiefs and kings could not promulgate laws without the concurrence of councils.

In general, two main types of political organizations could be distinguished in traditional African societies. There were, of course, variations or different forms in different tribal societies but the structures and foundations were essentially the same.

In the first general type, Group A, tribes existed as separate political entities and governed themselves independently. In the second, Group B, some came under the hegemony or rule by others either through conquest or voluntary submission. Within each grouping, there was further differentiation in political organization.

In Group A, there were societies with centralized authority (chiefs), administrative machinery and judicial institutions - chiefdoms or states.[1] Ethnic groups, which had such central figures, included the Fanti of Ghana, the Yoruba of Nigeria, the Mossi of Burkina Faso, the Swazi and the Zulu of South Africa.

African societies that dispensed with chiefs and governed themselves are called acephalous or stateless societies ("tribes without rulers").[2] Among them were the Igbo of Nigeria, the Kru of Liberia, the Tallensi of Ghana,

---

[1] Anthropologists define a state as a bureaucracy organized specifically to carry out political activities (Bohannan, 1964). In a state, there is an interlocking system of offices or positions that must be filled by officials. Authority is then made inherent in these positions. A few anthropologists, however, lump empires and autonomously ruled tribes with centralized authority together as "states."

[2] There were a few exceptional tribal groupings which exhibited the characteristics of both and are called polycephalous. One such tribe was the Kpelle, who had no single king or chief to serve as the head of state for all Kpelle. Instead, there was a series of paramount chiefs, all of equal authority. Serving under them were district chiefs, town chiefs and quarter officials (Gibbs, 1965; p.216).

the Konkomba of Togoland, the Fulani of Nigeria, the Somali, the Jie of Uganda, and the Mbeere of Kenya.

The distinction between "states" and "stateless" as a pedagogical device is itself often subject to controversy. After independence, there was an understandable urge to expunge "colonial" biases from historical writing about Africa. Special emphasis came to be placed on the African achievement in the precolonial era, highlighting precolonial African states. The emphasis was supposed to refute the idea that all Africans once lived in "tribes" and that Africans were incapable of building structures that approximated those of Western nation-states. The distinction between states and stateless societies subsequently became politicized.

But,

> In the 1970s, as the afterglow faded under the dark clouds of poverty and dependency, African nationalist historiography came to be seriously questioned. The glorification of states was shown to be misguided, and the state-stateless dichotomy to be misplaced. As Lonsdale has remarked, 'The first African histories after the colonial era tended to be. . .studies in state-formation as achievement. In more recent years, it has been objected that these were really chronicles of injury, not, as was thought, of pride; for states were and are engines of oppression, not civilization.' In the Marxist analysis the state contains the coercive apparatus required to secure and sustain the dominance of a class of non-producers over an exploited class of producers (Maylam, 1986:64).

However inadequate and controversial the dichotomy, it has been used in this book for heuristic purposes. Less controversial but confusing perhaps is the term "chief." It is often used indiscriminately to represent a king, a chief, and even a headman.[3] Strictly speaking, the chief is the person next to but subordinate to the king. When there are several chiefs subordinate to the king, then the principal chief would be paramount or head chief. The rest would be just chiefs and those under them would be sub-chiefs. Properly speaking the leader at the village level would be a headman, but he is called a "chief" by many.

In this study, however, the term "king" will be used to denote the head of a kingdom and the heads of constituent village governments will be called "chiefs." "Headmen" will be reserved for heads of tribal societies without centralized authority. A kingdom will be used for a political entity composed

---

[3] In modern Nigeria, the title "chief" has lost its meaning. It can be conferred upon a prominent person for exemplary service to the community. It can even be purchased by wealthy businessmen. Others simply confer it upon themselves: "Chief M. K. O. Abiola, Nigeria's biggest publisher, has nearly 2,200 chieftaincy titles and is still yearning for more" (*West Africa*, March 18-24, 1991; p.409).

of a homogenous stock although the size of the kingdom may vary. An empire will be used to denote a political configuration in which different tribes are ruled under a single monarch.

Chiefdoms were perhaps more numerous as political entities than any other. Although the basic nucleus of a chiefdom was formed by the chief and his relatives, it could include people who had no family links with the chief. Some chiefdoms were independent; some appeared to be in relations of overlordship or subordination to other chiefdoms; others might acknowledge overlord by one chiefdom but at the same time subordinate themselves to another. Thus, there were various grades of independence and subordination.

Chiefdoms varied in population size from a few hundred to several thousands. Chiefdoms and other political entities always had a tendency to split and segment. From time to time, a member of a ruling lineage would break away with his age-mates and other followers to establish his own chiefdom. Several factors - economic, political and even religious — underlay this fissiparous tendency: unwillingness to submit to dictatorship; the desire to become an ancestor (founders of a settlement automatically become ancestors); rivalries in the royal lineage over the choice of the chief.

External forces or agents could also spark the fragmentation of chiefdoms. Population growth and consequent over-crowding on the land forced migrations. Ecological factors or lack of arable land or pasture induced others to migrate. Aggression or conquest by a foreign enemy (Arabs, Europeans and other African tribes) broke up many chiefdoms. Maylam (1986) provided this example:

> The present demographic structure of South Africa owes much to events that occurred in the two crucial decades between 1820 and 1840. The arrival of British settlers and Boer migrations within the subcontinent considerably altered and expanded the distribution of the white population. But more dramatic were the cataclysmic changes in Nguni and Sotho society wrought by the *difaqane* (wars and violence). The overall impact of the *difaqane* was varied: some societies were severely devastated; some were forced to migrate and establish themselves in other parts of Africa; others withstood the traumas and even consolidated their position.
>
> The chain reaction of attack, counter-attack, devastation and dispersal that constituted the *difaqane* had its origins in Dingiswayo's time (p.55).

The turmoil unleashed by the *difaqane* caused many communities to be uprooted. Many chiefdoms were dislocated and their subjects scattered. The impact on the Tswana was particularly devastating. Some Bantu communities migrated to new lands to escape the turmoil; others broke up into groups of refugees to seek protection inside stronger, surviving chiefdoms.

> The most well-known northern Nguni refugees to migrate south-wards were the Mfengu. They were a heterogenous group, comprising people of diverse origins. One section of the Mfengu was made up of those Hlubi who fled to the south after being defeated by the Ngwane in the early 1820s. Remnant groups from the Bhele and Zizi chiefdoms also joined the ranks of the Mfengu. The Mfengu arrived in southern Nguni territory not as a cohesive community, but as small groups or individuals. Initially, they came to Gcaleka-land where they approached petty chiefs or headmen and requested food and shelter. The Mfengu attached themselves to the Xhosa in various ways. Some became incorporated into Xhosa society, perhaps by intermarriage. Other Mfengu became Xhosa clients, performing services and paying tribute in return for the use of land and the loan of cattle (Maylam, 1986:61).

This Mfengu behavior was also characteristic of the Ga and the Yoruba in West Africa. After migrating to new lands, they submitted to or ingratiated themselves with their new hosts. Over time, however, in contrast to the Mfengu, the Ga and Yoruba succeeded in dislodging the original inhabitants and establishing their own political systems.

In many cases throughout African history, the original inhabitants so dislodged also moved to subjugate the aborigines elsewhere rather than submit to "foreign rule." Some succeeded in imposing their suzerainty; the others failing were expelled to settle somewhere else. Villages were easy to set up. But even in the absence of external aggression or threats, there were inherent fissiparous tendencies as the villages grew beyond their optimum sizes.

The optimum size of a village depended upon the area, on available land for farming or grazing, and on the motivation keeping the group together. At some point however, the tensions which arise in a growing community prove stronger than the bonds uniting the community, and the village splits. Occasionally, when the headman was autocratic or was not able to inspire sufficient confidence, a small group of the community might hive off to start a new settlement elsewhere. Often, they were soon followed by others in the original community. *Freedom of movement* (or the exit option) often served as a check on despotism. A despotic headman soon found himself abandoned by some of his people.

Through this process of abandonment, migration, conquest and overlord-ship, numerous chiefdoms were created in Africa. Some lasted a few decades but others grew powerful to absorb others in kingdoms and empires —

Group B.

In this group, there were also two discernible political cultures. One was an imperial rule under which extensive domestic independence and autonomy were granted to the vassal states, as in the Asante and Zande empires in the nineteenth century (Indirect Rule). The other type of imperial rule was predicated upon assimilation of the "superior foreign culture" by the subjugated. Notable examples include the Mandinka, Fulani, Hausa, or in general, the Islamic empires in the eighteenth and nineteenth centuries in West Africa.

The following summarizes the general types of political structures:

GROUP A	GROUP B
INDEPENDENT RULE	EMPIRES
1. Stateless Societies (Without Chiefs)	1. "Assimilation"
2. Kingdoms or States	2. Indirect Rule

In virtually all traditional African societies, political organization began at the lineage or the village level. When migrating families formed a village, the original leader became the *odekuro* (owner of the village) in the case of the Ashanti and *samusha* in the case of the Shona. The political organization of the Akan was typical.

The Akan peoples of Ghana consist of the following sub-groups: Ashanti (or Asante), Fante, Agona, Brong, Akyem, Akuapem, Kwahu, Denkyira, Assin, Ahanta and Nzema-Evalue. But they all possessed more or less similar political structures. The structural units were the large settlements known as *nkuro* (*kuro* for singular). The *kuro* was normally the capital town or settlement of the state (*oman*). It consisted of wards, *abrono*, which were inhabited by a mixed number of family groups or lineages. "The lineages were scattered segments or sections of the 7 or 8 Akan clans (*nton*), one or more of which were to be found in all Akan states" (Arhin, 1985; p.14).

Members of one of the lineages were the *adehyee*, royals, who had the right to the headship of the town and sometimes of the whole state. The head of a town could be an *ohene*, head of a division (*omansin*) or head of the state (*omanhene*).

> Each Ashanti village consisted of a number of lineages which formed a political community under the *odekuro*, who belonged to one of the first lineages to settle there. The affairs of the village were managed by the *odekuro* and the heads of the lineages of the village. But the *odekuro* was also responsible to an elder who lived at the capital in Wenchi (Busia, 1951:6).

Similarly elsewhere, the lineage was the most powerful and effective force for unity and stability in early Africa (Williams, 1987; p.165). Each lineage had its head, chosen according to its own rules, who became the chief's councillors. Some chose their heads upon the basis of age, maturity and relation to ancestors. The Fanti of Ghana seldom used wealth as a criterion (Oguah, 1984). The old, venerably referred to as "elders", were often chosen as lineage heads since there was a tendency to associate old age with wisdom.[4] However, a lineage head, most often a male, could be replaced if the families felt he had "brought shame to the lineage" by acts of public misconduct or moral turpitude.

Busia (1951) gave this account of how the Asante chose their elders:

> When an elder died, the chief sent a message to the senior woman and the senior man of the lineage, requesting them to elect a man to be the head of their lineage. This man would on his election also become the chief's elder. All the grown-up men and the senior women of the lineage then held a meeting to select a candidate. They considered the sons of all the women of the lineage whose children had a kinright to the office. When they had decided on one they sent to the father and mother of their chosen candidate to 'beg them for their son.' If the parents agreed they said, 'We give him to you.' The members of the lineage, including all the men and women, met again in the house of the senior woman. The candidate was informed that he had been selected to become the head of the lineage. 'We put you in the place of our ancestors.' The senior man then sent to tell the chief that they had chosen a man to be head of their lineage. If the chief accepted the nomination, a day was fixed when the lineage could present their head to the chief and his elders. If the chief did not like the nominated candidate, he gave his reasons and asked the lineage to elect one with whom 'I could look after the state' (p.8).

After an acceptable Asante candidate was chosen, oaths of allegiance were sworn. A stool (a wooden chair) was given to the new head and he paid *aseda* (thanksgiving fee) of four pounds sterling and ten shillings plus a bottle of rum. The new head was then carried away from the chief's house on the shoulders of his relatives and friends to the music of the *fontomfrom* drums and the singing of *ose*. He was now the head of his lineage and an elder or councillor of the chief.

Structurally, an African chiefdom was composed of four basic units of government. The first unit was the chief, the central authority. The second was the "inner or privy council" which advised the chief. The third was the

---

[4] The characteristic is not peculiar to Africa alone. In the United States, for example, justices in the Supreme Court are appointed for life and are generally "wise old men and women," The original motive was to preserve "judicial independence". But life appointment does not necessarily mean "judicial despotism" since the judges can be removed by Congress.

"council of elders." If there were ten lineages in the village, for example, their heads would form the "council of ten elders." The fourth institution was the "village assembly" of commoners or meeting:

1. The chief, central authority
2. The Inner or Privy Council
3. Council of Elders
4. The Village Assembly

The various lineages or extended families in the village chose their own heads, as described of the Asante and they subsequently constituted themselves into a council of elders. The elders then chose the chief or approved the selection of a candidate nominated to be chief by someone else. The chief chose his own inner circle of advisers from among prominent and respectable citizens in the community. He needed no formal approval from the council of elders. However, since without the council the chief was powerless in enacting legislation, he was careful not to offend the councillors with his choice of advisers. More will be said on the selection of the chief, advisers and councillors in a later section (chiefdoms).

The repository of the greatest political power or influence was the Village Assembly of Commoners, giving true meaning to the phrase: "power lay with the common people." In most African villages, the commoners could freely form their own associations: political, economic and social. In other words, they had (*freedom of association*). Meetings were not necessarily regular but whenever any matter of importance was to be discussed by the elders, the commoners would meet and deliberate on such matters.

Their recognized leaders or spokesmen would present the views of the commoners to the elders. Among the Asante, this spokesman was called the *Nkwankwaahene*. He was not a member of the chief's official council, and his office was not a hereditary one. The commoners chose anyone of themselves whom they considered brave, eloquent and intelligent. When so chosen he became their recognized leader and the arbiter of disputes among them.

According to Busia (1951),

> Although he had no official place in the council of elders, the *Nkwankwaahene* was recognized as the representative of the commoners, and the elders considered any representations he made to them. His position was of political importance as it enabled the commoners to criticize the Government. . .Public opinion or criticism of the Government was therefore expressed through the *Nkwankwaahene* (p.10).

B. STATELESS SOCIETIES

A stateless society or "nonstate" would seem almost a contradiction in terms to Westerners, who may see the institution of the state as necessary to avoid tyranny, although recognizing that a "bad" state can impose tyranny. They see the absence of the state as a recipe for chaos. On the other hand, "Africans who live in stateless societies tend to see the state as unavoidable tyranny; they seek and find order in other institutions" (Bohannan, 1964; p.195).

Autocracy was always a theoretical possibility in government, a fact which concerned many ethnic societies. To guard against this, many elected not to have chiefs or any centralized authority at all. For example, "the Tiv of Nigeria were a people who lived in fear of power and were compelled to place themselves under the possessors of power for protection against its abuse by others" (Carlston, 1968:211).

Other stateless societies went a step further by institutionalizing a social habit of impugning or deriding centralized political authority through its oral narratives. Yelpaala (1987) noted that, through mythic, metaphorical and mimetic structures, leadership roles such as kings and chiefs in some stateless societies were cast in negative paradigms, while the ideal leadership was accented. To reinforce this cultural aversion to leadership roles, Igbo society also imposed such onerous obligations and religious restrictions on titleholders that their power was effectively neutralized or kept in line with notions of ideal leadership. The Dagaaba oral narratives are similarly replete with mythic and metaphorical images of kingship. "Kings and chiefs are often portrayed as unimaginative, unintelligent, lacking common sense, and likely to use brute force" (Yelpaala, 1983; p.357).

Yelpaala concluded:

> It is therefore obvious from the way societies like the Tiv, the central Igbo, and the Dagaaba were organized that they were well aware of the political structure of the centralized systems, but tried to eliminate them as much as possible. For instance, they recognized the tremendous advantage of centralized power during war and used a limited form of it only then. Leaders were given the power to command and carry out operations, but during peacetime, they became, like Cincinnatus, common people and ceased to exercise that power (p.357).

Similar tendencies were also observable among the Ga of southern Ghana. The Ga *mantse* only united his people and led them in times of war. Politically and in peacetime, he had no role in government.

There is evidence to support the thesis that ecological factors and livelihood also played a role in the choice of political systems; especially among pastoralists. The nature of their livelihood made centralized systems of government unfeasible. To govern themselves, they formulated viable social systems with their own values, skills and wealth and successfully maintained their societies.

Organizational Structure

In stateless societies, two principles from their descent system permitted them to govern their affairs with minimum of administrative burden and tedium:

> The first might be referred to as the structural regulation of internal affairs. A quarrel between members of two sublineages is an exclusive matter of the immediate parent lineage, and a dispute between two members of the same minimal lineage is of concern to that unit only. This principle tends to limit the arena of concern to the smallest relevant unit. However, despite the efficiency with which this limits relations, it tends to work against large-scale leadership.
>
> The second principle from the descent system which influences organization in segmentary (stateless) societies is related to the *political* functions of the groups and might be referred to as the rule of political practicality. Political units must be viable in ways that lineages need not; as a result, considerations of size and contiguity, which are irrelevant to descent as such, are important to a political organization. For example, a political unit must defend itself, which implies a minimum size, and it must have internal cohesion, which implies both a maximum size and a local arena of such size that interaction is possible. Political units, thus, are perceived as though they were units of the lineage system, even though the organization does not coincide with the lineage system (Vaughan, 1986; p.177).

Accordingly, the maintenance of justice as well as of cultural and territorial integrity were effected through the extended family organizations and the invocation of kinship behavior, not only in domestic but wider spheres. This was characteristic of the hunting and pastoral peoples such as the !Kung, the Pygmies and the Fulani. But precautions were taken. A system of checks and balances was instituted in which two or more power centers were balanced against each other and applied in all levels of the community so that no single center predominated. There was a wide dispersion of this system across Africa, adopted by such ethnic societies as the Tiv and Igbo of Nigeria, the Nuer of Sudan and the Bedouin Arabs throughout North Africa. Both types generally used kinship idiom and the norms of kinship behavior in their system of law and order. In general there were no officeholders; only representatives of groups. Such societies reached compromises in conflict resolution rather than making judgments and applying sanctions.

A few of these societies had leaders. The headman among the !Kung is called *kxau*. Among the pastoral Somali he is the *suldaan*. He is not a ruler; he is a leader only because he executes the collective will of the people (Williams, 1987; p.171). In !Kung society, the headman is the oldest son of the previous headman. If the male line is cut off for a generation, headmanship passes through the eldest daughter to her eldest son.

If a headman is too young, too old, or lacks personal qualities of leadership, the people would turn quite informally to some other man for leadership in their daily life, asking him for help and advice (Gibbs, 1965; p.268). But as Marshall (1958) pointed out:

> Headmanship is different from leadership, which is not hereditary. Leadership depends heavily on a man's character, his hunting prowess, and especially his ability to focus people's opinions. Usually headman and leader are the same person but, should a headman be too young - perhaps still in his mother's womb - or very old, a band will have a separate leader. . . Neither leadership nor headmanship implies any coercive power over the other members of the band. Only as a coagulation of group opinion can headmen or leaders exert a control - which, even then, is not final. The leader, being the kind of person to whom others come when decisions must be made, is often an arbiter, in quarrels, a focal point in discussion of plans, a comfort to the bereaved and a strength for those in doubt.

Yelpaala (1983) also found a similar situation among the Dagaaba:

> There are four types of authority: the *tendaana* (owner of the land), the central authority of the village; the lineage head; and the elders of the lineage. Age appears to be the most important criterion in all four types of authority. Personal attributes come next. . .The *tendaana* is legal authority, even though he does not have the power to compel obedience. The power to induce but not compel obedience is not attached to the office but depends on his personal attributes. However, his power to compel obedience or enforce decisions is linked to his spiritual role as *tendaana*. The same applies to other forms of authori-ty. . . The actual leader authority may be too old, too preoccupied, or too uninterested in the position or lack some vital attributes of a leader. Under any or some of these situations the legal authority may delegate the functions of the office to another. Sometimes the legal authority may be functionally weak and a failure but still serves the important

purpose of providing the basis for unity of divergent personalities and interests in the face of internal or external conflict (p.368).

Thus, in many acephalous societies, there was a clear separation between power (defined as the ability to influence events in a desired manner and direction) and authority (meaning the acknowledged or recognized right to exercise power). One did not necessarily flow from the other.
Williams (1987) concluded:

> It was therefore in the societies without chiefs or kings where African democracy was born and where the concept that the people are sovereign was as natural as breathing. And this is why in traditional Africa, the rights of the individual never came before the rights of the community. . .These self-governing people did not have a Utopian society in any idealistic sense. Theirs was a practical society in every way. Their laws were natural laws, and order and justice prevailed because the society could not otherwise survive. Theirs was, in fact, a government of the people; theirs was, in fact, not a theory, but a government by the people; and it was, in fact, a government for the people. That this kind of government did 'pass from the earth' is another fact we now call 'modern progress' (p.170).

The colonialists had the most difficulty in dealing with stateless societies. The colonial authorities sought responsible office holders with "power" in such societies. Finding no such power figures, the colonialists then "created" them. But these "leaders" lacked authority since they were not part of the kinship group and were treated as external representatives of an alien government. Within the tribe they had little authority and what little they had was considered tyrannous by the people under them.

In the following section, we examine the political organization of selected stateless societies.

The Igbo Government

The Igbo occupy what was formerly Eastern Region of Nigeria but is now broken into four separate states: Anambra, Cross River, Imo and Rivers. They belong to the Niger-Congo dialect but subdivided into two sub-family groups: the Benue-Congo sub-family and the Kwa sub-family (Olaniyan, 1985; p.21). The Igbo subscribe to a set of beliefs which conflicts with centralization of authority.

> The Igbo were individualistic and egalitarian, every man consider-
> ing himself as good as everyone else and demanding a voice in his

local affairs. Since everyone had a right to rise in society Igbo culture emphasized competition, competition between families, between lineages and between clans (Webster and Boahen, 1970:166).

Consequently, they adopted a flexible democratic political system which, though based on the lineage structure, was characterized by autonomous federations of lineages or villages organized through lineage heads, age grades and title societies. The policy-making body was composed of representatives of lineages within the autonomous political groups.

The Igbo village was divided into wards. The wards were grouped around a large village market which operated every four or eight days depending upon its size and importance. Each ward was made up of sections and each section of a number of extended families whose compounds were close together. A meeting of the village was held in the main market or inside an elder's compound.

The Igbo village government consisted of two basic institutions: the *Ama-ala*, made up of the heads of the extended families or lineages, and the "Village Assembly of Citizens."

> The lineage head in the east Niger Delta was elected and he sat in court with adult male members of the group. Among the EfikIbibio, the bond of lineage and the village did not lie strictly in kinship or blood as among the Igbo and the Annang, because the lineage and the village members were of diverse ancestry who had moved into the site from different settlements. Unity lay, however, in the political autonomy, obligations of mutual aid and the territorial isolation of the lineage or village (Olaniyan, 1985: 26).

Other persons were co-opted into the council. They were usually wealthy personages and some title holders, particularly the *ozo* title holders. The council was presided over by the senior *okpara*, the head of the family whose ancestor either founded the village settlement or first acquired the *ozo* title. "He was a 'ceremonial' head of the council and his authority did not extend outside his own family group. His status outside the council was of the same nature as that of any other member of the council" (Amoah, 1988; p.173).

The council was the controlling authority in the village. It performed all the functions which a chief and his council of elders performed in a chiefdom. But other groups, such as ritual functionaries and age-grades, helped with the maintenance of law and order. With regard to government of the village group as a whole, the controlling authority was the general body of the heads of families in each of the villages forming the group. This body was presided over by the senior *okpara* of the village in the village group which was the first to be founded in the locality.

At the village level, every adult Igbo male had the right to sit in on the council meetings. "In council meetings the matter to be decided is brought before the group and any member is free to voice his opinion" (Gibbs, 1965; p.24). But, as with the Fanti of Ghana, this right was seldom exercised unless a decision was to be taken which affected the individual in an important way.

> In routine matters the elders ruled by decree and proclamation but where decisions likely to produce disputes were to be taken, the *Ama-ala* could order the town crier to announce a village assembly in the market place or in a ward square.

> At the assembly, the elders laid the issues before the people. Every man had a right to speak, the people applauding popular proposals and shouting down unpopular ones. Decisions had to be unanimous. . .If the *Ama-ala* acted arbitrarily and refused to call the assembly, people could demand it by completely ignoring them and bringing town life to a halt (a VILLAGE STRIKE!). By ignoring and refusing to speak to an unpopular elder, social pressure often compelled the elder to bend to the popular will. The village assembly was considered the Igbo man's birthright, the guarantee of his rights, his shield against oppression, the expression of his individualism, and the means whereby the young progressive impressed their views upon the old and the conservative (Boahen and Webster, 1970:170).

This view is supported by Harris (1987):

> The village assembly characterized Igbo democracy. It was there that the elders presented issues to the people, everyone had a right to speak (*freedom of expression*), and decisions had to be unanimous. The village assembly therefore was a body in which the young and old, the rich and poor could be heard. Every citizen's participation was possible and important. Decision-making could often be time-consuming, but the slow procedure guaranteed greater individual participation (p.121).

After a close study of the various power bases (decision-making) in the Igbo political system, Olaniyan (1985) discovered five general features:

1.   The traditional archetype whereby decisions are reached by consensus among the lineage representatives among whom age, wealth or privilege have no overriding influence.

2.   A slight modification of the above is found among the Awka Igbo where members of title societies and lineage elders constitute the political decision-making group.

3.   Among Cross River Igbo, in Abriba, Ohafia, and Arochukwu, secret societies dominate the political scene.

4. Among the Asaba, Aguleri and Abriba Igbo, age-grades and lineage heads form the decision-making body.

5. Among Ogbaru, Oguta, Aboh, Onitsha and Osomari Igbo, the political structure is hierarchical.

In all these categories the essence of government remained the same. "Even in the fifth checks and balances are so employed that autocratic tendencies do not exist" (Olaniyan, 1985; p.27).

The Fulani Of Northern Nigeria

The Fulani are pastoral people who live mainly in northern Nigeria and many parts of West Africa, along the fringes of the Sahara. They herd their cattle for hundreds of miles in search of water and grazing land. Thus, they come in constant contact with other ethnic groups in their migrations. Consequently, they adopted a political system that adapted to the vicissitudes of their occupation. Such must necessarily be fluid, to guarantee their own economic welfare by maintaining links not only with alien groups of similar order whom they encountered in their pastoral life but also by rendering allegiance to states in whose territory they pastured.

The basic political unit of the Wodaabe of West Bornu consisted of the males of a small agnatic descent group and their families. This group associated with other like groups in the wet season but separated from them as the dry season approached and they began their search for water. In the wet-season when they were together, they had a political leader, the *ardo*.[5]

The *ardo* was charged with general responsibility for his group's social, political and economic affairs. "His exercise of authority was mostly

---

[5] In ancient times, the *maudo laawol pulaaku* (Guardian of the Fulani Way) exercised jural control over the clan. There were a few general principles which prescribed the "Fulani Way" (*laawol pulaaku*). According to Gibbs (1965):

For a Wodaabe man, right conduct is still mainly the exercise of familial virtues. Fulfillment of duties toward elders, wives, and coevals ensures the smooth working of the family and the lineage groups as economic and cooperative units. Fecundity means herdsmen and milkmaids. Good husbandry ensures that the next generation is provided for. Proper arrangement of children's marriage secures them in a social system in which they can count on the same satisfactions their fathers had. . .There are three other components of *pulaaku*. These are *seemteende* (modesty and reserve), *munyal* (patience and fortitude), and *hakkiilo* (care and forethought) (p.368).

The "Guardian of the Fulani Way" was the judge and had the power of banishing from the tribe any one who infringed the "Fulani Way." The Fulani Way was related to the human organism in that shame was felt in the belly, the place of secrets, the heart was the place of patience and fortitude, and the head the place of care and forethought. "It was from the exercise of care and fore-thought that a man succeeded in the possession of wives, children, cattle, and the esteem and cooperation of kinsmen" (Carlston, 1968:151).

dependent on consultation with members of the group, weighing their views and experience, and reaching conclusions which were announced in terms of advice rather than command" (Carlston, 1968:150). He was the spokesman of his group in dealing with like groups within Wodaabe society, and with all those outside Wodaabe society.

Gibbs (1965) provided a similar view:

> An *ardo* does not command, he advises, as is best seen in the conferences preceding pastoral moves. The *ardo*'s duty is to elicit all forms of evidence from the youngest herdsboy to the oldest herder, and to sum up the feeling of the group. Thereafter, any householder can go where he will without restraint and with no ill feeling (p.394).

The Somali

The Somali, like the Igbo, are highly egalitarian but, unlike the Igbo, are pastoralists. In accordance with the shifting nature of their lineage divisions, the Somali possess no formal hierarchy of firm political offices. At every level of lineage grouping, political leadership lies with the elders of all the constituent lineage segments. Occasionally, there may be a clan head (the *suldaan* or sultan). However, at every level of the segmentation, all adult men are classed as *oday* (elders) with the right to speak in the *shir* (ad hoc councils), which deliberate matters of common concern and decide policy. In addition, there are men of religion and *wadaad* (sheiks) and *waranleh* (warriors) who play a rather passive role in administration. The men of religion are expected to bless and guide council proceedings of the warrior lineages. Besides that,

> All adult men have in principle an equal say in the formulation of lineage policy. Naturally, however, the words of different men carry different weights, for respect is given to such factors as, wealth, inherited prestige, skill in oratory and poetry, political acumen, wisdom, and age. . .Council meetings are called when the need arises; there are no set times or places of assembly nor offices connected with them. Usually the participants sit in the shade of a convenient tree, in the central clearing of a hamlet, or they may meet in a tea shop in a trade village or town. Decisions reached follow the consensus (Gibbs, 1965; p.345).

It is important not to misintepret "equal say" and "words of different men carry different weights" as a contradiction. The essential point is that there is the right or freedom to express an opinion. Of course, how successful that opinion is in influencing others is a different matter.

The Gikuyu Of Kenya

After a people's revolution (*itwika*) which overthrew their despot in the 19th century, the Gikuyu people formed a revolutionary council (*njama ya itwika*) to draft a constitution. The constitution enacted laws and affirmed the rights of the Gikuyu people in government. According to Kenyatta (1938), these included the following:

1. Freedom for the people to acquire and develop land under a system of family ownership.

2. Socially and politically, all circumcised men and women should be equally full members of the tribe, and thereby the status of a king or nobleman should be abolished.

3. The government should be in the hands of council of elders (*kiama*) chosen from all members of the community, who have reached the age of eldership.

4. In order to keep up the spirit of the *itwika* (people's revolution), and to prevent any tendency to return to the system of despotic government, the change of, and the election for, the government offices should be based on a rotation system of generations.

5. No man should be allowed to hold a responsible position other than warrior, or become a member of the council of elders (*kiama*) unless he was married and had established a homestead. And that women should be given the same social status as their husbands (p.182).

Under the Gikuyu constitution, each family group formed a family council (*ndundu ya mocie*) with the father as head (a lineage head). The heads of several lineages formed the village council (*kiama gia itora*) which was headed by the eldest of the lineage heads. Over the village council was a wider district council (*kiama kia rogongo*) in which all the elders of the district participated. The district council was presided over by a committee (*kiama kia ndundu*) composed of the senior elders of the villages. From these elders, the most advanced in age and wisdom was elected as a judge and president (*mothamaki* or *mociiri*) of the *ndundu*. From the district council a national council was formed, comprised of several *ndundu*, representing the whole population. "Among the judges, a president was elected at the meetings of the national council" (Kenyatta, 1938:187).

The Gikuyu system of government was unique in several respects. First,

In the whole governmental organization there was no inheritable position, everything depending on personal merit. Elevation to high office was based entirely upon the behavior of an individual to his group and to the community at large. The group had the right to recall and dismiss or suspend any of its representatives whose behavior was contrary to the well-established rules of conduct. In fact, it was the voice of the people or public opinion that ruled the country. . . In the eyes of the Gikuyu people, the submission to a despotic rule of any particular man or group, white or black, is the greatest humiliation to mankind. The spirit of *itwika*, namely, the changing of government in rotation through a peaceful and constitutional revolution, is still ingrained in the minds of the Gikuyu people (Kenyatta, 1938:189).

The second feature of the Gikuyu system of government was its rotational system of succession among the generations. The community was divided into two categories: (a) *mwangi*, (b) *maina* or *irungu*. Membership was determined by birth. If one generation was *mwangi*, their sons would be *maina* and their grandsons would be *mwangi* and so on. One generation would hold office for a period of 30-40 years, at the end of which the *itwika* ceremony was performed for the young generation to replace the old. After the proclamations and feasting, a new government was formed and the revolutionary council (*njama ya itwika*) was dissolved and the delegates returned to their villages (Kenyatta, 1938:186).

It may be recalled that the Yoruba and the Lunda rotated kingship among lineages. Rotation of headship of a state, within lineages or generations, was one effective way of dealing with destructive competition for the throne.

Third, the Gikuyu system had no chief endowed with supernatural and religious sanctions as in the other tribal systems. Hence its classification here as stateless although the system had a head (*mothamaki*).

The !Kung Of The Kalahari

The !Kung are a San subgroup who live in the Kalahari Desert of Namibia. They organize themselves into autonomous nomadic bands, made up of a group of nuclear families who live together. They are linked to one another and to the headman by kinship bonds. Each band has its own territory and owns the resources within it. Sometimes, two or more bands may belong to the same territory. Hunting is their main means of livelihood and they hunt with the use of little unfeathered poisoned arrows.[6]

Each band has its own headman, called the *kxau* (owner). He leads the band in migration and represents it in dealings with other bands. "It is an office with few specific duties, no privileges, but grave responsibilities"

---

[6] There are four kinds of poison: a root, two grubs and the pod of a tree. One of the two kinds of grub is the larva of a beetle identified as *Diamphidia simplex*. After preparation the poison is smeared on the foreshaft of the arrow. Depending upon where the arrow pierces, a small buck can die in the morning, a man in a few hours, a giraffe in four to five days (Marshall, 1957). The amazing aspect of the poison is that it has no effect on the game's meat which can be eaten with relative impunity. The poison must enter the bloodstream directly to be deadly. Perhaps, medical scientists may want to investigate this mystery further.

(Vaughan, 1986; p.176). He does not own the resources per se, but merely oversees their fair distribution and exploitation by all members of the band. He also coordinates the movements of his band in relation to its consumption of resources, but his chief duty is to plan when and where the band will move (Gibbs, 1965; p.267). The headman is much like the head of an extended family and must coordinate the activities of the family units as they eke out a living.

When the band moves, the headman's position is at the head of the line. He chooses the site for the new settlement and has the first choice of a spot to put his hut. For his duties, he receives no rewards or tributes. In contrast to other social systems, the headman is not the judge. Wrongdoing is judged and controlled by public opinion, usually expressed in talk.

> Most decisions are reached by *consensus* and the headman does not need to arbitrate disputes. In the final analysis, cooperative behavior and consensual agreement upon norms and values hold the band together with the headman acting as their 'presiding officer' (Vaughan, 1986; p.176).

Headmanship is inherited by the eldest son from the father. If that son dies or leaves the band, the headmanship passes to the next oldest son. As noted earlier, if a headman is too young or too old, or lacks leadership qualities, people may turn to some other person for leadership. Such a leader has no authority and receives no honors or rewards.

Over the years, !Kung society has been buffetted by various ecological and political exigencies. In the late 1980s, the !Kung (or Bushmen) were wrestling with a pressing problem. Their future was uncertain with imminent grant of independence to Namibia. *The Wall Street Journal* did a story about them, and it would be instructive to follow the details of this story as it reveals some insights about their indigenous political culture and how it has adapted to modern times:

> In the precious shade of a gnarled Combretum tree, two dozen Ju/ wa Bushmen, squatting in the dust like baseball catchers, pass around metal pipes stuffed with tobacco and talk about forming a government. In Bush politics, this is as close as you get to a smoke-filled room. 'The white man has spoken for us too often. We must have a government to speak for ourselves,' says one of the men in the gentle clicking language of the Bushmen. 'Yes, yes,' clicks another. 'We must be organized, we must make our own laws'. . .

> For many millenia, the Bushmen had no need for governments or laws, or even for leaders, as they roamed freely across southern Africa, hunting and gathering in the Kalahari region of what is now Botswana and Namibia. But in the past several decades, the

politically mute Bushmen have seen their once-vast foraging territory whittled down to a rectangular-shaped piece of earth called Bushmanland, in northeastern Namibia.

They lost 70 percent of their territory with a stroke of a white man's pen when South Africa applied its apartheid policy to Namibia and carved out homelands for various non-white ethnic groups. Now, with these homeland borders sure to fall away as Namibia gets its independence from South Africa later this year (1989), the Bushmen fear that their little rectangle will be grabbed by covetous trophy hunters, conservationists and cattle ranchers.

This is what brought the wizened elders together under the spreading shade tree. They represent about 1,000 Ju/wa (one of the seven linguistic groups among the Bushmen) who are struggling to make a go of sedentary village life on the hardscrapple plains of eastern Bushmanland - the last group of Bushmen in southern Africa still living independently on a slice of their ancestral land. . .

'We must have a law among ourselves to protect our land. This will give us strength,' says Tsamko Toma, who is emerging as the spokesman of the Ju/wa. He is 49 years old and can neither read nor write. But, in his clicks, he speaks with the eloquence of a Jefferson or de Tocqueville. 'We do not seek the strength of the strong arm,' he tells his people, 'We seek the strength of thought.'

The deep furrows in Mr. Toma's wrinkled face suggest that this will be a difficult quest, for it requires a fundamental change in this ancient culture. For the *supremely individualistic* Bushmen, *seeking consensus* beyond the immediate hunting party and extending their everyday concern beyond the next meal is as foreign as snow.

'Each of us just can't think of his own problems as we have in the past,' warns Mr. Toma. 'We must begin to think together. We must think as a group for our own survival.' He shakes his head, out of both frustration and desperation. Those gathered under the gnarled tree don't all fit the image of Bushmen popularized in the film 'The Gods Must Be Crazy' - bow and arrow hunters dressed only in loin cloth and beads and so out of touch with the modern world that a Coca Cola bottle is a mystery. These Bushmen are fully clothed; some of them wear ties and jackets for the occasion. They smoke Winstons and Benson & Hedges (in addition to the metal pipes). Crushed Coke cans litter Bushmanland as they do other parts of the world. Bushmen still hunt, but mainly to supplement their farming and cattle raising. . .

Trophy hunters and conservationists alike want to claim a chunk of Bushmanland for a wildlife reserve, and the Herero cattle ranchers to the south covet a wide area of Bushmanland for its virgin grazing land. 'Everyone wants a piece of Bushmanland,' says Megan Biesele, an American anthropologist who is the project director of the development foundation.

To keep these hands off their land the Ju/wa are trying to stake a claim to their villages now. They have drafted the preamble to a Bushman constitution - 'The land of our villages belongs to us because it belonged to our fathers' fathers and our mothers' mothers - and invited Namibia's two main political parties, the South West Africa People's Organization (SWAPO) and the Democratic Turnhalle Alliance (DTA), for discussions under the Combretum tree. There, they have tried to reserve a place for themselves in post-independence Namibia and have sought to ensure Bushmen representation in whatever government is formed.

So far, neither party has committed itself to a firm land-use policy, but they pledge to keep the Bushmen in mind. 'All of us have become conscious of the fact that the Bushmen have been pushed around for too long,' says Katuutire Kaure, a DTA leader. Daniel Tjongarero of SWAPO says the Ju/wa made a good case under the Combretum tree. 'Everyone was sitting around, participating in the discussion,' he says. 'It was democracy.'

Still, it's taking a while for the Bushmen to learn the new political language. 'What does SWAPO and DTA mean?' asks an old man named Xashe. 'I think they are all my enemies' (*The Wall Street Journal*, July 13, 1989; p.1).

The key words and phrases to note in that story were: "gathering under the Combretum tree", "consensus", "ancient culture", "supremely individualistic" and a "Bushman constitution." The statement by the old man, Xashe, ("I think they are all my enemies") was particularly noteworthy. After independence in most parts of Africa, the nationalists and their political parties indeed turned out to be enemies of the indigenes or peasants.
Jane Perlez also provided this account of the Gabbra of Kenya:

GUS, Kenya — The new moon was due in several days, a signal on this occasion for the twice-a-year ceremony known as *sorto*, for sacrifices, marriages and reconciliations.

The Gabbra, one of Kenya's last nomadic tribes, unpacked the makings of their dome-shaped dwellings — from the skins and twigs and cloth — from the backs of camels to form family clusters for the special occasion.

Goats were being selected for the sacrifice on the first night of the new moon, when the men smear sap on their brows and the blood of the killed goat on their foreheads.

Among the 30,000 Gabbra who traverse this buff-colored sandscape east of Lake Turkana and north to the Ethiopian border, life goes on much as it always has. The nomadic instinct is still paramount, the elders say. . .

But a transition has started. . .

Lawrence Boxio, a tall, 30-year old dressed in Western trousers and shirt, says he is fairly typical of the changes. Just married, he says he intends to have 10 children.

'Five for the town and five for the nomadic life,' he said. . .

Mr. Boxio explained that he still wanted to have animals, the basis of Gabbra life. But he didn't want to be totally nomadic himself, thus his plan for dividing his family between the traditional and the new. Even as money enters the economy and a few well-to-do Gabbra own Land-Rovers, it is still the number of animals a Gabbra owns that matters.

'*Under the tree where the decisions are made*, it is a man's animals that count,' Mr. Boxio said (*The New York Times*, August 15, 1990; p.A.4).

Once again, note where the decisions were made — under the tree. Unfortunately in modern times, African elites, figuratively speaking, could not sit under a "national tree" to reach consensual decisions:

Johannesburg, Aug. 15 — Troops moved in today to try to restore order as fighting between rival black groups swept through three densely populated townships southeast of Johannesburg, leaving a trail of devastation and more than 100 people dead on South Africa's bloodiest day in many years.

Police spokesman Eugene Opperman confirmed that the overall death toll in the fighting, which began Sunday night (Aug. 12) but reached a crescendo today, was at least 140, and estimated the number of injured during the period at more than 1,000.

The cause of the fighting remains unclear. Police describe it as a clash between members of the Zulu and Xhosa tribes, but leaders of the African National Congress (ANC) and its allied organizations said it was an extension of the black civil war in Natal province between their supporters and members of the Zulu-based Inkatha movement (*The Washington Post*, Aug. 16, 1990; p.A17).

Selection And Role Of The Headman In Stateless Societies

Heredity did not play a prominent role in the selection of the headman in most stateless societies. Among the Afikpo Igbo, the criteria for leadership are seniority, good oratorical skills, and personal achievement, as expressed in such activities as titles or honors received and the giving of second funerals. Titles can be "bought" and second funerals, often considered a very sanctimonious offering to the departed, are costly. In this sense, wealth may enter as a qualification for leadership. However, Gibbs (1965) argues that,

> For a man to be a respected and persuasive leader he must be an elder (that is, a member of one of the village-group age grades), he must be a good orator, and he must have established his claim to a position of leadership by his achievement; one or two of these qualities are not enough. Hereditary factors are not completely absent here, for if a man's father or grandfather was a respected leader his position is enhanced by this fact, but only if he himself successfully fulfills the qualities of leadership (p.24).

For example, several criteria governed the selection of the Fulani *ardo*. He must have established a herd and a household and he must have wives and children of his own. Being prosperous helps, but he must have demonstrated skills in animal husbandry. Agnatic relation to the previous *ardo* is crucial. Consequently, it is an advantage to be the son or younger brother of the predecessor. "The most important factor, however, is that he commands the support of his entire group" (Gibbs, 1965; p.394). Without this support, the group will split, as it usually does over internal dissension over leadership.

B. GOVERNMENT IN CHIEFDOMS

> According to traditional ideals, a chief could never force his people to do what they did not want to do; *he was a leader rather than a ruler*, relying for his position on influence rather than force.

— Michael Bourdillon (1976).

At the village level, many African societies had chiefs or centralized authority. The chief, in most cases, was a male. He was the political, social, judicial and religious head of the people. As such, he had wide-ranging powers. But, "although the Bantu chief has the right of final decision, he always acts in council, i.e., machinery exists whereby he is assisted in his work as chief administrative and political organ by other members of the tribe" (Olivier, 1969).

The chief was assisted by a small group of confidential advisers called the inner or privy council. Membership was not limited but was drawn mainly from the inner circle of relatives of the chief and personal friends who may include influential members of the community. This inner council served as the first test ground of legislation. The chief would discuss privately and informally with this inner council all matters relating to the administration of the tribe. He might consult his advisers severally or jointly and form an opinion before placing an issue before the people. The meetings might be held in the privacy of the chief's home or in some secluded spot and after dusk when there was little chance of disturbance.

The chief was not bound to follow their advice and might ignore it if he wished. But he would not deliberately do so and risk the withdrawal of their support. This inner council, thus, constituted the first line of defense against despotism.

Among the Bantu, the duty of the advisers was not only to keep the chief in touch with happenings in the tribe but also "keep a check on his own behavior, and when he does wrong should speak to him privately and if necessary reprimand him. A man feeling aggrieved by some action or decision of the chief can lodge his complaint with any one of them (advisers), who is then expected to intercede on his (the complainant's) behalf" (Olivier, 1969). The role of the advisers was to see that the chief governs the tribe properly. If the chief ruled incompetently, the tribe would reproach the advisers for failing in their responsibility (Olivier, 1969). In fact, Busia (1951) reported two cases where two Ashanti elders "lost their stools and were fined in the one case sixteen pounds sterling (*ntanu*) and two sheep, in the other twenty-four pounds sterling (*ntansa*) and two sheep" for failing to advise their chief of his wrong-doing (p.73).

After placing an issue before his inner council, the chief might take it to the council of elders or headmen. This was a much wider and more formal body made up of all the hereditary headmen of the wards or lineages; in essence, representatives of commoners. "The village council thus represents the fountainhead of the common life, and its determination finds expression in the popular voice" (Mensah Sarbah, 1897:20). The chief might nominate to the council of elders, with the concurrence of other councillors, a few other men, usually young, of competence and intelligence who could help in the public deliberations of the community.

The chief presided over this council and sought its opinion. Essentially, it had two functions. The first was to advise and assist the chief in the administration of the tribe and the second was "to act as a brake on the chief, preventing abuse of power, voicing dissatisfactions, criticising and generally to keep the Chief under the necessary control" (Olivier, 1969). Amoah (1988:172) formulated the duties of the council of Akan elders,

> Besides selecting or approving of the nomination of the paramount ruler (chief), the council of elders advised him on the policies he pursued in both internal and external affairs of the chiefdom. In executing those policies and in running the general administration of the chiefdom, the paramount ruler constantly had to consult the elders. *He was forbidden to do anything which affected the interest of the chiefdom without the knowledge, approval and concurrence of the council.* Excepting emergencies he acted only on the advice of the council. *Without the authority of the council no new law could be promulgated.* He could not even receive foreigners unless a member of the council was present. In this way the council controlled the actions of the ruler and if he showed any disposition to make himself independent of the council, he was either deserted by the elders or deposed.

Arhin (1985) provided further elaboration:

> The second duty of the council of elders (the first being helping choose the ruler) was to advise the head of the unit in all matters affecting the people. These matters were *economic* and included the allocation of rights in land to needy subjects and strangers, and the establishment of markets; *religious*, that is, the performance of religious ceremonies, such as was done at the three-weekly *Adae*, and the annual *Odwira* festivals, and other ceremonies said by the priests to be necessary for 'prospering' the land; *judicial*, the settlement of private and public offenses; and *military*, the making of defensive and offensive warfare. The head of a political unit swore on his accession to act in all matters with the advice and consent of his council (p.19).

In turn, the councillors too were subject to checks. With the Asante, it has been stated:

> A councillor holds his office for life. So long as he behaves himself, it is not customary to remove him. . .The Council, when duly constituted, is the ruling voice in all matters political as well as judicial in the community. The head of the community (the king) can do no legal act affecting the interests of the community without

the knowledge, approval and concurrence of the Councillors.' They represent the sovereignty of the people, the King being their Head and the embodiment of the sovereign idea. As such they pay him homage and respect, but he must in turn respect their time-honored laws, customs, traditions, and sentiments. If he goes contrary to any of their well-cherished ideas of proper government, they can call him to account, and in serious cases, may in due course demand his deposition (Casely Hayford, 1911:23).

According to Amoah (1988:172):

The deposition was a check on traditional rulers. The council could destool the ruler either on its own volition or at the instigation of the subjects. In Ashanti and other Akan societies of Ghana any subject might lay a complaint before one of the elders regarding the conduct of the ruler. In Yorubaland, generally, complaints could be lodged by only the nobles and their families. If the complaint were found to be genuine the elders would inform the ruler and he could be admonished. Persistence in that offence might result in deposition.

Day-to-Day Administration

Though the African chief was often been characterized as "dictatorial" by European colonialists, he rarely made policy in day-to-day administration and legislation. If there was a social problem in the village, say rebellious youth, the chief would pose the issue to his council for proposals and debate. Under normal governance, the chief would introduce the subject to the council of elders and those wishing to do so would then debate it. Usually, he would remain silent in the course of the debates and assess the various positions. He would then determine the general majority opinion, if there was no unanimity, for further action. His role was to weigh all viewpoints and assess any emerging consensus. It was not his function to impose his decision on the council. That would defeat the purpose of the council debates. In this sense, the chief did not rule; he only led or assessed — an important distinction. "According to traditional ideals, a chief could never force his people to do what they did not want to do; *he was a leader rather than a ruler*, relying for his position on influence rather than force" (Bourdillon (1976).

Occasionally, however, the chief would, in the course of debate, attempt to make the councillors accept the opinion previously reached by him and his inner council. "But if the majority of the headmen are against it, he must abide by their verdict, unless he is looking for trouble" (Schapera, 1955; p.78).

Generally, routine matters were resolved by acclamation. Complex matters were debated until unanimity was reached. Decision so arrived at was sure of acceptance by the rest of the people since the council was made up of important men who were influential in the community. By himself, the chief could not act alone. Busia (1951) noted:

> The (Ashanti) chief was bound by his oath to consult the elders on all matters, and to obey their advice. The government thus consisted of the chief and the elders. They met regularly, for it was the duty of every elder to visit the chief every morning. In this way the elders met informally to discuss the business of the day and others of State. Each elder was interested in matters affecting the lineage he represented and the villages under him. The chief, on the other hand, was responsible for the whole Division. He therefore had to reconcile the sectional interests of the elders (p.14).

It was obligatory for every elder to call at the chief's house every morning "to greet the chief." Failure to do so without explanation was regarded as disaffection toward the chief. Often the chief and his elders discussed matters of a general nature: the prospects of the yam harvest, the meat supply, the state of the paths and roads. In matters of serious consequence, all the members of this council must be summoned. Such matters included additional tributes, market tolls, proposed new laws, the declaration of war, serious quarrels, and other matters of importance to the community.

Busia visited a few of these sessions in 1933. One matter discussed was the encroachment on Wenchi lands by the neighboring people of Kyeraa. After much discussion, the chief and the elders decided "to send reliable messengers to the spot to ascertain what had actually taken place. The *Gyasehene* was asked to provide two men. These were called at once to the chief's house, and were given their instructions by the *Okyeame*" (Busia, 1951:14).

On another morning, the matter was the increasing number of deaths that had taken place within a short time at the village of Koase. Some of the elders shared this alarm. "They asked the Akwamuhene to go to Koase and meet the *Odekuro* and his elders and find out more about the cause of these deaths."

One morning was spent in settling a dispute between the Adontehene and the *Okyeame Panyin*, each of whom claimed some palmtrees to be within the land of their respective lineages. "The elders discussed the matter, and decided that the palmtrees were on the *Okyeame's* land."

When there was no other business to discuss for the rest of the day, the elders went to work on their farms or visited one of the villages directly under them. If other meetings were imperative in addition to the morning meetings to discuss an urgent matter, the chief sent a messenger to summon the elders, usually in the evenings, after the day's work had been done. "The chief had to keep strictly the injunction that he was to act only on the advice of his elders" (Busia, 1951; p.15). Only rarely, did the chief act alone.

After meetings of the chief and his elders, decisions about which the people had to be informed were made public by the beating of the *gonggong* in the evenings, when all the people had returned from their work on the farms. The town crier began these proclamations, "All you people, *Nana* (the chief) bids you good evening; he says. . ." Then followed the information.

The elders were responsible for seeing that orders or decisions affecting the villages under their direct rule were made known to their people. They sent messengers to inform the village headman (*odekuro*), who summoned meetings of their elders and told them; and then in the evening the villagers were informed by the village crier. But when important proposals or laws had to be passed, the chief was obliged to summon a village meeting for the people to ratify them. The Ashanti call this meeting *asetena kese* which literally means "a big sitting-down."

This process of governance was also observed by Oguah (1984) among the Fanti of Ghana:

> The Fanti chief has to consult his councillors on all decisions affecting the society. . .His council usually consists of the elders of society. . . The elders are not appointed as councillors because of their wealth but because of their maturity. Thus both rich and poor find themselves on the council. . . The reason why the councillors are not elected is that there is no need for them to be elected. For all adult members of the society have a right to be present at the meetings of the council, participate in the eloquent debates, and to vote by exclaiming approval or disapproval. In practice only the inquisitive few attend the meetings of the councillors. But when there is a controversial issue, hundreds of citizens turn up at the meetings to ensure that the will of the people prevails.

Neil Henry of the *Washington Post* Foreign Service provided this recent account of a village meeting presided over by a chief:

> Awutu Breku, Ghana — It was with great solemnity that Amakuade Wyete Ajeman Labie II, paramount chief of the Awutu tribe, called his subjects together one day last month (June, 1990) to impart some very important news.
>
> 'The light is coming,' the ruler announced, standing before his

people in a robe of green and gold. 'The government people say they will bring wires to Awutu Breku and everyone will have (electric) power.'

Murmurs of surprise and appreciation swept through the crowd of mostly corn and cassava farmers, whose wood-frame shacks in this coastal village 25 miles west of Accra, Ghana's capital, have never had either plumbing or electricity.

Then the chief held up his hand for quiet.

'If you want the light,' he said sternly, 'you will have to pay for it every month.' And with that, leaving his people to ponder their pocketbooks, Amakuade strode back to his palace of painted mortar and stone, his kingly duty done (*The Washington Post*, July 27, 1990; p.A29).

Note that the chief did not dictate or decree that *he* had ordered electricity to his village. He placed the issue before the people and allowed them to discuss it. Then he said, "*If*, you want the light, you will have to pay for it." The point of note is the use of "if," implying that the decision was theirs to make, not his. Further, if they so made that decision, they (not the tribal government) would have to pay for it.

From West Africa, all the way to southern Africa, the same procedure could be observed. As Olivier (1969) asserted:

Time and time again we see this procedure applied to the conduct of public affairs in these Bantu tribes: The chief, in the exercise of his various functions, is assisted by a consultative body; theoretically he has the right to ignore their advice, but in actual practice he follows the consensus of opinion; should he act contrary to such advice, he does so at the risk of losing favor with his tribe and, in the final instance, of losing the chieftainship.

Consensus was the cardinal feature of the indigenous African political system. Majority opinion did not count in the Council of Elders; traditionally, unanimity was the rule in most tribal systems; hence, the African political characteristic of debating, sometimes for days, to reach uninamity.

Kendall and Louw (1987) also noted of the Nguni of South Africa:[7]

All council matters were subject to lengthy discussion (or indaba) by all adults. Decisions were usually based on unanimity, so govern-

[7] Nguni is an all-inclusive term used for black Africans in South Africa. It includes a large number of groups and sub-groups. In the Cape area, there are the Xhosa, the Thembu, the Mbo, and the Mfengu. Further north are the Zulu and the Dlamini.

ment was by consensus. On the rare occasions when unanimity was
not achieved, majority rule was invoked (p.7).

The primary reason for unanimity was survival. For the tribe to survive,
council members espoused and strove for unity or unanimity. If a councillor,
a head of a lineage, was irreconcilably opposed to a measure, he could leave
the village with his lineage to set up settlement elsewhere. This, of course,
was a frequent occurrence in African political history, evidenced by
migrations of families and even whole tribes. To prevent such break-ups of
the tribe, unity of purpose was always advanced.

Coercive powers were generally not employed by the chief to achieve
unity. Unity of purpose was achieved through the process of consensus-
building. In addition, persuasion and appeals, rather than force, were used by
the chief and councillors to win over recalcitrant members on an issue. Quite
often, such lobbying included visitations to dissident councillors to influence
their opinion in the privacy of their homes. If the council was still
deadlocked and could not reach a unanimity on a contentious issue, then a
village assembly would be summoned and the issue placed before the people
for debate. Thus, the people served as the ultimate judge or final authority
on disputatious issues.

The second feature of the indigenous traditional system was "decentralization." As Busia (1951) put it:

> The chief communicated directly with the elders, they in turn with
> the headmen of the villages under them and they with their
> subjects. When the system functioned well it was democratic. There
> was an aristocracy of rulers, but they were constitutionally elected,
> and they were under popular control through the right of destool-
> ment (removal) vested in the electors. Everyone was represented on
> the council through the lineage system. Legislation and major
> executive or administrative proposals were submitted for the
> approval of the representatives of the whole people meeting in the
> Divisional Council (*asetena kese*) (p.22).

This view is corroborated by Amoah (1988:173),

> The ruler together with the council made laws and decided all
> ordinary affairs. But if any question of great importance to the
> nation arose the whole people were assembled for its discussion and
> settlement; *every individual, regardless of his position, was allowed to express
> his view.* (Italics mine).

In many tribal organizations, the village assembly served important
functions as well. Among the Bantu, "all new laws must be ratified at such
meeting before they come into force, and action on all important issues can

only be taken after discussion at the tribal assembly" (Olivier, 1969). Though the laws were not recorded, they were often very well known to the people. As Schapera (1957) observed with respect to the Tswana:

> After deciding upon by the chief in consultation with his confidential advisers, the laws are merely announced to a tribal assembly; but as a rule, they are first referred to such an assembly for discussion and approval before being put into force. In any event, they receive wide publicity at the time of promulgation.

Most tribal laws were straight-forward prohibitions or injunctions. For example, "No one may drive a wagon through the village on Sundays" and "The heirs of an estate should share the property (of the deceased father) with their mother and sisters" (Schapera, 1957). These were promulgated and openly discussed at the village assemblies.

For the Tswana, Schapera (1955) distinguished four types of popular assemblies:

(a) The *phuthego*, an assembly to discuss matters of relatively minor importance or to listen to formal announcements from the Chief,

(b) The *pitso*, an assembly to discuss matters of major importance, such as taxation and levies, the undertaking of new public works, the formation of new regiments, and tribal disputes, or to celebrate some outstanding occasion,

(c) The *letsholo* (a tribal hunt), an assembly held only for exceptionally important and controversial matters, such as trouble between the chief and his brothers, or any serious cleavage in the tribe, or friction with some other tribe. In former times, tribal enemies of the chief were disposed of in the course of such a hunt.

(d) The *lekgotea*, that is, the tribe sitting in court.

The procedure followed at such village meetings was for the chief to begin by explaining its purpose. He would not announce any decision reached in council meetings, but he would merely state the facts involved and request discussions to begin. His advisers would open the debate, followed by headmen or elders. Then anybody else wishing to speak or ask questions might do so. If two men stood up together, precedence was given to the more elderly. Speakers stood bare-headed or bowed as a sign of respect, and faced the chief. "They are usually allowed to speak fully and freely but may occasionally be interrupted by a comment or question. The senior advisers and headmen finally sum up and express their opinion after which the chief announces his decision" (Olivier, 1969).

It is important to note the tradition of *freedom of expression* at such gatherings. Everyone — even including non-tribesmen — expressed their views freely. Their freedom of expression was assured. Sensible proposals or ideas were often applauded and inappropriate ones vocally opposed. Dissent was open and free, with due respect to the chief, of course. Dissidents were not harassed, arrested or jailed. If a dissident made an intelligent argument, he was praised for having offered an idea which could help the community. If he made a silly remark, he set himself up for ridicule. Or if he offered a proposal with little merit, it was rejected by the assembly. People could make fools or heroes of themselves at the village assembly and face social derision or win accolades. But the choice was theirs to make and they had the liberty to do so. Olivier (1969) put it eloquently:

> In theory great freedom of speech is permitted at these meetings. In practice, fear of subsequent reprisals by the chief often acts as a deterrent. But if feelings are running high, the Chief and his advisers may be openly criticized or reprimanded, often in very strong terms. Should most of the speakers express views different from those favoured by the Chief and his advisers, the latter will try to argue them round.

The chief, however, could not take arbitrary reprisals against those who expressed an opinion unless speakers used abusive language or acted in disrespectful manner. However, if opinion was sharply divided in the course of the debate, the chief might order the assembly to divide into groups according to their opinions. The relative strengths of the two parties would then be seen (Olivier, 1969; Schapera, 1955). Note the unique way of taking "votes." There was no counting; the voting was "visual."

At village meetings, majority opinion was the rule. Unanimity was not the objective. It could not be insisted upon since the meetings were often called because the Council of Elders themselves could not reach a unanimous verdict. As Flt.-Lt. Rawlings of Ghana observed in a recent interview with the New African (Dec. 1988):

> Traditionally, decision-making in Africa is done by *consensus*. The chief and elders create a *forum*, at which every member of the community can *make his or her voice heard*. As the discussion goes on and new points are made, *a majority position* emerges. (Italics mine).

Other African leaders would agree. Julius Nyerere, for example, once said: "The very origins of African democracy lay in ordinary oral discussion. The elders sat under a tree and talked until they agreed." (Cited in Mazrui, 1986; p.75).

At the village assembly, if the chief saw that he had sufficient support after lengthy debates, he would regard the decision as favorable and proceed with his policy. "But if his own supporters are in the minority, he must accept defeat as graciously as he can. The Chief is in strict theory able to override the wishes of his people, but in practice he rarely ventures to do so. Their co-operation is essential for the successful government of the tribe;

and should any Chief act contrary to the public opinion as here expressed the result would be disaster" (Olivier, 1969).

It should be noted that for a consensus to be possible, two fundamental requisites must be met. First, reaching a consensus requires *participation in the decision-making process* by ordinary tribesmen. The indigenous African systems ensured this by allowing all adults to sit in on the deliberations of the traditional Council of Elders to participate or voice their opinion. Further, Village Assemblies or Meetings offered ordinary tribesmen the opportunity to participate in the legislative process and reach a consensus. This was an *indigenous African political tradition*.

Second, by sheer force of logic, a consensus could not be reached without some freedom of expression. The process of reaching a consensus required that people be allowed the *liberty* to present their various viewpoints. These various positions were then debated until a consensus emerged. Clearly, a consensus would be impossible to reach if people were afraid to express their opinion for fear of being brutalized for their viewpoints. This point cannot be over-emphasized.

Even today, the tradition of reaching consensus is still very much alive among the illiterate peasants in Africa. The following is a description of this process in two villages, Boabeng and Fiema, in rural Ghana, that raised a modest amount of money through voluntary contributions by the villagers and fund-raising activities for development. The chiefs, prominent members of the village community as well as ordinary villagers assembled to determine what to use the money for. In a dictatorship, clearly such an assembly would not be called in the first place. What follows, taken verbatim from the *West Africa* magazine, provides an illuminating insight into the traditional decision-making process. Though it is rather lengthy, it was thought a paraphrase would leave much substance out.

> There were many suggestions, as there are bound to be on such an occasion. The village headteacher suggested a health post. Somebody suggested a post office. Another thought they should tar the main street of the town. 'Electricity for the villages,' somebody said. Pipe-borne water, a community center, a day nursery where farmers could keep their kids while they went about their business were among the many suggestions which followed. When all available suggestions had been made, it was agreed that they be taken one by one and examined. The headteacher's health post was first put for discussion. The argument for it was overwhelming: their sick have to travel long distances to clinics and hospitals at Nkoranza, Techiman and Kintampo. He recounted many instances in which lives would have been saved if a medical officer was around, and concluded by saying that he was 'speaking on behalf of pregnant women, children and generations unborn.'

Judging from the nodding of heads among the village elders and the womenfolk, the headteacher's argument went down very well.

Yaw Owusu, the blacksmith (who plays the guitar when Agya Ko Nimo comes to visit) then got up and replied that the importance of health cannot be gainsaid, and he would be 'the last person' to stand in the way of a health post.

But, he continued, we must learn from the mistakes of our neighbours. Take the district capital itself, he said. Five years ago they built a health center. They had a grand opening and it was even reported on the radio. But how does the center look like now? The nurses have left. And there is no medicine to be had. Except for the benches and things like that, the building is empty. I could name you every town in this district where health posts have failed, but you know this as well as I do. What makes us think we could fare better where all have failed?

The problem, he went on, is that we are tackling the question quite wrongly. He concluded that the thing to do would be to get community health nurses to go round the houses telling people how to avoid disease.

After a few more speakers, they closed the matter. The health post will have to wait. Even the headteacher (whose daughter was in a nurses' training school, and the obvious choice for 'officer-in-charge' of a new health post) was seen to nod in approval of the decision. Pipe-borne water followed. It didn't lack advocates. Pipe-borne water killed germs. Germs make you sick. Time is saved. Our women can be free, and our children too, from running too often to the stream.

So the thing to do is to buy one of these generators to pump the water to our homes. The same machine would give us electricity. And thus we kill two birds at one stroke. The attack was led by the old fetish-priestess. She was the kind who drove everything before her. No, you did not mess around with her. She declared it was out of the question to build one of these 'monstrous noise-making things' in the middle of the quiet stream. It would disturb the monkeys in the sanctuary, pollute the stream with grease, shoot chemicals to kill centuries-old, venerable trees. Drive the monkeys into extinction. When all these harms have been done, the engine would break down. There would be no spare parts to be had and no engine oil. And within two years the generator would be rotting away: a waste and a curse.

The conclusion of her speech excited a lot of interest. Wagging a finger at them, like a mother scolding irresponsible children, she told them that if any electricity or pipe-borne water project were to be undertaken by the villages, it must not be the kind which would belch smoke. She concluded: 'The best thing is to build a small dam. It can be done, though I am not suggesting by this that we commit the present money for that purpose.'

After much deliberation, the schemes involving electricity and pipe-borne water were struck off the list. Nobody wanted to be held responsible for polluting the stream. And come to think of it, had the report from the university not said that the stream is the healthiest stream in the world? The assembly similarly dismissed the scheme to tar the town's portion of the main trunk road.

When they reached the end of the list, it was obvious to them that though they wanted the amenities the cities enjoyed, they didn't want them at the expense of the environment.

The question still remained. 'What is to be done with the money at hand?' Somebody suggested the purchase of a bus to shuttle between the villages. The older members of the villages, who were quite suspicious of the way young people handled money, voted the proposal down.

Indeed for a while, the meeting digressed as the younger and older generations began calling each other names. But old Agya Yaw firmly brought things to an end.

It was then that she spoke. She told them about bee-keeping. The village knew about bees. School children went looking for honey during the weekends. It fetched good money in the neighbouring market towns. Well, she continued, instead of going looking for honey, you could actually build a bee hive right inside your backyard.

The woman was respected among the villagers. Although she was a stranger by colour and language, they had accepted her and given her an honorary citizenship.

In the weeks which followed, two members of the Youth Association came to the Consultancy Centre of the University of Science and Technology, in Kumasi, Ghana, and participated in a workshop for would-be bee keepers. They went back to the villages and started a bee-hive going. Two more were established in course of time.

The whole neighbourhood is buzzing with news of the success of the bee farming project. Other villages are sending people to come and study their methods. And the money is rolling in (*West Africa*, Nov. 1, 1982; p.2818-19).

A few instructive points may be noted from this story. Villagers freely suggested various proposals. These were debated freely, indicating freedom of expression. The debate got heated at times but order was restored by chief Agya Yaw. The final project adopted, the bee-hive, was proposed by a stranger, someone who was not a tribesperson, which indicated a process in which anyone could participate, regardless of their tribal origins. More importantly, the chief remained silent throughout the entire deliberation process. It was the people who determined what the project should be. He did not dictate that and ask the assembly to rubber-stamp it.

Now compare how Ghanaian elites reached their decisions:

Parliamentary Privileges Committee has been directed to investigate the exchange of blows between Mr. Yaw Frimpong, a Deputy Minister of Local Government and Cooperatives and a trade unionist, Mr. C.K. Atriable, in the Parliament building last Friday (*Daily Graphic*, Accra, August 12, 1981; p.1).

Even the peasants displayed greater political maturity and upheld each person's right to free speech. But as we shall see in Chapter 10, many "modern and educated" African leaders, with all their degrees and army titles, still do not appreciate the necessity of freedom of expression and the indigenous African political tradition of reaching a consensus. For starters, consider:

Panicked crowds raced through Nairobi's slums, as police gunfire rattled the air. Stone-throwing youths shouted freedom slogans. Scattered violence spread beyond the Kenyan capital and dissidents warned that unless he bends, President Daniel arap Moi could go the way of Romania's Nicolae Ceausescu. . .

The showdown began building on New Year's Day, in the aftermath of the Romanian government's collapse. A protestant leader asked Moi to lift a ban on political parties he formally imposed in 1982 – and was promptly threatened with arrest. . .

He made good on those threats on July 4, 1990, when police arrested Kenneth Matiba and Charles Rubia — former cabinet ministers who had led the call for change — and held under laws permitting indefinite detention without trial (Newsweek, July 23, 1990; p.28).

In Africa's own traditional systems, this right (of free speech) was fiercely defended, especially among the Igbo, the Yoruba, the Ga, the Asante and the Abesheini. Any adult had the right to express his/her opinion but exercised this right with due respect to the chief and the elders. The chiefs did not incarcerate those who held different opinions. People could disagree with their chief. It was the collective survival of the whole tribe, not the chief's individual survival, which was at stake. If the chief would not tolerate or pay heed to criticism, he was either removed, abandoned or killed.

Fed up with the antics of government officials, a group of Ghanaian intellectuals, calling themselves the Movement for Freedom and Justice (MFJ), held a press conference on August 1, 1990, and issued this statement:

We consider as highly dangerous to the political health of our country and to the national development effort that decisions affecting a whole country are not subject to the will of the people and that a group of individuals who have no mandate and are accountable to no one wields the powers of government and are free to take policy decisions in the name of the people.

We of the MFJ believe that the local MASS MEDIA SHOULD BE LIBERATED FROM THE GRIP OF THE PNDC GOVERN-MENT!

The atmosphere of fear, suspicion and intimidation and the existence of the culture of silence caused by the ready application of such oppressive laws as the Preventive Custody Law (under which an individual can be detained indefinitely) cannot make for a free and fair debate.

We ask and demand that our movement should be given the same chance and opportunities as are accorded the 31st December Women's Movement, the June Fourth Movement and other organizations associated with the government which are free to organize and advance their objectives through a free access to the mass media and without state security harassment and repression. . .

The only way to find out what the true views and feelings of the people are is through a genuine national debate culminating in a NATIONAL REFERENDUM organized by an independent body.

Under the existing political climate of the country, however, it is neither possible to ascertain what Ghanaians truly think about the future political system of our country nor arrive at a national consensus on this vital question.

The Selection And Traditional Role Of The Chief

"A nation without a culture has no soul. We are the custodians of our culture"

— Nana Kwame Nyi XII, Paramount Chief of the Assin Apimanim tribe of the central Ghana and also president of the Central Region's House of Chiefs (July, 1990).

In the chiefdoms, or states, rules for selection of chiefs varied from one ethnic group to another. Chieftaincy, in most tribal systems, was hereditary and reserved to certain lineages by right of genealogical link to the founding ancestors. In the Akan political communities of Ghana, these clans or lineages *(mmusua* or *mmusua kuw)* numbered eight in Ashanti and seven in Fante.[8]

The "ancestral" lineages chose the chief but succession was not always automatic. The hereditary principle was combined with greater or lesser degree of selection as most often competition for the office emerged. "The Tallensi (of Ghana) normally resolved the competitive struggle by *rotating* the position among the heads of those lineages" (Arhin, 1985; p.28).

While alive, the chief may appoint a vice or heir apparent with the advice and consent of the Queen-Mother and the council. In the Akan systems, the heir apparent was known as *abadiakyire*. The ruler may choose not to appoint one, or if he did appoint one, he might leave the village or die before the ruler himself. In these cases, the choice of the heir would be left to a Queen-Mother subject to approval by the "royal" lineage members.

Most often, the chief's eldest son would be nominated but could be blocked from succession if he was found to be unfit or mentally incompetent to govern. Other considerations taken into account included how he comported himself in the past, his mannerisms, capacity to lead, valor, and his popularity.

In some tribes, where such a royal lineage did not exist, different lineages

---

[8] In Ashanti, these were: Aduana, Agona, Asona, Asinie, Asokore, Beretuo, Ekuona, and Oyoko. In Fante, they were: Nsona/Dwimina, Annona/Yoko/Aguna/Eguana, Twidan/Eburotow, Kwonna/Ebiradzi/Odumna, Aburadzi/Eduana/Ofurna/Egyira, Ntwa/Abadzi, Adwinadzi/Aowin (Arhin, 1985; p.29).

offered candidates for the position. A group of elders would then choose the chief from a number of contestants or rotate chieftaincy among the lineages.

In general, the chief was never elected by balloting. He was appointed and did not appoint himself —a fundamental difference modern African heads of state should be aware of. However, there were cases where the office was usurped or acquired by chicanery, subterfuge or force. Such usurpations inevitably led to schisms in the royal lineage and subsequently to civil wars, break-ups of tribes and migrations by factions. The general rule of succession, at any rate, was appointment.

Busia (1951:9) provided the following account of how the *Wenchihene*, chief of Wenchi Division (a sub-division of the Ashanti Kingdom) was chosen. He was selected from the Suffoase lineage of the Yefrefo which traces its descent from Affia Atoa, the founding ancestress. The selection process of divisional chiefs, it should be pointed out, was almost identical to the one by which the *Asantehene*, the head of the Ashanti Kingdom, was himself chosen. (The selection of the *Asantehene* is discussed in the next chapter).

When the chief of Wenchi died and a new one had to be appointed, the elders held a meeting at which the Krontihene, a sub-chief and commander of the "national" army, presided. At this meeting the elders would select two among themselves to approach the Queen-Mother and ask her to nominate a candidate for the stool.

> The Queen-Mother then held a meeting with all the adult men and the senior women of the branches of the royal lineage (*afiepanyin*). They considered the eligible candidates in turn and chose the one they thought most suitable. The necessary qualities were intelligence (*adwem pa*), humility (*ahobre-ase*), generosity (*ne yam ye*), manliness (*abooduru*), and physical fitness (*dem biara nni ne ho*). When they had decided on a candidate, the Queen-Mother sent to inform the *Krontihene*. The latter summoned a meeting of the elders and told them of the Queen-Mother's nominated candidate. The elders sent a message back thanking the Queen-Mother, and adding that they could not say whether or not the candidate was acceptable, but that a meeting of the whole Division (*Oman*) would be summoned to consider the candidate. A day was appointed for this meeting, and the Queen-Mother was informed (Busia, 1951; p.9).

Note that the choice of the Queen-Mother was *subject to approval* by the entire Division or tribe. There was no guarantee that her chosen candidate would automatically be made chief. In fact, to avoid rejection, the Queen-Mother "usually held informal consultations with the elders and other influential persons to find out their wishes and those of the public" (Amoah, 1988:168).

In making their selection, the Queen-Mother and the elders of the royal family were bound by three rules:

> These were, firstly, that the eligible candidates of the generation of the deceased stool-holder should succeed before members of the next, younger, generation. Secondly, that where the family group was clearly divided on the basis of descent from several women, the succession should *rotate* among the descendants of those women. To ensure that the second rule was observed, there was a third rule that the male and female stool-holders should belong to different sections of the family group (Arhin, 1985; p.33).

The council of elders could reject the nomination if the Queen-Mother fails to observe the three guiding rules. In case of rejection, the whole nomination and consultation process had to start all over again. "The *ohemma* (Queen-Mother) had three chances to produce a candidate acceptable to the political community. If she failed, then representatives of the political community could select a candidate" (Arhin, 1985; p.33). Nor could the Queen-Mother or the chief flout the established procedure and impose their chosen candidate on the people. That inevitably would lead to a fracturing of the community, with "dissidents," who refuse to accept the new ruler, hiving off to set up settlements elsewhere or even starting a civil war.

According to Arhin (1985),

> Members of the royal family were (generally) not in a position to influence the electoral process through bribery. . .Without a standing army, the means of physical coercion or force was not a monopoly of the *ohemma* or of the royal family. The "army' of the political community consisted of *all adults armed with their own purchased muskets, powder and shot*. A 'people's army' of this sort could resist impositions, when led to it by the heads of the various sections. . .

> (Indeed, this happened) in Asante in 1885-1888, when the *Asantehemaa*, Yaa Akyiaa, insisted on having her own son as the *Asantehene* in contravention of all the three rules. Some Asante *amanhene* objected to this, saying that a man called Atwareboana, not Kwaku Duah, Yaa Akyiaa's son (later Prempeh I), should be king. The consequence was that the people of Asante fought a civil war that lasted for three years, ending with the defeat of Atwareboanah's supporters (p.34).[9]

---

[9] The point about "standing army" is worth noting and will be explored at length in a later section of this book. Most indigenous African societies had no standing armies. The people were the army. But modern Africa is rife with military dictatorships, some of which, like the Amin, Bashir, Doe and Mengistu regimes, were characterized by savage brutality and

Generally, after the Queen-Mother's choice was made known, the *Krontihene* then conveyed a message to all the heads of the various villages through their respective elders, asking them to be present for the election of the chief. On this important affair, all the headmen, elders and commoners came to the meeting on the appointed day. Thus, social conditions compelled the selectors to respond to the wishes of the community at large.

The spokesman (*Okyeame*) informed the general meeting of the Division (*Asetena Kese*) the name of the candidate the Queen-Mother had nominated. On the announcement of the name, the people expressed their approval or disapproval through applause, grunts, hisses, laughter, or silence.

> The elders would appear to deliberate over the matter, and then ask the commoners what they thought about it. The *Okyeame* would say: 'Thus has the Queen-Mother said. What do the people say?' The commoners would reply, 'We would like to hear what the elders have to say first?' The commoners would then approve or disapprove of the decision of the elders. If the candidate was not accepted, the Queen-Mother was informed and the royals (members of the royal lineage) proceeded to make another nomination. If after three nominations the Queen-Mother's candidate was still unacceptable, the Divisional Council nominated a candidate from the royal family. It was the Queen-Mother to say whether or not the popular candidate had a kin-right to the stool. Both parties usually agreed on one of the eligible candidates. In case of disagreement, the popular candidate, that is, the one who had the backing of the Divisional Council, won. '*Odehye nsi hene*' is the Ashanti maxim on such a situation: 'A royal does not install the chief!' That is the privilege of the commoners who have to serve him (Busia, 1951; p.11).

After a candidate had been selected and accepted, all the adult men and women of the royal lineages held a meeting with the chief-elect in the Queen-Mother's house. They settled any disputes or differences there might be between the chief-elect and any member of the royal family. After this the adult male members each swore an oath of allegiance to the chief-elect, promising to serve him as the chosen occupant of the stool of their ancestors, and to support him in his administration as chief of the Division. According to Busia (1951), "This precaution, besides expressing the solidarity of the royal lineage, imposed the moral and religious sanction of the oath on any member of the royal lineage who might feel injured on being passed over, to prevent him from working against the chief" (p.11).

A day was appointed for the installation of the new chief. All the elders

---

repression. Standing armies were introduced into Africa by the colonialists to suppress African aspirations for freedom. Therefore, military rule is as alien as colonial rule itself.

and headmen and their followers assembled in Wenchi. The *Krontihene*, through the *Okyeame,* formally sent for the chief-elect, who came to the assembly dressed in an *adinkra* cloth, signifying that he was in mourning, accompanied by the members of the royal lineages. The *Okyeame* addressed the chief-elect thus:

> Konti, Akwamu, Bokoro, Konton, Asere, Kyidom, Benkum, Twafo, Adonten, Nifa — all the elders say that I should give you the Stool. Do not go after women. Do not become a drunkard. When we give you advice, listen to it. Do not gamble. We do not want you to disclose the origin of your subjects. We do not want you to abuse us. We do not want you to be miserly; we do not want one who disregards advice; we do not want you to regard us as fools; we do not want *autocratic* ways; we do not want bullying; we do not like beating. Take the Stool. We bless the Stool and give it to you. The Elders say they give the Stool to you (cited by Busia, 1951; p.12).

After this admonition, the chief-elect thanked the elders and gave them their *aseda* (token of thanks) of 20 or 25 pounds sterling. He also gave 4 pounds and seven shillings for the *afona* (ceremonial sword) with which he took the oath to his elders. Standing before the *Krontihene* and Akwamuhene he said:

> I ask your permission to speak the forbidden oath of Thursday. I am the grandson (i.e. descendant) of the Anye Amoampon Tabra-ku. Today you have elected me; if I do not govern you as well as my ancestors did; if I do not listen to the advice of my elders; if I make war upon them; if I run away from battle; then I have violated the oath (cited by Busia, 1951; p.12).

The chief would be destooled if he broke any of the quote-mentioned oaths or taboos; for example, cowardice, chasing women, drunkenness, refusal to listen to advice or acting autocratically. The elders then each in turn took the oath of allegiance to the chief. Libation was poured. Rum and palm-wine (*nsua-nsa*) was passed around. The chief was then carried shoulder-high and paraded through the town with people following behind singing the *ose*.

The following day, the actual act of enstoolment took place in the stool-house (*nkonuafieso*) where the blackened stools of previous stool-holders were kept. The elders and important officers were present. The candidate took a stool name and the *Okyeame* informed the ancestors whose stools were in the stool-house that a new chief, their own descendant in the matrilineal line, had been elected to take their place and govern the Division. The *Krontihene* held the right hand of the chief, the *Okyeame Panyin* his left, and the Queen-Mother his waist. They then gently lowered him *three times* on to Anye Amoampon's stool and raised him again. Anye Amoampon came from the Suffoase Yefre line and was the first Chief of Wenchi.

Arhin (1985) explained the significance of this procedure thus:

> Lowering him onto the stool was meant to convey to him the idea of continuity of the office and the political community; he became, thereafter, the one who sat on the stool of 'so-and-so.' This legitimized, or made valid his occupancy of the office. In only lightly touching the stool with his buttocks, the elected power-holder was again informed, in an indirect way, that he was distinct from the stool or the nation for which it stood: the nation was believed to be immortal; he was mortal. In being lowered onto the stool his person became sacralized. He was granted immunity while he occupied the stool. But his sanctity flowed from the stool and the office. Hence, he could be *de-sacralized* or *de-sanctified*, and therefore destooled. . .

> To destool a stool-holder, then, the Akan de-sacralized the person by hitting him, forcibly touching the ground with his buttocks, and removing his sandals so that his naked feet touched the ground. Sheep was then slaughtered in order to pacify the spirits of the stools and the Earth as a 'witness' that the person was no longer the occupant of the stool of 'so-and-so.'

At any rate, after the enstoolment, the *Okyeame* then poured libations, and prayed for the new chief, and for prosperity and increase for the Division during his reign. A sheep was killed, and its blood sprinkled on the blackened stools. It was then cut up and distributed: one hind-leg to the chief, the waist to the Queen-Mother, the head and legs to the stool-carriers; the rest was shared among the elders.

After this the chief was the acknowledged successor of his ancestors and head of the Division. He visited each town in his Division in turn to thank his people, and to show himself to the gods at Gyansoso, Akrobi and Droboso.

The Queen-Mother's role in the indigenous African political process has been subject to much scholarly interest. The granting of this role was perhaps in recognition of the positive role women could play in the political process; especially the astuteness of women in modifying behavior and acute perception of political events.

In the Ashanti, Ewe and other African communities, the Queen-Mother was, or is, the stool mother of the chief. She could be the uterine mother, an aunt, a sister or a cousin of the reigning chief. Though she was not necessarily next in importance to the chief, she could wield more authority than many of the sub-chiefs. Amoah (1988:174) observed that,

> She played an active part in the business of government of the chiefdom. She sat with the chief in court and in council and always to the immediate left of the chief. She maintained linguists and councillors of her own who could be either males or females. She could hold a court of her own, settling mainly divorce cases. She, like the chief, owned a stool.

She was, in addition, regarded as the authority on kinship relations and chieftaincy matters and thus had the privilege to nominate a successor when the chief's stool was vacant. It was, therefore, her duty to educate the chief in the history and the custom of the chiefdom. She was also expected to advise the chief about his conduct. She may scold and reprove him in a way none of his councillors can. Like the chief himself, she too could be destooled if she failed to perform this duty. Indeed, "Two queen-mothers of Juaben, Ataa Birafo and Afua Kobi, were destooled for not advising their sons (i.e. the chiefs) well" (Busia, 1951; p.19).

Two observations about the selection process in Ashanti must be made. The first follows the general tendency evident in indigenous systems to replicate at the village level what obtains at the state level. Thus, the construction and arrangement of the village court may be identical to that of the king's court. Similarly, the process by which the Ashanti choose their village or Divisional chief is the same by which they choose their king, the supreme leader. According to Arhin (1985):

> The village council and the *Obaapanyin* (Queen-Mother at the village level) selected the *Odikro* from among the members of the village *adehye* group (royal family); the divisional council and the divisional *Ohemma*, selected the *Ohene*, and the state council and the state *Ohemma* selected the *Omanhene* (p.17).

Second, this selection process was not unique to the Ashanti. Other ethnic groups employ the same process; the Ga of Accra, for example, as discussed later in this book. Note also that the selection of the chief differs from the Western concept of "election" in that multiple candidates are not offered simultaneously to the "voters" to choose among them. Nor can the candidate be anybody. He is chosen from the royal lineage. This is a privilege reserved exclusively in most indigenous African systems to the lineage of the founders of the settlement (called the ancestors).

In the Akan states of Ghana,

> Members of the royal family were accorded a collective hereditary right to the stool. But the representatives of those who were to be

ruled were conceded *the right to have a say in whether they agreed to be ruled by a particular member of the group* (Arhin, 1985; p.31). (Italics mine).

For purposes of comparison, perhaps a description of how the Shona chief is chosen may be useful. In the Shona inheritance system, a position is inherited only through males and circulates in one generation before passing on to the next. In succession to the chiefship, the position alternates between a number of family houses in the chiefly family *and* then generationally. Recall that this system is similar to the Gikuyu of Kenya where after one generation, *maina*, holds the office of government for 30-40 years, an *itwika* (revolution) ceremony was performed to declare an end to the old generation's term of office. The younger generation, *mwangi*, the sons of the *maina*, then take over the reigns of government. Also note that in other African societies, chiefship rotates among the various families in the royal lineage.

The Shona add a proviso to their generational system of rotation. "A man cannot be chief while he has a 'father' alive over whom he has to rule" (Bourdillon, 1976:125). This is intended to ensure that the chief is always an elderly and senior man. But after a number of generations, the question of seniority becomes extremely confused. As a result, upon the death of a chief a number of claimants appear to succeed him.

> In a dispute I witnessed, there were as many as 10 claimants from five branches of the chiefly family each of whom could produce a case in his favor; although there are usually fewer claimants, this case is not unique and succession to the chiefship rarely takes place without debate. . .

> Although theoretically the Shona system involves clear rules to be followed and enforced by the spirit mediums, in practice succession is very flexible. The complexity of the rules provides for an element of choice. The arbitrators are members of the community and depend upon the community for their position and their livelihood to the effect that the needs of the changing community can influence their decision. In practice a suitable and popular candidate can usually be appointed with popular consent on the grounds of qualities of character associated with the chiefship. This practical democracy is not, however, generally recognised by the Shona themselves: for them their chiefs are not elected by anybody, but are born chiefs with the blood of their fathers and the power of their ancestors to help them (Bourdillon, 1971:128).

The last sentence in the quote should be of note as very often an erroneous impression is created by placing what native Africans say in the Western context. In this instance, the Shona say their chiefs are born chiefs, giving the impression of an "undemocratic" system when in practice the selection process may in fact be very "democratic."

Within this broad system of selection (generational rotation), there are additional provisions. For example, Karanga chiefs are often nominated by descendants of senior branches of the chiefly family which have been eliminated from the chiefly succession. Among the Ndau-Shangaans of the Chipinga district, possession of the medium of *Musikavanhu*, the rain spirit, is an important requirement.

Often a Shona chief must undergo some trial or ordeal before succession.

> The chief elect of the Korekore chiefdom of Chesa has to keep a handful of meal dry while he is carried into a pool and held submerged by the senior medium's acolyte for about half a minute. Other reported ordeals include carrying the corpse of the predecessor over a slippery rock to lower it gently into a pool, standing all night in some sacred and dangerous place, smearing sacrificial blood over the grave of a predecessor, and climbing blind-folded a steep bare rock. Successful completion of the ordeal, which is normally believed to involve grave ritual dangers, is taken as further sign that the ancestors and spirits of the land approve of the appointment. In practice, the ordeal shows the courage and good faith of the chief elect (Bourdillon, 1976:130).

At the installation ceremony, all sections of the chiefdom must be represented. The chief elect is seated in a prominent position in front of all his people. He takes up or is given the emblems of office associated with the chiefship: a handful of soil to indicate ownership of the land, a ritual head-dress and a spear or staff of office. All ward headmen, village headmen and important members of the chief's family must give the new chief a formal gift, whether a substantial present or a mere token, as a sign of recognition, and neighboring chiefs may send gifts in order not to appear hostile. The accession is a festive occasion accompanied by music and dancing and feasting on millet beer and meat supplied by the new chief.

This process has not changed much in modern times. Commenting on the indigenous process, Neil Henry of the *Washington Post* foreign service wrote of the Awutu people of Ghana:

> While one's candidacy for the chieftaincy is usually determined by blood-line — most often matrilineally — a remarkably democratic procedure is generally followed in choosing a chief from among the contenders.

> 'There are many who believe that the traditional system of chieftaincy in Ghana was more just and more democratic than any

modern form of government that has ever come to power in Africa,' said sociology professor J. Max Assimeng of the University of Ghana.

A chief, he said, traditionally was chosen by a panel of elders. Those elders acted as advisers and served as a counterbalance to the chief's authority, a relationship much like that between the US Congress and the president. 'The chief was ultimately in charge, but he never acted alone. He had to consult the elders,' Assimeng said.

'If a chief acted against the interest of the village or behaved unethically or irresponsibly, he could be dethroned, or in the case of Ghana's chiefs, 'destooled,' as Assimeng put it. Today, lunacy, theft and adultery represent a few of the leading grounds for a chief's certain dismissal by his people (cited in *The Washington Post*, July 27, 1990; p.A34).

But claiming that the African chief ruled for life, many "educated" African heads of state used this alibi to declare their countries to be "one-party states" and impose themselves as "presidents-for-life." No such vacuous justification for the egregious one-party state systems and military dictatorships that proliferate in Africa can be found in the indigenous system.

As noted earlier, the chief was chosen by a Queen-Mother; he did not appoint himself. Second, he was chosen from a royal lineage, upon which the *people* themselves have conferred the royal status and the privilege of supplying them with chiefs. By contrast, nobody has conferred upon the military in Africa, or one particular political party the privilege of supplying Africa with heads of state. Third, the people voiced their approval or disapproval *openly* of the choice made by the Queen-Mother who had three chances to produce an acceptable candidate. No peasant was arrested or "disciplined" for voicing his opposition to a candidate. Nor did the peasants have to belong to one particular lineage or "party" to "vote" their opinion. Ultimate approval lay with the people; they all did not have one political ideology. More importantly, even though the indigenous African chief is appointed for life, he can be destooled at any time if he breaks any of his oaths and taboos.

The Functions Of The Chief

The African chief was more of a leader than a ruler. Packard (1981) observed that,

Bashu chiefs can be seen as political leaders. They have the right to claim and receive tribute, to determine the distribution and use of land, and to levy fines for the transgression of certain social and religious prohibitions. In addition, they often act like politicians. They acquire their position by competing with existing chiefs or by engaging in succession struggles with rival kinsmen, and they strengthen their subsequent authority by competing with neighboring chiefs or potential rivals within their own chiefdoms. In other words, they participate in competitive political activities (p.3).

The traditional African chief performed many functions. First, as the political (administrative) head of the tribe, he was responsible for the maintenance of good order, the handling of public affairs, the ultimate authority in all matters affecting the welfare of the state as well as its administration. Among the Buganda, the chief was also responsible for certain kinds of public works: for cutting and keeping open roads, and for building and maintaining the compounds of senior chiefs, of the king, and of some of the gods, as well as for making and servicing places for drawing water, and for hunting down dangerous wild beasts (Gibbs, 1965;p.89).[10]

Second, the chief presided over the Chief's Court, which was the final court of appeal. Among the Shona, presiding over his court was "the most significant task of a chief" (Bourdillon, 1976; p.131). The word for this is *kutonga*. A chief at a Shona court was not so much a judge as chairman or president of his court. When a case was being tried any man present who felt he had something to say on the matter had a right to express his opinions. It was the chief's duty to uphold his right.

Traditionally, the Shona chief was the guardian of the fundamental values of *rupenyu* (life) and *simba* (strength, vitality, well being). Life came from the land of which the chief was the custodian and strength or power from the chief's status and accession rituals. Both life and strength were necessary for the prosperity of the people. The chief was responsible for the prosperity of his people and particularly for the land and its produce. Thus drought may be blamed on the general incompetence of the chief or on the fact that the wrong person was appointed.

Third, the chief was the religious head of the tribe, the presumed direct and living representative of the ancestral spirits which guarded the tribe and whose goodwill and cooperation were essential to the every-day existence of the tribe. It was the chief's duty to pay homage to or placate these ancestral spirits by rituals, sacrifices and offerings, to obtain their blessings in tribal

---

[10] The potential role the chiefs can play in current economic development, by being responsible for the construction and maintenance of rural infrastructure (roads, piped water) becomes all too apparent. Unfortunately, many modern African leaders, after independence, never utilized this traditional resource. The late Dr. Nkrumah of Ghana, for example, stripped the chiefs of much of their traditional authority. The state then assumed the traditional developmental roles of the chiefs.

undertakings (as in war), mediate between them and his people, and to prevent them from punishing the tribe (because of disobedience or non-adherence to traditional customs) with pests, droughts, sickness or hunger. Such rituals often included the pouring of a libation and the slaughter of sacrificial lamb.

In the exercise of these religious duties, it was not unusual for many chiefs to claim supernatural or divine powers and assert that their reign was ordained from without. Such exaggerated claims, however, were more reflective of the operative checks against despotism. Artificial instruments of social control were generally lacking for the effective establishment of autocracy. As a matter of expediency, many chiefs resorted to superstition or spiritual powers to inspire awe and social control.

Fourth, in military matters, the chief was the supreme commander, with the right to decide finally on matters of peace and war, and on strategy. Fifth, "although in most tribes the land legally belongs to the tribe, the people usually refer to the land as belonging to the chief" (Olivier, 1969). Thus, the chief was the final authority on matters pertaining to the use and possession of land. He had the right to distribute land not already occupied and also the right to "expropriate" land, that is to instruct people to vacate the land occupied and used by them because it was required for some public or general purpose. "A member so dispossessed has the right to demand other land in exchange" (Olivier, 1969).

Sixth, as the governmental head of the tribe, the chief had the right to admit foreigners or strangers into the tribe and to act against anyone in the community suspected of sedition, espionage or public mischief. Such actions were often decided in court with the defendant given a full public hearing and a chance to defend himself. Furthermore, the chief was the representative of the tribe to the outside world and in that capacity entrusted with all "foreign affairs."

Schapera (1955) also gave the following description of the Tswana chief:

> The Chief, as head of the tribe, occupies a position of unique privilege and authority. He is the symbol of tribal unity, the central figure around whom the tribal life revolves. He is at once ruler, judge, maker and guardian of the law, repository of wealth, dispenser of gifts, leader in war, priest and magician of the people. His exalted status is reflected in the ceremonial surrounding him and in the obligations of his tribesmen towards him. . .It is a serious offence for any tribesman to use abusive language about him, or to speak or behave improperly towards him or in his presence (p.62).

The chief received tributes, court fines and market tolls. As the main repository of wealth, the chief's other function was to assist members of the tribe who were in need, to treat visitors to his place in regal fashion, to supply food and drink to all those who were at his place on official business; for example, members of his council, regiments of his army who have been called up.

It is crucial to note, however, that such wealth did not belong to the chief as a person but to the "stool" or the office of chieftaincy. The chief merely held the wealth in trust for the tribe as a whole. He could not loot the tribal treasury or dispose of it in any way he pleased. When the chief died, this wealth was not divided up among his children. Instead, it passed on to the next chief. For example, among the Bantu, the chief's most important source of wealth is cattle. As a rule, he possesses by far the largest herds in the tribe. "But it is maintained that they are tribal cattle, in the sense that, the chief merely holds them in trust for the tribe as a whole, and cannot use them recklessly for his own ends" (Olivier, 1969).[11]

Koyama (1980) provided this corroboration:

> There are, in the Elliotdale district of the Bomvanas, certain cattle numbering roughly 40 which are for all time the subject of great curiosity in that area. They are said to be the cattle of the chief of the Bomvanas, Chief Zwelenqaba Gwebindlala. But on closer examination it transpires that the chief, at any given time, holds them not for himself but for the Royal family of the tribe. They are never slaughtered for private purposes, only for tribal purposes. They are known as *inkomo zomlambo* —cattle from the river (p.63).

This was indeed the general rule in many other African ethnic societies. In West Africa, whatever was sent as gifts or wealth to the chief was not regarded as the chief's own personal property but as "stool property" to be held in trust. In Asante, Fante and Ga societies, the chief could not dispose of this wealth in the manner he pleased. Busia (1951:51) opined that,

> The chief was not allowed to have personal property of his own. He could not own land in a private capacity. Everything he possessed — gold dust, wives, slaves, farms — became stool property on his becoming a chief. 'No one places leaves inside the elephant's mouth and takes them out again' is the Ashanti maxim governing this custom.

The specific levies collected and paid into the chief's treasury

---

[11] Olivier (1969) also cited a 1934 dispute between the Kgatla and their chief, Molefi. The dispute was ended when Chief Molefi publicly proclaimed that such cattle would be regarded in the future as the property of the tribe and used for tribal purposes. It may be noted in passing that there were three main repositories of tribal wealth or savings: the family pot, revolving rural credit schemes, and the chief's wealth.

circulated again to the people. . .The services and tributes which the chief received were to enable him to fulfil the obligations of his office, but not to enrich him personally.

This crucial distinction was not made by many analysts and historians. The "wealth of the chief" was misinterpreted as evidence of unequal distribution of income. It is true that some chiefs lived well and were better off than commoners, as custom required them to live "royally" and to entertain guests in a manner that enhanced the stature of the tribe. However the chief was wealthy in terms of *services* which he received but he could not accumulate capital for his personal use (Busia, 1951; p.50).

Gaudy extravagance by the chief in face of deprivation could constitute sufficient grounds for divestiture. Furthermore, in most tribes, modesty was the characteristic feature of the village chief's life. Writing in *The Washington Post* (July 27, 1990), Neil Henry observed:

Unlike most other monarchies, a village chieftaincy does not necessarily mean material wealth. Each year during harvest festivals, the faithful sub-chiefs donate funds to their paramount leaders, but the donations usually do not amount to more than token living expenses. Indeed, many of Ghana's paramount chiefs, including Amakuade of Awuku Breku, seem to live humbly and labor in the fields as long and hard as any commoner.

The power and respect they command from their followers seem to derive from their intelligence and wisdom and the model of behavior they set for the community.

Amakuade, for instance, lives in a fairly simple house that is not much different from or more comfortable than neighboring dwellings but is nevertheless called a palace because he lives in it. A gentle man with sun-wrinkled skin and rough calloused hands, Amakuade, who is known affectionately as Nai Odefi or Old Chief, and says he is the father of 'about 15' children, works six days a week in his corn field (p.A34).

The contrast between the "primitive" traditional leadership and the "modern" is striking. Modesty does not exist in the vocabulary of many African heads of state. In fact, some of them are reputed to be among the richest in the world:

President Mobutu's fortune approached $5 billion in a Swiss bank account, a fortune larger than Zaire's $4.4 billion foreign debt. . .The President's official salary alone amounted to 17 percent of the annual budget, while the country's foreign debt amounted to 70 percent of GNP (*West Africa*, November 30, 1981; p.2881).

Although it was known that Houphouet-Boigny, Africa's longest running dictator after 30 years in power, was siphoning off French aid funds to amass a personal fortune assessed as high as 6 billion *pounds sterling*, the French President happily paid for the Ivory Coast leader's crippling whims that now inspire popular protest (Paul Webster in *Guardian Weekly* (U.K.), June 17, 1990; p.9).

Over 3,000 Nigerians were operating a Swiss bank account, according to the Christian Association of Nigeria (CAN). The names of Nigerians 'operating Swiss bank accounts with ill-gotten money' are to be published this year by CAN. It said it would do so because the country's economy was crippled by this capital flight. . .CAN was particularly concerned that Nigerians were near the top of the list of Third World patrons of Swiss banks (*West Africa*, April 10-16, 1989; p.570).

The Zambian President, Kenneth Kaunda (the architect of Zambia's socialist ideology of 'humanism'), dismissed as 'a big lie' recent allegations that he had transferred $6 billion in state funds to personal bank accounts abroad (*The New York Times*, August 15, 1990; p.A6).

These heads of state would never dream of *sharing* their wealth with their poor fellow citizens. Yet, they are the very ones who insist that the rich countries should share theirs with the poor nations.

"Corruption As A Cultural Trait" — A Digression

One of the recurrent myths about Africa is the notion that corruption is culturally ingrained among Africans. The traditional practice of offering a "dash" has often been used by scholars to provide a "cultural" explanation to the pervasive incidence of bribery and corruption in Africa. In most West African countries, a bribe is often called "a dash." This appellation, however, is a misnomer that reflects a confusion or misunderstanding of the traditional practice.

In the Vais court case which was cited in Chapter 2, the plaintiff called upon the chief and presented him with a "dash." In that context, the "dash" constituted an advance payment for a service to be performed by the chief, who was not paid for his judicial services. By contrast, today's bribe is demanded or extorted by civil servants, prior to the performance of a service they are paid to render.

More importantly, historical evidence suggests that African natives themselves made a clear distinction between a "dash" and corruption. Diop (1987) revealed that:

> Ghana probably experienced the reign of a corrupt dynasty between the sixth and eighth centuries. Kati tells of an extremely violent revolt of the masses against it. The members of that dynasty were systematically massacred. In order to wipe it out completely, the rebels went so far as to extract fetuses from the wombs of the royal family (p.65).

Also recall that:

> Fishermen at Kromantse Number One in the Central Region destooled their chief fisherman for diverting about half of their allocation of fishing gear and selling it to others outside the town at *kalabule* prices. The ex-chief fisherman, Opanyin Kow Mensah, also allegedly sold 0.9 meters of the net at C200 (*cedis*) to some of them, while he had enough to build for himself a complete fishing net. Announcing this at a meeting of the local branch of the National Canoe Fishermen Council, the branch secretary, Mr. John Kwame Ennusin, said Opanyin Mensah was found guilty at an arbitration presided over by the Odikro of the town, Nana Kwansa Panyin II (*West Africa*, Jan. 10, 1983; p.113).

In southern Africa, where indigenous legal systems were more developed than elsewhere, the legal code on corruption, bribery and extortion by public officials was explicit. The Rolong, the Hurutshe and the Kwena of Botswana prohibit bribery in order to protect their communities against corruption by the use of public office to further private interests. Observing these societies, Myburg (1980) wrote:

> Bribery consists in presenting or accepting patrimony as a private reward for a public service. The nature of the service is irrelevant as long as the official concerned uses his public position to grant it. Thus the consideration for the bribe may be the allocation of a choice piece of land or a favorable judicial verdict.

> The general term for bribery is said to be *go raela* (to tempt); a descriptive term for an administrative service such as the allocation mentioned could be *go haposa tshiamo ka neo* (to avert righteousness with a gift) and for a judicial one *go duela tsheko* (to reward for justice).

> The crime is committed by the person paying the bribe *and* the

official accepting it. The punishment is a fine of one or more bovine animals.

Extortion. Extortion is coercion for patrimonial gain on the part of an official by a threat or threats of unwarranted public action or inaction. Where, for example, a headman declines to perform an administrative or judicial duty unless he is given a bovine animal, he commits the offense of extortion, *bogagapa*.

The punishment for extortion is *more severe* than for bribery, for the coercing official is more severely punished than the tempted one or the tempting private individual. The headman, in the example given, could be fined 5 head of cattle in addition to being deposed and ordered to return what he had received (p.103).

Note that in the commission of bribery and extortion, both parties are punished under indigenous African law. Evidently, the "primitives" had a better sense of justice. What one irate Nigerian wrote was perhaps more ominous:

You need to know that: 6 Nigerians are billionaires; 6,000 are multi-millionaires; 55,000 are millionaires; 22 million Nigerians earn less than 10 *naira* a day (7.88 *naira* = $1 as of July 1990); and around a million Nigerians earn less than 5 *naira* a day.

You also need to know that Nigeria is a country that has petroleum but has a scarcity of petrol.

You also need to know that over 70 percent of Nigerian land is arable, but less than 5 percent is cultivated.

You also need to know that we Nigerians have a potential for revolution (*BBC Focus on Africa*, December 1989; p.66).

Checks Against Abuse Of Power By The Chief

Perhaps no other area of study is as fascinating as the checks Africans built into their indigenous political systems to prevent or punish abuse of power or misuse of power, due to lapses or departures from the accepted standards of conduct. In theory, the African chief wielded vast powers which led many observers to characterize him as "autocratic." But according to Bourdillon (1976):

It is in court that the authority of the Shona chief is most often seen in practice, and the limitations on his power to judge reflect the limited political power of a traditional chief. Many old men say that in the past no chief could impose his own will on unwilling subjects; if he tried they would simply move elsewhere and the chief would be left without a following. Also, a chief needed supporters to protect him against jealous rivals (p.132).

Olivier (1969) observed that the Bantu chief "is surrounded and supported by various bodies and institutions which prevent him from becoming an abusive ruler and makes of Bantu government a peculiar type of democracy, although it is not based on the principle of free elections and on individual or communal voting." Furthermore, in exercising his powers, "the chief cannot ignore the feelings of his people, nor the influence of those who are expected to advise him, otherwise he will be riding for a fall" (Olivier, 1969).

Testimony before the South African Government Commission of Native Law and Custom was particularly telling. Asked to describe the Bantu system of government, Sir Theophilus Shepstone replied:

It is a form of Government at the head of which is the chief, who is apparently arbitrarily supreme, and who possesses all power, but, practically, that power cannot be exercised by him safely, except with the consent of the people. That consent is given at assemblies of the chief men of the tribe. These men are not always entitled councillors, but they have the right of meeting at these assemblies, owing to personal influence, or the possession of riches, or to their being the heads of large families, or of hereditary descent in the tribe. These headmen again rely upon the opinions of their constituents, or people under them (Cited by Olivier, 1969).

As a central figure in the village, the chief played many other roles, least of which was autocracy. The survival of the people was the imperative and, by dint of reason, as well as custom, consultation with his people was mandatory. He listened to as large a variety of viewpoints and proposals as possible, seldom dismissing any out of hand. His primary duty was to determine a consensual position, not to impose his own. He was required to explore every possible avenue since his foremost prerogative was the preservation of his people. He acted as an "umpire" to ensure fair play and equal justice for all. He mediated in disputes and thus had to be impartial, weighing all sides to a dispute. As we saw in Chapter 2, native courts existed to assist the chief in fair dispensation of justice. But as a judge, he was not infallible. His decisions at court could be overruled or even overturned. Bourdillon (1976) observed of the Shona: " a domineering chief is also disliked and quickly loses respect and influence, as would a wealthy yet close chief" (p.135).

In his duties, the chief traditionally solicited and encouraged dissenting or alternative viewpoints. Such solicitations were never considered demeaning. In fact, he was serving his traditional political role in making them. He frequently asked his people "to bring their minds." That was the vernacular invitation "to express an opinion." And those who "brought their minds" did so, in other words, expressed their opinion, willingly and freely, without fear of arrest.

Under this traditional system of government, it was generally unthinkable, not feasible, for the chief to impose his will on his people or act despotically toward his people. But most indigenous African societies did not take chances and actually instituted safeguards against arbitrariness and misuse of power by rulers. Broadly speaking, there were three types of sanctions that could be brought against an erring ruler: religious, institutionalized and spontaneous (peasant reactions).

Religious Or Supernatural Sanctions

The office of chieftaincy was sacred. It was the repository of ancestral spirits. Most Africans believed that when a person died his body decayed but his soul remained and lived with the ancestors in the world of spirits. The ancestral spirits watched the living constantly. They rewarded good men and rulers but punished them with epidemics, calamity and other catastrophes on the earth and ostracism of their souls after death for wrongdoing. The fear of incurring the displeasure of the ancestors by misrule checked chiefs and kings against becoming cruel and inhumane toward their people. Thus, the chief could not oppress his people and expect the blessing or cooperation of ancestral spirits. He was supposed to be the guardian of his people, not their oppressor. The African chief was expected to be humble toward his people but belligerent toward rival tribes. It was very rare to see an African chief shout at his people. That would be contrary to royal conduct laid down by the ancestors.

Although the strength of this belief varied from tribe to tribe, it was most deep-seated among the Akans of Ghana, the Yoruba of Nigeria, and the Limba of Sierra Leone. "Thus the Limba, who did not have any custom of deposing or killing a bad chief, relied on this belief as a sanction against misrule. They believed that the ancestors would kill a bad chief for them" (Amoah, 1988; p.178). Muslims also believed in retribution from *Allah* against misrule.

Arhin (1985) noted that, "Among the Tallensi, the Dagomba and the Akan peoples (all of Ghana), there was belief that powers felt but unseen by normal human beings would punish those who misused the power or authority that men reposed in them" (p.79). For the Tallensi, the most important elements in their religion were the spirits of the Earth and of the dead ancestors of the people. The *tendaana* was a priest of the Shrine of the Earth and he had authority by virtue of that position. The *kpeem*, or elder, head of the a family group, or the *na'ab* had authority as the custodian of the family shrines, and of *nam*, power residing in the relics or material symbols of authority handed down from the ancestors. The spirits of the Earth and of the ancestors were the guardians of the wellbeing of the living men and women. The custodians of the shrines of the Earth and of the ancestors were their interpreters. These spirits actively intervened in the affairs of men. They could be pleased or displeased by the acts of men. They showed their pleasure by granting the living plentiful fruits of the earth and rain. When angered, they blighted the earth and withheld its fertility, so that human life was endangered. When displeased, the ancestors visited illness upon the living and, in extreme anger, they threatened the extinction or disappearance, through death, of the wrongdoer and his entire family. Authority-holders, as well as ordinary men and women, were believed to be liable to retribution for offenses against the spirits.

Similarly for the Akan, both rulers and subjects were "watched" by the various deities and spirits of the ancestors. Certain taboos and prohibitions were laid down to avoid their displeasure.

> A ruler who committed a breach of the taboos was liable to both supernatural and human sanctions. The gods might kill him before his subjects could remove him from office. The oath the Akan ruler swore to his people on his installation was believed to carry its own sanctions (Arhin, 1985; p.79).

The Temne of Sierra Leone took their spiritual injunctions a step further. The corpse of a bad chief was dragged along the ground and mocked by those who hated him. By defiling the corpse, the Temne believed they would prevent his soul from joining the spirits of the ancestors. Most often, "that indignity of funeral ceremony acted as a check on bad chiefs" (Amoah, 1988; p.178).[12]

Institutionalized Sanctions

Most indigenous African communities institutionalized various checks against tyranny and abuse of power by office-holders. Of these checks, there were several.

---

[12] Unfortunately, modern African heads of state seem to have drawn little lesson from this. Since 1957, over 150 African heads of state were booted out, shot and their corpses paraded for their citizens to mock at. Still, they cling to power as if their respective countries were their own personal property.

Private and Public Admonitions

Dictatorial tendencies in a ruler always caused disaffection among the people and brought shame to the royal lineage. A founding lineage member might be provoked to replace the "dictator." As Busia (1969) observed: "Those who elected (appointed) the chief also had the power to depose him if he did not perform the duties of his office satisfactorily" (p.23).

Before a despotic ruler was removed from office, most indigenous African systems gave him ample opportunity to reform. Often, the ruler was reminded of the oath he took upon assumption of power, in particular, to "listen to advice" which stated the standard of conduct expected of him. The advice was cautionary but with a hidden threat of removal in case of lapses of behavior. In addition to the advice, the newly elected ruler was isolated for a number of days and given *instructions* on proper code of conduct.

It was the duty of the Queen-Mother to scold and rebuke the ruler for transgressions. If she failed in this duty, she herself, as we saw in the Ashanti system, could be destooled. The next check was the inner or privy council of advisers. These advisers gauged public opinion and passed the information on to the chief. If the chief persisted in his despotic ways, the advisers might abandon him. If this check also failed, there was a third, and the most important, line of defense: the council of elders.

The council was the representative body of the commoners. Without this council, the chief was powerless and could not make laws. Council approval or unanimity was needed on all matters affecting the community. The chief could not dismiss the councillors, since those offices were hereditary and restricted to non-royal lineages. In other words, the chief could not use family ties to suborn the councillors. The officers came from different lineages.[13]

It may be recalled that, among the Akan peoples of Ghana, one of the duties of the council was to act as a court for examining the conduct of the head office-holder of the political unit.

> If the examination showed him to have been only slightly at fault, the members of the council warned him and reminded him of the rights and duties attached to his position. If they found him grievously at fault, they caused his destoolment (Arhin, 1985; p.19).

[13] The analogous situation in the United States is to imagine the existence of three political parties: the Republicans, the Democrats, and the Libertarians. The presidency in modern times is often drawn from the Republican Party while the Democrats and Libertarians make up the Congress. Although the President of the United States is one of the most powerful in the whole world and could theoretically bring an end to the human race, without Congress he is powerless and cannot impose his will. The African Council of Elders is to the chief what the U.S. Congress is to the President of the United States.

If the councillors failed in this duty, they themselves might be subject to removal. If the chief overran the Council of Elders, the people themselves would show their opposition to despotism.

The Akan provided their people with an opportunity to admonish their rulers at certain festivals. For example, the Ashanti had the *odwira* festival at which the ruler gave a public account of himself. The people could express displeasure at his misrule by boos and hisses. In fact, they could do more: take legal action against the oppressive ruler.

A ruler's subjects, acting through their representatives on the council, could present grievances concerning lapses in his conduct. The council would then constitute itself into a court and hold an enquiry into these grievances. If found at fault in respect of any of the grievances, the ruler would normally be cautioned, and he would have to pay what the Akan call *mpata*, a pacification fee, which also served as a mark that an enquiry had been held into the case and appropriate steps taken. If it were found that the grievances were without factual basis, and therefore frivolously presented, those presenting them would be declared at fault, made to pacify the ruler and also to produce sheep and drinks for the performance of religious ceremonies in order to pacify the spirits.

Grievances generally related to a breach of one or the other of the contents of the advice a ruler's council offered to him on enstoolment (Arhin, 1985; p.81).

Prohibitions Against The Office Of Chieftaincy Or Kingship

Most indigenous African societies applied various restrictions against the office of chieftaincy so that whoever occupied the "stool" would act "properly." Of course, the restrictions varied from tribe to tribe. In some tribes, the king was not to venture out of his palace into town except under the cover of darkness. The king was never to speak to his people directly, except through a linguist (*okyeame* as in the case of the Akan). The Akan chief or king was forbidden to meet with any foreigner except in the presence or company of a member of the council of elders. The paramount chief was forbidden to see the burial place of chiefs; two paramount chiefs could not shake hands nor should a chief exchange clothes with another man or eat from the same dish with him.

Some of these injunctions were intended to enhance the sanctity of the office. But there were others which were clearly designed to check despotic tendencies and misuse of power. One that is of interest which was adopted by many indigenous West African societies was the prohibition against property holding.

As Amoah (1988) explained,

> In some societies, especially the Akans of Ghana, the danger of a ruler using his position to amass wealth for himself was obviated by the custom that the king could not, except in a few circumstances, own any personal property while he was in office. Everything that the ruler acquired while he was in office, unless the elders knew that he was acquiring it for himself and consented to it, automatically became stool property. That rule applied to the wives of the ruler as well. To make the rule effective, the administration of stool funds and property was put in the hands of the *Sanaahene* (treasurer). The ruler was debarred from any close contact with the stool finances. He was neither permitted to hold the scale used for weighing out gold dust nor to open the leather bag in which the gold was kept (p.177).

While this prohibition is fascinating and akin to requiring an American president to place his private holdings of stock in a "blind trust," it may have contributed to the myth of communal ownership. When the Akan said, "The chief does not own anything. Everything he owns belongs to the stool" it was easy for Europeans to take that practice to imply "communal ownership" rather than as an injunction against personal aggrandizement.

Even in modern times, chiefs are still held accountable and corrupt chiefs are destooled:

> An unspecified number of members of the 'Oyoko' clan, King-makers of the Okumaning stools, have been rounded up by Kade Police for allegedly beating up their chief, Nana Karikari Appau II. The King-makers have preferred 13 destoolment charges against the chief. These include the alleged embezzlement of C50,000 ($18,182) land compensation belonging to the entire Oyoko family at Okumaning and the signing of a land agreement with an Italian firm, Greenwhich Chemicals Company, involving some 16,000 acres without the consent of the entire family (*Daily Graphic*, 28 October, 1981; p.8).

The "primitive peasants" of Africa had the sense to institute and enforce these injunctions, destooling chiefs who flouted them. But not so the "educated" elites of modern Africa:

> Togo's former Security Chief, Colonel Senyi Memene, accused of diverting a staggering $1.5 million into foreign bank accounts, has been compelled to regurgitate part of his loot from Switzerland.

In addition, a minister of state, Kawo Ehe, ex-minister of Commerce and Transport, and a prominent Trade Union leader, Nanbog Barnabo, have been forced to refund a total of CFA27.5 million (about $94,000) to the national exchequer (*New African*, Jan. 1990; p.19).

Political Pressure From Various Groups And Associations

In June, 1990, Kenya's President, Daniel arap Moi, threatened to hunt down "like rats" those who were calling for political reform (*The Economist*, June 23, 1990; p.39). The African chief *never* threatens his people. Nor does he talk thus to his people:

Lusaka, Zambia. August 14, 1990 (Reuters) — President Kenneth D. Kaunda of Zambia, under growing pressure from advocates of democratic change, mounted a campaign against the revival of multiparty system in his country.

Mr. Kaunda, who abolished political pluralism in 1973, accused the democracy movement of receiving funds from outside the country and of abusing the freedom to campaign in a referendum on multiparty rule.

'I have bent backward in the spirit of patience and tolerance and have allowed multiparty supporters to behave as though they were a registered party in Zambia,' he said at a news conference. 'I am now going to unleash UNIP forces,' he added, referring to the ruling United National Independence Party, 'to go and explain the dangers' of multiparty government in Zambia.

The 66-year-old President, who has ruled his country of 8 million since independence from Britain in 1964, said advocates of political pluralism are bent on destroying Zambia (*The New York Times*, Aug. 15, 1990; p.A6).

First, it was not the role of the African chief to "unleash" his forces "to go and explain the dangers" of a particular political course. Rather, it was the *governed* who told the ruler how they wished to be ruled. Second, it was not the function of an African chief "to bend backward" and allow a political movement to exist. Freedom of association was a *right* in traditional Africa.

In fact, freedom of association was so common a feature of indigenous African systems that it was taken for granted. The commoners could form associations, religious, economic or political, with whom they wished and when. The chief or king had no power to ban these associations. Some of them brought political pressure to bear on despotic rulers and to check misrule or abuse of power.

As noted earlier, the Akans had a commoners' association whose leader was called the *Nkwankwaahene*, which was not a hereditary position. Qualities for this position were eloquence and bravery. Through him, the commoners complained to the council of elders and forced the elders to consider any representation he made on behalf of the commoners. "In this way, the office of the *Nkwankwaahene* provided an effective channel for expressions of popular criticisms against the ruler and his government. It enabled the elders to take action against the ruler without being charged with disloyalty or jealousy" (Amoah, 1988; p.175).

There were various other associations and commoner societies: for example, *asafo companies*, age-grades, and secret societies. The *asafo* companies of the Akans of Ghana were primarily warrior organizations of the common people or the youth. They were often organized in the face of external aggression to defend the chiefdom. But the *asafo* companies also performed a number of social services such as road work, sanitation and other duties that arose during annual festivals. They might refuse to perform these services to show their displeasure at a tyrannical chief. Moreover, they became an effective political force in the enstoolment and destoolment of chiefs. "No chief would remain on the stool for long if the *asafo* companies were united against him" (Amoah, 1988; p.176).

The age-grade system of the Igbo provided a variety of checks against despotism. The age-grades were arranged in order of seniority. Members of each age-grade stood together and acted together as one body in public affairs. Each age-grade controlled the moral conduct of its members. "If a member stole, for example, the rest of the age-grade called on him to restore the stolen articles to the owner and to pay a fine in kind to the grade" (Amoah, 1988; p.176).[14]

These age-grades were ranked in an order of seniority. There were the senior, intermediate and junior grades. Within the society as a whole, the power, authority, rights and duties of each person depended on the position of his age-grade in the hierarchy of the age-grade system. Thus, the senior age-grade of the elders constituted the governing class of the society, while a number of intermediate grades combined to act as the executive organ of the government.

> Members of each grade jealously safeguarded their own status and the correct relationship that should exist between their grade and those subordinate and superordinate to theirs. The age-grade

[14] This self-policing aspect of the age-grade system might be of interest to African Americans in combating the soaring crime rate in black neighborhoods. Africa's age-grades play a more positive role in society than the destructive black American youth gangs.

system, therefore, provided an effective balance of power in the society especially in those societies which had no centralized machinery for political and administrative control like the pre-colonial Igbo societies (Amoah, 1988; p.177).

Political checks were also applied against African chiefs by secret societies. The African continent in the pre-colonial days was the home of numerous such societies, many of which continued to exist even during the colonial period. "One writer enumerated about 150 of such societies in 1929" (Amoah, 1998; p.177). They were abolished in Nigeria in 1978.

Some were mystic societies, some patriotic and a few others were subversive and criminal. For example,

> In order to gain admittance to the society of leopard-men of Cameroon and Central Africa (Manja and Banda), the applicant had to kill a close relative (mother, son, or first wife in preparation for a ritual festivity. The members of this society, citing the need for vengeance as their justification, abducted and murdered people who had been accused of witchcraft. For these rituals they disguised themselves as leopards, either wearing skins of that animal or tattooing their bodies with colored mixtures in imitation of leopard skins. They walked on all fours, touching the ground only with their toes, so as to make their footprints resemble the leopard's, and they voiced similar cries. The same atmosphere of tension and collective terror, leading to self-destruction, prevailed in Zaire among the *amiotes* and leopard-men of the northeast, by the Ubangui River, and, in the crisis of the 1930s, in the Wamba and Bunia regions (Coquery-Vidrovitch, 1988; p.191).

Most secret societies, however, were founded to enforce, maintain and teach tribal tradition, the custom and beliefs of their respective ethnic groups. More importantly, they "could bring pressure to bear on the rulers and restrain them from pursuing unpopular measures" (Amoah, 1988; p.177).

Olaniyan (1985) noted that,

> Exclusivist clubs, otherwise called secret societies, operated among all the peoples of south-eastern Nigeria. The most prominent were the *Ekpe* and *Ekpo* of the Cross River (*Ekpe* - leopard, *Ekpo* - ghost). The clubs were graded, each grade having its peculiarities in dress, dance and ritual. Admission and promotion into and within any club involved elaborate ritual and monetary investment.

Among the Igbo the masquerade (*Mmuo*) clubs operated while the

delta and other riverine people used the *Owu*. Again membership was
restricted. . .

The *Ekpe* or *Ekpo* was the supreme authority in the maintenance of law
and order. The societies/clubs were a form of insurance policy for
living members and a source of elaborate funeral ceremony for dead
members. The *Ekong* club added intelligence and security duties to
those of law and order (p.28).

Perhaps the best known of the secret societies were those of Sierra Leone
and Liberia. The principal secret societies of the people of Sierra Leone were
the *poro*, known largely among the Mende, Kono, Temne and other
chiefdoms near the coast; the *gbangbe* and *doweh* among the Koranko in the
north; the *gbangbani* among the Limba; the *wunde* of the Kpa Mende and
bundo, a female society in virtually every ethnic group. Among the Vai of
Liberia, the *poro* was known as the *beri* and the female society was the *bundu*
secret society. But they were all practically identical in their organization
and functions.

Local village chiefs paid allegiance to a paramount chief. He,
however, had very little real power over the chiefdom unless the
secret societies were in agreement with their paramount chief's
policies. . .For the most part the main secret society for men, the
poro, exerted its power within a chiefdom. But on occasions the *poro*
operated across chiefdom boundaries, thereby linking territories which
were politically independent. Chiefs, on the other hand, could not
influence events outside their chiefdom by peaceful means as the *poro*
could. And so secret societies really had more say in public matters than
paramount chiefs (Stride and Ifeka, 1971; p.227).

The name *"poro"* means "laws of the ancestors," implying the force of
supernatual authority of the ancestors to back up *poro* power. The *poro* never
had any formal central organization and operated through independent local
lodges. Each had a sacred spot in the bush where initiation took place. Boys
were taught native law and traditions, singing, dancing and craft work. They
were also hardened by sleeping out in the open and by being put through
rigorous tests to develop physical courage.

The *poro* society, like the *sande* for girls, taught boys how to behave as
responsible men; it handled the problem of initiating or guiding boys
into manhood. But the *poro* also had important functions in government
of a chiefdom. The society was divided into two grades of senior and
junior officials. It was the members of the senior 'inner' council who
really controlled public affairs; these senior men bought their right to
hold senior positions in the *poro*. The inner council of the *poro* was the

paramount chief's executive body. This council also acted as a legal tribunal which tried delinquents and criminals. In fact, such was the legal standing of the *poro* that it, and it alone, tried certain cases which involved important citizens. (Stride and Ifeka, 1971; p.229).

Though a secret society could not provide the basis for political unity, it was politically useful. "For example, it upheld the authority of rulers but at the same time helped checked the abuse of power by rulers" (Boahen, 1986:99). The rulers were bound to observe moral and religious laws laid down by the *poro*. Major decisions such as those of war and peace were made by the secret societies, not by the rulers or their councils.

Destoolment Of The Chief (Removal From Office)

Most African societies had customary and established ways of removing a ruler from office. A few did not. The emirate was one such example, but then the Sultan of Sokoto could be removed. Another was the constitutionally irremovable Ga *mantse*. Where the rulers could not be deposed, the people relied upon the council of elders and supernatural or religious sanctions to curtail the excesses of the ruler. However, if a despotic chief dominated the council, he was either killed or abandoned by the people. In some cases, the chief himself might abdicate voluntarily.

Busia (1951) reported such a case among the Aowin people in the western province of Ghana, where a chief had never been destooled in their history. In 1946, however, all the elders except those who were closely related to the paramount chief concurred that his administration was unsatisfactory and that he should give up his stool. He agreed.

> A public meeting was held at which the Gyasehene, on behalf of the elders, gave the reasons why they had all agreed to destool the chief. The chief in reply said that he was the direct matrilineal descendant of the founding ancestress of Enchi, and that his ancestors had always ruled the State. He had never heard of such an incident. But he did not wish to be the cause of any disturbance in the State and he was willing to hand over the stool since all the elders were united against him. The Gyasehene walked up to the chief, took off his sandals so that his feet touched the ground, and declared him thereby destooled (Busia, 1951; p.37).

Also in 1969, the paramount chief of the Kaffu Bullom chiefdom in north-western Sierra Leone, Bai Shebora Kombanda II, was destooled.[15]

---

[15] He took up farming after his divestiture. In July, 1990, he was farming 2 hectares (5 acres)

In theory, the African chief ruled for life. But in practice and under normal circumstances, he so ruled as long as his people allowed it - an important distinction. He could be destooled (removed) at any time if he failed to perform his traditional duties or if his people so wished, irrespective of how long he had been in office. Oguah (1984) observed this with respect to the Fanti of Ghana:

> Though the chief is not elected by popular vote, he has to govern in accordance with the popular will. For the people retain the right to destool their chief at any time. When he is appointed to lead the community he becomes a leader for life but only insofar as he remains an *ohen pa* (a good chief). The moment he begins to exhibit dictatorial tendencies the people initiate a destoolment suit against him. What shames the Fanti ruler most is to hear the expression '*Woetu no egua do*' [He has been removed from the stool (throne)]. Thus, the fact that the Fanti ruler holds his appointment for life does not mean that he is licensed to dictate for life. For the Fanti chief's rule is not autocracy but consultative system of government.

The African chief was held accountable for his actions at all times. Olivier (1969) pointed out the following:

> Of course, even in those days, there were foolish chiefs, who thought they were brave and could do as they pleased. They did strange things without consulting anybody, such as eating their peoples' cattle, killing without just cause, waging war, and seizing young girls of the tribe. In such cases, when it became evident that the tribe was discontented and not likely to tolerate such oppression much longer, the fathers (or advisers) of the tribe would hold a great *pitso*, and in the presence of the tribe denounce the chief for his wrong-doings, and intimate that some other member of the royal household had been elected to act in his stead. A chief so deposed would be murdered if he remained to contest the position.

There was one such "foolish" chief. Van der Kemp, the first missionary to the Nguni in 1800, gave the following description of the Xhosa chief Ngqika:

> He has counsellors who inform of the sentiments of his people, and his captains admonish him with great freedom and fidelity, when he abuses his authority to such a degree, that there is reason to fear

of swampland and 3 hectares (7.5 acres) of upland. On the latter, he grew trees such as mangoes, oranges and oil palms while on the swampland, he grew rice during the rainy season and onions and other vegetables during the dry season (*African Farmer*, July 1990; p.45).

that the nation will show him their displeasure. This is done if he treats the admonition with contempt, not by way of insurrection, or taking up arms against him, but most effectually, by gradual emigration. Some kraals break up, and march towards the borders of the country.. They are successively followed by others, and this seldom fails to have the effect wished for. . .(Cited in Kendall and Louw, 1987;p.6).

This process actually took place when Chief Ngqika passed two laws: one forbidding a man with an unfaithful wife to take the life of her seducer, and another making the chief the heir of any of his subjects who died without heirs in their direct line. "Ngqika was forced to retract both these laws when his people demonstrated their disapproval by leaving" (Kendall and Louw, 1987;p.6).

For the Ashanti (or Asante), Busia (1951) noted:

The Ashanti people ultimately had the constitutional right to destool a chief. As the fundamental principle was that only those who elected a chief could destool him, a destoolment required the consent of the elders. Sometimes they initiated a destoolment themselves when, for example, a chief repeatedly rejected their advice, or when he broke a taboo, or committed a sacrilegious act. The kind of offences for which chiefs were destooled may be gathered from the following instances of destoolments recounted in the traditional histories of the Divisions.

Chiefs Kwabena Aboagye of Asumegya, Kwabena Bruku, and Kwasi Ten of Nsuta were destooled for drunkenness; Kwame Asonane of Bekwai for being a glutton (*adidifurum*); Kwame Asona, also of Bekwai, for dealing in charms and noxious medicines; and Akuamoa Panyin of Juaben for his abusive tongue, and for not following the advice of his elders. In Kokofu, Osei Yaw was destooled for being fond of disclosing the origin of his subjects (i.e. reproaching them with their slave ancestry), and Mensa Bonsu for excessive cruelty (p.22).

It was against one of the seven laws of the Asante to disclose the tribal origin of any citizen. Nor could the Asante king refer to anyone as *"odonko"* (slave). Slaves were war captives who often played important roles in royal affairs. The Asante were particular in creating a society in which people of different tribal origins could assimilate and feel secure. Revealing the ethnic origin of an Asante subject was therefore regarded as a grave offense which automatically resulted in the destoolment of the Asante chief or king.

An Asante chief or king was also destooled if he became blind, or impotent, or suffered from leprosy, madness, or fits, or if his body became disfigured. "Cowardice, theft, adultery, drunkenness, cruelty, extravagance and disobedience to the elders were also grounds on which the ruler could be destooled" (Amoah, 1988; p.175).

When the king committed a serious transgression and a removal was necessary, two rules had to be observed in his destoolment. First, only those who enstooled him could destool him. This meant that only members of the ruler's council could make formal statement of grievances and start the procedures for destoolment. Council members normally acted in response to public opinion and pressures from the villages, districts or the state as a whole. If the council failed to act, the people could rise up in open, large-scale rebellion.

Second, potential successors to the stool were not allowed to be involved in destoolment proceedings (conflict of interest). Among the Akan states of Ghana, members of the royal family were debarred from these procedures. Enstoolment and destoolment were the right of the people.

The Akan had an elaborate system of divestiture. To initiate a destoolment proceeding, any aggrieved party would file charges against the Akan ruler to the council of the ruler next higher in rank, except in the case of the *omanhene*, when a committee of the state council constitute the court. Charges against the *odikro* (village chief) were presented in the *ohene*'s (paramount chief's) council and against the *ohene* in the *omanhene*'s (the king or supreme ruler's) council.

The council or committee would hear evidence from both parties, cross-examine witnesses and pronounce judgement. The ruler was given ample opportunity to defend himself. If found at fault, he would be asked to "beg" the council to apologize on his behalf. But if the spokesperson of the aggrieved party refused to accept this apology, the judge presiding over the case pronounced the ruler destooled. Thereupon, functionaries present at the hearing removed his sandals, so that his bare feet touched the ground and lowered his buttocks to the ground. He was thus desanctified, losing the immunity derived from the stool. After this, sheep were slaughtered to pacify the spirits of the Earth and dead ancestors of the ruler who may believe they have been defiled.

> A destooled ruler was normally asked to leave the town. His people would make a village for him. He was allowed to take a wife and a boy to settle in this new village. He had no access to the village treasury. Nor could he dip his hands into the treasury and take whatever loot he could for his exile. He would remain in this new village until the elders of the town decided his presence would no longer pose a threat to their peace and tranquility.

> In the case of the headships of the large Akan political communities, formal charges were often not made for destoolment purposes. If

the council agreed to destool the head of state, they informed the Gyase division. Then at a major festival, after the ruler had been carried in a palanquin through the town, he was not conveyed back to the palace but to a place already agreed and prepared as his new and future home. This was done to avoid protracted political strife and acrimony as it was believed the ruler's supporters would accept the accomplished fact of his removal but would 'fight' vigorously against any destoolment proceedings (Arhin, 1985; p.84).

Modern scholars may object to this procedure of "quiet removal" as undemocratic. But the council was a representative body of the people and such important decisions as removing a ruler could not be taken without prior consultation with the people or popular approval.

The Asante people in this way destooled three kings — Osei Kwame in 1799 for, among other reasons, absenting himself from Kumasi and failing to perform his religious duties during the Adae festivals; Karikari in 1874 for extravagance, among other failings; Mensa Bonsu in 1883 for excessively taxing the Asante people. Numerous other destoolments occurred among the Akan and Ga peoples.

Spontaneous (Peasant) Responses

There was always a possibility that the religious sanctions may fail to restrain a tyrannical ruler. Or a council of elders bereft of moral courage may succumb to a despot with a strong personality. In any of these eventualities, the commoners or peasants could resort to various remedies. Arhin (1985) refers to these as "diffuse" sanctions:

> Diffuse sanctions were not institutionalized. They were dispersed or unorganized, not given a definite form or arrangement, and not operated in any regular manner. They included gossip, ridicule, and the spread of rumor about the conduct of rulers; this hurts them, when they hear the rumors, without their being able to trace the source of the information that led to the gossip, ridicule and rumor. These could affect power-holders in such a way as to make them change their ways.

> Diffuse sanctions included the spontaneous avoidance of the ruler by his subjects. 'Avoidance' of this sort was like the passive or non-violent resistance movement (against colonialism) of the modern period. A *tendaana*, a *Na* or an *Ohene* could find himself isolated by his subjects in consequence of his misrule.

> Another diffuse sanction was the withdrawal of services by certain

officials of the ruler. Services included the performance of duties at the palace, communal labor on the ruler's palace or on his farm, and the refusal of this subordinate rulers to attend his summons (p.80).

The Igbo of Nigeria have an interesting way of dealing with autocratic officials. A village strike might be called and the elders shunned. Quite often, this forced the councillors to mend their ways. But when these measures did not remedy the situation, the people revolted. The Akan peoples of Ghana call this *adom ye* (rebellion); the Yoruba of Nigeria *kirikiri*; and Gikuyu of Kenya *itwika*.

According to Amoah (1988):

> Revolt was used as a weapon against misrule. The history of many tribes in West Africa provides numerous examples of rebellion against their paramount rulers. Indeed the history of the disintegration of West African kingdoms and empires before the advent of colonial rule is a story of revolts by aggrieved subjects against their rulers. In Ashanti, for example, the people rebelled against the Asantehene in 1827 and again in 1875.

> It is again recorded that in 1748 in the reign of Opoku Ware I, his war captain (i.e. *Nsafohene*) rebelled against him for introducing laws which aimed at reducing their powers. The king fled to Juaben for refuge. From there he sought reconciliation and that having failed a battle ensued which terminated in favor of the king's armies (p.178).

Stride and Ifeka (1971) recounted another case:

> Serious internal conflict occurred in the Wolof empire in 1481 when Burba Birain was deposed. This revolt was led by his half-brothers because he had advanced the interests of his full brother at their expense. The first serious blow to Wolof territorial integrity did not come until 1513. In that year, Dengella Koli, the son of an unsuccessful Fulani rebel against the mighty Askia Muhammad of Songhai, led a strong force of Fulani and Mandingo into Futa Toro. With the aid of its Serer and Tukulor inhabitants, he wrestled Futa Toro from Wolof overlordship and set up a Fulani dynasty which lasted until 1776 when it was overthrown by a Tukulor Muslim movement (p.23).

The traditional rulers were well aware that if they ruled cruelly, their people would rebel against them, which often served to keep them in check. But even if they could put down rebellions, there was one final peasant weapon they were powerless against: desertion.

Aggrieved or oppressed subjects could always "vote with their feet," as there was no shortage of land in Africa's wide frontiers. According to Amoah (1988):

> If a ruler was tyrannical his people might want to go away and settle somewhere else or put themselves under the protection of another ruler. That was not difficult in the pre-colonial days when there was plenty of land. In 1827, and again in 1875, the people of Juaben (in Ashanti, Ghana) for example, rebelled against the king of Ashanti, fought him and a large number of them moved into the sphere of influence of another paramount ruler, where they later founded a new independent chiefdom of New Juaben with its capital at Koforidua in the Eastern Region. In those days when chiefship was of people and not of land, rulers tried to have populous chiefdoms. Movement or threats of it of people away from the chiefdom was, therefore, a strong sanction against misrule (p.178).

Among the Sukuma of Tanzania, "control of the abuse of power by a chief existed through the practice of emigration to another chiefdom, together with the respect for tradition imposed upon him by his elders" (Carlston, 1968:438). In southern Africa, there were many migrations of communities to escape Zulu subjugation or "puppet" Zulu chiefdoms.

> Thus Mzilikazi, from 1821 to 1823, created an empire in Southern Rhodesia (now Zimbabwe), making an entirely new nation around his capital, Bulawayo, out of people of very varied ethnic origins. These were the Ndebele (or Matabele), who first fought the Shona and then, at the end of the century, fiercely opposed European intrusion. Another example was Shoshangane, who, before crossing the Zambezi in 1835 to found the Ngoni kingdom on the western bank of Lake Malawi, created the kingdom of Gaza in southern Mozambique, which was destroyed only at the very end of the century, by the Portuguese. Finally, Zwangendaba — who in 1821 to 1825 took flight in the direction of Lake Victoria — completed the destruction of the old Shona civilization of Monomotapa (Zimbabwe) and, continuing as far as Nyasaland, Zulufied Burundi and Rwanda.

> Migrant groups in turn left these Zulufied kingdoms, spreading out, in a single generation, over more than 3,000 kilometers and effecting profound internal changes (Coquery-Vidrovitch, 1988; p.74).

LEMMA: The oppressive African chief soon found himself without a tribe and his chiefdom collapsing, politically and economically. The chief did not possess the means to prevent the people from leaving. From this observation, witnessed innumerable times, may be enunciated an inviolable African peasant law: *oppression instigates flight of people*. This was not only evident in pre-colonial Africa but also during the initial stages of colonial conquest and even in modern times.

> Among the forms of passive resistance, the flight of *individuals* was a classic peasant reaction, typical of the first colonial phase. It proved the simplest way to avoid payment of taxes or being commandeered for work in porterage and was employed as long as the somewhat lax control of the colonial administration allowed it. By the time of World War I (in some of the remote areas, somewhat later), however, individual flight gave way to *collective* migrations. . .

> First, to avoid conscription during the massive recruitment campaigns for the European war at the end of 1915 and the end of 1917, entire villages of southern Senegal (at least 35,000 peasants) left for Portuguese Guinea and Gambia, and the peasants of Guinean Fouta Djallon went to Sierra Leone and Liberia (between 5 and 13 percent of the population). The populations of whole provinces disappeared, and others halved their numbers.

> Second, migrations took place in response to the demand for laborers. . .The Mossi laborers of Upper Volta (Burkina Faso) fled from the prospect of underpaid forced labor in the Ivory Coast and went to work on the cocoa plantations of the Gold Coast. As long as the system of forced labor existed – that is, until 1946 in the French colonies and until independence in the Belgian Congo and the Portuguese territories — the villagers' desire to flee was at least as strong a motivation as the inducement of better wages in a neighboring country (Coquery-Vidrovitch, 1988; p.183).

Migrations or collective flights are still occurring in modern Africa after independence from colonial rule, producing an ever-growing refugee problem. From less than 1 million in the 1960s, Africa's refugees have swelled to a count of over 10 million by 1990, with 3 million illegally settled in apartheid South Africa. Many factors have contributed to the refugee problem: droughts, famine, economic hardships but not least of these have been political oppression, persecution, endless and senseless civil wars.

What comes out of this discussion are, firstly, indigenous political systems had their own built in checks and balances against despotism. When these checks failed, the peasants exercised their final *inalienable* option: exit.

Writing about the Bantu, Olivier (1969) best summed up its native system of government,

It is evident that the principle of free elections is unknown in Bantu society; that the tribal chief (who usually owes his position to the fact that he is the chief representative of the ruling clan) is neither autocrat or despot, but is continuously assisted, in the exercise of his various functions by advisory councils and by the people themselves; that the tribal and territorial sub-divisions effectively curb the unitary power of the chief, and also form the basis of tribal government and in addition ensure active participation on all levels of the population in such government.

This system was not that much different from what obtained in the rest of indigenous Africa. For example, summing up for the Ashanti, Busia (1951) wrote:

Chiefship in Ashanti was based on the lineage system. Each lineage was a political unit, and the lineage head represented it on the Council of Elders. The chief was chosen from one of the lineages by (either a queen-mother or) the heads of the other lineages. Kin-right and popular selection were often combined.

The chief was bound by custom to act with the consent and on the advice of his elders, who were themselves representatives of lineages, and were subject to similar restraints from the members of their own lineages.

The chief was subject to checks from the elders, with whom he was responsible for the administration of the Division (tribe). They formed the Government. Public opinion and criticism were expressed by a loose association of commoners, *mmerante*, through their leader, the *Nkwankwaahene*, or through the elders (p.21).

When Africa came under colonial rule, the traditional political authority of the chief was reduced. He was thrust into the difficult role of acting as an intermediary between the people and foreign invaders. On one hand, the chief was the traditional representative of the people. On the other, he was a government employee. In many cases, the colonial government, especially the French, deposed uncooperative chiefs and appointed their own. Such government-appointed chiefs acted autocratically because they felt they had the colonial government behind them. Others became corrupt. Most of these "government" chiefs were frequently destooled.

As Busia (1951) noted:

Before 1900, chiefs were mostly destooled for failure to consult the elders or the breaking of custom, though there were other causes.

Nowadays the most common cause is that of 'misappropriating stool funds.' This has become a prominent charge against chiefs since the 1920s. . .Some subsidiary charges also recur: that the chief has violated native custom; that he has broken the laws to which he assented on his enstoolment; that he does not add to stool property; and that he does not keep up appearances befitting his rank (p.14).

Many destoolments arose from the confused role of the chief occasioned by colonial subjugation and the destruction of the old correlation between the chief's political power, religious authority, economic privilege and military strength, with the consequent decline in prestige and authority. The frequency of destoolments in Ashanti may be gleaned from the following table:

Name of Chief	Native Jurisdiction	Year of Destoolment or Abdication
Akuamoa Boaten	Juaben	1942
Kwadwo Apawu	Agona	1942
Kwabena Kunadu	Suma	1943
Kwabena Kakari	Essumenja	1943
Kwaku Jarko II	Techiman	1944
Kwame Affram	Kumawu	1944
Kwaku Nkansa	Adansi	1944
Yaw Gyamfi	Bekwai	1945
Osie Akoto	Kuntanasi	1945
Asum Gyima III	Ejisu	1945
Yaw Boakye III	Bekwai	1946
Amoako Agyeman	Adansi	1946
Kwabena Wiafe II	Offinsu	1946
Kwabena Asubonteng	Dormaa	1946

Source: Busia, 1951; p.216.

Since independence in the 1960s, there have been some improvements in the native system of government. A chief can be removed in several ways: by the people according to traditional procedures; by Kingmakers and traditional councils; or by a House of Chiefs - a body composed solely of chiefs. The House of Chiefs was created by the British colonialists in an attempt to formalize the native system of government.

There has been a tendency among African elites to denigrate chiefship as an outmoded institution despite the fact that there are still chiefs in many parts of Africa today. Their roles and functions have been changing, however, showing chieftaincy to be a dynamic and adaptive institution. Neil Henry of the *Washington Post* foreign service made a study of Chief Amakuade Wyete Ajeman Labie II of Awutu Breku of Ghana. He wrote:

In modern Africa, the life of a village chieftain — or the king, as he is also known here — is not an easy or simple one.

Once upon a time, a Ghanaian king needed to know only a few things well — how to lead his warriors in battle, punish miscreants, settle disputes between villagers and apportion the richest farmland fairly enough to keep most of the peasants happy. A wise chief also made sure there was enough liquor or fruit juice on hand to pour regular libations to the revered ancestors.

But nowadays, a chief must know how to lobby the state for public works, how to get emergency assistance in times of epidemics or other hardships and how to interpret and explain the government's policies to the people.

'You must not be a drunkard. You must not be a prison convict. You must be sober, wise, fearless and bold,' said Amakuade, 55, calmly explaining the essential attributes of a good king as he sat one recent night in his palace in the glow of his kerosene lantern. 'You must enforce customary laws of the village, but you also must understand the rules of the government.'

He sighed. 'As a chief, I have many worries.'. . .

When asked to name a few of his predecessors, Amakuade, paramount chief of the 70,000 Awutu people, rattled off 15 names, some of them dating back to the arrival of the Portuguese explorers in the 15th century. Upon invoking each hollowed name, the chief poured a drop of gin onto the floor of his office as expression of respect.

A former stenographer who was chosen chief in 1956, Amakuade ensures the observance of customary laws, such as the provision of two fowls by a father to his neighbors exactly eight days after the birth of his child. But Amakuade says the modern tasks are more difficult. For two years, the chief has been trying to get the government to send a machine to dig out and empty the village's two overflowing and useless latrines, but without success (*The Washington Post*, July 27, 1990; p.A34).

Other African chiefs have similar problems in their dealings with government, which caused one Lesotho chief to observe: "We have two problems: rats and the government."

In addition, today's African traditional rulers are not "illiterate and backward." In fact many of them are highly educated and have held enviable careers in the civil service. As the *West Africa* discovered in the case of Nigeria's traditional rulers:

> In Bendel State, the Cambridge-educated *Oba* of Benin, Omo N. Edo, Uku Akpokpolo Erediawa, was BA (Hons) and a federal permanent secretary before his resignation and coronation in March 1979. The Olu of Warri, Godwin Toritseju Emiko, ran a highly successful legal practice in Warri between 1982 - 1987, and Charles Abangwu held an LL.B. and had been commissioner of agriculture in the East-Central State before his appointment as Igwe of Isienu. Among Yoruba *obas*, the *Ooni*, *Oba* Okunade Sijuade Olubuse II, was a qualified accountant and one of the country's most affluent businessmen, while the *Alaafin* of Oyo, *Oba* Olayiwola Adeyemi II, was in the insurance business in Lagos until his appointment as *Alaafin* in 1972. Other notable Yoruba *obas*, such as the *Alake* of Egbaland, *Oba* Lipede, the Shoun of Ogbomosho, *Oba* Oyewomi, and the *Olofa* of Offa, *Oba* Ariwajoye, were all successful businessmen in Lagos, Jos and Offa respectively. The late Deji of Akure, Olsa Ademuwagin, Adesida II, and the reigning Awi of Ado-Ekiti, *Oba* Adelabu, both gave up lucrative careers to become *Obas*.

> A renowned school teacher and writer, the *Owa* of Ijeshaland, *Oba* Aromolarari, had already embarked on a Ph.D. degree when he was elected the Owa, while *Oba* Oyekan gave up a promising career as NCNC politician in order to become *Oba* of Lagos in 1964. The Eze of Ururu Ikendiri, R.E. Mbalewe, holds the HND and was an executive director of SCOA before his elevation, while the Nze-Obi of Egbema, Sunday Uzo, was an aeronautical engineer who had been general manager of the Rivers State Transport Corporation.

> In the Northern states, where the myth of undereducated feudalism needs even greater demystification, the following list speaks for itself as a challenge to the misleading image of the past: The Sultan of Sokoto, Ibrahim Dasuki had been First Secretary in the Foreign Service and later Federal Permanent Secretary; Emir of Kano, Ado Bayero was an Ambassador; Emir of Gombe, Shehu Abubakar, was Permanent Secretary in Bauchi State; Emir of Gumel, Ahmad Sani, holds a masters in Public Administration and had been commissioner for local government; the Etsu Nupe, Umaru Ndayako, holds a BA and was federal deputy permanent secretary; the Tor Tiv,

James A. Orshi, is a qualified lawyer with LLB and had been Secretary to the Government and Head Civil Service, Benue State (20-26 March, 1989; p.432).

Arhin (1985) provided the following list of highly educated Akan traditional rulers:

Ashanti Region

Otumfuo the *Asantehene*: Nana Opoku Ware II, Barrister-at-Law, Commissioner of Transport and Ambassador to Italy under the NLC government; Nana Otuo Sereboe II (*Juabenhene*), B.Sc. Engineering; Nana Oduro Numapau II (*Esumegyahene*), Chartered Accountant, former Secretary, Bank of Ghana.

Brong-Ahafo Region

Nana Agyeman Badu (*Dormaahene*), B.Litt. (Oxford), a former Research Officer of the Chieftaincy Secretariat; currently President of the National House of Chiefs.

Eastern Region

Nana Kuntunkununku II, (Akyem *Abuakwahene*), Medical Practioner; Nana Ampem Wireku (*Amanokromhene*), formerly Lecturer in Economics, University of Ghana, Chief Government Statistician, Commissioner for Finance under NLC Goverment, 1978 Chairman of the National Economic Advisory Committee; Nana Akuamoa Boateng II (*Omanhene* of Kwahu), Barrister at Law.

Western Region

Nana Kobina Nketiah IV, D.Phil. (Oxford), former Vice-Chancellor of the University of Ghana, and Member, Executive Council of the International African Institute, London.

To remove a chief nowadays, the first step entails bringing up "destoolment" charges against him. He is then given ample opportunity to answer the charges. He is destooled if he cannot respond satisfactorily without leaving any shadow of doubt. To guard against capricious vendettas, the chief is also given a chance to appeal a destoolment verdict. Consider these incidents from Ghana:

- The Eastern Region Chieftaincy Tribunal of the House of Chiefs at Koforidua has upheld an appeal filed by Nana Mireku Ababio II, *Asakrakahene* and *Krontihene* of Kwahu Traditional Area, against his destoolment. In June, 1984, the Judicial Committee of the Traditional Council, declared Nana Ababio destooled after some kingmakers, led by Nana Bamfo Asenso II, preferred destoolment charges against him.

Nana Ababio was accused of failing to defend the people in a stool land dispute between the people of Asakraka and Nkwatia-Kwahu and pouring libation on the black stool to curse an elder of the town. The Chieftaincy Tribunal, chaired by Nana Oware Agyekum II, *Omanhene* of Akim Bosome, awarded C30,000 costs against Nana Asenso and his elders (*West Africa*, October 20, 1986; p.2235).

– A five-member committee appointed by the Ashanti Region House of Chiefs to go into the Mampong Stool Affairs has submitted its report that Nana Atakora Amaniampong, the *Omanhene* of Mampong Traditional Area, should abdicate peaceful-ly.

The five-member committee, chaired by Nana Yaw Gyimah II, *Omanhene* of Asokore, in the report said Nana Atakore Amaniampong had broken a pledge to *Otumfuo* Opoku Ware II, the *Asantehene*, and violated an oath to keep peace with his divisional and sub-divisional chiefs (*West Africa*, December 1, 1986; p.2528).

– Nana Atakore Amaniampong II, *Mamponghene*, has been des-tooled by the Ashanti Region House of Chiefs.

A uninamous decision on the *Mamponghene* was taken by the House at its first meeting at Manhyia Palace, Kumasi. The House based its decision on recommendations by a five-member committee of enquiry, under the chairmanship of Nana Yaw Gyimah II, Asokorehene, appointed to go into the Mampong Stool affairs.

The committee recommended that the *Mamponghene* should heed the popular and good counsel of the *Asantehene*, *Otumfuo* Opoku Ware II to abdicate (*West Africa*, March 2, 1987; p.442).

– The *Adansihene*, Nana Kwantwi Barima II, has been destooled by the Asanteman Council after 23 years reign.

The destoolment took place at a meeting of the Council at the Manhyia Palace in Kumasi, after the Council had found Nana Kwantwi Barima guilty of violation of the great oath of Ashanti.

The Council, presided over by *Otumfuo* Opoku Ware II, the

Asantehene, also imposed a fine of C24,000, which was later reduced to C12,000.

According to evidence before the Council, when the *Asantehene* left Ghana in August, 1983, for medical treatment in the United Kingdom, it was the *Mamponghene,* Nana Atakora Amaniampong, who should have acted. At the time, however, the *Mamponghene* had also sought permission to seek medical treatment and and the third in line, Nana Oduro Numapau, *Essumejahene* was asked to act.

The *Adansihene* was said to have refused to attend Council meetings because they were not summoned by the *Mamponghene.* When the Council summoned another meeting on the return of the *Asantehene* from the United Kingdom, Nana Kwanti Barima again failed to attend. He also did not attend a recent meeting between Ashanti chiefs and the Ashanti Regional Secretary, Mr. F.A. Jantuah (*West Africa,* May 7, 1984; p.1001).

One of the most disgraceful aspects of governance in modern Africa is the fact that the elites have not been able to establish procedures by which an African head of state can be removed from office peacefully. Nor have they been capable of building checks and balances into their modern political systems. The only way to remove modern African heads of state is by military coup d'etat or assassination. Few showed the political wisdom to step down voluntarily when their people had tired of them. In an editorial, the *West Africa* (Nov. 5-11, 1990) rebuked:

The most damning historical fact of the past 30 years is that no independent country on the Afrian continent has ever thrown out its leader in a free and fair election, not even the so-called models like Senegal, The Gambia and Botswana. Presidents have changed only through retirement, death, or coups. Is it any wonder that, the world, observing this phenomenon, may feel disposed to marginalise Africa? (p.2773).

CHAPTER 4

AFRICAN KINGDOMS

A. ORGANIZATIONAL STRUCTURE

Beyond the village level, there were the provinces and ultimately the kingdom. Among the Asante, the rulers were the village chief, the paramount chief and the king (the *Asantehene*). The sizes of African kingdoms varied enormously and dispersed geographically although there were some regional concentrations. For example, most of the East African kingdoms were located north and west of Lake Victoria, while small chiefdoms and self-governing lineages predominated over much of present-day Kenya, Tanzania, and northern Uganda. In some kingdoms, there were no provinces, and the political entity did not amount to much. Nevertheless, nearly all the societies of central Africa had kingdoms (Vansina, 1987).

African kingdoms have been characterized as "divine kingships," a concept based upon the assumption that the king is the actual embodiment of the kingdom and that there is a mystical union between the two (Vaughan, 1986; p.177). Divine kingship has often spawned myths of royal despotism but, as we shall see subsequently, though always a theoretical possibility royal absolutism was seldom practiced.

An emerging view, propounded by Kopytoff (1989) among others, suggests that African natives were far more politically sophisticated and pragmatic or functionalist than given credit for in kingly affairs. The following paraphrases the work of Kopytoff (1989).

Africans recognized a duality in constitutional legitimation. "This duality is vividly illustrated by Benin's political culture, whose central tenet was that while the king had an intrinsic right to rule, the kingship had come into being by the will of the subjects" (p.62).

The king was the soul and embodiment of the kingdom. The prosperity of the kingdom was intimately tied up with the physical vigor, health and even sexual potency of the king.

> Under a satisfactory ruler, who had lived up to his nurturing obligations, the subjects would present the patrimonial perspective

on rulership, in which the ruler is the absolute 'owner' of everything. Similarly, the good ruler would state publicly that his rule rested on the happiness of the people and on their consent. In this respect, the early colonial observers of Africa, who tended to focus on the ideology of the ruler's despotism, and the later liberal observers, who tended to stress the reciprocities between the rulers and the ruled, each gave half of the correct story (Kopytoff, 1989; p. 68).

Kopytoff continued: "The crucial point in Africa was that legitimacy had been conferred by the people by way of the 'consent' of their symbols (a notion that modern secular democratic ideology finds difficult to grasp)" (p.65). Therefore, "being the creation of subjects, the African ruler's legitimacy rested on an implicit contract that could be withdrawn" (p.66).

The king was accepted by Africans as a necessary evil. He was necessary for the preservation of the social order. But he was a potential danger; he could abuse his powers and be all intrusive, expending the independence and freedom of his people. Africans faced a dilemma: how to have an authority to assure order and yet keep his royal fingers from interfering with their daily lives. Though solutions to this conundrum were varied across Africa, they were two in general.

The first was statelessness, by which some societies such as the Igbo and the Nuer elected not to have kings or centralized authority at all, as we saw in the previous chapter. Order was maintained informally through kin groups. The second solution — the ideal — which many African tribes strove for, with various degrees of success, was to have someone hidden from public view but whose awe-inspiring authority could be invoked to maintain order and harmony. This is akin to the "tooth fairy" or "Santa Claus" in Western culture which awe Western children. The equivalent in traditional African political systems was the divine king.

He was secluded and his every day life planned to the minutest detail and loaded with socially useful burdens.

The outward signs of his sacredness were onerous personal tabus, which he had to keep in the interests of the polity. His sex life, symbolically fused with his fertility and vigor, might be severely restricted. His most elementary physical functions, such as crying, eating, drinking, or defecating, were ritually controlled. And his movements were hemmed in by tabus, such as those against touching the soil in fields or seeing a corpse. And sometimes he might not even be allowed to reach the frailty of old age or, when at the point of death, to expire naturally by himself. Tabus of this sort applied, it should be noted, not only to secluded and unmistakably "sacred" kings but to all African chiefs and kings (Kopytoff, 1989; p.66).

Most of these restrictions were designed to reduce the king to an executive nonentity, curtail the discretionary use of political power and confine him to his palace where he would be safely out of people's private lives. They served primarily to take the gold out of royal glitter. At the extreme, as in the Ga kingdom, the king could become a remote, secluded, depersonalized, politically powerless, and utterly ritual figure. Thus, kingship, totally desecularized was a symbol, a puffed-up but hollow office which could also serve as a convenient scapegoat if things went wrong. As long as the king was prepared to obey these restrictions, some tribes in fact did not care who the king was or from where he came. To the Goba of Namainga (Central Africa), their "kings, *qua* rootless immigrants, were useful 'slaves'" (Kopytoff, 1989; p.66). Along the Nile-Zaire divide, some small states requested the Alur people to furnish them with chiefs and kings. In Benin, "the Edo elders were said to have requested the *One* of Ife to send them a king" (Kopytoff, 1989; p.65).

This pragmatic view of the king was well described by Kopytoff (1989):

> The pragmatic proposition was elaborated into a legitimizing and culturally believable complex. As a constitutional proposition, it was present in almost every African traditional polity. To capture its essence, scholars, focusing on the cultural strangeness of the idiom, have made it more religious than political by resorting to such terms as 'sacred chieftainship' or, in the case of its more dramatic and very specialized manifestations, 'divine kingship' (p.64).

> The patrimonial chief, in brief, was expected by his non-kin subjects to live up to his side of the bargain, and the subjects were not interested in his motives but in his performance. This indifference to motivations was congruent with the fact that many of the tabus which the ruler might breach were quite beyond his volitional control — tabus against physical weakness, illnesses, and old age. Personal moral blame and punishment for moral transgressions were beside the point here. What was expected was outwardly visible performance and an essentially mechanical correction of failure. . . .Among the the Rukuba of Nigerian Jos Plateau, while the sacredness of the king made him 'divine,' it also made him into a 'scapegoat king' (p.67).

If he failed to perform, he was disposed of. Regicide was a noted characteristic of divine kingship although it has been outlawed in most traditional societies since the beginning of the twentieth century.

In its classic form, divine kingship sanctioned killing the king when he became infirm or when things were going badly in the kingdom. The custom stems directly from the belief in the unity of the king and kingdom, in that the prosperity or failure of either may be regarded as that of both, and a king can thus be held responsible for conditions in the kingdom. Should he be ill or weak, the kingdom will be in danger; or should conditions in the kingdom be bad, there must also be something wrong with the king. Further, it follows that a change in the person of the king will change conditions in the kingdom (Vaughan, 1986; p.177).

Kingship, then, was a cleverly disguised deception. Naturally, such a ruse could not be perpetrated for ever. But to ensure its survival, a ritual was crafted. The interregnum in most traditional African kingdoms was a period of institutionalized lawlessness. With the law in suspension, markets were looted, traders beaten and homes vandalized. The objective was to remind the population of the chaos that would result if there was no king. Why keep up these deceptive appearances? Perhaps for the same reason that Santa Claus and his reindeer must leave the North Pole ritualistically in December.

What follows is a discussion of some selected African kingdoms to isolate the commonalities among them while noting the aberrations in some cases.

The Serer State/Kingdom (Senegal)

The Serer people at present make up about 16 percent of the population of Senegal. They originally occupied the states of Sine and Saloum. Around 1420, a group of invaders, the Gelowar, won control of these states. The Gelowar are generally believed to have been a Mandingo clan. Although in the 16th century these states came under the domination of the Wolof empire, discussed in the next chapter, they remained Serer in character.

Serer society was stratified into a caste system similar to that of the Wolof and most members remained members of the group into which they were born. The highest class was the *Tiedo* (or *tyeddo*). This was the warrior caste which included rulers, soldiers, judges and tax-collectors. Of these, only men of pure Gelowar descent were eligible for election to the kingly office of *Bur*. Sons of Gelowar fathers by women of insufficient rank were known as *Domibur*; and although they could not inherit royal power, they were usually given lesser chieftainships in the kingdom. Slave members of the *Bur*'s household could attain this status if they held important offices in the royal service.

Below this aristocracy was the *Diambur* (or *jambur*) class of freemen. Composed of peasants and craftsmen such as blacksmiths, leather-workers, weavers, woodcarvers and *griots*, it was at once the largest class in Serer society and the principal source of regular state revenue. At the very bottom of the social scale came domestic and agricultural slaves. Even these were divided into two categories: those captured in war by their owners, and those born into the service of their master. Although the former were mere chattels of their owner and could be sold at will, they could gain their freedom through good behavior, intermarriage or by flight. The latter were regarded as members of their master's family and could own personal property.

The head of the Serer state was the *Bur*, as he was also called in the Wolof empire. He was selected from among the Gelowar, the founding group; again, as in virtually all indigenous African political systems. On his accession, he was invested with divine status by important religious ceremonies "but this did not safeguard him from lawful deposition if the Serer did not prosper under his rule" (Stride and Ifeka, 1971:28). He personally appointed leading state officials and district heads and could appoint people of servile origin whose loyalties were to him alone. However, an all too powerful *Bur* could be checked by the *Diaraff Bundao* and a council of leading noblemen. With the advice of the council, the *Diaraff Bundao*, the single kingmaker, could depose the *Bur*.

Other important men in Serer politics included the *Burmi*, the *Grand Farba*, and the *Farba Birkeur*. The *Burmi*, the man named as the next *Bur*, was usually required to live away from the capital in order to prevent his becoming a source of serious political rivalry and intrigue to the reigning *Bur*. The *Grand Farba*, the chief of the royal slaves, and the *Farba Birkeur*, master of the royal household, were the great personal officials of the *Bur* on whom the success of royal administration largely depended. Another highly influential courtier was the *Linger*, the Queen-Mother, who played the same role as her Wolof counterpart.

The Kingdoms Of Sierra Leone (Temne And Mende)

Until the 16th century the vast majority of the people of Sierra Leone belonged to communities speaking West Atlantic languages: the Temne, Limba, Bullom, Shebro, Fula, Kissi, Gola and Krim. The Bullum lived along the northwestern coast and the Krim along the coast south of them. The Temne lived in the western interior and the Kissi in the east, with the Limba occupying much of the northern interior. But by the early 19th century the pattern of settlement had changed dramatically.

Large numbers of Mande-speakers (Mende, Koranko, Kono, Loko, Vai, Susu or Soso and Yalunka) had migrated into the country to occupy much of the southeast and had expanded further into the area in the north. Subsequently, the small Mende states began to emerge into a number of

larger confederacies, such as the Kpa-Mende confederacy and the group of
states under the authority of King Makavoray of Tikonko. "The confederacies emerged out of several needs: to protect people from the raids of coastal
slave-trading states ruled by the mixed race rulers like the Caulkers,
Clevelands and Rogers; to secure and maintain control over trade routes
between the further interior and the coast, and to compete successfully in the
growing palm oil trade" (Boahen, 1986:98).

The largest Mende confederacy was that of the Kpa-Mende originally
centered in the town of Taiama, which actually was 16 towns making up a
metropolis. There were 9 stockaded towns and 7 open villages where farms
provided food for the fortress towns. Many of the inhabitants of the open
villages were slaves. But they owned farms, often married into the master's
family and could even become headmen or chiefs.

> Mende chiefs and kings were elected and chosen on merit by the
> elders after a long process of consultation. Kingship was not
> hereditary. It was important to select a man with a proven record in
> warfare and/or trade. Such a man was Gbanya Lango, king of the
> Kpa-Mende confederacy (Boahen, 1986:98).

The king exercised authority over all the settlements. A Mende ruler,
apart from having to protect his subjects in war and famine, also played an
essential role in ceremonies and rituals. He entertained strangers and judged
cases as president of the court of elders. In return, his subjects were obliged
to perform services for the ruler; for example, making a rice farm (*manja*) for
him, keeping his compound in good repair or building a new one and
clearing the roads. In addition, the ruler was entitled to a portion of the rice
and palm oil harvest of each extended family (*mawe*).

The king ruled with the aid of officials. One was the speaker, who had
three principal functions: to act as the ruler's deputy in times of illness or
absence; to act as the main intermediary between the ruler and his subjects
(all complaints and disputes were first brought to the speaker); and to pass on
the ruler's orders to subordinate officials. This role was similar to that of the
okyeame in the Ashanti kingdom or the modern-day prime minister.

The Temne were divided politically by the beginning of the 19th century
into 12 or more kingdoms. Each however was independent of the other, an
arrangement which was similar to the constitution of the Ga Kingdom
discussed below. Temne kings were elected, as among the Mende, by the
elders who in practice were the senior grade of the local lodge of the secret
societies. Rulers were believed by their subjects to be sacred, and they
underwent long and complex installation ceremonies.

According to Boahen (1986),

> In theory, once elected, a Temne king could not be deposed and

could even act as a tyrant; in reality, his powers were limited in various ways. After election, a king was confined in *kantha*; he would be secluded with his subordinate officials for several months to be made aware of his duties and responsibilities to his people. Subordinate officials could not be deposed either; therefore, the king was obliged to listen to their views and advice and to try to work with them in a co-operative manner. Top policy decisions were made not by the king alone but by the king's council or by the *poro* society (p.99).

The council contained officials who resembled modern cabinet ministers: the *kap kabin* or speaker, who acted as a prime minister, *the kapr masm* or chief priest, the *kapr loya* or chief prosecutor, the *kapr soya* or army commander, the *kapr kuma* or custodian of the kingly articles of office and the *kapr fenthe* with responsibility for health. The council also included subordinate officials, *mamy* queens and leading officials of secret societies.

Cooperation between Temne kingdoms took the form of military alliances. As we shall see shortly, the Ga kingdoms similarly united only in times of war. In peace times, the Temne kingdoms pursued their own independent courses of action.

A few points worth noting are, firstly, that kingship was not hereditary in the Kingdoms of Sierra Leone. The second was that Temne and Mende kings could not make important decisions without the concurrence of the king's council — a requirement which was characteristic of many indigenous political systems. Third, the king could not remove the councillors, as their positions were hereditary.

The Mossi States/Kingdoms

The kingdom of Mossi occupied much of what is Burkina-Faso today. In the 14th century, it was made of five "core" kingdoms: Ouagadougou, Yatenga, Fada-Gurma, Mamprussi and Dagomba. Like the Ga Kingdoms described below, the Mossi kingdoms were fiercely republican and independent of one another.

Each was a constitutional monarchy. The king, the *moro naba*, came by heredity from the family of the previous *moro naba*, but his nomination was not automatic (Diop, 1987; p.43). He was chosen by an "electoral" college of four dignitaries, presided over by the prime minister, the *togo* (or *ouidi*) *naba*. The king was assisted, in addition to the prime minister, by three others: the *rassam naba*, the *balum naba*, and *kidirange naba*. Each of them governed one region. The *togo naba* was in charge of four royal districts.

After the prime minister, the *togo naba*, came the *rassam naba*, chief of the slaves of the Crown. He was also the minister of finance, guardian of the treasury of precious objects (cowries, bracelets, etc.). "Though himself a slave, the *rassam naba* ruled over free men, and held power over full-fledged citizens" (Diop, 1987; p.44).

The *balum naba* was third in rank. He was the mayor of the palace, in charge of introducing ambassadors and distinguished visitors. The *kidiranga naba*, head of the cavalry, came from an ordinary Mossi family.

In fact, the ministers who assisted the king were not members of the high nobility. Instead, they were chosen outside it and from among the common people and even slaves. They represented, at the royal court, the different social categories, professions and commoners. Even slaves and laborers or those without nobility were represented at the royal court, not symbolically but organically. According to Diop (1987), "the non-absolute nature of the Mossi monarchy is revealed by the fact that, once invested, the ministers cannot be removed by the king" (p.45).

Williams (1987), highly enthralled by the Mossi system, wrote:

> Their political system, highly democratic, was unsurpassed by any state anywhere in the world. That system was developed by Africans. The family was the smallest socio-economic and political unit. The extended family council, for example, settled all cases involving offenses by members which affected only the family or were not serious enough to be carried to the village court. Bad behavior by one member was a reflection on the rest of the family. The Western creed of fierce individualism had no place in the society. What one did was either a credit to his family or a dishonor.
>
> The village council was the next political unit with an elected headman and a Council of Elders. The elders were the representatives of the various family sections or wards that made up the village. The village council was the center of authority, subject to the will of the community. The districts were the next and larger divisions, varying in size, and having many villages and towns (p.213).

The Ga Kingdom

This "kingdom" was unique in the sense that it was never a state with one central organization. Like the Mossi Kingdoms, up to 1840, it was made up of six coastal towns along the Gold Coast: Accra, Osu, Labadi, Teshie, Nungua and Tema. "Each was an independent republic with its own territory and its own unique set of customs. There was never any political association between the towns and they never had a paramount chief" (Field, 1940:72).

Some of the people were aborigines; others were immigrants. The Ga-speaking immigrants arrived as extended-family groups of persecuted refugees. Neither they nor the aborigines had any military organization. They were all farmers, and the newcomers settled peacefully among the aborigines wherever there was vacant territory. There were no towns, no centralized government, no military organization, and no chiefs beyond the priestly heads of the extended families and their active assistants, the hunters. They all formed discrete settlements and lived by farming.

When slave-raiding became rife, the farming settlements were threatened with extermination. They, therefore, gathered themselves together in "towns" for mutual protection (Field, 1940:72). Tema was a confederation of four extended-families, Nungua of four, the others more than four. Accra was a confederation of seven extended families: *Abola, Alata, Akunmadzei, Asere, Gbese, Otublohu,* and *Sempi.* "Though they became allies in times of war, they never had any say in one another's affairs in times of peace and never had one Paramount Chief (or King)" (Field, 1940:158).

Every activity had to have a fetish or supernatural assistance. Agriculture had its priests; so too did hunting and warfare. The "medicine" for warfare was the war stool. Consequently, every little town "confederacy" set up a stool to carry into battle. As Field (1940) admonished: "To ignore the supernatural significance of the Ga stool is not only to play *Macbeth* without the witches, but to ensure complete failure to understand the curious position of the stool and the *mantse* in the constitution" (p.75).

Associated with the magical war stool was the *mantse*, literally "townfather" or "father of the military confederation." The word "chief" or "king" does not express the meaning and in the past did much to mislead the Europeans. The *mantse* was "medicined" to make him supernaturally brave and invincible.

> As a human being a *mantse* had - and has - no authority. He 'has no mouth.' Magically useful in war, in peace he is only 'a small boy.' Even in war, he was not a military leader. He never went right into the fight, but he and his stool stood apart protected by a special bodyguard. The director of operations was the *akwashontse*. The *akwashontse*'s court is a military court and the *mantse* is subject to it. An unsatisfactory *mantse* could be beheaded by its order (Field, 1940; p.73).

When the towns were formed as coalitions of extended families, the heads of these families became the heads of all civil affairs and one of them became the head priest of the whole town. In the days of warfare, the *mantse* was chosen partly for his physical vigor, for he had to travel to war. He was therefore seldom old enough to be regarded as the head of his family.

The real government of each of the six Ga towns was in the hands of the elders - "a democratic gerontocracy." The *mantse*, unless he was also a priest, had no integral part in it. He had no means of support: he lived on either the fitful charity of his relatives or, if made *mantse* later in life, on his own savings. "He is the vestigial survival without function, like the vermiform appendix in the human body, and is of embarrassment rather than use to the organism" (Field, 1940:74).

The Kingdom Of Ife

In the 19th century, the Kingdom of Ife was of a moderate size, stretching about 70 miles long and 40 miles wide. Ife was its capital in the southwestern part of Nigeria. It was the original founding state of the Yoruba kingdom and remained its nucleus kingdom after the "dispersal."[1] The king, the *Oni*, ruled over the capital through town chiefs; over the provinces through palace chiefs and over the villages through local town chiefs (*bale*). It should be remembered that the greater Yoruba kingdom or empire was composed of kingdoms which were internally autonomous. Some called their ruler the *Oni*, or *Ooni* while others called theirs the *Oba*. Thus, *oni* or *oba* refers to a Yoruba king.

Ife was divided into five wards (*adugbo*), each comprising a number of precincts (*ogbon*) headed by ward chiefs and precinct chiefs. Each precinct was made up of a number of compounds headed by the eldest male clan member. The compounds were large, complex, rectangular structures, housing up to several hundred inhabitants, with rooms arranged around one or more open patios (Bascom 1984; p.30).

There was a royal court made up of the *Oni* and eight palace chiefs (*Wole*) who served as intermediaries between the *Oni* and the provincial chiefs. Each chief was responsible for certain duties. The provincial chiefs collected tribute from the town chiefs within their jurisdiction and divided it with the *Oni*. The ward chiefs were responsible for the young adults in their wards.

The Kingdom Of Kongo

This kingdom was founded around the 14th century. It had a hierarchical structure originating from the basic village under a headman, a hereditary position. The core of the village was a localized matrilineage (Vansina, 1975; p.41). Several villages combined to form a district under an official appointed by the king, who could also remove him. District officials carried administrative duties and served as judges in the district courts. Several districts formed a province under an official, also appointed and subject to

---

[1] The Yoruba kingdom is discussed at length under imperial governments.

removal by the king. The center of the kingdom, of course, was occupied by the king, or *mani Kongo*.

The Basoga Kingdom Of Uganda

The ruler, *Zibondo*, commanded a large administrative staff of household and territorial officials, headed by the *katikkiro*, the "prime minister", who had direct control over the palace and its environs. The outlying area of the state was divided into a number of major subdivisions, each under the administration of a prince (*mulangira*) or a commoner chief (*mukungu*) appointed by the ruler. Subordinate to the chiefs and princes were the headmen of the villages (*ab'ebisoko*) (Fallers, 1965).

The Ganda of Uganda also had a similar hierarchical governmental structure. The country was divided into ten territorial districts or *ssazas*, the chiefs of which were appointed by the king, the *kabaka*. Within these territories and representing a second level of authority were a number of great chiefs, or *bakungu*, who exercised authority over a third level of chiefs, known as the *batongole* and *bataka*, except such lesser chiefs as were appointed by the king directly (Carlston, 1968:250). The lesser chiefs were chosen by traditional methods, that is, by hereditary.

The Swazi Kingdom

The Swazi Kingdom is surrounded by South Africa and is the home to the Swazi, a Bantu-speaking people. The kingdom is unique because it is a dual monarchy. The monarchy is built on a network of ties betwen the royal *Nkosi Dlamini* and commoners. The clans, over 70 in number, fall into four major grades. At the apex is the *Nkosi Dlamini* in which the lineage of the king, known as the *Malangeni* (Children of the Sun), is preeminent. The king, *Ngwenyama*, is the recognized lineal descendant of the first leader of the conquering *Nkosi Dlamini*. He performs executive, legislative and judicial functions, holds land in trust for the Swazi nation and allocates its usage, performs sacred rituals, and is the symbol of national unity (Libby, 1987; p.154).

The king is chosen by the rank of his mother and, together with her, he symbolizes the Swazi state. Honors are fairly evenly distributed between them, and though the king, as male, is dominant in legal and executive activities, the mother — the source of his selection — exercises complementary rights (Gibbs, 1965; p.498).

> But this is not to say, however, that he monopolizes all power. His authority is, in fact, balanced by the *Ndlovukazi* (the queen mother),

and it is shared by two traditional institutions — the *Liqoqo* (inner or family council) and *Libandla* (General Council or Council of the Nation). The *Liqoqo* functions in much the same way as a cabinet in a parliamentary or presidential system of government. It is a small group of ten to twenty senior princes (that is, descendants of the king's royal Dlamini line), important representatives of the queen mother's Nxuma-lo clan, senior chiefs from outside the Dlamini, and Nxumalo clans and a few commoners of outstanding importance in the country (p.156).

The king is guided by *non-Dlamini tindvuna* (councilors), both civil and military. The relationship between the king and his councilors is expressed in two frequently quoted axioms: "The king is king by the people" and "The king is ruled by his councilors" (Gibbs, 1965; p.499). The civil councilors act as governors of royal homesteads and are chosen from a limited group of clans. The emphasis is placed on ability and respect for people so that within the general structure recognition is accorded individual qualities.

The *Liqoqo* meets informally, and certain of its members are consulted frequently by the king. However, while the king is supposed to be guided by its advice, he is not bound to follow its recommendations. "The *Libandla*, by contrast, is regarded as having binding authority on actions taken by the king on behalf of the Swazi nation. It is comprised of the *Liqoqo* members, all of the chiefs, their counselors, and all adult men in the country. Although it normally meets only once a year, in principle its approval is required for all important new laws and decisions" (Libby, 1987; p.156).

Commoners may participate in discussions with the king and their chiefs through regional forums called *Tinkhundla*. Gibbs (1965) stated:

> The people (can) voice their opinion through two councils. The *liqoqo* (inner or privy council) is composed primarily of senior princes; merit is also a qualification. They rarely number over twenty and their discussions are private. . .

> Whenever the *liqoqo* thinks necessary, it reports its discussions to the second council, the *Libandla Laka Ngwane* (Council of the State) composed of chiefs and headmen and open to all adult males. The members hold no regular sessions, follow no clearly stated agenda, and as their guiding principle make every effort to achieve agreement before action is taken. Should a consensus not be possible, the matter is generally shelved; organized opposition parties are not part of the traditional system. The *liqoqo* may never override the decision of the *libandla*, and the king, who is usually the last speaker, should try to reconcile the wishes of both councils (p.500).

The Swazi kingdom is a modern African state and occupies a special place in the history of British colonial Africa because it remained largely intact on account of the reluctance of the British to assume reponsibility for its financial management. There was incessant friction between the British colonial power and the traditional authorities over land and mineral rights. But the kingdom was allowed to govern the Swazi people according to their traditional laws and customs. Despite being placed under British colonial administration, being forced to adopt a British-imposed constitution, and being required to hold democratic elections in 1964 and 1967, the traditional kingship remained the effective government of the Swazi people. After independence, the British-crafted constitution was abandoned and the system of government reverted to the traditional. Libby (1987) put it well:

> From the standpoint of the traditional Swazi authorities, there is no confusion or ambiguity in the existence of modern institutions of government under the political control of the chieftaincy. Positions in the Western administrative hierarchy complement rather than replace the traditional offices. Persons possessing the qualities appropriate for each position are selected. Taken as a whole the political elite hold overlapping positions in the governmental, and traditional hierarchies (p.155).

The Zulu Kingdom

In many respects, the Zulu Kingdom, in southeastern South Africa, was also unique in African history. It was one of the African kingdoms that devised a political system as a direct response to an environmental crisis.[2]

In the 18th century increasing population density in the sub-continent made migration to new areas difficult. In ancient times, this was the principal way Africans relieved population pressures on the land and restored soil fertility. In southern African this was no longer possible. Furthermore, since it was becoming difficult to convert forest and bush to grass and arable land, there emerged constraint on the rate of increase of production under the existing modes of exploitation of the land and environmental resources.

There was a major famine in the region during the early years of the 19th century. That inevitably led to conflicts and struggles between the major groups (or chiefdoms) in the region - the Mthetwa, the Ndwandwe, the Ngwane and the Zulu - to gain access to diminishing arable and grazing

---

[2] Guy (1979) noted: "While it would be an over-simplification to argue that the environmental crisis of the late 18th century led to the creation of the 19th century kingdom which solved this problem, the evidence does suggest that we should study the early existing production techniques on the physical environment and the problems caused in such an environment by the pressure of population on existing resources" (p.12).

land. Out of these wars and violence (the *difaqane*), the Zulu chiefdom under Shaka emerged victorious. Some chiefdoms were annihilated, dispersed, but those which survived the struggle were incorporated into the Zulu kingdom and assimilated.

The Zulu kingdom was greatly expanded through military conquest. Its success rested on the use of a strictly disciplined, mobile army whose warriors, well protected by large shield, engaged in effective hand-to-hand fighting, using a short stabbing spear. The army grew in size and incorporated young men from conquered chiefdoms. But military prowess alone explains only part of the story.

Shaka expanded his power by the use of existing ruling lineages, the exploitation of rivalries within them, and between them and their subjects and their subordinates, much as the colonialists later did. Subjugated lineages came under Zulu hegemony in varying degrees and forms. Those lineages close to the Zulu heartland were fully incorporated in the kingdom. Other lineages on the peripheries of the kingdom seem to have had fewer rights and heavier obligations.

> Transcending these varying forms of incorporation was a loose sense of Zulu nationhood. This was fostered by Shaka's emphasis on national ceremonies, and by the use of national symbols, notably the *inkatha*, a woven grass coil (Maylam, 1986; p.28).

Statehood was further enhanced by vesting strong authority in the Zulu king. Shaka made key decisions of state, wielding wide-ranging executive, judicial and military powers. Religious systems were reorganized to focus on the king at the apex. There was an attempt at central intervention in the economy to enable Shaka to accumulate abundant material resources. But Maylam (1986) cautions that the degree of centralization in the Zulu kingdom should not be exaggerated:

> The size of the state necessitated the delegation of authority. Heads of pre-existing chiefdoms, although ultimately subject to Shaka, retained a degree of autonomy. Some of these were allocated land and cattle by Shaka to ensure their loyalty. Shaka entrusted key advisory and executive roles to senior members of the ruling lineage, both men and women. And he appointed a large number of *izinduna*, state officials who performed various administrative functions (p.28).

The basic structure of the kingdom was the result of social integration of two systems (Guy, 1979; p.21). On the one hand, there was social power based on production, coming from the production units - the homesteads (*umuzi/imizi*) - and expressed in terms of kinship and the clan. On the other hand, there was the power of the state coming from above, and based on the extraction of surplus, mainly in labor through the military system.

Under the Zulu military system, all men and women in the country, on reaching the age of puberty, were gathered into age-set, *amabutho*. Members of the female age-sets remained within their fathers' homesteads, but were not allowed to marry until the king had given his permission.[3] The male age-sets were housed in the royal homesteads - the *amakhanda* - and served and labored for the king directly. They served as regiments of the Zulu army, responsible for raiding beyond Zululand's borders, maintaining law and order in the kingdom and cultivating crops for the royal homestead. In the *amakhanda*, the men, as the king - the head of the army - said, were occupied in "building military kraals, planting, reaping, and making gardens for the king. These are the men who look after the king" (Guy, 1979; p.29).

The king ruled with *izikhulu* - the great ones - of the kingdom. The *izikhulu* represented the great pre-Shakan chiefdoms, incorporated by the founder into the kingdom. The king with *izikhulu* comprised the *ibandla*, the highest council of state.[4] Without the *izikhulu*, the king could make no decisions of national importance. Membership of the *izikhulu* was determined primarily by birth (lineage association) but political acumen was also a factor considered as well.

The *ibandla* represented the authority of the state at its highest level. However, there were frequent and more widely based state meetings in which younger chiefs, men of note within the kingdom, the large number of officers in charge of the homesteads, and the regiments of the state, and the confidential advisers to the king participated (Guy, 1979; p.30). The control and administration depended on a vast number of state officials of differing rank and status. These were the *izinduna* (singular, *induna*) of the kingdom, the army commanders, regimental officers, personal attendants to the king, messengers, tribute collectors, and so on.

State power was devolved from the king to the *izikhulu*, to the heads of the administrative areas within the kingdom, with local affairs being the responsibility of the resident homestead-heads (*abanumzana/umnumzana*). All married men in the kingdom were homestead-heads, and these men were also state officials. The *abanumzana* were responsible for the allocation of

---

[3] When the men of a regiment were well into their thirties, and the women of the age-sets associated with them perhaps ten years younger, the king gave them permission to marry and set up their homesteads. This was interpreted by a number of scholars as a necessary measure to check population expansion in the face of dwindling resources. But, Guy (1979) argued that, "Marriage in Zulu society did not signal the onset of sexual relations; these had been taking place long before, although they were of a kind which did not lead to conception" (p.11). This kind of sexual activity in Zulu should be a matter of urgent investigation by population control experts.

[4] The *ibandla* was similar in structure to the *Libandla* (the inner council or privy council) of the Swazi discussed above.

clan land, the implementation of law and resolution of disputes in their areas. They also served as intermediaries between the people and higher authorities.

Exceptional Kingdoms

A few African kingdoms departed from the norm in the forms they took although the basic king-council structure was the same. A couple are discussed below. These exceptions of course should not be taken as the rule. It may be recalled that, although a few states such as Asante and Zulu had standing armies, this was not the general rule. The people were the army. It is important *not* to confuse the exceptions with the general rule.

The Kingdom Of Dahomey

The ascension of this kingdom was strikingly similar to that of the Asante. Like the Asante, the kingdom of Dahomey was created by a clan or ruling dynasty known as Fon or Aja, which continued to rule until the very end of the 19th century. Secondly, like Asante, Dahomey also started out as a small inland kingdom and subsequently expanded southward. Both the capitals of Asante and Dahomey (Kumasi and Abomey) are almost on the same latitude. Thirdly, both Asante and Dahomey began to emerge in the 17th century and in the second half of the 18th century had attained great prominence. The kings of Asante, Osei Tutu and Opoku Ware and the Dahomean kings Agaja II and Tegbesu IV were not only contemporaries but also brave and victorious. There were, of course, differences between the kingdoms: internal organizations, systems of administration, military organizations and sources of income.

The founders of Dahomey were part of the Aja people, who also include the Ewe of Ghana and Togo, the Fon, the Gun and the Popo of Dahomey. The Aja migrated southeastward from Tado and founded the kingdom of Allada around 1575 on the Abomey plateau.

Dahomey was forged into a strong kingdom from the Abomey plateau by the military prowess and dynamic personality of Wegbaja who ruled a small chiefdom between 1650 and 1685. He re-organized the war-bands of the Fon monarchy, instituted military training and adopted the tactic of night attacks by which he overran neighboring tribes mainly to the south and southeast of Abomey. He strengthened the position of the Fon monarchy, and won the political support of the people by lavish hospitality and open-handed generosity. People under his jurisdiction were forbidden to kill thieves, even those caught red-handed; nor were they allowed to take personal revenge on someone who had harmed them. All such serious cases were reserved for judgment and punishment by the ruler. "So insistent was Wegbaja on upholding of royal authority that he is said to have executed his own son for a breach of one of these new laws" (Stride and Ifeka, 1971; p.277).

He elevated the status of the Fon ruler over his subjects and sub-rulers alike. Further strengthening of his position required the provision of adequate revenue to support his personal courts and power. Accordingly came the institution of a regular poll tax and the introduction of the practice that a dead man's property reverted to the ruler. In effect, all property in the state belonged to the ruler.

The inheritance of all property was validated through the king's court. In addition, he monitored events of all kinds throughout his kingdom with the help of *agbadjigbeto*. This was the equivalent of a modern-day secret service, which combined war intelligence with public information service. Wegbaja and later Dahomey kings (Akaba and Agaja) used this for spying on other tribes and for spreading propaganda with Dahomey.

The kingdom was structured into perhaps the most rigid and highly centralized governments in all of Africa, rivaling even the Zulu kingdom. The system controlled by Dahomey kings was directed toward military efficiency and royal absolutism. Military and civil discipline were strict and there was a clearly defined chain of command.

The kings of Dahomey were assisted by a cabinet which consisted of the *migan* (prime minister); the *meu* (finance minister) created by Tegbesu; *yovo-gan* (viceroy of Whydah); the *to-no-num* (the chief eunuch and minister in charge of protocol); the *tokpo* (minister of agriculture); the *agan* (general of the army); and the *adjaho* (minister of the king's palace and the chief of police). The most interesting and unique feature of the cabinet was that each of these posts had a *female* counterpart who complemented him but reported independently to the king.

Furthermore, Dahomey had a large army consisting of full-time soldiers, and a militia which could be called up at any time. This army was believed by European observers to be the strongest and best organized on the west African coast.

> During his reign, Gezo increased the number of the full-time soldiers from about 5,000 in 1840 to 12,000 by 1845. This army consisted not only of men but also of women, the famous Amazons 'devoted to the person of the king and valorous in war.' This unique female section was created and organized by Gezo and consisted of 2,500 female soldiers divided into three brigades. Commanders of this army were also top cabinet ministers in charge of the central government thus enhancing the position of the army in decision making (Boahen, 1986; p.86).

The provincial system of government was also markedly different from what obtained in most other African kingdoms such as Asante and Oyo. The kings of Dahomey usually abolished the ruling royal lineages of the states they conquered (as the French colonialists did in Africa), suppressed their laws and customs, imposed Dahomean laws and customs and then appointed governors of such states. It was a policy of "Dahomeanization" or total integration of the conquered states.

The whole kingdom was divided into 6 provinces, each controlled by a royal official appointed by the king. All subordinate chiefs and tributary rulers were appointed by local hereditary custom but no appointment was valid until royal approval was formally given. Communication between the king and the provincial governors was swift and was ensured by a strong body of runners, stationed at relay posts throughout the kingdom. This institution was comparable to the *ilari* system of Oyo and was introduced by the Dahomey king Tegbesu. Provincial governors could be summoned to the capital at any time.

Each province was required to submit regular reports to Abomey in person enabling the king to maintain close watch over responsible officials. In addition, each governor had a spy attached to his office.

Much of the revenue the Dahomey kings collected was directed toward the purchase of firearms, the ownership of which was a royal monopoly. Subsequently, other royal monopolies were declared: trade in slaves, the cultivation of certain agricultural crops and certain European imports such as gold, coral, and ammunition.

Unknown in other African kingdoms was the Dahomean poll tax or head-money paid according to the rank, reputation and income of the person. Agriculture was also taxed. Taxation was about one-third of the total production. The tax on palm oil, the largest single source of revenue after the 1850s, was bartered at Whydah for guns and powder. Boahen (1986) disclosed that:

> The farmers in each village were counted by officials of the minister of agriculture and the tax paid in kind by each was fixed according to the assessment made of the villages' total production. Livestock were also counted and taxed. The kings of Dahomey regularly conducted a population census to get an accurate estimate of the number of people to be taxed and also to be conscripted into the army when necessary (p.87).

The annual census also provided figures for the distribution of the population by sex, occupation, province and village. There was even a census of all goats, cows, sheep and pigs and a strict account of slaughtering. Each village chief reported the number of pigs slaughtered. The butcher's guild kept all the skulls of pigs sold in the market. Both reports went to the king at Abomey, who sent out market inspectors, called *zangbeto*, not only to make periodic checks but also to fix prices.[5] Oral records of negotiations and important statistics were kept by women specially appointed for their good memory. Many of these were royal wives known as *Kposi*. Several accompanied the king at every interview he gave, and royal ministers also had a staff of women recorders.

Summing up, Stride and Ifeka (1971) observed:

> The entire administrative machine was ruthlessly efficient. Headed by rulers of rare political talent and backed by a people of great military skill and courage it was a dynamic political organism. Furthermore, the dangers that accompanied Dahomey's rise to importance had impressed upon its people the urgency of unity. They expressed this idea in vigorous and emphatic symbolism: the life of the nation was a pot with many holes. Only if all citizens kept their fingers firmly over the holes could the life-giving force, that of the royal power, be prevented from draining away. Nor did it drain away until finally faced by the superior military technology of France (p.287).

The Dahomey Kingdom was the extremely rare case in African history that approximates the modern example of rigidly controlled society. Yet, modern-day African leaders, nationalists, intellectuals and even Marxists mischievously used the Dahomean example as "a general African model" to defend ill-conceived schemes to restructure African societies to suit their whims. For example, that all property in the kingdom of Dahomey belonged to the king was taken as the precursor of "African socialism" whereby ownership of all the means of production was placed with the state. But no such justification is acceptable.

First, the kingdom of Dahomey was the *exception* and exceptions do not make the general rule. Second, the population of Dahomey was ethnically homogenous which is not true of modern African nations. Third, the kingdom was small.

> The kingdom was only about 160 kilometers from north to south and from east to west it never extended anywhere beyond 80 kilometers; it was indeed much narrower near the coast where it was about 45 kilometers wide. Thus Dahomey occupied an area of only

[5] The *zangbeto* watched the merchants and if they found that a woman had violated the price law, members of the secret association could walk through the village for seven nights cursing the woman who had disregarded the "customary price." If she did not comply, the *zangbeto* would come out again and curse her for 16 more nights and carry through the village a banana tree wrapped in a white cloth representing a corpse in a shroud. It was believed the lawbreaker died shortly thereafter (Bates, 1983:40).

6,400 square kilometers, about a tenth of the size of the modern Republic of Benin. It was therefore much easier to defend or hold together than the sprawling empires of Oyo and Asante (Boahen, 1986).

Fourth, Dahomey was hemmed in by powerful states: on the west flank by the Asante and the west by Oyo. This forced the Dahomeans to "stick together" against powerful external aggressors. Oyo however began to crumble in the 1820s, providing Dahomey with an opportunity for expansion.

Fifth, royal absolutism of Dahomey kings was *not* the main feature of the original Dahomean constitution. According to Curtin, *et al.,*

> The original Dahomean constitution was similar to those of the Yoruba states. That is, the *oba*, or ruler, was the supreme official, but he was not free to act on his own. Instead, his powers were strictly circumscribed by a set of councils, some representing lineages, others professional groups. One council normally chose the *oba* from among eligible members of the royal lineage. Another usually had the power to order the *oba* to commit suicide. Once in office, an *oba* could appoint some officials and councillors, but these royal appointees were always balanced by others who represented particular interests or particular lineages. The personal ties that counted most in this society were first of all the ties of kinship, secondly the ties to fellow members of a professional or occupational group. Only after that was the individual bound to give loyalty and obedience to the *oba*.
>
> The Dahomean constitution began to depart from this pattern early in the 18th century, intentionally subverted by a succession of rulers who used their control over firearms to convert the state into despotism (p.242).

The last sentence in the quote should be of particular note and applicability to many African nations today. Pre-independence constitutions were "intentionally subverted by a succession of (military) rulers who used their control over firearms to convert the state into a despotism": Benin, Burkina Faso, Burundi, Central African Republic, Ethiopia, Ghana, Guinea, Liberia, Mali, Nigeria, Rwanda, Somalia, Uganda, Zaire and many others.

Sixth, and perhaps more important, the kingdom of Dahomey collapsed under the weight of its own stifling regulations and controls — a poignant lesson to all modern state-controlled African economies. The collapse of Dahomey began in 1883, when the French took over Porto Novo and Cotonue. To evade excessive rates of taxation, trade, goods and people moved to Cotonou from the state-controlled port of Whydah. Cotonou flourished and became the commercial center of the French colony which was also named "Dahomey."

The Dyola Kingdom

The Dyola, who have lived for many centuries near the mouth of the river Casamnce on the fertile plains of Senegal, should not be confused with the Dyula, a Mande group. They speak different dialects.

One section of the Dyola had a system of fairly centralized government by kings and priests. But another section only obeyed one ruler when they were at war with other tribes. In peacetime, secret societies, age-groups and local chieftains maintained law and order.

Stride and Ifeka (1971) remarked that:

> Among the centralized Dyola the king is appointed for life, while a secret council of chiefs help him to govern. There is a reasonably straightforward division of authority between the king who is a ruler and priest rolled into one - a divine king - and the secret council. The council deals with the affairs of state, but in theory the king has the final word. The council is solely concerned with administration, but the king has important religious duties in addition to his work as a political ruler. This kingship *rotates between two to four royal clans*: in this respect the Dyola resemble some of the savanna states where certain lineages take it in turn to provide a ruler. In theory, rebellions are less likely to occur when several lineages supply kings because power is more evenly distributed between the main contenders (p.200).

Among the less centralized Dyola, secret societies have an important part to play in governing the semi-autonomous villages in much the same way as the *poro* in the Temne and Mende societies in Sierra Leone. Secret societies worship ancestral spirits which sanction the authority of the society's members. There are also associations like age-groups, as we saw in the Igbo system, which provide collective labor in the village as, for example, the *compins* or work groups of the Gambian Wolof.

The intensely unique Dyola system of government provides yet another indication of how diverse and flexible the native systems of government were. In this case, although one section of the people chose to have centralized administration while the other opted for semi-independent villages, they all constituted the kingdom.

Despite the great diversity and variations in size, African kingdoms possessed remarkable similarities. Curtin, *et al.,* for example, observed that:

But great diversity in size masked fundamental similarities, for lineages were as important in large states as they were in areas of decentralized political authority. Almost everywhere in Africa the lineage rather than the individual paid tribute or answered to the court of law. In East Africa as in West, the right to supply the ruler or to exercise some other political function was often assigned to a lineage (p.157).

Other similarities were also noted by Kopytoff (1989):

The ethnographic literature shows strikingly similar themes in royal rituals across the map of Africa, even if there are arguments among scholars about the specific nature of their integrative action. Similar themes occur among peoples as widely scattered as the Swazi, the Asante, the Fon of Dahomey, the Yoruba, the Jukun, the Ndembu and the Shilluk. The royal installation ceremonies always involved the active participation of the symbolic representatives of the people whose role it was to admonish the new king on his responsibilities and to remind him that he was king by the will of the people; sometimes, the king was dressed in rags, or beaten, or made to crouch before the people's elders and harangued by them. At the same time, however, it was clear — from the very intensity of these preventive harangues — that the power, once conferred on the new incumbent, was in theory absolute and, publicly at least, unquestioned (p.69).

One other general commonality was the hierarchical structure, at the apex of which sat the king. Relatives, friends or individuals with exceptional abilities were appointed by the king as provincial governors. Administration of the kingdom was decentralized. Provincial governors transmitted the orders of the king and collected tributes. The provinces exercised various degrees of autonomy and could — in fact many did — break away to establish their independence.

In virtually all African kingdoms, the king was semi-divine, playing a rather limited role in the political affairs of the kingdom. He was burdened with a cornucopia of restrictions on his behavior and lifestyle. In fact, his whole life was planned to the slightest detail. In some societies, the king was forbidden to shake the hands of strangers. He could not even speak to his people, except through a linguist. He was surrounded by layers of advisers and councils. He was obligated to listen to their advice, although he was not bound to follow it. But only a foolish king would not do so.

Of course, various forms were possible within this general framework, and extremes could be found. At one end was the Ga *mantse* who had virtually no political role; he was only useful in times of war. At the other extreme were the Dahomey king and Muslim *emirs* who exercised far greater control over their kingdoms/sultanates. But despite these exceptions, the general rule was limited monarchical intervention or participation in political affairs. The king's main role was spiritual and religious as discussed below.

B. THE TRADITIONAL ROLE OF AFRICAN KINGS

The African Concept Of The Universe

An understanding of the role of kings necessitates a brief discourse on the African concept of the universe. As underscored earlier in Chapter 1, Africans believed their universe was composed of three elements: the sky, the world and the earth. The sky and the earth embraced the world which was the place of the living. The world was run in a strictly orderly manner, metaphysically speaking (Diop, 1987; p.59). The universe was ruled by only one set of hierarchic forces: every being, animate or inanimate, could occupy only a specific place according to his or its potential. These forces were cumulative; thus, a living person who had a fang or claw of a lion, in which the vital force of the animal was concentrated, increased his own power by that much. In order to overcome him in battle, one had to have a sum of forces greater than his own plus the lion's.

Therefore, to the African, the world was ordered like one vast equation; human animation corresponded to the animation of nature and each gesture extended back to its mythical precedents. African art, dance, music and other human activities reflected the rhythms of the universe.

The three orders of the sky, the earth and the world comprised the cosmos. The sky was the domain of spirits of both the living and the yet to be born as well as powerful forces: lightning, thunder, rain, drought, etc. The earth was the domain of the dead ancestors, other dead tribesmen as well as the the activities of the living: agriculture, fishing, hunting, etc. The world was peopled by the group and other tribesmen as well and therefore the domain of war, peace, trade and relations with other tribes. In most indigenous African societies, each of the three orders was represented by a god.

The King's Link To The Universe

In the ethnic societies considered kingdoms, the king had a precise function and a definite role: to "maintain harmony between society and its natural environment by means of ritual action" (Davidson, 1970; p.192). Several studies on the ideology of African kingship have also shown that "kings were frequently defined by the members of society as ritual mediators between society and the forces of nature, and that they were closely associated with the well-being of land and society and with the problem of ecological control" (Packard (1981; p.6).

For example, the duties of the Nigerian Junkun king in this sphere were threefold: to perform the daily rites for which he was uniquely qualified by office; to provide for and direct the activities of other cults; and to sustain and control his own spiritual potency. And the Swazi king, through the annual *ncwala* ceremony, mediates between the world of the living and the world of supernatural beings, taking on to himself the "filth of the nation" and thus purifying and renewing his kingdom (Beidelman, 1966). On the Swazi king thus falls the onerous task of reproduction of the social order.

For comparative purposes, the kings of medieval Western Europe also had three fundamental duties: to ensure the spiritual welfare of their people by acts of piety and the protection given by the true faith; to defend their people against outside enemies; and at home, to safeguard justice and peace. "The forms of kingship might be different: the content in Africa and Europe was essentially the same" (Davidson, 1970; p.193).

To perform his functions, the African king must be the one only with the greatest vital force in the whole kingdom. Only in this way can he serve as mediator with the superior universe, without creating any break, any catastrophic upheaval within the ontological forces (Diop, 1987). His powers were expected to be enhanced by those of the dead ancestors as well as his people because he sat on a sacred stool, the repository of the powers of the kingdom.

The king thus had two roles to play: political, as head of the kingdom, and spiritual, as the link to the universe. Kings had certain fundamental duties, such as serving as ultimate judicial appeal. However, in practice, it was the provincial heads who made the laws and even waged wars. "The Asante King never directly interferes in the internal government of a province, but he can bring external pressure to bear in suitable cases" (Casely Hayford, 1911). The kings, like most chiefs, were not rulers; they were leaders. The spiritual function of the king was always paramount and eternal:

> For what the kings did was to subsume in their persons the many ancestral powers formerly invested in a more or less large number of lineage leaders, and so enable a people's unity to survive. They were, in other words, the guardians of guardians of a social charter which contained a network of otherwise separate charters. Willingly accepted only when legitimate, they could not become kings except when recognized as standing at the ritual apex of their people's socio-moral order. Hence the accent on "divinity." For the king's

existence as a political person or military was a secondary thing. (Davidson, 1970; p.191).

Vansina (1987), who extensively studied the kingdoms of Central Africa, also found that, "the king's role is small: he is the representative or symbol of the chiefdom and may have some religious duties, but his participation in the political decision-making process is insignificant" (p.29). In fact, the king hardly made policy or spoke. He had a spokesperson, called a linguist, through whom he communicated. He hardly decided policy. His advisers and chiefs would determine policies and present them for royal sanction. His role in legislation and execution of policy was severely limited. The Ga people of Ghana took this to the extreme. As it may be recalled, the Ga *mantse* (king) had no role in political affairs or authority except only in times of war. In many other ethnic societies, however, the king was the physical symbol of his kingdom, a personification of sacred ancestry and the religious head of his tribe as well as the link to the universe.[6] As such, the vital force of the king must never decline; nor must the king die, since he embodies the spiritual and therefore material well-being of his people. The consequences would be devastation: droughts would occur, women would no longer be able to bear children, epidemics would strike the people. Great care, therefore, must be taken to prevent a break in the line of transmitted power. To inculcate the indispensability of kingship, some tribes adopted customs of organized disorder when their king died and during the interregnum period. For example, among the Gonja of northern Ghana, at the death of a divisional chief, the market of Salaga would become bedlam. Young men rushed in, overturning tables and stealing wares.[7] Among the Mossi, the market was also violently disturbed upon the death of the king. Peace and order was restored when a new king was installed. Many other tribes simply did not announce the death of a king until a new one had quickly been enthroned and the old one buried.

The emphasis on the spiritual meant a separation of kingship and the political leader. Kingship as an office was regarded as the spiritual repository of the collective soul of the people as well as the powers of ancestors. As such, the office was sacred, protected by many taboos and rules. The king

[6] Ogot (1967) argued that kingships evolved almost regularly when an incoming minority, marching for new land, had to extend their rule over settled people who lived within different lineage frameworks. For example, the dynasties which appeared after the Luo invasion of Uganda, "evolved as a result of a small well-organized group successfully imposing its rule over a disorganized majority." Under these circumstances, any political set-up based upon kinship ties cannot work. The minority group, in order to maintain its rule over what is usually a hostile majority, must present a united front. Their means of doing this is kingship.

[7] Originally, this custom was not supposed to result in larceny. But there were always those who took advantage of the custom.

and kingship would be identical only if the king obeyed these rules. As the Ga say: "If the big man does not respect, the small man will not respect."

Once the king departed from the rules, he corrupted or endangered kingship and therefore the state or the soul of the people, by transgressing the boundaries of the right and natural, thereby allowing the intrusion of evil. For example, the Barotse "emphasize that the king was bound by the law, and that if a king ruled cruelly his council and people were entitled to rebel against him and to try to dispose of him" (Gluckman, 1965).

Usurpers could not seize the throne. To remain as legitimate, kings must not only provide the vital link but also obey the taboos and the rules. "And the rules - the constitutional rules - were repeatedly developed in the direction of 'checks and balances' to control the growth of centralising power. There is perhaps no more fascinating subject in the history of African institutions" (Davidson, 1970; p.198).

It was, however, not possible to lay down the exact qualifications the king must have to provide the vital link with the universe. When an "electoral" council met to assess the legitimacy of claimants to the throne, it did not select the wealthiest but in accordance with tradition, the one who had the requisite qualities of providing the vital link.

Ideally, the king should be strong, generous of mind, humble, bold in warfare and devout in everyday life. Descendancy from the founding ancestors was desirable. He should epitomize a people at one with its moral order, at peace with itself, at every point in harmony with the ancestors "who brought us into our land and gave us life" (Davidson, 1970; p.193). His life was strictly regulated by custom to fit this role.

Among the Mossi, the monarch's schedule was planned down to the slightest detail. He once did not have the right to leave the capital. In many tribal societies, the less public exposure of the king the better. His primary function was to deal with the universe and ancestors. He was not expected to perform terrestrial functions, except the ceremonial. The *Oni* of Ife "could return home to visit his relatives only incognito and under cover of darkness. He appeared in public only once a year" (Bascom, 1984; p.31).

This was also the case with other Yoruba *obas*.

> The Yoruba *oba* is usually described as a sacred or divine king. His coronation and installation were performed with solemn and lengthy rites which set him apart. He lived a life thereafter of ordered ceremonial, secluded in his palace, subject to many ritual restraints and approached only with infinite respect and by designated persons of the Court. He rarely appeared in public, and then always robed and, in the case of the great *oba*, wearing a beaded crown whose fringe hid his face. He was not only the head of the town and kingdom but their personification, reincarnation and also all his ancestors back to the origin of the dynasty, and he was the titular head of all religious cults in

the kingdom. *This sacred aspect of Yoruba kingship did not lead to the oba's becoming an autocrat but rather the reverse* (Smith, 1969; p.111). (Italics mine).

The Suku of southwestern Congo also surrounded their king with a number of taboos and restricted his activities in order to instill awe or enhance his divinity. No one could see him eat; he could not walk in cultivated fields, lest the fertility of the soil might be affected. He could not see a corpse nor cry over the dead. He must not be allowed to die a natural death, for that would affect the power of his sacred "medicines." It has been claimed: "When the king drank, those present had to cover their faces while one of the attendants recited proverbs and sayings recapitulating historic events, praising the king for his good deeds and also hinting at those where he had shown himself to be unjust" (Gibbs, 1965; p.460). The king of Loango of Central Africa went one step further: "If he was thirsty, he would order his attendant to ring a bell, and all present, even European guests, would fall flat on their faces so as not to behold the king drinking" (Birmingham, 1981:42).

An apparent incompatibility may be noted between the sacred role of the king, the divinity of the office and his other role of chief representative of the people who must have access to him. How could a king interact with the people if they could not see him eat or drink? This dilemma was resolved in many tribal systems by providing the king with a "spokesman." Among the Asante, this spokesman was called the linguist.[8]

The linguist was the mouthpiece of the king or chief in every public function as well as judicial proceedings. He was generally an intelligent, bright, and witty individual, skilled in the use of language, especially proverbs and idioms. This intermediary role was important. The linguist, in a sense, served as a buffer between the king and the people. Criticisms of kingly actions could be vented at the linguist and it would be his duty to smooth down angry words to the king. Similarly, when they came from the other direction.

To lead his people well, the king must obey the rules and save his people from such calamities as droughts and famine. When such evil occurred, the king had not ruled well and was to be deposed or killed (regicide). Among the Kerebe of northwest Tanzania,

Kings were expected to regulate rainfall and the inability to conform to these expectations over an extended period of time was

[8] Linguist is a misnomer since this spokesman spoke not many but one language. Casely Hayford (1911) explained that, "he was called a linguist first by a half-educated native interpreter, asked to explain his position to the white man, and as 'linguist' he has been known ever since in the language of law and politics on the Gold Coast."

a major reason for deposing an *omukama*. Two kings are said to have been deposed in this manner at the beginning of the nineteenth century: Ruhinda, who was unable to prevent an excessive amount of rain from falling, and his successor, Ibanda, who fell victim to an extended period of drought (Packard, 1981; p.6).

The Junkun of Nigeria however believed "kings were supposed to be killed if they broke any of the royal taboos on personal behavior, fell seriously ill, or ruled in time of famine or severe drought: whenever they could no longer be regarded as fit guardians of the 'right and natural'" (Davidson, 1970; p.201).

The king was also put to death when the level of his vital force was perceived to have declined. For example, among the Serer, "A Bur (king) who reached old age was subject to ritual murder because it was believed he could no longer guarantee that cattle and women would remain fertile" (Klein, 1968:13). Similarly, among the Shilluk of the Nilotic Sudan, a sick or old king was to be killed.

Although regicide has been abolished, the belief in the practice generally reflected the existence of a ideological relationship between political authority and the problem of ecological control (Packard, 1981; p.6). In the Kingdom of Cayor, the king could not rule when he was wounded. In other societies, an old king was not killed but revitalized when old. He would symbolically die, be born again, regain the vigor of his youth and be fit once again to rule. This ritual was found among the Yoruba, Dagomba, Tchamba, Djukon, Igara, Songhai, Wuadai, Hausa of the Gobi, Katsena, and Daoura, the Shillucks, among the Mbum, in Uganda-Rwanda, and in what was ancient Meroe (Diop, 1987; p.61).

In other tribes, if the king failed to provide the vital link to the universe, he was dethroned. There were various procedures for divestiture. While the Serer tribe of Senegal adopted a distinctive drumbeat to signal the end of a king's reign, the Yoruba of Nigeria demanded the king's suicide "by a symbolic gift of parrot's eggs" (Isichei, 1977; p.71). In the Kingdom of Cayor, "the prime minister was the one who could initiate the procedure which would lead to the deposing of the king, if the latter disagreed with him, that is, with the people; if, in fact, he ceased to rule wisely" (Diop, 1987; p.76).

Monarchical divinity is often confused with either absolutism and tyranny or given too much importance in politics. Packard (1981) offered this caution:

> While indigenous ideas about the nature of sovereignty come into play on specific occasions —the most important of which involve periods of ecological crisis — at other times, cosmology appears to have little significance for politics, and both motivations and actions

are ascribed either implicitly or explicitly to universal categories of thought and behavior. Political actors thus appear to take on and divest themselves of cosmological notions as the situation dictates, operating at one moment by universal rules of political behavior, and at others in a culturally defined mode (p.8).

Furthermore, most of the political organizations which had a king surrounded him with councils and with courts. "Almost all have institutionalized means to keep him from abusing his power" (Bohannan, 1964; p.191). Vaughan (1986) also noted:

It may be suspected that divine kings and such panoply of government might tend to authoritarianism, but several institutions militate against this in African states. In some kingdoms, such as the Ashanti, village and regional divisions were sufficiently organized so as to decentralize the secular authority of the king. In many instances, the dependence upon the *rule of law* and a respect for law seems to have inhibited ambitious rulers. Nor should it be forgotten that regicide itself was an ultimate check upon the excesses of a king (p.178). (Italics mine).

Under the African scheme of things, despotism could not be reconciled with the traditional role of the king. Philosophically, the one who was supposed to provide a vital link to the universe for his people could not at the same time sever this link by repressive measures or distance himself from his people. Inevitably, a big gap between apparent despotism and reality developed.

Though Africans delighted in telling foreigners how "powerful" their kings were to ward off foreign aggressive intentions, the kings were severely restrained in the exercise of those powers against their people. The Asante king appeared absolute. "Yet, he had to procure the consent of the chiefs, and the chiefs the consent of the elders, in order to bring about group action" (Carlston, 1968:127). Even in the rigidly-controlled Kingdom of Dahomey, Boahen and Webster (1970) found that,

Although the king's word was the law of the land yet he was not above the law. Dahomeans like to recount how king Glele was fined for breaking the law. When gangs of men were working co-operatively either on state roads or building a house for one of their members, it was a law that a passer-by must approach the leader and make an excuse as to why he could not break his journey to assist in the work. Permission was almost inevitably given, the law being largely designed to reinforce courtesy. King Glele's procession passed one such group without asking to be excused. He was stopped by the headman and fined many cases of rum and pieces of cloth for breaking the law. . .The fact that the kings of Dahomey (now Benin) were prepared to obey the laws they themselves created was the difference between arbitrary despotism and despotism which realized that its power and position rested ultimately, no matter how indirectly, upon the will of the people (p.108).

Note once again the *rule of law* even in the Kingdom of Dahomey. The Zulu King also had to obey the law of the land. At the South African Government Commission on Native Law and Custom in 1881, Zulu King, Cetshwayo, was asked why he did not use his vast authority to prevent girls from being given in marriage sometimes without their consent. The Zulu King replied thus, through an interpreter:

> If the father tells a girl to do something that was not the custom of the country, then the people would support her, but in this case it is the custom of the country.

> The King says he cannot alter a law like that, because it has been the custom, in Zululand ever since the nation was created. Every king has agreed to the law and so must he. The nation would say that anyone who tries to change that law was a bad king.

> Yes, the king would change it if the chief of the land were willing to make a change in that way.

> If there is a certain law which the king wishes to be known in the country, he declares it at the feast of the first fruits.

> The king has a discussion with the chiefs about it, and they give out the law, but he cannot make a law without their consent. He consults the chiefs and gives his reasons, and if they conclude to agree to it, it is the law, but he cannot make a law against the wishes of his chiefs (Olivier, 1969; p.145).

The *rule of law* thus prevailed in the Zulu Kingdom. The Zulu king could not arbitrarily change the law without full council consent. In most African kingdoms, the king seldom exercised his authority except in cases of judicial appeal. His authority was usually delegated through the bureaucracy to the heads of smaller territorial units, the provinces or principalities. In central Africa, delegation of authority usually amounted to delegation of almost all authority save religious - and on a few occasions, even religious authority was delegated (Bohannan, 1964; p.192).

In African kingdoms, chiefs held whatever authority was delegated to them by the kings to rule their chiefdoms. One of the functions expected of chiefs in the kingdoms was raising tribute for the king. All the kingdoms investigated by Vansina (1987) utilized some sort of "taxation" in the form of tribute and labor. Tribute was collected at one level of the system and transmitted up to the next higher level so that ultimately a part of it from everywhere reached the top.

The lines of communications between chiefs and kings varied. The most common, however, was for the chiefs to form councils, or to send representatives as intermediaries on the councils of the king. Membership of the councils were the primary deterrent to tyranny of kings and varied from one kingdom to another (Bohannan, 1964; Vansina, 1987).

There was another subtle check. In many African kingdoms, an individual may be designated as an immediate kin of the king, though the person may not necessarily be related to the king. Thus, the king has a "mother" as in the Ashanti and Swazi kingdoms; a "sister" as among the Lozi; or a "father" as among the Margi. This kin may rule jointly with the king but in most kingdoms this person is expected to treat the king in a familial rather than a political manner.

He or she is expected to speak to the king and advise as a mother or a father would to an irascible child. Thus, he or she is in a unique position to scold, criticize the king, even publicly on occasion. Further, "this individual may usually give sanctuary to anyone believed to be unjustly abused by the king" (Vaughan, 1986; p.179). But this individual may be removed if he or she fails to perform expected duties and sides with the king. As we saw earlier, the Ashanti removed several Queen-Mothers in the nineteenth century for neglect of duty. The removal of this individual generally sent a clear message to the king of public displeasure of his reign. In most cases, it was enough to cause the king to mend his ways. Vaughan (1986) noted this uniquely African institution "which serves as a restraining force upon many African rulers for both its subtlety and for the emphasis it places upon the importance of the family in African society" (p.178).

C. THE SELECTION AND REMOVAL OF AFRICAN KINGS

Like chieftaincy, kingship was also restricted to certain lineages in most African societies. Such lineages were often those that founded the settlement — the original settlers of the land, or the ancestors and their descendants. As we saw earlier, certain duties and standards of performance were expected of African kings and failure to perform them could result in deposition. A king could be removed if he failed to bring prosperity to his people. He could also be overthrown for failure to govern according to the will of the people or for pursuance of policies inimical to the interests of the state after all counsel had been ignored. This was precisely the fate of King Gikuyu of the Gikuyu of Kenya:

King Gikuyu was the grandchild of the elder daughter of the founder of the tribe. He ruled many moons and his method of governing was tyrannical. People were prevented from cultivating the land, as he commanded that all able-bodied men should join his army and be ready to move with their families at any time and to wherever he chose. Thus the population lived a sort of nomadic life and suffered many hardships from lack of food. At last, they grew tired of wandering from place to place and finally decided to settle down. They approached the King and implored him to let them cultivate the land and establish permanent homes, but owing to his autocratic power he refused to hear or consider their plea. The people were very indignant with him for turning a deaf ear to their appeal, and in desperation they revolted against him. The generation which carried out the revolt was called *iregi*. . .After King Gikuyu was dethroned, the government of the country was at once changed from a despotism to a democracy which was in keeping with the wishes of the majority of the people. This revolution is known as *itwika*, derived from the word *twika*, which means 'to break away from' and signified breaking away from autocracy to democracy. This achievement was celebrated all over the country; feasting, dancing and singing went on with intervals for a period of six moons which preceded the new era of government by the people and for the people (Kenyatta, 1938; p.180).

What follows is a discussion of the process of selection and removal of various African kings.

The King Of Cayor (Former Province Of Ghana)

Between the third and the tenth centuries, most of tropical Africa was part of the empire of Ghana. Cayor was a former province which broke away and established itself as an autonomous kingdom, south of the estuary of the River Senegal, with Damel as its king. Around the 15th century it was overrun and absorbed into the Wolof empire. As a tributary state, however, Cayor continued to govern itself and choose its king by traditional methods which were similar to those used in the neighboring states of Baol, Sine and even Jolof. By the 16th century, Cayor had been emancipated from Jolof imperial rule to become an autonomous kingdom.

The king of Cayor was chosen and invested by a government council which was composed of the following, according to Diop (1987:46):

Lamane Diamatil
Botal ub Ndiob ~   Representatives of free men, men of castes or without
Badie Gateigne   castes

Eliman of MBalle
Serigne of the ~   Representatives of the Muslim clergy
Village of Kab

Diawerigne MBul Gallo
Diaraf Bunt Ker ~   Representatives of the *Tieddos* and prisoners of the
                    Crown

This council was convened and presided over by the *Diawerigne MBul Diambur*, the hereditary representative of free men. The *Tieddos* was comprised of all the individuals attached to the king, whether as soldiers or courtiers. This constitution was similar to that of neighboring Saloum and Wolof, all of which together with Ghana were part of the Wolof empire.

There is not much historical account of actual depositions of Cayorian kings. That this was possible however can be gleaned from the fact that in 1481 Burba Birain, the supreme ruler of the Wolof empire, was deposed. It can safely be assumed that the deposition of the king of Cayor followed the same procedures in Wolof or Saloum described below.

The Bur (Serer King)

The Saloum Kingdom in Senegal was inhabited by the Serer peoples. The *Bur* was their highest political and religious personality. He was the embodiment of state power, and the personification of the ancestors. Klein (1968) noted:

> The *Bur* was chosen by the second-ranking chief, the *Grand Jaraf*, after consultations with the major titleholders, who formed an inner council. According to Diagne, the consent of *Farka*, a chief who was chosen from among the *tyeddo* (warriors) to speak for the servile classes, was also necessary. The man selected as *Bur* was then confirmed by an assembly of *tyeddo* and *jambur* (the commoners), which probably included village chiefs and family heads for all parts of the kingdom. . .
>
> Just as the *Grand Jaraf* alone theoretically chose the *Bur*, so too he alone could order the distinctive drumbeat that meant that the *Bur* had been deposed. In practice, he could give this order only when he had the support of a large part of the community. . .The *Grand Jaraf* was chosen by the *Bur* from among the leading *jambur* chiefs, but the choice had to be approved by an assembly of *jambur*. The *Grand Jaraf* was the leader of the *jambur*, as well as their judge and their spokesman in royal councils. His authority could be revoked only by the *jambur* assembly,

and thus he was an independent voice in royal council, a check on royal power (p.14).

Stride and Ifeka (1971) expatiated on this intricate system of checks and balances:

> The actual nomination of a new *Bur* was the function of a single king-maker known as *Diaraff Bundao* (*Grand Jaraf*). In strict theory, he had the sole right to select or depose a *Bur* but in practice always acted on the advice of a council of leading noblemen. The *Diaraff Bundao* himself could never have a claim to the throne for he was of non-royal blood, being the head of the *Diambur* (*jambur*) caste. His own appointment was made by the reigning *Bur*, whose choice was influenced by the wishes of a council of *Diambur* chiefs. During the interval between death of one *Bur* and the installation of another, the *Diaraff Bundao* actually governed the kingdom (p.28).

The Ga King

With regards to the Ga stool, it is a fact that "no one, however normal or probable his election would be, has any inherent *right* to succeed" (Field, 1940:51). The appointment of the Ga *mantse* ("king") involved two steps. The first was the selection of a nominee by the members of the stool House (known as *dzase*), akin to a "royal lineage." Though some Ga towns selected the nominee on a rotational basis among the constituent clans, the town of Accra restricted the choice to the Abola clan. The second step was the election proper of the nominee by the representatives of the people called *manbii*. Field (1940) described the procedure thus:

> The *manbii* first send to the *dzase* asking for a candidate. The *dzase* meet under the presidency of the *dzasetse* and elect a nominee. The *manbii* meet again and consider the nomination. If they reject the candidate, they demand another. They go on demanding and rejecting till they get an offer they can accept. Differences of opinion in any of these meetings are put to the vote. The elected candidate is privately enstooled by a small group of officials and is afterwards publicly exhibited to the town in his new capacity of *mantse* (p.51).

Technically speaking, the Ga *mantse* could not be destooled.

> A *mantse* is made a *mantse* by a magical process, and that process cannot be undone. That is to say, he cannot be 'destooled' and replaced by another *mantse*. He can be removed only by killing. This used to be the treatment if he were sufficiently bad, but if insufficiently, he was simply

deserted, ignored or 'sent to Coventry.' Tribal business was carried on without him and, moreover carried on satisfactorily, for he was not essential to it (Field, 1940; p.76).

Destoolment was never part of the Ga political culture until European arrival and patronage:

> From those early days Europeans had it in their heads that an African tribe must necessarily be under a single ruler, monarch, or 'chief', and that this ruler must be the most suitable agent to go between themselves and the tribe, whether they are giving orders to the tribe, trading, or otherwise negotiating (Field, 1940:75).

Thus in dealing with the Ga *mantse*, the Europeans conferred upon him political authority and privileges which he did not have. In the indigenous system, the *mantse* was only useful in times of warfare. He had no political authority or executive function and was never an integral part of the native government. However, European patronage and obsequiousness emboldened a few Ga *mantses* to act autocratically. The incensed Ga people dissuaded the Europeans from dealing with such despots but to no avail. In response, the Ga people destooled many of these "European" *mantses*. One was *Mantse* Obli Taki who was destooled in 1918 by his Labadi people "for a number of offences, chief of which was the selling of Ga land in the name of the Ga people without consulting the owners of that land, and the pledging of the stool itself as security on a loan" (Field, 1940:183).

The Asante King

Called the *Ohene*, the Asante king is the chief magistrate, the chief military leader, and first executive officer of the state. He is the first in councils of the state and his influence is measured only by the strength of his character. He represents the state in all its dealings with the outside world; and, "so long as he keeps within constitutional bounds, he is supreme in his own State" (Casely Hayford, 1911). The king is also the president of the legislative board but he seldom, if ever, initiates any legislative act. Casely Hayford (1911) continued:

> It is the province of the people through their representatives, the Councillors, to introduce legislation, and say what law shall direct their conduct. Hence, when a law is to be promulgated, which is done by the 'beating of the gong-gong' the formula, in the mouth of the Linguist is, 'The King and his Councillors and Elders say I must inform you ——'; then follows the particular command and the

words, '*par hi*,' an emphatic exclamatory phrase, and a loud rattle of the gong, by way of general proclamation.

The Asante king is also the chief military commander of his forces and in time of war directs the forces. He is also the chief magistrate and presides over the hearing of all important cases and serves as the final judge of appeal. But he can be destooled by established procedures in cases of serious misconduct. In fact, the Akan peoples of Ghana, of which the Asante are part of, have a very elaborate system of king selection, succession and removal. This process, it may be noted, is identical to that used in selecting divisional chiefs discussed extensively in the previous chapter.

For the Asante, the *Ohene*, was selected from the Akwuamus, considered to have "the best blood in the land." This made the Akwuamus the aristocrats of Kumasi, the capital of the Asante Kingdom, and conferred upon this lineage the right to be consulted in all internal matters (Casely Hayford, 1911:36).

Upon the death of a king, the council of elders would meet and request a successor from the Akwuamus, the royal family. The royal family would then nominate a successor, who might be the cousin, or nephew, of the deceased king. With matrilineal descent, such a cousin would be the son of the sister of the deceased king's mother or the nephew would be the son of the sister of the late king. The choice of the nominee "was probably determined by the personal valor, intelligence, and capability of the individual to lead the forces of the community in time of war" (Casely Hayford, 1911).

The person nominated would be presented to the Council of Elders, and upon being approved, placed by the councillors "on the stool" (enthroned). The process, however, might not always be smooth. During the reign of the old king, there might be several heirs apparent, each favored by different groups: the royal family, the king himself and the councillors. But the councillors retained the final right of veto.[9] Upon being "enstooled", a nephew would be allowed to govern so long as he was a man of character and capacity and could lead the people. But as Casely Hayford informed:

> The community would still continue to possess the power of veto in case a given member of the royal family was found incapable of performing the kingly functions. They would say, in effect, to the incompetent aspirant, 'We appointed your ancestor to the kingly office as a reward for uncommon abilities, and we are prepared to

---

[9] Casely Hayford (1911) cited a 1900 court case, Enima v. Pai, in which the plaintiff (Enima) sought to be declared the rightful successor to the Kwimbontu's stool in the Wassaw district to which the Werempims or the Councillors had elected Pai and upon which they had actually placed him. The plaintiff and defendant were cousins and as such both were qualified. The court upheld the Councillors' choice and recognized Pai as the legal king.

honor his family by seeking election to the kingly office from and by it; but we must object to being ruled by any unfit person. We will, through the (royal) family council, decide which member of the family shall govern us, if we are dissatisfied with the family's own selection.'

Casely Hayford (1911) continued that, "no Asante king was born a king." There were a number of circumstances which might prevent the nearest to the "stool" from ever occupying it. "A junior heir may be selected to sit upon the stool if a senior heir is a profligate, or otherwise incapable of maintaining the kingly dignity. Nor does a king acquire an indefeasible title to the stool when once he has sat upon it. It is the right of those who placed him thereon to put him off the stool for any just cause" (Casely Hayford, 1911).

The Asante king is the one in whom the various lineages that comprised the society found unity. He is the symbol of their identity and continuity as a society and the embodiment of their ancestral values. His golden stool, the symbol of his power, is also the "soul of the nation", the sacred emblem of the tribe's permanence and continuity. Since the Asante place supremacy on the spiritual world, the king is the link, the intermediary between the living, the dead, and those yet to be born.

When the Asante king was installed, he was raised and lowered three times over the blackened stool of his ancestors. By this ritual, his person and the office were sanctified. "Persistent failure to meet his responsibilities and obligations resulted in his destoolment. In other words, the stool was a symbol of office and role, analogous to the crown in Western cultures" (Carlston, 1968:128).

The *Asantehene* could also be destooled for any of the following reasons: drunkeness; abusing his people; disclosing the origin of his subjects, especially slaves; not listening to advice; cowardice, theft, adultery, cruelty, extravagance, disobedience to the elders and physical or mental impairment such as blindness, impotence and disfigurement due to leprosy.[10]

Should such a cause arise, certain laid-down procedures were followed:

Firstly: The authority which, in accordance with the Customary Law, called the King to the stool, is the only authority which can call for his destoolment.

---

[10] In modern parlance, grievous acts detrimental to the state that would provide sufficient ground for deposition would include corruption, embezzlement of state funds, looting state treasuries for deposit in Swiss banks, building basilicas, imposing Marxism or an alien ideology on the people, refusing to sit under "the tree" to negotiate peace, incompetent leadership, economic mismanagement, oppression and slaughter of citizens of the state, as well as arbitrary arrests and detention of citizens without due process of customary law. The elites of modern Africa have much to learn from the "backward" peasants.

Secondly: To render the destoolment of a king valid, he must have
             been properly destooled; and before he can be properly
             destooled, he must have had a full opportunity of
             showing cause why he should not be destooled.

Thirdly: It is not for every petty act of misconduct that a king's
             destoolment can be called for. He must have been
             convicted of acts seriously detrimental to the State, or
             otherwise gravely unbecoming the kingly dignity.

Fourthly: The proper tribunal, in accordance with the Customary
             Law, must try the king, and the law is jealous of the
             procedure on such occasions.

If found at fault, the ruler was immediately "destooled" (deposed). A
destooled ruler was normally asked to leave the town to a new village
prepared for him. He was allowed to take a wife and a boy along and
remained banished until the elders decided his return would not disturb the
peace. The people of Asante destooled three kings in 1799, 1874 and 1883.

They destooled Osei Kwame in 1799 for, among other reasons,
absenting himself from Kumasi and failing to perform his religious
duties during the *Adae* festivals. They destooled Karikari in 1874 for
extravagance, among other failings. They destooled Mensa Bonsu in
1883 for excessively taxing his people (Arhin, 1985; p.85).

The *Oni* Or *Oba* (Yoruba King)

Yoruba kings were distinguished by the right to wear beaded crowns, the
symbols of their authority. In many respects, they were divine. The *Oni* was
chosen from the royal patrilineal clan; the largest clan in Ife.

The position is hereditary but does not pass from father to son.
Males of four lineages or branches of the royal clan are eligible to
become king in rotation, but lineages are skipped if they have no
suitable candidates, and the same lineage may even provide two *Oni*
in succession. Each of the eligible compounds may campaign for its own
candidate by spending money in entertaining the town and palace chiefs
who select the king, and by deferring to all who may influence their
final choice. . .

Wealth is important in these campaigns but it is not an essential
qualification for a king or a chief; nor is a candidate selected simply
on the basis of how much he and his family spend, although this is a

measure of his generosity and of how well he is liked by those who
know him best. The main objective is to select the best candidate;
and the qualities which are most important are good character,
unselfishness, and *willingness to listen to advice.* . .Seniority is not a
factor, although it may have been in earlier times. The candidate must
be at least about thirty years of age, he should be married, and his father
must be dead; no chief should have a father to whom he must bow
(Bascom, 1984; p.32).

This was also true of other Yoruba kingdoms but with some slight
variations:

There is a tradition that the kingship at Oyo originally descended
by primogeniture in the male line, and this may have been the case
in other kingdoms of the Yoruba. But at some period, apparently in
the 17th century, the patrilineal hereditary system was modified at
Oyo so that the choice of *Alafin* (the supreme ruler of all Yoruba
states) was exercised by the *Oyo Mesi* among a number of candidates
from the royal house. This system was followed in most of the
kingdoms and towns, with the notable exception of Egba Alake and
Oke Ona, where all freemen were theoretically qualified to be chosen
as *oba* by divination. The royal family in most cases divided into two or
more branches occupying different compounds in the town (and the
usual practice in the present day is for the branches to take turns in
presenting candidates to the leading chiefs as king-makers on each
vacancy). With one or two exceptions (for example, the reputedly
Borgu dynasties of Saki and Kisi), the royal lines claim descent from the
founders of the town who were of the same Yoruba stock as their
followers. There is thus no trace of a ruling caste in these kingships,
such as obtains in the Hausa and Nupe states since the establishment of
Fulani states in the 19th century. . .

Many considerations determined the king-makers' choice of an *oba*,
but a guiding principle was to select a ruler who would respect and
conform to the constitutional conventions of the kingdom. This would
usually be a man neither youthful nor elderly, and in certain circumstances the king-makers deliberately avoided a candidate whose presence or personality seemed too commanding; at Ado Ekiti in 1910, for
example, a prince was rejected because he was so tall he would have
looked down on his subjects. The rules governing the succession varied
from kingdom to kingdom. At Oyo there was a custom, broken on the
death of Atiba in 1859, that the *Alafin*'s eldest son, the *Aremo*, who was
associated with his father in the government, should take his life on his
father's death. In Ijebu and Owo it was held that no prince was eligible

for the throne unless he had been born to a reigning *oba*. In early times it was not necessarily a male who was chosen as ruler, and the traditions of Oyo, Sabe, Ondo, and Ilesa record the reigns of female *oba* (p.113).

Generally, the Yoruba *Alafin*, *oni* or *oba* ruled for life but each could be deposed for misrule. There were two procedures. The leader of the *Oyo Mesi*, the *Bashorun* had the duty to choose and depose the supreme ruler (the *Alafin*) with the full concurrence of the *Oyo Mesi* and the *Ogboni*, a cult society. The process started with the despatch of symbolic parrots' eggs to the *Alafin*. Upon receipt, he was expected to commit suicide as he had been rejected by his people and the ancestors. The first recorded rejection and suicide was that of *Alafin* Ayibi (Smith, 1969; p.45). Subordinate rulers, *oba*, could be removed by similar procedures. The chiefs would start the process by boycotting the *oba*'s palace. If he did not change his policies, a deposition would be contrived or even his suicide required.

In modern times, however, a suicide is not demanded:

> Okunade Sijuade, the *Ooni* of Ife, angered by the role played by *Oba* Lamidi Adeyemi, the *Alaafin* of Oyo over the conferment of the Akinrogun title on Chief Tom Ikimi, chairman of the National Republican Convention, has threatened to withdraw Adeyemi's crown and render him an ordinary citizen.

> Sijuade who was speaking at the conferment of Akinrogun on Ikimi claimed that as the representative of Oduduwa (the Yoruba's progenitor) he could remove the *Alaafin* because the *Alaafin*'s crown, which qualifies him to be a traditional ruler, was given to him by the *Ooni*. 'I can withdraw his crown by the special powers conferred on me,' the *Ooni* said.

> *Oba* Adeyemi had earlier petitioned the Oyo State government over the Akinrogun Chieftaincy saying that the *Ooni* had no right to confer such a title. The Oyo State government acting on that petition first stopped the conferment but later allowed it to go ahead on the condition that it was made a local Ife affair and not a Yoruba tribal title.

> But the *Ooni* said he could not be queried. 'No individual or council can query me and my power to create a traditional rulership. . .no Yoruba council or individual can dispute this.'

> It was very unfortunate he said that the Oyo State government panicked over an issue 'which it should have taken all necessary steps to investigate' and if possible gone into the archives to find about the powers of the *Ooni*.

He appealed to the Oyo State government to always be sure of its facts before making pronouncements (*West Africa*, March 18-24, 1991; p.408).

The second procedure was a "People's Revolution," if the council of chiefs failed to act to remove an incompetent *oba*. The Yoruba king could be deposed from his office as a result of arbitrary or tyrannical action by a procedure known as *kirikiri*. "A mob would parade through the town or country-side loudly abusing him and ending at his residence, which was pelted with dirt and stones. If he did not leave the country or commit suicide within three months, then a select band of men seized and killed him" (Carlston, 1968:182).

This Yoruba procedure (*kirikiri*), as well as the Gikuyu *itwika*, were genuinely indigenous African revolutions. Note that they were not copied from abroad. Further, they met the salient definition of a "revolution." A true revolution occurs when the oppressed rise up and overthrow their oppressors. But in modern Africa, it is rather the oppressors who chant "revolution." When France celebrated the bicentennial of its 1789 Revolution, many African tyrants showed up in Paris for the celebrations which prompted this wry editorial from the *West Africa* magazine (July 24-30, 1989):

> Some of the African guests, such as President Mobutu of Zaire, whose human rights record is grim, looked out of place at such a ceremony, although Zaire is one of the African countries which, ironically, has the word 'Revolution' in the name of its ruling party. . .

> Most of the African leaders present barely related to the anniversary in any case, and would have been on the *wrong* side in 1789. For the challenges it still embodies are far from being met in Africa, and the spectres of chaos and bloodshed that haunted it, still lurk in the background (p. 1199).

The Kongo King

In the Kingdom of the Kongo, every male descendant in every line of descent from Wene, the ancestor, could make a claim of succession to the throne. By 1700, these descendants were so numerous that they formed a social class, *infantes*. The selection of the king rested with an electoral council of elders who chose the most popular candidate from one of the two dynastic families (Harris, 1987). This was supported by Vansina (1987), who studied the kingdom extensively, corroborated:

There was, then, no royal clan and there was room for genuine
election. There was an electoral college of nine or twelve members
in which the *mani Kabunga* held a veto and of whom the *mani Soyo* and
the *mani Mbata* were the only other members we know by title.
Candidates to the throne usually began to prepare for their candidacy by
seeking support years in advance, and when a king died there were most
often two factions at the court backing the two important challengers.
The electoral council would then usually nominate the prince who
seemed to have the strongest backing (p.42).

Diop (1987), however, cautioned that the use of the term "electoral
college" may be improper. For the council or "college" were compelled to
appoint, after thorough examination of each candidate, not according to
their preferences but in accordance with tradition, the one who had the
requisite qualities (p.61).

The Luba King In the Luba society of central Africa, kingship was
forged on the concept of *bulopwe*. This was a sacred quality that was
vested in the blood and transmissible only through males. It endowed
the carriers with supernatural powers and therefore the right and the
means to rule. Without *bulopwe*, nobody could have ruling authority
and all *bulopwe* stemmed from the Kongolo or the Kalala Ilunga
lineages.

The Luba king was believed to have supernatural powers and was thought
of as a *vidye* (a nature spirit). Compared to other African kingships, the
special feature of the Luba kingship was the connection between ancestor
cult and divinity through the bloodline. In theory, the Luba king exercised
absolute authority since there was apparently no superior council to
counterbalance his power. But, Vansina (1987) argued:

> His power was tempered by the fact that he had half-brothers who
> might rise against him, supported by their mother's patrilineage,
> and that they would be backed by the court and the people if he
> were a tyrant (p.74).

The Zibondo Of Basoga

The king of the Basoga kingdom of Uganda was called the *zibondo*. He
could choose his own heir but "his testament had to be reviewed - and
might well be altered - by the council of his lineage. There was a bias in
favor of the senior son, but this was not a fixed rule. In consequence, there

was room for conflicting claims and ambitions among potential heirs (Fallers, 1965:99).

Due to the possibility of rivalry among siblings or potential heirs - which could tear apart a kingdom - many African societies adopted the practice of not announcing the death of a king until a successor was chosen and installed. For example, in 1964 when the ruler of the Shambaa Kingdom (in northeastern Tanzania) died,

> The leaders of the subject lineages of Vugha (the ancestor) called a meeting to discuss succession. It was a quiet meeting; its existence was mentioned only where responsible elders gathered in private, for the children were not to know the king was dead until a new king had been installed. . .Two names were seriously discussed. The first was Kinyashi and the second was Limo. The elders of Vugha finally agreed to make Limo king (Feierman, 1974:94).

The Kabaka Of Buganda

The Kingdom of Buganda, which is part of Uganda, lies along the northern and western shores of Lake Victoria near the headwaters of the White Nile and stretches about 200 miles along the lake shore. Buganda was never conquered by the British, but came under British protection through treaties and agreements. As a result, its indigenous political system was almost wholly preserved. However, it was reformed to serve new purposes. The ruler of the kingdom was the Kabaka. As an exception to the general African belief in divinity, the kabaka was not regarded as a god, nor was he closely associated with the gods. He was neither a divine king nor a priest, but his authority was derived partly from the conquest of Kintu, the first king of the dynasty, from whom he was descended, and partly from the power he held in the nation.

> The kabaka was elected from among the Princes of the Drum, that is, men whose father had been a kabaka. The choice was made by the Katikkiro (prime minister) who survived from the previous reign, in consultation with other senior chiefs. There was no such rule as primogeniture to indicate one prince as heir apparent; and although a king might indicate a preference for one prince to be his heir, this choice was not binding. The electors chose a prince partly on the basis of his personal character, and partly in relation to the strength of support for different candidates among the chiefs. Once a prince had been chosen and proclaimed and had passed through the accession ceremonies, he was kabaka until his death; there was no constitutional means for deposing him (Gibbs, 1965; p.90).

The *kabaka* has often been described in the literature as a brutal tyrant:

> The supremacy of the king's will in peace and war was maintained
> by a continual display of his absolute power over the lives, bodies
> and fortunes of his subjects. The palace was the scene of constant
> killings and mutilations of courtiers, wives, concubines, and servants
> of the king who had incurred his disfavor. Men and women were
> casually selected for sacrifice in ritual carried out to safeguard the
> king's health and to prosper the kingdom. Men were killed
> arbitrarily merely to show the king's power. Cowards in war were
> burned (Carlston, 1968:245).

But Gibbs (1965) argued that: "If the *kabaka* angered too many important
people at one time, he was liable to be overthrown by rebellion, as many
kings were: there were always ambitious princes ready to seize the throne,
and dissatisfied chiefs to support them (p.91).

To sum up, what emerges from this discussion is that most African
kingdoms had definite rules of succession or selection of their kings. No one
wielding a bazooka just emerged to impose himself as "king" on the people.
Although kingship was hereditary, rules of descent did not necessarily place
rigid constraints on the selection of rulers. Gluckman (1959) offered this
assessment:

> Rarely in Africa do we find rules which indicate clearly and
> definitely a single heir. . .Or if the rules themselves were clear,
> they operated uncertainly in practice. The result was that almost
> every succession could raise rival claimants (p.46).

Competition took place during succession disputes, which were contested
by branches of the royal clan, by the sons and nephews of former kings, or
by prominent regional chiefs or between segments of the royal lineage.
Contestants often "campaigned" for supporters to buttress their claims.
Cohen (1970) observed:

> The major internal opposition to the monarch lay within the other
> segment of the royal lineage, that is to say, among his competitors
> for the royal office. These men and their followers, using whatever
> support they could obtain among the titled nobility, presented a
> constant danger of usurpation and even assassination to the ruling
> monarch. Excessive tyranny, continual lack of military success, local
> uprisings, or even weakened physical condition through ill-health or
> old age stimulated such opposition (p.192).

Upon selection, the African king was expected to perform certain duties:
assure the prospertiy of the nation, foster peace and act as the mediator

between the cosmological forces. Failure to perform these duties resulted in deposition or regicide. Rule of law prevailed and even the king, in contrast to modern African heads of state, had to obey the law as laid down by the people. Of final note, the role and office of the African king were not that much different from those of the kings of medieval Europe or the emperor of modern-day Japan. The Japanese emperor, a hereditary position, performs analogous functions. He is deified and installed according to an ancient Shinto ritual called *Daijo-sai*, or Great Eating Festival, which is a closedly guarded secret.

In October 1988, when Emperor Hirohito was gravely ill, his son Akihito was readied to undergo the ritual. Following the death of the emperor the following year, preparations began in February 1990 with auguries on a turtle shell. The shell revealed the locations of two holy rice fields. Then, under conditions of strict ritual purity, came the sowing, cultivating and harvesting of the rice, and the construction of two thatched-roof shrines on the imperial palace grounds.

Before ascending to the throne in November 1990, Emperor Akihito, the 125th emperor in a dynasty that traces its roots to the 7th century, performed a solitary all night vigil of prayer to his divine ancestress, the goddess Amaterasu (the sun goddess) in each of the two thatched-roof structures. He prayed for peace and abundant harvests. Then wearing white silks and a plumed headdress, Akihito dished out food for his numerous "guests" — Japan's 8 million *kami*, or gods. Afterwards, he retreated behind a screen, where the spirit of the sun goddess invited him to enter her womb. When he emerged, according to Shinto belief, he was no longer an ordinary human but an *arahito gami*, or living god — the living embodiment of *Ninigi-no-mikoto*, the god of the ripened rice plant — and the newly deified emperor of Japan.

African scholars and leaders may note that Japan, an economic superpower, did not have to renounce its ancient Shinto beliefs to achieve that status.

CHAPTER 5

GOVERNMENT IN NATIVE AFRICAN EMPIRES

African societies that were independent or autonomous governed themselves with or without chiefs or kings. Others came under the hegemony of stronger political groups in the ancient empires that were once numerous in Africa. There were differences in imperial rule; generally in the degree of independence or autonomy allowed subjugated people as well as flexibility and liberty to preserve their cultures. At one end of the spectrum were the Asante and the Zande who adopted the "indirect rule" paradigm, allowing their vassal states extensive autonomy. At the other end were the Islamic empires such as the Mandinka, where conscious efforts were made to supplant existing cultures. Each type is now described in detail.

A. BY ASSIMILATION

The Mandinka (Islamic) Empire, 1870-98

This empire, at its zenith, occupied much of what is today Mali and the northern part of the Côte d'Ivoire. The basic Mandinka stock was the Diula, who were Muslims. They were also "long-distance traders and because of the foreign goods they sold and their skill as craftmen, weavers and blacksmiths, they moved freely throughout Mandinka country and beyond, trading among the Mossi, with French merchants on the Senegal and on the coast of Monrovia and Freetown" (Boahen and Webster, 1970:42).

The Mandinka Empire was notable for its hierarchical structure and decentralization. It was divided into 162 cantons, each of which consisted of twenty or more villages. The cantons were grouped together to form ten large provinces. The empire was governed by three parallel lines of authority: the traditional, the military and the religious, leading to the *almani* and his State Council.

The village chiefs were chosen by traditional methods of lineage, but their power was limited by the *almani*'s appointee. Canton chiefs were also chosen by traditional methods but held mostly honorary positions. The provinces were headed by relatives or close friends of the *almani* who was the supreme political, judicial and religious head of the empire as well as its military commander. He ruled through a State Council composed of the provincial heads of the three lines of authority. His rule was based upon assimilation of local cultures:

> The major aim of Samori's (the *almani*) administration was to destroy tribalism and promote national loyalty among the Mandinka. He did this by placing less emphasis on the village groups and more on the canton which brought villages together irrespective of their past relations. . .Images, ancestor houses and sacred groves were replaced with mosques and schools, the major agents in creating new values and goals of the younger generation (Boahen and Webster, 1970:46).

Eighteenth Century Zande Kingdom

This kingdom adopted a type of "mixed" imperial rule. It came into existence in the eighteenth century and occupied much of central African Republic. It flowed southward into Belgian Congo and northward into Sudan. The ruling stock was the Ambomu people under the leadership of the Vongara royal house which at its pinnacle had subjected over twenty different ethnic groups to its rule.

The grand Zande kingdom was a collection of small kingdoms of the Vongara dynasties all of whom descended from King Ngura, the first ruler of the Ambomu people. Each kingdom was divided into provinces: the central one was reserved for the king and the surrounding ones given to his sons or representatives to rule in his name. The central province had a royal court for the administration of the entire kingdom.

The prince or governor in his province replicated this pattern, constructing a court on the same model as the royal court. A collection of villages made up a district, to which a deputy was appointed. The deputy was responsible for maintaining good order, paying of tribute in kind and labor, supplying military service and settling disputes. Village governments were generally left unaltered. Evans-Pritchard (1963) emphasized:

> It was the policy of the Avongara not only to leave a submitted people in their territory but also to entrust authority over them to their own chiefs, demanding only acknowledgement of their paramountcy and tribute in labor and produce. The prominent commoners of Mbomu or assimilated stocks were encouraged to settle in the conquered territory, thus making for further dispersal of their clans and for intermingling of clans in general. . .In the

Sudan, there were no attempts on the part of the conquered peoples at rebellion, and their lot was by no means harsh.

What gave coherence and stability to the heterogenous amalgram of ethnic and cultural elements was the superior political organization of the Avongara - Ambomu which enabled them to impose their language and institutions on the subjugated peoples. Nevertheless, there was a curb on despotism.

If a prince tried to exact too much from his subjects, went after their wives, or was cruel there were sanctions they could apply. They would cease to visit him at court, isolating him, and if they found that they were no longer able to feel secure in person and property they moved their homes to another province and transferred their allegiance to its governor. An unpopular prince would also find that when it came to civil war or the death of his father, he would not receive the support of his subjects. . .(moreover) kings and princes felt obliged to behave according to the traditional pattern of their status, to be courteous to their subjects and not to go beyond what custom prescribed for them, to do nothing shameful. All in all we may say that, though the royal power might appear to have been unlimited, as in theory it was, in practice it was limited by the fact that a ruler had to exercise it through others, and these others could only exercise it if they retained the confidence of those over whom they represented royal authority (Evans-Pritchard, 1963).

The Zulu Kingdom

This kingdom, which was discussed extensively in an earlier chapter, is mentioned only briefly here as an example of an imperial rule which sought the near total absorption or incorporation of conquered tribes into Zulu culture. There was a strong centralized authority vested in the Zulu king who made key decisions of state and wielded enormous executive, judicial and political powers. However in practice, he was not an absolute ruler, as his decisions were subject to the approval of his state council, as discussed below in comparison with the *Alafin* of the Oyo empire.

B. BY INDIRECT RULE

The Ancient Empire Of Ghana

In 1068, a learned Arab scholar of Cordoba in southern Spain, by name of
Al-Bakri (El-Bekri), wrote a glowing account of an empire of great wealth
and power in the western Sudan. Although Al-Bakri never visited the
western Sudan himself, his book was based on information gathered from
Muslim merchants who traded across the Sahara from Morocco to purchase
gold, ivory and other items of trade.

Ghana was by 1068 the largest, wealthiest and most powerful state in
West Africa. Situated in the vast savanna area between the Senegal and the
Niger, its authority extended from the frontiers of Tekrur to the western
banks of the Niger, and from the Mandingo area in the south to beyond the
fringes of the desert in the north.

Its ruling people were the Soninke, the indigenous inhabitants of the area,
who had established their capital at Kumbi, the greatest trading center of the
western Sudan. Their ruler at the time that Al-Bakri wrote was Tunkamenin, who commanded great devotion from his subjects and respect from
foreign visitors. The Soninke followed a matrilineal system of succession and
Tunkamenin became king because he was the son of the former ruler's sister.
Note that the Asante to this day follow the same system of succession.

The imperial city of Kumbi was a twin city with two separate centers six
miles apart. Although linked, they were distinct in terms of character and
function. One formed the Muslim quarter where North African merchants
resided during their trading missions to Ghana. This was the main
commercial area and the influence of North Africa was pervasive in the
many stone-built houses, the twelve mosques for Muslim prayer and the
presence of many scholars learned in Arabic, Islamic theology and Islamic
law. The other town, known as Al-Ghaba, was the more important for it
was the administrative center of the Soninke empire.

The Ghana, the ruler, lived in Al-Ghaba. Despite the outward signs of
Islamic presence, the vast majority of the Soninke were not converted to
Islam at the time of Al-Bakri. In matters such as succession to the throne and
the appointment of various ministers and functionaries, the old African
tradition was strictly observed. In fact, Diop (1987) asserted that,

> The seven Cayorian dynasties never embraced Islam. It seems that
> one of the last Damels of Cayor (which was a province of the Ghana
> empire), Latdjor Diop, the very one who had offered such
> determined resistance to Faidherbe, the symbol of national struggle
> in Senegal, converted to Islam for diplomatic reasons, in order to
> find new allies in Saloum, such as the Tuculor marabout Ma Ba
> Diakhu, and in Trarza (p.47).

The Soninke people worshipped a variety of traditional gods and believed that the spirits of their ancestors guided the fortunes of people — the same beliefs held by many other native Africans. The ruler of Ghana himself acquired a semi-divine status once he had undergone the necessary religious rituals at his accession and was regarded as the direct link between living man and the supernatural. It may be recalled that the *Asantehene*, the Ga *mantse*, the *Alafin* of Oyo and other African kings were similarly consecrated.

As a semi-divine ruler of Ghana, he could appeal to a vital combination of both the religious and political loyalties of his people. He could manipulate the pronouncements of the various religious cults and act dictatorially towards the Soninke people. But as Stride and Ifeka (1971) reminded:

> (His semi-divine status) could practically exclude him from personal influence on imperial policy. Since his semi-divine nature required that he received all official communications second-hand through the medium of his Interpreter, who also transmitted his orders to his people, he could be kept largely ignorant of government business or policy could be changed by the officials applying it. Equally, if the cult priest gave political advice contrary to his personal wishes, he had little alternative but to follow it. Perhaps the glory of the Ghana system of government was that for such a long period it was able to provide stable and efficient administration irrespective of the character of the rulers (p.35).[1]

The Ghana empire included many areas whose people were not Soninke and therefore had religious loyalties to gods of whom the ruler of Ghana was not the earthly representative. This, in the interest of imperial unity, produced a dual system of provincial government.

> In the Soninke areas, the head of local government was a Soninke governor, possibly a close relative or trusted companion of the Ghana. In the non-Soninke areas, the local ruler was the *natural ruler* of his own people selected by their customary procedures and confirmed in office by the ruler of Ghana (Stride and Ifeka, 1971:35).

Both provincial governors of Soninke areas and tributary rulers of conquered peoples had the duties of loyalty to the ruler of Ghana, the provision of annual tribute and the contribution of bands of warriors to his imperial army when they were required for active service. In return, the ruler of Ghana provided protection against external enemies, facilities for

---

[1] Unfortunately, such a statement can not be made of modern Ghana, wracked by chaos, political instability and administrative ineptitude since it gained its independence in 1957.

sharing in the prosperous trade of the empire and the provision of justice to settle serious quarrels in the empire.

This system of government was not much different from the Asante or the Oyo or even the Benin empires. In fact, across the region constitutions were similar and showed remarkably little change. Diop (1987) concurred: "The Mossi and Cayorian constitutions reflect a political organization which must have been in effect since Ghana, and therefore probably dominated the African states for nearly two thousand years (p.47).

The ruler of Ghana was assisted by ministers, two of which were the *Vizier* (or *Waziri*), whose role was similar to that of a modern prime minister, and the Interpreter, who was the official means of direct communication between the ruler and his people or foreign visitors. This was essentially the same role played by the *okyeame* in the Asante kingdom. Similarly,

> The legal system of Ghana was not divorced from the executive. Each village head tried straightforward cases in his own village but people discontented with his judgment could appeal to the provincial governor or tributary state ruler. In the last resort, a man could appeal to the justice of the ruler of Ghana himself or his trained judges. Serious law-suits could be judged according to Soninke custom or, if the discontented party was a Muslim, according to Islamic law (Stride and Ifeka, 1971; p.36).

The Wolof Empire

The Wolof people today form about 35 percent of the population of modern Senegal and are loosely related to the Serer who comprise a further 16 percent of the country's people. About 80 percent of the Senegalese speak the Wolof language and it has been said that to be Senegalese is to be Wolof.

The Wolof state was formed by the voluntary association of a number of small independent village states. By oral tradition,

> The story starts in Walo where the inhabitants of a number of village-states, each ruled by a king with the Serer title of *Laman*, quarrelled violently over the distribution of wood collected along the shores of a lake. Before bloodshed could occur, a mysterious figure arose from the lake, shared the wood fairly among the villages and then disappeared. The amazed people feigned a second quarrel and, when the stranger reappeared, they detained him and offered him the government of their states. At first their captive refused to eat but, tempted with the prospect of marriage to a beautiful girl, he became more human in his ways and accepted their offer to kingship.

When these peculiar happenings were reported to the ruler of Sine, who was himself the greatest magician in the land, he exclaimed 'Ndyadyane Ndyaye', an expression of utter amazement. He then suggested that all rulers between the Senegal and Gambia should make voluntary submission to the remarkable stranger. This they did; and the first ruler of the Wolof state became known as Ndyadyane Ndyaye with the title of Burba Jolof (Stride and Ifeka, 1971:22).

At its zenith in the 16th century, the Wolof empire comprised the following provinces or states: Jolof, Walo, Kayor, Baol, Sine, Barra, Kular, Baddibu, Saloum, Lower Niani and Wuli. The first successful break-away movement by a Wolof state occurred in the mid-16th century when the Damel of Kayor revolted, overran Baol and repulsed the efforts of the Burba Jolof to restore him to obedience. This internal division enabled the Moors of Mauretania to inflict a severe blow on the Wolof states in the 17th century. Although the empire subsequently began its collapse, the Wolof, as a people, continued to this present day to be the dominant people of Senegal.

Each of the Wolof states was governed by its own ruler appointed from the descendants of the founder of the state. Each enjoyed practical autonomy in the administration of the affairs of his own kingdom but was expected to cooperate with the Burba Jolof in matters of common imperial interest such as defense, trade and the provision of imperial revenue. The authority of the Burba Jolof was bolstered by his traditional descent from Ndyadyane Ndyaye and the consequent divinity of his office.

An important feature of Wolof government was the strong position of the nobility. Neither the Burba Jolof nor the rulers of the other Wolof states held office by hereditary right alone. Although each had to be descended from the founder of his state in the male line of succession, and be born of a noble woman, actual appointment was made by elections conducted by the great nobility. Once appointed, the Burba Jolof, or the sub-ruler, went through elaborate religious rituals to inform him on the duties of his office and to elevate his status to that of a divine monarch. Thus sanctified, the Burba Jolof was expected to lead his people to victory and bring them prosperity. If he failed in these key functions, his exalted nature could not save him from deposition, although his personal army might (Stride and Ifeka, 1971:25).

Relations between Wolof sub-rulers and the Burba Jolof were based on voluntary cooperation, even the payment of tribute for the upkeep of the imperial dignity and power being voluntary.[2] Women played an important

---

[2] Oddly, Stride and Ifeka (1971) concluded that, "This voluntary element produced one of the most autocratic systems of government known in West Africa" (p.25). Unless other factors

role in Wolof government and society. The *linger* or Queen-Mother, was the head of all Wolof women and was influential in the state. To maintain her dignity she owned a number of dependent villages which cultivated her farms and paid her tribute. There were other female chiefs whose main task was to judge cases involving women. In the state of Walo, a woman could aspire to the office of *Bur* and rule the state.

The Mali Empire

The creators of the great ancient empire of Mali were non-Muslims: the Mandingo, a Negro people whose homeland was the Madinka plateau between the upper streams of the Senegal and Niger. Mansa Musa (Mansa Kankan Musa) is generally regarded as the great conqueror who founded the empire of Mali. He ruled from 1312 to 1337. During his reign, Timbuktu came under his suzerainty.

One of Mansa Musa's contributions to Mali history was the spread of its fame and prestige abroad. He did this largely by his famous pilgrimage to Mecca between 1324 and 1326.

> He was not the first Mansa of Mali to go on a pilgrimage, but no West African ruler ever went to Mecca on such a lavish scale. He took an escort of about 60,000 courtiers and servants, richly dressed and carrying 3 million pounds' worth of gold in modern value. Everywhere he went, he became legendary for his generosity and the extravagant spending of his retinue. Wherever he halted on a Friday, he paid for the construction of a mosque; and his party spent so much gold in Cairo that the value of the precious metal fell there. So much did Mansa Musa disburse in charity, gifts and purchases that he had to borrow gold to pay the cost of his homeward journey. Every opportunity of advertising the great extent and power of his empire was taken. As a result, the power and wealth of Mali became known not only throughout the Islamic world but also in Europe (Stride and Ifeka, 1971:52).

Ibn Battuta, a Berber of Tangier (Morocco), who visited Mali in 1532 provided a detailed account of life in the empire of Mali when the empire had already passed the peak of its greatness.

> Accustomed to seeing African peoples only in the role of slaves, he was amazed to find them governing an empire which rivalled

were at play, it was hard to imagine the continuation of *voluntary* payment of tribute in the face of despotism. Generally, tribute payments were withheld to check the excesses of autocratic rulers.

anything he had seen in North Africa and on his extensive travels in Asia. Ibn Battuta was immensely impressed by the ceremony and majesty that surrounded the Mansa, a true reflection of his exalted status and the wealth at his command. . .

Equally, he noted that Mali women enjoyed a freedom and importance not accorded to their sex in North Africa. Married women were not confined in *purdah* and were allowed to associate with other men besides their husbands. . .

Possibly, the thing that impressed Ibn Battuta most was the character of the people and the quality of their government. He records that the people were of exceptional honesty and that the government strictly punished anyone who engaged in dishonest practices. The corrupt governor of Walata, for example, was completely stripped of his possessions and privileges. Equally, law and order were so well maintained that a man laden with valuable goods could travel the length and breadth of the empire without fear of molestation. The whole atmosphere of the empire was one of peace and prosperity (Stride and Ifeka, 1971:57).

Boahen (1986) also noted:

Ibn Battuta was also struck by the order and racial tolerance that prevailed in Mali, and the care with which people observed prayers in the empire:

The Negroes are seldom unjust, and have a greater abhorrence of injustice than any other people. Their Sultan shows no mercy to any one guilty of the least act of it. There is complete security in their country. Neither traveller nor inhabitant in it has anything to fear from robbers or men of violence.

Surely, this could be said of only very few contemporary European or Middle Eastern states in the middle of the 14th century (p.31).

Nor could this be said of contemporary African countries in the 1990s, even Mali today. But the system of the government in the ancient empire is our immediate concern. The governmental system was essentially the same as that of Ghana. The Mansa was a semi-divine ruler whose political power was based on the spiritual headship of his people. Note that the semi-divine status of the Mansa, as in many other indigenous systems, could be invoked to seclude him from effective contact with political life. Most African kings played an insignificant role in politics.

Associated with the Mansa in the central government of Mali were a host of councillors and officials, some the inheritors of traditional titles from their forebears, others possibly the appointees of the Mansa. Some were non-Muslim and others Muslim. Although not much is known about the details of the various "ministries" of Mali, "obviously no successful Mansa could ignore the advice of his leading noblemen" (Stride and Ifeka, 1971:60).

Local government was more clearly defined. The Mandingo areas, being directly ruled by the Mansa, were divided into provinces, as the Wolof, Kanuri and Songhai. Each was governed by a *Dya-Mana-Tigi*, who was either a relative or trusted friend of the Mansa. Each province was subdivided into districts composed of a number of villages, the district head being entitled *Kafo-Tigi*. At the bottom of the scale, but in some ways the most important, was the village community under a *Dugu-Tigi* who was head of the village cults. The duties of the local government officials were to see that the annual tithe on produce and livestock was properly assessed and collected, ensure that local levies were forthcoming for the army in time of need, preserve law and order and administer petty justice. Serious cases would be referred to higher authority and the Mansa himself was the supreme court of appeal.

> The conquered peoples of tributary states were *indirectly ruled*. Their natural rulers, once appointed by their own people, were confirmed in office by the Mansa or his representative at investiture ceremonies where the tributary ruler did pay homage and took an oath of allegiance. The sub-ruler was responsible for the provision annually of a block tribute, the local assessment and collection of which was left to him. Tributary states also had the obligation of providing quotas for the imperial army and of accepting the Mansa's justice. In some cases, a tributary ruler had to accept at his court a Mandingo resident known as a *Fari-ba* whose function was to safeguard imperial interests, especially in commercial cities (Stride and Ifeka, 1971:60).

Nineteenth Century Asante Empire

This empire, which stretched over much of what is now called Ghana, consisted of two parts: Metropolitan Asante and Provincial Asante. Metropolitan Asante included the *amanto* or "true" Asante states clustered around Kumasi. The principal *amanto* were the five Oyoko states of Kumasi, Nsuta, Juaben, Bekwai and Kokofu; an important non-Oyoko *amanto* state was that of Mampong. Most of these states lay within about 30-40 miles radius from the capital, Kumasi, and its inhabitants considered themselves to be of the Asante tribe; that is, owing allegiance to "the golden stool." Provincial Asante consisted of vassal tribes.

Bowdich, an Englishman who spent four months in Kumasi in 1817, was the first observer to describe the relationship of the amanto to Kumasi. "Up to the reign of Osei Kwadwo, amanto chiefs were of equal rank; the Asantehene was primus inter pares with amanto chiefs" (Stride and Ifeka, 1971:267).

Each amanto state was largely self-governing with regard to internal affairs and was organized on similar lines to Kumasi. Each chief or omanhene had his council of hereditary advisers (elders); held his own Odwira ceremony after he had attended the Asantehene's Odwira at Kumasi to confirm his allegiance to the sovereign; maintained his own treasury and raised revenue; ran his own courts from which an appeal could be made to Kumasi; and possessed his own military organization which could be put at the disposal of the Asantehene when necessary.

The central government of Metropolitan Asante consisted of the Confederacy Council, made up of all the kings or Omanhene (properly designated as paramount chiefs) of the various states, presided over by the Asantehene (the king). It also had an executive council (an inner council) or cabinet, made up of a few of the principal wing-chiefs of the Kumasi division and some of the divisional chiefs.

In Kumasi, the Asantehene sat on the golden stool. In addition, there were 77 stools, representing 77 public functionaries, as for example, the Bantuma Chief, the Ateni Chief, the chief of the Royal Burial Grove or the chief of the Lamplighters. Many were the chiefs of the states within Metropolitan Asante, each of which had its own state council. The local government of Kumasi was in the hands of the Kwintsirs, a body of men who were the keepers of the golden stool. They also formed the Department of War.

Boahen and Webster (1970) pointed out:

> Though all these Councils were advisory rather than policy-making bodies, neither the Asantehene nor any Omanhene enjoyed uninhibited dictatorial powers. On the contrary, each of them would be destooled whenever he was considered to have abused his power. . .(In provincial Asante), all these states continued to govern themselves in exactly the same way as they were doing before their conquest and annexation. All that they were expected to do was to accept one of the wing-chiefs of Kumasi, who seldom visited the provinces, as a friend at Court, to pay an annual tribute and contribute to the army when called upon to do so (p.118).

This kind of rule was rather benign imperialism and conquered tribes could make a bid for independence if they so wished. Indeed, many did so throughout the eighteenth century but, "it was the superior military techniques and the bravery of their army that enabled the Asante to crush all these rebellions and to preserve the empire intact" (Boahen and Webster, 1970: 118).

More importantly, the internal structure of the Asante governmental organization was one of confederacy. "The first feature to note about the Asante system is that it was based on decentralization, which gave a large measure of local autonomy to the smaller units" (Busia, 1967:29). The reason, according to Kobina Sekyi was "the need to give the small states a new force which led to the creating of the Ashanti Confederacy and the Fanti Confederacy which were both conceived on the basis of federal systems of government" (cited in Langley, 1979:442). But Carlston (1968) argued that, since the authority of the *Asantehene* depended upon consultation with his chiefs, the procedure "was closer to a confederacy than to a federal union" (p.127).

Of greater significance was the fact that this system of government was apparently quite widespread on the former Gold Coast in the 19th century.

> In the Gold Coast proper we have, for example, the native states of Asante, Fanti, Ahanta, Insima, Ga, Wassa, and others, having more or less the same laws and customs, and speaking generally the same language, or dialects of the same language. Each federal State takes rank in the order of its importance in the native State union, and its composition and constitution is the same as that of the principal or premier State, which is usually the State of the paramount King (Casely Hayford, 1911).

The Oyo Empire (Yoruba)

The political structure of the Yoruba Kingdom in the 18th century when it was in its heyday, resembled that of the Asante and Zande Kingdoms. Its development also bore a close resemblance to that of the Zulu kingdom as well, suggesting strong similarities in the constitution of African kingdoms.

According to Yoruba traditions, the original founder of the kingdom, Oduduwa, settled in Ile-Ife at some time in the 14th century. Before his arrival, about 13 semi-autonomous settlements had organized themselves into a loose confederacy. Oduduwa settled among them and subsequently subjugated them, imposing his authority over them. The pre-existing groups organized themselves into a resistance group known as the Igbo and harassed Oduduwa and the new settlement until accommodation was reached around the middle of the 14th century.

Indeed, population expansion and pressures on the land induced migrations out of Ile-Ife. The migration intensified when Ile-Ife was struck by a prolonged drought that caused great famine and malnutrition for a protracted length of time. As a result,

A decision was taken that the best way to solve the problem was for some people to emigrate. A meeting was summoned at a place which still bears the name of *Ita Ijero* (place of deliberation) where a decision was taken as to what direction each party should take, and how future contacts were to be made with Ile-Ife and among the migrants, who were led by princes who belonged to the Oduduwa group (Olaniyan, 1985; p.37).

The Zulu state, it may be recalled, also encountered similar famine and environmental crisis. While the Zulu solution was to raid or conquer neighboring states, the Yoruba solution was emigration. Although it is not known how many kingdoms the Oduduwa princes established after the dispersal, Olaniyan (1985) surmised that "not fewer than 16 kingdoms are known to have been formed after the Ife model in various parts of Yorubaland" (p.37). Among them were Ado, Ara, Egba, Egbado, Ijero, Ikole, Otun, Oye and Oyo. Each of the dispersing groups built their kingdoms by displacing the heads of pre-existing communities and instituting a political system patterned after the Ile-Ife model with slight modifications.

The hub of the Yoruba empire was metropolitan Oyo, the home of the Yorubas who spoke the Oyo dialect and who were for practical purposes identifiable with the people of Old Oyo. This area was divided into 6 large provinces, three to the west of the River Ogun and three to the east. South of metropolitan Oyo, there were other Yoruba kingdoms such as Egba and Egbado, whose peoples spoke different Yoruba dialects.

The Asante kingdom, it may also be recalled, had a similar structure: metropolitan Asante, provincial Asante and the vassal states. Like the Asante, the sway of Oyo extended over non-Yoruba areas to the southwest: the Aja states of Dahomey and the Ewe of Togo. But, "imperial policy toward these non-Yoruba states was to allow them almost *total* local independence provided that they did not seek to escape from their tributary status" (Stride and Ifeka, 1971:296). This imperial policy of "indirect rule" was identical to the Asante's.

Although autonomous, the kingdoms were bonded closely together and continued to share ideas. Since all were sons or grandsons of Oduduwa, the succeeding rulers of the kingdoms (as well as their subjects) considered themselves kinsmen (*Ebi*). Periodic renewal of contacts with the ancestral spirit at Ile-Ife were maintained.

The sizes and complexities of these secondary kingdoms varied considerably, ranging from Oyo, covering over 10,000 square miles, to the miniature states of Ekiti, where, for example, the Ewi of *Ado* ruled over only some 17 small towns and villages. The larger kingdoms were subdivided into provinces. In addition, there were city-states, such as Badagry and Egbado towns. But all of these were "internally autonomous in a quasi-federalism" (Smith, 1969, p.110).

Among these states Ife enjoyed seniority and prestige. Its ruler, *the Oni*, commanded respect not so much as the ruler of one of the Yoruba group of kingdoms, since Ife is not remembered as having attained political or military importance, but as the king of a town which was regarded as the cradle of the race and whence the rulers and leading elements in the population of most of the other kingdoms traced their origins. . .Each of the Yoruba states was a sovereign entity, though related by tradition and sentiment to Ife and the other states of the Ife family (much like the ties between the 7 Hausa Bakwai of northern Nigeria) (Smith, 1969; p.108).

The Yoruba system of government was extremely complex and might appear confusing to outsiders. But the political systems of the various constituent kingdoms were in general similar. The basic political unit was the town (*ilu*), which was made up of lineages. A typical Yoruba kingdom was made up of many towns, villages, markets and farmsteads. One of these served as the capital town where the king (*oba*) lived. This leading *oba* was the wearer of a beaded crown, bestowed on his ancestor, according to legend, from Ife and his town was defined as *ilu alade* (crowned town) to distinguish it from other towns. Subordinate towns were classified as *ilu ereko* (literally, "towns on the fringe of the farmland"), which in turn ranged from *ilu oloja* (a market town with an *oba* not entitled to wear a beaded crown) to the *ileto* (village), *abule* (hamlet) and *ago* or *aba* (camp, settlement).

Each settlement was organized in a hierarchical form. The component lineages were headed by male adults called *Baale* (or *Bale* — father of the house), who oversaw the administration of the town. At the apex was the head-chief or *oba*, who claimed descendancy from Oduduwa.

The *oba* was the natural head of his own people and selected according to purely local custom. However, his appointment had to be confirmed by the central government at Oyo. Thus,

> Yoruba towns were ruled by their own *obas* chosen from the local ruling lineages and their policies had to be confirmed by local councils made up of heads of non-ruling families and local societies. Yet even with the full force of local opinion behind him, it would be a brave *oba* who dared offend the imperial government at Oyo (Stride and Ifeka, 1971; p.297).

As the head of government, the *oba* was politically supreme, and as the executive head, he exercised considerable powers: he could arrest, punish or reward any of his subjects. But Olaniyan (1985) further argued:

> In practice, however, the *oba* was not an absolute ruler. His powers were checked in a number of ways and more importantly, he did not rule singlehandedly but in conjunction with a council of chiefs known

generally as the *Iwarefa*. The chiefs on the council were usually grouped into two parallel lines representing commoners' interests and princely interests (p.43).

Smith (1969) reached similar conclusions:

> The sacred aspect of Yoruba kingship did not lead to the *oba* becoming an autocrat but rather the reverse. Not only was he bound by rules and precedents in his personal life but these also required him to submit all business to councils of chiefs and officers, and only after consultation and deliberation by these bodies could a policy be decided upon and proclaimed in the *oba*'s name.

> Every *oba* had at least one council of chiefs who formed a powerful, usually hereditary, cabinet, and in most kingdoms there were lesser councils for the regulation of the different aspects of government. *Thus the oba was at least as much fettered by constitutional procedure as a ruler in a modern democracy.* Moreover, the chieftaincies were hereditary with the 'descent group' or extended families which made up the population of the town. Thus the chiefs were representatives of their family groups as well as being officials of the king and the kingdom (p.111). (Italics mine).

The supreme king over all was the *Alafin* (or *Alaafin*) at Oyo. His duties to sub-states were as considerable as those owed to him by the sub-rulers, so that "the essential basis of the empire was mutual self-interest" (Stride and Ifeka, 1971:298). Both tributary kings and provincial governors (of metropolitan Oyo) had the duty of collecting tribute due to Oyo and for contributing contingents of troops under local generalship to the imperial army in times of major war. All sub-rulers had to pay homage to the *Alafin*. The acknowledgment of the duty of allegiance was renewed yearly by compulsory attendance at important religious ceremonies. The most important of these was the *Bere* festival, which was celebrated to mark public acclamation of successful rule by an *Alafin*. After a *Bere* festival, there was supposed to be peace in Yorubaland for three years.

For his part, it was the responsibility of the *Alafin* to protect tributary states from external aggression, particularly from the north (Muslim). It was also the duty of the *Alafin* to settle internal quarrels between his sub-rulers and between individual sub-rulers and their peoples. He was thus the supreme judge of the empire; his court was the final court of appeal.

> The *Alafin* was carefully selected and commanded enormous respect. No man could be considered for elevation to the imperial throne unless he was directly descended from Oranyan, the founder of Old Oyo. Yet

the office did not automatically pass from father to son for there were several distinct lineages of royal descent (Stride and Ifeka; p.298).

The actual selection of a new *Alafin* was in the hands of the *Oyo Mesi*, a supreme council of state, whose seven members were collectively recognized as king-makers. They consulted the Ifa oracle as to which of the candidates was approved by the gods. The new *Alafin* was then proclaimed as the appointment of the gods. He was consecrated in his office by important religious and political ceremonies during which he was initiated into the mysteries of kingship and control of the sacred cults. Once these rituals had been completed, he was no longer regarded as an ordinary mortal: he was "*Ekeji Orisa*", companion of the gods, a semi-divine beyond the reach of ordinary mortals. He was the head of his people in the inseparable sphere of administration, religion, and justice. (This consecration of the *Alafin* may be compared with that of the *Asantehene* who was lowered three times, lightly touching a blackened stool with his buttocks, or to that of the Japanese emperor in the *daijo-sai* ritual.)

> The *Alafin*'s power, in theory, was unlimited by human agency. Cult priests and government officials were alike appointed by his command; and the usual practice was for the *Alafin* to appoint eunuchs loyal to himself.

> In practice, the *Alafin* did not have such absolute power. He could ill afford to offend the members of the *Oyo Mesi* or the *Ogboni* (earth cult). Although he could not be deposed, the *Alafin* could be compelled to commit suicide. If both the *Oyo Mesi* and the *Ogboni* diapproved of his personal conduct or policies, or if the *Oyo* peoples suffered serious reverses, they would commission the *Bashorun* to present the *Alafin* with an empty calabash or a dish of parrot's eggs. On handing over these meaningful symbols, the *Bashorun* pronounced a fearful formula: 'The gods reject you, the people reject you, the earth rejects you.' The *Alafin* was thus informed that his political position had been completely undermined and his removal decided. Custom demanded he take poison (Stride and Ifeka, 1971:299).

Smith (1969) maintained that:

> The *Alafin* was not always the dominant figure or wielded autocratic power; he was in fact subject, like all Yoruba *oba* to elaborate restraints embedded in the custom (which can justifiably be called the constitution) of the kingdom. He had to submit his decisions in the first place to his council of seven notabilities, the *Oyo Mesi*, whose principal officer was the chief known as the *Basorun*. In turn, the *Oyo Mesi* were checked by the council of *Ogboni*, a society which, in its worship of the earth,

embodied both religious and political sanctions. An *Alafin* of strong and resolute character could initiate and carry through a policy, obtaining the support and perhaps sometimes overruling the opposition of his counsellors. But not all *Alafin* were of this calibre, and the constitutional restraints on them were always stringent. The *Oyo Mesi* were even entitled to pronounce a sentence of rejection on an *Alafin*, upon whose receipt (it was sometimes tactfully conveyed by a symbolic gift of parrots' eggs), the king was bound to commit suicide. The first recorded rejection and suicide seems to be that of *Alafin* Ayibi. Another rule, apparently established during the reign of Ojigi, provided that the *Aremo*, the *Alafin's* eldest son, should take poison on his father's death, the intention being doubtless to protect the *oba* and his officers against the possible ambitions of a prince who was usually associated with his father in the Government (p.45).

The *Bashorun*, head of the *Oyo Mesi*, was a sort of prime minister. He was in charge of the religious divinations held annually to determine whether or not the *Alafin* retained the approval of the gods. This may be considered an "annual performance review" or spiritual "vote of confidence." The *Bashorun* was in a position to influence important decisions of the *Oyo Mesi* and the *Ogboni*. In fact, for a period in the 18th century, the *Bashorun* wielded more authority than the *Alafin*. This was largely because the *Alafin* could be divorced from politics by strict adherence to religious taboos that seclude him from his subjects whereas the *Bashorun* was always in the center of power.

The *Ogboni* was a very powerful secret society composed of freemen noted for their age, wisdom and importance in religious and political affairs. The *Ogboni* was concerned with the worship of earth, and was thus responsible for judging any cases involving the spilling of blood. The leader had unqualified right of direct access to the *Alafin* on any matter. Even the most important decisions of the *Oyo Mesi*, especially the rejection of an *Alafin*, could not be carried without *Ogboni* approval.

As Stride and Ifeka (1971) put it:

> Whereas the *Oyo Mesi* represented the great politicians of the real, the *Ogboni* was the voice of popular opinion backed by the authority of religion. Although the members of the *Oyo Mesi* were ex-officio members of the *Ogboni*, they were not its senior members even though their informed opinions must have commanded respect.

> The *Oyo Mesi* and *Ogboni* thus provided important constitutional checks on the personal authority of the *Alafin*. He was bound to listen to their advice and to ignore their opinions was to invite rejection. . .

These constitutional safeguards eventually worked against the

interests of strong central government. Except in times of exceptional danger, there was an unfortunate tendency to select a weak
Alafin to succeed one of strong character and marked achievements lest
a succession of autocratic rulers should transform the constitution into
an absolute despotism (p.300).

It is a little baffling why the authors should describe this tendency as
"unfortunate." But what comes out clearly is yet another evidence of the
fear of the African people of the ever-present threat of despotism and their
fervid desire to curb the powers of their rulers through various constitutional
and religious checks. It is also remarkable how the *Alafin* was enjoined to
listen to the advice of his councillors or face rejection (removal) — an
injunction characteristic of most indigenous systems of government. More
astonishing is the absence of similar injunctions in modern systems of
government in Africa.

The royal court formed one of the three pillars of government at Oyo, the
two others being the *Oyo Mesi* and the *Ogboni*. In addition to the *Ogboni*,
other cult organizations, usually of lesser importance, existed in all towns
and kingdoms; at Oyo, the *Egungun*, a masked association led by the *Alapini*,
a member of the *Oyo Mesi*, exercise an important influence on government
by virtue of its function of recalling ancestors. Overlapping and parallel with
all these bodies were associations of chiefs concerned with particular aspects
of government and daily life, especially the conduct of war, trade, and of
hunting. Among the *Egba* the leading chiefs were members of the *Ogboni*;
the *Parakoyi* were the trade chiefs, while the hunters, who in war acted as
scouts for the main army, were grouped together as the *ode* (or *Eso*). Under
Lisabi a fourth order was created in the towns, the *Olorogun*, the leaders of
the militia or war chiefs. They were individually appointed for their military
skill and valor in war, and their rank was not hereditary. At the head of the
Eso was the *Are-Ona-Kakanfo*, supreme commander of the imperial army.
This official was customarily required to live in a frontier province of great
strategic importance in imperial defense. "Thus he was well placed to
guarantee imperial security against attack and was too far removed from the
capital to interfere directly in central politics" (Stride and Ifeka, 1971:300).
In fact to ensure this, he was debarred from entering the capital except with
permission. This minimized, if not precluded, the possibility of military
coup d'etats.

On all major campaigns, the *Are-Ona-Kakanfo* personally commanded in
the field. He was obliged to win victories, as a defeat carried with it the
punishment of committing suicide. He could escape the consequence of
failure by fleeing to found a separate state a safe distance away from imperial
retribution. "Thus did Oyo protect itself against hesitant generalship in the

field and 'retire' those generals who clung to military command when their martial vigour was declining" (Stride and Ifeka, 1971:300).[3]

> The system of government of the capital was repeated on a smaller scale in the provincial towns of the kingdom, and paralleled also in the subject kingdoms. There are many indications that these later were allowed by Oyo to retain a large measure of independence, although regular tribute had to be paid and the *Alafin* sometimes assumed the right to nominate a new ruler, and his confirmation of one was required. (Much like the Asante kingdom). Oyo authority was expressed in a form of *indirect rule* by the stationing all over the empire of resident political representatives known as *ajele - asoju oba* (the eyes of the king) - who in turn were supervised by the *ilari*, the royal messengers from Oyo (Smith, 1969; p.45).

For example, in the Ijebu kingdom there were three main councils, occasionally overlapping in membership. The highest, the *Ilamuren*, consisting of the great magnates and officials under the presidency of the *Olisa*, discharged legislative, executive, and judicial functions relating to the whole kingdom. Next came the *Osugbo* under the dispensing of justice, and then the *Pampa*, composed of the younger men and overseeing administration and warfare.

> The government of a Yoruba kingdom and its capital thus presents a complex and somewhat confusing picture, mainly because of the fusion of political, judicial and religious concepts and the division of responsibilities. Even in so small a kingdom as Ikerre (in Ekiti), for example, the Government exhibited this Byzantine (?) quality; there were two groups of leading chiefs, each divided into three grades, and four main councils: the *Iyare Mefa*, or inner council, meeting daily; the *Ajo Iyare*, meeting every 8 days to discuss town affairs; the *Ajagun*, or war council, and the *Ajo Ilu*, or general council of the town held four times yearly. Yet, in practice all seems to have worked smoothly enough in these delicately balanced governments, except when some external pressure or crisis intervened to overthrow the slow and deliberate processes of the constitution.

---

[3] One cannot fail to notice the contrast between the organization of the Yoruba army and the military in modern Africa. How professional are modern African soldiers? A retired Nigerian army chief, General Hassan Usman Katsina, supplied the answer: "The problem with the armed forces today is their lack of dedication to duty and the duty of professionalism. Perhaps no profession is as abused" (*The Africa Report*, July-August, 1990; p.52). Could they even fight a war? According to Brigadier Benjamin Adekunle, a retired general: "Nigerian soldiers of today are so inexperienced that they are scared of war" (*New African*, July, 1989; p.58).

Naturally each kingdom developed different mechanism for dealing with its individual problems, so that it would be futile to postulate any "model" constitution for a Yoruba kingdom. On the other hand, with the notable exception of the new states of the 19th century, the main features of government - the town, the sacred *oba* at its center, the hierarchy of hereditary chiefs and priests with their jealously guarded responsibilities — remained constant.

This form of government was not confined to the capital, but was repeated through the kingdom, every town forming a microcosm of the central government. The place of the crowned *oba* was taken by a less ruler, generally entitled to wear only a simple crown or coronet (called *akoro* in Oyo) or a cap of office. Usually these rulers were chosen like the greater *oba* by kingmakers from royal houses and presented for approval to the *oba* of the kingdom, while in some cases the latter nominated the provincial rulers (Smith, 1969; p.117).

To the outsider, this system of government may be "Byzantine" which was the typical reaction of many foreigners to the indigenous African systems. Though traditional African societies might have appeared "chaotic," there was order. In African philosophical scheme, there was perfect harmony among the seemingly anarchic and unrelated events in a giant natural equation. The king's role was to preserve the harmony. Perhaps the closest modern-day analogy is a jazz quartet. Separately, each plays "horribly." The guitarist seems to be "way off on a discordant tangent." The trombonist is "blowing his head off." The drummer seems to be "summoning the devil" and the cymbalist is "creating confusion." But when all this "confusion" is synthesized or fused, out comes some beautiful music. To the untrained ear, jazz music is simply "total confusion." The African king's role may be likened to that of a synthesizer or conductor — to produce harmonic music out of the confusion.

Similarly, the components of indigenous African systems may seem "Byzantine," but together with the others, they may produce "beautiful music." Indeed, Smith (1969), perhaps inadvertently, reached this conclusion: "Despite its hierarchical character, Yoruba society was in practice surprisingly *democratic*" (p.118).

Additionally, there were striking similarities between the Yoruba and other governmental systems. For example, the powers of the Zulu king, like the *Alafin*, were similarly curtailed. He was powerless without the *izikhulu*, an inner council made up of the chiefs of pre-Shakan chiefdoms. He could not take any decision without them. Both the Oyo and Zulu kingdoms instituted checks against royal absolutism. Both also assimilated pre-existing ethnic groups. But there were slight differences however. While the Zulu kingdom was centralized, the Oyo empire was a confederation of smaller autonomous kingdoms, all of which traced their ancestry to Oduduwa.

The development of the Fante kingdom on the Gold Coast (now modern Ghana) also paralleled closely that of the Oyo. The original founders of the kingdom lived for centuries at Mankessim (cf. Ile-Ife for the Yoruba). But, "during the last three decades of the 17th century, as a result of population pressures, they moved out to carve out kingdoms for themselves in the areas left virtually empty by the decimation or assimilation of its original inhabitants, the Etsii" (Boahen and Webster, 1970; p.119). By the beginning of the 19th century, the Fante kingdom consisted of about 17 sub-kingdoms which organized themselves into a Fante Confederacy under the rule of Brafo (cf. the Yoruba *Alafin*), the king of Mankessim, and the High Priest of the national god, *"Bora Bora Weigya"* or in Fante as *"Nnanom Mpow"* (cf. *Oduduwa* of the Yoruba). Like the Yoruba, the Fante kingdom broke up into parts in the middle of the 18th century.

The Kingdom Of Benin

Also known as the empire of Great Benin, this kingdom emerged among the Edo peoples of the midwestern region of Nigeria. When it reached its zenith in the mid-sixteenth century, parts of Ishan to the north, the Urhobo and Isoko of the lower Niger delta, southern Yoruba country and western Igboland were under the rule of Benin. World famous for its cultural artifacts, especially masks and wooden sculptures, Benin emerged in the very area of the present day city of Benin around the tenth century, under a ruler with the title of *Ogiso*. The growth of the kingdom has attracted a great deal of scholarly attention because it was one of the most important empires of the southern savanna, forest and coastal regions of West Africa that owed its early developments neither to Islam or European influence. More important for our purposes, however, is the fact that the structure of Benin society and government followed almost identical patterns observed in other indigenous African systems.

Unlike the Yoruba, the Edo did not live in towns or urban centers but in small communities and villages close to each other. Though the dense tropical rain forest compelled the Edo to live in small close communities, it also afforded protection from external attacks. Each Edo community or village for purposes of administration was divided into three age grades, the elders (*edion*), the adults *(ighele)* and the youths (*iroghae*).

The grade of elders, the oldest of whom was the head of the village or community (*odionwere*), was responsible for the making of laws, settling disputes and religious affairs and rituals. The adult grade constituted the warrior and executive group while the youth grade performed public works such as clearing the roads and footpaths. These communities were welded into a kingdom by the Ogiso dynasty in the 14th century, whose first king was called Obagodo.

At the peak of its power, the kingdom of Benin, like that of Oyo, consisted of two parts. The first was the kingdom proper, or metropolitan Benin, which was the capital or principal town of Benin City and a number of subject towns, villages and hamlets around the city. The second consisted of the states, towns and kingdoms that had been conquered and converted into tributary states. These were provincial Benin.

At the head of both parts of the empire was the *Oba* or king, who, unlike the *Alafin* of Oyo, was not selected for this office, but succeeded directly as the eldest son. The *Oba* could not be deposed, as could the *Alafin* by the *Oyo Mesi*. But according to Boahen (1986), "although he wielded enormous religious power and was regarded by his subjects as semi-divine, in practice, the *Oba* of Benin exercised his powers and governed the metropolitan kingdom in cooperation with not just one group of senior title-holders or estates, as in Oyo, but rather three" (p.78).

These were the *uzama* (hereditary nobles and kingmakers), the *eghaevbo n'ogbe* (palace chiefs), and the *eghaevbo n'ore* (town chiefs). For major decisions of state, such as the declaration of war or the promulgation of new laws, consultation of a state council made up of these three groups by the *Oba* was mandatory. Once again, note that even though the *Oba* was vested with extraordinary powers he could not act alone without the state council. In fact, it was this council which passed laws and carried out executive and judicial functions at the central government level.

The *uzama* were the highest ranking and oldest of the orders dating from the Ogiso period. Next in rank to the *uzama* was the *eghaevbo n'ogbe*, or the order of the palace chiefs. The chiefs of this order were the principal administrative officers of the state and the *Oba*'s closest advisers, and they lived in the palace quarters of the town. Their specific duties relating to palace administration included looking after the *Oba*'s finances, wives and children. In addition, the palace chiefs could be sent out to gather information, investigate complaints and represent the *Oba* at village rituals.

The third order was that of *eghaevbo n'ore* (town chiefs) whose leader, the *Iyase*, has been described as being both Prime Minister and leader of the opposition. With only one exception, all the posts or titles of this order, like those of the palace chiefs, were in the *Oba*'s gift. In other words any freeborn commoner not heir to any hereditary office and who had acquired wealth and prestige through trade or warfare or farming, could be appointed as a member. (Note once again that in traditional Africa, wealth was *not* evenly distributed.)

Besides being members of the supreme council, the town chiefs performed many important religious, military and administrative functions. First, the four senior members, as a duty, performed the rite of *zematon*, which was to purify, renew and release the mystical powers of the *Oba*. Like the palace chiefs, they controlled many fiefs and therefore the *Oba* depended on them for tribute, labor and troops. Furthermore, no state chiefs appointed by the *Oba* could be installed without their approval since it was their leader, the *Iyase*, who had to perform the installation ceremonies. Finally, the *Oba* needed their support to prevent him from coming too much under the control of the palace chiefs.

None of the posts in either the *uzama* or the *eghaevbo n'ogbe* was hereditary; they were all open to competition by all freeborn commoners from any part of the kingdom and not confined to particular lineages or families as was the case in Oyo. Moreover, the *Oba* could create new titles any time and confer them on whomever he pleased. But taking a title or being initiated into a grade was an expensive exercise as fees had to be paid to all title holders of the orders except the *uzuma*. The *Oba* could literally "pack" the councils with "yes-men." But as Boahen (1986) pointed out: "it is evident from all these roles that the *Oba* could not impose his will on or dictate to the town chiefs and the interest of the state could best be served by active cooperation among the *Oba*, the town chiefs, and the palace chiefs" (p.79).

The administration of provincial Benin was rather flexible. There was no single system; some vassal states were governed more effectively and directly than others. The rulers (*enigie*) of the nearest Ishan states to the northeast had to be approved by the *Oba*; had to pay annual tribute and above all participate in the wars of the *Oba*. In other words, they were governed in much the same way as the states within metropolitan Benin. On the other hand, distant vassal states of the northwestern Edo peoples, such as Akoko, Ivbiosakon and Afenmai were governed rather loosely. "It would appear that most of them were left alone so long as they paid their tribute regularly" (Boahen, 1986:79).

But Benin's rule over the Yoruba vassal states to the northwest, especially that of Owo, was very strict. A resident Benin official was stationed in Owo, through whom the *Olowo* of Owo sent his annual tribute to Benin. Owo also was required to send its princes as "hostages" to the Benin court. This was mainly for educational purposes: to instruct the Owo of Benin in culture and religious rituals.

Over its provincial domain, then, Benin had no uniform system of government. The degree of control varied according to the distance from the center and the strategic importance politically or commercially of the area (Boahen, 1986:80).

The Kanuri Empire (Northern Nigeria)

This Islamic empire came into existence in the ninth century, when the Kanuri succeeded in imposing their authority on the politically disunited and scattered communities of the Lake Chad basin. "The *girgam* - Kanuri's oral traditions - credit this achievement to Say'f b. Dhi Yazan (or simply Saif) who established the Sefawa dynasty, the longest-lived in Africa" (Olaniyan, 1985; p.57).[4]

Like Ghana, another ancient Islamic empire, the Kanuri empire, the first at Kanem and the second at Borno, survived for almost one thousand years. The first empire at Kanem began to collapse from 1259 to 1472 due to struggles for power and internal dissension. The empire was revived by Mai Ali Ghaji (1472-1504) who reconstructed Kanuri power at Bornu rather than at the ancestral capital of N'jimi.

The political organization of the empire (both the old and new) operated at two levels, central and provincial. At the head of the empire was the *Mai*, a hereditary sovereign chosen from the descendants of Saif. He was the personification of the empire and the wellbeing of his subjects was identified with his state of health. Originally divine rulers, the *Mais* were sacrosanct and preserved all the outward attributes of sacred monarchy long after their conversion to Islam. They ate in seclusion, appeared ceremonially before the public gaze on very rare occasions and gave audiences to strangers from behind a screen of curtaining. "In strict theory, their position as both political and religious leader of their people gave them absolute power in all spheres of government. In practice, they were constitutional rulers who had to heed the advice and ambitions of their councillors" (Stride and Ifeka, 1971; p.128). One notices again and again the wide gap between royal absolutism in theory and despotism in practice.

Olaniyan (1985) was more emphatic:

> The *Mai*, like other sacred monarchs in other Nigerian states, was not an autocrat. He had to take cognizance of the existence of two bodies of title holders. The first was the council of state, made up of twelve men selected from the nobility and great men of servile origin. These twelve dignitaries, together with the *Mai*, formed the supreme ruling body. It was very unlikely for a *Mai* to take any decision without consulting them (p.61).

Besides a few councillors who held hereditary titles, the *Mai* appointed court and state officials and assigned responsibilities to them. All important activities of the state took place in his palace. But the official organ of government was the Council of Twelve, which advised the *Mai* on policy and saw to its implementation in his name.

This council was composed of the great officials of state who were

---

[4] Other durable lineages included the rulers of the central kingdom of the Mossi in Burkina Faso, the Keita lineage of Mali and the Mwanamutapa of central Africa.

selected both from the royal family and influential men of servile origin. *Without their cooperation, the Mai was practically powerless*; they, on the other hand, could govern the country with little reference to his wishes (Stride and Ifeka, 1971; p.128).

The second important political institution was a body comprising three women title holders: the *Gumsu* (*Mai*'s first wife), the *Magara* (*Mai*'s senior sister) and the *Magira* (the Queen Mother). These three women performed important activities in the palace and they trained the princes. They exercised great influence in the politics of the empire and they also exercised wide-ranging powers during an inter-regnum or when there was a weak *Mai* on the throne. By the threat to withdraw their services, this council of women could force a *Mai* to change his policies. The *Magira* had complete responsibility for the provision of royal food and the *Magara* for care of the royal children. "The extent of the Queen-Mother's influence can be seen in the fact that *Mai* Biri was imprisoned on the *Magira*'s order and *Magira* Aisa controlled Kanuri political life before the accession of Idris Alooma" (Stride and Ifeka, 1971:129).[5]

For administrative purposes, the empire was divided into four provinces and placed under four governors selected from the twelve councillors. The *Galadima* was in charge of the west; the *Kaigama* the south; the *Yerima* the north; and *Mestrema* the east. The governors defended their provinces from attack, prevented them from secession, mobilized their citizens for war and collected tributes for the *Mai*. They were also responsible for the preservation of law and order and for extending Kanuri influence beyond their frontiers. The governors, except for the *Galadima*, did not live in the provinces and had to appoint representatives known as the *Chima* to perform their functions. "The day-to-day administration of the provincial villages and towns was left in the hands of their hereditary rulers, (known as *Chima Gana*), an arrangement which made it possible to govern *indirectly* and reduce instability" (Olaniyan, 1985; p.61).

The Kanuri empire and the Sefawa dynasty owed their success and longevity to a number of factors. For the empire, the first was the strong and effective leadership provided by such *Mais* as Saif, Dunama II, 'Ali Ghaji and Idris Alooma. Second, membership of the Council of Twelve was not hereditary and the four great officers in charge of the major sub-divisions of the empire were appointed to govern areas where their families had no vested interests. What is more, with the exception of the *Galadima*, they and other important noblemen were required to live in the capital under the eye

[5] This role of women in government was similar to that of Queen-Mothers in the Asante, Fanti, Edo, and other states. It may be recalled that in the kingdom of Dahomey, cabinet ministers even had female counterparts and there were female battalions in the army.

of royal authority. Only in times of emergency did they visit the areas they governed and assume personal control.

> While this lessened the danger of their building up independent local power, it had the further value that as new areas were added to the empire, their natural rulers could be appointed *Chima Gana* to their own people. This reinforced their authority over their people, guaranteed a high degree of local autonomy and at the same time brought them under the supervision of one of the great Kanuri noblemen at Ngazargamu (Stride and Ifeka, 1971:129).

Third, "the *Mais* did not keep large standing armies" (Stride and Ifeka, 1971:130). The military therefore did not act as a drain on imperial budget. The bulk of the troops were local levies that could be called up and commanded by local officials. Yet, this imperial military machine was able to overcome small-scale uncoordinated resistance from the neighbors and repel invasions. Fourth, administration was decentralized though the Kanuri "absorbed the socio-political features of pre-dynastic (i.e. pre-ninth century) inhabitants" (Olaniyan, 1985; p.61). The inhabitants managed their own local affairs under their hereditary rulers. Fifth, Islam provided a unifying force. "The Sefawa dynasty was one of the longest-lived in the history of the world, having ruled Kanuri states for about a thousand years" (Stride and Ifeka, 1971:125). A number of factors accounted for this. First, great precautions were taken to avoid dynastic struggles, preserve the balance of the constitution and minimize rivalries withing the ruling classes of the empire. As the *Mai's* sons reached manhood, they were despatched to the provinces to prevent them from becoming centers of political rivalry and intrigue within the capital.

Second, the Sefawa deliberately intermarried with the women in the conquered areas in order to minimize feuds and rebellions. The number of offspring of such mixed marriages became members of the ruling dynasty (Olaniyan, 1985; p.57). Third, the Sefawa dynasty introduced Islam gradually and peacefully. For example, although 'Ali Ghaji employed Islam to consolidate his bureaucracy, "he never used force to spead Islam" (Olaniyan, 1985; p.59).

The administration of the Kanuri empire was very similar to that of another Muslim empire, the Songhai which Stride and Ifeka (1971) described as "the greatest indigenous empire in the history of West Africa" (p.67). The progenitors of the Songhai empire were peoples living in small communities on both sides of the Niger river in the Dendi area. They included the Da (sedentary farmers), the Gow (hunters) and the Sorko (fishermen and canoe-men). They were invaded from the northeast and conquered by bands of dark-skinned Zaghawa nomads. Over time, they were forged into a powerful empire which reached the peak of its power in the 16th century under the Sunni dynasty.

One notable Songhai ruler was Sunni Ma Dogo, alias Muhammed Da'o, who reigned around 1420. He was followed by Sunni Ali (1464-1492), who within a period of 28 years transformed the little kingdom of Gao into the huge Songhai empire, stretching from the Niger in the east to Jenne in the west. After the Sunni dynasty came the Askia, the first of which was Askia Muhammad, which reigned between 1528 and 1591.

Askia Muhammad "did not implement Islamic models but merely improved upon or expanded the existing traditional system" (Boahen, 1971:39). He divided his empire into provinces, like the Kanuri empire, and each ruled by a governor called *koi* or *fari*. These provinces were comprised of a metropolitan Gao and 4 major provinces: Dendi to the south of Gungia; Bal, north of the Niger bend and including Taghaza; Benga in the lacustrine area; and Kurmina in the important grain-producing area south of the Niger from Timbuktu.

The ruler of the eastern province was the *dendi-fari* while that of the western province was *gurman-fari* or *kurmina-fari*. Each was advised by a council of ministers. Thus the *kurmina-fari* was advised by a council consisting of the *balama*, the commander of the Songhai forces in the west, the *binga-farma* and the *bana-farma*, all of whom were royal princes.

At the center, Askia Muhammad established a council of ministers to assist him in all aspects of government. Most of these central posts, as well as the governors, were carefully selected from the Askia's family and circle of friends to ensure maximum loyalty. There were enormous powers in the hands of these governors. But their offices were not hereditary. They served at the pleasure of the Askia who could both appoint and remove them at will.

One important feature of the reign of Sunni Ali needs to be noted:

> All the rulers of the second dynasty, the Sunni dynasty, were attached to their traditional religion more than to Islam, and paid far more attention to their idols, priests and diviners than to the Koran and the mallams. Indeed, they became known as magician-kings, as Levtzion has pointed out: "even after they had lost temporal power, the Sohantyr, descendants of Sunni Ali, retained their prestige as powerful magicians." Sunni Ali himself, though generous to the Muslims, did not hesitate to punish or persecute them if they stood in his way. Throughout his reign, the traditional Songhai religion remained the basis of his authority, and it was only because Islam was gaining ground in the western part of his kingdom that Sunni Ali had to keep up an outward Muslim appearance by saying prayers, fasting and so on.

Thus, during the period of the Sunni rulers, Islam never became the religion of the state (Boahen, 1971:34).

This flexibility and tolerance of traditional religious practices were also evident during the reign of the Askia dynasty. Each great official was allowed to have his own distinctive dress, his own personal allocation of drums for use on ceremonial occasions and some distinguishing privilege.

> Such privileges included the right of the commander-in-chief (*Dyina Koy*) to sit on a carpet and sprinkle himself with flour instead of dust when prostrating before the *Askia*; the exemption of the governor of Gurma from removing his turban when kneeling before his ruler; and the distinction of the Governor of Benga who was allowed to enter the city of Gao with all this drums beating (Stride and Ifeka, 1971:79).

Stride and Ifeka (1971) continued with the observation that, although great stress was placed on the Islamic character of the towns with crowded mosques and Islamic judges, traditional African practices, such as the use of an "interpreter" as an intermediary between ruler and the people and African religious influences remained pervasive.

> Thus, it appears that the Askias were either essentially Muslims who for political reasons paid lip-service to the traditional religious forms to retain the loyalty of non-Muslim subjects, or they gradually became re-absorbed into the ethnic religion while maintaining a Muslim gloss that propitiated indigenous and foreign Muslims alike. Whichever was the true state of affairs, it is clear that successful Askias *drew political support and religious approval from all quarters. This was a remarkable feat of statesmanship* (Stride and Ifeka, 1971:79). (Italics mine).[6]

The Lunda Empire

In the 15th century, this was a small kingdom in central Africa, situated somewhere around the southeastern part of present-day Zaire. As with the Oyo empire, "from this nucleus small groups of villages would break off whenever the population increase warranted it and would settle on the plains to the west, conquering and bringing the resident population under their

---

[6] Unfortunately, that "feat of statesmanship" has not been replicated in modern Nigeria, Mauritania, Sudan, Tanzania and other Moslem African countries. Recent events prompted one irate Nigerian, Mr. Aloysius Juryit of Calabar, to write: "Events in the Sudan and Mauritania, to mention only a few, have shown that the worst racists are Arabs, especially when it comes to dealing with blacks" (*New African*, March 1990; p.6).

leaders, the 'chiefs of the land' (the *mwaantaangaand*). The relations between the villages were maintained by the notion of perpetual kinship between the leaders" (Vansina, 1975; p.78). By the 19th century, this kingdom had grown into an empire, comprising several chiefdoms that stretched from southeastern Zaire into Angola and northern Zambia.

The political structure was based on the village, which was ruled by a council of elders (*ciyul*) and by a headman (*mwaantaangaand*) These villages would be grouped according to the nature of the ties of perpetual kinship existing between the headmen and would be ruled by the *mbay* (elder of the headmen). The *mbay* in turn would be grouped into a political district that was governed by a *cilool*, appointed by the king.

At the capital, the king, the *mwaat yaav* (the "Lord of the viper"), and his titleholders comprised the centralized government. The king had sacred attributes, nominated court officials, created new titles, could depose officials of all ranks, and presided over the *citentam* (a national council and court of the highest titleholders). He was assisted by three types of officials:

a. Fifteen *acubuung* (headmen of the fifteen oldest villages in the land). Included in this group were other religious titleholders.

b. Residents of the capital who were closely linked to the king by ties of perpetual kinship.

c. Tributary chiefs who lived in the countryside but were represented at the capital by permanent delegates, the *ntomb*. The *ntomb* would pay the tributes they received from the provincial heads (*cilool*) who in turn received them from the local chiefs.

Provinces that were farther away would pay tributes once a year, in the dry season, whereas those closer to the capital did so several times a year. "The outer provinces could do as they pleased as long as tribute was paid" (Vansina, 1975; p.82).

The Lunda had no regular standing army, in contrast to the Asante, except for a small police corps at the capital. Yet, they were able to expand their empire over a large part of Africa in the 16th century.

Vansina (1975) attributes their imperial success to the fact that the Lunda developed a political "system that could be adapted anywhere in Africa." There were two aspects of this system that were noteworthy. The first, the political structure rested on the twin mechanism of positional succession and perpetual kingship. A successor inherited not only an office but also the personal status of the deceased, including his name and kinship relationships. This divorced the political structure from the real descent structure. One did not have to descend from any one particular lineage in order to hold titles. Privileges and status were vested in the office rather than in individuals. This enabled resident populations to be ruled and absorbed into government without necessitating any changes in the existing social structures.

The second aspect of government in Lundaland was "indirect rule." Vansina (1975) explained:

Local chieftains could be assimilated to *mwaantaangaand* and the newcomers would be *cilool*. They would settle and found a Lunda colony (*iyanga*) which would become a neutral place from the point of view of the non-Lunda residents in an area, a place where one could go for arbitration, a place to which one was ultimately subjected without the use of force (p.83).

The Kingdom Of Kuba

The kingdom was south of Zambia in Northern Kantanga, covering the Province of Kasai between the Sankuri and Kasai rivers in present-day Zaire. It gained its prominence in the 15th century and was a federation of several African tribes. Its history is important because it offers yet another example of an indigenous system in which different ethnic groups coexisted peacefully under one ruler — a task many African heads of state face today.

There were five rulers during the short period of 19 years between 1568 and 1587, one being a woman, and each ruled with the concurrence of a Council. It is not known whether the Council, sitting as an electoral college, set what seems to indicate four-year terms. After 1587, longer but still fixed terms for kings (or queens) also seem to be indicated. It appears that these limited terms of office by kings continued during the supremacy of the Council. For a long time ten years in office seemed to be the limit.

The core or central organizing group was the Bushoong, which formed a federation with voluntary kindred groups and other tribes, numbering eighteen at the outset. The Cwa and the Kete were the aboriginal settlers. They offered no opposition to the invaders and welcomed them all, becoming members of the federal union under an elected king called Woot (Williams, 1987; p.224). Other members were the Mongo, Pende, Llebo, Shoowa, Kel, Kaam, Kayilweeng, Lulua, Luba, Ngeende, Maluk, Pyaang, Ngoombe, Byeeng, Coofa and Mbeegi gongo.

From the very beginning the core group of Bushoong set an example for nation-building for all Africa, but few African states ever followed it, as Williams (1987) lamented. First of all, the total population at the formation of the federal kingdom was estimated at between 75,000 and 100,000, of which number the Bushoongs were 80 percent. All the other tribes combined, therefore, were only one-fifth of the total population. This meant that even under the most liberal democratic system the Bushoongs could have dominated and ruled all the other tribes by the sheer weight and power of overwhelming numbers.

Here was what might be considered to be a justifiable occasion to depart from the traditional African constitution with its all-embracing democratic system. Quite to the contrary they followed it to the letter by simply transforming the Village Council of Elders into a council of State in which each tribe, now constituting a constituent province, was represented as an equal by its own chief or a representative of its choice. The members of the state council were the electors who chose the king. As it was throughout Africa, the Council represented the people and, therefore, all powers not delegated rested with the Council. The significance of this was that the smallest tribe or province, which might be only 2 percent of the population, was equal in the Council to the Bushoong group that was 80 percent of the population, a situation which head-counters might criticize as the very antithesis of democracy (Williams, 1987; p.224).

The numerically dominant Bushoongs seem to have been statesmen with a larger view of what democracy meant if it were to operate as a unifying force with divergent and formerly independent groups. "What they did in effect was to make a frontal attack on tribalism not by futile denunciations or exhortations, but by actually detribalizing themselves first of all" (Williams, 1987). They not only treated all of the different language groups as equals, but they promoted a national policy of glorifying those cultural variations in any groups which were so outstanding that they should be adopted nationally. Hence, every tribe that in isolation had developed something noteworthy but peculiar to itself, no matter how "strange" or different from all others, could see its unique culture pattern become a national institution and be filled with both pride and gratitude. If the Pende had a different kind of dance and excelled in it, theirs would become the national dance of Kuba. If the Luba excelled in the architectural arts, they would be the leading planners and builders; and so on in all human endeavors. Each group could win national distinction in one way or another for excellence in one or more fields, including agriculture and cattle breeding.

The political structure actually began with the family council or clan council, which was the basic social unit of kinsmen. During the formative period of the state each clan had its own village. As new immigrants swelled villages into towns and cities, these became divided into clan sections or wards. Each ward sent its elder as a representative to the village, town, or city council, over which presided the village headman, town subclass, or city chief. These chiefs, in turn, served as representatives of their areas on the provincial council over which the Paramount Chief of the whole tribe presided. The Paramount Chiefs of the central provinces or states, the original eighteen founders, represented their provinces in the Central State Council over which the elected King of Kuba presided.

Williams (1987) presented this outline of the Government of Kuba:

1. The Council of State

(a) The King presiding
(b) The Linguist (interpreter and special aide to King)
(c) The Chief of Chiefs (Prime Minister. The title "Chief of Chiefs" actually is that of the King. Here it means to say to all the chiefs of Kuba: When you see and speak to my Chief Minister, you see and speak to the King.")
(d) The Governors of Provinces (Paramount chiefs). Each paramount chief or one of his elected generals was in supreme command of all military forces in his province. The King, who was also a governor of his particular tribal province, had only the soldiers of his province under his command.

2. Administrators not members of the State Council
(a) First Chief of the Treasury
(b) Chief of Border Defenses
(c) Supervisor-General of Tax Collection, Goods and Services
(d) Chief of the King's Household and Protector of Ancestral Tombs and Regalia.
(e) Chief of Roads and Markets
(f) Collector-General for Tributary States (This office was created in the wake of Mboong Leengn's imperialist expansion in 1650.)

There were twenty-six kings during the 342 years of Kuban history, or from about 1568 to 1910. As in the cases of other states studied, the founder or founders of a nation constituted the specially honored group, and it was the source of royalty itself. Kuba was following the African tradition when it made the central or nuclear group of 18 founders the permanent ruling council to the exclusion of "strangers" (in Africa, all those who came after the community or nation is established). Yet it is equally clear that as newcomers increased the population, and as the nation expanded by conquering neighboring societies, the basis for future conflicts was also being expanded. Such factors, as noted in other African empires, were the source of internal conflicts in the old African states. They still exist in the new African states today, even though not all discontent has come to the surface (Williams, 1987). And, as in the case of Kuba, the problem stemmed from the failure to include every segment of the population in a national program of absolute equality, and the opportunity to participate so fully in every phase of the national life that a sense of patriotism and belonging to the nation would gradually outweigh that of belonging to a tribe.

The irony of the Kuba kingdom was that its original program of uniting many language groups into one national one was very successful. Many tribes, including the Bushoong group, merged so completely that they lost their individual tribal identity and language and became one people, speaking one language derived from all the others, the Bakuba or "People of Kuba." But there were two internal structural defects which spelt the doom and break-up of the kingdom.

First, conquered states and tribes which came after the federal union was formed were not eligible for representation on the State Council, and their chiefs, therefore, could not participate in the election of kings. Second, there were other special benefits and privileges enjoyed by the eighteen elector-chiefs which other chiefs did not have or, more pointedly, the newcomers had burdens and responsibilities from which the elector chiefs were free. The heaviest of these were the tributary taxes levied on all chiefs except the "original eighteen." Thus, in the end, the kingdom began to practice "tribalism" by excluding newcomers or conquered people from the affairs of government. The people of Kuba might have adopted this for survival reasons.

> In short, what we do deprecatingly call "tribalism" is, in fact, the necessary cohesive and social mechanism for survival and defense against threats to survival. The tribe is the unit through which the race itself has survived during all of its migrating and scattered circumstances. The enemies that beset it were black as well as white. This the tribes of today know as well as their black brothers outside of the "Circle of 18" knew four hundred years ago in Kuba. Tribalism will disappear only when the reasons for its existence in the first place disappear (Williams, 1987).

This historical lesson should not be lost to modern African heads of state. Most railed against the "cancer of tribalism" and exhorted their people to eschew the tribalistic proclivities. Yet, they, the leaders, surrounded themselves with members of their own ethnic and religious groups: Banda of Malawi with the Chewa; Babangida of Nigeria with Muslims; Biya of Cameroon with the Boulou; Houphouet-Boigny of Ivory Coast with the Baoule; Mobutu of Zaire with the Gbande; Moi of Kenya with the Kalenjin; and Rawlings of Ghana with the Ewe.

The Empire Of Mwene Mutapa (Great Zimbabwe)

Great Zimbabwe was a city-state and the capital of the Mwene Mutapa Empire which flourished for three hundred years beginning in the 12th century. This empire was a *confederation* of numerous states, of which Great Zimbabwe was one. These states were scattered across the region, including modern Mozambique.

The rulers of the empire bore the title *Mwene Mutapa* and appointed their male brothers as provincial governors. But the governors, or rulers of the city-states took no direct orders from the king as would be the case in a highly centralized system of government. The governors had extensive local autonomy and in fact, by the end of the 15th century, some of them had asserted their independence.

A flourishing trade existed between the African interior and the coast. Traders from Great Zimbabwe journeyed to the coast to trade ivory and gold for ceramics, beads, faience, glass and celadon. This trade was free, and the natives participated freely. Gold mining, upon which the fortunes of Great Zimbabwe was built, was open to all. Peasants could mine and sell gold. This activity was not restricted only to the *Mwene Mutapa* to the total exclusion of the people. One needs to ask why modern Africa has all these state monopolies, controls and government enterprises that exclude their own people? But there is a more mundane reason why Great Zimbabwe is mentioned here if only cursorily.

When Rhodesia, after years of struggle against colonial rule, finally attained its independence in 1980, President Robert Mugabe vowed to restore the country to its old glory. He changed the name to Zimbabwe. But then very strangely, he also vowed to transform Zimbabwe into a "one-party Marxist-Leninist state." Every student of African history knows that the ancient empire of *Mwene Mutapa* was definitely *not* a "one-party state." And certainly *Mwene Mutapa* was *not* Marx or Lenin.

O African tradition. What great travesties have been committed in thy name!

CHAPTER 6

THE NATIVE SYSTEM OF GOVERNMENT: A SUMMARY AND AN ASSESSMENT

A. SUMMARY

1. Chiefdoms And Kingdoms

In spite of their multitudinous variations, Africa's native political institutions showed a remarkable degree of structural similarity.

> While a hallmark of African civilizations is their stunning cultural pluralism and tremendous diversity, there is also a basic traditional continuity that provides, simultaneously, a suprising degree of similarity between even widely separated African societies. . .

> Communities formed, evolved, disintegrated, and were transformed. And yet, throughout these complex processes of evolution and change, a deeply rooted belief system often survived. Typically, the unity of the universe, with a harmonious interaction of human beings with their environment, together with the vitality of natural and supernatural forces, was stressed. New social and political forms were grounded in a traditional world view (Lamphear, 1986; p.72).

In view of their diversity, it is useful to place African polities on a continuum along which they change from a solidarity group based on a corporate kinship model — as in a stateless society — to one based on an implicit contract between the rulers and the subjects as in kingdoms (Kopytoff, 1989; p.67). The legitimacy of the African ruler rested upon the consent of the people to be ruled and was contingent upon the ruler's satisfactory performance of certain duties (an implicit contract). This consent or contract could be withdrawn for non-performance. Failures were blamed on the ruler (scapegoat king), not on the ancestors, foreigners or imperialists. If the harvest was poor because the ancestors were "angry," the ruler was faulted for failure to perform the necessary propitiating rituals.

The ruler was seen as necessary for the social order and therefore desired by the people. But by embodying a power that, to be effective, had to be vast and unquestioned, he was also potentially dangerous. For, being unquestioned, the power was subject to abuse and it could betray the expectations of those who conferred it. Accordingly, various mechanisms were devised to prevent this abuse of power: constitutional checks (Queen Mothers, advisers, councillors, assembly of freemen, etc.), religious sanctions, spontaneous peasant revolts, etc. Their efficacy is of course debatable but not their existence. A few of the features of the indigenous system of government may now be discussed.

Busia (1967) observed that: "A noteworthy feature was that there were traditional political systems, like those of the Ashanti (also, Fanti, Yoruba, Suku, Lunda, Zulu and many others) which allowed the people to choose their own rulers, and, as we have seen, there were alternatives to choose from." It was not possible for a lunatic to take a gun, dethrone the king and make himself king or chief.

The king or chief had to be acceptable to the people because he had specific roles to play. Acceptability required the possession of certain qualities, among which were descendancy from ancestral lineage, good judgment, intelligence and willingness to listen to advice. Without these qualifications, anybody who seized power through the barrel of a gun would lack the legitimacy and the authority to rule, regardless of the number of bazookas he wielded. There were guns in Africa as far back as the 15th century. Yet, the history of Africa is noticeably bereft of instances where an individual, with the aid of a gun, overthrew the king and imposed himself on the people.[1]

Even by the indigenous succession rules, there was no guarantee that the king's eldest son, often the heir apparent, would automatically ascend to the throne. The candidate or the choice of a successor was subject to ratification by an assembly of provincial leaders or "Kingmakers." Similarly with the selection of chiefs, the choice was subject to approval of the council of elders. In some societies, the whole village participated in the selection process.

The second characteristic of the indigenous political system was the fact that the king's role in the day-to-day administration of the kingdom was severely limited by tradition. Although he was vested with absolute authority and power, in reality he exercised little of it. Much of that authority was delegated to provincial heads (princes, paramount chiefs) with further delegations to junior-ranked officers (sub-chiefs and village chiefs).

---

[1] The colonialists also discovered that the "chiefs" they appointed and imposed upon the people in many parts of Africa were not accepted by the people as legitimate. In Somalia, these colonial government appointees were known as *akils*.

Every little decision or measure in every village in the kingdom did not have to await the approval of the king. Administration was highly decentralized.

Concomitantly, there was much devolution of authority. The exceptions, such as the Kingdom of Dahomey and Kongo, were very few.

In most empires and kingdoms, chiefs and provincial heads had considerable leeway in the exercise of their discretion in making decisions. The wisdom in this practice should be noted. The chiefs were closer to the people and therefore better understood them as well as the local situation. Consequently, they were most qualified to determine what was best for their people and how best to achieve it, given the prevailing local circumstances.[2] If the village chief made a miscalculation or poor judgment, he was held responsible by the council of elders and ultimately by the people who removed him. If a provincial head exercised poor judgment, he was removed by the king. In most African societies, it was the king who appointed and removed provincial heads. Generally, those who made the appointment were also invested with the power of divestiture.

Third, the political structures were not rigid but *adaptive* to economic and environmental exigencies as well as *responsive* to local needs, circumstances and the wishes of the ruled. They were reformed when social conditions required it. It may be recalled that in the settlement of disputes, there was seldom the application of precedents or rigid adherrence to a strict code of impartial laws. The primary objective of court decisions was to reconcile the disputants while pursuing justice at the same time. The emphasis was not so much on compensation or punishment as on promoting social harmony. And so it was with the political system.

The principle of central government was combined with greater degree of local autonomy. This practice was also evident in the selection of chiefs and kings: the hereditary principle combined with various degrees of selection. The type of political system was adjustable. There were several examples where neighboring states with the same hierarchical political structures adopted different rules of governance to suit their own particular needs and desires. The Fanti, Ga and Asante kingdoms are one set of examples. The Oyo and Benin empires are another. And even more dramatic example was the Dyola where one section of the people opted for centralized authority while another section chose to live without it.

Fourth, corruption was not a common feature of the indigenous system of government as we saw in Chapter 3. The traditional practice of offering a "dash" has often been used by scholars to provide a "cultural" explanation to

---

[2] As we shall see in a later section, modern African governments after independence tried to dispense with the chiefs and dictated agricultural and development policies from their capital cities.

the pervasive incidence of bribery and corruption in Africa. But no such "cultural" basis exists. From Chapter 1, we noted that the wealthy in traditional Africa acquired their fortune on their own initiative and ability within the bounds prescribed by social mores and religious precepts. There is not much evidence to suggest the use of political office for self-enrichment. It is true the chief or king was "wealthy" and "lived royally." He was expected to. But the wealth was not his personal but "stool" or "tribal" property.

Fifth, the native system was also very stable and fairly democratic in the sense that the people could participate in the decision-making process. This is attested to by the fact that many kingdoms lasted for centuries (Diop, 1987). There were few recorded episodes of violent revolutions in Africa's history by exploited "serfs" against paunchy "lords" even though there were classes in Africa.

Stability

In most African societies, there were three general social classes: the nobility, the freeborn, and the slaves. In Senegal, for example, the society was divided into slaves, the *djam*, and freemen, *gor*, including both *ger* and *neno*. The *ger* comprised the nobles and all freemen with no manual profession other than agriculture, which was considered a sacred activity. The *neno* consisted of all artisans; for example, shoemakers, blacksmiths, and goldsmiths.

The *djam*, or slaves, included the *djam-bur* (slaves of the king); the *djam neg nday* (slaves of one's mother); and the *djam neg bay* (slaves of one's father). The *ger* constituted the superior class.

Similarly, "delta society (Nigeria) from the sixteenth century distinguished between royalty, freeborn and slaves born within the community and slaves brought from outside" (Olaniyan, 1985:24). Slaves as a social class were common in many West African societies, including the Asante and Fanti of Ghana as well as the Suku of Congo.

Contrary to the assertions of many historians, slavery was not a Western institution that was foisted on Africa. Mazrui (1986), for example, declared that, "slavery was at once the consequences of racism and the mother of new forms of racial degradations" (p.104). But as Diop (1987) observed, even "white men were in the habit of reducing their own fellows to slavery" (p.152).

Before the twentieth century, many societies in the world practiced some form of slavery. Prisoners of war, political opponents and religious dissidents were often enslaved in Old England. For example, in 1530, in England, under the reign of Henry VIII, a vagrant picked up for the second time was whipped and had half an ear cut off; taken for a third time, he was "to be executed as a hardened criminal and enemy of the common weal" (Marx, 1915; p.806). Seventy-two thousand vagrants were thus executed during that reign. In the time of Edward VI (1547), "if anyone refused to work, he shall be condemned as a slave to the person who denounced him as an idler" (Marx, 1915; p.806). The owner of such a slave might whip him, chain him, and brand him on the cheek and forehead with a letter "S" (for Slave), if he disappeared for two weeks. If he ran away a third time he was executed. An idler vagabond caught on the highway was branded on the chest with a "V" (for vagrant). The same laws were in effect during the reigns of Elizabeth (1572) and of Louis XVI in France. The supporters of Monmouth's rebellion in England were sold by the Queen.[3] Cromwell's Irish and Scottish prisoners were sold to the West Indies and non-Muslims who opposed the Sokoto jihad were sold to North Africa.

Criminals in Europe and Africa could be executed, transported or sold. Europeans favored execution; Africans favored sale.

> In the eighteenth century there were 300 different offences in Britain for which one could be executed. In Dahomey, there were only two, for the king preferred to sell rather than execute his troublemakers. Those who could not pay their debts were sold for life or until the debt was paid. Among the Yoruba, debt slaves (pawns) were called *Iwofa*, among the Asante *Awowa*, and among the Europeans *indentured servants*. About a quarter of a million white debt slaves entered America before the nineteenth century (Boahen and Webster, 1970; p.69).

In pre-colonial Africa, social conditions were such that,

> All the white minorities living in Africa might own Black slaves, but slaves and white masters alike were all subjects of a Black Emperor: they were all under the same African political power. No historian worth his salt can permit the obscuring of this politico-social context, so that only the one fact of Black slavery emerges from it (Diop, 1987; p.92).

There was, however, an important distinction between the slave/master relationship in Africa and that in Europe between serf/lord, which is often overlooked. In Africa, slavery was more of a social distinction without economic consequence than fact. The African slave, "instead of being deprived of the fruits of his labor, as was the case with the artisan or the serf

---

[3] Diop (1987) contends that, "because of all these European-originated deportations, it can be asserted without exaggeration that present-day America is populated in part by citizens of slave (or indentured) origin, whether they be white or black" (p.147).

of the Middle Ages, could, on the contrary, add to it wealth given him by the 'lord'" (Diop, 1987: p.2). Slaves of the kings of Mali and the Askias of Gao "enjoyed complete liberty of movement. Thus an ordinary slave of Askia Daud, a native of Kanta, was able to carry out a pilgrimage to Mecca without his master's knowledge" (Diop, 1987; p.153).

To avoid the ugly connotations associated with commercial slaving, Vaughan (1986) suggested the use of *limbry*: "Existing data, albeit tenuous, suggest that about 80 percent of African societies had limbry" (p.174). In contrast to commercial slavery, African "limbries" 'were not on the whole mistreated, dehumanized or exploited" (Vaughan, 1986; p.174).

In Nigeria, the treatment of slaves was by no means harsh; nor was their lot deplorable. The majority were integrated into the society and the respective families of their owners in order to retain their loyalty, prevent rebellion and get the best out of them (Falola, 1985; p.99). The slaves were free to some extent; they could intermarry among themselves, own property and redeem themselves if they had the means.

More importantly, Boahen and Webster (1970) pointed out that:

> Slaves had many privileges in African kingdoms. In Asante, Oyo and Bornu, they held important offices in the bureaucracy, serving as the *Alafin's* Ilari in the subject towns of Oyo, as controller of the treasury in Asante, and as Waziri and army commanders in Bornu. Al-Hajj Umar made a slave emir of Nioro, one of the most important of the emirates of the Tokolor empire, and in the Niger Delta states slaves rose to become heads of Houses, positions next in rank to the king. Jaja, who had once been the lowest kind of slave, became the most respected king in the delta, and was no exception; one of the Alaketus of Ketu, and Rabeh of Bornu, rose from slave to king (p.69).

In Senegal also, slaves were closely associated to power. They were represented in royal courts and many became *de facto* ministers (Diop, 1987:2).

Since slaves faced few barriers to occupational mobility or economic advancement, there was hardly any need for a tumultuous social revolution, such as the French Revolution in which the exploited overthrew their lords.[4] Blatant exploitation of one class by another was not common. Even feudalism was rare, confined to only a few states such as Ethiopia, Rwanda and Burundi. Thus, revolutions, where they occurred at all in Africa, were

---

[4] Slavery, of course, was never under any circumstances an ideal institution and there were cases of slave revolts. One example was the revolt under Afonja in the Oyo empire. Another was the Koranko revolt in 1838 against the Susu of Sierra Leone. Led by Bilale, the Koranko ex-slaves built a fortified town to offer freedom to runaway slaves. In Calabar, the slaves united in an organization called the Blood Men, and forced the freeborn to respect their human rights (Boahen and Webster, 1970; p.70).

mostly initiated from above (palace revolutions) rather than from below. Open revolutions by the people against their indigenous rulers were not common; operational checks against despotism, as we shall see shortly, worked. Even when they failed, the people, as a last resort, could always exercise their inalienable right to move. Consequently, over the centuries, indigenous "African societies remained relatively stable" (Diop, 1987; p.2).

Stability, to a large extent, owed its origin primarily to the design and operation of the indigenous political system in which anybody — even including slaves — could participate in the decision-making process. There was representation of slaves, the freeborn and the nobility at the royal court in most African states. There was even foreign representation. The kings and chiefs of Angola and Asante, for example, allowed European merchants to send their representatives to their courts. No one was "locked out" of the decision-making process, to use modern phraseology. "The Dutch despatched an embassy to the *Asantehene's* court as early as 1701" (Boahen, 1986; p.58). In Angola, King Alfonso allowed the Portuguese merchants to send their spokesman, Dom Rodrigo, to his court.

Furthermore, the emphasis was on reaching unanimity or consensus. Individuals could voice their opinion and debate freely. To all intents and purposes, such a system was inherently democratic. It was not an oligarchy, plutocracy, stratocracy or autocracy in which only a few made the important decisions affecting the community.

In addition, stability was enhanced by decentralization. Lamphear (1986) noted:

> Recent research has proved that decentralized communities were far more complex and sophisticated than was at first commonly supposed by foreign observers. Moreover, these communities often were marked by a stability far greater than that of the centralized states. Certainly, centralization did not necessarily imply any "superior" political or cultural development (p.72).

Indigenous Curbs Against Despotism

> In the eyes of the Gikuyu people, the submission to a despotic rule of any particular man or a group, white or black, is the greatest humiliation to mankind
>
> - Jomo Kenyatta, late president of Kenya.

An intensive study of indigenous African political culture reveals an obsessive fear, on the part of the African natives, of state tyranny. In fact, most Africans considered the state as necessarily tyrannous and consequently structured their political institution to provide an effective bulwark against this threat. So fearful were such groups as the Igbo and the Nuer that, rather than risk state tyranny, they elected to dispense with a state or centralized bureaucracy altogether. According to Yelpaala (1983), "the oral traditions of some of these societies suggest quite clearly that decentralization was conscious and designed to curb the concentration of power in any individual or institution" (p.356). It was a useful check on the abuses or excess in the use of centralized political power.

Centralized leadership roles were also impugned through derogatory oral narratives and cast in negative paradigms. In such societies, when the elders acted arbitrarily, they were shunned. If they persisted, a village strike was called. When that failed to persuade the elders to mend their ways, they were abandoned; their people just moved to a new location to start a settlement. The burning fear of tyranny was also much evident even in those ethnic groups which chose to constitute themselves into states. The evidence for this is afforded by, first, their highly decentralized systems of government; second, by the detailed devolution of authority and assignment of responsibilities; and third, by the institution of a complex system of checks and balances to curb autocracy. Busia (1968) emphasized:

> The Asante were careful to prevent their chief from becoming tyrannical, and they developed a delicate balance between central authority and regional autonomy. If the chief abused his power, his subordinate chiefs, the members of his Council, could destool him. On the other hand, if a subordinate chief or Councillor tried to become too powerful, the chief could destool him. In each case, there were constitutional procedures to protect the individuals concerned, and to check against arbitrariness or vindictiveness (p.24).

Indeed, several *Asantehene* were deposed in the course of history. Among them were Kofi Kakari, who was deposed in 1874, and Mensa Bonsu, removed in February 1883 for his avarice and refusal to raise an army and reconquer Gyaman (Boahen and Webster, 1970; p.128). *Itwika*, the Gikuyu equivalent of the French revolution may also be recalled at this juncture. Gluckman (1965) also observed:

> The Barotse (Central African Republic) are apparently terrified of giving away power and always think of the dual pressures of the ambivalence of power on an individual. If royalty be seated among commoners to protect the people, its bearer may become puffed with power and abuse of it. He cannot be checked by another prince, since princes are in theory rivals for power; therefore when [one] has a deputy who restrains him and who acts in his

absence. . .this deputy is drawn from the ranks of those who interlink commoners and royalty. . .No one who has studied or worked in any political system can fail to be impressed by the Barotse's penetrating insight into relations of power.

Every position, according to Gluckman (1965), was balanced by another: the king against his council, ranked members of the council against each other or against their deputies. The leading executive official, the state *ngambela*, also had his own *ngambela*: this deputy or "second" was a councillor holding a permanent title who was specially charged, beyond other councillors, with restraining the state *ngambela* (Davidson, 1969:199).

The Oyo Empire of the Niger Delta (Nigeria) also developed an elaborate system of checks and balances to guard against despotism as may be recalled from the previous chapter. The political system centered around four powerful figures: the *Alafin*, the *Bashorun*, the *Oluwo* and the *Kankafo*. Theoretically, all power came from *Alafin* who was considered semi-divine.

Next to the *Alafin* was the *Bashorun*, the leader of the *Oyo Mesi* or Council of Notables, made up of seven prominent lineage chiefs of the capital. Furthermore, the councillors held judicial power with the *Alafin* in the capital. But the *Alafin* had no control over the appointment of the councillors since, as chiefs, they were lineage-appointed. Thus the *Bashorun*, who dominated the *Oyo Mesi*, had an ultimate check upon the *Alafin*.

The third power in the empire was the *Ogboni* headed by the *Oluwo*. The *Ogboni* chiefs, like the *Oyo Mesi*, were lineage-appointed. They also had judicial functions, but their primary function was the preservation of the Ife oracle which could accept or reject the *Bashorun's* decision to command the *Alafin's* suicide. But the *Alafin's* representative sat on the Ogboni council and his opinion carried considerable weight. Thus, he could use this position to check ambitious *Bashoruns*.

The *Kakanfo* was the field marshal with his seventy war chiefs, the *Eso*, who were expected to be loyal to the *Alafin*. The army was responsible to the *Oyo Mesi* who appointed and promoted its officers. But wouldn't the *Kakanfo* overthrow the *Oyo Mesi* and seize power? That was not possible, according to Boahen and Webster (1970):

> Civil authority feared the potential power of the Kakanfo and in order to isolate him from politics he was usually of humble (slave) origin and was forbidden to enter the capital city. The political system was thus a complex and delicate balance with checks and counterchecks against concentration of power in one man's hands (p.90).

Among the Tutsi of Rwanda, political power was delicately balanced between two constituent bodies to prevent abuse.

Although the king was theoretically absolute, there were some structural checks and controls on his power. Thus royal power was somewhat limited by the pressures that the influential Nilotic lineages - often holding hereditary offices - were able to exert on the central government. The association within the royal institution itself, of two equally assertive Tutsi groups, the royal *nyiginya* and matridynastic patrician also kept a certain precarious balance (Gibbs, 1965; p.422).

Native Freedom of Expression

The traditions of free speech and interchange of views do not support any claim that the denial of free speech or the suppression of opposition is rooted in traditional African political systems

- Dr. K.A. Busia, late premier of Ghana.

Freedom of expression was not only anchored in the African tradition but also taken for granted by most Africans. Consensus was the cardinal feature of the indigenous system of government, and this freedom was a *sine qua non* for consensus to be reached. The Igbo, for example, considered this freedom to be the birthright of every adult. Any member of the community could take part in public discussions of community affairs as was also the case in many other ethnic societies. Even in native court hearings in many African societies, anyone present at court could express his opinion freely. More than a century ago on the Gold Coast (now Ghana), Cruickshank (1854) noted: "anyone - even the most ordinary youth will offer his opinion, or make a suggestion with equal chance of being heard, as if it proceeded from the most experienced sage." The freedom to express an opinion was a fundamental right of the African people.

In most societies, Africans could attend the meetings of the Council of Elders if they so wished. They could raise objections to proposals or offer alternative ideas. The Councillors would then debate and assess their merits. Busia (1968) stressed:

The members of a traditional council allowed discussions, a free and frank expression of opinions, and if there was disagreement, they spent hours, even days if necessary, to argue and exchange ideas till they reached unanimity. Those who disagreed were not denied a hearing, or locked up in prison, or branded as enemies of the community. . .

The traditional practice indicated that the minority must be heard, and with respect and not hostility. The traditions of free speech and interchange of views do not support any claim that the denial of free speech or the suppression of opposition is rooted in traditional African political systems (p.29).

Besides freedom of expression, criticisms of the actions of tribal leaders and government were the daily features of public discourse. As observed repeatedly, the chief's imperative was the survival of the *whole* community, not his own individual survival. He was merely the leader of the people and did not constitute the whole community himself. Any action he contemplated that would impinge on the life of the whole community needed to be subjected to scrutiny by his people. Critical reviews were inevitable. Again, Busia (1968) observed that,

The Asante provided opportunities for 'commoners', those who were ruled, to express criticism, either through their lineage heads, or through a chosen leader recognized as spokesman for the commoners; through him the body of free citizens could criticise the government and express their wishes when they thought that undesirable measures were being contemplated or enforced; in the last resort, they could depose their rulers (p.26).

The kings could also be criticized. The traditional practice was not direct criticism, as it was imperative to defer or show respect to the royal highness. However, the king was criticized through the use of proverbs, hints and allusions. The wise kings listened and rectified errors of judgment. The others were poisoned, assassinated or abandoned by the people. Recall the case of Xhosa Chief Ngqika, who in 1800, passed two unpopular laws and was forced to retract them when his people started leaving.

At village assemblies, when issues were placed before the people, debates and criticisms were allowed. But once a majority decision had been made, no further debate or criticism was permitted. At this stage, the decision reflected the will of the community, arrived at through the participation by all members. To criticize it meant going against the wishes of the whole community and not just the decision of the chief or the king alone.

Those deeply offended by the community decision could always exercise their right to exit: leave the village to found a new settlement or kingdom elsewhere. The history of Africa is filled with such instances. Those who stayed were obliged to go along with the group decision. To foreigners, it gave a deceptive appearance that the ruler dictated policy which was humbly accepted by a docile people without question or criticism. Clearly, this was not the case. Modern African leaders also misinterpreted this as "unity" behind the chief. But the decision was not imposed by the chief or one single individual. It was reached collectively by consensus. Everyone participated in that process. Perhaps a Western example would help clarify this crucial issue.

Suppose a university professor takes a group of students on a study trip to Washington, D.C., London or Paris. The professor's responsibility is to ensure that no harm comes the group's way so that they could all return safely to their educational institution 190 miles away from the big city.

After a tour of places of "educational interest", the group decides to take a recreational intersession. One student suggests the theater, but another is more interested in patronizing a restaurant. Museums and art galleries are also suggested. After much debate and wrangling, they opt for the marina. Richard however is not happy. He is much opposed to the marina idea. He may decide to "stick with the group" and not be seen as "going against the wishes of his class." Or he may decide to go off by himself, if the professor would allow it. On his own, he could get lost in a strange city. He could fall victim to daylight robbery. Or he could fail to rejoin the group, in which case they would leave without him and he would have to pay for his way back. After contemplating all these possibilities, he decides to "stick with the group." So they all board the bus and depart for the marina.

Someone meets this group at the beach and comments that they are all meekly following the professor like a herd of lambs. Since no sustained, vigorous or organized opposition to the professor could be seen, he must have been an autocrat, dragging the students to the beach against their wishes in a very undemocratic manner. Obviously, such comments would be misinformed and inappropriate. Unfortunately, some foreign comments about the indigenous African political system were along similar lines as no vibrant opposition to the chief was seen.

Modern African leaders also pointed to the "docility" of the group and the deference shown to the professor. He was not challenged or criticized. The group was "united" behind the professor. There was no dissent. This too was a misinterpretation of the situation.

In the traditional African political systems, there was thus no sustained criticism or opposition as in the Western sense. Once a majority or group decision was reached, everyone "stuck with it." Those virulently opposed could go off by themselves and many did.

Peasants' Power

One fact which is often overlooked in pre-colonial African history was the strong relative bargaining power of the ruled vis à vis the rulers. True political power, due to a combination of factors, rested with the people or the masses and emanated from the people to the ruler. The chiefs and kings were, more appropriately, leaders and not rulers.

The first factor was the land tenure system. Except for deserts and lacustrine areas in central Africa, land was relatively uniform in quality and abundance. Further ownership of land resided with ancestors, not with the state or rulers. This factor established what may be regarded as complete independence of the ruled from the rulers. The king or chiefs could not exercise control over the people through the dispensation of land ownership titles as the lords of old England could over the serfs. In Africa, the monarchs held the land only in trust.

Second, the abundance of land meant that those who derived their sustenance from farming could move from one place to another if they did not want to live under a certain political system. As one historian noted, "Given provocation, subjects could migrate beyond the borders as well as within the boundaries of a kingdom. Malcontents [could] join. . .some [other] polity" (Bates, 1987; p.41).

Williams (1987) also noted this for the Mossi:

In addition to these councils on various local levels, the Mossi developed another way of controlling the behavior of rulers. This was the practice of moving from one unsatisfactory village or district to a more favorable one. Whole villages might move from one district to another. No district chief could afford this direct reflection on his ability to 'keep the people', the most important of his inauguration oaths. It also tended to undermine the economy of his area (p.214).

The right to move was a universally recognized fact and option across Africa. Witness the fact that there are over 10 million refugees in Africa today. In indigenous Africa, mobility was a political tool the people could use to extract and bargain for favorable treatment from their rulers. For example, among the Ganda of Uganda, control over the abuse of power by chiefs was effected by a number of mechanisms:

The leading *ssaza* chief, the one holding the highest degree of precedence, had the title of *Sabadu* in his service of the king. . .The *Sabadu* of a chief, could not only advise, but he could criticize his chief for abuse of authority. Peasants who felt that they had been mistreated could complain to him so that he might reason with the chief concerning their complaint. The king, through his royal council, heard cases involving charges that chiefs were failing to carry out their duties properly in governing their people and were abusing them. The king would remove such a chief from office. In fact, the king had the power to discharge a chief from office, other than the chief of a clan, without a trial. Finally, peasants always had the refuge of leaving the service of an arbitrary chief and entering that of another (Carlston, 1968:252).

The Sukuma of Tanzania, as well as many other Bantu tribes, exercised the option to exit when faced with despotism. "Control of abuse of power by a chief existed through the practice of emigration to another chiefdom, together with the respect for tradition imposed upon him by his elders" (Carlston, 1968:438).

Third, commoners possessed institutionalized means of giving voice and thereby securing more favorable policies from their governments (Bates, 1987; p.41). Commoners often controlled particular offices, such the "prime ministership", the principal administrative office in the nation. Chiefs often had to rule through councils dominated by non-royals. The Oyo Mesi of the Oyo Empire is one extreme example; it could depose the Alafin and compel his "suicide" (divestiture).

In many cases, commoners kept the selection and appointment of administrative personnel out of the hands of the king. The rule of hereditary succession to headmanships and chieftainships insured that lineage elders could control the selection of administrative personnel.

Fourth, most states had no standing armies. The people were the army and commoners also exerted considerable influence upon public officials through the agency of secret societies (as in Yoruba, Igbo and Kpelle). Weapons were not monopolized by the royal army where there was one. Anybody could make or own spears, bows, arrows and even powder and shot. Nor could the king ban the importation of weapons. Trade routes were open and free. The chief or king could not use an army to back his rule or enforce unpopular policies. An army, where it existed, was under full control of the council of elders, not the chief or king and it was only useful externally to ward off external aggression or subjugate other people. But internally, the army served no useful purpose which explains why most African societies disbanded the army after the cessation of external hostilities. Where they were not disbanded, checks were set in place. Recall that the *Kakanfo* (field marshal) of the Oyo empire was prohibited from entering the capital city.

The citizenry thus possessed both the option to exit and the capacity to give voice to their interests. Their political position was further enhanced by the level of competition for office within the political elite. As we saw earlier, though kingship was hereditary, it was not automatic. In most cases, there were several claimants to the throne. Contestants for office had to gather a following. In competing for supporters, they obviously had to make pledges to generate benefits if they should win the office. Bates (1987) concluded:

> The evidence suggests that while there was inequality in the states
> of pre-colonial Africa, those who held positions of privilege had to
> insure that the benefits created by the states were widely shared.
> For the bargaining power of the masses, relative to the elites, was
> strong, and to retain power the elites had to serve the interests of

their followers, if only because they would otherwise lose their followers physically or politically, or other elites would displace them (p.42).

African natives did not go on demonstrations, waving placards and chanting "People's Power" in front of the chief's hut. There was no need to do so. For they already had the power: to leave the village, to voice their opinion, to participate in government, and to play a role in the selection and removal of government officers. This is what peasants' power or empowerment is all about.

2. The Empires

African imperial cultures were suffused with a great sense of hierarchy which made decentralized decision-making possible. The general hierarchical structure may be presented as below:

THE HIERARCHICAL STRUCTURE OF AN AFRICAN KING-
DOM OR EMPIRE
KING
INNER COUNCIL
STATE COUNCIL
PROVINCE PROVINCE PROVINCE
PRINCE
INNER COUNCIL
PROVINCIAL ASSEMBLY
VILLAGE VILLAGE VILLAGE
CHIEF
COUNCIL OF ELDERS
PEASANTS

At the apex sat a supreme ruler, a hereditary position but subject to contest within the ruling dynasty. Competition among ambitious princes could open up fractures. Such fissions did indeed occur, resulting in the splintering of many empires.

The supreme ruler, a semi-divine figure, was assisted in the administration of the empire by an Inner Council (cabinet). This Council handled the day-to-day administration of the kingdom/empire with a State Council. Its composition was mixed. The ruler could appoint relatives, friends or persons of acclaimed repute to serve on the Council but with full Council consent; that is, appointees were not "imposed" on the Council. The rest of the councillor positions (representatives of the various provinces) were of a hereditary status which precluded the possibility of "packing" with the ruler's appointees.

Without the State Council, the ruler was impotent. He could not legislate or take any decision of vital importance to the community without the expressed approval of the Council. Such unilateral decisions could result in deposition or regicide. In any case, the executive functions and political role of the supreme ruler were severely restricted by the divinity of his office. He could technically be excluded from government administration and even political influence by the insistence on strict compliance of various behavioral taboos and the performance of numerous religious rituals.

The next lower layer of government in the hierarchy was provincial. Each empire was divided into provinces (or cantons) and was ruled by the siblings or offspring of the ruler (princes). Each prince would have his own inner council and rule through the Provincial Assembly made up of representatives of the various chiefdoms that formed the province. There was a tendency to duplicate every function of government at the lower level. The local capital would become a replica of the central capital when local chieftain duplicated the king's apparatus for collecting tribute, judicial organization, and his army. Curtin *et al.,* (1978) noted: "This pattern contrasts sharply with the government of any 20th century nation, in Africa or elsewhere, in which particular functions are specifically reserved for central or for local government" (p.164).

> At its maximum extension, the pattern may be represented as a structure of concentric 'circles' of diminishing control, radiating from the core. The core, usually the area of earliest political consolidation, continued to be ruled directly by the central authority. Then came an inner area of closely assimilated and politically integrated dependencies. Beyond it was the circle of relatively secure vassal polities who enjoyed a certain degree of autonomy. This circle merged with the next circle of tribute-paying polities straining at the center's political leash. Beyond, the center's control became increasingly symbolic, confining itself to fewer and fewer functions. . .And beyond a certain point, control became erratic, ineffective and, finally, impossible. The center would only practise political intimidation and extract sporadic tribute through institutionalized raiding or undisguised pillage. Finally, came the potential frontier — areas beyond the effective reach of the metropolitan power which nevertheless sometimes conceitedly claimed to control it (Kopytoff, 1989; p.29).

Several reasons may be adduced for this duplication: exhibition of bond (or common ancestry) with ruler at the capital; recognition of suzerainty; or a bid for total local autonomy to assure less reliance on the capital; or a practical response to the limitations of power by distance. Whatever the reason, however, this feature meant the king or supreme ruler was *dispensable*. A subsidiary or tributary state could break away more easily as virtually all the king's apparatus and even regalia had been duplicated at the local level.

The duplication was also a reflection of another operative constraint — "the technology of reach" —which imposed clear limits on the political penetration that the center could achieve both in geographical extent and, locally, in depth (Kopytoff, 1989; p.29). Transportation difficulties, lack of effective means of communications, and paucity of military resources conspired to weaken the center's control as the polity expanded.

At the local or village level, traditional political structures of the vassal states were generally left undisturbed. Traditional local rulers, chiefs, retained their authority but saw their duties expanded to include the payment of annual tributes and the provision of local levies for the imperial army. In return, the imperial government fulfilled such obligations as defending the local community against external aggression and keeping existing trade routes open for commerce.

The imperial administrative system of government was highly *decentralized* and the political configuration was of the *confederate/federal* variety. Imperialism or subjugation, thus, was more nominal than real. "Subjugated" communities enjoyed considerable latitude and autonomy to handle their affairs and rule themselves with little imperial interference.

There were of course numerous variations and modifications of this general paradigm. The specific duties of the imperial ruler, the exact composition of the State Council, its powers, its selection process, the nature of constitutional checks against the ruler, the executive powers of provincial governors, and the degree of autonomy enjoyed by the subjugated all varied from one empire to another. But the building blocks or the structure remained fundamentally the same and the exceptions to the general norm were very few.

One was strong centralized imperial administration which occurred in only few empires such as the Zulu and the Yoruba. Still, these centralized systems possessed checks against the supreme ruler. Another exceptional imperial doctrine was assimilation, occurring in few empires such as the Zulu, the Yoruba, the Zande and the Islamic empires (Mandinka, Mali, and Kanuri). Even then, assimilation in the Islamic empires was religious rather than cultural — an important distinction.

Converts to Islam retained most of their tradition and cultural practices. Additionally, the introduction of Islam was gradual. Little evidence exists in African history to support forcible imposition of Islam on the local people. At least in West Africa (in the Ghana and Kanuri empires), many ethnic groups which refused to accept Islam were allowed to follow their own traditional religious beliefs. Islam was forced to adapt itself to the political and social practices of African natives. Some Muslim rulers also intermarried with the natives and adopted native African customs. It was this *adaptability* which enabled the Ghana (Muslim) empire and the Sefawa dynasty of the Kanuri empire to enjoy the longest reigns in Africa. Further, coversion to Islam was voluntary and relatively easy.

African religion, it may be emphasized, did not differ radically from Islam, Christianity and other religions in tenets. Each religion recognized a Supreme God and the cosmological division between the living (mortals) and the superhuman (spiritual). What differed among them was the provider of the *link* between the two worlds. The principal intercessor was Jesus Christ for the Christians, Prophet Mohammed for the Muslims and deities, ancestors and kings for the Africans. Conversion to a new religion essentially amounted to accepting a new intercessor. The conversion did not require a profound alteration of the conception of the two worlds or fundamental adjustments in societal relationships. Only the provider of the link was different. Thus, it was relatively easy to persuade Africans to accept or substitute for their own a new intermediary, purported to be more potent, holy and saintly. The new intercessor, when so accepted by Africans, played exactly the same mediating role in the African religious scheme of things. Thus, religious assimilation in the Islamic empires did not result in any violent reordering of social relations and dramatic alterations in behavior.

Cultural assimilation, by contrast, was far more difficult to accomplish. This required the shedding of centuries-old beliefs, the uprootment of cultural practices, the complete overhaul of ideological and value systems, and radical transformations in social behavior, expectations and allegiances. But in Africa, the pull toward local particularism and kinship — the articulating idiom of social relations — has always been very strong. As a result, complete cultural assimilation, where attempted in African history, was generally not successful. A notable example was French colonial policy of cultural assimilation — a miserable fiasco. In indigenous Africa itself, only the Zulu, the Yoruba and to a smaller extent the Zande empires achieved some success at cultural assimilation. The general failure of cultural assimilation is attested to by the fact that over 2,000 ethnic groups preserved their cultural identities.

Checks Against African Imperialism

There were a number of factors which checked any measure of African imperialism and rigid central control. The first was, of course, the language barrier. In the absence of written literature and formal education, it took a considerable amount of time to learn the language of the imperial overlords. This difficulty constrained rapid assimilation of the subjugated group. The second factor was the fact that lines of authority in indigenous Africa were based upon kinship and ancestral connections. It was difficult to supplant these and substitute authority from imperial officers who lacked kinship relations and, thus, legitimacy.

The third check was geographical. Africa was sparsely populated in the past. Ethnic groupings were fluid. Ethnic groups that found themselves under alien tyranny always moved into Africa's great expanses of unoccupied land to uphold their independence and protect their cultures. Those who could not move because they were hemmed in by the sea and powerful ethnic groups on their sides, such as the Fanti of Ghana, either revolted or transferred their allegiance to an adjacent and stronger kingdom and sought its protection. Many groups formed such alliances even with European traders who declared protectorates over them. Indeed, much of the colonization of West Africa began with these protectorates.

The fourth check against African imperialism was logistical. Despotism necessitated the possession of efficient population control instruments. These were unavailable due to the underdeveloped state of technology, transportation and communication networks in the early days (Busia, 1968). When a subjugated people on the outer reaches of an empire broke away, it often took several weeks for the information to reach the capital by footpath. Talking drums reduced the informational lag somewhat but not by much.

Rwanda and Burundi, however, appear to be the few exceptional places where the conditions for despotism over subjugated ethnic groups were fulfilled: only two tribes (the Watutsi and the Hutu) were involved and there were no unoccupied areas to escape to. The history of these two countries has been marked by bloody tribal atrocities.

The Watutsi originally migrated from the north and established their sovereignty over the local ethnic group, the Hutus. Centuries of subjugation made the Hutus feel inferior and held in serfdom by the Watutsi minority. In Rwanda, the Watutsi made up 10 percent of the population and the Hutus 89 percent. In 1959, the Hutus overthrew their Watutsi masters, killing an estimated 100,000 and subsequently winning majority rule, in 1962 (Lamb, 1984: 13).

In neighboring Burundi, which also gained its independence from Belgium in 1962, the Watutsi worried that power might be transferred to the Hutu majority. It has been suggested that:

> The minority Watutsi government came up with a simple solution: it set out, in 1972, to massacre every Hutu with education, a government job or money. In a three-month period, upwards of 200,000 Hutus were slain. Their homes and schools were destroyed (Lamb, 1984:12).

Such rule, however, was generally the exception in pre-colonial Africa. Traditionally, persecuted groups always moved. But colonialism, independence and population growth substantially reduced the number of unoccupied spaces oppressed people could escape to. Furthermore, the acquisition of more and better means of coercion after independence radically altered the logistics of population control. Modern and sophisticated arms and aircraft now afford African leaders much tighter control over a great number of people and over a much wider geographical area than in pre-colonial times. The potential for despotism, therefore, became much greater in modern than in pre-colonial Africa.

Back in the 18th and 19th centuries, the main weapons were the bow and arrow, or the spear, which everybody could make. They were, in that sense, democratic weapons. "No man [could] be a despot for long, especially where the technology [was] relatively primitive. It was only in the latter part of the last century, after the introduction of guns, that the *kabaka* [of Buganda] had even a small standing army" (Gibbs, 1965; p.91). Most societies disbanded their armies after a war or cultivated food to feed themselves or the king as in the Zulu kingdom. Bauer (1984) put it succinctly: "Despotism and kleptocracy do not inhere in the nature of African cultures or in the African character; but they are now rife in what was once called British colonial Africa, notably West Africa" (p.104). Analysts would probably do well to look for the causes of these elsewhere, other than in indigenous African culture and character.

Despotism will emerge in *any* political regime which lacks an effective system of checks and balances. Common sense also suggests that the design of any such system of safeguards ought to be left completely out of the hands of the ruler. A president of an African country cannot be expected to hand over power or create a "watch dog" to police his own activities. Even "primitive" peasants recognized this common-sensical fact when they created councils of elders to check autocratic tendencies. The chief or king could not remove the councillors as their positions were hereditary. Modern African elites have much to learn from the "backward" peasants.

Absence of Strong Centralized Rule

Devolution of authority was the common feature of ancient African empires. This was particularly evident in such states as the Zande and the Oyo empires. Very few African empires had rigidly centralized administrations. These exceptions included the Kingdom of Dahomey, the Asante Empire, the Kingdom of Kongo and the Zulu Kingdom. But even so, the degree of centralization tended to be exaggerated, as was noted of the Zulu kingdom (Maylam, 1986:28).

Historical evidence further suggests that those empires characterized by strong, centralized administrations were inherently unstable and chronically threatened by internal revolts. Although superior military might have kept rebellious vassal states in check, it was only a matter of time before the subjugated states successfully asserted their independence or bolted for freedom.

This was also the conclusion reached by Williams (1987):

> The actual fact is that the traditional African political system was fundamentally and structurally *anti-empire*. The very circumstances of the endless process of segmentation, of forever splintering off to form little independent mini-states, developed a built-in disunity, reinforced by the attending growth of different languages. But self-government or chiefdom was a way of life, not a theory (p.283).

Chiefs and elders, as we have seen, were leaders and not rulers. The cultural imperative was independence. The same operating principles applied when a group of states united to form a kingdom and kingdoms to form an empire. But the assertion of central control often led to rebellions and the break-up of the kingdoms and empires. Wickins (1981) was emphatic in his conclusions:

> Strong centralized government was exceptional in sub-Saharan Africa. Poverty of communications made it difficult to prevent states from breaking up, and it is no accident that some of the most stable and enduring ones had navigable rivers, notably the kingdoms of the western Sudan, served by the middle Niger. Secondly, even relatively wealthy rulers, like the Mwene Mutapa, could not maintain a professional army of any size to enforce commands. Executive weakness and bad communications, together with total or general illiteracy, necessitated a devolution of powers of administration, either to appointed officials or to subordinate rulers, and in the absence of currency those exercising such powers had to be paid in kind. This meant in effect that they had either to be granted the right of appropriating a share of locally collected tribute or taxes (such as market dues and tolls) or to be given non-heritable cattle or, if it was coveted and not freely available for the taking, land (p.228).

In Bunyoro subordinate chiefs were allowed to distribute land, conscript labor and collect tribute, part of which had to be passed on to the king. The provincial governors of the Kongo kingdom had to collect taxes on behalf of the king. Similarly, among the Nguni authority was divided among subordinate chiefs. They retained a portion of the death duties and taxes collected on behalf of the king. In the western Sudan empires taxes and tolls were levied by local rulers who passed on a share of the proceeds to the central government.

In the 15th century onward, however, there was a brief trend, often promoted by the influence of Islam, toward greater power at the center, closer control over official positions and extended use of forced labor, slave labor and the establishment of servile standing armies, as in the Hausa states in the 15th century and Asante in the 18th and 19th. But,

> Such empires could fall apart as suddenly as they were built up, as did Oyo in the first half of the 19th century and Akwamu on the Gold Coast in the 18th. Neither had a literate bureaucracy. Even Asante, with its rudimentary and partially literate bureaucracy, was subject to internal tensions and never obtained complete control over some of its constituent parts.

> In African states, as in medieval Europe, appointed officials tended to become hereditary, and hereditary subordinate rulers to become less zealous in carrying out the wishes of the paramount ruler. Control became more nominal and less real, the more remote the center was. Dispersal of taxing rights invites — indeed, constitutes — fragmentation of sovereignty: land set aside for the support of public officials is likely in practice to become hereditary and likewise to cause loss of power and even collapse at the center (Wickins, 1981; p.229).

Perhaps to overcome the danger of uncontrollable officials, members of the royal family were sometimes given administrative, or at least tax-collecting, duties. This was the case in the Ovimbunda states of the Benguela highlands in the 19th century, the Hausa state of Nupe, the empire of Mwene Mutapa and the sultanate of Fez in Morocco, the Asante and the Zulu kingdoms. But then, the royals or local rulers given this privilege could accumulate resources and demand their independence from the center.

Perhaps to obviate this potential threat, some kingdoms employed the services of slave officials for collecting tribute, each with his own administrative staff as in the medieval empire of Ghana. The Asante employed the services of eunuchs for tax-collection purposes while the Hausa state in Zaria entrusted these duties to slave generals. But even this was no insurance against the diminution of the authority of the center. Because of functional mobility of slaves, it was not impossible for the exceptionally able ones to establish their own states, like the celebrated Ja-Ja of Opobo in the latter part of the 19th century (Wickins, 1981; p.229).

The factors making for centralization of authority were lacking in indigenous Africa. In fact,

> Some of the large territorial states - Funj is an example, the kingdom of Mwene Mutapa (of which Great Zimbabwe was a part) another — *were virtually confederations of autonomous areas.* Poor

communications, together with local particularism and dynastic intrigue, made it frequently difficult for a central government to assert its
will. This was to be seen even in Ethiopia, a region subject to the
unifying force of religion and faced with threats from both Muslim
pastoralists, chiefly Galla and Somali, and Muslim sheikdoms, which,
however, were themselves constantly at odds with one another despite
the bond of Islam (Wickins, 1981; p.229).

In addition, there was always the tendency of a kingdom to splinter upon
the death of the king for practical reasons. Quite often, the king chose his
eldest son to succeed him. But as Curtin, *et al.*, (1978) reminded,

> When such a king had ruled successfully for a period and finally
> died, the senior son who became the next king found himself in a
> difficult position. He tried but invariably failed to become a
> centralizing father-king. The existing chiefs were his half-brothers,
> who saw no reason to obey someone of their own generation. They
> knew that if they united in resistance to his authority, they would all
> survive in power. Their close kinship made combined action easy.
> They paid no tribute, kept completely independent armies and
> maintained their own courts of final appeal. In effect, the kingdom
> broke up into a number of temporarily self-sufficient minikingdoms
> (p.165).

Various ethnic societies tried to overcome this problem of succession.
Many rotated the kingship among the royal lineages. Dahomey adopted a
unique rule: only princes born of royal wives during their father's reign were
eligible to succeed to the throne. The Oyo of Nigeria went further:

> Until the early 19th century the eldest son of an *alafin* (king) was
> debarred from the succession by a curious custom probably designed to
> prevent political intrigue against an *alafin* by an impatient heir-
> apparent. During the father's life, an *alafin*'s first-born son filled the
> important office of *aremo* but at his father's death he too had to die. Nor
> was he the only one to accompany the deceased *alafin* on his journey to
> the spirit world: all the *alafin*'s personal officials had to perish with their
> master. Thus a newly-appointed *alafin* had a free hand in selecting his
> own executives in the spheres of administration, religion and justice and
> could appoint officers loyal to himself (Stride and Ifeka, 1971:298).

But the Oyo system of government was not autocratic. The *alafin*'s
authority was balanced by those of the *Oyo Mesi* and *Bashorun*.

In spite of these precautionary steps, kingdoms and empires were
constantly fracturing, largely due to situational factors and cultural obsession
for independence. Of course, some historians, especially those with a tinge

of African nationalism or those imbued with an inclination to "redeem Africa's past glory," have emphasized African capability to build states and to run a centralized bureaucracy. But logistical and situational barriers stood in the way, compounded by lack of effective systems of communications and population. Besides, state-building is not the only yardstick by which "African achievements" can be measured.[5] Besides, "If we condemn European imperialism as imposed on unwillingly subjected peoples, should we not also condemn African imperialism?" (Isichei, 1977; p.64).[6]

Naturally, there has been considerable disagreement among historians about the extent of centralization of power in the native African empires or kingdoms. Some historians argue that, though its vassal states had some degree of autonomy, the Kingdom of Ashanti was rigid in its demands for tribute and was highly centralized. For example, Isichei (1977) asserted:

> The state was financed by tribute from conquered areas, a poll tax levied in Kumasi, death duties and tolls. A large sector of the economy was controlled by the state, including the royal mines, worked by slave miners, ivory hunting and much of the area's trade. . .

> The king had a deliberate policy of limiting the growth of the merchant class since this might ultimately challenge his authority. He restricted the accumulation of capital by imposing heavy rates of interest and exacting heavy death duties (p.63).

Daaku (1971), however, argued that there was little evidence to suggest that the kings, chiefs and elders of Asante exercised such complete monopoly over large sectors of the economy. The Asante people were free to engage in trade and other economic activities without much interference from the state. Busia (1951) was more emphatic:

> In spite of the bonds of clanship and the possession of common

---

[5] For example,
      The So people (who live in the Lake Chad area in Nigeria) were mainly settled farmers but among them were craftsmen of considerable industrial and artistic merit. They were able to work in both clay and metals to manufacture household utensils, tools, and works of art for religious purposes. Impressive objects found by archaelogists include burial urns and naturalistic figures of animals and human beings both in clay and bronze (Stride and Ifeka, 1971:115).

[6] There is a further lesson in this. Because of age-old rivalries between Asante and the other Akan tribes, an assertive action by the Asante often made other tribes nervous. Ghana would have been torn apart by secessionist wars if after independence in 1957 its government had been dominated by the Asante. Fortunately, its first president, the late Dr. Kwame Nkrumah, hailed from the small Nzima tribe. Zaire and Nigeria were not so lucky: Katanga war of secession under Moise Tshome in 1960; Biafran war under Ojukwu. By extension, Zulu nationalism has no place in post-apartheid South Africa any more than Afrikaner or Xhosa domination.

social and political institutions, language, and religion, the Ashanti Union was, as far as can be ascertained, *a loose confederation.*

Each of the segments had had a previous existence as a distinct community before the Union, and had developed in its own region a well-established form of government through the lineage, village, and sub-division, which enabled it to manage its own affairs. . .

The history of the Ashanti Union in the 19th century gives the impression that the Union was a loose one in which the separate States exercised a wide degree of autonomy, and showed a tendency toward complete independence (p.88).

In fact, despite the superior Asante military strength, there were persistent revolts against Asante imperialism by the Fanti in the southern states and also in the northern states such as Gyaman and Gonja. The Fanti, for example, objected to the annual tribute in slaves demanded by Asante. There were similar revolts against the Tukulor of the Bambara empire (western Sudan), the Samori of the Mandinka empire and the Zulu in southern Africa. When Shaka succeeded Dingiswayo, who was killed in 1818, as Zulu king, he proceeded to build an efficient military and highly centralized state. He established his headquarters at Bulawayo. Though he governed with a small group of loyal councillors, Shaka remained the source of power and decision because of his leadership ability, the loyalty of the army, his power to appoint and dismiss subordinate rulers, and also because he laid the basis of an evolving unity. This was manifested by the fact that Zulu became the basic language and the absorption of outsiders as citizens, provided they swore allegiance to Shaka. The trend was toward nation-building, but fear was the main cohesive factor:

Because of this fear on the part of some, but mostly because neighboring states were disrupted by the rise of the Zulu kingdom, widespread migrations carried refugees in all directions. Many sought refuge nearer the coast where European power was increasing. Others broke away and founded their own states. The Nguni ruler, Sobhuza, organized a group which resisted Shaka for a time but eventually withdrew to more defensible terrain in the mountains overlooking the Pongola River. Here, during the 1820s and 1830s, Nguni and Sotho peoples laid the basis for the Swazi Kingdom. Resistance also came from Mzilikazi, a subordinate who defied Shaka and fled with Ndebele people to the eastern Transvaal in 1823, and near Pretoria in 1825. There Mzilikazi and the Ndebele became a dominant kingdom including Nguni and Sotho peoples (Harris, 1987; p.144).

Other groups successfully broke away and founded other states such as LeSotho. In 1828, Shaka was assassinated, marking the end of only a ten-year rule. This was inevitable according to Maylam (1985):

> The potential for internal conflict and disintegration was built into the Zulu political structure. The Shakan state system had been superimposed upon a pre-existing structure of autonomous communities. . .

> Shaka had striven to build a centralized state, but he lacked both adequate administrative machinery and an effective communications system to be able to maintain centralized authority throughout the realm. This deficiency carried two implications. Firstly, the relative weakness at the center enabled local chiefs to exercise considerable autonomy. Secondly, in an effort to offset this decentralizing tendency, Zulu kings were compelled to delegate authority to members of the royal family. While it was intended that these should become instruments of royal power throughout the state, in practice they could become rivals to the king by building up power bases in their own areas and challenging royal authority (p.76).

There were striking similarities between the rise and fall of the Zulu and the Asante empires. Both were characterized by strong, centralized tendencies and an expanded role of the military in administration. But neither succeeded or endured. They were each plagued by persistent revolts, suggesting that this type of rule was inappropriate given the conditions that existed in indigenous Africa.

All in all, strong centralized rule was not the characteristic feature of government in native African empires and kingdoms. Attempts made in this direction came to grief, which should serve as lesson to modern-day African governments. Devolution of authority, decentralization, and a loose confederate-type of relationship with constituent parts have proven to work best in an African political entity composed of different ethnic groups. Obviously, a modern African government that insists on "a strong, unitary state and constitution" and obedience of orders from the center would only be courting disaster. Unfortunately, this was the type of governmental system that many African nationalists sought to establish in their countries under "one-party states" after independence from colonial rule. The disastrous results are now there for all to see.

B. A SUMMARY OF THE FEATURES OF THE INDIGENOUS POLITICAL SYSTEM

African political systems and languages may be diverse and multitudinous. However, there were many basic beliefs, practices and institutions which were common to them. These may now be summarized.

BELIEFS

- A strong sense of family values was pervasive. Kinship was the article of social organization. The community's interests anteceded those of the individual for purposes of survival. However within the community, the individual was free-born politically, economically and socially. He was free to do what he chose with his life. Life was what he made of it in the community.
- The African philosophical tenet of "I am because we are" did not preclude individual achievement, prosperity or accumulation of wealth. The philosophical tenet, social mores and obligations merely set the parameters within which the individual could freely operate.
- There were differences in wealth, social status and power. The wealthy were revered. Their success was attributed to a blessing by ancestors, luck or sheer hard work. Industriousness was admired and valued but laziness was abjured.

NATIVE COURTS

- Virtually all the indigenous African states had courts to settle disputes and uphold individual and property rights within the community. Court hearings were open and any adult could attend them. Those present at court could air their opinions freely. The chief, who served as the judge, would weigh all viewpoints and reach a verdict.
- The judge was not infallible. His decision could be appealed or overruled by popular opinion. There was no written law and precedents were not important. Each case was adjudged upon the prevailing circumstances. Thus, native law was not rigid but adaptive to new situations.
- Decisions could be appealed from the family court to the village court and ultimately to the royal court.
- There was a detectable bias in favor of parents and the elderly as in disputes between a son and his mother or grandfather. However, native law came down more heavily on erring elders, for they were supposed to know better and set a good example for the youth.

- In the stateless societies, disputes were settled by moots. Although there were no sanctioning bodies, settlement was enforced by the rule of public opinion.

POLITICAL SYSTEM

- Tribal governments began at the village level. The founding lineage chose the chief. Chieftaincy was hereditary but not automatic. The choice of an heir was subject to the approval of the "royal" lineage or the Council of Elders," and, in some tribes, by the "Village Assembly." Even so, there were always rival claimants and competition for kingship, which generated the search for supporters. The chief was a leader, not a ruler. He was chosen to execute the will of the people and could not usurp such a will.
- The chief had an inner or privy council of advisers to assist him in administration. The duty of the advisers was to gauge public opinion and reprimand the chief, if need be, when he erred.
- The second unit of government was the "Council of Elders," who were the heads of the various lineages and thus representatives of the commoners, the majority. Council meetings were open and any adult could sit on them, participate and air their opinions freely. Dissidents were not jailed or massacred. Unanimity was the rule and when an issue proved contentious, a village meeting was called to put the issue before the people.
- The third unit was the "Village Assembly" - public assembly of all citizens. At the village meetings, individuals exercised their freedom of expression without fear of harassment. It was up to individuals to make sensible suggestions or fools of themselves. But their right to freedom of expression was respected and upheld. At such meetings, however, every effort was made to reach a consensus.
- Despotism was a theoretical possibility but not a practical fact. There were four checks against autocratic tendencies: the "royal" lineage, the inner council of advisers, the council of elders (headmen) and the village assembly. Without the councils, chiefs were powerless. Further, new laws had to be promulgated and ratified at the village assemblies for full debate by the people. Thus, in many states, there were checks and balances to curb despotism and the chief's power.
- The people always retained an inalienable power to exit. When all the checks against despotism failed, an unpopular or autocratic chief was abandoned through emigration beyond the boundaries of the chiefdom or state.
- The traditional role of the chief was not autocracy but to ensure the survival of his tribe, serve as an arbiter of disputes, act as caretaker of

ancestral land and govern by consensus. He had to be impartial and be willing to listen to and encourage alternative viewpoints. The oppression and slaughter of his own people did not make sense. Nor did brutal despotism fit into this traditional role and the social system where there was intense competition for supporters and retainers.

- In the empires and kingdoms over subjugated tribes, the imperial rule was one of confederation. Strong centralized government was rare, and where it came into existence, did not last long because of the African's cultural passion for independence.

- There were two types of imperial rule: indirect rule with extensive local autonomy, and rule by assimilation. Assimilation, in turn, was of two types: religious and cultural. Religious assimilation, as in the Islamic empires, was not forced but gradual in the initial phases and spread over long periods of time. But cultural assimilation, as in the Zulu and French colonial policy, achieved little success.

- Under either type of imperial rule, there was a marked hierarchical political structure, radiating from the state council through provincial heads down to the village government. As in chiefdoms, the kings and emperors were also surrounded with councils without which they were powerless. In normal daily administration of kingdoms and empires, the kings played little political role. Much of their authority was delegated to provincial heads and subsequently to village chiefs. The kings occupied themselves mostly with spiritual and religious duties of the office of kingship. They were rarely seen in public and spoke through linguists.

- The village government in the empire was not radically altered. The tribes retained a large measure of autonomy and governed themselves as before and chiefs continued to be chosen by traditional methods. That is, the chiefs ruled through the inner council, the council of elders, and the village assembly.

- The military played little or no role in day-to-day government administration. In fact, most African states did not even have standing armies. The people were the army. Only in a few African kingdoms, such as the Asante, Dahomey and Zulu, were the military given a prominent role in governance. In the Islamic empires, military officers were appointed as nominal provincial heads. But other than that, the role of the military was to defend the tribe or empire against external threats, not to rule. Historical evidence does not show Africans being ruled by soldiers under the native system of government. Military rule, therefore, is without question as alien and *un-African* as colonial rule.

C. THE INDIGENOUS AFRICAN CONSTITUTION

The seeming diversity of the native political institutions derived principally from modifications in administrative procedures and different local names for the component structures, rules of succession, powers of regional heads, checks and balances of royal power, and the degree of autonomy under which the villages and the provinces were administered. Despite these differences, sufficient generalities can be gleaned to draw up an indigenous African constitution.

Acceptance of some general rules of governance or a "constitution" can be discerned from the various peoples of Africa. Williams (1987), after 16 years of research and field studies covering 26 African nations and 105 language groups was able to distil an indigenous African constitution from customary law and practices:

ANCIENT AFRICAN CONSTITUTION AND LAW

I.   The people are the first and final source of all power.

II.   The rights of the community of people are, and of right ought to be, superior to those of any individual, including chiefs and kings who are under the law, not above it.

III.   Kings, chiefs and elders are leaders, not rulers. They are the elected representatives of the people and the instruments for executing their will.

IV.   Government and people are one and the same.

V.   The family is recognized as the primary social, judicial, economic and political unity in the society; the family council may function as a court empowered to try all internal (non-serious) matters involving only members of the extended family group.

VI.   The elder of each extended family or clan is its chosen representative on the Council.

VII.   Decisions in council are made by the elders. The chief or king must remain silent. Even when the council's decision is announced, it is through a speaker (Linguist). Decrees or laws are issued in the same manner to assure that the voice of the chief or king is the "voice of the people." (This is an example of a provision that had wide variations.)

VIII.   The land belongs to no one. It is God's gift to mankind for use and as a sacred heritage, transmitted by our forefathers as a bond between the living and the dead, to be held in trust by each generation for the unborn who will follow, and thus to the last generation.

IX.   Each family, therefore, has a right to land, free of charge, sufficient in acreage for its economic well-being; for the right to the opportunity and means to make a living is the right to live.

(a)   The land, accordingly, cannot be sold or given away.

(b)   The land may be held for life and passed on to the family's heirs, and so on forever.

(c)   The chief is the custodian of all land, his principal duty being to assure fair distribution and actual use.

X.   All moneys, gifts, taxes and other forms of donations, to chief or king still belong to the people for relief or aid to individuals in times of need.

XI.   Every member of the state has the right of appeal from a lower to higher court. (In some states appeals could be taken even from the king's court to the "Mother of the Nation.")

(a)   The procedure was from the chief's village court to the district court, to the provincial court, the king's court.

(b)   Such appeals were allowed in serious or major crimes only (those affecting the whole society).

XII.   Fines for offenses against an individual accrue to the victim, not the court.

(a)   Part of the money received from the loser was returned to him as an expression of good will and desire for renewal of friendship.

(b)   Another part was given as a fee to the trial court as an appreciation of justice.

XIII.   "Royalty" in African terms means royal worth, the highest in character, wisdom, sense of justice and courage.

(a)   He who founded the nation by uniting many as one must be the real leader, guide and servant of his people.

(b)   The people, in honor of the founder of the nation, therefore will elect chiefs from the founder's family (lineage) if the heirs meet the original test that reflected the founder's character, whose spirit was supposed to be inherited.

XIV.   The trouble of one is the trouble of all. No one may go in want while others have anything to give. All are brothers and sisters. Each is his "brother's or sisters' keeper."

XV.   Age grades, sets, and classes are social, economic, political and military systems for (1) basic and advanced traditional education (formal); (2) individual and group responsibility roles; (3) police and military training; (4) division of labor; (5) rites of passage and social activities. In chiefless societies the age grades are the organs of social, economic and political action.

XVI.   Bride Price or Bride Wealth is the gift that signifies mutual acceptance on the part of both families and is intended as a family security bond which may be returned in part if the wife turns out to be worthless or utterly unsatisfactory. (Bride Wealth tended to stabilize the institution of marriage. This was not "wife-buying.")[7]

XVII.   The community as a whole is conceived of as one party, opposition being conducted by leaders of various factions.

    (a)   Factions of opposition are usually formed by the different age groups.

    (b)   Debates may go on indefinitely or until a consensus is reached.

    (c)   Once a consensus is reached, and the community's will determined, all open opposition to the common will must cease.

    (d)   Those whose opposition is so serious that they are unwilling to accept the new law may "splinter off" either individually or in groups under a leader (to form a new state or the nucleus for it).

XVII.   In warfare the object is not to kill the enemy, but to overcome him with fear, if possible, such as screaming war cries, loud noise, hideously masked faces, etc. Where killing is unavoidable it must be kept at a minimum. In case of defeat there must be some kind of ruse to enable the enemy to retire in honor.

XIX.   The African religion, not being a creed or "articles of faith," but an actual way of thinking and living, is reflected in all institutions and is, therefore, of the greatest constitutional significance.

    (a)   Politically, the role of the chief as high priest who presents the prayers of the people to his and their ancestors in heaven, is the real source of his influence, political or otherwise.

    (b)   Socially, the "rites of passage," songs, and the dances (to drive away evil, etc.), as well as the purification and sacrificial rites for the atonement of sins, are important.

XX.   Since religious and moral law must prevail and the race survive, a man may have more than one wife; for he is forbidden to sleep or cohabit with his wife either during the nine months of pregnancy or during the suckling period of one or two years thereafter.(1) The wife may not prepare meals for the husband or family during the menstrual period. (2) The husband is strictly forbidden to have any kind of relationship with one wife during the set period that belongs to another wife.

XXI.   The supreme command of the fighting forces is under the council, not the king. If the king becomes the commander-in-chief, it is through election by the council because of his qualification as a general or

---

[7] There are ways in which a wife can deal with "a worthless or utterly unsatisfactory" husband. She could withdraw her services, haul the errant husband into a family court, consisting of elders of the extended family or as a last resort seek a divorce, which is recognized in many tribal systems.

field commander. This position ends with the war and the armed forces return to former status under the council or, more directly under the respective paramount chiefs. There were no standing armies" (pp.170-173).

Williams "constitution," though broadly accurate in its description of traditional African governance, contains one factual error in Article 17: "The community as a whole is conceived of as one party, opposition being conducted by leaders of various factions." More accurately, Africans conceive of themselves as members of the *same* community rather than of one party. A political party is an association of individuals who share the *same* ideological beliefs whereas a community is composed of people sharing a common residence (locality), history, kinship, language and other social ties. Africans may mutually share a sense of community but not necessarily the same ideological beliefs. In fact, Williams' own statement, "opposition being conducted by leaders of various factions," refutes the conception of the community as "one party."

Additionally, Williams' "constitution" is rather over-expansive, covering virtually all aspects of traditional African society: the family, government, law and even defense. A constitution, as understood today, specifies the nature, the functions and the *limits* of government. Alternatively, a constitution is a *guarantor of freedom.*[8]

With these strictures in mind, we may now sketch the broad outlines of an African constitution:

THE INDIGENOUS AFRICAN CONSTITUTION

A. THE NATURE OF GOVERNMENT

I.   The people, the source of all power, shall be ruled by a chief or a king (not a soldier) and chosen by the founding or ancestral lineage. This criterion must be combined with others such as intelligence, bravery and pleasant disposition. The choice of the "ruler" is subject to the approval of the people since the legitimacy of the "ruler" rests upon the consent of the people to be ruled (implicit contract).

II.   The chief or king, who is not a ruler but a leader, shall perform the following duties:

1.   Provide a vital link between the living and the ancestors.
2.   Maintain order, balance and harmony among the cosmological elements: the sky, the earth and the world.

---

[8] For example, a "good" constitution is one that limits the powers of the government. Only when the intrusive powers of the state are curtailed can freedom of the people be assured. Too much power in the hands of the state leads to abuse. As Lord Acton once said: "Power corrupts and absolute power corrupts absolutely."

3. Promote peace, justice, social harmony and prosperity among the people.

4. Respect the laws of the ancestors and abide by the will of the people. (Rule of law).

III. Failure to perform these duties could result in "destoolment" or regicide. In addition, the "ruler" shall be deposed for the following failings:

1. Drunkenness   4. Physical disfigurement
2. Cowardice in war   5. Oppression of the people
3. Failure to listen to advice 6. Looting the tribal treasury

IV. There shall be no standing army. The people are the army. In the event of imminent external threat, members of the young age grade or the warrior class shall be called up to defend the community. The army shall be disbanded when the threat subsides.

V. The "ruler" shall govern with a Council. The chief or king must remain silent as Council deliberates on an issue.

1. Important decisions must be debated until unanimity is reached. If not, the issue shall be placed before a Village Assembly of commoners and debated until a *consensus* is reached.

2. The "ruler," together with the Council, shall ensure that the will of the people, arrived at by *consensus*, is carried out. The "ruler" shall not unilaterally abrogate the expressed will of the community.

3. The "ruler" shall not entertain or enter any contract with a foreigner or a stranger without the full approval of the Council.

4. All decisions initiated by the "ruler" must be approved by the Council.

VI. Councillor positions are "hereditary." Councillors are chosen by their respective lineages and cannot be removed by the "ruler." The "ruler" may nominate persons of high regard to the Council but with the concurrence of the Council.

VII. The primary duties of the government are to defend the community against external aggression, maintain law and order, and ensure the survival of the tribe by promoting peace, justice, harmony and economic prosperity. It is not the function of the tribal government to operate commercial enterprises to the total exclusion of the subjects. The chief may operate a farm or business if he so wishes. But he cannot prohibit others from engaging in the same economic activity.

VIII. **Bill of Native Rights**

The people shall enjoy the following rights which cannot be questioned or nullified by the "ruler":

1. The right to economic livelihood to support the family without interference by the chief or the king or the govern-

ment. The occupation of the individual is his/her own determination to make. It the individual's prerogative to determine whether to become a farmer, a hunter, a fisherman or a market trader. And how much he/she sells a produce for on the village market is for the individual to determine. It is not the duty of the chief or king to fix prices or debar any individual from entering any commercial transaction or contract if he/she so wishes.

2. The right to the use of land. Land belongs to the royal ancestors, not the chief or the king. The "ruler" only holds land in trust to ensure the fair distribution and equal access by all. The chief or king cannot dispossess or deny tribesman the use of the land without full Council review.

3. The right to defend the family against intruders, even against harassment by the chief.

4. The right to live anywhere a person so chooses and the right to leave the community unmolested.

5. The right to an open and fair trial in case of wrongdoing and the right to appeal to a higher court.

6. The right to participate in government and the decision-making process, regardless of a person's status, sex, age, ethnicity or religion.

7. The right to comment on and criticize government policy, since the legitimacy of the "ruler" is based upon the consent of the people.

8. The right to express an opinion freely and the right to be heard are fundamental to African culture and participatory democracy.

9. The right to associate with any group — socially, economically and politically — if a person so chooses. A person may belong to an age group, a social club, a secret society, a guild or a political faction if he/she so wishes. It is not the business of the chief or king to ban these associations.

10. The right to practice any religion of his/her own choosing.

IX. These rights specified above are enshrined in the following *freedoms* upon which the chief, the king or the government must not infringe:

1. Freedom of Choice (to live anywhere, to engage in any occupation, to trade goods at whatever prices).

2. Freedom of Expression (required to debate, criticize policies and participate in the decision-making process).

3. Freedom of Association in the social, economic and political arena.

4. Freedom of worship and

5. Freedom of Movement.

X.   These freedoms shall be enjoyed within the boundaries defined by the community as a whole, not by the chief or king.

The above Bill of Rights is a compression of the 20 Fundamental Rights of the African People listed by Williams (1987; p.175).

D. THE INDIGENOUS AFRICAN POLITICAL SYSTEM: WEAKNESSES AND STRENGTHS

Like other systems, the indigenous systems too had their weaknesses and strengths. It may however be useful to keep in mind that "weaknesses" and "strengths" are not invariant to changing circumstances, time and locality. What may be deemed as a "weakness" or an obstacle can in fact be a blessing in disguise or an asset at a different time and place.

One weakness was the restriction of chieftaincy and kingship to certain lineages. Not everyone could become a king or a chief unless he had *bulopwe* (royal blood). In that sense, the native system could be considered "undemocratic." But that is too restrictive a definition of "democracy." Moreover, this criterion was not of overriding importance in all cases. The Igbo, for example, considered other qualities such as leadership abilities, good character and oratorical skills. It can also be argued that government based upon kinship in fact served a very useful purpose of checking despotism. Authority was derived from kinship relationships. For that reason, an outsider who did not possess such a relationship could not arbitrarily impose his rule on strangers unless such rule was accepted. Imposition by force could not endure as the ruler would lack legitimacy.

The second weakness pertained to the general absence of a cohesive agent to hold the polity together. Though kinship was politically expedient, it was a rather poor cohesive force beyond the village or the town boundaries. It is true the Oyo and the Zande kingdoms were welded together on this basis. The kings of the subsidiary Oyo kingdoms traced their descendancy from their ancestral home of Ile-Ife. However, it is doubtful if the average citizen in the outlying kingdoms could make such a connection.

The Asante, on the other hand, glued their kingdom together through a required allegiance to the "Golden Stool", which was alleged to embody the collective soul of the Asante people. Tradition holds that Okomfo Anokye caused this stool to descend from the sky and provided the Asante with a powerful means of cohesion. But the frailty of this cohesion was demonstrated in the latter part of the 19th century when British forces launched raids to capture the "Golden Stool." These incursions threw the kingdom into disarray, since not all the subjects of the Asante empire rallied in defense of the "Stool."

By contrast, Islam provided a more cohesive pull and a stronger basis for empire-building. It was no accident that the Islamic empires, such as Ghana and Kanuri, lasted the longest in Africa's history. The Luba Empire must also be mentioned as having successfully found a satisfactory solution to the "cohesion problem." They combined positional succession with perpetual kinship.

But the lack of cohesion was a reflection of the cultural passion for independence. Even though many African groups converted to Islam, they still retained their indigenous cultural identities. The endless process of segmentation and splintering off to form little independent states all attest to the African cultural desire for independence. By nature, Africans are rebellious of authority and fundamentally anti-imperialistic.

It is a myth that Africans of various ethnicity have always been united behind their leaders. African history does not bear this out. Fiercely independent kinship groups have always been the constituent parts of an African society. And far from being a "negative" as they are often portrayed, feuding clans can in fact be transmuted into an asset. The trick is to channel their rivalries and energies into *productive* endeavors, rather than into destructive (warring) avenues. Let clans show off their ethnic superiority by the number of roads, hospitals, and markets they can build, rather than by the number of men they can keep under arms.

The third alleged weakness was that indigenous African polities hardly qualified as nation-states in which citizens shared a common national identity and a language. The proliferation of ethnic groups in Africa was often taken by European writers as proof of the incapability of Africans at building states. Perhaps in an effort to refute this allegation, various African intellectuals and nationalists, after independence, sought to emphasize state-formation in indigenous Africa. In fact, a few of the newly independent countries took the names of old African empires (Ghana and Zimbabwe). Unfortunately, this quest was rather ill-conceived. Glorification of the old was one thing; understanding why was another.

The case of Dahomey clearly illustrated that Africans were capable of building highly centralized and efficient state bureaucracies. Their general absence in much of Africa was not so much proof of the "incapability" of Africans at state construction. Rather, their very absence was indicative of a high degree of political awareness or sophistication.

Abundant historical evidence reveals unequivocally that the peasants recognized the state as necessarily evil. Indeed, the state in recent times has unabashedly proven itself to be an instrument of oppression and the raider of the public treasury. Recall the quip of the Lesotho chief: "We have two problems: rats and the government." Africans have known for centuries, even before the arrival of the Europeans, that highly centralized government and concentration of power invariably breed tyranny.

A close study of the organizational structure of chiefdoms and kingdoms unmasks a frightening obsession with the need to curb the powers of the ruler and prevent him from acting cruelly toward his own people. Africans, of course, distinguished between their own kinship groups and others. But most Europeans made no distinction. To them, all Africans were the same.

In the indigenous political systems, chiefs and kings were encircled with advisers, and councils, without which the rulers could not make laws. Most instructive was the elaborate system of checks and balances to curb any autocratic tendencies of the ruler. Many of these checks were in place well before 1776 when America gained its independence. As noted earlier, so intense was the fear of tyranny that many African societies, such as the Igbo and Tiv of Nigeria, elected not to have any state or centralized authority at all. They were called *stateless* societies. Why then do modern African elites stress state-formation? Clearly, the absence of highly centralized states in the indigenous system was not a failing of Africans. Rather, it pointed to their politically astute desire to avoid tyranny. What modern Africa needs is not emphasis on state-formation but a dismantling of the oppressive state behemoth. The illiterates realized this.

Hereditary positions are the fourth weakness, often decried as "anti-democratic" structures; for example, the elders on the ruler's council were not subject to periodic selection. This unfortunate interpretation arose from the application of Western standards to a native institution. To the Westerner, hereditary positions gave an impression of ossified autocrats who, secure in their offices, were unresponsive to popular opinion or demands. This was not necessarily the case in indigenous Africa.

It is true hereditary positions, combined with the principle of hierarchy, could cause difficulties. The most senior wielded the most authority until he or she died.

> It made removal from office, and especially demotion, a culturally difficult operation. One consequence was that the easiest option for a junior competitor was to secede from his superior or to kill him. For the same reason, a king wishing to remove the head of a subordinate chieftaincy would often find it easiest to kill him (Kopytoff, 1989; p.37).

This however was not the norm in many African societies. The king was chosen from a royal lineage and could appoint his relatives and friends as ministers or governors. The strength of the indigenous system lies in the fact that not all the officials of government came from the same family or lineage. That was important. The councillors were a potential source of opposition or checks on his power. He had to deal with them whether he liked it or not. The king may not like the views of the councillors but he could not replace them with his own appointees.

Hereditary councillors were chosen by their own extended families or lineages. Even where a position passed from father to eldest son, succession was not automatic in most indigenous systems. Hereditary positions, in addition, played a vital role in the system of checks and balances. This particular feature was rather "democratic" in that it sought to curb the excesses of the ruler. He could not dismiss the councillors who disagreed with him. The councillors did not owe their positions to the ruler in most cases. They were chosen by their respective lineages and could be destooled by them, not by the ruler. The council was secure from ruler subversion. Thus, hereditary positions were an insurance against royal absolutism.

To provide a modern analogy, members of the United States Congress may be considered "hereditary" in the sense that they are *not* appointed by the president, although their offices are not "inherited." This is the "positive" aspect of hereditary positions. Theoretically, there was little chance of the ruler turning the council into a "rubber-stamp" parliament. In practice, however, a ruler with a strong will and personality could bend the councillors to his wishes. But there were constitutional checks and in addition, such pliant councillors risked incurring the wrath of the people and a rebellion.

The tendency to dwell on the "negative" aspects of hereditary positions, i.e., the primogenital rules of succession, produced recommendations for reform, one of which was replacing them with appointments. Such an action, however, would only increase the danger of autocracy, as the Asante learned during the reign of Osei Kwadwo.

> In 1764 Osei Kwadwo began a series of radical reforms, which were followed up by his successors Osei Kwame and Osei Bonsu. Osei Kwadwo embarked on a plan to change hereditary positions into appointive posts. He also created new stools and chiefships. A key office, for instance, was the new post of Minister of Finance. In this way a class of appointive officials developed, men appointed to their post by the *Asantehene* on the basis of their merit. Obviously such procedures increased administrative efficiency and encouraged individual mobility: some posts were filled by men from outside Kumasi and the *amanto*. . .

> (But) an important result of this revolution in government was that the *Asantehene increased his own power at the expense of hereditary chiefs and the amanto*. By the reign of Osei Bonsu in the early 19th century the *Asantehene* was no longer *primus inter pares* with the *amanto*: he was the supreme sovereign of metropolitan and provincial Asante (Stride and Ifeka, 1971; p.268).

But then, soon after "these reforms" the people of Juaben, one of the divisions of the Asante kingdom, rebelled against the *Asantehene* in 1827. Boahen (1986) offered this assessment:

> It is true that the great reformers, Osei Kwadwo and Osei Bonsu,

did introduce some administrative changes by imposing on the existing provincial administration a network of Asante resident commissioners hierarchically organized at regional and district levels; but the very fact that revolts and rebellion were *so common* in the 19th century shows that these administrative changes did not prove particularly effective (p.61).

Centralization of power may enhance efficiency, but it goes against the grain of cultural tradition and the imperative for independence. The African people will oppose any such concentration of power at the center.

It has also been argued that the native political system possessed a structural bias toward despotism since the amount of personal authority exercised by the ruler depended upon the strength of his personality and political skills.

The factors which determined the exact degree of personal authority the ruler of Ghana exercised were his own character and powers of leadership (Stride and Ifeka, 1971; p.35).

The exact amount of influence exercised on the government of the Kanuri by any individual *Mai* depended on the strength of his personality, his administrative wisdom and ability to manage his councillors. The weak *Mais* could be practically excluded from contact with the problems of government, while the strong ones could dominate their councillors, exploit differences of opinion among them and exercise a controlling influence on the adminstration of their empire (Stride and Ifeka, 1971; p.128).

In the traditional systems of government, there were various checks against possible abuse of power by the rulers. The effectiveness of those checks, however, depended to a large extent, on the moral courage of the council of elders, the leaders of the commoners and the personality of the ruler himself.

Thus where the personality of the ruler was stronger than those of the members of his council and the leaders of the common people he could easily get them to compromise to his excesses and in the process he would become a tyrant (Amoah, 1988; p.179).

This tendency, however, is not unique to the native African system alone but reveals itself even in modern Western systems as well. Certainly there were differences in the personalities and characters of the Carter and Reagan administrations in the United States, even between administrations of the *same* Republican party (for example, Reagan and Bush administrations). Similarly, the Thatcher and Heath governments in Britain were not of the same political character. But these various administrations were not operating under different constitutions in the same country.

There were of course bad chiefs and councillors in the traditional system. As in most societies, there were instances of corruption and abuse of power in Africa's history also. But "the machinery was devised, and when it functioned well could check those in power and protect those who were ruled, and regulate behavior for the peace and well-being of the community" (Busia, 1969; p.27). Moreover, African chiefs and even kings in many societies could be "destooled." If not, they were abandoned.

Astonishing as it may seem to some, the indigenous African political system at the state or empire level did not differ radically from a modern day Western political system, except for a few differences.

The African System	**The Western System**
King (not chosen by universal suffrage)	President (popularly elected)
Inner Council/Cabinet (appointed)	Cabinet (appointed)
State Council (Hereditary officers; Appointees)	Parliament/Congress (elected)
Provincial (Governors appointed)	Provincial/State (elected)
Village Chief (Chosen from a royal lineage)	
Village Council (Hereditary councillors)	

The strengths of the indigenous political system lie in its stability and consensual democracy. These attributes were enhanced by the tradition of participatory democracy and decentralized administration which allowed the various ethnic groups the autonomy to preserve their own culture. Clearly, a lugubrious attempt by a modern African head of state at cultural imperialism (to transform his people into Marxists, Leninists, Maoists and other alien "ists") is doomed to failure. Similarly doomed in modern Africa is a misguided policy to create a unitary state with a highly centralized administration.

The shape of a modern African government must of course be adaptive to local conditions and the desires of the governed. But it must also reflect the time-tested, traditional norm: federal/confederate type of political association, the presence of a State Council (or Constituent Assembly in modern parlance, not a military junta) as well as the existence of checks and balances to curb the powers of the head of state and any drift toward dictatorship.

The modern African head of state, like the supreme ruler of an ancient African empire, presides over a political configuration of heterogeneous ethnicity. For example, the modern state of Zaire has no less than 200 ethnic groups. The imposition of a strong unitary and highly centralized administrative system of government is most likely to exacerbate ethnic divisions, disunity, political strife, chronic instability, civil wars and even secession attempts. Abundant evidence from Africa's own pre-colonial history attest to these lessons. But tragically, African elites and intellectuals, dismissing the indigenous system as "backward" and "archaic," scoffed at these lessons and erected political and leadership systems which were not only a far cry from the traditional but also produced interminable chaos since independence in the 1960s.

Profiling the typical Mr. Big Man — His Excellency the African Leader — Blaine Harden wrote:

> His face is on the money (the national currency). His photograph hangs in every office in the realm. His ministers wear gold pins with tiny photographs of him on the lapels of their tailored pin-striped suits. He names streets, football stadiums, hospitals and universities after himself. He carries a silver-inlaid ivory mace or an ornately carved walking stick or fly whisk or a chiefly stool. He insists on being called 'doctor' or 'conqueror' or 'teacher' or 'the big elephant' or 'the number-one peasant' or 'the wise old man' or 'the national miracle' or 'the most popular leader in the world.' His every pronouncement is reported on the front page. He sleeps with the wives and daughters of powerful men in the government. He shuffles ministers without warning, paralyzing policy decisions as he undercuts pretenders to his throne. He scapegoats minorities to shore up popular support. He bans all political parties except the one he controls. He rigs elections. He emasculates the courts. He cows the press. He stifles academia. He goes to church (*The Washington Post*, Dec. 9, 1990; p.K5).

As should now be clear, this vulgar caricature of leadership is an elite contraption and was never an integral part of indigenous African political culture. But unbelievably in modern times, various intellectuals, experts, scholars, governments, multi-lateral institutions, and aid agencies, *both* African and Western, serenaded and supported such grotesque leadership as "authentically African."

Various Western donor governments showered him with munificent provisions of aid because he was "the big elephant" — the "strongman." Black Americans waxed in adulation of him because he was black and blasted away at colonialism and racism. And last but not least, sycophantic African elites sold off their scruples and obsequiously lavished praises upon him to assure their perquisites and Mercedes Benzes. The elite of all should have known better. Even "backward" peasants never created such hideous leadership in their indigenous system.

CHAPTER 7

THE INDIGENOUS ECONOMIC SYSTEM

A. THE "ECONOMIC PROBLEM"

People have unlimited wants; they want many things, ranging from autos, TV sets, clothes, houses, to trips to the moon. However, the resources required to produce these goods are limited. These resources, in economic jargon, are termed *factors of production*. Economists identify four of them: labor, land, capital and the enterpreneur. Because factors of production are either limited or scarce, economics is the study of the allocation of scarce resources to meet the infinite and competing wants of people.

Every individual and society, at one point or another, faces what is alternatively called "the economic problem" - allocating scarce resources to satisfy many wants. An individual's income, for a time, is fixed and must be allocated among many needs. One may choose to spend more on food and less on clothes or vice versa. Similarly, a society may choose to allocate more of its limited resources toward the production of bombs and less on the provision of bread or vice versa.

The nature of this economic problem for a society is encapsulated in the following questions:

1. What to produce? Guns or butter?
2. How much?
3. For whom?

At one extreme, a central planning agency may attempt, without much success, to make these decisions for society as a whole in what would be called a *planned* or *command economy*.[1] The former eastern-bloc or socialist countries in Eastern Europe, the Soviet Union, China and Albania are examples of such economies. In such an economic system, the state owns the

---

[1] There are other variants of this paradigm of which one is statism (or *dirigisme*). It is tantamount to state direction of economic activity. Statism is not necessarily associated with one particular ideology and can occur under socialism, Marxism and even right-wing fascism. For example, the economies of Ivory Coast, Malawi and South Africa, often characterized as "capitalist," have all been *dirigiste* because of the pervasive presence of the state.

means of production, determines what to produce and establishes state enterprises to produce them. Commodity prices are fixed by the state or government. If a commodity is in short supply, it is rationed by the government by means of chits or ration coupons.

At the other extreme, no central agency but, instead, private individuals determine for themselves what to produce, how much and for whom in what is called *pure capitalism*. Capitalism, by the strict economic definition, simply means an economic system whereby the ownership of the factors of production and decisions pertaining to production and distribution are made by private individuals, not the government or the state.[2] Individuals interact *freely* at the *marketplace* to sell commodities or services they produce and purchase those that they need. Through these interactions, the "economic problem" is solved.

The actual solution does not take place overnight or under the supervision of one individual or government agency. Rather, the market solves the "problem" by trial and error, through a signalling process. The market transmits price signals to millions of consumers and producers who make or adjust their economic decisions (how much to purchase and produce) on the basis of these price signals. For example, if there is not enough of a certain commodity, say gasoline, that consumers want, its price would rise.

The rise in price would send signals to both consumers and producers. The high price would induce consumers to reduce purchase or economize on the use of gasoline; for instance, drive less and at lower speeds, use the public transportation system, purchase a fuel-efficient automobile, etc. Producers, on the other hand, would see in the high price an opportunity to make greater profits. This will induce them to produce more of the respective commodity.

The curtailment of consumption coupled with expanded production, would, other things being equal, drive down the price. If the price falls sufficiently, consumption would be stimulated and supplies would be somewhat reduced. The lower price would not provide much of an incentive to sell greater quantities of gasoline. The increased consumption and reduced supplies would start pushing prices up. Through this constant upward and downward movement of price, how much of a commodity should be produced is brought into balance with how much consumers are willing to purchase. In this way, the "economic problem" is solved. The process never ends, but is aided by continuously adjusting prices.

The process can be interfered with by preventing prices to adjust through the imposition of maximum prices (price ceilings or price controls) and minimum prices (price floors or price supports). Such interferences, oftentimes unwarranted and ill-conceived, obstruct the balancing of what

---

[2] Marxists, however, define capitalism differently: as an economic system based upon the exploitation of labor for the creation of surplus value (profit).

consumers want (demand) with what producers offer (supply). The results are either chronic shortages or surpluses. The existence of these imbalances in *any* economic system is indicative of a waste of resources.

The focus on the price of gasoline alone does great disservice to the vital role the market plays in a society. It is not only a place where prices of commodities are determined but also, more importantly, a place where goods are *exchanged*. This was the *original* function of the market.

If individuals produced everything they needed (self-sufficiency), there would be no need to engage in economic transactions or exchange and a market would not exist. Such an economy would be termed a "subsistence economy." But individuals cannot produce all their wants and must necessarily exchange some of what they produce for what they do not.

The original purpose of a market was precisely to facilitate this exchange of goods between people. In fact, the earliest market was a place a person could go to barter one commodity for another. Today, the use of money conceals this role of the market: to permit the direct exchange of goods. When one sells chicken at the market and uses the proceeds to purchase bread, one in effect trades the chicken for bread. The sale of chicken was really an exchange of chicken for money and the purchase of bread was an exchange of money for bread. The money only acted as "a medium of exchange" (chicken — money —bread).

The advantage of using money is that one does not have to "search" for someone who had bread and wanted exactly chicken in exchange (what economists call "a double coincidence of wants"). The chicken could be sold to anybody. Another advantage is intertemporal allocation of purchase. The proceeds from the sale of chicken can be "saved" temporarily and spent at a different time.

If people want more fish instead of chicken, the price of chicken would fall on the market. In other words, your chicken would exchange for *less* bread. On your next trip to the market, you might want to take some fish.

In this way through price gyrations, the market "communicates" with people, helping them determine whether to produce more fish and less chicken. And society as a whole determines "what to produce." But these decisions cannot be made unless there is a market. The market, then, is indispensable to the operation of the capitalist system and explains why capitalist economies are called "market economies." Today, however, pure capitalism economies do not exist. Most Western countries are characterized as *mixed economies*, exhibiting characteristics of both systems. In the United States, for example, the government operates a postal and rail service (Amtrak). Such government-run commercial operations would not exist under pure capitalism.

It is necessary to spell out the definition of capitalism because it is a term which is misunderstood by many. From popular usage, capitalism connotes evil, exploitation and the avaricious pursuit of profit. This is *not* the connotation or definition ascribed to the term by Western economists. The popular conception of "capitalism" is more akin to the Marxist definition.[3]

Each system has its own inherent merits and defects. To help underpin these, consider a society (Batanga) made up of 10 families. Assume that the gross national product (GNP) of Batanga is 10 dolls. Thus, what to produce (dolls) and how much (10) have been determined. The next question is: "for whom?" or who gets what?

Under capitalism, distribution is effected through the *market*. Depending upon the demand for dolls - the supply is fixed at 10 - the price may be anywhere between $15 and $50. Suppose the price is $50. Those who can *afford* dolls at $50 apiece will not have any difficulty purchasing them. Those who cannot, must go without dolls. The price serves as an allocative tool to determine who gets what. You might say, "That's unfair!"

The key word is *"afford"*. Since not everyone has the same means, the market necessarily possesses an inherent bias or a built-in element of inequity. Those who have lots of money, the rich, will always have "unfair" advantage or access to market goods. Therefore, there will always be inequities in the distribution of commodities under capitalism.

Second, the type of commodities individuals want may not always be socially desirable; for example, automatic rifles, bazookas, uzis, child pornographic material, hard drugs, etc. In some neighborhoods in Los Angeles, Washington and New York, one would be safer driving a tank. But then there would not be much road left if everybody drove around this way.

Third, market psychosis can degenerate to an animalistic level. In the phrenetic and avaricious quest for profit, human values and the environment may become constant casualties. The obsession with quick profits may not make industrialists think about polluting the environment unless social pressure is brought to bear on them.

These were the defects of capitalism that prompted Karl Marx to devise an alternative economic order. The outline of his "socialist" system may now be sketched. Recall that in Batanga there were 10 families and 10 dolls. Why not let the state take over the production of dolls (the supply) and distribute them according to the formula: one doll per family at a price of

---

[3] It is also important to note that there are various forms of capitalism. Japanese capitalism is different from American capitalism or South African capitalism. The economic system in South Africa may be called "dirty" or bastard capitalism. It is a free market and capitalism for the whites only but "socialism" for the blacks. Black South Africans live in a world in which almost everything is owned and controlled by the state. Where they must live, what type of occupations they can engage in, and how much they should be paid are all determined by the state. Though not on par with the Soviet Union, the South African economy is one of the most statist and heavily regulated in the whole world. More than 200,000 prices are controlled by the government. Even with timber, "a permit is required to plant trees, to cut, process, transport, sell, and export" (Kendall and Louw, 1987; p.58).

$1, instead of the outrageous $50. Sounds appealing? But distributional inequities and problems also occur under the socialist system.

The first is determining what *rationing criterion* to use. Suppose Family A is headed by the secretary of the Communist Party and Family B is headed by a farm laborer. Should Family A get 3 dolls and Family B 1 doll? Notice that this is a profound question with philosophical ramifications.

If the answer is in the affirmative, then the capitalist system, which uses prices as a rationing device, is being replaced by one which uses *status* as a rationing tool. Should prices or status be employed for rationing purpose? If by status, then inequities are bound to occur since not everyone has the *same* status. If so, then why replace an inequitable system with one which is equally inequitable?

How about allocating one doll per family, regardless of who is the head of the family? Easier said than done, for this allocative rule too is unworkable. Family C may have no children, Family D may have 15 children. A further complicating factor is that boys do not use dolls. What if Family E has 4 boys? Some might suggest that the state must determine the gender of each child in each family before making the allocation rule. There goes individual privacy and there enters government intrusion.

The second problem is determining how many dolls to produce. The object of production is to satisfy needs. That is, the supply (what is produced) must equal what is needed (demand). If production is undertaken by the state, the government must know what the demand will be. If the government overestimates the demand, there will be an excess supply. Too many dolls will be produced than wanted; an obvious waste. If, on the other hand, the state underestimates the demand, there will be a shortage. Assume that the state was able to forecast this year's demand accurately at 10 dolls. What about next year?

To make an accurate prediction, the state must be able to forecast how many babies will be born in each family and how many will be girls. But that is not enough. Some families may have the tendency to produce more girls than boys. The reason for this should be investigated. That would call for a scrutiny of sexual practices in each household. Wait, there is more! Also needed will be information about contraceptive use, the probabilities of conception, and the reliability of contraceptives. Give up?

Third, the state must decide the price of the dolls. Should it be $1 or $50, the outlandish capitalist price? If the state fixes the price too low, there would be far greater demand than the government anticipated and a shortage will result. If the state sets the price too high, it will have unsold dolls on its hands. Now, extend this analysis from dolls to tomatoes, beef, apples, shoes, automobiles, and the myriad of commodities produced today.

Given the nature of this problem, it is *impossible* for the state to know accurately what the demand for these commodities will be at various prices. Even the U.S. government, with all the sophisticated computers at its disposal, would find it a herculean task to determine *exactly* what the demand for tomatoes, one commodity, will be at 89 cents a pound, let alone an African government, manned by a small cadre of incompetent bureaucrats. Needless to say, the socialist systems do not have this capacity either. Consequently, there will always be chronic demand/supply imbalances whenever the state attempts to solve the economic problem.

Often, the state is unable to produce enough commodities owing to poor planning, mismanagement and corruption. The results are chronic shortages, long queues and black markets.[4] Witness the chronic shortages of commodities in pre-revolution Eastern Europe. One characteristic feature of socialist systems is the incredible amount of time *wasted* in chasing scarce goods. All that time could obviously be more productively used to increase the supply of the commodity everybody is chasing.

Worse, capitalism's distributional inequities that provided the initial impetus to devise an alternative system also exist under the socialist model. Under capitalism, the rich have unfair advantage. Under socialism, the ruling elites have the unfair advantage even if allocation is not by status. The elites use their governing authority to allocate to themselves a disproportionately large share of the national pie through the control of distribution networks and corrupt practices. Worse still, the commodity distributed by the state ends up costing the consumer far more than the official price, not to mention anything about the quality.

Suppose a pound of beef costs $5 on the free or black market - a "capitalist" solution. The same pound of beef is offered at the government shop at $1 a pound - a socialist solution. On the free market, beef is always available, if you are prepared to pay the price. At the government shop, supply is irregular. Some days they have beef; some days, well, tough luck.

Assume that you are a taxi driver who makes $20 a hour and have heard on the car radio that the government shop will have some beef today for sale at $1 a pound. You race to the shop, but a long queue has already formed. You join the queue. After 3 hours, you are sold 2 pounds of beef - the maximum allowed per customer. Now, how much did those 2 pounds of beef cost?

The average person would say $2. Wrong. The true cost would be $2 plus the money you lost while the taxi was idle. The 3 hours wasted in the queue could have been used to generate $60 in taxi fares. Therefore, the true cost of the 2 pounds of beef was $62, or an incredible $31 a pound which is worse than the "capitalist" price of $5 a pound.[5]

---

[4] A black market is one in which a commodity is illegally sold above its official price. For example, dolls being sold for $5, instead of the official (legal) price of $1.

[5] Economists call the $60 the "opportunity cost." That is, the opportunity to make $60 that was lost because you were standing in line. Quite often, this opportunity cost is not added by those who queue in line for things. Consequently, they think they are getting a commodity

There are problems with *both* the capitalist and the socialist systems. It is not our intention here to show how these problems can be resolved under either system. Our purpose is to clear up some technical and definitional confusion before proceeding to describe Africa's indigenous economic system. It is however important to keep in mind certain words such as *ownership of the means of production, central planning bureau, state enterprises, exploitation of labor,* and *markets.*

B. PRODUCTION

Organization and Occupations

Africa's indigenous economic system is probably the area least understood by non-Africans. The myth of "hunters and gatherers" persists, giving the impression that there were no economic institutions or culture in Africa before contact with the Europeans. Inexorably tied to the land, Africans eked out oppressive living from primitive "subsistence" agriculture. Trade and exchange were unknown since self-sufficiency and subsistence farming were the operative commands.

Books that covered pre-colonial Africa dwelt excessively on the "backwardness" of African technology. A similar obsession with the external characteristics of Africa's indigenous political institutions was lamented in the previous chapter. Such obsessions detract attention from the more substantive issues - the *existence* and *purpose* of the indigenous institutions. The commonly held view that traditional African economies were "subsistence" economies is now being questioned. Schneider (1986), for example, observed:

> While Africans often conducted their economic affairs in ways not identical to those of Europeans and Americans, their behavior can still be considered economic and commensurate with a market process. What is meant by the market process? It does not necessarily mean taking goods to a marketplace, although traditional African societies, especially in West Africa and in the Congo or Zaire basin, had highly developed marketplace systems. It does mean that people engage in producing things in order to obtain other goods in exchange. In America this is represented by the worker selling his labor for wages, or by the manufacturer

"cheaply" when in actual fact they are not. Notice that even if you spend only half an hour in the queue and purchase 2 pounds of beef, the real price per pound would still be higher than "the capitalist" price. In this case, it would be $6 per pound against the free market price of $5 per pound.

producing goods for profit and then using that profit to obtain other desired items. In a society where the market process operates, goods are produced to one degree or another for exchange and not for direct consumption alone (p.181).

The following discussion of the indigenous African economic system will focus on these issues: *how* production was organized, *how* goods were exchanged or distributed, *how* the natives obtained finance and *what* role, if any, the chiefs or native governments played in the economy, notwithstanding the "primitive" technologies.

West Africa was particularly noted for its indigenous economic development. As Skinner (1964) put it:

> The peoples of (pre-colonial West Africa) had economies which made agricultural produce available in amounts large enough to be sold in rural and urban markets, craft specialization often organized along the line of craft guilds, whose members manufactured goods to be sold in these markets; different kinds of currencies which were nearly always convertible one to another and, later, to European denominations of values; and elaborate trading systems, external as well as internal. Goods produced in even the smallest West African societies were circulated in local market centres, and ultimately by porters, caravans, and boats, to the large Sudanese emporiums from which they could be shipped to Mediterranean areas in exchange for foreign products.

Africans engaged in quite a wide variety of economic activities. Though mostly primary - agricultural, pastoralism, hunting, fishing and woodworking - there were also crafts and other industries such as cloth-weaving, pottery, brass works, mining and smelting of iron, gold silver, copper and tin.[6]

Agriculture was the primary occupation of Africans, and the basic unit of production was the extended family. Each family constituted itself into a working unit or labor force and acted as an operative economic entity which produced goods together and shared the fruits of their labor as they saw fit, allowing for individual discretion and reward. Within the family, there was specialization of labor and sexual division of occupation. Different crops were raised by different members and certain tasks were reserved for women. For example, the cultivation of food crops (domestic staples) was almost

---

[6] Archaelogical discoveries at Nok, near Jos suggest iron-smelting in Nigeria as early as 500 B.C. (Olaniyan, 1985: 103). "Nor is there anything specially mysterious about the outburst of engineering activity that clearly took place in many parts of east and central Africa between 500 and 1500 A.D." (Wrigley, 1960).

everywhere a female occupation. In Ethiopia, however, the raising of goats was done by women.

Land for cultivation was readily available. Members of the extended family farmed their own lineage land but strangers could also readily acquire land. As we shall see shortly, strangers, upon the presentation of a token gift - goats, kola nuts or a bottle of rum - and in some cases, upon the payment of an allotment fee, could obtain land from the chief to farm. A person could also borrow land. Nominal gifts would be made by the borrower and thereafter the borrower would pay tribute at intervals. "But even this was voluntary" (Falola, 1985).

What a person grew on the land was his own free choice to make. The produce was private property. Even among the Kalahari Bushmen, "all that a woman gathers belonged to her alone, and of course was shared with her family" (Marshall, 1958). How much a person shared with his kinsmen and how much he kept for himself was an individual decision. There was rarely mandated, proportional distribution of produce among the extended family. As Field (1940) observed of the Ga people of Ghana, "in farming every married man has his own farm though all help each in clearing, so problems of division of produce do not arise" (p.62). Families may live together in a compound. But each wife cooks for her own nuclear family. She will feed the hungry children from other families, knowing that her children too will be fed when she is absent. At times, the wives in a compound may take turns cooking.

One hard fact of reality was that a man could not produce all the ingredients needed for a meal on a farm. By necessity, some farm produce had to be exchanged for the ingredients the man could not produce. Thus, even if a man wanted to feed only his immediate family, the reality was that he had to produce enough surplus on his farm to exchange for something else, say meat. Consequently, it became the traditional duty of the wife to exchange, barter or trade any food her husband produced over and above the amount required to feed husband, wife and children. The wife might make the trade herself or if she could not, leave that task to her older daughters. This explains why in Africa trading activities are still dominated today by women and young girls. Thus, although household self-sufficiency was the rule, agricultural surpluses had to be produced by the extended family to exchange for the good it could not produce. Exceptionally bountiful harvests were partly stored, partly traded. The existence of indigenous food preservation systems attest to this. Perishable root crops were stored in earthen silos. Some were prepared into products that could keep longer. For example, cassava was made into garri or konkote which could keep for months under the humid and hot tropical conditions and still be safe for human consumption.

In many of the more highly developed societies, surplus agricultural products were produced by serfs and slaves. In Benin, there was a class of men known as the *gletanu* (great cultivators) who even produced crops especially for sale to middle-women. "The farms of these men, cultivated by their relatives and slaves, comprised areas of 15 to 25 kilometers in length and several kilometers in breadth, and specialized in the raising of some single food staple such as millet, maize or yams" (Skinner, 1964). The Yoruba of Nigeria also used slaves for the specialized production of foodstuffs for resale in the markets.

One misconception about African peasant farmers has been that they make no "economic decisions" or respond to economic stimuli and grow crops as dictated by "tradition." But according to Schneider (1986):

> Recent studies show that Africans, like farmers all over the world, are in fact faced with complicated decisions about what to produce. . .The number of possible ways a Kamba farmer (of Kenya) can combine his resources (land and seeds of various types, labor, and other elements of production) to achieve different end results was investigated using a method of linear programming. It was noted that if, as is true of the Kamba, various mixes of maize and beans, peas, millet, sorghum, and finger millet can be planted, if the various combinations are affected in different ways by different patters of rain during the season, if the amount of land available to each farmer varies, if the time of weeding varies with the crop and the pattern of growth of that year, and if the amount of labor that can be used varies with each farmer, then, in order to get the best return from whatever opportunities are available to him, the farmer must select among more than 240 possible combinations. There is no way for him to act "traditionally." Similar conclusions have been drawn concerning economies in the Congo or Zaire basin (p.187).

Contrary to past beliefs, traditional African agriculture is both complex and diverse. "It is not uncommon for a farmer to grow thirty or more different crops (as many as sixty are recorded) and to have several varieties of many of them" (Schneider, 1986; p.188). Even methods of fertilizing are complex, involving the use of ash, compost and manure in various combinations. Nor are African peasant farmers, for lack of advanced technology, necessarily succumbed to environmental determinism. Schneider (1986) noted how the Haya, southwest of Lake Victoria, ingeniously met an environmental challenge with the cultivation of bananas in that region. Ordinarily, bananas are raised on solid ground of extremely high fertility, moisture and warmth. The Haya lived in an area of with high moisture and warmth but unsuitable soil.

> Nevertheless, the enterprising Haya overcame the problem by constructing compact circular villages inside which they dump

mulch, mainly cattle manure but also the leaves of dead banana trees, whereby they have built up the soil to the texture and fertility necessary for growing bananas. Rather than being determined by the habitat the Haya have overcome a constraint to achieve their goal. But why did they do it?. . .The answer surely must be that for reasons peculiar to the Haya situation it was worth the cost in terms of the "profit" to enrich the soil (Schneider, 1986; p.189).

There were also industries in pre-colonial Africa: metalware, pottery, glass, iron-working, gold, silver-mining, basketry, leatherworks, woodwork, clothing and others. In Benin, "the glass industry made extraordinary strides" (Diop, 1987; p.136). In Nigeria, "the cloth industry was an ancient craft" (Olaniyan, 1985). Kano attained historical prominence in the 14th century with its fine indigo-dyed cloth that was traded for goods from North Africa. Even before the discovery of cotton, other materials had been used. The Igbo, for example, made cloth from the fibrous bark of trees. The Asante also were famous for their cotton and barkcloth (kente and adwumfo).

Craftsmen, artisans, goldsmiths, blacksmiths produced all types of goods in Africa. In many communities, the craftsmen organized themselves into guilds. These guilds recruited and trained apprentices, disciplined members, controlled the production of goods, set the standards of goods and made laws against undercutting and inflating prices for its members. Craft guild production and guild organization reached their greatest development among the Nupe, Hausa, Yoruba and Benin (Olaniyan, 1985; Skinner, 1964). There were guilds of carpenters, masons, wood-workers, potters, weavers, glass-makers, iron-ore miners, blacksmiths, brasssmiths and silver-smiths.

A person was free to join any guild he or she desired. There was *freedom of association*. No African chief or king would dare ban a guild. It was unthinkable. The right to form an association was inalienable.

Most guilds were organized on a family basis, a son belonging to his father's guild, but outsiders were free to join. Each guild had its leader who, in consultation with the members, set rules and standards. "In Benin, the members of the craft guild, *so*, worked on one another's raw material, but the marketing of the finished product was left to the individual" (Wickins, 1981: 112). They also helped one another in sickness and one another's family in the event of death. In many communities, guild leaders served as members of the King's Council. This facilitated communication between the ruler and the guilds and provided a conduit to channel the concerns of guild members to the king as well as seek royal protection for that craft industry.[7] The protection sought was more of a military nature than

---

[7] It is instructive to note that membership constituted representation of "special interest" on

economic. For example, the king could not control or prevent the movement of gold in trade but could use the royal army to defend gold mines or shops of goldsmiths should they come under siege from neighboring states.

The guilds were interdependent; the blacksmiths supplied the hunters and carpenters with tools, the carpenters supplied wood to sculptors, and the hunters supplied skin to leather-workers (Falolan, 1985). The scarcity or shortage of one item, say pig iron, would affect many other craft industries.[8]

The Factors Of Production: Supplies And Ownership

In indigenous Africa, *all* the factors of production were owned by the natives, not by their rulers, the chiefs, or by tribal governments. Feudalism was not commonplace in Africa, except in Abyssinia (Ethiopia). That means, in popular language, that the means of production were privately owned. The hunting spears, fishing nets, cattle, pots, huts, farm produce, fish, textile looms, gold jewelry shops, and various tools and products were all privately owned. Gray (1962) observed this of the Sonjo of Kenya:

> Generally speaking, property is privately owned among the Sonjo. The only important exception is the building plots upon which houses are built. These are owned communally. . .The other forms of property are owned by individuals. Thus, a piece of property such as a field, a beehive, or a goat, at any given time can be traced in ownership to an individual. . .According to Sonjo law, a man has ultimate ownership rights in his own property and in all property possessed by his patrilineal descendants for as long as he lives. When he dies, these rights are inherited by his heirs.

the King's Council. The American or Western political system lacks this representation. As a result, special interest groups in the United States spend millions to lobby Congresspersons to advance their agenda. Much has been written about the corruption of the political process by lobbyists. Perhaps, the ultimate and logical solution might be direct representation of special interest groups in Congress.

[8] This interdependence is today referred to by economists as "inter-sectoral linkages." It was formally studied by Wassily Leontief, culminating in the well-known "input-output" tables. The idea was adapted and extended by Hirschman (1958) in his celebrated "forward and backward linkages" as a strategy for development. This strategy was adopted in Africa by the experts and African leaders but in the in the wrong place - the small "modern" sector where few linkages existed - and consequently failed. Chances of success would have been enhanced had the strategy been applied to the indigenous sector where the inter-sectoral linkages were extensive. For example, the development of the native iron-working industry would, through inter-sectoral linkages, "pull" along many other sectors.

Ownership of land, however, was an issue over which there was a great deal of confusion among experts.

Land Tenure

The land of our villages belongs to our fathers' fathers and our mothers' mothers

- Preamble to the Constitution of the Saan (Bushmen of Namibia).

Land was widely regarded by the experts as "communally owned." This characterization, however, was a misnomer and tended to obfuscate the general issue of property ownership. As we saw in Chapter 1, in indigenous Africa, the ocean, lakes, forests and rivers did not belong to anyone. They "belonged to all," Africans would say. But this was often misinterpreted as "communal property." A river "belonged to all" but a dam across the river was private property. Once someone applied his labor to something, it became a personal property. The same attitude was extended to land.

Westerners consider land as something that can be cut up into parcels and traded on a market with property rights attached to them. In indigenous Africa, land was an important aspect of the social group and its use was governed by social relationships (kinship, ancestral descendancy) and religious beliefs. In most indigenous African systems, as we noted in an earlier chapter, the earth was regarded as possessing a spirit or power of its own which was helpful if propitiated, and harmful if offended or neglected but the land was also regarded as belonging to the ancestors. It was from them that the living inherited the right to use it. The spirits of the ancestors constantly kept watch and saw to it that it was used properly and fairly.

Busia (1951:42) provides us with an account of how deeply held these beliefs are among the Asante:

A farmer cut himself while felling trees on his farm at the village of Gyansoso, near Wenchi, and died shortly after he had been conveyed home. The *obosom* (god) of the village, when consulted, declared that the farmer had died because his ancestors who had farmed there before him were dissatisfied with him. He was a greedy person who did not share his food with his relatives, and had even neglected his sacrifices to the ancestors (p.43).

In virtually all traditional African societies, there was a widely held belief that the land belonged to the dead ancestors. The living only exercised a

right to use it. Thus the land served as a link between the ancestors and the
living descendants. Since the chief or king acted as the human intermediary,
he naturally became the custodian of the land. Even so, the king did not
have unlimited jurisdiction over land.

> The African king, however powerful, was easily persuaded that the
> soil did not belong to him; this is especially applicable to emigrant
> kings: they easily accepted the sacred authority of the original
> occupants, even if the latter were presently without any material
> power. . .He (the king) received the land in trust; he never sells it -
> he would not dare to do so for religious reasons - he allots only the
> use of it. The sale of land, properly speaking, seems to have been
> unknown in traditional pre-colonial Africa (Diop, 1987; p.150).

> The King, qua king, does not own all the lands of the State. The limits
> of his proprietary rights are strictly defined. There are first of all lands
> which are the ancestral property of the King. These he can deal with as
> he pleases, but with the sanction of the members of his family.
> Secondly, there are lands attached to the stool which the King can deal
> with only with the consent of the Councillors. Thirdly, there are the
> general lands of the State over which the King exercises paramountcy.
> It is a sort of sovereignty oversight which does not carry with it
> ownership of any particular land (Casely-Hayford, 1911).

> In Ashanti, the object which symbolized the unity of the ancestors
> and their descendants was the stool which the chief occupied. In any
> Ashanti village the inquirer was informed, 'The land belongs to the
> stool,' or 'The land belongs to the chief.' Further investigation
> revealed that both expressions mean the same thing: 'The land
> belongs to the ancestors' (Busia, 1951:44).

Of the Shona, Bourdillon (1976) stated:

> 'Ownership' or 'proprietorship' do not exactly convey the Shona
> idea of the relationship between the chief and the land.

> People often say the real 'owners' of the land are the spirit
> guardians of the chiefdoms, the spirits of founders or early rulers of
> the chiefdom and their immediate kin. In most chiefdoms, the
> ancestral spirit guardians of the chiefly dynasty have joint dominion
> over the chiefdom, and sometimes the spirits of a previous, ousted
> dynasty are believed to exercise some control over the country
> (p.87).

Newcomers to a Shona chiefdom would offer a gift to the spirit owner with millet beer after building a homestead. Any project of significance, such as building a dam or a school, should have approval of the spirits of the area. The living representative of these spirits (of the ancestors) is the chief. Thus the Shona chief is closely associated with the land precisely because as the senior descendant of the original owners of the land he is the man who should intercede with their spirits.

> 'Ownership' of the land by the spirits is bound up with the relationship between the spirits and the living community. 'The land forms a close and enduring bond between the living and the dead: through their control of the fertility of the land they once cultivated, the spirits are believed to continue to care for their descendants and the descendants are forced to remember and honor their ancestors. Chief Sileya says, 'The owners of the soil are the whole tribe, more especially the deceased members' (Bourdillon, 1976:88).

The ancestors were the *original* founders of the settlement or the first settlers on a piece of land on which the village subsequently grew. The Gikuyu of Kenya did not have chiefs but interestingly they also shared similar beliefs:

> The Gikuyu consider the earth as the 'mother' of the tribe, for the reason that the mother bears the burden of about 8 or 9 moons while the child is in her womb, and then for a short period of suckling. But it is the soil that feeds the child through lifetime; and again after death it is the soil that nurses the spirits of the dead for eternity. Thus the earth is the most sacred thing above all that dwell in or on it. Among the Gikuyu the soil is especially honored, and an everlasting oath is to swear by the earth (*koirugo*).

> Owing to the importance attached to the land the system of land tenure was carefully and ceremonially laid down, so as to ensure to an individual or a family group a peaceful settlement on the land they possessed. According to Gikuyu customary law of land tenure every family unit had a land right of one form or another. While the whole tribe defended collectively the boundary of their territory, every inch of land within it had its owner (Kenyatta, 1938:22).

The following are the various types of holdings under the Gikuyu tenure system:

1. *Mwene ng'ondo* or *githaka*, the individual owner of land who has acquired it either by purchase or through inheritance or by acquiring first hunting rights.

2. *Moramati*, a trustee, who acts as the guardian to the younger members of his family group.
3. *Mohoi*, one who acquires cultivation rights on the *ng'ondo* or lands of another man or family unit, on a friendly basis without any payment for the use of the land.
4. *Mociarwa*, a man who is adopted into the family of a clan other than his own by means of a special religious ceremony.
5. *Githaka kia mgwataniro*, land held by two individual families as joint property. (This practice was not very common).
6. *Mothoni*, a relation-in-law of the first degree, who acquires cultivation or building rights or both.
7. *Mothami*, a man who acquires cultivation and building rights on the *githaka* of another man or clan.
8. *Borori wa Gikuyu*, territory of the Gikuyu. This term denotes the political unit of all lands within the tribal boundary.

In pre-colonial Africa, there were great expanses of land and constant migration of people. Many moved to escape oppression, to relieve population pressures on the land or to seek better pastures elsewhere. Because of the ever-present dangers from slave raids and wild animals, people moved in groups or parties.

There were four main modes by which land could be acquired: by right of first occupation, by conquest or by way of gift and by purchase. For example, among the Hausa and Gikuyu land could be purchased although purchase was not very common in traditional Africa.

In those early days, land could be wrested from those occupying it by war. The victorious chief could give parcels of this conquered land to his warriors as reward. But unoccupied land belonged to no one. Natural waters and pastures could be used by anybody. But as soon as a man sank a well or built a dam, he could exercise exclusive rights over the water it contained (Schapera, 1953). "The man who first came with his followers to settle in a previously unoccupied area was usually termed the 'owner of the land' and his heir would continue to receive respect for his primacy" (Colson, 1953). Among the Tonga, who occupy the plateau of southern Zambia, the owner was called *ulanyika* and among the Dagaaba of northern Ghana, *tendaana*.

To understand this process, let us call the *tendaana* Ntonji and assume the year was 1860. Suppose Ntonji and his party (his sons, their wives and children - a minimal lineage) staked a claim to 100 acres of unoccupied land. A year later, he was joined by his brother Areji and his followers. They found an adjacent but unoccupied piece of land, say 50 acres and laid a claim to it. Over time, there would be the Areji, Kwartey, Usumang and other lineages, all tracing their ancestry to Ntonji. Each would have its own plot of land. Together, they would form the Ntonji village with Ntonji as the chief.

The Ntonji lineage would increase the size of their land holdings to say

200 by taking possession of other unoccupied plots of land. This was necessary to allow shifting cultivation.[9] In theory, there was no limit to the size of land they could own. There were two ways in which land size could be increased. An individual could go out and stake a claim to distant lands, but establishing ownership rights over such land was problematic. In addition, the individual and his family may not be able to resist encroachment from warring neighboring groups.

The second way was to seek additional land under the protective umbrella of the chief. For example,

> From the central village the chief sent out his hunters to view the surrounding country. A large area usually distinguished by natural boundaries such as rivers, rocks or trees was demarcated. The chief made a sacrifice to the Earth and the rivers of this locality on behalf of the community. The areas thus demarcated became stool land, under the care of the chief. It was tribal land. This is how, according to the tradition, Mampong was founded.
>
> From the central village, a lineage group, or a man and a few of his kinsfolk, went out to found a new village within the tribal land in order that they might farm there (Busia, 1951:47).

A lineage obtaining a piece of such "tribal land" could farm it forever, passing it down from generation to generation. Essentially, there was little difference between farming a piece of the "tribal land" and lineage land. Each could not be sold; only usufructural rights were exercised. Perhaps the only apparent advantage with acquiring "tribal land" was that the chief was duty bound to defend it. In addition, the chief may set aside a portion of the tribal land for communal usage, grazing for example, just as in the West portions of the land can be set aside as public parks, forest reserves, etc.

> In every Kikuyu district there were pasture lands where livestock grazed in common. There were also salt-licks (*moonyo*) and mineral springs (*irori*), the access to which was free to all those in the district. In addition to these were public places (*ihaaro*) reserved for meetings and dances. And also public roads and paths (*njera cia agendi*), as well as sacred groves where national sacrifices were offered to *Ngai* (Kenyatta, 1938:36).

Assume that the Ntonji lineage did not seek any distant land and was content with their 200 acres of land in two or three plots scattered around

---

[9] Shifting cultivation, or land rotation, is a traditional farming practice whereby a plot of land is cultivated continuously for a period of time and then left fallow, in some cases for eight years, to permit the soil to regenerate its fertility.

the village. Upon his death in, say 1923, Ntonji's 200 acres would be divided among his ten children. With the Mbeere tribe of Kenya,

> Once an individual has inherited land from his father or begun cultivation of land gained from his lineage, his agnates do not interfere in these use rights. That is, a person freely uses the land as he wishes, determining what sort of crops to plant, including cash crops. Further, the lineage exercises no rights to any part of the harvest nor to money gained from the sale of tobacco, cotton, or food crops. Use rights gained from inheritance within the domestic group or from acquisition of lineage land (assigned by the trustee on behalf of the group) are indissoluble and provide the cultivator with wide latitude in the ways he will exploit the land (Glazier, 1985: 196).

Ntonji's sons could also acquire unsettled land and add this to the original 200-acre lineage land. However, after colonialism and independence, all unoccupied land became government property.

On the inherited land, Ntonji's sons exercised only usufructural rights. A son had the right of use but could not sell the land. Ownership and control remained within the lineage. Lineage control over the land was exercised by the elders and in some small tribes by the chief:

> Among the Kwena of Botswana, a man named Sephuthabakwa was in 1938 fined by the chief's court for having demanded and received cattle from men to whom he had given part of his arable land, and he was ordered to restore the animals to their former owners. It was explicitly stated that he had behaved very badly: land belongs to the chief and tribe and cannot be sold (Schapera, 1957).

If a son wished to sell an inherited piece of land, he must inform the elders. They would discourage him by references to Ntonji, the ancestor, who enjoined subsequent generations not to relinquish land outside the lineage. If the purpose of the intended sale was to raise money, the elders might offer him the cash or livestock that he required (Glazier, 1985:198). If he persisted in selling, the sale would be permitted on condition that it was redeemable. That is, the seller (the son) would reassume his use rights in land by returning the original amount of livestock or money to the purchaser.

Kenyatta (1938) provided this interesting account of how the Gikuyu acquired their land, taking a typical man and wife situation:

> From the beginning of things, *Ngai* or *Mogai* (God or Benefactor), when he was dividing the world into territories and giving them to the various races and nations that populate the globe, gave the man Gikuyu

a territory full of the good things of nature. The *Mogai* commanded Gikuyu to establish a home for himself and his descendants. Gikuyu and his wife, Moombi, built their first homestead at a place called *Mokorwe wa Gathanga*, and had many children. As time went on, the people increased rapidly owing to the multiplicity of wives and good nourishment from the soil. Soon the land, which was held as the family land, became densely populated. For this reason some of the people decided to move southward and try to acquire more lands from the forest dwellers called the Gumba (pigmy). . .

As the time went on the Gikuyu started to buy lands. All the lands which were bought in this way were held under private ownership or as a family joint property. . .

For example, if a man whom we will call A bought land before he was married, that land was his own private property during his bachelorhood. When he married B, the land became the joint property of husband and wife. In this case we will assume that A had no relatives or he was independent of such relatives. He cleared a part of his land for his wife to cultivate; that part cultivated by his wife became her own or she had full cultivation rights, while the soil still remained the property of the husband. Let us say that a man had 60 acres of land. The first wife might have cultivated 2 acres; she would refer to this part as 'my garden' (*mogonda wakwa*), and the rest as our land (*githaka giito*). Next A married a second wife, C, and cleared another part of his land for her the same way as for B. The land which remained uncultivated belonged to all three. The wives could call it 'our land,' while their husband called it 'my land' (*githaka giakwa*). Now each wife had her garden or gardens according to her capacity in cultivation. No one, except perhaps the husband, would encroach upon her cultivated pieces of land. If any of the wives wanted a new garden, her husband would clear another piece from the uncultivated land. After some time the family began to increase. Let us imagine that each wife had 3 sons and perhaps some daughters. . .

Mr. A with his two wives B and C had six sons. The sons following the father's example married two wives each. In this way the land which used to be the private property of Mr. A, and of which he had absolute ownership, was now shared by several persons who had full cultivation rights, namely, the father, the two wives, the six sons with their twelve wives, making a total of 20 persons who called the land 'ours,' and the father who retained the title of 'my land' (*ng'ondo yakwa*).

For our analysis let us suppose the twelve wives followed the example of their mothers-in-law and had an average of 3 sons each. This would bring the number of the land claimants to 56 persons, all having full cultivation rights, and each regarding the piece under cultivation as 'my garden.' The other uncultivated land or fallow land would be regarded by all collectively as 'our land,' while Mr. A still called the whole of the land 'my land.' If we take the daughters into consideration, as they also had to use land before marriage, we will find that while Mr. A was still living he might have had about 70 or more people of his own as nucleus of his *mbari* or clan unit.

As time went on this group of people became a big community and the land which all regarded as 'our land' could no more support them. When a family group reached this point, the more prosperous members of it went and bought lands somewhere else and started the same procedure; but those who were not in a position to buy land became *ahoi* or *athami*, i.e., they acquired cultivation or building rights on the lands belonging to another family group or clan unit.

The above description gives a clear picture contradicting what is called communal ownership of land, a term which presupposes that the land belonged to every Dick and Harry in the community. This could not be the case for, as we have shown, the land did not belong to the community as such, but to some individual founders of various families who had the full rights of ownership and the control of the land (pp.27-31).

Communal ownership is a misleading description in other tribal systems as well. Open access by all in the village to any piece of land is certainly not the case as evidenced by the practice of shifting cultivation. For if what obtains is communal tenure, then shifting cultivation would only be possible when the whole community moved to another location. As Bohannan (1968) contends, "Communal tenure is an illusion that results from viewing the systematic exploitation by kinship groups of their environment through the distorting lens of western market-oriented and contract-dominated institutions of property and ownership" (p.88).[10]

In fact, there was not in any part of the Gikuyu, as far as memory goes, any land that belonged to everybody, or what is called 'no man's land.' The term 'communal or tribal ownership of land' has

[10] Hill (1987) also observes that, among the Yoruba of Nigeria, land is held by descent groups or corporate lineages. "Although such land is 'corporately owned' it is always farmed by individuals. Communal cultivation is not only unknown, but formed no part of traditional memories" (p.100n).

been misused in describing the land, as though the whole of it was owned collectively by every member of the community.

> The Gikuyu defended their country collectively, and when talking to a stranger they would refer to the country, land, and everything else as 'ours,' *borori wiito* or *borori wa Gikuyu*, to show the unity among the people. But the fact remained that every inch of the Gikuyu territory had its owner, with the boundary properly fixed and everyone respecting his neighbor's (Kenyatta, 1938:26).

The misconception of communal ownership could also have arisen out of innocent Western misinterpretations of statements made by African chiefs. For example, asked about customary law regarding land tenure in Transkei (South Africa), chief Mgudlwa replied:

> According to native custom the land belongs to the chief and is his property. He might sell the land if he were moving away with all the people. He could leave to other people to settle on the land after consulting with the magistrate, but if the *amaphakathi* (council of elders) objected, he would leave it alone.

> Under the tribal tenure, the chief would have the power to dispossess any person and put another in possession. I have heard of this, but I have never done so myself. The way in which land is allocated is this. A man goes to the head chief, who allots him a place in the section occupied by himself. The man does not give the chief anything for this, but he has to work for the chief when called upon without reward, and generally to obey his wishes. In the case, however, of any trespass upon the land allotted, there is no claim for damages, even if the trespass took place in the night. They may thrash the parties trespassing, but this is no formal offense. This was our law, but the magistrate has now made regulations against trespass committed at night (in Koyama, 1980:141).

The use of such terms as "our land," "tribal land," and "land reserved for communal usage" have created much confusion. "Our land" or "tribal land" is used by Africans only in the military sense, as men were required to defend the territorial integrity of the tribe. Additions to the "tribal land" may be made through conquest or by staking a claim to unoccupied land. Of this "tribal land," part may be set aside for communal usage, as in salt licks for all cattle. But not all "tribal land" is subject to such communal usage.

Westerners might have assumed that "tribal land" meant "land belonging to all the members of the tribe" in the economic sense of common usage. But Africans rarely use the expression "the land belongs to us all." Rather, the land belongs to the ancestors and each individual or group has a different ancestor.

Most of the "tribal land" is lineage-owned or controlled and the composition may vary. For example, of the total "tribal land" area, 80 percent may be lineage owned, 10 percent reserved for communal purposes and the rest placed under the custodianship of the chief. To help understand land use for "communal purposes," it would be useful to discuss that of the Dinka of the Sudan.

The territory of a Dinka community is usually comprised of two geographical divisions technically known as *baai* and *toc*. Each of these land divisions has its special significance to Dinka pastoral life. *Toc* is generally low land. This is the area where lakes or rivers overflow their banks and flood the adjacent plains during the rainy seasons. Most parts of the *toc* may be described as open plains or vast areas of land covered by a variety of water plants and grass. The lowest parts of the *toc* remain swampy throughout most of the year. Scattered trees may be found in areas which are relatively high. The "Sud" region along the White Nile is a typical example of *toc*.

Toc is very vital to the life of the Dinka for a number of reasons. First, the Dinka rear cattle in the *toc*. It is very suitable area for their cattle to graze, as it consists of large and rich pastures. Besides the pastures, there is always plenty of water throughout the year for cattle use. Second, the fishing areas are in the *toc*. Third, the *toc* attracts a variety of wild game because of rich pastures and water. It therefore constitutes a good hunting area. Consequently, the life of the Dinka is very much adapted to the *toc* and a Dinka person cannot imagine life without a *toc*.

Baai, on the other hand, literally means "home," meaning land suitable for building homes or permanent settlements. It is also suitable for farming or agriculture. Furthermore, because the *baai* is high ground, it has many forests from which many advantages can be derived.

The real legal importance of the division between *toc* and *baai* rests on the fact that land use in the two areas is different.

> In the *toc* area the whole land is subject to communal usage (with very few exceptions). Private rights are overriden by communal rights. But in the residential area (*baai*), apart from those areas which are reserved for communal use, private interests in land or rights are recognized and respected; for example, the community does not tamper with the rights of an individual to have a residence, or agricultural land around his house (Makec, 1988; p.153).

Among the Nilotes Dinka, Nuer and Shilluk, a man and his family have the exclusive right to use a piece of arable land or residential land. It is inherited from generation to generation. The right of the individual member of the tribal community over his residential land is so strong that even if he abandons it, it must be kept unoccupied unless he gives consent to a relative to take it over (Makec, 1988:156).

The consensus of opinion is that the right of ownership of a given territory is always vested in the community. The problem however is the identification of the nature of the individual's interests or rights in the land, as there are different types of rights: "possessory right," "right of ownership" and "usufruct right." The native African law does not define precisely the nature of the individual's rights. But "despite the vagueness, the general opinion of all the writers is that an individual enjoys ownership rights over his residential and arable land" (Makec, 1988:165).

The exclusive right of a man and his family to use the land, the inheritance of such land from generation to generation, the right of the individual member of the tribal community over the residential land even if such land has been abandoned, all point to the fact that the individual Dinka right in land may be expressed as a right of ownership.

In our earlier example, all those who trace their ancestry to Ntonji were entitled to use his original 200 acres.[11] At any other place in the village, say at Areji's homestead, Ntonji's descendants would be considered "tenants" or "strangers" - those not related to Areji's lineage.

If Ntonji died without leaving heirs, or in the event that the lineage moved temporarily elsewhere, their original 200 acres would be placed in the custody of the chief. He would not be the owner but a mere caretaker. The chief would be at liberty to allot portions to anyone, including non-tribesmen or "tenants", upon the performance of customary rites. "Strangers" may gain access to such a piece of land from the chief by making a token gift of say, a bottle of "schnapps" and two goats.[12] For example, among the Busoga of Uganda, a "tenant" seeking land to cultivate would see the village headman. An allotment fee and time of payment would be agreed upon.

> The allotment fee, *nsibuzi* or *nkoko* (literally a 'hen') was traditionally merely a symbolic payment of a hen or a bark-cloth made in recognition of the headman's authority. . .Once the allotment fee has been paid, the tenant and his heirs have perpetual, rent-free use rights in the land. Under the traditional political system, the tenant would be called upon to pay tribute in produce to the headman and it is said that failure to make such payments was cause for eviction. In 1904, the Council of Soga Chiefs agreed that so long as the tenant cultivated his

[11] Among the Yoruba, land rights were granted only if one were an effective member of the lineage. Rights were forfeited when one left the lineage but could be restored by returning and participating in lineage affairs, thus becoming an effective member.

[12] In some places, tenants may pay a fifth or tenth of the harvest for the right to use the land. This may fall closer to the Western concept of renting or leasing.

holding and paid his poll tax, he could not be evicted. He was, however, required to pay a fixed sum in money tribute to the headman and chiefs in commutation of his former tribute obligations. . .

Although the payment of the allotment fee (non-refundable) assured usufructuary rights in the holding to the tenant and his heirs, the tenant must fulfil certain conditions in order to maintain these rights: otherwise the headman may assert his reversionary right to the holding. The tenant must either live on his holding or cultivate it or, if he desires to rest it must state his intention to do so to the headman in the presence of witnesses. If these conditions are not fulfilled, the headman may reclaim the land (Fallers, 1965: 165).

Among the Dagaaba, the *tendaana*, the custodian of the land, performed certain functions.

As 'owner' of the land, one of the most obvious functions of the *tendaana* has always been the administration of land. He was an active administrator of the land, particularly at the establishment of each village, and was instrumental as a witness to the acquiring of unoccupied land as individual or family land by new settlers. It was his duty to establish boundaries and recall them in land disputes. It was always the duty of the *tendaana* and his family to keep mental records of various individual and family landholdings and to police the boundaries of the village against encroachment by surrounding villages. When village boundary problems arose, all its members were expected to support the *tendaana* and his family (Yelpaala, 1983; p.370).

Among the Ashanti,

The custodianship of the chief entailed certain rights and responsi-bilities. The chief was responsible for the defense of the land at law or by arms. He had also certain defined rights which were coexistent with the rights of lineages and individuals in his Division. In case of extreme need he could sell the land, but not without the consent of his council and a sacrifice to the ancestors. The chief had a right to certain portions or skins of certain wild animals killed on the land of the Division. He was entitled to tributes of fish from those who fished in its rivers; to a certain amount of work on his farm from his people, and to an annual tribute of food, meat, or fish at the *Odwira* ceremony.

But over the same piece of land his people had rights of usufruct. Any piece of land to which no lineage had the claim of usufruct came directly under the chief in his official capacity. Strangers wanting land on which to settle or farm would ask the chief, who would give them portions of these lands. . .

When an Ashanti said that the land belonged to the chief or the stool, he meant that the chief had these rights, but he was also aware that the subjects of the chief, grouped according to lineages, had recognized rights in the land too. These were the principles of Ashanti land-tenure (Busia, 1951:45).

One observes the same practice among the Shona:

The chief's dominion over the land finds practical expression in that only he can give permission for a group of foreigners to settle in the chiefdom and cultivate its soil. In the past, various hunting tributes were payable to the chief in recognition of his dominion over the land in which the kill was made: the chief received the elephant tusk nearest to the ground when the elephant fell, the skin or heart of any lion killed in his territory, a portion of certain kinds of big game, and he could claim any scaly ant-eater (believed to have strong medicinal properties) killed in his territory. In the old days, when a chief travelled through his country he received tribute from the crops of his subjects in recognition of the fact that they grew on the chief's land. . .

In return for his dominion, the chief has the duty to ensure good rains and good crops by performing the appropriate rituals to the spirit guardians of the chiefdom and in the past he had also to protect his people from invaders and raiders (Bourdillon, 1976:87).

The African chief is in some sense owner of the land, but this "ownership" is restricted to very limited rights over the land and certain duties towards it. Once the chief has granted cultivation rights to an immigrant, these rights are inalienable; the grantee has indisputable rights to the produce of his land, his herds and their offspring and he has the right to keep away trespassers. But he cannot sell his land rights and should he leave the territory these revert to the chief. Even when the chief was paid tribute, he was not entirely free to use it but was bound by customary rules and especially by his obligation to help subjects in need.

Tenant rights were enforced and the headman could not arbitrarily repossess the land.

The sovereign's right of appropriation and confiscation was not exercised lightly or recklessly. Only in cases of, for example, the commission of a grave offense against the community, abandonment of the land, or when the chief required the land for himself or for another chief, was this right exercised. There could therefore be 'despotic acts' giving evidence of an unbridled exercise of power, but there was always the safeguard that the powers were not exercised recklessly. I submit that public opinion would always be taken into account. There were also always the councillors whose advice was as a rule taken into account by the chief. In practice, therefore, the rights of the individual were never nullified (Koyama, 1980; p.69).

Yelpaala (1983) noted the special circumstance under which the chief could expropriate land among the Dagaaba:

The *tendaana* and his family could unilaterally terminate a person's farming rights to a particular parcel of land for defiling the *tengan* (the earth deity) by erecting a wet ebony stick in the farm. The occupant of that land is then expected to abandon the farm straightaway or death will immediately follow. However, the *tendaana* cannot and does not transfer someone's land to another unilaterally (p.370).

When this happened, a tenant could seek redress. Fallers (1965) reports a village court case between a tenant and a headman. The plaintiff (the tenant) accused the headman "of chasing me from my land, which I bought from him for thirty-five shillings, without refunding the money which I paid him for it" (p.264).

The court ruled in the tenant's favor and the headman was fined thirty-seven shillings to be given the plaintiff: thirty-five shillings for restitution and two shillings for the court fee paid by the plaintiff. The land reverted to the headman.

What the individual farmer cultivated on the land was of his own determination. But in some tribal societies, his farming activities must synchronize with those of his agnates. In Yoruba, Nigeria, for example, the *ebi* was traditionally the agnatic descent group which shared a common residence. This body of agnatic kinsmen, with their wives, had an estate - a precisely determinable area within which they traditionally farmed, and which they protected from encroachments by others. Within the *ebi*, the members farmed not in specific areas which they considered their own, but the group moved its farms about within the area so that they could remain as a unit to take advantage of the best soils and to control the system of fallowing (Bohannan, 1964; p.180). Nobody "owned" anything, but every member had a right to a farm sufficient to support his immediate dependents. These rights to a farm were inalienable. The *ebi* had a head and council which ran the agricultural affairs of the *ebi*.

A plot of land worked by a man would pass on to his heirs in Yorubaland.

But they would only own the crops they grew on it. "Trees like oil palm, kola trees, and cocoa are private property, owned by the person who plants them and later by his heirs (Bascom, 1984; p.24). Thus, one man may own a kola tree when another has the right to plant beneath it but no right to touch the kola nuts. Outsiders are permitted to lease clan land for farming on condition that they pay an annual fee (*ifo, ishakole*) as an acknowledgment of the clan's ownership. But when a tenant plants a cocoa tree on the land, the clan may have to go to court to protect its right to it (Bascom, 1984; p.24).

In some parts of Muslim Africa, land can be bought and sold. According to Hill (1987),

> The fact that in Hausaland (Nigeria) all land 'ultimately belonged' to the crown did not prevent ordinary farmers from behaving as though they were the outright owners of their farmland which, if it were *karakara* (annually cultivated manured land) could be freely sold or mortgaged as it had been previously: The Muslim courts recognize individual rights and compensation was paid when the government requisitioned farmland. . .The sale of *karakara* was an ancient practice, certainly preceding the colonial conquest of northern Nigeria by at least a century (p.147).

A powerful influence was the Koran, which recognized private property and laid down rules for inheritance. In Muslim Egypt and the Maghrib, the theoretical ownership of all landed property remained vested in the state. But in practice, it was alienated through such devices as grants of tax-collecting rights and grants of land to religious foundations (*waqfs*). During the reign of Muhammad Ali, pasha of Egypt, in 1812-1814, full legal private land ownership was established in Egypt. Islamic law did not, however, forbid undivided family property nor "tribal ownership" of land as was the case in Upper Egypt.

But in neighboring Ethiopia,

> Private ownership was commonplace and a method of land-holding very much like it was found in Rwanda. Its development was frequently associated with strong central government and the emergence of classes, separate religious institutions and personnel, intensive agriculture (especially irrigation and plough-cultivation) and a high ratio of people to land. . .Even in Ancient and Macedonian Egypt, where the government was particularly power-ful, individual and institutional property in land existed. Theoretically, all land belonged to the crown; practically, although the king was by far the biggest landowner, with estates in every administra-tive district (*nome*), private and temple ownership was common.

Temple estates, for the maintenance of the priests and the support of religion, and mortuary endowments, for the cult of the dead, were sometimes very large indeed. Ramases II (1198-66 B.C.) gave nearly a thousand square kilometers, inhabited by 86,000 people, to Amun, the god of Thebes. Private estates varied considerably in extent, from a few hectares (granted, for example, to a veteran) to great multiple land-holdings. Some were run as a unit of production, others broken up into plots and cultivated by tenants (Wickins, 1981:50).

In southern Ghana, migrant cocoa farmers were able to buy the land outright during the 19th century. In fact, "it is well over a century since the Krobo of the southern Ghana started buying forest land on a large scale for the purpose of establishing oil-palm plantations" (Hill, 1987:146).

In the traditional Gikuyu system, land could also be bought and sold outright. Kenyatta (1938) provided this riveting account of this process of sale:

After land was bought from Ndorobo, any man who held such land, through purchase or inheritance, had full rights to sell it outright or give it to any one as he liked without consulting any one, except the elders who acted as the ceremonial witnesses in all land transactions. . .

In the Gikuyu system of land tenure the most important aspect and deciding factor as to the ownership of land is the ceremony of marking the boundary. This was performed only when absolute land sale took place. In the case of a *mohoi* or *mothami*, *mociarwa* or *mothoni*, no such ceremony could be performed between them and the landlord, for they had only been given cultivation or building rights.

It was only when the purchaser had paid or agreed to pay the number of sheep and goats required as the price of the land, that the two parties concluded an agreement in the form of a ceremony. This was done in the presence of the principal elders of the district who acted as witnesses. Before buying and selling of land took place, there was a preliminary ceremonial discussion between the seller and the buyer.

According to etiquette of the people, no man could go directly to another and tell him that he wanted to buy his land. The same applied to the seller, he could not advertise the sale of his land publicly; the reason being that the land was regarded as the mother of the people, and as such the selling or buying of it must be treated matrimonially.

Therefore, the correct approach was that when a man wanted to buy another man's land, he would brew a small beer and take it to the landowner in the same way as if he were proposing marriage to his daughter. After sipping the beer ceremonially, the two men would then join in a conversation, talking in parable something like this: 'Well, son of So-and-So, I brought you this small beer to tell you that within your homestead I have seen a beautiful lass. I hope you will excuse me when I say that I am madly in love with her. My great desire which urged me to come here today is to ask you if you will accept me as your son-in-law. I am sure that you, being a man of great experience, will not fail to see the admiration I have in my heart for your beautiful lass. And I know that you will not fail to give your consent to my humble request.'

Through such a conversation the landowner would know at once what the guest really wanted. Then, in the same parable language, they would agree or disagree. If they agreed about the price of the land they would fix a date and invite the elders of the district to be present as ceremonial witnesses.

On the appointed day, the elders gathered on the land in question, where the two parties wishing to enter into symbolical matrimony awaited them. The seller of the land was asked to testify by an oath that the land he was selling was his own property, that he or his ancestors were the original and rightful owners. And that he was satisfied with the number of sheep and goats he had asked as the price of his land, and that later he would not ask the purchaser to give him more than what had been already agreed to. Then the elders turned to the purchaser and asked him to take oath and declare that he had willingly agreed to buy the land and to give the number of sheep and goats asked for it; that the animals he was giving were his own or family property, and that there was no dispute as to the ownership of such property in his family group or outside it.

When the above declaration was concluded, the purchaser provided a ram, which was slaughtered on the spot where the declaration was made. The contents of the stomach were taken out, then the elders formed a procession with the seller and the purchaser at the head of it. They moved slowly chanting a ceremonial melody connected with the fertility of the soil. The landowner pointed out the boundary of his land which he was selling, at the same time the ceremonial elder sprinkled the contents of the stomach along the line, while the rest planted trees and lilies (*matooka*) as a permanent boundary mark.

The elders, in their ritual tones, uttered curses against anyone who should cunningly or maliciously remove the boundary mark of his neighbor. When the marking of the boundary was completed, all sat down at the center of the land, two small pieces were cut from the skin of the ram, the purchaser put one on his right wrist and so did the seller. This act of uniting the two men in the land transaction, who now regarded one another as relatives-in-law, concluded the ceremony of marking the boundary.

After the elders had finished their official duty they joined in a meat feast and sometimes in beer drinking. The elder who sprinkled the contents of the stomach along the boundary line was given a ewe as the reward for his laborious duty. The official name of the ritual gift is known as '*mwate wa kuhura njegeni*,' i.e., a ewe for dusting off aching caused by a stinging creeper called *njegeni*.

According to the Gikuyu system of land tenure no man could claim absolute ownership of any land unless he or his ancestors had gone through the ceremony of marking the boundary, which was the Gikuyu form of title-deed. The boundary trees and lilies so ceremonially planted were highly respected by the people. They were well looked after and preserved. The history connected with such lands was passed from one generation to another. No man dared remove his neighbor's boundary mark, for fear of his neighbor's curses and out of respect for him.

If one of the boundary trees or lilies dried out, fell down, or was rooted up by the wild animals, the two neighbors would visit the spot and perhaps replace it, but if they could not agree as to the actual place where the mark stood, they called one or two elders who, with a little ceremony, replanted the tree or lilies. But in case of a big dispute, especially where a fire had destroyed boundary marks, a full council of elders was called to replant the tree and lilies (pp.38-41).

Wickins (1981) noted that similar "sales" occur among the Chagga in East Africa, the Nupe and Tiv of West Africa and the Bemba of Central Africa (p.48). In most tribal systems, however, the concept of land sale was an alien one. Land could not be sold because of the universal belief that it belonged to the ancient ancestors and those living on it held it only in trust. To part with it was to invite the wrath of the ancestors. Land could not be alienated by sale to foreigners.

Land was also deified and selling it was considered sacrilegious. "Among the Igbo, the earth-deity or the spirit-force of the land, was the 'fount of all fertility and the guardian of public morality" (Olaniyan, 1985:98). A family or an individual could not alienate the land. There were religious beliefs and sanctions to back up this practice.

Similar beliefs were found among the Asante and many African societies. The soil was regarded as a deity, a goddess who could be neither bought nor sold. "Thus, when a stranger 'purchased' or was allocated land, he came into possession only of the *use* of the land" (Hull, 1976; p.83). African strangers to traditional towns and cities understood this principle that produced the most difficulty for the Europeans, who operated on the erroneous assumption that the chiefs were the "owners" of the land, rather than trustees. Consequently, when the chiefs granted land concessions in return for gifts, the transfers were misinterpreted by the Europeans as "sales."

It is not difficult to speculate why the sale of land was forbidden in rural Africa. Its use and rights were an integral part of the web of lineage relationships. The land was ancestral property. It was deified since ancestry provided the article of social cohesion. If the land was sold, the social group would disintegrate. Furthermore, for the natives, land was their only asset that afforded them income and security. In their uncertain world, they could at least rely on their land to produce food. Under the traditional system of government, they received no subsidies or income supplements from the government. They fended for themselves.

Second, sale of land was prevented to afford the elderly a place to stay. If land sales were permitted, the younger generation might sell to new owners who might evict the elders — mostly the old and the infirm. Third, saleability of the land would establish the complete independence of the heirs from the elders. Preventing land sale allowed the elders to retain some form of social control over the younger generation. Fourth, land sale was not allowed to prevent purchases by rival ethnic groups.

For these and other reasons, land sale, in general, was not and is still not permitted in much of traditional Africa. However, access to land is readily available, even to "strangers." Moreover, what is produced on the land is an individual decision to be made by farmers of their own free will and choice. More importantly, the harvest is private, not communal or government property. Busia (1951) was emphatic on the Ashanti:

> Individual members could cultivate farms on the lineage portion of the land, and own individually the crops they grew. They could do what they liked with these. But they could not sell the farmland, or any economic trees like kola or palm-trees standing on it without the consent of the lineage (p.48).

Many other African customary laws have a system similar to the Roman right of usufruct. For example, the Dinka word for this is *oor* under which "the one who cultivates the land of another owns the farm produce" (Makec, 1988:162).

Land Reform - A Digression

In the 1960s and 1970s, the land tenure system came under increasing attack from development practitioners who considered it "an obstacle" to agricultural development. Private or individual ownership was widely advocated as necessary for the "green revolution." Over-zealous experts drew up "Land Reform Programs" and could not rest until they saw peasants brandishing title-deeds to their own little plots of land. Without private ownership, the experts argued, there would be little incentive to improve the land. The result would be over-grazing, over-cultivation, exhaustion of soil fertility and soil erosion.

These arguments provided African governments with the pretext to seize unoccupied land for development purposes. Part of the state land was allocated for sale to private developers. There were some merits in the arguments in favor of private ownership. But problems inevitably arose when the "private ownership solution" was imposed on the rural economy with little understanding of its existing tenure and production system.

Traditionally, food has been produced in Africa under a system of shifting cultivation. Though land has always been plentiful in Africa, the practice was rapidly becoming untenable. Increasing population pressures on the land reduced the length of the fallow period. Further, the appropriation of unoccupied land by the state made it difficult for peasant farmers to rotate their land. The combination of these factors resulted in intensive cultivation, the exhaustion of soil fertility, and consequent soil degradation, erosion and increasing desertification.

Clearly, soil maintenance and land improvements are needed in Africa. The natives themselves realised this; hence, the old practice of shifting cultivation. But communal ownership was not the problem for which an immediate "private ownership" solution was required. "Communal ownership" never stopped the spectacular successes of the cocoa farmers of West Africa, nor Africa's other cash crop producers. The native land tenure system did not preclude land improvement and innovative uses of it:

> The view that traditional rule prevents land reform is not very sound. In the last half of the 19th century, people from the Krobo and Akuapim areas succeeded in obtaining land for the production of palm-oil and the cultivation of cocoa in Akyem Abuakwa. In the present century, farmers from other parts of Ghana have migrated in increasing numbers to the central and western regions and

obtained land for the cultivation of cocoa, palm-oil and other crops. The control of land by traditional rulers has not prevented the use of land by other people.

Secondly, it is doubtful that if the Central Government assumes control of the lands of the various political communities, and the officials of the Central Government become the allocators of land, people will become any happier. The officials of the Government of Ghana distribute plots of land in the cities of Accra and Kumasi for building purposes. But only those who have succeeded in acquiring some plots would say that the officials distribute them on a fair basis (Arhin, 1985; p.128).

However, to improve the situation, one needs to adopt schemes with less socially disruptive effects. For example, tribal land reserved for common grazing could be fenced in and managed in much the same way as a national park in the West is managed: charge a fee (say $2 per head of cattle) and use the proceeds to fertilize, irrigate and provide rich pasture. It would save the pastoralists days of wandering in search of pasture. At the same time, it provides them with a sense of sharing which is so important to them. If properly managed, such a project could provide employment and revenue for the tribal treasury.

With farming, of course, it would be preferable to have individual peasant farmers themselves take improvement measures through the application of fertilizers and compost, and cultivate a plot of land continuously at one fixed place. Imprecise ownership rights, however, prevent individual improvements to the land. But outright private ownership of rural land would be neither a feasible nor a desirable solution because of the complexity of traditional tenure systems.

In the 1970s when Kenya instituted a program of private ownership of rural land, the result was a chaotic explosion of land disputes between tenants, strangers and hosts or lineage owners (Glazier, 1985; p.197). A more feasible alternative would treat the lineage as a "corporate entity" and award this body the ownership title. As argued in Chapter 1, it would be more useful to treat peasants as corporate groups rather than as individuals in the Western scheme of things. For example, it would make more sense to extend an agricultural loan to a clan head than to an individual peasant; likewise, title deeds for land ownership.

The advantages of this alternative are twofold: first, it would permit land-users to retain some of their valued facets of the kinship group. Kinship serves as the peasant's insurance society, his old-age pension, as well as his community. Second, it would permit them to constitute themselves into "corporations" - sole or aggregate - which are units of modern societies.

This "solution" was tried with remarkable results elsewhere. According to Bohannan (1964):

> The Osage (An American Indian tribe), when they struck oil, turned their tribe into a limited corporation under the laws of the State of Oklahoma. The Yoruba people of the western region of Nigeria turned their extended-family compounds (*ebi*) into landholding units before the law, under the 'Communal Land Rights (Vesting in Trustees) Law' of 1958 (p.180).

That law, in effect, transformed the Yoruba lineage group, the *ebi*, into a legal entity before the laws of Nigeria. As such, the "corporation" could own land, complete with property rights. As a corporation, the *ebi* would have less difficulty borrowing money for land improvements. This, it seems, would be a much more appropriate solution to the land tenure problem.

Labor

Work on the land necessarily demanded labor, which was supplied from within the extended family. The larger the extended family, the more self-sufficient the unit was in its labor requirements. This fact partly explains the cultural tendency to have many wives and children. Philoprogenitive propensities were socially acceptable and in fact considered an investment in human capital that yielded results especially at harvest time.

Planting and nurturing Africa's staples required little labor. Cassava (manioc), for example, merely required breaking its stem and pushing it into the ground. Crops were fed by rain. But the two stages in the food-production cycle making the greatest demands on labor were harvesting and transporting the produce to the villages. For these tasks, peasant farmers relied on their children and kinsmen. Occasionally when labor needs exceeded the capacity of the extended family, recourse was made to "cooperative work groups."

Such groups were organized for heavy farm work or for a specific project such as clearing a piece of land for farming or putting up a structure. Generally, work groups involved the pooling together of members of the same age group, kinsmen, or all male or female members of a village. In Benin, the cooperative work group was called *dopkwe* and was used by the peasant farmer when his "fields were too extensive to permit them to be hoed by his own labor and the labor of those whose services he has at his disposal" (Skinner, 1964). The Afikpo Igbo had two types of cooperative work groups. The first, *ozi aho*, (work-everybody) was a men's group organized most commonly for house-building and for yam heap-making. The second was *ozuzu* (committee), formed by young women on the basis of friendship for mutual help in weeding during a farming season (Gibbs, 1965; p.9).

Among the Yoruba,

> A man can invite his relatives, his friends or the members of his club, depending on the size of the task, to form a working bee (*owe*). He provides food and drink for the group at the end of the day's work, but this is not considered payment; others participate because they earn the right to call upon their host for help under similar circumstances. No strict accounting is kept of an individual's participation; but if someone calls for working bees without taking part when others hold them, it is noticed and others will fail to respond to his invitation (Bascom, 1984; p.20).

The Nupe used a larger cooperative unit called the *egbe*. The cooperative working party was also used for purposes other than agricultural. Among the Ngwato of Botswana, men's regiments may be called upon to build huts or cattle kraals and women's regiments to thatch or weed.

There were other ways in which additional labor could be obtained. Among the Yoruba, farmers may agree to a labor exchange (*aro*), working together an equal number of days or hoeing the same number of heaps on the farm of each in turn. The host would provide only food. Through a system of peonage, the wealthy had others working for them as pawns. The pawns (debt slaves) served as collateral security for loans borrowed by their parents or themselves. They worked for the creditor until the loan was paid. This practice has long been abolished in many parts of Africa.

Clientage was another means by which additional labor could be secured outside the extended family. Ordinary citizens would voluntarily attach themselves to a patron and offer their labor services in return for protection, education or instruction in some trade or craft. This practice was widespread in South Africa among the Xhosa, the Thembu, the Zulu and Dlamini. A person would be lent cattle by a wealthy community leader or chief. He herded the cattle and drank their milk, and received some of their offspring. In exchange, he assisted the owner in building or fencing or attended him in a court case or in war (Kendall and Louw, 1987; p.5).

The institution of domestic slavery provided additional labor, although this was largely used by the wealthy and powerful. "Slaves were obtained as captives in wars or raids, and as commodities bought in the market" (Falolan, 1985). However, as we saw in the previous chapter, the treatment of African "limbries" was by no means harsh. To a large extent, slaves were free to own property and participate in government. Some even rose to prominent positions in government. Further, not all African societies had slaves. For example, the Bantu-speaking Nguni never dealt in slaves nor enslaved their own people for debt (Wickins, 1981: 61).

Capital

Economists define "capital" as anything that is not wanted for its own sake but aids in the production of further goods. Thus, Robinson Crusoe's fishing net was a capital good; similarly tractors, industrial machines and scythes. By popular usage, however, capital has come to mean funds or money needed to operate or start a business. In indigenous Africa, capital funds were generally scarce. There were banks in colonial Africa, but the natives lacked the collateral to obtain credit. To secure their initial start-up capital for their fishing and commercial operations, they turned to two traditional sources of finance. One was the *"family pot."* As was discussed in Chapter 1, each extended family had a fund into which members made contributions according to their means. Coercion was not applied but non-contribution effectively extinguished one's access to the "pot."

The fund was used for a variety of purposes: consumption and investment. For example, to cover funeral expenses, weddings, the educational costs of the more gifted among them, to finance extension of the family house or to provide capital. Among the Ewe seine fishermen of Ghana, the family pot was called *"agbadoho."* Members borrowed from this pot to purchase their fishing nets and paid back the loans.

The second source of finance was a revolving credit scheme which was widespread across Africa. It was called *susu* in Ghana, *esusu* in Yoruba, *tontines* or *chilembe* in Cameroon and *stokfel* in South Africa.[13] Typically, a group of say 10 people would contribute say $100 into a fund. When it reached a certain amount, say $1,000, it was handed over to the members in turn. Such a scheme required a liberal dosage of trust among members to be operational and somehow the natives managed to make it work. In fact, for many businesses in the indigenous and informal sector, the loan club was their primary source of capital.[14]

---

[13] The *skokfel* (or *stockvels*), however, was more than a rural credit scheme. It was an institution of mutual aid that provided support in case a member suffered a bereavement or went to jail. The support was invariably extended to the member's family (Iliffe, 1987; p.136).

[14] Three observations regarding the *tontines* may be instructive. First, they are not unique to Africa alone. Similar schemes exist in other parts of the Third World. These are called *hui* in China and Vietnam; *keh* in Korea; *tandas* in Mexico; *pasanaku* in Bolivia; *san* in the Dominican Republic; "syndicate" in Belize; *gamaiyah* in Egypt; *hagbad* in Somalia; *xitique* in Mozambique; *arisan* in Indonesia; *paluwagan* in the Philippines; *chit fund* in India and Sri Lanka; *pia huey* in Thailand and *ko* in Japan. Second, if the same *susu* scheme of the African natives were organized in the United States, it would be called a credit union! A credit union is simply an association of individuals who pool their savings together to lend only to themselves (the members). Third, these indigenous saving clubs still exist;

"In Cameroon, a survey of 360 businesses showed that more than half started with help from the *tontines* or *chilembe*" (*South*, Feb 1989; p.25).

A sample of 398 village households in rural Niger in 1986 indicated that informal credit accounted for 84 percent of total loans and was equal to 17 percent of

One could also borrow money by pledging farms, a practice which was common in Ghana and Nigeria (Hill, 1987; Von Pische, 1983). If borrowing was not possible, one could form a partnership with a person with capital.

A common arrangement involved three partners who shared the returns from a venture equally. In trading ventures, one partner supplied the capital, one transported the goods and braved the hazards of the trail, and the other organized the partnership, which in some cases involved little more than getting the capitalist in touch with someone who had the stamina and courage to make the trip (Miracle, 1971).

In commerce, middlemen or agents were able to secure trade credit solely on the basis of trust. A producer or importer would advance some goods to a trader for repayment to be made in a few months in a medium acceptable to the supplier. In Senegal, for example, thirty barrels of flour was payable in four months; bars of iron had 5 months credit in the 19th century (Newbury, 1971).

At Old Calabar in 1851, the British Council estimated that at least 70,000 pounds (sterling) of imported goods were in the possession of brokers and a further 13,000 pounds (sterling) had been advanced and already traded to suppliers. Another observer found that 'with the utmost confidence a fellow nearly naked will ask you for three, four, or even five thousand pounds (sterling) worth of goods on credit, and individuals are often trusted to that amount. I have trusted more than one man goods, the returns of which were worth between two and three thousand pounds.' Trust formed the essential part of the agreements between Sierra Leone traders and King Docemo of Lagos in 1854. . .In the Gambia, the scale of trust in the 1850s was about 200 to 2,000 pounds sterling per agent, and there were eight or ten agents for each French firm (Newbury, 1971).

In West Africa, much of the palm-oil trade, like the slave trade, operated on the trust (credit) system (Boahen and Webster, 1970; p.187). European

agricultural income. Informal *tontines* (rotating savings and credit associations) predominate. . .

Out of a sample of 56 *tontines* in 22 villages, some had only 4 members, others more than 40. The average member contribution ranged from 100 CFA francs (25 cents) to CFA 25,000 ($70). The total size of all 56 *tontines*, as measured by member contributions per meeting, was the equivalent of $72,000. This suggests a promising base for deposit mobilization in rural Niger (World Bank, *World Development Report*, 1989; p.113).

merchants advanced goods on trust to House heads who in turn gave them out on trust to their buying agents in the interior. When a ship arrived the captain expected that the merchants to whom he had given trust would have a cargo of oil ready so that there would be little delay in returning to Europe.

It must be pointed out, however, that the trust system did not always work out satisfactorily. Africans could receive the goods and abscond with them. Though there were frequent complaints about cheating, few Europeans were willing to give it up since it was an effective weapon against commercial rivals. As Boahen and Webster (1970) put it:

> An African was compelled to sell all his oil to the European whose trust he held. The European never wanted his trust totally repaid by a reliable merchant because the African would then be free to sell to the European's rivals. Europeans tried every method, honest and dishonest, to keep Africans in debt to them. To break the monopoly hold on Africans, new firms would offer either higher prices or trust on easier terms. If the Africans supplied the new merchant with oil the old firms would forcibly seize it. The king would then declare a boycott of all trade until the dispute was settled. *The king also declared a trade boycott when the European firms combined to fix prices.* Nevertheless, despite its imperfections, the trust system did supply Africans with some credit to begin commercial operations. (Italics mine).

Notice the punitive action by the African king against European firms when they colluded to fix prices. After independence, as we shall see in Chapter 10, it was not the European firms or African kings but rather African nationalist governments who fixed prices.

Entrepreneurship and the Profit Motive

The enterpreneur, in economics, is the person who assesses the market situation, sees a profitable opportunity, marshalls the resources (factors of production) necessary to produce a product or service and then sells this to the public. In these activities, the entrepreneur bears considerable risks. The market opening may evaporate without warning or the product may not turn out to be exactly what consumers want. If he/she errs in the calculations, there will be losses to be borne out of the entrepreneur's own pocket. If he/she is successful, there will be profits.[15] Consequently,

---

[15] Those who rail against excessive profits often fail to consider the other side of the coin. When a business fails, the losses are absorbed by the entrepreneur. If excess profits must be taxed, would the government be prepared to subsidize private losses?

evidence of risk-taking, occupational specializations and profit/loss may be taken as hallmarks of entrepreneurship.

Before the advent of Europeans, the three listed attributes could be found in indigenous Africa. It was true Africans were overburdened with an institutionalized leviathian of social obligations and mores. But as Smith (1962) observed for the Hausa:

> The pressure of these demands on Hausa traders stimulates them to increased exertion. No margin of profit is too great or too small for their notice: no type of exchange is unsuitable providing it gives a good return and is not forbidden by Islam. With this ethic, the Hausa are indefatigable traders, having a special flair for bargaining. They are willing to take high risks for the chance of commensurate profit.

Although kings and chiefs opened markets, in some ethnic societies they were founded by individuals. For example, among the Guro of Ivory Coast, "The founder of a market was usually a pre-eminent and rich individual, a *fua*, who sought social recognition. The opening of a market was the occasion of a celebration: cattle were killed and people from the neighboring villages were invited to share the meat. It was usual to give the market the name of its founder" (Meissalloux, 1962). Such a venture was risky, as people might not patronize it and use a nearby market instead.

There were other risk-taking ventures. Africans also travelled great distances to buy and sell commodities. In fact, there was the existence of whole groups devoted specifically to commerce. Diop (1987) mentioned the ancestors of present-day Djula and Sarakolle (p.132). But the Kwawu of Ghana and the Yoruba of Nigeria were particularly known. Yoruba traders were almost everywhere in West Africa: in Kano, Katsina, Whyddah, Elmina, Bamako and Ouagadougou (Gibbs, 1965; p.558).

There was also craft specialization. Certainly, those who produced pottery did not expect to eat it. Neither did the Yoruba sculptors. Production was predicated upon the existence of a market for the finished product - a market which could vanish at any time. Producing for a market necessarily entailed risk-taking and entrepreneurship, traditions which were there in pre-colonial Africa.

The gold rush that occurred on the Gold Coast in the 1880s could scarcely be dismissed as "subsistence agriculture." Indigenous mining was flourishing with simple tools (shovels, hoes, picks, hammers, chisels and pans). Tarkwa, in the southwestern part of the Gold Coast, was booming with immigrants from many parts of West Africa. One such entrepreneur was Thomas Hughes, a Fanti of Cape Coast, who was "represented as the pioneer of modern mining: he imported heavy machinery and worked in Western Wassaw" (*West Africa*, April 11, 1988; p.628).

Europeans also took part in the gold rush. Between 1877 and 1883, over 100 such concessions were granted by the chiefs in the Tarkwa area on which they drew rents and royalties. Little historical evidence suggests the existence of malpractices or overt discrimination in the grant of these concessions. The natives and the Europeans were treated equally by the chiefs. By 1880, the natives had formed the Wassaw and Ahanta Gold Mines Syndicate in the Tarkwa area to compete with the European mining operations. Another Fanti Syndicate - the Gold Coast Native Concession Purchasing Company - was set up in 1882 by such dignitaries as J.F. Amissah, F.C. Grant, J. Sarbah, J.H. Brew and J.W. Sey. There were also many indigenous small-scale operators whose activities involved panning alluvial gold. Those who could not participate in the panning of gold saw profitable opportunities in acting as middlemen between the chiefs and the Europeans. Africanus Horton was said to have participated in 31 of the first 108 concessions granted (*West Africa*, April 11, 1988; p.629). These operators were essentially free enterprisers. But European mining companies saw them differently.

In the 1890s, they persuaded the colonial administration to pass two ordinances to restrict the activities of the indigenes. The first was the "Mercury Ordinance," which required that a Gold Coast citizen secure a licence to "import, have possession, buy, sell or transfer" the mercury used in gold processing. The second, the "Rivers Ordinance," stipulated that an indigene must get a licence before dredging or diverting water in "certain scheduled rivers" (*West Africa*, April 11, 1988; p.630). The natives could not meet these requirements and *galamsey* (panning of alluvial gold) declined as an economic activity.

A similar episode occurred in South Africa. According to Kendall and Louw (1987), in 1835, 16,000 Mfengu with 22,000 head of cattle formally entered the Cape Colony and settled in the Peddie District. On arrival, they raised cattle and engaged in agriculture, tilling, ploughing, and reaping. They used their wages to invest in sheep, wagons, and tools. Before long, they were engaged in trade and transport. During the 1840s and 1850s, they were selling tobacco, firewood, cattle, and milk, and disposing of surplus grain for cash or stock. As Kendall and Louw (1987) put it:

> By the 1870s, black farmers in the Eastern Cape were active and prosperous. The Mfengu competed against white farmers at agricultural shows and won many prizes. A Wesleyan missionary told the 1865 Commission on Native Affairs: 'Even this year (after the drought) I think their exhibition far surpassed that of the Europeans. It was a universal remark in the district that the Mfengu exhibition far excelled that of the Europeans both as to number and quality of the articles exhibited.' A Cape statistician noted: 'Taking everything into consideration, the native district of Pedie surpasses

the European district of Albany in productive prowess.'. . .Commentators of the time described the blacks as 'very
industrious,''very thrifty,' 'greatly progressing,' with 'a desire to
have their children educated.' It was observed that *freedom from
restraint is a ruling passion in them*.'. . .By 1890, there were between
1,000 and 2,000 affluent commercial farmers (p.11). (Italics mine.)

White South African farmers felt threatened by blacks. Not only were
blacks better farmers, according to Kendall and Louw (1987) but they were
also competing with white farmers for land. As a result, a series of laws were
passed, as in the case of the Gold Coast, that robbed blacks of almost all
economic freedom. But the worst came after independence, as we shall see in
Chapter 10, when African elites and nationalist governments, under various
misguided ideological postures, enacted laws stripping away the economic,
political and intellectual freedom of their own people.

Profit was never an alien concept to Africa. Throughout Africa's history,
the activities of traders and numerous brokers or middlemen clearly
indicated the pursuit of profit and wealth. Opinions about African traders'
profits were divided. But,

> One observer thought they made as much as 40 percent profit in a
> season's operation. Another analysis in 1841 indicates that the
> trader bought the guinee (blue bafts) at about 16.5 kilos of gum per
> piece and sold it to the Moors at between 24 and 30 kilos to cover
> cost and leave the African trader about 6 kilos or 7 fr. 80 c. per
> piece (Newbury, 1971).

In the brokerage business, the middlemen kept a fixed proportion of the
proceeds. For example, among the Egba and Ijebu brokers of palm oil in
Nigeria in the 1850s, a quarter of the price went to the broker and three-
quarters to African suppliers (Newbury, 1971). Profit calculations were
always on the mind of African traders. For example,

> The Nupe saw to it that the prices of goods corresponded closely to
> variations in supply and demand, above all, to seasonal fluctuations.
> They also made sure that distance between the area of production
> and market, and the additional labour and loss of time involved in
> transport, enter into the calculation of price and profit (Skinner,
> 1964).

If a profitable opportunity presented itself, African traders exploited it.
They kept accounts "in their heads," of course, but they could "read" prices
and how price differences between markets offered opportunities. As McCall
(1962) observed in regard to the women traders of Koforidua of Ghana:
"Traders keep their accounts in their heads, including credit and debit items

with a number of individuals; everyone who has had anything to do with them has commented on their remarkable facility." Newbury (1971) also remarked that West African traders took advantage of inter-market price differentials: "The circuit traders made small profit by transporting staples - salt, gold, ivory, kolas or cloth - between markets where price differentials were high." About 1822, the explorer Laing noted an interesting circuit in tobacco, cloth and rice between the Temne of the Rokel River and the inland Koranto of Sierra Leone:

> The natives who reside near Sierra Leone, through whose country [cloth] passes to the market, gain in a three-fold degree more than the manufacturers. They purchase tobacco at the waterside for about one shilling and sixpence per pound; and travelling to Kooranko, will barter one hundred pounds, or bars, of that commodity for two hundred country cloths; returning to Rokon, they exchange their cloth for rice at the rate of one cloth, or nine-pence sterling, for a tub of rice, the average price of which used to be at Sierra Leone, from five to six shillings (Cited by Newbury, 1971).

At Laing's quoted prices, this meant an outlay of 7 pounds (sterling) and 10 shillings purchased some 50 pounds (sterling) worth of rice at the end of the circuit. Profit by arbitrage was also undertaken by the natives of Gambia as far back as the 17th century. According to Curtin (1971),

> Both gold and slaves were exported across the Sahara, and both were sold on the Gambia for export by sea. In this case, a difference in price between the seaport and the desert port apparently made it profitable to take gold to Tarra instead of the Gambia, even though the distance from Bambuk was greater. The movement of slaves from Tarra to Gambia was a shipment from one port of export to another, again made economic by price differences. The profitability of these moves may also partly be explained by the fact that slave caravans on the march carried headloads, offering by-product transportation for heavy goods.

Curtin also related the exploitation of another profitable opportunity by the Diakhanke of Bundu. When cloth currency was used on the Senegambia, the Diakhanke,

> organized cotton production in their own villages, having the cotton grown by slaves and then woven by slaves or Fulber weavers (*maabube*). After having literally made money, they could spend it anywhere in the region or convert it to gold in nearby Bambuk.

Skinner (1962) also found similar entrepreneurial activity among the Mossi:

> Around 1904, a trader paid about 50 francs or 50,000 cowries for a head of cattle in Mossi country and sold it for about double the price at Salaga. With the proceeds of this transaction, he bought kola nuts at the rate of one franc or 100 cowries per hundred. Thus with the sale of one cow a trader could obtain 10,000 kolas, these being valued at about 500 francs or 500,000 cowries in Mossi country.

There were of course indigenous speculators. Tardits and Tardits (1962) found that:

> In South Dahomey villages, women speculate mostly on corn; the shrewdest buy and store corn in March and April and sell it during the period of scarcity in June and July before the new harvest, when the prices are at their highest. In the head town of Porto-Novo or the port of Cotonou, if they hear a ship will be delayed, women may agree to buy all the stocks of sugar and cigarettes from the stores. The pound of sugar then may climb from 40 to 100 francs, the package of cigarettes from 30 to 110 francs. The rise in price will often be felt in village markets two or three weeks later.

Obviously, it is not only Western "capitalists" who engage in speculative economic activities. One may object to such speculative activities on the grounds that they exploit consumers. However, speculation could mitigate price increases in times of scarcity when hoarded commodities are disgorged. It is true women traders could hoard commodities and drive up prices. Hoarding also represents taking advantage of an abnormal situation. But the fault lies not with the women traders but the *conditions* which gave rise to the hoarding. First, hoarding is risky. Traders cannot predict *how long* a ship will be delayed in arriving. They could lose money, and many often do, if a ship docks earlier than expected. Second, there would be no need to hoard if ships arrive *regularly*. Third, it should be pointed out that consumers, too, hoard; euphemistically referred to as "stocking up." One cannot condemn hoarding by traders and ignore that by consumers.

The people of Africa also proved themselves as capable of complex commercial transactions. Again, according to Curtin (1971),

> In 1689, the principal markets for purchasing slaves was the town of 'Tarra' in the Sahel. Slave-traders from the east and south brought slaves there for sale to the Moors against salt. The Diakhanke tapped into this trade, but in a round-about way. They had tried taking European goods to Tarra, to find that only textiles were

directly exchangeable for either salt or slaves. The non-textiles had first to be traded for textiles. Textiles could buy salt, and salt could buy slaves. But this process required a long stay in Tarra, with high costs for lodging, provisions and probably brokerage as well. The Diakhanke settled on a better method. They took the European goods directly to Bambuk for exchange against gold, then took the gold to Tarra, where it could be exchanged for slaves, and a full complement could be assembled in a few days.

Schneider (1986) provided an interesting account of another such complicated trade but involving the Acholi, Didinga, Dodoth, Kokir, and Tirangori of northeast Uganda in the early part of the twentieth century:

> The Kokir bought goats from the Tirangori in return for cattle. The Kokir then traded the goats to the Didinga to their south for cattle. The Didinga, in turn, shipped grain to their south to the Dodoth to get goats. And the Didinga traded goats to the Acholi to their west to get grain and iron goods. . .What must be happening is this: the Kokir are buying cattle from the Didinga to resell to the Tirangori for profit in cattle. That is to say, they are middlemen in the livestock trade. Similarly, the Didinga are selling goats to the Acholi for grain to resell to the Dodoth for a profit. Looked at its entirety, this is an elaborate, interlocked, international (or regional) system in which goats, cattle, grain, and iron goods are being redistributed to achieve a maximized balance of preferences, and the redistribution being accomplished by a profit system (Schneider, 1986; p.190).

Profit made in traditional Africa was private property; it was for the traders to keep, not for the chiefs or rulers to expropriate. On the Gold Coast in the seventeenth century, there were men of wealth. "The lines of men like Akrosang Brothers and Edward Barter of Cape Coast, Aban and John Kabes of Komenda, John Kurankye of Annomabo, Asomani and Peter Passop of Akwamu and Accra, and John Konny of Ahanta; and their rise to prominence in coastal societies may be cited" (Kwaamu, 1971). Their wealth was not sequestrated by chiefs for equal distribution to all tribesmen.

What the natives did with their profit was their own determination. The traditional practice was to *share* the profit. Under the *Abusa* scheme devised by the cocoa farmers of Ghana at the beginning of this century, net proceeds were divided into three: a third went to the owner of the farm, another third went to hired laborers and the remaining third was set aside for farm maintenance and expansion. Under the less common *Abunu* system, profits were shared equally between the owner and the workers. Variants of this profit-sharing scheme were extended beyond agriculture to commerce (Miracle, 1971) and fishing.[16]

Perhaps it would be fitting to conclude this section with a brief account of the legendary Abi Jones, a successful female entrepreneur in Sierra Leone in the 1860s. This account is paraphrased from White (1987).

She was born on May 12, 1868. When her mother died nine years later, she attached herself to her paternal aunts as an apprentice and secured her business training. The aunts had founded the Ships Chandlers and General Contractors Company after "years of painstaking work building up an extensive network of suppliers of palm produce, vegetables, and fruit." The aunts stood out among the women at the "Big Market" in Freetown by their reputation for reliability in their contacts with European shipping companies.

The company was eventually split in two and Abi Jones was given half to manage. She kept intact the network of produce suppliers and established close personal relationships with the many carriers who brought produce to her.

In addition, she even got to know many of the producers, establishing deals that encouraged her producers to sell their goods exclusively to her. An example of such a supplier was Sarah Cole of Leicester, who sold all her garden vegetables to Jones. Besides close ties with suppliers and carriers, Jones developed relationships with European importers and shippers. Continuing her aunts' reputation for reliability, she was able to gain substantial credit concessions from the European firms. The firms seemed to trust her despite the fact that she was beginning to rival them, for she established direct import and export relations with British, German, and American firms trading in tropical produce or exporting manufactured goods to West Africa (White, 1987; p.96).

By the late 1890s, Abi Jones was exporting piassava, a coarse fiber used to make brushes, to Britain, Japan and the United States. She had eleven sons but no daughters, unfortunately, to carry on her business. The seven sons who survived infancy served as Jones's apprentices however.

---

[16] Profit-sharing schemes, it may be noted, underlie the success and stability of Japanese corporations today. These schemes are currently in use in many parts of Africa. For example, the native fishing enterprises in Accra, Ghana, use an abusa-type of scheme. Consider a fishing canoe with a crew of seven, a roll of fishing net and an outboard motor. Since there may be different owners of the canoe, the net and the outboard motor, each is considered as a "person" and added to the crew of seven to give a total of ten "persons." Profits of the operation are then divided ten-ways, with each "person" receiving a tenth. If the owners of the canoe, the net and the motor happen to be the same individual, his share of the profits would amount to 40 percent.

"From the family *profits* three of the sons went to Britain for their education. Upon his return the eldest and most famous son, Dr. Radcliffe Dugan Jones, built a nursing home and offered free treatment to poor people." The Jones family were able to sustain their successes despite Lebanese competition. Operating on a grand scale of a family firm and maintaining ties to her loyal producers, Abi Jones was able to compete with the Lebanese and successfully built a business enterprise that spanned three generations.

She lost the piassava business during the 1940s however. But when she died in 1942, she left her sons a healthy business. Her sons continued to operate the business successfully. In the 1970s, they began facing increasing difficulties. By 1980, the business had closed.

There is more to the Abi Jones story than mere proof of the existence of African entrepreneurship. The year of the closure, 1980, was particularly significant. Notice that the closure did not occur in pre-colonial times, nor during the colonial era but in the post-colonial era. As we shall see in a later section, many African governments, after independence, adopted policies that insidiously strangulated indigenous entrepreneurship. The Jones family business was one such victim.

CHAPTER 8

THE INDIGENOUS ECONOMIC SYSTEM: DISTRIBUTION

A. FREE MARKET AND FREE TRADE TRADITION

Market Types And Organization

Part of the goods produced by Africans were consumed, the rest traded or sold in markets. Much has been written about trade and markets in indigenous Africa, but dismissingly. For a variety of reasons, it has been argued that trade and markets could not have developed in Africa. For one thing, household subsistence agriculture was assumed to be the norm. Surplus agricultural produce therefore was unavailable to trade. For another, climatic conditions posed grave problems of storage, and technical difficulties seriously hampered bulk transportation of goods. And "those who do not believe that traditional African societies had market systems suggest that evidence of such systems is a reflection of colonial and Western contact, especially in the last hundred years" (Schneider, 1986; p.186). Yet, trade and markets there were.

The development of markets was inevitable even if self-sufficiency was assumed to be strictly operative. It was physically impossible for a homestead to produce all its needs on the farm. By necessity, a surplus over its needs was required to exchange for what it could not produce. In earlier times, such exchanges were done by canvassing from hut to hut, a time-consuming process. A market was simply a place where these exchanges could be made more easily. Where exchanges occurred regularly, a marketplace would develop. The institution of a marketplace, then, was a natural evolution. "Though people like the Hausa have adopted new types of currency, there were indigenous currencies consisting of cowrie shells, livestock, copper bars, and iron goods which made indigenous markets possible" (Schneider, 1986; p.186).

> Markets were ubiquitous in West Africa. There were a few regions where aboriginal markets were absent - in parts of Liberia, southwestern Ivory Coast, and in certain portions of the plateau

regions of Nigeria. Nevertheless, even here people engaged in trade, and benefited from the markets of contiguous areas. The markets served as local exchange points or nodes, and trade was the vascular system unifying all of West Africa, moving products to and from local markets, larger market centers, and still larger centers (Skinner, 1964).

There were two types of markets and trade: the small village market and the large markets which served as long-distance, inter-regional trade centers. Most markets tended to be situated on the border between different geographical zones - forest and savanna, coastal belt and interior - or between different ethnic groups - Gikuyu (cultivators) and Masai (pastoralists), and on inter-regional trade routes, providing travelling merchants with food and shelter, as well as facilities for exchange (Wickins, 1981).

Rural markets were often sited at bush clearings or at the intersection of caravan routes. As Hill (1987) asserted: "Rural periodic markets are such ancient institutions in many parts of West Africa and the literature on African markets is vast" (p.54). Skinner (1964) concurred:

> The first Europeans to arrive at the lower Niger River in the eastern coast of West Africa reported that they saw Igbo traders from inland bringing yams, cows, goats and sheep for trading with such coastal peoples as the Ijaw in exchange for salt. . .Markets of the societies in the middle zone between the eastern coast of West Africa and the Hausa states in the north were important centers of exchange in the period prior to European incursion.

Though indigenous markets in southern Africa were not as well developed as in west Africa, they were not entirely absent either (Bohannan, 1964; p.206). It is only in South Africa that historical accounts seem to indicate the introduction of organized markets by the colonialists. "Unorganized" markets however existed before the arrival of the colonists in South Africa. The difference between the two resided in the use of paper currency introduced by the Europeans. This distinction is important since there were numerous places where the people of South Africa exchanged or bartered goods. The absence of paper currency did not mean "unorganized" markets did not exist in much the same way as the absence of paper currency did not mean the institution of money was unknown to Africans.

Wickins (1981) also supported this view:

> The African peoples of the southern part of the continent traded among themselves both before and after the advent of European settlement, sometimes apparently over considerable distances. Some were more active traders than others, the Tsonga, for example, a coastal people living between Kosi Bay and the Save (Sabi) River.

There were accustomed to travelling hundreds of kilometers by canoe on the Limpopo.

The great bulk of African internal trade was in foodstuffs and livestock (Newbury, 1971). Traded commodities included plantain, maize, kola nuts, salt, palm oil, dried or smoked fish, goats and cattle. In East Africa, however, a few commodities dominated local trade.

The staples of internal trade were salt, copper and gold. Salt was the basis of trade at Ingombe Ilede, an iron-using agricultural settlement near the confluence of the Zambezi and Kafue Rivers, occupied during the last two or three centuries of the 1st millenium A.D. and reoccupied, according to archaelogical evidence, in the 14th and 15th centuries. It commanded large salt deposits. Another salt trading center was Ivuna, near Lake Rukwe in modern Tanzania. Artifacts of copper, gold and iron excavated at Ingombe Ilede and Sanga indicate the existence of a trade in these materials, since there were no local sources (Wickins, 1981: 177).

Many of the pre-colonial rural markets of West Africa provided for the needs of local producers, consumers and traders as well as serving as foci for long-distance traders. Some rural markets operated daily, depending upon the volume of trade. In Nigeria,

Every village and town had markets which were attended in the morning or evening and in some cases, throughout the day. These markets were held either daily or periodically. The daily markets were local exchange points where producers, traders and consumers met to sell and buy. The periodic markets were organized on a cyclical basis of every three, four, five and sixteen days to feed the daily markets. Every community had a market cycle which enabled traders and buyers to attend different markets on different days (Falola, 1985:105).

Opening a rural market entailed two steps. The first was to bring a group of traders together at least once weekly in some open space at which some shelters had been erected. The open space may initially be cleared by an individual entrepreneur. If it attracted attendance from other communities, then the village chief would be called upon to establish the market officially. The officiation, the second step, involved the performance of certain rites. The Hausa *ardo* called upon Allah to prosper the new market, while devotees of the ancient cult of spirit-possession (*bori*) carried out supplementary rituals to propitiate the spirit of *Inna* whose support was essential for the success of the market.

The establishment of a new market was more elaborate among the Mossi.

When a new market is to be established, the chief gives out the order for the ceremony:

> First of all he speaks to his *Raga Naba* (market chief), usually a non-Mossi slave, about the need for the market or the desirability of changing its location. This man then consults a *tengsoba* (earth priest) who must be also a *barga* (soothsayer) to find out where in a certain area it would be most propitious to locate the new market. After the *tengsoba* has ascertained the number and nature of the spot, he tells the *Raga Naba* what type of sacrifice would be appropriate. A few days later, the *Raga Naba*, his young assistant and the *tengsoba* take *zom kom* (milletflour), *dam* (sorghum beer) and a chicken (or goat) of a designated color, and go to the new market place. . .The *Raga Naba* takes the millet water and pours some on the ground saying: 'Good God, take this water, drink it, and take this other water (here he pours the beer), and give it to all the *tengsoba* in the village so that the market will always be good and there will be no fighting in the market!'. . .Only after this ceremony is completed can the market be opened (Skinner, 1962).

The local markets had two important characteristics. The first was their cyclical periodicity (Skinner, 1964). Market days were rotated among a cluster of villages. Yoruba, Dahomey and Guro markets operated on 5-day cycles. Igbo rural markets were on a 4-day or multiple of 4-day cycle while Mossi markets ran on a 3-day or 21-day cycle. The cycling served a dual purpose. It was an adaptation to a situation where the volume of goods to be exchanged was too small to carry out on a daily basis. It also promoted intercourse between villages and further served to stabilize prices in neighboring markets and redistribute supplies among them.

The second characteristic of rural markets was the segregation of vendors or merchants according to the products sold. Tomato sellers were seated at one section of the market. The object was to promote competition. "It (segregation) made it convenient for buyers to locate the regular section of each commodity, to choose from a wide variety of goods and to buy at a fair price since the traders had to compete with one another at the same time" (Falola, 1985; p.106).

In Mossi markets of Ghana, there was a further segregation by reference to the trader's place of origin (Skinner, 1962). For example, a large number of sellers of one type of product, say tomatoes, formed an open circle in which each trader sat facing the point of origin. Inside this circle, separated by a few feet, was another circle of traders of another produce with their backs toward the general direction from which they came. This configuration performed a social function by making it easier to find one's friends, to converse, to drink with them, to find someone through whom to send messages to specific villages, to find help needed in the event of a fight and to find an escape route by which one could leave in the event of trouble.

The markets were well organized and structured. Some specialized completely in certain product lines (agricultural produce versus handicrafts) while others carried general wares. Each market had its own rules and customs regarding settlement of disputes and the quality of the products being offered for sale. Disputes inevitably arose in market places and violence and fights occurred. For these reasons, the Guro of Ivory Coast located markets outside the village.

Generally, most African markets had market chiefs, often appointed by a political chief or elected from among the traders, to maintain law and order at the marketplace. Among the Kuba of Zaire, the market chief "saw to it that no armed persons were allowed on the market place, and that the dealers in similar products were grouped together. His policemen repressed any uproar and settled on the spot any dispute about transactions" (Vansina, 1962).

Many other ethnic societies established courts at the market place to handle disputes (Bohannan, 1964; p.214). For example, the 19th century explorer Clapperton found that in the Hausa markets of Nigeria, "if a purchase was later found to be defective, the broker or seller was obliged by the laws of the market to refund the price paid for it" (Skinner, 1964).

Each Hausa market, *kasuwa*, had a headman (the *Sarkin Kasuwa* or *Magajin Kasuwa*) who was responsible to the village or town chief. He had a number of deputies: the *Sarkin Awo* (chief of the grainsellers, often a woman), the *Sarkin Pawa* (chief butcher), the *Sarkin Dillalai* (chief broker), and so on. Each craft leader was chosen by the group he/she represented. The *Sarkin Pawa* was responsible for the market meat supplies and also controlled the rotation of killings among the butchers.

The chief of the grain sellers was responsible for maintenance of fair measures and prices. Since grain used to be sold in various measures there was the potential for cheating. The *Sarkin Awo* enforced the use of standard measures such as the *mudu*, a metal bowl of standard capacity.

Generally, each craft headman remained with his/her various group to settle minor disputes about payment or quality of goods, price and the like, before they became serious, or brought them to the market chief, who could refer them to higher authority. Perhaps for this reason "quarreling and blows were very rare at these markets" (Gibbs, 1965; p.128). In other tribal systems, "a committee of elders took it as one of their most serious civic duties to maintain a market place so that their part of the world would be 'kept on the map' and prosperity would reign" (Bohannan, 1964; p.213).

In the Guro markets of Ivory Coast, fines were imposed in cases of fights or insults and there were men responsible for maintaining peace. Palm wine drinking was not allowed at Guro markets, except on very special occasions. Among the Igbo, the youngest age-grade, the *ekpe uke isi* (society-grade six) acted as the market police. They settled minor disputes, referring the serious ones to the *ekpe uke esa* court (grade seven). In the Konso markets of southern Ethiopia, petty complaints and disputes were taken up by the *pokwalla* (head man) and judges selected from the ranks of the *Orshata* (group of elders). The market area was patrolled by members of the local *Xella* (an age-grade), whose function it was to maintain order under the direction of other members of the *Orshata*.

Market Regulations And Controls

Generally, African markets were not rigidly and centrally controlled by chiefs. Each craft or trade policed itself. Rules and regulations that existed were aimed more at the preservation of law and order, the collection of market tolls, the use of standard measures of quantity and the supervision over the slaughter of cattle.

> Aside from these activities there was little regulation of the Igbo market, though in order to prevent fighting there was a strict rule against carrying machetes or large knives in the market. While traders generally sat with others of their village-groups, there was no strict regulation as to where they should remain, and *there apparently were no price controls* (Simon and Ottenberg, 1962). (Italics mine).

In the Mossi markets,

> There are no official restrictions on the kinds of goods which may or may not be sold. In pre-European times slaves and eunuchs were the common stock-in-trade of the major markets and of some of the smaller ones as well. The only active supervision that existed and still exists concerns the butchering of meat. Every person who sells meat in the market must exhibit the skin of the butchered animal in a public place so that there will be no question as to the ownership of the animal. If the meat in question is the remains of a cow killed and half-eaten by a lion, then the village or district chief must be notified before the meat enters the market (Skinner, 1962).

Yelpaala (1983) also found that, in Dagaaba markets,

> There was the freedom to buy and sell any commodity within the market environment (*daa*). Free and voluntary interaction between buyers and sellers produced a market-determined price. When this condition was violated, the transactions were said to result in *fao* (robbery) in the sense that the buyer or seller might extort a price lower

or higher price than the market-determined price, thereby reducing social welfare (p.370).

Note from the above quotes the absence of price controls or price-fixing by chiefs. There was the *economic freedom* to buy and sell. Several attempts were made by African traders and chiefs to corner and control markets. But most of these attempts failed and even where they succeeded, they were temporary. It is important to discuss the reasons why such attempts were doomed. First, with respect to agricultural produce, there were many producers and sellers as well as substitutes. The yam-seller could not subvert the market since there were many competitors and numerous foodstuffs to choose from.

The possibility of control did exist with respect to imported items. But even here, and as we shall see shortly, control was spurious. There were many alternative routes over which an item could be imported. These served to check against excessive profits and consumer exploitation. Competition, *as is always the case*, protected native consumers and kept profits down.

Second, markets operated on cycles and rotated among villages. The chief in Village A could not decree a price for an item and enforce that ruling when the market moved to Village B, over which he had no jurisdiction. Third, as we shall see below, the market performed important non-economic functions as well. A strict regulation of markets in indigenous Africa would necessarily mean obtrusive interferences with social, political and religious activities as well. Such intrusions were bound to raise the ire of the people. Fourth, freedom of movement severely limited the scope for regulatory action. Traders could always rebel against onerous market tolls and regulations by moving to markets in other locations.

Centuries ago, the chiefs realized that they could not control markets or rigidly regulate trade. Nor was it in the interest of their community to do so. This point is worth emphasizing since modern African governments refuse to appreciate it.

Market Tolls And Taxes

Originally, long-distance traders passing through a market town paid tolls to the local chief. The tolls varied according to the nature of the goods to be sold. High-valued items attracted heavier tolls. For example,

Every trader who came to Katwe (eastern Zaire) had to pay a tax to the *muboza* (market master). If a person chose to mine salt, he paid one-third of his accumulated salt to the market master. If he brought his own goods to trade, a third of the goods would go to the market master (Packard, 1981; p.90).

Quite often, the locals were exempted from such "heavy" taxes. But the outside traders registered little complaint since revenue from the tolls was used to maintain law and order at the marketplace, to keep the market clean and to protect them by providing them with armed escorts towards the outskirts of the village. In the course of time, however, local traders of important items such as livestock were taxed if they requested certain services from market officials.

One of these services was debt collection. To collect a debt from someone who has persistently refused to pay up, a trader would wait for an important function at the market place at which many people had gathered. For a few hundred cowries, the trader would approach the market chief who would assign the task to the town crier. He would seek out the recalcitrant debtor, shout insults at him amid threatening gestures and publicly curse the debtor, who normally paid up after a few days of this hospitality.

Another service was the provision of custody for lost and found articles at the market place. Still another was the making of announcements about lost relatives, runaway wives, or other important events. The announcement could be made by the person himself with the permission of the market chief or have the chief himself do so. In earlier times, the *Raga Naba* of the Mossi would climb a tree and make the announcement.

As to be expected, a few misguided kings and chiefs tried to exact exorbitant market tolls and taxes for these services. For example, in the 19th century, a Mossi market had the following taxes:

> The *Kos Naba* (the sales chief) collected 250 cowries in taxes for every beef cattle slaughtered at the market and took their humps and gave them to a palace official called the *Nemdo Naba* (meat chief) for distribution in the royal household. He also collected 250 cowries on every cow sold there, but did not usually tax goats and sheep. In lieu of this he occasionally took a head or two of these animals from each herd that passed through the market and sent them to the palace kitchens. Donkeys were also taxed at the rate of 200 cowries per head sold in the market. Horses sold to the nobility were not taxed, but those exported were taxed about 300 cowries (Skinner, 1962).

The response was predictable: market activity declined and trade was shifted to less taxed areas to evade the oppressive taxation. For example, in 1881, the Mossi found the market taxes to be prohibitive and moved their market activity from Wagadougou to Mane. Heavy taxation also led to the decline of Whyddah in 19th century Dahomey and the ascendancy of Cotonou. Further, in the 1890s, horse traders from the Yatenga, in the north of Mossi country, and the Hausa caravaneers were sometimes forced to sell part of their wares to the *Moro Naba* at one-hundredth the purchase price. "Not all the caravaneers submitted to extortion, and at one period many of them traded with Mane instead of passing through Wagadougou where the tariffs were too high" (Skinner, 1962).

An even more poignant example was provided by Smith (1962):

At first the Kano rulers seem to have left its markets in peace, but early in the 18th century, Muhammad Sharefa began to collect taxes there, and in the next reign, the market was nearly killed, the Arabs left the town and went to Katsina, and most of the poorer people fled to the country. Kano's commercial decline brought Katsina prosperity.

The Importance Of Markets In Indigenous Africa

No African chief can refuse to hear a case brought to his attention at market

- Skinner, 1962.

The village market performed vital economic, social and political functions that were well understood by the chiefs and the people. The marketplace was the central nervous system of the community. In fact, as Skinner (1962) observed for the Mossi of Ghana,

Of great importance is the fact that whenever and wherever there is a large gathering of Mossi there is a market. . .

The rural market is the center of Mossi social life, and friends as well as enemies meet within its confines. What Mangin wrote some 40 years ago is still true: 'Every self-respecting Mossi - man or woman, child or elder - must go to market at least once in a while were it only to look. . .and to be looked at, if he can put on some handsome clothes.' Except for the Moslems who are now experimenting with a form of *purdah*, there are few persons who do not go to market. The absence of someone from the market for more than two consecutive occasions is a sure sign of illness, travel, or family crisis. As one man said to me, 'I must go to market, and when I get there I look for three persons: my girlfriend, my debtor and my enemy. If I do not know whether any of them are at the market I am ill at ease. And when I go to the market and do not see them all, the market is not good.'

Among the Akan of Ghana,

> The market place plays an extremely prominent part in the life of
> Koforidua. Besides being the source of food and clothing for the
> family, it is the place where the wife and mother spends most of her
> waking day (McCall, 1962).

In the 1850s, an American missionary, T.J. Bowen, provided a vivid
description of the importance of Yoruba markets:

> The most attractive object next to the curious old town itself - and it
> is always old - is the market. This is not a building, but a large area,
> shaded with trees, and surrounded and sometimes sprinkled over
> with little open sheds, consisting of a very low thatched roof
> surmounted on rude posts. Here the women sit and chat all day,
> from early morning till 9 o'clock at night, to sell their various
> merchandise. . .The principal marketing hour, and the proper
> time to see all the wonders, is the evening. At half an hour before
> sunset, all sorts of people, men, women, girls, travelers lately
> arrived in the caravans, farmers from the fields, and artisans from
> their houses, are pouring in from all directions to buy and sell, and
> talk. At the distance of half a mile their united voices roar like the
> waves of the sea (Cited by Bascom, 1984; p.25).

In East Africa, studies by Gulliver (1962) also showed that markets were
extremely important to the Masai and the Arusha. "For the Arusha, it [the
market] gained a particular importance for it provided the main opportunity
for personal contact with the Masai in the conscious efforts to learn and
imitate all they could of Masai culture" (Gulliver, 1962).

The rural market served many purposes. First, it provided the people with
the opportunity to exchange goods or occasional agricultural surpluses and
to purchase what they could not produce themselves. Second, the market
provided an indispensable avenue for social intercourse: to meet people, to
gossip, or to discuss and keep abreast of local affairs. "In West Africa and the
Congo, [markets] were major centers of entertainment" (Bohannan, 1964;
p.215). Dancers, singers, musicians and other artists often went to the
market to display their skills. Work parties and weddings often took place at
the markets. Third, markets served as centers of inter-ethnic contact and
channels of communication (White, 1987; p.41). It was at the market that
important information about foreign cultures, medicine, product improvements, new technologies were exchanged. Thus, it acted as an integrative
force, or a place for cultural and normative exchange.

Fourth, the market area often served as *the* meeting place for important
political events such as durbars and village assemblies convened by the

traditional rulers. Fifth, the market served as an important area for communication and dissemination of information.

> A market place is also one of the best places to look for news of a runaway wife, or of any stranger in an area. The Mossi say that women have footprints like an elephant in that they can be found quite easily, but that the footprints are always clearest in the market. What this means is that the market is the main communication center of Mossi society and news of happenings in the region can be heard there. If a person is in an area one can be sure that the people in the market will know about him, or that he will sooner or later visit the market (Skinner, 1962).

Sixth, "in traditional Africa, almost all market places were associated with religious activities" (Bohannan, 1964; p.215). Markets were consecrated with shrines associated with them. The consecration emanated primarily from the need for peace and calm at the market place. It was believed "such consecration would guarantee that supernatural sanctions would back up the political authorities in their maintenance of peace in the marketplace" (Bohannan, 1964; p.215).[1]

It hardly constitutes an exaggeration to assert that the marketplace was the heart of indigenous African society. It was the center of not only economic activity but also political, social, judicial and communication as well. Perhaps, the most pernicious punishment that could be inflicted on an African society was to destroy its market, as this would assail its inner sanctum.

The importance of the market was well recognized in traditional African culture and folklore. For example, "The traditions of Efidwaase and Edubiase in Asante are full of the praises of those of their chiefs in whose time the markets grew in importance" (Daaku, 1971). The high regard of markets in Yoruba life is suggested by the fact "in Ife the days of the week are named for the markets held on them: *Oja Ife*, the market of Ife in front of the *Oni*'s palace, *Ita Iremo* in Iremo ward; *Aiyebgaju* precinct in Ilode ward; and *Ita Ikogun* in Ikogun ward. Days are named after markets in other Yoruba towns as well as after deities (*Ifa, Ogun, Shango*, and *Orishala*)" (Bascom, 1984; p.25).

So important was the market to the Mossi of Burkina Faso that it was sanctified: "The (Mossi) marketplace was not simply a place for the

---

[1] It is important to note one general trait of native behavior. Things that were of crucial importance to the natives were deified: land, kingship, marketplace, and among the Igbo legal cases through consultation with oracles such as *Ibini Ukpabi*. At first blush, the divination may appear as superstition but was more reflective of the absence of the means of enforcing order and stability. The assumption probably was that, a deified article would not be desecrated. Thus, if the king or the market-place was revered, peace and order would prevail.

exchange of goods; it was an area of security and order, the equivalent of the world, at whose centre the king reigned with ancestral sanction" (Davidson, 1970; p.197). This was also true of the Hausa:

> Traditionally, the center of a rural community was a walled town at which the chief, *imam*, and market were found. Even today, when population or other changes lead the authorities to establish a new village and village-chief, one of his first tasks is to promote the development of a regular market at his headquarters. If this fails and another settlement in his area has a viable market, the chief will go to live there (Smith, 1962).

The market was so significant in indigenous Africa that Skinner (1962) asserted emphatically that: "No African chief can refuse to hear a case brought to his attention at market (though he may postpone it until a regular court hearing). These courts may be the same as - but are often different from - the arbitrating facilities for settling disputes which arise among sellers and customers within the market place itself."

The inter-regional trade and market, on the other hand, was more highly developed in pre-colonial Africa. The writings of early travellers to Africa documented a dense and complex web of continental trade traffic and inter-regional exchanges.

> The main circuits are fairly easily identified from early nineteenth century evidence and can be extrapolated from later sources; The Senegal-Gambia-Casamance basins linked to the Upper Senegal and Niger markets; the South Rivers, Sierra Leone linked to the Futa-Jallon and Upper Niger; Liberia, Ivory Coast, Gold Coast, Volta, Dahomey complex linked to Mossi-Dagomba and Niger markets; the Gun and Yoruba coast and Hausa-Fulani markets; the Delta and Niger complex linked with Hausa-Fulani markets. Old and important trade routes provided lateral communication, particularly between Mande and Hausa trading circuits (Newbury, 1971).

The most notable of these inter-regional trade routes was the Trans-Saharan. Early trade across the Sahara was by caravan, whose conductors were the Sanhaja, desert nomads and Berbers. Their main route ran from Sijilmasa in the oasis of Tafilelt in southern Morocco to Aoudaghast, just north of the ancient empire of Ghana. It took fifty-one days by caravan (Diop, 1987; p.141).

By the beginning of the 19th century, the caravan trade across the Sahara had coalesced on four main routes. One route began in Morocco and ran through Taodeni to Timbuktu on the Niger. The second began in Tripoli and passed through Ghadames and the oasis of Air to the Hausa states of Katsina and Kano in Nigeria. The third also began in Tripoli, then trailed through the oasis of Fezzan to the kingdom of Bornu (Nigeria). The fourth linked Tripoli with the kingdom of Wadai and Darfur.

The northern termini of the trans-Saharan trade routes remained more or less the same for centuries - Fez and Marrakesh in Morocco, Constantine in Algeria and Kairouan (Tunis) in Tunisia and Tripoli in Libya. The southern end-points were Timbuktu, Katsina, Kano, Birni, Ngazargamu, Wara and Abeche, all on the southern edge of the Sahara desert. Because of the dense tropical forest and prevalence of tse-tse flies, the trans-Saharan caravans never reached the West African coast. Human porterage was the mode of transporting goods from the southern termini to the forest and the coast. In its initial stages, the exchange of two commodities dominated the trans-Saharan trade - gold from the Ghana empire in exchange for salt from deposits of rocksalt in the Sahara, notably at Teghaza, Taodeni and Taotek. It was gold which first attracted foreigners to black Africa. As this trade developed, cowrie shells, horses, aggrey beads, figs, dates, tobacco, copper and iron bars were added to the imports from North Africa. Exports from western Sudan were expanded to include cloth (from Kano), ivory, gum, ostrich feathers, craft products, shea butter, dried fish, kola, and slaves.

Elsewhere in Africa, other trade routes flourished. The important ones in south-eastern Africa were along the Zambezi River and the Sabi Valley. On the East African coast, Kilwa and Mombasa grew up as important entrepots serving the coastal trade. Goods imported (cloth, glassware, porcelain, perfume and beads) came from Arabia, Persia, India and China. These goods were traded for ivory and gold from the interior. By the early 14th century, an important Sofalan gold trade had developed linking Sofala, Kilwa, Mogadishu and Malindi.

Historical evidence does not suggest any widespread adoption of exclusionary rules in trade or at the rural markets. There were occasional attempts by some powerful merchants and Europeans to control trade or corner markets. But such attempts were short-lived and unsuccessful, as was to be expected.

There was not one long-distance trader or caravan but several, as well as numerous caravan routes. Further, there were many traders of foreign origin: Spanish, Portuguese, Dutch, English and the French. Thus alternative routes, competitors or interlopers always existed. This point was driven home hard to the Dutch traders in the 17th century at Elmina on the Gold Coast when they attempted to establish exclusive trading rights over gold and fined the natives if they traded with other Europeans. One Dutchman, William Bosman, bemoaned the ineffectiveness of the trade restrictions:

> The Negro Inhabitants are generally very Rich, driving a great Trade with the Europeans for Gold, which they chiefly Vend to the English and Zealand Interlopers, notwithstanding the severe Penalty they incurr thereby; if we catch them, their so bought goods are

not only forfeited, but a heavy fine is laid upon 'em: Not deterr'd I say by this, they all hope to escape to effect which, they Bribe our Slaves, (who are set as Watches and Spies over them) to let them pass by Night; by which means we are hindered from having much above an Hundredth part of the Gold of this land: And the plain Reason why the Natives run this Risque of Trading with the Interlopers, is, that their Goods are sometimes better than ours, and always to be had one third part cheaper; whereby they are encouraged against danger, very well knowing, that a successful Correspondence will soon enrich them" (Cited in Langley, 1979; p.440).

What can be gleaned from this was a rebellious African attitude toward trade controls. The African people understood competition. Two centuries later, it may be recalled, a Cape statistician discovered to his rude awakening that "freedom from restraint is a ruling passion in them." Foreigners who did not express any hostility toward African natives or mercantilist pretensions were free to engage in trade and live freely. In some tribal societies, they were even integrated in normal governance. For example, in the 16th century King Alfonso of the Kingdom of Kongo had Portuguese advisers. Among them were Alvare Lopes, Manuel Pacheco and Francisco Barbudo. They informed the Kongo kings about Portugal and represented the Portuguese segment of the resident population. "They even acquired a *de facto* seat on the electoral college with a veto" (Vansina, 1975; p.43). King Alfonso had a permanent bodyguard made up of mostly foreign soldiers. Also in the Asante Empire, Dutch nationals and Muslims served as advisers and officers during the reign of Mensa Bonsu and Osei Tutu in the 19th century.

As long as they were willing to abide by the local market rules, foreigners were welcome in indigenous Africa and free to participate in trade. According to Diop (1987):

At the market towns of Timbuktu, Djenne, Biru, Soo, Ndob, Pekes, foreign nationals could live in utmost security with their goods, while pursuing their business. For the most part these were Arabs from North Africa, Egypt, and Yemen, and Europeans, especially Spaniards. Some of them were even students in Timbuktu. Black Africa was hospitable to foreigners (p.133).

It has often been argued that long-distance trade was the prerogative of royalty, nobles and rich men. But Dickson (1969) argued that the main reason was economic. Trading at distant places in those times of great insecurity required heavy outlay which only the wealthy could afford. Consequently, the "poorer sections of the population were effectively excluded from large-scale long-distance trade although there was no law expressly forbidding their participation in it" (Dickson, 1969).

The importance of free trade was long recognized by the chiefs and the natives. First, "through trade, people shared, exchanged and borrowed ideas on cultural, political and religious institutions and promoted inter-group relations and interactions among the various Nigerian communities" (Falolan, 1985). Second, trade was the means by which people could acquire the weapons to defend themselves against marauding neighboring groups. Third, trade was the means by which Africans could acquire other commodities they could not produce themselves and even wealth. Packard (1981) noted of Bashu of Zaire:

> Whether a man engaged in salt trading on a regular or an occasional basis, it provided a way of acquiring important nonsubsistence goods. Moreover, because salt could be traded for goats, participation in the salt trade was a means of acquiring bridewealth and thus a road to social advancement. The absence of any initial capital expenditure requirement meant that it was a road that was especially attractive to young men who had not had time to acquire other forms of wealth. Participation in the salt trade was thus an important aspect of Bashu economic and social life (p.89).

Fourth, trade was recognized as the engine of economic growth. Free trade provided the basis for the growth of many African empires in earlier times. Examples of such empires included Ghana, Mali, Songhai, Bornu in West Africa and Great Zimbabwe, Chokwe and Nyamwezi in central and east Africa. The rise and fall of these empires were very much tied to the vicissitudes of trade. The empire of Ghana in the 10th century, for example, derived much of its fortunes from being the southern terminus of the western trans-Saharan trade route. Deserving special mention was the Empire of Oyo or Yorubaland.

Basing its early commerce on the trans-Saharan trade, Yorubaland developed into an empire by the 15th century. The empire's wealth was based not only on long-distance trade but also on trade between its numerous small towns and local markets. An extensive network of periodic markets evolved to support this trade. "In some towns, a male secret society, the *Parakoyi*, regulated trade. Among the Egba, for example, this society of 'trade chiefs' met every 17 days to consider the town's trading interests, settle disputes, and regulate prices and standards" (White, 1987; p.28).

The traditional role of chiefs was also to *encourage* trade and create the environment needed for trade to prosper peacefully. Casely-Hayford, the African scholar from the Gold Coast (now Ghana) wrote in 1903 of the Ashanti Kingdom:

It was part of the State System of Ashanti to encourage trade. The King once in every forty days, at the *Adai* custom, distributed among a number of chiefs various sums of gold dust with a charge to turn the same to good account. These chiefs then sent down to the coast caravans of tradesmen, some of whom would be their slaves, sometimes some two to three hundred strong, to barter ivory for European goods, or buy such goods with gold dust, which the King obtained from the royal alluvial workings. Down to 1873 a constant stream of Ashanti traders might be seen daily wending their way to the coast and back again, yielding more certain wealth and prosperity to the merchants of the Gold Coast and Great Britain than may be expected for some time yet to come from the mining industry and railway development put together. The trade Chiefs would, in due course, render a faithful account to the King's stewards, *being allowed to retain a fair portion of the profit*. . .Important Chiefs carried on the same system of trading with the coast as did the King. *Thus every member of the State, from the King downwards, took an active interest in the promotion of trade and in the keeping open the trade routes into the interior* (cited in Busia, 1951; p.80). (Italics mine).

Note again the use of "profit" and also the fact that this was *before* the scramble for Africa in the 1880s. Bowdich, an European visitor to the Ashanti Kingdom in the mid-1850s, corroborated:

It is a frequent practice of the King's, to consign sums of gold to the care of rising captains, without requiring them from them for two years or three years, at the end of which he expects the captain not only to restore the principal, but to prove that he has acquired sufficient of his own, from the use of it, to support the greater dignity the King would confer on him. If he has not, his talent is thought too mean for further elevation (cited by Busia, 1951:81).

In South Africa also, the Zulu chief, Dingiswayo, was especially noted for his efforts to develop and promote trade in the late 18th century:

In the first year of his chieftainship, he opened a trade with Delogoa Bay, by sending 100 oxen and a quantity of elephant tusks to exchange for beads and blankets. Prior to this a small supply of these articles had been brought to that country from Delagoa Bay by the natives. The trade thus opened by Dingiswayo was afterwards carried on, on an extensive scale, though the Portuguese never in person entered his country. The encouragement held out to ingenuity brought numbers around him, liberal rewards being given to any of his followers who devised things new and ornamental. His mechanical ingenuity was displayed in the carving of wood. He taught this art to several of his people (Wickins, 1981:227).

There was also a strong and powerful economic incentive for the chiefs to promote trade. For example, though West African societies were based on agriculture, West African polities derived the bulk of their incomes not from agriculture but from trade (Bates, 1987; p.30). Ensuring that peace and order prevailed at the marketplace served not only the interests of the traders but those of the chiefs as well.

Toward this end, markets were consecrated and supernatural sanctions invoked against those who disturbed the peace, as noted earlier. Weapons were generally forbidden at marketplaces (Bohannan, 1964; p.217). In some societies, there were informal sanctions and customs to ensure that a peaceful atmosphere prevailed. In Nigeria,

> The custom in every community forbade killing, molestation and kidnapping of fellow village or town dwellers. Thus, trade within the same community was assured. In inter-community trade, there were some established institutions which promoted peace. Some communities entered into mutual agreements never to attack one another. Marriage ties cemented the relationship between many places. Many traders deliberately chose wives in commercial centers and towns along the trade routes and this strengthened the relationship between communities. Finally, religion was used to promote trade. Muslim traders regarded themselves as brothers who must not harm one another. Among the Igbo, the oracle system helped to promote trade (Falolan, 1985).

Other societies relied on the lineage system to afford security of exchange. For example, among the Tonga of Zambia,

> A person wishing to make exchanges could travel safely for considerable distances provided he exercised caution by moving along a chain of kinship. In the event that a claim was not met, the lineage had obligation to take vengeance. Those who wished a further safeguard could initiate a 'bond of friendship' with prominent men along the route or at the place of destination. The man who accepted such a pact agreed to guarantee a friend's person and prosperity while he remained within the neighborhood. An attack upon either was considered an attack upon the host who could then summon kinsmen and supporters to retaliate against the offender (Colson, 1962).

A similar system of protection was found by Lewis (1962) among the Somali:

To reach the coast in safety a caravan had to have protection on its journey among many different and often hostile clans. This was achieved by an institutionalized form of safe-conduct. The leader of the caravan. . .entered into a relationship of protection with those amongst whom he passed on his way to the coast. . .Attacks on a protected caravan are attacks on the patron and his lineage whose honor and 'name'. . .can only be upheld by prompt retaliatory action.

The need for protection drove home ever so pertinently a realization that peace was indispensable for trade to prosper. Laws were passed to assure this. On October 11, 1867, the Egba United Board of Management of Yoruba (Nigeria) promulgated an ordinance. Its first stipulation was quite explicit:

That it shall be lawful for any person or persons, without exception, to have free access in Abeokuta for the purposes of trade, and to export therefrom any goods or produce, passing from Abeokuta to Lagos by the River Ogun, or elsewhere (Cited by Nicol, 1969:53).

Although the ordinance was for the collection of custom duties, it upheld the principle of free and open trade. In the same region of Nigeria, a group of traders constituted themselves into the *Aro* to dispense justice in trade disputes (by taking recourse to the "oracle") and offer military protection for trade (Northrup, 1978). So successful were the *Aro* in establishing peace that villages would contract their services or offer them permanent settlement in the hope of ridding the host society of criminals and other undesirables (Bates, 1987; p.24).

Media Of Exchange

To effect trade, direct barter was the medium of exchange in early times. Goods were exchanged directly. In many communities, however, certain commodities soon began to be used as money. "Most African societies had money of some sort, although they used credit extensively, especially among close friends and relatives" (Schneider, 1986; p.189).

Technically speaking, any commodity could serve as money so long as it was generally acceptable (in continual demand), durable, and inexpensive to keep. Thus, in Africa, grain could not be used as money but a multitude of other commodities served as money in pre-colonial times: cloth; cattle, goats and other livestock; salt, iron, copper and brass bars; cowrie shells, beads, fire-arms; mats; and gold dust.[2] Not all of these served as "money" everywhere since acceptability varied. Nevertheless,

> A combination of them composed a currency system, as in East Africa where cattle, sheep and goats, iron goods and beads and cowries, in that order of value, made up the system. Cattle, and sometimes camels, were, of course, the big bills in the system.

> Some Africans even had something known as a 'unit of account.' For example the Kru of West Africa had the 'round.' The round was like money in that the value of a product, like a gun, could be quoted in rounds, but there was no physical object, like a dollar bill, to which the round referred. At any given instance a collection of goods, such as a length of cloth, some iron, and some utensils, might be designated as one round. The value of a unit of account, like the value of money, was that in the absence of a monetary object, it allowed traders to calculate and exchange a miscellaneous mix of goods with ease (Schneider, 1986; p.190).

On the Gold Coast,

> Gold dust was the currency in local and regional markets among the Akan. Normally, people weighed their gold dust at home before they went to the marketplaces. But to facilitate trade, there were always special people with their scales, *futuo*, to be called upon to weigh gold for doubtful buyers for a small fee. . .

> There is no doubt that the use of gold weights pre-dated the arrival of the Europeans. This is evidenced by the fact that all the names of gold weights used on the Gold Coast at the time of De Marees were in Twi except for *quinta* (Daaku, 1971).

---

[2] One important effect of using a commodity as money is the dimunition of its original value status. For example, when cattle are thus used, they are no longer judged according to their beef or milk-producing abilities but rather by their "monetary" properties such as durability to serve as a store of value (wealth). "Hence African cattle tend to be small, tough and low in milk production. Another effect of the predominance of their monetary function was a reluctance on the part of Africans to kill their cattle even though beef was a very desirable food" (Schneider, 1986; p.190).

It was not so much "religious taboos" which prevented certain African natives from consuming their cattle but their monetary quality. Obviously, various "educational lectures" would miss the mark unless a different form of money was introduced to "release" the cattle. Unfortunately, the various paper currencies introduced by modern African governments were poor substitutes as they were often rendered worthless through overprinting.

Gold dust could be used in small quantities. On the Gold Coast, the smallest quantity in trade or for general use was a *pessua*, or equivalent to the English farthing.[3] Busia (1951:79) provided these common gold weights in Ashanti:

Name in Ashanti	Equivalent in English Currency
Soaafa	3s. (shillings).
Dommafa	3s. 6d. (three shillings and six pence).
Soaa	6s.
Fiaso	6s. 6d.
Domma	7s.
Nsaanu	13s.
Surupa	1 pound.
Dwoa	1 pound 10s.
Asoaanu	4 pounds.
Peredwan	8 pounds.
Peredwan asia	9 pounds 6s.
Ntanu	16 pounds.
Ntansa	24 pounds.

Early trade with foreigners was "silent." Stories of such trade abound in history books. One was reported by Diop (1987):

> After crossing the desert separating Ghana from Upper Senegal, the Arabs reached the banks of the Faleme, unloaded their goods in small bunches (varied products from the Orient), gave a signal, and then retreated ; the Africans then came out and in front of each bundle placed the quantity of gold dust they judged it to be worth, then withdrew. The Arabs came back and collected the gold if they found the amounts satisfactory; if not, the cycle was repeated, still without any contact (p.131).

With ships, sailors would unload their cargo at the shore and retreat to their ship to light a smoking fire. The people of the country would see the smoke and come and lay down gold to pay for the cargo and withdraw. The sailors would disembark and examine the gold. If it seemed a fair price to them, they would take the gold and leave; but if not, they would go aboard and wait till the people came back and added more gold.[4]

Archaelogical excavations at Naucratis in Egypt revealed bronze and silver coinage as early as the 8th century. Coins and currencies were generally

---

[3] The units of currency that Ghana now uses are the *cedi* and *pesewa*.

[4] Many sociologists and historians have argued that this form of exchange was "unfair" and fraught with the potential to "cheat" the natives. But as Diop (1987) argued, "If they were swindled, they could without loss to the essentials of their life, suspend relations with any given group of traders so identified" (p.132).

convertible into one another. For example, in West Africa, the conventional quantity of gold dust was the *mitkal*, which was approximately 4.6 grams. The *mitkal*, depending upon the rates of exchange in the 13th century, was worth anywhere from 500 to 3,000 cowries (Diop, 1987; p.134). Evidence exists that identical weights of gold or heavier ones were turned into coins with embossed designs at mints for commercial purposes, as a visitor to Ghana noted:

> When the river returns to its bed, everyone sells his gold. The bulk of it is bought by the inhabitants of Wardjelan (in present-day Libya) and by those from the tip of West Africa, wither this gold is transported to the mints, coined into dinars, and traded commercially for goods. This is how it happens each year. This is the principal product of the land of the Blacks; great and small, they make it their livelihood (Cited in Diop, 1987; p.134). Thus, in West Africa, there existed a whole gamut of currencies used in commercial transactions. There was even a curious sort of cloth currency, manufactured in the form of squares of fabric (four spans to each side) at the textile center of Terenka. These squares, called *chigguiya*, were in use at Silla, also on the Senegal, along with other currencies such as salt, copper rings and *dora*, a cereal (Diop, 1987; p.133).

Market Prices

Every African native today will declare that prices in the village were historically or traditionally not determined or fixed by the village chief or king. This fact has been true for centuries and must be stated emphatically, since many modern African governments are ignorant of it.

Prices in indigenous markets have traditionally been influenced by several factors: the forces of demand and supply, scarcity, time of day, status of the consumer, relation with the seller, quality of the product, its degree of necessity, bargaining skills and competition. In general, prices are determined by the normal forces of demand and supply while the other factors merely shave off or add a few pennies to the price so that two different consumers do not pay exactly the same price. That means there is price discrimination in indigenous African markets.[5] This has always been the traditional practice.

Skinner (1964) noted that "the Mossi merchants were very aware of the principles of supply and demand and held goods out of the market when

[5] Price discrimination, technically, means charging different prices to different customers for the same product.

prices fell, in order to obtain later higher prices." One of the essential ingredients of a market economy is that producers "calculate" what to produce and how much in relation to the cost of resources and prices of the final products. Schneider (1986) found that:

> The Hausa (of West Africa) have a real market economy. Goods are measured by the standard measuring bowl (*tiya*) and information about prices is disseminated daily by word of mouth, especially by children. . .They acquire their wants not merely by raising for themselves what they need and desire, but also by using the forces of the market to get the best quantity for the best price relative to cost. In this respect, they are no different from an American farmer who sells all his milk to the dairy and then purchases some for family consumption at the local supermarket. . .Some rural Hausa communities seem unusually market oriented, even to the extent that most farmers do not save seed grain but prefer, like American farmers, to buy or borrow seed each year (p.185)

Vansina (1962) also discovered that on Kuba markets in Zaire:

> The most important characteristic of prices in Kuba is that they behave in exactly the same way as prices do in European markets. The price is set by the relation of supply and demand. When shrimps first appear on the market, they fetch a high price. Later on, the price falls.

On the Konso markets of southern Ethiopia, Kluckhorn (1962) discovered that, "supply and demand was the basic adjustment mechanism for prices." If a commodity was scarce its price rose. Dupire (1962) observed this on Fulani markets:

> The price of millet and of salt, essential elements in the life of the nomad, vary in proportion to their scarcity. That of millet is at a minimum after the harvest and at a maximum just before the next harvest - variations on the order of one to four - while salt is less expensive at the return of the caravans which bring it back from the salt mines of the Sahara.

The status of the buyer also affected how much one paid for a commodity. According to Meissalloux (1962):

> Even today, it is frequent that, when asked about the 'price' of a product or a service, the seller sets different rates according to the status of the buyer. To members of one's family, it is gift. From fellow-villagers, a token gift is expected in reciprocity and food

during the period of work. To members of other villages, it depends on matrimonial alliances or friendship. To alien Guro a bargaining is offered and alien people a still higher 'price,' unless prestige or hospitality requires it to be a gift. Conversely, we are told that it was proper for a rich and prominent man to pay highly for some goods as guns, slaves, etc., in order to exhibit his wealth both to his fellow villages and to foreigners.

Europeans knew that in indigenous markets, they paid higher prices than the natives. That was one reason why many sent servants to make purchases for them.

The price of an item was often influenced by the time of day. Toward the end of the market day, most traders were in a hurry to get home or reluctant to carry home unsold goods. Africans knew that was the best time to obtain good bargains. On markets in south Dahomey, Tardits and Tardits (1962) found that,

Prices of all goods are at their highest in the morning. Sellers, though they know at which prices they will agree to sell, wait to see what their clients look like. The first customers make proposals, the merchants watch their colleagues and, after a few sales, prices tend to be set. Around 9:00, the market comes to a peak. An *akasa* seller told us: 'If by 8:00, half of my pot of *akasa* has been sold, it is going to be a good market day; if not, it looks bad.' When sales are slow, women will extend some credit or give bonuses rather than reduce prices. Nevertheless, the price falls slightly at the end of the day unless the balance between demand and supply remains favorable to the sellers.

On Abyssinian markets in Ethiopia, price declines toward the end of the market were accelerated by the operation of a complex social factor. Amhara traders were particularly concerned about their "honor" and wary of being mocked by the Coptic peers. Messing (1962) commented:

Unlike Arabs, the Amhara are too proud and not so intent on economic 'maximizing' as to resort to badgering a customer. Amhara basket-makers may refuse to admit that their wares on display are for sale, claiming they were previously ordered and are waiting to be picked up by the customer. Then, to avoid having to carry unsold goods home, they sell cheaply when the market begins to close at about 4.00 pm, two hours before dusk. Hence the proverb advises the buyer: 'To church [go] early, to market [go] late.'

Under normal circumstances, that is, barring any exceptional conditions with regard to closing time or prestige of customers, the forces of demand

and supply determine prices but only within certain limits. For example, a pound of herring may cost between $2.00 and $2.50. If herring is relatively scarce, that is, there is greater demand than supply, it may sell at between $3.00 and $3.60. How much exactly one pays will depend upon two additional factors. The first is one's bargaining skills and the second is the level of competition on both the consumers' and sellers' sides. A skillful bargainer may obtain herring at $3.00 a pound whilst another customer may pay $3.75. Or if there is a great deal of seller competition an individual may purchase herring at $3.00 a pound.

African market women, of course, wanted to make a profit while consumers were desirous of obtaining commodities at the lowest possible prices. Such opposing interests are inevitable in *any* exchange transaction. The "conflict" is resolved through bargaining. The purchaser would make a bid. The seller would lower the price a little. The purchaser, in turn, would raise the bid. The seller would then lower the price some more. Through this bidding and discounting process, they would settle on a price acceptable to both and the transaction would be consummated. Economists call this price the "equilibrium price."

In most indigenous African markets, higgling and haggling was the process by which prices were determined. It is fallacious to suggest that prices were fixed by chiefs, kings or any village government authority. People bargained over prices. Haggling over prices was the rule (Skinner, 1964). "Bargaining was the standard feature of Yoruba economic transactions" (Bascom, 1984; p.26). Similarily in Ethiopian markets (Kluckhorn, 1962).

African consumers and traders were both adept at bargaining. Each group employed various tricks to enhance its bargaining position and interests. Consumers used various stratagems to secure commodities more cheaply. Africans, today, would affirm that one's bargaining position is influenced by a number of non-market factors; for example, past patronage, relations with the seller and "bluffing." As a "special customer," the seller may offer "a good price." Or a discount may be offered if the purchaser were a relative - a cousin or a niece. It was not unusual to see a buyer feign injury, with an arm in a sling. The hope was that the "injury" would evoke compassion. Or instead of making the purchase themselves, they would send somebody who "knew" the seller. Others employ the "tease" or the "bluff"; they feign interest in purchasing and then suddenly turn to walk away, hoping that the seller might call them back and offer them a lower price.

The standard trick of market women was the lament that, all day long, they had not sold a single item or business had been poor. Some claimed that they would only make a little profit, say a dollar, if the item were sold at a particular price. Then there were those market women who were always dressed in black. Traditionally, a bereaved woman (through loss of a husband, child or a relative) wore black to elicit sympathy; at the market place to educe compassion.

Traders also "tease". They may ask a potential customer to sample a cooked food item in the hope that the customer might be impressed enough to make a purchase. Traders, like consumers, employ deceptive practices as well. For example, a corn merchant would use narrow vessels which customers themselves use to measure the quantities they want to purchase. The problem with those vessels is that they are usually hard to fill. Many customers are often seen wrapping their arms around these vessels and piling up corn with the feeling that they are receiving more than they are paying for it. Salt merchants use similar techniques; they sell salt in cigarette tins, the bottoms of which have been filled with paper, and the salt is stacked above and over the edges of the tin. "Garri" and flour merchants also use peculiar cigarette tins; their bottoms have been knocked in. Some tins even have holes in them which the traders deftly cover with their fingers before measuring quantities. Then in the proces of pouring the contents into a customer's bag, they quickly remove their fingers.

Oil merchants dig their fingers in the bowl while filling it; then add a small quantity as if they are giving the customer a bonus. The usual trick of fish sellers is to slip a few large ones into a bunch of little ones. That makes it difficult to characterize the collection as "small" or "large". But prices vary according to the size of the batch.

Each side is aware of these tricks and takes appropriate precautions and devises strategies in bargaining. Buyers, of course, are not always fooled, nor do the sellers always succumb to bluffing. Tardits and Tardits (1962) provided a description of such a bargaining process on South Dahomean markets:

> Bargaining is the rule. Prices asked by sellers as well as buyers are always higher or lower than those which are finally agreed upon. Long debates ensue in which praise and insults have their place. The merchant seldom loses money since she may always refuse a disadvantageous bargain, whereas a buyer may be unaware of the market prices or become impatient and lose money. . .

> A customer looks at a fish tray; the merchant asks 425 francs for 40 fish; the customer offers 350 francs. After a short discussion, the merchant is ready to sell. The customer then withdraws the offer and proposes 300 francs; the discussion goes on till the seller has accepted; the buyer thinks it over a second time and says: '275 francs.' The merchant finally agrees but the customer drops the proposed price down to 200 francs. At this point, the merchant refuses to sell. Discussion starts again until at last the bargain is concluded for 225 francs. Customers who might have watched the

scene could also have bought fish at the last price. In this case, there were none and the next customer to come along undertook the bargaining anew and finally paid 235 francs for 40 fish.

Since the Amhara of Ethiopia are imbued with a social propensity to uphold their honor, bargaining is conducted with a slightly different twist.

The Amhara seller may refuse to state a price and ask the buyer to make an offer. If the offer is reasonable and the purchaser is on the same socio-economic level so that no problem of 'honor' is involved (which would require a foreigner to be charged at least double), the transaction will be concluded promptly. If a social problem is involved, the seller has to guess how high he must increase the price (*waga asarrara*) to avoid being mocked. This makes him uncomfortable and he tries to disconcert the customer with veiled insults. The customer can play the same game; when buying sheep for food he may remark, 'I am not expecting a hyena for dinner,' (i.e., the animal you are trying to sell me is so lean, sick and old that it is close to death and would soon be fit only for a hyena). As is clear, two different individuals generally do not pay the same price for an item. How much each paid was determined by how far one was prepared to go with the bidding or the discounting process. And how far one was prepared to go was influenced by many factors: the intensity of the need for the commodity, the number of sellers of the commodity at the marketplace, and the availability of substitutes. If one 'desperately' needed a commodity for which there were no substitutes and for which there was only one seller at the market, obviously one's bargaining position would be relatively weak. Similarly, the fish seller would be less unyielding at the close of the market where there were numerous other fish sellers (Kluckhorn, 1962).

Competition often influenced prices, but the degree of competition varied from one village market to another. For example, Skinner (1962) observed that,

There is little competition about someone else having 'stolen' a customer. The reason for this is that every person in the market is a potential customer of everyone else. Normally, a buyer simply moves from seller to seller sampling the goods if that is possible (some unscrupulous men can even get drunk in the process of 'sampling' beer) and trying to get the best bargain. No seller would think of running after a customer, and customers seldom, if ever, move away from a vendor in the hope that he would be called back to be sold the article at a lower price. The result is that the pace of commerce in a Mossi market is somewhat relaxed, but the lack of intense competition prevents a great deal of hostility and quarreling among the market people.

This of course is in sharp contrast to markets on the West African coast where competition is keen. Tardits and Tardits noted that "competition is hard in Dahomean markets. Merchants sell either the same goods or products for which there are ready substitutes. The appearance of the goods is the first factor that will be taken into consideration by the customers. Sellers will insist on the fact that the food offered had just been made. They advertise 'crispy fritters,' 'freshly made akasa,' 'nicely cooked mashed beans' or 'juicy croquettes.'" Miracle (1962) also discovered that on the copperbelt of Zambia and Zaire, "many commodities found in market places are sold competitively, often approaching the classical pure competition with many sellers no one of whom can affect price through his activities alone."

The scale of competition, of course, varies not only from one market locality to another but also with respect to the nature of the commodities as well. For example, the intensity of competition is less for sugar cane and some fruits since there are only a few sellers and collusion is possible. Indeed, there are attempts to corner rural markets but such attempts more often than not fail.

Effective collusion or market cornering requires effective control over supply. For example, OPEC can corner the oil market because of the control it exercises over oil supplies. Furthermore, the nature of the resource is such that not everyone can produce it. Only those countries which are geologically endowed with this resource.

By contrast, barriers to entry generally do not exist in indigenous Africa, particularly with respect to the production of agricultural produce. Anybody can cultivate sugar cane, gather fruits or go fishing. Therefore it is not possible for fishermen to collude, corner the market and "gouge consumers" for any lengthy period of time. Even if they succeed in forcing up price by such action, sooner or later, some enterprising individuals would enter the fishing industry and provide fish at lower prices. It is this competition, not orders, decrees or price controls, that keeps prices down. The best defense against consumer exploitation is *more* competition, not less.

When competition is operative, one generally observes a reluctance on the part of sellers to raise prices. They employ various gimmicks to fool the customer into believing that the price is still "cheap." This reluctance to raise prices can be detected in pricing practices in America where commodities usually sell for $9.99 or $9,999.99, a penny shy of $10,000. Such pricing may have the psychological effect of suggesting that the item costs $9,000 instead of the $10,000 a competitor may be charging.

African traders, however, have a different way of responding to competition. They also show a reluctance to raise prices, choosing instead to do one of two things whichever is appropriate, depending upon the nature of the commodity. One is to reduce the quantity and maintain the old price. The same cigarette tin used to sell flour or garri will continue to be used, but if a price increase is necessary, it is achieved by knocking the bottom in further and keeping the old price. Ghanaians have been lamenting about the "shrinking ball of kenkey" for decades. A ball of kenkey, a cooked ground maize, used to sell for one *cedi* in the late 1960s. Back then, it could feed an average person. By 1978, that ball, still costing a *cedi*, had so shrunk that the average person needed four!

Miracle (1962) offered two explanations why prices tend to remain fixed while the size of the measure or heap is varied:

> One reason for this is that the quantity sold in African markets is, for many commodities, so large relative to the smallest monetary unit that price changes dictated by economic conditions, or bargaining, often can be achieved only through altering the quantity offered. . .A second reason probably is that sellers can more easily conceal price changes if the adjustment is through quantity.

These days, with escalating inflation in many African countries, however, it may be noted that sellers have been more willing to raise prices. For example, the cost of a ball of kenkey in Ghana is no longer one *cedi* but ten *cedis*.

The other technique of effecting price increases is by varying the amount of bonus (variously called *basela* in Zambia, *matabish* in Congo, *ntosu* in Akan) which the seller adds at the end of a transaction. For example, a fish seller may throw in a couple of fish after a purchase as *basela*. The oil merchant may add a few half-cupfuls after a purchase. Consumers expect this bonus and often demand it. The Ga of Ghana ask: "*Owoo min?*" while the Akan order the seller: "*Tosu!*" To keep his price low, the fish seller may throw in 4 fish. To raise his price, he may add only two at the end of the next transaction.

In sum, prices on indigenous markets generally fluctuated in accordance with the forces of demand and supply. When tomatoes were "in season," the price fell and vice versa. These price oscillations were understood by the peasants and chiefs.

If the price of an item was too high, the traditional response was to bargain down the price. If it did not come down sufficiently, purchase was withheld and a substitute purchased. This was especially true of the agricultural economy. For farm produce, there was a whole range of substitutes. For example, one could substitute cocoyam, cassava or plantain for yam. Nobody was "forced" to buy yam who could not afford it. When the price of a commodity remained persistently high, the natives either produced it themselves, as often happened in the case of yams, or travelled to the source to obtain it more cheaply. Tales of traders trekking long distances to buy goods more cheaply at the source are legion. Similarly, there were many meat substitutes: beef, mutton, lamb, chicken, duck, wild game and fish. Again, nobody was "forced" to buy chicken.

African chiefs did little to interfere with the day-to-day operations of the village market. Nor did they impose price controls on the market. It was never the traditional role of chiefs to police how prices were set. Even wages were not fixed by any village authority (Hill, 1987; p.110).[6] To all intents and purposes, the African village market was an *open* and *free* market, however "primitive." Cases of market intervention by chiefs were few. These generally occurred when there was a market breakdown or failure as in times of severe drought and famine.

During such times, the chief or king might limit price increases and make available to the needy food stored in his own farm. These price "controls" however were limited to agricultural produce - essential for survival. In indigenous African society, it was considered unethical and anti-social to profit by charging exorbitant prices in times of food shortages. When conditions returned to normal, prices of agricultural produce were free to vary. Price controls or market intervention was not a regular feature of indigenous African society in normal times.

It may sound strange to the reader why such an obvious point is being belabored here. But as we shall see in Chapter 10, many post-colonial African governments did not understand this facet of indigenous economic culture. They imposed price controls on peasant farmers and traders and arrested violators, charging them with "economic sabotage." In fact, in such African countries as Ghana, violators were threatened with death by firing squad.

Role Of Women In The Distribution System

A study of Africa's indigenous economy reveals the vital participatory role played by women. This role has not changed historically. As we saw earlier, the majority of Africa's peasant farmers today are women. "In Africa women produce, process and market up to 80 percent of the food," according to a report by the United Nations Development Fund for Women, 1988-1989 (Cited in *World Development Forum*, December 15, 1990; p.1).

Rural markets and trade are also dominated by women. In Yoruba, "local farm produce - either cash crops or food crops - are marketed at the local market, almost invariably by women" (Hodder, 1962). These are not recent

---

[6] This practice is not extinct. Visitors to an African village market today would still observe bargaining over prices. The chiefs do not fix the prices.

phenomena. Female participation in market activities has always been the rule due to the traditional division of labor upon the basis of sex.

In early times, activities considered dangerous and physically strenuous such as waging wars, hunting, fishing, manufacturing (cloth-weaving, pottery, leatherworks, iron smelting, sculpturing, etc.) and building were male occupations. Food cultivation and processing were traditionally reserved for women. Since the family's entire needs could not be produced on the farm, a surplus was necessary to exchange for those items. It was only natural that trade in foodstuffs and vending came to be dominated by women and for market governance to lie in their hands. Indeed in many localities, market rules were generally laid down and enforced by "Market Queens", usually selected from the women traders who were often affectionately called "market mammies".

There was no indigenous African law that debarred men from engaging in market activity. The men just felt "uncomfortable" at the market. Similarly, there were no occupational barriers that forced women to remain as traders. Despite the traditional division of labor along sexual lines, women of exceptional ability could and did compete successfully with men in other fields. Yaa Asantewaa, for example, was a woman who led the Asante to inflict a humiliating defeat on the British forces in the 1870s. Women could also become chiefs and queens; an example was Queen Nzinga.

There was no particular occupation that expressly restricted entry to women. Where such barriers existed many proved to be porous. Long-distance trade for example was one such occupation where entry was not blocked because of women's reproductive responsibilities.

> No Ga woman who wishes to leave her town for a few weeks' trading is ever prevented by domestic ties. There are plenty of women in her compound who will cook for her husband and children in her absence - she will do the same for them some day. If she has an infant child it goes with her, sitting unnoticed tied to her back while she uses her hands or carries loads on her head. As for the husband, some other wife engages his attention. Let no one think that wives object to polygamy. To be sure, when a careless husband invites two wives to his compound for the same night there are often ructions audible to all the neighbors - the most spirited terms of abuse in my collection were garnered on such occasions - but carelessness will cause friction in any good institution (Field, 1940; p.68).

On account of the risks involved as well as the capital required, however, long-distance trade in its inception remained the domain of wealthy men, especially nobles. But by the 19th century, enterprising women were taking an active part in this trade. The Nuer and Yoruba women traders were particularly noted in West Africa.

In Sierra Leone, women proved themselves to be assiduous and enterprising in trade. In 1879, Governor Rowe of Sierra Leone expressed his admiration of these women:

> The genius of the Sierra Leone people is commercial; from babyhood the Aku girl is a trader, and as she grows up she carries her small wares wherever she can go with safety. The further she goes from the European trading depots the better is her market (Cited by White, 1987; p.27).

J. Africanus Horton, the distinguished African doctor and writer, was also favorably impressed: "The (Aku) women make excellent traders, within a very short time they would double, treble, and even quadruple a very small amount" (White, 1987; p.27).

Most women traders acted as intermediaries between European or Arab traders and the indigenous producers and consumers. The women usually bought produce from small farmers and bulked them for sale to the Europeans for export. For the backward flow, they purchased manufactured goods in bulk from the Europeans and broke them into small pieces for distribution to the remotest village, using a vast network of indigenous middlemen. Quite often, by the time an imported commodity reached the final consumer in the village, it would have passed through the hands of scores of middlewomen.

The object in trading was to make a profit. The Yoruba women "trade for profit, bargaining with both the producer and the consumer in order to obtain as large a margin of profit as possible" (Bascom, 1984; p.26). And profits made from trading were kept by the women in almost all of the West African countries.

> A Ga woman also makes money by her trading. . .A man has no control over his wife's money, but any extra money she can extract from him for herself can never be reclaimed (Field, 1940:54).

> In South Dahomey, commercial gains are a woman's own property and she spends her money free of all control. . .Trade gives to women a partial economic independence and if their business is profitable they might even be able to lend some money - a few thousand francs - to their husbands against their future crops (Tardits and Tardits 1962).

Though the amount of profit was often small by international standards, many women traders were able to accumulate enough for a variety of purposes: to reinvest and expand their trading activities, to cover domestic and personal expenses since spouses have to keep the house in good condition, to replace old cooking utensils, to buy their own clothes and to educate their children.[7]

Another important use of trade profits was the financing of political activity. As Herskovits put it: "Support for the nationalist movements that were the instruments of political independence came in considerable measure from the donations of the market women." In fact, there is no black African leader, past and present, whose mother or grandmother, did not engage in trade. Trading was the traditional occupation of women in Africa. It is important to keep in mind the support women traders provided the liberation movements when we examine in Chapter 10 how the nationalists, who assumed power in Africa in the 1960s after independence, paid back these market women.

Women traders were particularly agile in transactions. They were quick to spot and exploit a profitable opportunity and to abandon a line of operation if it was unprofitable. Tardits and Tardits (1962) gave the following description of the planning by a typical woman trader in South Dahomey, assuming she had sufficient capital and had chosen to sell *akasa* (a corn porridge):

> First, she observes the market conditions carefully. She buys *akasa* from several women, noticing the quantities and prices. She then buys two or three basins of corn. She discovers rapidly where to find the best quality of corn, the lowest prices in the village or on other markets, and will try to make good bargains. She knows her cost prices and manages to keep steady profits by decreasing the quantities of food sold when corn prices go up so as to avoid any change in the market prices. An experienced woman knows in advance how much gain she will derive from a market day, and if she finds that her trade is tiresome or unprofitable, she gives it up for a more lucrative one. We asked a number of women if they had changed trading activities during their lives: 79 out of 100 had made a change, and among the 21 who had not, there were 7 young girls.

A 1602 Report on market activity on the Gold Coast (Ghana) found these women traders "very nimble about their businesse" (Cited by Skinner, 1964). Field (1940) also found that:

> The market in every Ga town is run entirely by women. No trading, except that initiated by foreigners is ever carried on by men. . .Many of the women are very shrewd and ingenious in their

---

[7] The case of Abi Jones was earlier cited where profits from her trading were used to educate her sons. Indeed, many of the post-colonial leaders of Africa were similarly educated - by funds accumulated from trading profits.

trading. One day when good catches of fish were coming in I saw a woman, who had no fishing men-folk, exchange a bowlful of fried *akpiti* cakes for a panful of fresh fish, and then hastily sell the fish to a 'stranger' who was trying to make up a load to take away. The sale of the fish brought her three shillings and fourpence. The sale of the cakes would have brought her one and sixpence. The materials out of which she made the cakes probably cost less than sixpence (p.64).

Similarly among the Akan of Ghana, McCall (1962) found that in Koforidua:

The market place is largely a woman's world. Except for the small percentage of traders who are men, the processes of trade are said to be mysteries to men. Men often seem uncomfortable in the market; they prefer to send a woman or a child to make purchases for them, and avoid entering it if possible. For women, the market place is not only a place of business but of leisure as well. Sales are sometimes slow and women chat and josh with each other.

To start trading, women often looked to their husbands for support or borrowed from the extended family pot. For example,

As soon as he is married the Ga husband is expected to set his wife up in trade (*'ewo le dzra'* - he puts her in the market). It is part of every woman's normal occupation to engage in some sort of trade and every reasonable husband is expected to start her off. . .When she is unlucky in her trading and loses her capital her husband is expected to set her up again, but if she loses her capital three times she is a bad manager and he has no further obligation in the matter (Field, 1940; p.55).

When additional capital was needed to expand, the women asked their husbands or employed various ways to establish or obtain credit. African women traders were particularly adept at establishing commercial relationships with European firms and there were four general ways in which the women secured trade credit. The first was the development of a close relationship with an employee of a European firm or an European customer they would call a "special customer." Often, the basis of this relationship was established at the market when the European customer was given special discounts. Over time, the relationship would grow and the "special customer" might be asked to provide contact with an European firm. Through this "special relationship" the European firm may advance large amounts of goods on credit to the African woman trader. As McCall (1962) found,

The European managers never complain about this part of this business. On the contrary, they eulogize the honesty of the women traders, who have an astonishing record of meeting their commitments on time and in full.

The second way was when "women came to know European employees by supplying other services, such as laundering, and subsequently asking to be advanced goods based on the trust established in this non-trading transaction" (White, 1987; p.41). The third was by introduction. Women traders often asked their relatives, or friends to intercede for them and guarantee their creditworthiness. These intermediaries were often traders themselves who had established a good reputation with the European firms. Fourth, some women traders joined together either to purchase in bulk or to seek credit collectively. They would usually have a "leader" or a spokeswoman who acted in their behalf in dealings with the European firms. Most European firms preferred dealing with a group leader, rather than on individual basis, as this reduced risks of default and deliquency. The group leader ensured timely fulfilment of repayment obligations of her associates.

At the indigenous level, women traders either bought goods on credit or with whatever currency that was in use. Some traders served as commissioned agents and dealt regularly with a particular producer.

> A weaver, for example, may show his agent cloths that he wishes to be sold and tell her the price he expects to receive for them. If she believes that the price is right, she takes them on credit; when they have been sold she pays the weaver what he asked and in return she receives a commission, usually about five percent. If she cannot sell the cloths at the weaver's price, she can return them to him; but if she can sell them at higher prices, she earns a profit in addition to her commission (Bascom, 1984; p.26).

In Yoruba, women who sold palm wine, a local drink, developed an interesting trade arrangement. Palm wine is tapped from the palm nut tree from which palm oil is derived. The wine, with a high yeast content, deteriorates rapidly after tapping. After two days, it is fully fermented and cannot be sold. After a day, it brings in only half price. Bascom (1987) noted how a commercial arrangement was devised to respect the "fermentation problem":

> Each palm wine tapper has a group of women who sell for him, each receiving the same amount each day to sell at the price set by the tapper. All the money received on the first two days belongs to the tapper, and that received on the third day belongs to his agent. If she should drop her calabash on the way to market, she or the tapper takes the loss depending upon whose day it is. A tapper is not concerned about how well an agent does on her own day, but he

demands that she be reasonably successful in selling on his days, and if she is not he refuses to deal with her again (p.26).

The importance of women in the indigenous market economy cannot be overemphasized. The market, as noted earlier, was the heartbeat of economic activity in many African societies. Food production, processing and trading were indigenous activities dominated by women. These women were *free enterprisers* who went about their activities on their own initiative, drive and interest the way they saw fit. They were *not* operating under orders from their chiefs or kings. As agents of distribution, women traders performed economically vital functions.

First, through their bulking operations for export and bulk-breaking of imports, women traders linked the indigenous economy with the international system. For example, imported sugar could be purchased in the remotest village by the smallest unit — by the cube (and cigarettes by the stick). Second, through their trading activities, they developed a distributional system or network based upon trust and reliability. This indigenous distribution system was by no means "spectacular." Commodities changed hands frequently in the transmission system. Yet, it was reasonably efficient in distributing goods over a wide area to isolated villages. It would not be an overstatement to offer that, without these women traders, the vitality and the throbbing of the indigenous economic heartbeat would cease.

From this follows the proposition that any event, whether government policy or a calamitous occurrence, which diminishes the scale of market activity would have a disproportionately adverse effect on African women. That in turn would have ramifications throughout the family structure and the entire indigenous society since the occupational system and the family structure were functionally related.

Traditionally, peasant farmers, mostly women, produced surpluses which they exchanged at the market for products they could not produce themselves. If for some reason, the market offered little incentive to trade or the market itself was destroyed, two types of responses might be expected. First, the women would take their produce to another market or elsewhere, where they could get a better price. This practice was observed innumerable times in Africa's history.

Second, if the traders could not take their produce elsewhere due to border closures, then they would either reduce the surpluses taken to the market or refuse to go to the market at all. The repercussions of this would be felt in the entire indigenous extended family system.

African women were not only procreators but also income earners. Their income came almost exclusively from market activity. Therefore, any event or policy (such as wars, violence, oppressive taxes and regulations) which destroyed an indigenous African market or reduced the scale of its activity hit hardest at women. It reduced their income-earning potential or, worse, threw them out of employment.

Female unemployment in traditional Africa hit hardest at the soul of the African family. If African women were forced to stay home because of disincentives to engage in market activity, several deleterious effects on the society could be imagined. The birth rate could explode. Malnourishment might occur if the family could no longer exchange its surplus commodities at the market for those it could not produce. Family stability could even be threatened.

Market trading generally made African women economically indepen-dent. Chatting at the market place also provided an important social release for pent-up emotions. Reducing the scale of market activity would make women more dependent on their spouses in Africa, a potentially troublesome prospect if the husbands themselves face hardships.

As we shall see in Chapter 10, many African governments, after independence, adopted *anti-market* policies under the guise of "socialism." The brunt of these fell disproportionately on African women in a tragic case of ideological malfeasance and stupidity. Capitalism was abhorred by many African nationalists because the colonialists were "capitalists." And because markets were a feature of capitalism, these "capitalist institutions" were to be eradicated. Never mind the fact that these markets were in existence centuries before the colonialists arrived in Africa. And never mind the importance of markets to traditional African societies and women.

Recall that it was the women traders who made donations and provided financial support to help the nationalist struggle for independence. The promotion of markets and commerce as well as government policies that create the environment for market activity to prosper *ought* to be the objective of every true African woman or those desirous of improving the lot of the native African woman. Mrs. Esther Ocloo — a Ghanaian entrepren-eur, co-founder of Women's World Banking and the 1990 winner of the annual Africa Prize for Leadership — said almost exactly as much: "From my several years' working experience with women farmers of Africa, I can assure you that if the *right* environment and *incentives* were created for women farmers, and the problems facing them now were addressed, the sustainable end of hunger would be a reality" (*World Development Forum*, Dec 15, 1990; p.1).

About a third of the food crops harvested in Africa by peasant farmers goes to waste because of poor storage and lack of motorable roads. African women carry on their heads harvested produce from the farm to the village. Because of physical limitations, whatever could not be carried was left to rot on the farm. Instead of improving this transporting of foodstuffs, creating the right environment and incentives as well as removing marketing obstacles, modern African governments meted out trade restrictions, price controls and economic repression to peasant farmers and traders.

In pre-colonial times and even during the colonial era, African women were free to travel and engage in trade. There were no "borders"; goods and people moved *freely* across Africa. Today, modern African leaders man artificial borders with uniformed bandits and decry the same activity as "smuggling." But the free trade spirit culturally ingrained in Africans refuses to be extinguished:

> Bilanga is a small stretch of no-man's land at the border post of Kasumbalesa, on the copperbelt, between Zambia and Zaire. By day it appears to be an ordinary border post carrying out its daily routine, but by night it is transformed into one of Africa's biggest smuggling conduits.

> After dark everyone becomes a smuggler. For the right price soldiers will allow anything to pass from stolen cars to everyday essentials. Recently an army fuel tanker, loaded with 300,000 litres of petrol (gasoline) crossed into Zaire where it disgorged its contents under the supervision of a senior army officer. . .

> Truckloads of mealie meal (maize meal) pour over from the Zambia side to Zaire where a 25kg bag of rolled meal fetches K500, twice the price on Zambia markets. The Zaireans want almost all types of Zambian manufactured goods like batteries, sugar, cement, petrol, paraffin, motor parts, detergents, soap, candles. . .

> Lubumbashi, the Zairean regional capital, is flooded with Zambian goods. The Zairean customs officials are even dependent on Zambian water.

> In exchange Zaire smuggles Far Eastern electronic goods that have been imported into the country at low tariffs. TV sets, videos, prohibited drugs, rare protected animals and birds, cross the Zambian border. Also digital watches, new and second hand clothes, shoes, plastic sandals, cosmetics, wigs and chitenge cloth, originally from Holland (*New African*, December 1990; p.35).

It was centuries ago that African chiefs and kings learned that controlling trade was impossible. It was also three centuries ago when the Dutchman William Bosman lamented the ineffectuality of trade restrictions against Africans. Despite heavy penalties and fines, the Dutch could not prevent "the Negro inhabitants from vending to the English and Zealand interlopers." What makes modern African governments think they can prevent Zaireans and Zambians or other Africans from trading with each other?

Means Of Transportation/Roads

Various modes of transportation were used in trade. Horse-drawn carts were crossing the Sahara as early as the 2nd millenium B.C., but the camel proved to be more effective (Wilkins, 1981; p.128). The use of the camel, for obvious reasons, spread fairly quickly in the arid and semi-arid regions of Africa.

In the savanna, donkeys and oxen were the chief pack animals and were found as far as the coast of Sene-gambia. In the forest, where trypanosomiasis (sleeping sickness) was rife and pasture scanty, the relay system by head porterage was the common means of transport. "But porterage was a particularly costly form of transport, and that is why porters were often slaves who were sold off at the end of the journey" (Wilkins, 1981; p.128).

River transport was often used, although this was impeded by cataracts and rapids. Canoes made use of the Niger, the Nile, the Zambezi, the Shire, the Senegal, parts of the Volta and many small rivers, lakes and coastal lagoons. There was heavy traffic along the Upper Niger River between Timbuktu and Djenne, Mali. A comprehensive system of roads was absent in pre-colonial Africa. However, there were pathways for overland movement of goods and people.

Quite often, traders carried the goods themselves or made use of family labor. To reduce the risk of falling prey to bandits and marauders, traders often travelled in caravans or convoys. To pass through a town, they often paid customary tolls. They varied according to the articles carried and were collected by the representatives of the rulers of each community. The primary purpose of the toll was to provide traders with armed protection thereby ensuring safe passage and a peaceful atmosphere for them to engage in their business. "It was not unusual for armed guards appointed by rulers to accompany traders or to patrol trade routes" (Falolan, 1985).

B. THE ROLE OF GOVERNMENT IN THE INDIGENOUS ECONOMY

Government Intervention

Indigenous African economies were based upon agriculture, pastoralism, markets and trade. The importance of these activities was appreciated by both the rulers and the natives. Most political entities were hierarchically structured. There was an almost universal principle that each unit had the right to manage its own affairs which concerned it alone. Only when its affairs impinged on other constituent units did authorities of the larger units or the kingdom as a whole feel the need to intervene. The role or functions of the larger government can be gleaned from the following:

The administrative function of the Ashanti officials - elders, *Adekurofo, Abirempon,* and chiefs – was to keep law and order in the community. This entailed defending the community from external attack, maintaining amicable relations among the persons and groups within and between the community and its ancestors and gods (Busia, 1951:65).

Both provincial governors of Soninke areas (of the ancient Ghana empire) and tributary rulers of conquered peoples had the duties of loyalty to the ruler of Ghana, provision of annual tribute and the contribution of bands of warriors to the imperial army when they were required for active service. In return, the ruler of Ghana provided protection against external enemies, facilities for sharing in the prosperous trade of the empire and the provision of justice to settle serious quarrels that might arise within the empire (Stride and Ifeka, 1971:36).

The main functions of traditional African governments were:
1. Defense against external aggression,
2. Maintenance of law and order,
3. The promotion of justice and social harmony within the kingdom, and
4. The promotion of trade and commerce.
The role of the indigenous government in the economy was very small. In fact, "The chief function of the Ashanti administration was to ensure harmony in the society rather than to provide services requiring expenditure" (Busia, 1951:78). Besides that, trade assumed primacy in peacetime.

One of the traditional roles of the African chief was to create a peaceful atmosphere for his people to engage in trade. It may also be recalled that when Asante military adventurism threatened commerce, a group of traders was formed in the 1860s to advocate peace, order and stability. Even in agriculture, it was not the role of the indigenous government to interfere or dictate what crops the peasants should raise. What a peasant farmer cultivated was his own individual decision to make. The role of the chief or kings in agriculture was to ensure that access to land was not denied to anybody, even strangers. Supervision or regulation of access did not constitute control over production.

In most cases across Africa, "there was no direct interference with production" (Wickins, 1981:230). Such an interference would have been in direct and obvious antipathy to African philosophy. This philosophy held that the individual was part of a community whose interests were antecedent. Within the community, the individual was completely free to pursue any avocation he/she so wished. The tenet of African law which maintained that any harmful action against another individual was a threat to the whole society was applicable to the realm of economics. A restriction on the economic activity of an individual could place severe restraints on the economic welfare of the whole society. If the individual prospered, so too did his extended family and the community. The individual could prosper so long as his prosperity did not conflict with the interests of the community. The society's interests were paramount. To the extent that such conflicts did not arise, the chief or king had no traditional authority or business interfering with an individual's pursuit of prosperity. Ultimately, the individual was answerable to the ancestors, not the chief or king who merely acted as the intermediary. This was a well-nigh universal African belief.

With trade, the historical evidence does not suggest obtrusive government interference either. It hardly made sense for the chiefs to prevent their own subjects from engaging in trade. Traders were free enterprisers, taking the risks themselves. Daaku (1971) emphasized:

> Those who so desired and ventured into distant places in pursuit of trade could rise to higher positions in the traditional setup. Along the coastal towns, successful traders began to display their affluence by surrounding themselves with a host of servants. Some were raised to the status of headmen or elders. They built themselves magnificent houses on which some of them even mounted a few cannon. The rise of these people was not only a coastal phenomenom. In practically all the forest states there came into prominence men like Kwame Anteban of Nyameso in Denkyira whose wealth became proverbial.

The kings and chiefs occasionally had farms and other economic enterprises. For example, the Asante kings had royal gold mines and the chiefs in east Africa and southern Africa had goats and cattle. But they were mainly for consumption by royalty and guests - not purposedly for the people. This point is crucial. The history of Africa does not provide evidence of chiefs and kings operating tribal government farms to feed the people. The natives fed themselves, built their own huts and provided for themselves.

In the event of a poor harvest, the king or chief was obligated to make some produce from his farm available to the needy. But it was not the traditional role of chiefs to use produce from his farm, if he had one, to feed his people under normal circumstances.

Nor did the kings and chiefs operate tribal government enterprises. The craft industries were owned by individuals or families, not by the chief or the state. The ruler might choose to have an enterprise but, again, it was mostly for his own benefit, not the natives'. It was the same with trade. Daaku (1971) noted in the case of the Akan of the Gold Coast that,

> Apart from the occasional trading organized for and on behalf of

the chiefs, trading, *like all other vocations*, was primarily an affair of individuals. Much of it was conducted by a man and his family, that is, his wives and children and/or with his sister's sons. It was *never* an affair of the state nor a few principal merchants who organized it on the model of the East Africa trade in which well-armed trading caravans were fitted out to journey into the interior. (Merchants in East Africa were also private individuals). Individual traders often set out on their own or with friends to try their fortunes on either the coastal or northern markets. (Italics mine).

Of the Bashu of eastern Zaire, Packard (1981) noted:

The salt trade between Isale and Katwe (in the early nineteenth century) was open to anyone who possessed the energy and desire to travel to Katwe. It was not even necessary to have goods to trade for the salt since it was possible to mine salt for oneself and then provide a portion of the extracted salt to the chiefs of Busongora.

The traders usually travelled in large groups armed with spears for protection against wild animals and occasional attacks by the inhabitants of the plains. By the end of the nineteenth century, by which time the valley had become a battle-ground for competing political and commercial groups, the number of traders in a salt caravan reached fifty or more. . .

Whether one extracted salt or traded for it, the transactions and activities took several days to complete. During this time the mountain traders camped at sites assigned by the market master, *muboza*, who oversaw all commerce at Katwe (p.89).

There were very, very few instances where trade was monopolized and controlled by the state. In fact, the number of commodities reserved strictly for chiefs throughout Africa's history is less than twenty out of thousands of commodities. According to Bates (1983), the most frequently mentioned objects of chief's monopoly were: ivory, kola, slaves, cattle, skins, and parts of game killed (p.55). The rest were free commodities.

Free trade and enterprise were the rule. The most frequently cited exceptions were the Kingdoms of Asante, Bunyoro, Mwene Mutapa and Mossi for example.

Sometimes trade was channelled through a single port, such as Whydah in Dahomey, where it was administered by the state in its own interest; or the production of staples, such as gold, ivory or kola nuts (in the case of Asante) was reserved by the state.. In the Kingdom of Mwene Mutapa in East Africa, the production and trade of gold was a royal monopoly. In the East African Kingdom of Bunyoro, there were royal markets and the right to purchase arms was restricted to a privileged group (Wickins, 1981; p.226).

It may be recalled from the previous chapter that Dahomey was the most centralized and planned economy in West Africa in the 19th century (Boahen and Webster, 1970). It declared a royal monopoly on salt and slaves. Agricultural production was centrally planned by the state. Livestock and food crop production were closely controlled and regulated. The basis for planning was the annual census which provided figures for the total population and its distribution by sex, occupation, province and village. There was even a census of all goats, cows, sheep and pigs and a strict account of slaughtering. Each village chief reported the number of pigs slaughtered. The butcher's guild kept all the skulls of pigs sold in the market. Both reports went to the King in Abomey, who sent out market inspectors, not only to make periodic checks but also to fix prices. The inspectors were drawn from the *zangbeto* society, a secret society which operated with the specific authorization of the state. Tardits (1962) gave a this description of their activity:

> *Zangbeto* watches the merchants and if they find that a woman trespasses the law, the members of the association walk through the village for seven nights, cursing the woman who disregarded the [customary price]. . .If she does not comply, *zangbeto* will come out again, curse her for sixteen more nights and carry through the village a banana tree branch wrapped in a white cloth representing a corpse in a shroud. . .

The tradition says that the lawbreaker dies shortly afterwards. The production of food crops was similarly controlled in Dahomey. Each province of the kingdom specialized in certain crops: Abomey in beans and maize, Zagnanado in millet, Allada in maize and cassava, Save in groundnuts and maize, and Adja in maize. Condiments - honey, red and black pepper, and ginger - were royal monopolies produced in restricted areas under supervision.

There were export, annual agricultural and palm oil taxes. All palm trees in the kingdom were counted and a constant check was kept on their annual yield. Taxation was about one-third of the total production. The tax on palm oil - the largest single source of state revenue after the 1850s - was bartered at Whydah for guns and powder. Livestock was taxed every three years. Artisans paid duties. In addition, there was a market tax and toll charges on all major roads.

The results of centralized planning was higher taxation and restrictions on personal liberty. Dahomeans were the most heavily taxed West Africans in the 19th century. This rigid centralization was possible because the kingdom was small and hemmed in by two powerful neighboring states — Asante and Oyo. Eventually, however, the Kingdom of Dahomey imploded under the weight of its bureaucracy and maze of regulations. The collapse began in 1883 when the French took over Porto Novo and Cotonou. To evade the excessive rates of taxation of trade, the natives migrated from the state-controlled port of Whydah to Cotonou under French protection. Cotonou flourished and became the commercial center of the French colony which was also named "Dahomey".[8]

The Asante Empire in the 19th century is also frequently cited as another example of a centrally planned economy. "A large sector of the economy was controlled by the state, including royal mines, worked by slave miners, ivory hunting and much of the area's trade" (Isichei, 1977: 62). But Daaku (1971) argued that, "there is no evidence to suggest that the chiefs and their elders exercised any monopoly over the coastal trade in the same way as the Aja kings established complete and absolute control over all aspects of trade in Dahomey." It was true that the Asante kings maintained a royal monopoly over trade in slaves and gold. However,

> [In the case of slaves], this was because the declaration of war and the conclusion of peace were vested in the chiefs and their elders. The chief could therefore reward some captains with the proceeds of war which were mainly slaves. But even in the slave trade, chiefly monopoly was not complete since rich prosperous merchants could travel to other trading centers like Salaga and Bontuku to buy slaves. . .It is has often been said that chiefs exercised virtual control over goldmining in their states. . .But however close the control, oral tradition seems to postulate a situation in which gold-mining was never completely brought under state control. The traditions of Adanse, Assin, Denkyira, and Mampong are emphatic that gold-mining was open to all. In the organization of trade the evidence suggests that no Akan state monopolized it to the exclusion of its subjects. On the contrary, all subjects were encouraged to take a hand in it. What was required by the rulers and what they always did was to provide a peaceful atmosphere within which trade could be transacted (Daaku, 1971).

When the state intervened in trade or markets, it was basically for two reasons. First, it "was aimed primarily at the acquisition of commodities required in some instances, for the direct support of the state - weapons for defense and offense, luxury goods for display - and, in others, for the indirect

---

[8] The demise of the Kingdom of Dahomey, in general, should serve as a lesson to present-day governments in both South Africa and independent Africa on the folly of excessive government control of markets, trade and freedom of movement of black Africans.

support gained through the prestige of liberal distribution of largesse" (Wickins, 1981:227). Even here, the intervention or control was in long-distance trade, not local trade and markets.

Second, intervention "was actuated by the desire to cut trading links of rival states" (Wickins, 1981). The Baganda were successful for a large part of the 19th century in preventing Arabs from trading with Bunyoro. In West Africa, there were frequent wars between Denkyira and Assin, Akwamu and Akyem, Asante and Denkyira and Asante and Fanti on the Gold Coast in the 17th and 18th centuries to prevent trade routes from falling into the hands of the other. In the 19th century, there were similar commercial feuds among the Delta states of Yorubaland.

In conclusion, state intervention in the economy was the exception rather than the rule in pre-colonial Africa. Bates (1983) stressed:

> In pre-colonial Africa, the states underpinned specialization and trade; they terminated feuds; they provided peace and stability and the conditions for private investment; they formed public works; and they generated wealth, if only in the form of plunder. In these ways, the states secured prosperity for their citizens (p.40).

Neo-Marxists have argued that pre-colonial African states also had the means for expropriation and redistribution. The rulers were relatively wealthy and the prosperity they generated were unequally shared. But there are several flaws in this argument.

First, the African people separated the king and kingship. Gifts and tribute paid were to the office of kingship, the sacred repository of ancestral powers. Such wealth was "stool property" to be used for "tribal purposes" and not personal property of the chief to be misused for his own benefit. When a chief was exiled, he could not take this wealth along with him. Or when he died, this "stool wealth" was not divided among the chief's heirs. It was transferred to the next chief.

It is important to cite a dispute which arose over this particular matter and its settlement. According to Olivier (1969):

> The Bantu Chief's most important source of wealth is cattle. As a rule he possesses by far the largest herds in the tribe. Most of them are offspring of cattle originally looted in war. Such cattle were all brought to the Chief, who divided some among the successful raiders or among men who had otherwise distinguished themselves, but always kept a generous number for himself. The cattle he kept back are sometimes held to be his personal property over which the tribe has no claim at all. But it is also maintained that they are tribal cattle, in the sense that the Chief merely holds them in trust for the tribe as a whole, and cannot use them recklessly for his own ends.

This point came up recently in the dispute among the Kgatha regarding Lentswe's estate (1934-35). In order to put the matter beyond doubt, Chief Molefi then publicly proclaimed that for the future he would set aside and regard these cattle as the property of the tribe, and not the Chief, and as such would utilize them only for tribal purposes. A similar conception of cattle is held by the Tlokwa.

The king or chief could live well and comfortably, befitting his royal status. But the wealth he displayed was "tribal property." Furthermore, since chiefship or kingship was not open to all, it was not a means by which any individual could amass personal wealth. Thus, the king or chief could not be considered as someone who used royal authority to extract wealth from the masses for his own benefit. If a king ruled incompetently, the tributes were reduced or the king was killed.

Second, redistributive powers were seldom coercive. Nor could the powers of expropriation be exercised without the approval of the council of elders. Even slaves owned property in many indigenous systems. Neither could the kings and chiefs have been able to control trade if they had had the desire. A multitude of alternate routes existed and the commodities traded were numerous. The cost of controlling the movement of so many items over a myriad of roads and bush paths was enormously prohibitive.

A major factor inhibiting state intervention was the absence of an effective government machinery. Africa generally lacked the skills of writing, measuring and keeping accounts, which are indispensable for a rigid control of trade. Only Dahomey had such a method. It used pebbles to record population size, classified by age, sex and district, as well as to record production, taxes and movement of goods mainly for fiscal and military purposes. The Asante also used Muslim record keepers. State intervention required a strong centralized government but this was "exceptional in sub-Saharan Africa" (Wickins, 1981:228).

The other factor was the nature of the indigenous system of government itself. Only politically powerless groups can be exploited; that is, those without any voice or representation in government. The indigenous system of government however was not constituted this way, as we saw in previous chapters. It was a participatory system of government in which any adult, even including slaves in some societies, could participate in the decision-making process.

Another factor was peasant "foot power." Tribal boundaries were ill-defined since there were no border guards, and goods and people moved freely across them. When peasants felt unduly restricted or exploited in their economic activities, they could always move or switch allegiance to a different chief. Historical accounts of such migrations are legion.

Taxes

Government expenditures in traditional Africa were small. "Financial matters did not bulk large in Ashanti administration, for there was no wage-earning system" (Busia, 1951:78). Of the four functions of government listed in the previous section, only defense had the potential of "run away" outlays in the event of sustained external aggression. But even then, tributary states were expected to supply, at their own expense, warriors to the imperial army where such an army existed. Very few states had standing armies. In most societies, the people were the army. After repelling external threats, the people's army was disbanded and the "soldiers" went back to their normal activities. Thus, military expenditures in peacetime were unknown. Where a permanent army existed, a contingent operated farms to feed the soldiers.

The practice of communal labor kept recurrent and developmental expenditures down:

> [In Ashanti] the women kept the village clean, (in Igboland, it was the younger age-grades) each of the women sweeping the area around her house. The men provided the place of public convenience by digging pits a few yards from the village and building huts over them. They also cleaned the roads and paths. It was left to each village to provide its own services under the direction of the *Odekuro* and his council.

> The chief's house was built and kept in repair by the various elders and their subjects and slaves. To feed his household there were stool farms managed by the subjects who came directly under the chief (Busia, 1951:79).

Revenue was however needed for the purchase of gunpowder, arms, royal regalia, to defray funeral and entertainment expenses. A treasury system accordingly evolved in each village or division. These local treasuries were financially independent of the center. They expected no grants or revenue sharing from the "central government." Rather, it was the central government that expected tributes and other revenue from the provinces. Since the central government made little expenditures, it was structurally geared to generate budget surpluses which cumulatively became the wealth of the kingdom.[9]

Revenue was obtained from several sources: from trade, market tolls,

---

[9] It may be objected that the central government (or federal government in most cases) acted parasitically. But in indigenous Africa, the state was not tyrannous. Further, wealth accumulated by the king was not the king's personal property. Thus, the king or senior government officials in many African societies could not use their offices for their own personal enrichment.

transit levies, court fines, pillage and gifts to the ruler. For the Ashanti, Busia (1971) enumerated these sources:

> One source was trade (batadie). Every chief or Birempon had men among his gyase subjects who traded for him. There were two trade routes, one between Ashanti and the Northern Territories and the other between Ashanti and the coast. To the north the Ashanti took kola, and brought back slaves, shea-butter, blankets, and livestock. To the south they took ivory, gold-dust, and slaves, and returned with metal rods (ntwaa), rum, guns and gunpowder, salt, and cloth. . .

> A second source was from atitode. This was what trangressors who had been found guilty by the court paid 'to buy their heads.' It was a fine in lieu of the death sentence(for such crimes as treason, adultery with the chief's wife, or having sex with a married woman in the bush-ahahantwe). The whole amount of such fines was paid into the chief's treasury. Also accruing from court cases was the aseda (thanksgiving money) from those whom the court had found innocent. . .

> The chief also received revenue from gold-mining. Two-thirds of all gold mined in his Division was paid into the chief's treasury, the remaining third being retained by the elder or Birempon in direct charge of the area in which it was mined.(This applied more to alluvial gold nuggets washed ashore on tribal land).

> Direct levies were also imposed for specific purposes such as funerals, regalia, war, ceremonial, or hospitality. Sometimes a special levy was collected for the chief's treasury when a new chief was installed (Yedi too bo Ohene fotoo: We raise a levy for the chief's treasury) (p.81).

In the Ashanti kingdom,

> There was strict control of public funds. The chief had his treasurer, Sannaahene (head of the leather bag), as did the Birempon whose treasury officer was the Fotosanfo (he who unlooses the bag). It was to the treasurer of the chief or Birempon that all revenue was paid. It was also the treasurer who paid out any money required, and the Okyeame (spokesman) or Dabrehene (chamberlain) witnessed all such transactions. The chief of Birempon himself might not hold the scales used for weighing out the gold, nor might he open the leather bag in which it was kept. If a levy was raised for a specific purpose, the Sannaahene's duty was to see that the levy was used for that purpose.

> The system of accounting was in the following manner. For

revenue, there were two boxes. One box, the *adaka dese*, had three separate compartments, each containing gold dust made up in 8 pounds sterling packets (*peredwan*). The box was kept in the chief's sleeping room, and the chief, the *Sannaahene*, and the head chamberlain witnessed withdrawals from it. A cowrie shell was put into the box whenever a packet was withdrawn.

The *Sannaahene* had another box in which smaller sums were kept. When he had enough to make a *peredwan*, it was weighed out and put into the larger box.

For expenditure there was a third box, the *apem adaka* (box of a thousand). This was replenished by the *peredwan* packets taken out of the large revenue box (*adaka kese*). The money was weighed out in small packets, (3 shillings, 3 shillings and 6 pence, 7 shillings, 13 shillings) which the *Sannaahene* used for his purchases. The payments were recorded by replacing each packet taken out with a cowrie shell (Busia, 1951:83).

After a week, a month or at the end of the financial period when accounts were tallied, the cowrie shells in *all* the three boxes must be the same in number. Any discrepancy alerted "accountants." The Ashanti could easily tell where the problem lay since the count which did not match up to *any* two was the suspect. For example, if the counts were 20, 20 and 15 (or 35) the third last box and the person in charge of it were the culprit. Perhaps the reader may want to devise a way of "cheating" this amazingly simple accounting system. "That the system worked well may be judged from the fact that the destooling of chiefs for 'misappropriating stool funds' was of very rare occurrence before the period of the British Administration of Ashanti" (Busia, 1951:82).

Market tolls and duties (indirect taxes) were other important sources of revenue. For example,

> The subjects of the Kanuri empires paid two main sorts of taxes, both paid in kind. One was a tax on the harvest to provide for the upkeep of the *Mai* and his court; the other was to supply the needs of local government officials. Both the *Mai* and important noblemen founded slave villages to further supplement their income. . .Other sources of revenue were the spoils of war, the profits of justice, the giving of presents to the *Mai* and taxes on trade (Stride and Ifeka, 1971:131).

These were used for the maintaince of law and order as well as to settle disputes at the market place. However, few states imposed direct or regular taxes in pre-colonial Africa. Only Asante and Dahomey were known to have had regular poll taxes. In 1898, when an attempt was made to collect a Hut Tax in Sierra Leone by the British colonialists, the natives revolted. The tax was five shillings on every house in the protectorate. The revolt was led by the famous chief, Kebalai, the *bai bureh* (Boahen, 1986; p.135).

Traditionally, the natives paid tributes to their kings. But these were dependent upon how well they ruled. If the king ruled well, they praised him and sent large tributes. Otherwise, they withheld or reduced their tributes to send the incompetent government a clear message.

The Bantu chief was entitled to several tributes. One was called *sehuba*, which was the breast-portion (*sehuba*) of every big game animal, and one tusk of every elephant, and the skins of every lion and leopard killed by his subjects, whether hunting alone or in a regiment, or in a *letsholo* (tribal hunt). Though the tribute was compulsory and failure to deliver it was a penal offense, this practice died out. Another tribute was the *dikgafela*. This consisted of a basketful of corn, required to be given to the chief by every woman in times of good harvest. The presentation was a ceremonial affair and from this corn, beer was brewed and shared by all the people. Finally, in most Bantu societies were a number of large "public" fields (*masoto*, *matsweta*, *mapasa*), cultivated for the chief by different segments of the people. The chief provided the seeds and the people did all the work. Produce from the farms was given to the chief.

In other societies, the people chose a certain day to work on the chief's farm, if there was one, as a form of indirect tribute. In the Akan states of the Gold Coast, all the gold mined privately on a certain day was turned over to the king but on a voluntary basis.

In the Ashanti Kingdom, the subjects of a chief were liable to perform service of an agricultural nature. They worked on the chief's farm several days each year. At Wenchi this service was performed every *Wukudae* (Wednesday *adae*); that is, about six times a year. At Enchi in Aowin, the surrounding villages took turns to work on the chief's farm. The number of days varied from place to place, depending upon the needs of the chief. He asked his men for help when he needed it and provided them with food and drink while they worked for him.

During the *Odwera* ceremony, the Ashanti chief received yearly tributes of "first-fruits" from his subjects: yams, rice, maize, palm-oil, meat and snails. A hunter who killed an elephant or an antelope on the chief's land sent his portion as fixed by tradition. In the case of an elephant, the foreleg, ear, tail, and one tusk were the chief's portion. If a hunter who was the chief's subject killed an antelope he gave the foreleg to the chief; if the hunter was a stranger, he gave the chief the hindleg. A hunter who killed a leopard gave the chief its skin. The chief's share of all the wild animals found on his land was known and fixed by custom.

The African chief was in a position to use his position to accumulate personal wealth. He could conscript labor and create wealth. But as argued earlier, such wealth was not regarded as his personal property but as "stool property or wealth" which he held in trust for the people. When a chief died or was exiled, this "stool wealth" remained for the next chief. In fact, "all moneys, gifts, taxes and other forms of donations to the Chief or King still belonged to the people for relief or aid to individuals in times of need" (Williams, 1987; p.171).

Ranked in accordance of importance, Bates (1983) found that the three sources of revenue for pre-colonial African states were:

> The ruler's own estates or gardens, his own cattle, or tribute, much of which was made up of agricultural products. Forced labor and confiscation were the next most frequently mentioned. Then came trade, with market fees representing the least frequently mentioned source of public revenue (p.30).

With the abolition of the slave trade, the second source of revenue was eradicated. The subsequent restoration of peace and order led to a spurt of market activity and, as a result, market tolls and fees increasingly became the primary sources of revenue. The market tolls, it may be remembered, were principally used to keep the marketplace clean and orderly.

C. SUMMARY OF THE FEATURES OF THE INDIGENOUS ECONOMIC SYSTEM

Land Tenure

- Land in the village did not belong to everybody as implied by "communal ownership." Land was lineage-controlled. The true owners of land were those who first settled on it - the ancestors. Although dead, their spirits were believed to be ever-present and guide the living.
- The chief or the lineage head was a mere custodian of the land. His role was to hold the land in trust. He could not deny a tribesman access to the land. Even strangers could obtain use rights upon the provision of a token gift. Use rights were virtually perpetual so long as a small tribute was paid, voluntary in some cases, and the land was not abused.
- Crops raised on the land belonged to individual farmers, not to the village chief or headman. What types of crops to cultivate was an individual choice.
- If a family abandoned their farmland and moved out of the tribal area, as was often the case, such unoccupied land fell into the custody of the chief for allocation. The chief would not claim ownership of this land even though the people might refer to it as belonging to the chief.

Economic Enterprise

- All the means of production were privately owned, not held by the state. Even land was not owned by the state or the chiefs. Lineage heads exercised control over land in most villages.
- The natives were free enterprisers, going about their economic activities on their own initiative, not at the command of chiefs. Profits made by them were theirs to keep, not for the chiefs to expropriate.
- There was *no* African law which prohibited the natives from making a profit or accumulating wealth in the course of their economic activities. Prosperity and wealth could be pursued but within the limits set by either Islam or social norms or both. Group loyalty or solidarity was generally held to be important and to the extent that there was no conflict the pursuit of wealth and prosperity was not debarred.
- The wealth of the rich was not sequestrated by the chief or king for equal distribution to all the people. All the wealthy were required to do was to *assist* their poor kinsmen.
- There were few direct taxes. Only tribute was paid to the chief voluntarily. The size of the tribute was determined by how well the chief governed. The kings derived much of their revenue from their own royal estates and gardens. In essence, the kings looked after themselves.
- After the abolition of the slave trade and with the restoration of peace, trade expanded and market tolls and duties increasingly provided the bulk of state revenue. But all taxes, gifts and other forms of donations to the chief or king still belonged to the people to be used in times of need or emergency to assist them.
- In general, there were no state or tribal government enterprises, except in very few cases such as Kingdom of Dahomey. A king or chief could operate a farm, a mine or some commercial enterprise. But it was for his own benefit, not purposedly for the welfare of the people. It was not his traditional function to use his farm, if he chose to have one, to feed his people. The people fed themselves and provided for their needs.
- In many indigenous systems, there was generally no direct interference with production or distribution of commodities. Agricultural production and trading trading were activities dominated by women. What these women cultivated and traded were their own decisions to make.
- Markets and trade were free and open. Though trade in some few commodities, such as slaves or ivory, was reserved for the king, in general no king or chief monopolized trade or markets to the total exclusion of his subjects. It would have been an *un-African* thing to do. Rather the chiefs encouraged their people to engage in trade and it was

the traditional function of the chief to create a peaceful atmosphere for his people to engage in free trade.

- Prices on native markets were not fixed or controlled by the chiefs. They were, in general, determined by market forces - supply and demand. These principles were understood by the natives and they bargained over prices. Markets were well structured and organized in West Africa under 'Market Queens.' At most markets, systems were in place to settle trade disputes.

- Though some powerful merchants tried to control markets and fix prices, open competition was the rule. Nor could such competition be eliminated. There were numerous suppliers, middlemen, brokers, trade routes as well as substitutes. Trade in indigenous products could not be controlled, but the possibilities existed for that over 'imported' items. However, even in these cases, control could not be complete, since alternative trade routes existed.

Kendall and Louw (1987) also reached similar conclusions:

> Pre-colonial African law and custom shared the following features with the free market system: Assets such as stock, crops, huts, handicrafts and weapons were privately owned and land was privately alloted and subject to private grazing rights;
> - There were no laws against free contract and voluntary exchange;
> - There was no coercive redistribution of wealth and almost no taxes;
> - Chiefs and headmen had few autocratic powers and usually needed to obtain full consensus for decisions;
> - Central government was limited, with a high degree of devolution to village councils, and there was no central planning structure;
> - There were no powers of arbitrary expropriation, and land and huts could be expropriated under extreme conditions after a full public hearing (p.21).

D. THE INDIGENOUS ECONOMIC SYSTEM: AN ASSESSMENT

A great deal of mythology and ignorance still surround the indigenous economic system, which was variously called "communism" and "socialism." Foreign observers who came upon the profit-sharing schemes of the natives hastily denigrated them as "primitive communism." Many African leaders also took the same profit-sharing schemes as proof that the indigenous system was "socialism." Much of this was, of course, mythology. There was no state direction of economic activity or planning bureau in many African societies. Nor were there state enterprises and widespread state ownership.

The means of production were privately owned. Huts, spears and agricultural implements were all private property. Wage labor was absent, but there was no widespread alienation of labor from the fruits of labor. What the peasant produced with his labor was his personal property which he shared with his family or anyone else in the manner he saw fit. Even slaves, in many African societies, were not completely dispossesed of the fruits of their labor.

The profit motive was present in market transactions. But this motivation was not overriding. The marketplace, as we have seen, served other important purposes as well. It was a place for social intercourse and the center of entertainment. Individuals went to the market not necessarily to shop but to interact and socialize.

Similarly, a trader might chat all day and not be perturbed by the fact that she had sold only one or two items. But she would not sell an item for *less* than she purchased it for. If a profit was made, it was shared with her family. Divisions of profit were not always proportional. Else, many traders would have not have been able to accumulate sufficient capital either to expand their trading enterprise or to send their children overseas for education. Nor could they have provided vital support to the nationalist movements for independence.

Free enterprise and free trade were the rule in indigenous Africa. Not every aspect of indigenous economic activity was planned and directed by the chief or the state. The natives of Africa went about their economic activities on their own initiative and free will. They did not line up at the entrance of the chief's hut to apply for permits or seek permission before engaging in trade or production. What they produced and how much were their own decisions to make. The African woman who produced *kenkey*, *garri* or *semolina* herself decided to produce these items. Nobody forced her to do so. Nor did anybody order the fishermen, artisans, craftsmen or even hunters to produce specific items. It may sound trivial to stress these points. But elementary as they may seem, they have been misunderstood by many scholars, experts and African leaders.

In modern parlance, those who go about their economic activities of their own free will are called free enterprisers. By this definition, the Kente weavers of Ghana, the Yoruba sculptors, the gold, silver and blacksmiths as well as the various indigenous craftsmen, traders, farmers were all free enterprisers. And this is the way the natives have been for centuries. The Masai, Somali, Fulani and other pastoralists who herded cattle over long distances in search of pasture and water to fatten them were also free enterprisers. So too were the African traders who travelled great distances to buy and sell commodities - an economic, risk-undertaking venture. Recall the Fanti proverb: "*Obra nyi woara abo*" - Life is as you make it within the community.

They could take these risks associated with entrepreneurial activity because of the security afforded them by the extended family system. This much-maligned system possessed some positive economic aspects that were overlooked by many development experts. Although this system entailed some "sharing" (not forced or proportionate), it also provided the spring-board for Africans to launch themselves into highly risky ventures. If they failed, there was always the extended family system to fall back on as a safety net. Conversely, if they succeeded, there was some obligation on their part to the system which supported them.

State intervention in the economy was not the general policy. The Kingdom of Dahomey and Asante were among the few exceptions. But rigidly controlled Dahomey crumbled under the weight of its own regulations. Even in commerce, there was a notable absence of state controls and ownership. In Gold Coast, for example, gold-mining was open to all subjects of the states of Adanse, Assin, Denkyira and Mampong. Some chiefs taxed mining operations at the rate of one-fifth of the annual output. In some states, certain days were reserved exclusively on which all gold mined was ceded to the throne. But the mines were in general not owned and operated by the chiefs. Rather, the chiefs granted mining concessions.

Much of the indigenous economic system still exists today where African governments have not destroyed it through misguided policies and civil wars. Women traders can still be found at the markets. They still trade their wares for profit. And in virtually all African markets today, one still bargains over prices - an ancient tradition.

Is this indigenous system "capitalism", "socialism" or "communism"? Since there is no one standard definition of "capitalism", the indigenous system may or may not be capitalism, depending upon whose definition is being used. Under the Western, economic definition, capitalism is an economic system by which private individuals, not the state, solve the "economic problem" (of what to produce, how much and for whom) through the market system.

By this definition, the indigenous African economic system can be characterized as "capitalistic" in the sense that peasants, not their chiefs or states, determine what to produce, how much and for whom. In most traditional societies, many of these transactions occur through the market-place. Even the behavior of kings and chiefs was not that much different from their subjects. Much of the king's revenue was derived from royal estates or farms. Produce from these farms was strictly for royal consumption, not to feed the people. In other words, the kings fed themselves.

The indigenous economic system, however, was a different kind of capitalism in one important respect. Profit was shared, in contrast to the Western system whereby profit was appropriated by the owners until recently, when some U.S. corporations adopted profit-sharing schemes with their workers. Furthermore, the indigenous African system was not one of unfettered capitalism. Individual economic liberties were always circumscribed or bounded by social norms and obligations for the survival of the group. For want of a better terminology, the traditional economic system may be described as *bounded capitalism* and the ideology as *indigenism*.

Profit could be made. There was *no* African law which outlawed the pursuit of profit, wealth or prosperity. Kings and chiefs propitiated gods, recited incantations, poured libations to ancestral spirits, and performed religious sacrifices in bids to seek supernatural help to make markets, towns or the society *prosper*. An individual too could prosper and accumulate wealth but not at the expense of his kinsmen. The pursuit of wealth had to be within the *bounds* or limits determined by Islam or social norms or both. Further, the rich were not to misuse their wealth against their kinsmen. Rather, they were to assist their less fortunate brethren. Smith (1962) said it best: "The Hausa set a high value on the freedom to pursue wealth, within limits set by Islam on the one hand and by customary norms on the other. Thus Hausa admire industry and commercial skill for the wealth and status they bring and for the generosity and display by which this wealth and status is demonstrated."

By the Marxian definition, on the other hand, the indigenous system was not capitalism. Marxists define capitalism as an economic system based on exploitation of labor to produce maximum surplus value (profit) which is appropriated by the few. The definition, by necessity, is couched in terms of classes: the few (capitalists) and the proletariat (the masses). According to Marxists, the indigenous African economic system could not be characterized as "capitalism" since, abstracting from slavery, there was generally no massive exploitation of labor. This could not have occurred, they continue, for two reasons. First, since wage labor was absent, there could not be alienation of labor from the fruits of its efforts. Second, peasants could always move and settle at another location whenever they were "exploited."

As the Marxian definition stands, the indigenous African economic system is easy to categorize as not being "capitalism." But further confusion is added when neo-Marxists associate free markets, free trade and free enterprise with the definition of capitalism. As we have seen, these institutions were in existence in Africa before the advent of the Europeans. That should make the indigenous system "capitalism" by neo-Marxian definition but not by the orthodox Marxian.

Could the indigenous system be termed "socialism"? There seems to be more agreement on the definition of socialism. Essentially, it is a system in which the producers possess both political power and the means of production. Further, distribution of commodities is effected through the state system, rather than through markets, and the emphasis is on "equity." It may be argued that the indigenous African economic system was "socialism" due to the fact that the producers, the peasants, possessed both political power and the means of production. But distribution was not made by the state. Government-mandated distribution systems did not exist in traditional African society. Furthermore, the Marxist definition of socialism tends to equate producers automatically with urban workers or wage-eaners.[10] Such a class did not exist in indigenous Africa. Therefore, by both counts, the indigenous system was not "socialism." Many experts and African leaders erred in characterizing the indigenous system as fundamentally socialist. According to Kendall and Louw (1987): "an examination of southern African tribes reveals political and economic systems based on individual freedom and private property rights, with considerable differences in levels of wealth and social status" (p.3).

Moreover, socialism as practiced by modern African leaders entailed pervasive state intervention and participation in the economy as well as the institution of a plethora of controls, regulations and price-fixing. As we have seen, these were not characteristic of the indigenous economic system. African chiefs do not fix prices or operate "state enterprises."

Nor could the indigenous African economic system be termed "communism." This is a system in which there are no classes (no reserve army of the unemployed, no proletariat or rich capitalists). There is common ownership of the means of production as well as subsistence. Distribution of goods is undertaken by the state according to principle: "To each according to his needs." The indigenous African economic system, clearly, did not possess these features. In fact, Maylam (1986:65) was emphatic:

> In the attempt to discover various modes of production in precolonial Africa, it has been discovered that Marx's schemata are not readily applicable to Africa. *No African society was as simply self-sufficient for it to be classified as a 'primitive community' in the Marxist sense.* Some years ago there were flirtations with the feudal mode, but this too has come to be seen as inappropriate. Thereafter the concept of the Asiatic mode seemed to offer analytical leverage. This mode presupposes the existence of semi-autonomous village communities which are exploited economically through the agency of a superimposed state structure. This too has been rejected by Coquery-Vidrovitch and others as inapplicable to Africa, although it might be seen to bear some resemblance to the 19th century Zulu state: while the Zulu state hierarchy imposed demands on local communities, notably for tribute and labor service, the homestead survived intact as a fundamental unit of Zulu society.

Finally, will the indigenous system inevitably pass through the stages of

---

[10] One glaring contradiction of modern "socialist" countries is the fact that peasants, the farmers and producers, are conspicuously locked out of the political process. Even more glaring is the lack of the political power of the urban workers themselves. Witness the travails of Solidarity in Poland and Ghana's Trade Union Congress.

feudalism, capitalism, socialism to communism according to the immutable laws of Marx? This is not only unlikely but practically impossible as well, no matter how much effort African leaders undertake at social engineering.

According to Karl Marx, in Europe, the feudal organization in the countryside and the corporations in the cities for a long time prevented money-capital, the result of usury and commerce, from being transformed into industrial capital. The 16th century feuds between parliament and feudal lords over political authority resulted in freedom for the serfs and a mass exodus to the cities. This exodus created a "reserve army of the unemployed" which laid down the conditions for the birth of capitalism. For sustenance, the peasant had to sell his labor for wages. There thus came into existence a separation between the worker and working conditions. Theretofore, the peasant produced at home what he needed for domestic use. In becoming a wage-earner in the city, he no longer had anything but the strength of his labor to sell to urban manufacturers.

These manufacturers found it to be in their interest to pay the lowest possible wages for the greatest amount of work however inhumane the working conditions. This form of economic activity - capitalism - was constantly motivated by the quest for profit and superprofit. Over time, the workers would become alienated and would rebel against the capitalist system, replacing it with a worker state in a socialist revolution. Eventually, a communist system would evolve in which there would be no class divisions and all the means of production as well as distribution would be owned by the state or the people.

There are two fundamental difficulties with stage theories such as this. The first is: where precisely does one place indigenous Africa in this scheme? As Wickins (1981) asserted: "Marx's writings on pre-capitalist economic formations are not very helpful for analysing African societies or for showing how they develop" (p.230). Second: Must all societies, by force of destiny, necessarily pass through these pre-ordained phases? One may not like the Western capitalist system and may wish it followed some alternative path. That is fine. But to dictate or impose this alternative trajectory upon Africa amounts to an offensive intellectual imperialism which must be denounced as vehemently as other forms of "imperialism."

It is the African people, not an empty-headed army sergeant or an "educated" fufu-head, who must determine what type of economic system is best suited for them. Free markets, free trade, and free enterprise have for centuries been an integral part of their indigenous economic heritage.

CHAPTER 9

THE INDIGENOUS INSTITUTIONS UNDER COLONIALISM

When the missionaries arrived, the Africans had the land and the missionaries had the Bible. They taught us to pray with our eyes closed. When we opened them, they had the land and we had the Bible.

— Jomo Kenyatta, the late president of Kenya (Cited in Lamb, 1983:59).

'*Ng'enda thi ndeagaga motegi*" (There is nothing that treads on the earth that cannot be trapped; in other words, you can fool people for a time, but not forever).

— A Gikuyu Proverb.

It has been said that the despotism of the chiefs was thus overthrown. But it appears that that despotism was immediately replaced with a new despotism — the despotism of the Governor-General who, overnight, stepped into the shoes of all the chiefs and became the 'Supreme Chief of Natives.' The power to allot land became vested in him via the various officers of the government, the most active of which was the Native Commissioner of the district, called the Bantu Affairs Commissioner after 1962.

— Digby Sqhelo Koyana of South Africa.

A. COLONIALISM

Early Contacts And Scramble For Africa

After the 1840s when the slave trade was finally abolished, commerce began to flourish in the ensuing calm and peace. Rivalries, however, continued between various African peoples. Cattle raids continued and hostilities intensified when one ethnic group fought another for control of lucrative markets and trade routes. Those who found themselves under siege from warring neighbors found it convenient to seek protection from the Europeans.[1] For example, in the 18th and 19th centuries, the Fanti and the Asante on the Gold Coast were frequently at war. When the Dutch allied themselves with Asante, the Fanti thought it wise to seek British protection. In March 1867, the Dutch and the British signed an agreement under which all Dutch forts and settlements east of the mouth of the Sweet River, near Elmina, were to be exchanged for those of the British to the west.

"The news of the agreement infuriated the Fante because they were not consulted. It also alarmed the rulers of the western districts because, since they knew the Dutch were the traditional friends of the Asante, they expected their states would soon be overrun by the Asante" (Boahen and Webster, 1970:210). On January 16, 1873, rioting broke out in Sekondi to protest the transfer of British protectorship. Until the 1860s, the Europeans were generally unwilling to extend protectorates over African natives as that required additional expenditures. In 1843, for example, the African Committee of the British House of Commons passed a resolution which disavowed any deep involvement in Africa.

"Their third resolution lays it down plainly that the policy of the British Government henceforth in Africa, 'should be to encourage in the natives the exercise of those qualities which may render it possible for us more and more to transfer to the natives the administration of all Governments, with a view to our ultimate withdrawal from all, except probably Sierra Leone'" (Cited in Nicol, 1969). But in the face of growing commercial competition, the British nevertheless were forced to act or face being squeezed out of Africa. Throughout the second half of the 19th century, the British, French, Dutch, Portuguese and other Europeans brutishly jostled one another for influence over trade and control of certain valued commodities. Numerous forts and castles were built, especially along the West African coast to defend commercial interests against foreign interlopers and to expand trade as well.

To secure commercial beachheads and advantages, pretentious friendship

---

[1] This led many African radicals to accuse the chiefs of collaborating with the colonialists. This charge, however, failed to recognize that the chief's prerogative was always the survival of his tribe. If an alliance with an European power assured their survival, the chiefs exercised this option, albeit reluctantly. It was, for many, the most prudent choice out of a set of options.

treaties were signed with African chiefs and kings. But not all of Africa's rulers were that naive. As Dappa Pepple in Bonny on the Niger Delta said in the 1840s: "One white man come and make book (treaty) and another white man come tomorrow and break it; white man be fool, but treaty is in my head" (quoted in Wickins, 1981; 274).

So intense was the competition for commercial hegemony that in 1884 Chancellor Bismarck of Germany found it necessary to convene a conference of European nations with the avowed purpose of reducing tensions among them. The effect of the conference was to establish rules for the recognition of spheres of commercial suzerainty. In the aftermath of this Conference began a frenzied scramble for Africa to establish such spheres of dominance where none existed before. Suddenly, the rules of the game had changed dramatically.

Tendentious treaties were this time yanked out of African rulers, in some cases by sheer military force. De facto protectorates became colonies. Various rationales were proffered to justify this transformation to colonialism. The "savages" of Africa had to be civilized in order to free them from the oppressive regimes of their traditional rulers. The missionaries' "duty" was to convert the pagans. These self-righteous objectives drew a few sarcastic comments. Said Herbert Macaulay in 1905: "The dimensions of 'the true interests of the natives at heart' are algebraically equal to the length, breadth and depth of the whiteman's pocket."

The Christian mission educed the following parody in a Gold Coast newspaper:

> Onward Christian Soldiers unto heathen lands,
> Prayer books in your pockets rifles in your hands,
> Take the happy tidings where trade can be done,
> Spread the peaceful gospel with the gatling gun
> (Cited by Boahen and Webster, 1970; p.225).

In the beginning, many Africans conceived of colonization as an alliance or a strengthening of friendship with the Europeans, rather than as an act of occupation. The kingdoms of the Tiv, of Porto-Novo and of Douala all had signed treaties, and their leaders complained bitterly when the treaties were violated (Manning, 1988; p.62). In East Africa,

> The Gikuyu gave Europeans building rights in places like Dagoretti, Fort Smith and others, with no idea of the motives which were behind the caravans, for they thought that it was only a matter of trading and nothing else. Unfortunately, they did not realize that these places were used for the preliminary preparations for taking away their land from them. They established friendly relations with the Europeans and supplied them with food for their caravans, taking it for granted that naturally the white wanderers must undoubtedly have their own country, and therefore could not settle

for good in a foreign land, that they would feel home-sick and, after selling their goods, would go back to live in their homesteads with parents and relatives.

The belief that the Europeans were not going to live permanently in Africa, was strengthened by the fact that none of them seemed to stay very long in one place. Therefore, reasoning from this, the Gikuyu naturally came to the conclusion that one day all Europeans in Africa would pack up bag and baggage and return to their own country in the same way as they came. It was a common saying among the Gikuyu that 'Gotire ondo wa undereri, nagowo Coomba no okainoka,' which means that there is no mortal thing or act that lives for eternity; the Europeans will, no doubt, eventually go back to their own country. This saying was taken up as a lamenting slogan, and was sung in various songs, especially when the wanderers started to show their real motive for wandering. . .

The natives were friendly, and even enlisted as porters to go to the coast, but these good relations received a disastrous check. Owing largely to the want of discipline in the passing caravans, whose men robbed the crops and otherwise made themselves troublesome, the people became estranged, and presently murdered several porters. . .(For this) the Gikuyu were 'taught a lesson,' they were compelled to make 'the payment of 50 goats daily,' and the free work of 300 men to build the fort they had destroyed.

After this event the Gikuyu, with bitterness in their hearts, realized that the strangers they had given hospitality to had planned to plunder and subjugate them by brute force. The chief, Waiyaki, who had entered into a treaty of friendship with the strangers, was afterwards deported and died on his way to the coast. People were indignant for these acts of ingratitude on the part of the Europeans, and declined to trade with them, thinking that the Europeans and their caravans would get hungry and move away from the Gikuyu country; but soon the Gikuyu were made to know that 'might is right'. . .

And the Europeans, having their feet firm on the soil, began to claim the absolute right to rule the country and to have the ownership of the lands under the title of 'Crown Lands,' where the Gikuyu, who are the original owners, now live as 'tenants at will of the Crown.' The Gikuyu lost most of their lands through their magnanimity, for the Gikuyu country was never wholly conquered by force of arms, but the people were put under the ruthless domination of European imperialism through insidious trickery of hypocritical treaties (Kenyatta, 1938:47).

But African rulers were not without options. They could collaborate and try to seek the favor of the new masters, resist to the end, surrender when defeat was imminent, or attempt to bargain for advantage. They also had a similar but independent set of choices to make in response to Western culture.

The choice was not usually a simple 'for' or 'against.' An African could choose Western weapons and reject Christianity, or the other way round. Nor was his response to Western power necessarily related to his response to Western culture. He could accept Christianity, yet fight to the end against Western rule; just as he could accept Western rule as inevitable and collaborate with colonial governments, yet remain all the more faithful to Islam (Curtin, et al., 1988; p.459).

Because of these choices, African reaction to colonialism was varied. Some chiefs protested and put up a vigorous resistance. Others passively accepted alien rule, while others tolerated it only as long as they had to, until they had the strength to throw it off.

Resistance Against Colonialism

In many parts of Africa, the resistance against colonial rule was ferocious. In north Africa, the Arabs of Mauritania revolted in 1905, killing the French governor Coppolani. In 1896, Ethiopians defeated the Italians at Adowa. The emperor's success was partly due to the fact that he was able to obtain a regular supply of modern rifles and artillery despite European embargoes.

In West Africa, historians have commended the spirited resistance of the Sarakolle kingdom of Mamadou Lamine (1885-1887), the *jihad* of ma Ba Tall (1861-1867) in Senegambia, and particularly, the Tukulor episode of Umar from Timbuktu to Fouta Jallon in Guinea and from Medina to Segu. Perhaps the most gallant resistance came from the Abe people of eastern Ivory Coast who fought for 27 years (1891-1918) to maintain their independence.

Between 1887 and 1889, the French negotiated tributary treaties with Abe chieftaincies under which the French bound themselves not to interfere with African customs, land tenure or government (Boahen and Webster, 1970; p.234). Almost immediately, the French violated the treaties by demanding slave porters, by meddling in the election of chiefs and by dispatching two military expeditions to strike at the Samori in the north.

Head taxes were levied on the entire population. In 1903, the French began the construction of a railway for which they seized African lands and demanded forced, slave labor. Fearing that the natives would rebel, the French in 1909 seized 100,000 guns, imposed 30,000 (pounds sterling) in fines and deported 220 African leaders (Boahen and Webster, 1970; p.235).

Irate and feeling threatened by a new railway line that ran through their land, the Abe rose as one in rebellion. They attacked railway stations and cut the track up at 25 points. In reaction, the French governor-general despatched 1,400 troops who squelched the revolt with merciless abandon. The colonial troops burned villages, executed prisoners and displayed the heads of rebels on pikes at railway stations and in villages. The killings and deportations over the 27-year period almost wiped out the chiefly class.

The Asante of Ghana also rebelled against colonial rule. In March 1891, the British sent an officer to Kumasi to invite the Asantehene to place his country under the British. The Asante king, Prempeh I, sent back a terse reply. In his own words: "My kingdom of Asante will never commit itself to any such policy. Asante must remain independent as of old, at the same time to be friendly with all white men. I do not write this with a boastful spirit but in the clear sense of its meaning" (Cited in Boahen and Webster, 1970; p.129). This prompted the British to send several military expeditions against the Asante.

On the East African coast, there was the *Maji-Maji* revolt in 1890. This was a mass movement that encompassed several ethnic groups - the Shambaa, Zaramo, Zigula, Yao, Ngoni, Ngulu, Kwere, Hehe, Kami, Sagara, Makonde, Mbugu, Arab and Swahili. A relatively large number of powerful entrepreneurs joined them to offer a vigorous opposition to the colonial powers. Such were Mirambo (1871-1884) on the great ivory route of Tabora (Tanzania), Msiri in Katanga (1860-1891), and, until he allied with the Belgians in the Upper Congo, Tippu-Tib in Maniema (Coquery-Vidrovitch, 1988; p.67).

In southern Africa, the Sotho and the Zulu (under Chaka) staged a remarkable rebellion against colonial domination in the 1880s. Using the *impi* formation, the Ndebele kingdom offered a serious military resistance between 1893 and 1894. In the years that followed, the Shona and the Ndebele alike were dissatisfied with British occupation, with the loss of their land and cattle, with forced labor, and other abuses that characterized European domination. The old political structures had been weakened, but rallying around the ancestral spirit of *Mlimo* they rose up in an open rebellion. Using guerrilla tactics, rather than open battle, they managed to kill about 10 percent of all the Europeans in the Ndebele kingdom. But the subsequent European repression was even more bloody in its destruction of African lives (Curtin, *et al.*, 1988; p.467).

Chief Mandume of the Ovambo (Angola) also provided stubborn resistance to the colonialists. He fought the Portuguese for four years, 1911 to 1915, to preserve intact the pre-colonial status quo. In the final battle, he managed to assemble some 50,000 men armed with some ten to twelve thousand late-model rifles and five Boer tanks filled with munitions. Elsewhere in Africa, there were sporadic revolts by the Gbaya of Congo, the Dende of Zaire and the Gikuyu of Kenya.

African resistance to colonial rule was in general weak, due to the vast military superiority of European weapons; in particular, the Maxim-gun, a machine gun, proved decisive. Frequently, African armies of 20,000 or more were routed by European-led armies of 2,000 or less. This led the overconfident Europeans to surmise erroneously that the weak resistance was due to the oppression of Africans by their rulers and to overestimate their welcome and acceptance.

The unfavorable military imbalance that operated against Africans could not be rectified because of embargoes on gun imports. By 1885, Europeans, had gained sufficient control of the import-export trade of the West African coast to ban the importation of guns and ammunition. But some guns and ammunition were smuggled and Africans developed new tactics that proved instrumental in some cases, even with the use of their existing inferior weapons. For example,

> The Samori avoided walled cities and massed cavalry. The Bauole of Ivory Coast adopted the strike and retire method of guerrilla warfare, which was especially suitable for foot soldiers in a forest region. Intelligent resistance required that the defenders never face the invader's machines (Boahen and Webster, 1970; p.228).

In the final analysis, however, the Maxim-gun triumphed and compelled respect, obedience, humiliation and subjection. As Manning (1988) put it:

> The early colonial years brought political humiliation for Africans. Scores of African rulers died on the battlefield; many more were executed or exiled after defeat. Those who signed treaties and remained as protected rulers soon found themselves demoted from king to chief and required to collect taxes or recruit laborers for their French and German overlords. At a later stage, most were dismissed altogether (p.57).

Africa was conquered with relative ease militarily. But culturally, the battle proved far more formidable and costly than the Europeans had anticipated. It was one thing to subjugate a people and demand obedience as well as taxes by military force. But it was quite another to force them to shed centuries-old traditions, adopt alien ways of doing things and to respond spontaneously and voluntarily to the dictates of a foreign culture.

Colonial Atrocities

Much has been written about the iniquities of colonialism and the atrocities perpetrated against African natives. In 1905, for example, two French officials, Gaud and Toque, were put on trial in Brazzaville for blowing up an African porter by dynamite for fun (Manning, 1988;69). Colonial atrocities, especially in Belgian Congo, now Zaire, was deplorable. In 1897, a British army advanced into Benin, burnt the capital and looted it of nearly 2,500 of its famous bronze treasures (Boahen and Webster, 1970; p.232).

Though some rudimentary checks existed, the potential for mischief and abuse of the natives was enormous. A Frenchman in his twenties, who had just finished school, would suddenly find himself posted to a colony as *commandant de cercle*, with complete authority over 200,000 African natives. He could literally do as he pleased since his personal powers were guaranteed by the *Statut de l'indigenat*, the most hated feature of the colonial system in French West Africa. The *indigenat* consisted of regulations which allowed colonial administrators to inflict punishment on African subjects without obtaining judgment of court or approval from the metropolis. This allowed the colonial officers to *jail any African for up to two years without trial*, to impose heavy taxes and inflict punitive fines or burn the villages of those who refused to pay.[2]

Colonialism was extractive, generally a for-profit operation. "The idea that the imperial objective is commercial profit is the theory of economic imperialism" (Boahen and Webster, 1970; p.219). But how profitable colonialism was is subject to controversy. "Profits rarely matched the costs of colonial rule very closely - being sometimes much higher, sometimes much lower. [Belgian Congo] was the only colony that paid off directly to an European government" (Curtin, 1988; p.477).

Nevertheless, colonialism was geared toward the generation of maximum revenue at the least expenditure. Where possible, the natives were to be forced to work without pay to keep costs down. Considerations of equity or ethics were not the salutary hallmarks of the colonialists. Ever so cost-conscious, they showed an avid reluctance to undertake new expenditures unless it was absolutely necessary or could yield returns sufficient to recoup the initial cost. Consequently, the colonialists were less tolerant of native activities that threatened this objective, either by raising the costs of extraction and administration or reducing revenues. Where such native

---

[2] It is useful to keep this in mind since, after independence in the 1960s, the black neo-colonialists who took over retained these repressive measures. In 1990, for example, a person in Angola, Ethiopia, Ghana, Kenya, Libya, Nigeria, Sudan, Uganda, Zaire and many other African countries could be picked up and detained without charge under heinous "Preventive Detention Acts."

activities occurred, as in the form of rebellions or civil disobedience, they were to be crushed immediately and relentlessly.

Belgian Congo was the epitome of this approach.

A unique feature of the Congo Independent State was the heavy investment by its sovereign, King Leopold, in the cost of administration in the early days. Leopold hoped for a rapid rise in exports (particularly ivory) from his colony which would repay his investment (Manning, 1988; p.68).

Unfortunately, trade grew slowly and Leopold could not impose import duties to raise revenue since the international agreements that underpinned the creation of the state prohibited such duties. By 1891, King Leopold had used up so much of his fortune that a new policy was necessary. He turned half of the colony over to concessionary companies. These companies, with a tiny amount of capital, undertook to guarantee the commercial profitability and the mineral exploitation of these areas. Naturally, they adopted forced collection of rubber by the inhabitants of the concessions (Manning, 1988; p.68).

In 1884, a young Englishman, Glave, wrote: 'Everywhere rubber and murder, slavery in its worst form. The missionaries are so completely at the mercy of the state that they dare not report these barbarous doings.' Murphy, an American missionary, writes to *The Times* (of London) saying that a Congo Free State corporal, collecting rubber, had asked an African woman where her rubber and husband were. The woman had answered that the man was fishing, but would bring the rubber when he came back. The corporal said: 'You are lying!' He shot her then and there. Her husband arrived with the rubber, and, on seeing the dead body of his wife, killed the corporal. This led to a punitive expedition, when the large town of Solima was burned to the ground and many prisoners were killed and wounded. In Bosira, because deliveries of rubber were not forthcoming, on the orders of a staff officer, 1800 prisoners were killed. The same month, some [African] soldiers deserted from the state steamer to the town of Bombumba. The officer demanded their return by the chief, but the soldiers had already fled farther. Thereupon, the chief was wounded, and his wife was slain before his eyes, her head being cut off to secure her necklet. Twenty-four other prisoners were killed. The armed 'police'. . .cut off the hands of seven fugitives, one of them a little girl, who survived. . .The soldiers drove the Negroes into the forests to collect rubber; anyone who refused to go was shot. The left hand of any person shot was cut off and brought to the commissary to show him that the soldiers did not waste cartridges. Among them were the hands of women and children. . .Fugitives who are caught are placed behind one another in single file, and shot with one bullet in order to save cartridges. . .Mr. Clark, a pastor, had been in Ikoko in 1893 when the population was at least 4,000; by 1903 he found it reduced to 600. Many had been killed by the [colonial] soldiers, most of the others had fled into the wilds (Bauer, 1934; p.187).

Such crimes made one wonder whether it was not the colonialists themselves who rather needed to be civilized. Declared Queen Nzinga of Angola: "The real savages in Africa were the whites" (cited in Williams, 1987).

The literature on the barbarities of colonial overlords and the exploitation of African natives is vast. Additions to it would only elicit diminishing marginal interest. Of substantive importance to our inquiry is how the native institutions fared under colonialism. This question is of crucial importance since many African scholars and leaders, as well as American experts, have claimed that the native institutions were obliterated by colonialism. Of particular interest are the political, legal and economic institutions of indigenous Africa.

African Chiefs Under Colonialism

At the political level, we have seen that kinship was the article of political organization in traditional Africa. Political authority was derived from kinship. Political structures could be destroyed but authority was inviolable or substitutable. Authority from the people was needed to rule and without it anyone who usurped the throne was illegitimate. The colonialists removed and exiled many African chiefs and kings. But those they appointed to replace them lacked the requisite traditional authority and legitimacy to command obedience and respect from their people.

It may be recalled that in indigenous Africa, there were two general types of political organization: states and stateless societies. The colonialists had the most difficulty with the stateless societies such as the Ga of Ghana, the Igbo, the Fulani of Nigeria, and the Somali. In these societies there were no chiefs or central authority for the colonialists to depose. The "leaders" the colonialists created were rejected and shunned by the people. Worse, many of these appointees, called *canton chiefs* in French West Africa and "warrant chiefs" in southern Africa, became autocratic because they felt they had colonial backing. A case in point was the Ga *mantse*, and it is worth discussing this in detail since the colonial government attempt to restructure this native institution not only proved futile but also created immense difficulties for both subjects and the colonialists. It even set the colonial government up for ridicule and exploitation.

As we saw earlier, the Ga kingdom in the 19th century was a confederation of six independent republics (Accra, Osu, Labadi, Nungua, Teshie and Tema) with no paramount chief. Each town governed itself independently of the rest and had a *mantse*. But the *mantse* was not a chief in the sense that was usually reserved for the term.

The Ga *mantse* was only magically useful in war. He had no political authority and was not part of the government of the Ga people. Even in war, the *mantse* was not a military leader. He carried his stool, supposedly endowed with magical powers, to war. He never directly entered into combat. In fact, he and his stool stood aside, protected by a special bodyguard.

When the Danes came to Osu in the 19th century, they insisted on dealing with a chief. There was none among the Ga people. But to the Danes, the Ga *mantse* was good enough and they started dealing with him as "chief." In response, an indignant people of Osu created a *mankralo* and transferred allegiance to this *mankralo* and deserted the *mantse*.

Adamant, the Europeans persisted in recognizing the *mantse* as "chief." The Ga people, in turn, responded by destooling such European-made "chiefs." In 1908, for example, the Labadi *mantse* was destooled when he made negotiations with the colonial government behind the backs of his people. A few years later, Taki Obli of Accra was also destooled for his unauthorized attempt to sell town lands and to appropriate for himself money and privileges which were not by native custom a *mantse's*. His successor, Taki Yaoboi, believing he had the awesome colonial power behind him, also acted arbitrarily without consulting his people. He too was destooled.

This was but one aspect of the problems that plagued the relations between the colonial government and the native institutions. Other problems emerged when the colonial governments insisted on having their way. This foolhardiness was berated eloquently by Field (1940) who found it imperative to issue a thinly veiled warning about the large number of new offices and posts the colonialists were creating:

> The danger of any (colonial) Government created or Government maintained council is that the consciousness that its existence and prestige do not depend on services rendered (as do spontaneous native institutions) will encourage it to become a mere instrument of corruption. No body of Africans tries cases justly unless there are automatic penalties, such as loss of position and loss of prestige, for dealing unjustly. Such sanctions do operate in a *mantse's* own little community in his own town, and there he can be relied upon to support the old tradition of decency to which he owes his position and to which his community owe its safety. But Government has assumed that he has an appreciation of abstract justice for its own sake. He has not, or if he

has it is such a flickering flame that it is at once snuffed out by the blast of bribery. The tendency of such a body as the State Council is to think, 'Government is behind us. Our people cannot touch us. We can do as we like. Plenty of people are offering to bribe us heavily, so let us make hay while the sun shines' (p.80).

When the British colonialists conferred new importance and authority upon the Ga *mantse*, the position became a plum rather than an irksome chore. A scramble for this position ensued whenever it became vacant, creating much confusion and turmoil. The responsible elders of the town would elect the new *mantse* constitutionally, but invariably a cantankerous party of agitators and opportunists ridiculed and exploited the colonial government's ignorance of native governance by producing a rival candidate - often a passive puppet - and declaring him to be the "rightful" *mantse*. As Field (1940) contended:

> In native constitution, there is no such thing as 'right' to the stool. No one has a right until he has been constitutionally elected. But the (colonial) Government does not know this and the District Commissioner, bewildered by a dozen different tales of 'native custom,' each invented ad hoc refers the matter to the State Council. This body, after years of delay, muddled discussion and complicated negotiation, decide in favor of one candidate. . .Government accepts the council choice, and regards him as chief. To his people, however, he is known as a 'Government's *mantse*,' and their own, or People's *mantse*, exists simultaneously. . .A 'Government's *mantse*' is, as often as not, merely the puppet of a small gang who have financed him from the first, and are running him as a speculation. Apart from Government, the only recognition he gets in his own town is from the disreputable band of hangers-on who invested in him and hope for an income from the investment (p.80).

Meanwhile, the elders would refuse to enstool the colonial government's *mantse* and shun him. Respectable people would also ignore him and take all their affairs to the elders. This state of affairs could exist because in the Ga system of government, the *mantse* was inessential. Trouble however erupted when the government *mantse* tried to extend his authority, of which he had none under the native constitution, or intervened in native affairs when he was traditionally restricted to military affairs. The people responded to his overreach by destooling him.

Problems with the colonial government-appointed Ga *mantse* manifested themselves elsewhere in colonial Africa. Whoever was chosen to exercise authority for the Europeans could not impose European government as it was understood in Europe. The appointees were allowed to rule but only with a rough guideline about the kind of rule to provide. When a colonial appointee entered the revenue system, he collected taxes from his subjects, retained a portion and passed the rest on to the "foreign infidels." So long as the Europeans were satisfied, he could do with his subjects as he pleased. Clearly, there was much room for abuse of power and corruption on the part of the colonial appointees.

Another example, besides the Ga's government appointed *mantse*, was the *akil* of the Somali. Although the *akils* were selected by the elders to represent them in their dealings with the colonial government, they were placed in an unenviable position of having to act in accordance with governmental interests while at the same time defend the interests of the group. Quite often, they acted more in their own personal interests, leading to their abandonment by their people. The *akida* appointed by the Germans in East Africa also suffered a similar fate.

In the Belgian Congo, African administrators were recruited from the ranks of African soldiers in the state service. "There, in their role as the principal agents enforcing the state demands for wild rubber collections, they became petty tyrants with the right to punish anyone at all on the spot by whipping. For collective resistance or simply for failure to meet their demands, they could call down a punitive expedition to destroy a village or punish a whole district" (Curtin, 1988; p.475).

There were similar problems with canton chiefs who were appointed and served under French colonial administrators as Manning (1988) recognized:

> By the 1930s the canton chiefs were often literate in French and many of them built significant fortunes. Although they had standing in the traditional hierarchy, their wealth and power came mainly from their position in the French government. One of the most famous canton chiefs was Justin Aho Glele, a descendant of King Glele of Dahomey who ruled Ounbegame canton near the old Dahomean capital of Abomey. His wealth, his power in the old royal family, his close ties to the French administration made him a target for constant political attacks by Dahomean critics of the administration.

> Another influential canton chief was Felix Houphouet-Boigny of Ivory Coast. His was a rare case of a man who became a canton chief despite administrative opposition. He was born in 1905 to a chiefly family. . .Houphouet was highly educated, widely respected, a traditional chief, a successful businessman, and a government official, whose conflicts with European planters were to become crucial in the postwar nationalist movement (p.84).

The colonial governments tried to reform the system by placing appointees on salary and removing corrupt or incompetent "chiefs." But it did not resolve the problem satisfactorily. As a group of headmen in Uganda put it: "If you pay me to wash my table, it will then become your table" (Cited by Curtin, 1988; p.476).

Some of the colonial appointees such as Felix Houphouet-Boigny served well and managed to gain the trust of their people. Others, however, became corrupt and tyrannical, leading several European observers to conclude erroneously that venality and despotism inhered in the African tradition. Many African scholars, in response, rightly pointed out that corruption and tyranny were not regular features of the indigenous African political system and, if anything, may have been reared under colonial rule. But finger-pointing served little purpose. The focus should have been placed on systemic accountability and checks. *Any* political system, regardless of its origins, that lacks these will degenerate into tyranny and corruption. Recall the warning by Field (1940): "The danger of any (colonial) Government created or Government maintained council is that the consciousness that its existence and prestige do not depend on services rendered (as do native institutions) will encourage it to become a mere instrument of corruption."

Colonial Policies

The issue of the fate of African chiefdoms and kingdoms under colonialism requires an examination of colonial policies and the strategies African rulers adopted to preserve their political integrity. Firstly, since colonial policies differed among the Europeans, some African chiefdoms had better chances of surviving under one colonial policy than another. The British and the Germans on the whole regarded their colonies as complete entities and therefore treated each one separately. The French and the Portuguese, on the other hand, saw their colonies as integral parts of the metropolitan countries and therefore as mere provinces overseas. "Thus, while the British did envisage a day when each of its colonies would become an independent state in its own right, the French did not recognise the possibility until the late 1950s; and the Portuguese never changed their unrealistic attitude" (Boahen, 1986; p.123).

Furthermore, according to Boahen (1986), even though all the colonial powers regarded the black race as inferior to the white race, "the British did show a great deal of respect for the Africans and for many aspects of their culture and institutions, while the French and the Portuguese condemned practically everything African as primitive and barbaric" (p.123).

Secondly, African rulers themselves adopted different survival techniques to combat colonialism. Some of these failed; others succeeded.

The British adopted a colonial policy of "indirect rule" by which they generally made no conscious effort to supplant the indigenous rulers. The policy largely left in existence the administrative machinery which had been created by the natives themselves. For example, "Carter in Yorubaland and Lugard in Hausaland thought in terms of a protectorate in which they would change little in the indigenous system, but would merely establish British paramountcy" (Boahen and Webster, 1970; p.231). Where there were no indigenous centralized authorities as in Igboland and southern Africa, the British created "warrant chiefs." In the 1860s, Britain was generally reluctant to extend direct rule over territories thousands of miles away, as this would entail considerable expenditures. Furthermore, Britain was more occupied with its Asian empire, in particular India, than their African possessions, which were to be prepared for eventual self-rule.

Under the British colonial system, each colony was divided into regions under regional or chief administrators, each region into provinces under provincial commissioners, and each province into districts under district commissioners. Each district was made up of one or more of the traditional states, and the day-to-day affairs and local ordinance came under the traditional rulers and their council of elders. According to Boahen and Webster (1970):

> The African chief was the instrument of local government. He appointed all officials who were responsible to him. He or his officials presided over the law courts which as far as possible applied African law. His agents levied taxes for the local treasury. Part of the revenue was sent to the central government and the remainder kept for local improvements such as roads, sanitation, markets and schools, and to pay the salaries of local officials (p.242).

The use of the existing native administrative machinery allowed the British to govern lightly and cheaply. More importantly, the use of traditional chiefs as intermediaries required that potential conflicts between the two cultures be identified and resolved. Under such a system, the indigenous institutions faced the least danger of complete annihilation under British colonial rule. Their chances of survival were somewhat more assured.

The colonial policies of the other Europeans, however, posed the gravest danger to indigenous Africa. They were highly centralized and authoritarian. "The French adopted a policy of deliberately destroying the great paramountcies and by 1937 only fifty of them were remaining, most of which had been deprived of their prestige" (Boahen, 1986; p.127). French colonial policy had two strands. One was *assimilation*, the approach taken by Louis Faidherbe in Senegal, under which the colony became an integral part of the mother country rather than a separate but protected state. Additionally, the colonized were expected to *assimilate* French culture. The rationale for *assimilation* was poignantly furnished by Boahen and Webster (1970):

The French (like the Arabs in Africa) assumed that their civilization and culture had attained the highest possible standard and set out to impose this standard on other nations whose civilizations they considered to be inferior to their own. They set out on this 'civilising mission' in the strong belief that the other peoples - be they white, black, brown or yellow - were capable of being assimilated into French culture, and assumed that what was good for the French as a nation was also good for the other nations. Thus, black peoples of Africa and the yellow peoples of Asia were to be transformed into Frenchmen, speaking, living, behaving and thinking like Frenchmen. The territories in which they lived were to be identical to the provinces in France, administratively, economically and politically. Assimilation was thus a comprehensive colonial theory which sought to influence every aspect of the lives of the colonized peoples, and also to mould the colony and its society in the image of France (p.252).

The other strand in French colonial policy was *association*. This concept was developed and applied by Savorgnan de Brazza in Central Africa. The associationists believed that, though *assimilation* was desirable, it was impracticable because non-Western people were racially inferior (Curtin, 1988; p.480). A more realistic objective was to aim for a mere association so that the subject people could develop within their own cultures.

Association was akin to the British policy of "indirect rule." The French version, however, differed in some fundamental respects. The French colony was considered part of France rather than a separate political entity. Nor did the French have any intention of using the traditional rulers as intermediaries. They allied themselves with African rulers to neutralize them until they could be eliminated or deposed at convenience. Those who remained were put in a position of serving as agents of the colonial state rather than rulers in their own right. For example, when the French conquered Dahomey in 1894, General Dodds dismembered the kingdom. Only the central province, the area around the capital of Abomey, remained, while the rest of the provinces were converted into new kingdoms and placed under direct French rule. Where there were no central authorities, as in the stateless African societies, such as the Fulani and Somali, new "chiefs" were created.

European governments sometimes ruled indirectly by subcontracting colonial government to private companies - rule by *incorporation*. Leopold of Belgium's private Congo Independent State was a form of company government.[3] Large portions of the colony, as we saw earlier, were administered by private concessionary companies. Belgian Congo was

---

[3] Incorporation was also used in the Portuguese colonies of Angola, Mozambique and French Central Africa.

governed by a triumvirate of Crown, Church (Roman Catholic) and large companies in which the Crown held substantial stock. While British officials out in the fields would use persuasion to get something done, Belgian officials would issue commands: "Plant 40 rubber trees here next month - or else!" Much brutality, exploitation and forced labor characterized the rule by the companies which forced the Belgian parliament to respond by annexing the Congo Independent State and bringing it under Belgian state control.

After 1908, Belgian colonial policy assumed a new shape of *paternalism* or *tutelage*. This envisaged a much tighter political and economic control over the colonies than under the French policy of *assimilation*. The new Belgian colonial policy of paternalism was harsher as well. Africans were treated as children, incapable of guiding their own destinies. Every aspect of their welfare had to be provided for by the colonial rulers.

Belgian Congo was administered directly from Brussels. The Governor General was the representative of the Crown, all edicts and directives came from Brussels, and the Congolese were not consulted in the administration of their own affairs. Belgian overlords felt free to interfere in the selection of African leaders in their protected states. The Governor General wielded vast powers which were often abused as there were no local legislative assemblies to guide or check him.

Though the French and Belgian colonial policies of *assimilation and tutelage* posed the greatest threat of obliterating indigenous African culture, in practice this did not materialize. *Assimilation* turned out to be a failure. For one thing, effective implementation required extraordinary expenditures which the French colonial government was unwilling to make. For another, there was African disenchantment with French citizenship and Belgian tutelage.

In the latter half of the 19th century, absolutism had noticeably retreated from the political arenas of France, Belgium and Germany. Politics were becoming increasingly dominated by republican ideals of legal equality of all citizens. As these nations sought to expand their colonies, a dilemma emerged as to the political status of the new territories and their inhabitants. If the colonies were part of the mother country, would their African subjects be regarded as citizens as well? And would African citizens be accorded equal rights as their European counterparts?

Because of perceived inferiority of African culture, most European nations were reluctant to grant citizenship to their colonial subjects. Citizenship, if necessary at all, was to be granted under special circumstances. Only when Africans had become sufficiently well educated and acculturated could they become French citizens with full political and other rights. Such Africans became known as *evolues*.

The Belgians imposed more stringent conditions since they generally held the African in abject disdain. He could not travel in the Congo without a permit, possess firearms and was not allowed to drink anything stronger than beer. He could become a carpenter or a mechanic, but not an engineer. He could be a bishop, a journalist, an accountant, a medical assistant, a teacher, a civil servant, or a druggist but not an architect or attorney. By the 1930s, while there were several lawyers in British and French West Africa not one could be counted in the Congo. To the Belgians, lawyers meant politics, and politics was one thing outlawed for the Africans.

One vital point of difference between the Belgian system and that of the British and French was that the Belgians did their utmost to keep their African subjects out of Europe and particularly out of Belgium itself. Africans in other colonies could attend British and French universities in Europe, but not Congolese. Belgians did not countenance citizenship for Africans — only under very strict conditions. In addition to education and acculturation, permanent employment with Europeans was required before Africans could become *immatricules* (registered) and live under Belgian law. Only a few Africans became *immatricules*.

In French West Africa, an opposition to citizenship quickly emerged. In 1908, French administrators and French settlers in Senegal began calling systematically for restrictions on the citizenship rights of the *originaires* (the inhabitants of the four communes of St.-Louis, Goree, Rufisque, and Dakar) because they were alleged to be "illiterate" in French. Accordingly, the government of French West Africa promulgated a naturalization decree which tightened the qualifications for citizenship. Until 1946, an African desiring French citizenship had to fulfil one of the following requirements: to have been born in any of the four communes; to have held with merit a position in the French service for ten years; to provide evidence of good character and possess a means of existence; to have been decorated with the Legion of Honor or the Military Award. In the Portuguese colonies, the African had to be well educated, a Christian and to have abandoned such African practices as polygamy. Once his application was accepted and he became a Portuguese citizen, he was saved from the indignity of having to carry a pass book and exempted from compulsory labor.

By 1922, less than 100 persons in all of French West Africa had qualified for citizenship (Manning, 1988:79). In 1936, the number of French citizens was 78,000 in Senegal and only 2400 in the remaining French West African colonies out of a total population of 15 million (Bell, 1986; Boahen, 1988). In the Portuguese colony of Guinea, for example, only 1418 out of total African population of 550,457 had become *assimilados* by 1950.

There was a great deal of borrowing back and forth among European administrators so that they all came to share a family resemblance (Curtin, 1988; p.481). British colonial policy, for example, increasingly took on a French character. As Boahen (1986) put it:

The traditional paramount ruler or sultan was no more the head of the social and political order but was rather a subordinate of the British overlord, who used him to implement such unpopular measures as compulsory labor, taxation and military enlistment for two world wars. Those traditional rulers who had armies lost control over their armies while they also had no say in the conduct of foreign affairs and legislation. . . Furthermore, the British could depose traditional rulers and replace them with their own nominees. Finally, the British often interfered with existing paramountcies by breaking some of them up and raising subordinate chiefs to the status of paramount chiefs as they did in Sierra Leone (p.126).

European colonial policies also went through various phases of reform. The first phase occurred in the period prior to the outbreak of the first World War. The exposure of colonial scandals by European anti-imperialists forced the expulsion of private companies as direct colonial administrators in the Belgian Congo. The next phase of colonial reform occurred after the second World War with introductions of constitutions to allow Africans greater participation in the colonial administration.

Thus, after the first and second World Wars, almost all the colonial policies, with the possible exception of the Portuguese, underwent revisions and modifications to put a more humane face on colonialism. For example, following the defeat of Germany in 1945, the German colonies of Togoland, Tanganyika, Rwanda, Burundi and Namibia were placed into the tutelage of other European powers. Rather interestingly, the colonial policies of the British and the French became switched. The failure of *assimilation* prompted the French to replace it with *association*. Thus, in the final analysis, when we "probe beneath the surface of formal structure and rhetoric, we find that the experience and internal processes of French and British colonial administration were not only similar, but also in many instances practically identical" (Berman, 1984:176).

Curtin (1988) reached similar conclusions:

Colonial governments, above the level of African intermediaries, was remarkably uniform, regardless of the European power in charge. . .

General administrative officers were amazingly few for the extent of territory governed. The whole of French Equatorial Africa in the mid-1930s was run by only 206 administrative officers, with 400 specialists and technical officers to assist. The whole of British tropical Africa at the same period (leaving aside Egypt, the Sudan, and southern Africa) was governed by about 1,000 general administrative officers, plus another four or five thousand European specialists, while the Belgians ruled the Congo in 1936 with 728 officers in charge of the 104 territories. In Rwanda and Burundi, however, they ruled with an administrative staff of less than 50 Europeans, because African kingship had been preserved there (p.482).

The Native Institutions Under Colonialism

To assure the survivability of their polities, African rulers adopted various measures. Some saw the weakness in their military positions and cooperated with the colonialists to prevent being overrun by either a stronger neighboring state or by the colonialists themselves. The Fanti states of Ghana, Rwanda and Burundi as well as the Ganda kingdom of Uganda acted in this way.

Far from being an act of cowardice or a sell-off of their people, the rulers of these states realized, it was the best policy for preserving their kingdoms under the prevailing circumstances. For example, at the time of the French annexation of Porto Novo in 1883, the Toffa chief was facing three enemies: the Yoruba to the northeast, the Fon kings of Dahomey to the north and the British on the coast. He saw an alliance with the French as a propitious opportunity.

Buganda also was never conquered by the British, but it cleverly placed itself under British protection through treaties and agreements. As a consequence, its indigenous political system was saved from destruction and was reformed to serve new purposes (Gibbs, 1965; p.88). In not opposing British annexation, the Buganda won many concessions for themselves. Significantly, they also enhanced their bargaining position since they possessed the latent power to make British rule either cheap and comparatively easy or extremely difficult. According to Curtin, *et al.*, (1988):

> Their great success was to translate their bargaining position into a written agreement, the Uganda Agreement of 1900, by which the British government spelled out the concessions it would make in return for Ganda acquiescence in British overrule. The political effect was to keep the title and office of *kabaka* intact but to assign real power to the *Lukiiko,* a representative body (p.460).

Many other African rulers managed to hold on to their power by timely surrender and collaboration. For example, the Muslim theocratic state in Futa Jallon and many Fulbe emirs of northern Nigeria retained a great deal of power by cooperating at the appropriate time with the earliest British officials. Similarly, the Mossi kingdom of Burkina Faso retained its existence. Zanzibar and the Muslim states of North Africa survived after colonialism for a rather special reason. Most of them had been recognized for centuries as political entities in European international law. In southern Africa, Lesotho and Swaziland kept their identities "through skill and luck in manipulating the rivalry between Britain and the Boer republics" (Curtin, 1988; p.461).

Other African rulers fought against colonial rule to the bitter end and saw their kingdoms destroyed. For example, Ba Bemba of Sikasso opposed the French until 1894 when he killed himself rather than surrender his sovereignty to the French. The Ndebele and Shona kingdoms as well as the kingdom of Dahomey were decimated when their rulers resisted to the end. Chiefs who disobeyed the Portuguese in Angola paid dearly with their lives:

> Chiefs failing to secure the required number of slaves were themselves enslaved. Over a hundred chiefs and notables were sold into slavery in a single year and another hundred murdered by the Portuguese. We may safely assume that the actual number of chiefs enslaved or murdered was greater than that stated above since the Portuguese, like other nations, generally cut casualty figures for the record (Williams, 1987; p.261).

The destruction of political structures in some regions of Africa, however, did not mean the complete obliteration of all African political cultures. When the British attempted to wipe out their chieftaincy system, the Ndebele and Shona rallied around the religious spirit of *Mlimo* and rose in rebellion. Similarly in Asante, the British captured and exiled the king to Sierra Leone in January 1897. But to the Asante, it was the golden stool, not the king, which was the symbol and soul of their nation. When the British made a vain attempt to capture the golden stool in April 1900, they met a stiff and humiliating defeat at the hands of an Asante woman, Yaa Asantewa, the Queen Mother of Edweso. Though this rebellion was finally crushed, the British never gained possession of the golden stool.

In eastern and southern Africa there were widespread cases of forced labor and expulsions of the natives from their land. But even so, the natives erected the political structures elsewhere. In spite of the meddling of political institutions, the appointments of government "chiefs" and the deposition of traditional rulers, the indigenous political cultures by and large survived. There was no doubt that the indigenous political structures had been weakened and the traditional rulers had much of their authority reduced. But the claim that the indigenous system of government was completely wiped out is fallacious. As most Africans in the ex-British colonies would affirm, in 1960, at the dawn of independence, the native institutions as exemplified by chiefs, kings and council of elders were still in existence.

This was also generally the case in French West Africa, since *assimilation* was a failure. In 1888, Gabon, Congo and the interior areas were combined into one immense colony, known as French Congo. But French presence in this great territory was so modest that local communities were little disturbed, except along major waterways and along the 400-kilometer porterage route from Loango on the coast to Brazzaville. Yet,

> Even where the old states lost their formal political power, they continued to exist, and the kings and chiefs could act as representatives of their constituents, not simply as tools of the administration. The *Mogho Naba* (king) of the Mossi kingdom of Ouagadougou, placed in office by the French in 1905 at the age of 16, gained the trust of his people. . .In the remains of the old Dahomean kingdom itself, the monarchy survived in a strange fashion. When the last king was deposed, the old central province was divided into several cantons. The canton chiefs were members of the royal family, so each had himself installed with the ceremonies appropriate to a king (Manning, 1988; p.74).

Importantly, there was one indigenous institution which the colonialists actually sought to strengthen: the native system of courts and law. In the field of property rights, civil and criminal matters, the Europeans drew a very sharp line. Europeans were to be governed by European law and Africans by African law.

> In both French West Africa and the Belgian Congo (but not in French Equatorial Africa), the colonial regimes sought to strengthen their legal foundations by drawing up formal codes of African law. For various ethnic groups or for whole colonies, government officials drew up written codes based on traditional law, on decisions made in the Native Courts, and on the needs of the colonial state. Their idea was to strengthen the Native Courts, to base decisions on a formal code and no longer on common law and judicial precedent, and to reduce the number of cases going before the courts of French or Belgian law. For Dahomey, the political activist, Louis Hunkarin, did much of the work of drawing up the manual of customary law (Manning, 1988; p.84).

The British made similar efforts and commissioned reports of the Code of Native Customs and Law. John Mensah Sarbah of Ghana, for example, wrote on Fanti Customary Laws. The jurisdiction of the native courts was recognized. In southern Africa, some attempts were made to provide the native courts with court registers and roofed buildings.

Regarding the indigenous economic institutions, it may be recalled that the indigenous economy was primarily agricultural, although there were such industries as textiles, iron-smelting, pottery and some craft enterprises. The means of production and distribution were privately owned. Land was controlled by the lineage group. All other unoccupied land in the realm fell under the custody of the chief. He merely held the land in trust. Commerce and markets were free. Market tolls and taxes were common but there was generally no direct taxation as represented by poll or hut taxes. Instead, tributes were paid to the king or chief. Generally absent in indigenous Africa were state or tribal government-run enterprises. Kings and chiefs in some cases had trade and farms operated for them, but they were mainly for the benefit of the royal family, not intended for the people. Direct government intervention in the economy was not a common feature of indigenous African society.

After the abolition of the slave trade in the 1840s, there was the need to provide alternative means of occupation to replace the trade in human cargo. Toward this end, cash-crops were introduced into Africa. About this time, the industrial revolution was gathering momentum in Europe. Factories needed raw materials and markets for manufactured products. Colonies could provide both: raw materials and markets.

In the 1880s, the scramble for Africa began in earnest for the acquisition of colonies. Almost simultaneously, an anti-imperialist opposition began to form in Europe. Much of this opposition centered on the necessity of colonies and the wisdom of using public funds to support military adventurism overseas. This opposition forced colonial administrators to be fiscally conscious. The colonies had to be self-supporting in order to stifle anti-imperialist opposition. Toward this end, the first priority in each colony was the generation of tax receipts to maintain the colonial apparatus. No large-scale expenditures in the colonies were envisaged.

To keep colonial expenses to the barest minimum, the utilization of the existing indigenous economic institutions was envisaged. There was no general colonial attempt to interfere with peasant agricultural production or to uproot the existing institutions. Such an attempt would have been foolhardy and illogical. The existing system was already serving the interests of the colonialists and industrial Europe by providing raw materials for the factories of Europe and providing markets for industrial products.

Moreover, uprooting the native system would have stirred up a rebellion from African rulers - a rebellion which would have played into the hands of anti-imperialist opposition in Europe. Negative risk-avoidance was a conscious part of colonial policy. Even abstracting from such a resistance, replacing the peasant system with a different regime would have been prohibitively expensive. The extraordinary difficulty of transforming Africans into French citizens may be recalled. As Fieldhouse (1986) observed: "Capitalism commonly found it more rewarding to maintain the indigenous structures and to articulate them with itself than to attempt to destroy them" (p.32).

In most places, all unoccupied land, however, was seized by the colonialists and became "Crown Lands." In many parts of eastern and southern Africa, the natives were driven off their land and the chiefs stripped of their traditional authority.

> The complete annexation of the Transkeian Territories by the British in 1894 saw also the completion of the transfer of sovereignty from the chiefs to the Cape colonial government and later (in 1910) to the government of the Union of South Africa. It has been said that the despotism of the chiefs was thus overthrown. But it appears that that despotism was immediately replaced with a new despotism — the despotism of the Governor-General who, overnight, stepped into the shoes of all the chiefs and became the 'Supreme Chief of Natives.' The power to allot land became vested in him via the various officers of the government, the most active of which was the Native Commissioner of the district, called the Bantu Affairs Commissioner after 1962 (Koyana, 1980; p.142).

Cash crops such as coffee, cotton and cocoa were introduced into Africa by the colonialists. Some scholars dispute this however, claiming that some of them were indigenous to Africa. At any rate, many of these were grown on plantations, mostly owned by Europeans, although the British on the whole disallowed Europeans from setting up plantations in West Africa and left the production of these cash-crops in the hands of the Africans. The African farmers established small farms using mainly family labor supplemented by hired migrants or labor. The French, Portuguese and the Germans, on the other hand, allowed both Africans and Europeans in the agricultural field, and in places like Ivory Coast, Guinea and Togo, large plantations were established by Europeans. Furthermore, while the French declared all vacant lands to be the property of the state, the British and the Germans left land under the control of the Africans (except in eastern and southern Africa) (Boahen 1986; p.128).

Contrary to radical orthodoxy, the introduction of cash-crops in general did not have much deleterious impact on food production. In many areas of Africa, the resources allocated to expanding cash-crops were not extracted from food-producing activities. In most parts of Africa, the cultivation of food crops was a female occupation, and it was men who took up cash-cropping.

Palm oil and peanuts proved to be least disruptive of the existing peasant production. They were already consumed by Africans and expanding production did not require any cataclysmic change in the organization of production. Cocoa and coffee rather proved to be complementary to food production. In the early stages of their growth, they required the shade of leafier plants such as plantains, cocoyams and bananas, which were also locally consumed foodstuffs. Thus, expanded production of cocoa and coffee tended to result in parallel increases in these foodstuffs. Cotton, however, was the most problematic. Cultivation cost was high. The plant was not edible and, in addition, could not be inter-planted with food crops as cocoa. Peasants were generally reluctant to adopt cotton cultivation. However, this reluctance was overcome in some cases by force and in others with sufficiently high price incentives since the Europeans, the French in particular, were desirous of reducing their dependence on American cotton.

Colonialism also had commercial objectives. Profit was the objective of the commercial companies operating in Africa. In the 19th century, a growing number of European and African merchants had established themselves on the coast. Access to the interior was under the control of African states. The coastal firms wanted European governments to support them in eliminating the African middlemen and gaining direct access to the interior. Political pressure was brought to bear on colonial governments to regulate trade and control its direction to ensure the steady generation of monopoly profits.

Many African middlemen were accordingly eliminated and commerce subsequently came to be dominated by a few large European firms. For example, by the 1930s, the whole import-export business in West Africa was controlled by three large European companies. The first was the United African Company (UAC) formed by the amalgation of the Royal Niger Company and the African and Eastern Trade Corporation Ltd. in 1920. By the 1930s, UAC was controlling fifty percent of the overseas trade of West Africa (Boahen, 1986). The second was the *Compagne Francaise de l'Afrique Occidentale* (CFAO) which was founded in 1887 and the third was *Societe Commercial de l'Ouest Africain* (SCOA) founded in 1906.

There was collusion among these firms. For example, shipping to West Africa was controlled by "conferences" in which the major British, German and French firms established uniform rates and penalized merchants who did not make regular use of their services (Austen, 1987; p.130). Markets and prices of cash-crops were also controlled either overtly or collusively. Despite all their efforts, the Europeans however could not keep competitors out completely. By the 1930s, Levantine, Arab, Indian and other Asiatic firms were providing vigorous competition.

There is no doubt that the benefit of trade flowed unequally to the Europeans. There is also no question that collusive and restrictive trade practices operated to the disadvantage and detriment of Africans. The issue that is of immediate consequence, however, is whether the indigenous economic institutions were destroyed under colonialism. The fate of the native institutions and equity in the distribution of gains of trade are two totally different issues.

In most of colonial Africa, the indigenous economic institutions underwent some metamorphosis and transformations and adaptations, but they were hardly destroyed. The rural peasant farmers did not suddenly disappear with their traditional practices under colonialism. Their farming practices such as shifting cultivation and land rotation were modified in the face of the new conditions. But they changed little from the pre-colonial era. Though there were numerous cases of forced labor, the peasants grew their foodstuffs on their small agricultural holdings, side by side, along the huge European plantations. The indigenous agricultural system was not snuffed out.

More noticeable were the periodic rural markets. They did not vanish under colonialism. Markets were regulated and controlled in colonial Africa. The rationale, degree and timing of official market intervention were extremely varied. East and Central Africa experienced the most sustained intervention while French West Africa witnessed regular but seldom overwhelming regulation. In British West Africa, the colonial government moved from relatively limited to very severe forms of market control. Justifications for market intervention were mixed, ranging from the promotion of metropolitan and commercial interests to the protection of "innocent natives" from the vagaries of world markets.

In most cases, however, regulations were applied to trade (import and exports) and cash-crops. Marketing boards were established to fix prices of cash-crops and produce-buying agents were required to have licences. Commercial firms also colluded to fix prices of imported manufactures. But in general, there was no colonial policy to control either the production, marketing, or the prices of native foodstuffs. Marketing and distribution of food crops by the natives were not disrupted or regulated. In fact, in many places, the indigenous market institutions were actually strengthened during this era. Markets were built by the colonialists. The few pieces of regulation and inspection routines were mainly for purposes of sanitation and revenue collection. Prices for local foodstuffs were left free to be determined by market forces. There were two reasons for this.

First, the commercial companies were not interested in native foodstuffs such as yam, cocoyam and garri. Cash-crops in demand in Europe were their primary concern. Second, the colonialists would have failed had they attempted to fix prices for the local foodstuffs. These items were produced by millions of peasant farmers, not only on the coast but in the interior as well. Controlling their prices would have entailed exorbitant expenditures and venturing into the interior as well - an undertaking which most of the Europeans abhorred. Further, the local foodstuffs were not consumed by the Europeans. It would hardly make sense for self-centered Europeans to control the prices of commodities which were of little physical or commercial value to them.

The indigenous industries did not disappear completely under colonialism. Imports of manufactured goods from Europe comprised such items as textiles, building materials, motor vehicles, bicycles, various household goods, and such food items as flour, sugar, tinned milk and sardines. With the exception of textiles, most of these goods were not being manufactured in pre-colonial Africa. Although there were a few clear instances where efforts at local industrialization were blocked, "for the most part, such efforts simply did not exist and the major shortcoming of colonial regimes was their failure to promote them (local industrialisation)" (Austen, 1987; p.133).[4]

On a much broader scale, Africans were forced to adjust their production systems to the new situation. Although easier access to imports eliminated the markets for such basic items as cheap textiles and locally smelted iron, imports also provided intermediate goods such as finished yarn, chemical dyes, scrap metal and rubber which could be converted for specific local uses by African craftsmen. Even with textiles, its importation into Africa did not wipe out the native cloth industry completely. The Asante *kente* cloth and Kano cloth industries still operated under colonialism. The native dress was required for certain ceremonial occasions and as such still had a market demand.

Nor did the indigenous entrepreneur vanish with the establishment of colonies in Africa. Colonialism introduced new rules of commerce and competition. To start a commercial venture, capital was required which many Africans could not raise. The colonial banks, for one thing, discriminated against African customers and, for another, insisted on large collaterals which many Africans could not provide. Nonetheless, various Africans were able to pool their resources together to raise sufficient capital to open village shops, operate transport trucks and timber companies. Some failed, but some were successful.

Large capital requirements kept many Africans out of various economic ventures. Mining and the operation of railways were examples. The capital-intensive technology required was well beyond the means of Africans to provide. At first blush, it would give the impression that such activities were reserved exclusively for Europeans. But the fact that automobiles were driven mostly by Europeans did not mean Africans could not own them if they could afford them. There was generally no colonial policy which expressly debarred Africans from owning automobiles. Nor were there explicit laws which prohibited Africans from commercial and industrial undertakings, except in a few areas in Belgian Congo and South Africa. Africans were clearly at a disadvantage and handicapped. But if they could raise the large capital often required, they could also compete with the Europeans.

Where capital requirements were modest, many artisans undertook new

---

[4] Austen (1987) further argued that the reason why the colonialists did not actively promote local industrialization was the absence of pressure from a local class of merchants and artisans, whether immigrant or indigenous, who identified their own interests with the development of internationally competitive industries. The lack of such pressure was not due to any lack of manufacturing enterprise but rather due to the structural barriers of finance and capital.

ventures. This was evidenced by the huge "informal sector" which encompassed carpentry, tailoring, bakeries, automobile and bicycle repair shops, and the production of new goods out of scrap metal (metal works, glass works, etc.). As Austen (1987) put it: "They successfully adapted their technology to deal with the products of modern mechanised industry but could not provide goods of their own which might substitute for complex imported commodities or even replace their vital working parts" (p.134). An excellent example of this adaptation of technology was provided by the "mammy lorries" variously known as 'tro tro' in Ghana and *mutatis* in East Africa.

Taking a simple truck chassis with a mounted engine, native artisans affixed a seating compartment with benches which were made completely of wood, an abundant local resource. Many of these mammy lorries were kept on the road for many years, in some cases as long as 50 years, by their owners who took great pride in operating them.[5] Since the 1930s, these mammy lorries have provided reliable transportation to the peasants. More importantly, they have been indispensable in penetrating the interior of Africa to evacuate cash-crops as well as foodstuffs. If these *tros tros* were for some reason completely taken off African roads, the urban areas would face serious shortages of food and possible starvation.

In sum, the indigenous economic institutions survived under colonialism and operated side by side with the new colonial system. The rural markets coexisted with the modern supermarkets in the European quarters. The peasants' small-scale holdings existed alongside the settler farms and expatriate-owned plantations. Peasant farmers were only partially integrated into the cash economy. Though they cultivated cash-crops for remote markets, "they continued to grow their own food supplies and organized their work around pre-colonial hoe-cultivation technology and the inherited social patterns of household, kinship and community" (Austen, 1987; p.138). The women traders continued their business side by side with the large European companies. The indigenous entrepreneurs and craftsmen also coexisted with their European counterparts.

The fact that the indigenous system proved resilient and little altered by colonialism was widely acknowledged by almost all scholars in the 1950s and 1960s. The state of development in the colonies was frequently referred to as "dualistic." And an underdeveloped country was routinely character-ized as possessing a "dual economy." It consisted of a small modern enclave

---

[5] Their owners always personalized their trucks by inscribing on them their philosophical beliefs. Visitors to Africa who have come across these trucks may have seen a few of these interesting inscriptions. For example, "Sea Never Dry," "All Shall Pass," "Man Is Suffering Ooo But Woman Don't Know." A particular favorite was this one: "K.K. Is Coming" which was inscribed on a board in front of the truck. Then at the back was: "K.K. Is Gone."

surrounded by a "sea of backwardness" as the indigenous sector was often derogatively referred to.

The colonialists lived in the modern enclaves or "European quarters" and the natives in the indigenous sector which attracted little colonial attention unless there was a rebellion or some act of civil disobedience. Most of the developments that took place under colonialism occurred in the European sector. The interior was left untouched unless the discovery of an important resource dictated the construction of roads and railways to exploit it. The railways that were built exhibited a dendritic system, i.e., a leaf-like network emanating from the coastal areas to the various regions of the African interior and not being linked to one another. Their sole purpose was to evacuate minerals or cash-crops, not for social development. As Nkrumah (1973) scolded:

> Under colonial rule, foreign monopoly interest had tied up our whole economy to suit themselves. We had not a single industry. Our economy depended on one cash crop, cocoa. Although our output of cocoa is the largest in the world, there was not a single cocoa processing factory. There was no direct rail link between Accra and Takoradi. There were few hospitals, schools and clinics. Most of the villages lacked a piped water supply. In fact the nakedness of the land when my government began in 1951 has to have been experienced to be believed (p.395).

Thus, the oft-repeated argument that the indigenous institutions were violently extirpated is without validity.[6] The rural or indigenous sector was virtually left untouched or undeveloped. Clearly, the native institutions, then, could not have been destroyed entirely by the colonialists.

As Austen (1986) put it:

> Through almost all of tropical Africa, the diplomats' 'paper partition' of the 1880s and early 1890s were followed by years and sometimes decades of relative inactivity. Only the most rudimentary, if any, administration was established outside the capitals, few roads and hardly any railways were built, *and for most Africans life had hardly changed.* The reasons for these hesitations were financial: private European investors were uninterested in Africa, metropolitan legislatures opposed major public expenditures on colonies, and even the

---

[6] Various scholars have advanced several arguments for the lack of social development of Africa's interior. Some have argued that the development of the interior would not have served the interests of European economic domination over Africans. Others have argued that, "traditional African production systems persisted not because of support or inhibition from outside but because they proved their efficiency against the competition of European private enterprise and allegedly 'expert' public technical advice" (Austen, 1987; p.143).

Western commercial firms already established at coastal entrepots refused to move inland ahead of piecemeal government 'pacification' (p.124). (Emphasis mine).

Similar remarks were made by Gellar (1986):

While the establishment of European colonial governments imposed a new political order in Africa, the impact of the colonial state on African societies should not be exaggerated. The European presence in many territories was, in fact, limited to small numbers of administrators, merchants, and missionaries concentrated primarily in the colonial capital and in the major trading centers. In many areas of rural colonial Africa, the people rarely came into direct contact with European officials. As late as the mid-1920s there was only one British administrator for every 100,000 persons in northern Nigeria. In some parts of Africa, the colonial state was not able to permanently impose its rule and had to rely on periodic military expeditions to 'pacify' the area. Thus, in the desert of several French colonial territories, for example, Algeria, Mauritania, Mali, and Niger, the Tuareg and other desert peoples managed to maintain a considerable degree of autonomy because their areas were largely inaccessible and ungovernable.

Because of the small number of European personnel, limited financial resources, and an undeveloped communications infrastructure, the colonial state had to rely heavily upon traditional African rulers, chiefs, and religious authorities to help govern the vast areas and populations under its control. Where the Europeans did not find local rulers, they often created their own chiefs *(chefferies* in Belgian Congo) to administer an area or named strangers or people of low social status to fill the role. The French, for example, who had less respect for traditional authority than did the British, would often name an interpreter, a guide, or even a cook as canton chief to replace a local authority when the latter's loyalty to France was in question. The system of Indirect Rule permitted traditional rulers and chiefs to govern certain areas under the careful supervision of the European authorities (p.132).

Almost all students of African colonial history assert that the African people were exploited economically and received little social development under colonialism. But their indigenous institutions were largely left intact, although there were some adaptations and modifications. It defies logic to accuse the colonialists of neglecting the indigenous sector and destroying it at the same time, when they hardly spent much time there except to exploit or evacuate mineral deposits or other resources.

B. AN ASSESSMENT

Colonialism in Africa constituted an imposition of alien rule on the people of Africa, under which they were subjected to degrading acts of human rights abuses and political oppression.

> The colonial state was autocratic, not democratic. While colonial rule has often been described as a 'School for Democracy,' this image did not reflect accurately the realities of political life in Africa. Before 1945, less than 1 percent of the African population had full political and civil rights or access to modern democratic institutions. Instead, most Africans were ruled by autocratic bureaucracies with little interest in promoting democratic ideals (Gellar, 1980; p.131).

Colonial atrocities and autocracy at once evoked an emotional response from most Africans. At one extreme were the majority of African leaders and intellectuals, exemplified by such personalities as Kwame Nkrumah of Ghana, Nyerere of Tanzania and Ali Mazrui (1986) to whom every aspect of colonialism was evil. At the other extreme could be found very few Africans, among them may be noted President Felix Houphouet-Boigny of Ivory Coast. In a recent statement, Houphouet-Boigny was quite explicit:

> Colonialism was a good thing for Africa. Thanks to it, we have one united Ivorien nation, rather than 60 tribes who know nothing about each other (*World Development Forum*, Vol. 5, No.9, May 15, 1987; p.3).

It is not particularly useful to assess colonialism in terms of whether it was "good" or "bad" for Africa. The real story is probably somewhere in between. It is rather more expedient to strip colonialism of its emotional and political rhetoric and regard it as *contact* between Europeans and Africans. The contact of course was not on equal terms and the benefits from it were lopsided. Nonetheless, there was contact. Couched in these terms, a fruitful and objective analysis of the consequences of the contact is possible. Some of the changes or effects of this contact were positive and some were clearly negative.

On the positive side, first, the abolition of commercial slavery and the slave trade must certainly be noted. Second, the subsequent establishment of peace and order, albeit by an iron hand and after brutal conquests, greatly enhanced commerce and contributed in no small measure to economic and social development. Third, the native systems of justice were strengthened and new forms of administration were introduced into Africa which have continued to function. Fourth, some rudimentary system of roads, bridges, railways, universities, schools, telegraph and other infrastructure were laid down by the colonialists, albeit insufficiently and reluctantly. These infrastructural facilities were new and generally nonexistent in pre-colonial Africa. Their introduction was vital for Africa's economic development.

Fifth, European trading companies and missionaries promoted the cultivation of cash-crops and set up botanical gardens where instruction could be given to farmers and from where seedlings could be obtained. Agricultural research stations and institutes were also established to study and promote the adoption of higher-yielding and disease-resistant varieties of seeds.

These positive developments produced a phenomenal expansion of trade and agricultural production. For example,

> The volume of cotton exports from French West Africa rose from an average of 189 tons in 1910-14 to 495,000 tons in 1935-39, while that of coffee soared from 5,300 tons in 1935 to 495,000 tons in 1936. The volume of groundnuts (peanuts) exported from Senegal alone increased from 500,000 in the 1890s to 723,000 tons in 1937. However, the greatest success story was that of cocoa production in Ghana whose volume of exports rose from only 80 lbs in 1881 to 2 million lbs in 1901 and 88.9 million lbs in 1911. This made Ghana the leading producer of cocoa in the world, and the quantity continued to rise until it reached a record figure of 305,000 tons in 1936 (Boahen, 1986; p.128). For all of Africa, the following Table shows a remarkable increase in exports.

**EXPORTS OF SOME COMMODITIES FROM AFRICA,
1908 - 1962** (Metric Tons)

	1908	1924-28	1934-38	1962
Palm Oil	121,000	188,700	243,500	303,300
Cocoa	48,429	325,901	469,352	854,060

Source: Wickins, 1981, p.272-273.

On the negative side were, first, the artificial nature of Africa's political boundaries. The boundaries partitioned same groups of people, resulting in social disruption and tension. For example, the Ewe were divided by the Ghana-Togo border, the Akan by the Ghana-Ivory Coast border, the Senufo by the Ivory-Coast-Mali border and the Yoruba by the Nigeria-Benin border. The Somali fared the worst. They found themselves in Somali, Ethiopia, Djibouti and Kenya.

Second, colonial rule weakened the traditional institution of chieftaincy by depriving the chiefs of effective authority. The third was the loss of African sovereignty and freedom for its people. The fourth, was the extent of economic exploitation. This view was offered by Gutkind and Waterman (1977):

> On the eve of the second World War, the peasants of French West Africa had to furnish each year, according to Governor-General Delavignette: 175,000 francs in poll-tax and cattle-tax, 21,000,000 days of statute labor and 12,000 soldiers. This catalogue is not complete. To the taxes were added supplementary payments, 'customary' or otherwise, levied by the canton chiefs; debts paid to the provident societies (in Senegal loans of groundnuts seeds were repayable with 25 per cent interest within *three months*; in fact, dishonesty often raised this to nearly 100 percent, and annual quotas even higher; sales of compulsory crops below cost price. . .Days of statute labor represented only a fraction of forced labor, excluding extra labor for the chiefs and recruitment for big public works and private enterprise (p.128).

Fifth, it has been argued that, though foreign trade expanded for Africa under colonialism, it was not an equal exchange. "There was a far greater instability in the prices of export goods as compared to imports. All shortfalls had to be borne by the African producer, while rises in prices were largely absorbed by African intermediaries" (Gutkind and Waterman, 1977; p.126).[7]

Sixth, it has also been claimed that colonialism extended exploitation to the soil and intensified land degradation in Africa. Under pre-colonial conditions, a prolonged fallow period generally ensured recovery of soil fertility. The obligation to produce more without being able to use supplementary acreage, and often over an area reduced by concessions to European settlers led to an acceleration of land rotation and a reduction in the fallow period resulting in a decline in yields and a permanent ruin of the soil along with a reduction in pastoral land.

Seventh, colonial rule established professional armies in Africa where none existed. It may be recalled that, in pre-colonial Africa, few states maintained standing armies. In the event of an imminent threat of war, the chief would summon all young men of a certain age grade to assemble at his residence. They were then organized into battalions to defend the village or led into war by the chief.

A discussion of the positive and negative effects of colonialism invariably provokes the question: How did Africa fare on balance? This has been one of

---

[7] It must be added, however, in the first half of the 19th century West Africa enjoyed increasingly favorable terms of trade (Wickins, 1981; p.286). While imports from Europe declined in price because of improved technology in manufacturing and the fall in marine transport costs, the price of palm oil, the main West African export continued to rise until the 1850s.

the most controversial and intractable questions that have plagued post-colonial Africa. Marxists and dependency theorists maintain that, on balance, colonialism pauperized Africa. African states ceased to be autonomous economies and were transformed into peripheral extension of the metropolitan and international capitalist economy. Colonial objectives were not to develop Africa but to undertake such forms of development that were compatible with the interests of the metropolitan powers. Since they were mostly industrialized, the colonies were envisaged to be nonindustrial appendages to the metropolitan economy: consumers of manufactured goods and providers of agricultural, sylvan and mineral commodities. As a result, the development of the colonial economies was perniciously "skewed": over-specialized in one or very few main cash-crops (mono-export culture), highly vulnerable to oscillations in commodity prices and a secular deterioration in their terms of trade which were beyond the control of the colonial subjects.

Specialization in cash-crops destroyed their ability to feed themselves and supply their other needs internally. Most domestic industries died from competition from cheaper and probably better imported manufactures. Because of collusion among foreign firms and discrimination from colonial banks, the modern sector was completely in foreign hands. Thus, most of the surplus profit generated by the economy flowed overseas and was not invested in the colony.

The opposite "conservative" view was that there was never any possibility of rapid or easy economic development in tropical Africa. Markets were small and local, technology was backward, and political and social factors checked development. The inherent capacity of Africa to develop was there but to be developed effectively, it needed to be integrated into the more dynamic world economy.

The incorporation did not necessarily depend on their becoming colonies; but given the circumstances prevailing in the 19th century, colonialism was the best way in which this could be done (Fieldhouse, 1986; p.28). The main contribution of colonial rule was that, in their own interests, the European rulers "opened up" the interior of Africa and linked virtually every part of the continent with the outside world. By imposing their own absolute rule over areas far larger than any single indigenous state, they removed political obstacles to the movement of goods, people and ideas. By building railways and improving river transportation, they facilitated commerce and trade.

Deficiencies and inaccuracies can be detected in *both* arguments. But at this point in time, the net effects of European colonialism on Africa as an issue is not particularly relevant. When 400 children die each day in southern Africa, according to the United Nations, it is silly to engage in sterile academic debates over European colonialism in Africa. Colonialism was an accident of history and cannot be erased or undone. Why then the ceaseless wail over "colonial legacies" as primary causes of Africa's economic predicament? Must the elites forever blame all of Africa's woes on colonialism? Even illiterate peasants are fed up with this lament over colonialism. Recall that in 1981 some of Ghana's peasants were calling upon the British to recolonize the country — an indictment of the leadership which had failed them.

Two bombs were dropped on Japan in 1945. Yet, the Japanese were able to put that dark episode behind them and get on with the task of reconstructing their economy. Today, Japan, with no known natural resources, is an economic superpower while Africa, with its tremendous natural resource wealth, starves and its elites wail over colonialism.

It is true the past must be studied to provide guidance for the future. But obsession with the past can be imprisoning. Ever so engrossed with the past, the individual becomes captured by it and fails to see opportunities that are currently available, let alone take advantage of them.

Everyone agrees that colonialism did not bequeath much to Africa by way of infrastructure and development facilities. One would have expected a retention of the "positive" legacies and a discard of the "negatives." But as we shall see in the next chapter, African elites and nationalists did precisely the opposite. They kept the negatives (repressive measures, guns, the army, artificial borders) and destroyed the "positives" (infrastructure, parliament).

The army, a colonial institution, was expanded enormously in post-colonial Africa. African governments railed at the "artificial colonial borders" and yet retained and manned them by uniformed bandits. Worse, we, the elites, could not maintain, let alone augment the little that we got. In fact, we destroyed it! When Zaire gained its independence in 1960, it had 31,000 miles of main, first-class, roads. Today, less than 3,500 miles are usable. In Uganda, Makerere University in the 1950s was the pride of Africa, dubbed "The Harvard of Africa." Today, it is in ruins. In exactly the same conditions of decrepitude are the University of Ghana, Ibadan University and other African universities left by the colonialists.

Even in spite of all the condemnation of colonialism, there was much peace and order as well as stability. There certainly was discrimination and denigration of Africans, but there was also much freedom for Africans to go about their activities. This freedom perfidiously vanished in most African countries after independence — a fact which was noted by Archbishop Desmond Tutu, a Nobel laureate:

> It is true God's children in Africa suffer because there is *less* freedom in their countries than during the colonial times. African leaders need to be reminded that there is totalitarianism and despotism nearly every-where in Africa (*Daily Nation*, Nairobi, March 26, 1990).

This is not a defense of colonialism. But scholars, obsessed with the iniquities of colonialism — abominable as they were — totally ignore preseant-day reality. For decades post-colonial Africa has not seen peace. Today, chaos, civil wars and social turmoil rage as military barbarians and "crocodile liberators" run amok in the region, leaving human debris and carnage in their wake.

Strictly from the African perspective, it is persiflage to romanticize about Africa's development under no European colonial rule. Foreign rule over Africa was inevitable. The Europeans and Arabs were battling to subjugate Africa. If the Europeans had not colonized Africa, the Arabs would have. By the 17th century, North Africa was already under Islamic conquest. West Africa was saved by the Sahara, which served as an effective bulwark against Islamic expansionism. In East Africa, Islam was poised to make inroads in the late 1880s. To determine the fate of Africa under Arab colonialism, one should take a good look at Lebanon, the Middle East, or Arab treatment of blacks in Mauritania and Sudan.

No black African will ever forget that in the 19th century, over 2 million black slaves were shipped from East Africa to Arabia, a slave trade dominated by Arabs.

> The Zanzibar slave trade, with an annual sale that increased according to some estimates from 10,000 slaves in the early 19th century to between 40,000 and 45,000 in the mid-19th century, was at its height during the rule of Sayyid Said (1804-1856 - born 1794), sultan of Muscat and Oman. . . Enslaving and slave trading in East Africa were peculiarly savage in a traffic notable for its barbarity. Villages were burnt, the unfit villagers massacred. The enslaved were yoked together, several hundreds in a caravan, and on their journey to the coast, which could be as long as 1280 kilometres. . .It is estimated that only one in five of those captured in the interior reached Zanzibar. The slave trade seems to have been more catastrophic in East Africa than in West Africa (Wickins, 1981; p.184).

Some of the African slaves were shipped to Iraq, where they were inhumanely treated. In the latter part of the 19th century, they revolted and were subsequently placed in the Iraqi army. As we noted in the Introduction, slavery of blacks and discrimination against them by Arabs still continue in this modern day and age - the 1990s - in such African countries as Mauritania and Sudan. For 17 years, a war still rages on between the Moslem north and Christian south in Sudan. It was Muslim domination of Nigeria that partly set off the Biafran War of 1967-70 which cost over one million Nigerian lives.

For black Africans, it is idle to speculate on whether on balance European colonialism was "good" or "bad" for Africa. Nor is it even useful to mull over how Africa would have fared under Arab colonial rule. The more pertinent question is how Africa has fared under elite colonialism since independence.

C. SUMMARY

Colonial rule was oppressive, destructive and exploitative but most of Africa's indigenous institutions survived under colonialism. In fact, many were not even touched by colonialism. Native courts and legal systems were actually strengthened in the beginning of the colonial period since Africans were to face African law while Europeans were judged by European law. The indigenous economic system was generally left intact, although there were instances of colonial interferences and intervention: forced labor, oppressive taxes, control and fixing of prices of primary exports as well as imports of manufactured goods. Other than these, there was economic *freedom*, circumscribed somewhat, for Africans to engage in their traditional means of livelihood.

Peasant farmers cultivated their plots of land, using the same pre-colonial techniques of land rotation and bush fallow. Surplus produce was sold on open, free village markets. Prices on these markets were determined during the colonial era in the exactly the same manner as they were determined in pre-colonial times — by bargaining. Profits made were for the peasants to keep, not for the chiefs to expropriate. The village markets continued to operate periodically, in cycle or rotation with other villages, during the colonial period as they did before colonialism. In fact, rather than uproot the indigenous economic system, the colonialists found it more rewarding and profitable to retain it, but to manipulate it to their advantage, since an alternative system would have been too prohibitively expensive to install.

It was in the political arena that the indigenous system of government came into violent clash with colonial rule by virtue of the fact that the articulating element was political authority. But even so, it may be recalled, the indigenous political structures faced different sets of circumstances under different colonial regimes. The indigenous political system was the least disrupted under the British colonial policy of "indirect rule", although the British increasingly became more authoritarian toward the waning years of colonialism. The greatest threat of annihilation came from the other colonial regimes — the French, the Belgian and the Portuguese. Some old kingdoms, for example in Dahomey, were completely destroyed by the French. Chiefs were appointed and removed by the French, Belgian and Portuguese colonial authorities. Nevertheless, the council of elders was left untouched. Furthermore, the indigenous structures adapted themselves to enhance their chances of survival under colonialism. In fact, colonialism initiated this very process of transformation and adaptation. These indigenous structures did not suddenly disappear —attested to by such references to African societies as "dualistic" and by accusations that the "colonialists never developed Africa." The clear implication from these is that indigenous Africa survived. In many parts of rural Africa, large areas were not radically transformed or even penetrated by colonial rule.

All in all, then, colonialism left the indigenous legal institutions somewhat fortified in the initial stages; the economic system was left generally intact; but the political structures were considerably weakened. The issue of paramount importance is *not* how oppressive or iniquitous colonialism was as agreement already exists on this. Nor how Africa fared *on balance* under colonialism. Rather, the more appropriate question to ask is how has post-colonial Africa fared under the nationalists, the champions of liberty and development? We examine this question in the next chapter.

CHAPTER 10

THE POST-COLONIAL DESTRUCTION AND BETRAYAL OF AFRICA

After independence, most of the black African countries entered a new era I would call 'Black Imperialism.' While many of the African leaders are addicted to shouting against imperialism and colonialism, they forget to recognise the existence of a new form of imperialism, the 'Black Imperialism.' Black imperialism, by definition is the exploitation of Africa by Africans and usually by top government officials, business men and women.

These people behave the same way as their former white counterparts used to. We all know that the whites drained Africa of her resources during the period of colonisation, but are these not the African leaders who are doing the same thing today? If one looks at the list of the rich leaders of the world, one finds many African leaders on the top! Most of them, if not all, keep their money in Western banks. So are they not continuing the same process started by their former masters? On the economic front, I am sorry to say that if one takes opinion polls in most African countries, over 50 percent of ordinary blacks will say they were living better during the white rule and they would not mind their returning! This is a big shame, but facts are usually bitter!

- Tony Moro, an African Student in *New African* (Feb. 1989; p.38).

A. BLACK NEO-COLONIALISM

As we saw in the previous chapter, colonial rule was humiliating and invidious. The object of European colonialism was the exploitation of Africa to develop European metropolitan centers. But there were some positive as well as negative consequences from contact with the Europeans. After independence, unforbidding pragmatism would have required a careful and an objective assessment of European colonialism. It was an act of history which will never be erased no matter how much African nationalists wailed over it. Common sense should have dictated retaining the positive aspects of contact with the Europeans and shedding the negative legacies or rectifying the mal-effects of colonialism. For example, a conscious effort should have been made to maintain the peace and order that were so vital for the expansion of trade and commerce. Required at the other end would have been a restoration of the dignity and freedom of the African people, a partial disbandment of the professional armies, and the eradication of artificial borders to permit freedom of movement of the African people as existed in pre-colonial Africa. But these measures were never undertaken by the nationalists in post-colonial Africa, 1960-1990.

Independence And Aftermath

Independence came to most Africans, but true freedom and development eluded them. With few exceptions, the nationalists who took over from the departing colonialists were no better. In fact, in many countries, they were worse.[1]

Three decades of independence and "freedom" have witnessed a steady increase in the incidence of hunger and a systematic deterioration of living standards across Africa. By 1990, income per capita for most African countries was less than it was in 1960. The economic decline was particularly serious in sub-Saharan or black Africa, as we saw in the Introduction. Even the World Bank, which characteristically abjured political commentaries, was alarmed enough to break its reticence. While noting earlier progress and a few exceptional countries, the World Bank in its report, *Sub-Saharan Africa: From Crisis to Sustainable Growth*, complained that: "Overall Africans are almost as poor today as they were 30 years ago" (Nov. 1989; p.1).

It is even painful to inquire about their political situations. At the Pan-African Congress in Mwanza in 1958, the delegates shrilly wailed over the fact that: "*The democratic nature of the indigenous institutions of the peoples of West Africa* has been crushed by obnoxious and oppressive laws and

---

[1] Many have difficulty with this comparative statement, misinterpreting it as a veiled justification for colonial rule. Nothing could be farther from the truth. Africans overwhelmingly rejected colonial rule and asked for *more*, not less freedom or tyranny after independence. Abhorrence for colonial rule does not mean Africans should not hold their leaders to the *same* ideals of liberty or make comparisons to determine their progress. In fact, the fixation with past colonial exploitation blinds many to the grotesque exploitation and treacherous oppression of the people of Africa today. It is this insensitivity to their plight which enrages most Africans.

regulations, and replaced by autocratic systems of colonial government which are inimical to the wishes of the people of West Africa." It demanded that: "The principle of the Four Freedoms (*Freedom of speech, press, association and assembly*) and the Atlantic Charter *be put into practice at once. . .Democracy must prevail throughout Africa from Senegal to Zanzibar and from Cape to Cairo.*"

The Congress stoically resolved to "*work for the establishment and perpetuation of true parliamentary democracy in every territory within the African continent.*" It vowed an "*uncompromising safeguarding of liberty of every citizen* irrespective of his race, colour, religion or national origin. The Conference declared publicly that it was "dedicated to *the precepts and practices of democracy.*" It made it plain that "*The safeguards and protection of citizen's rights and human liberties will be buttressed by*:

(i)   Uncompromising *adherence to the Rule of Law*;

(ii)   Maintenance of the *absolute independence of the Judiciary*;

(iii)   *The exercise of the right to vote or stand for any office*; and

(iv)   The *constant observance of the declaration of the Universal Human Rights and the United Nations Charter.*

Further, the Congress called "*upon the Government of East and Central Africa to remove all legal restrictions against the freedom of the press and particularly condemns the unjust prosecution and convictions which have taken place in some of these Territories against the African press in particular.*"

Treacherously, the Pan-Africanists failed to establish these lofty principles and ideals (democracy, the vote, freedom of the press, of assembly, etc.) after independence. In 1990, less than than six countries of the 52 African countries had multiparty democracy, freedom of the press, of speech and of political association.[2] Nor did the nationalists build upon the "democratic nature of the indigenous institutions of the peoples of Africa."

Back in 1919 in Paris, the maiden Pan-African Congress eloquently issued a series of resolutions, one of which demanded:

> The natives of Africa must have the right to participate in the Government as fast as their development permits, in conformity with the principle that the Government exists for the natives, and not the natives for the Government. They shall at once be allowed to participate in local and tribal government, according to ancient usage, and this participation shall gradually extend, as education and experience proceed, to the higher offices of states; to the end that, in time, Africa is ruled by consent of the Africans. . .Whenever it is proven that African natives are not receiving just treatment at the hands of any state or that any State deliberately excludes its civilized citizens or subjects of Negro

---

[2] These six countries were Algeria, Botswana, Egypt, Mauritius, Senegal and The Gambia. Namibia is excluded as it gained its independence in March 1990.

descent from its body politic and culture, it shall be the duty of the
League of Nations to bring the matter to the notice of the civilized
world (Cited in Langley, 1979:740).

For thirty years after independence, Africans were denied this participation, and the League of Nations shirked its responsibility to bring this
broken promise to the attention of the rest of the world. This perfidy is the
subject of my book, *Africa Betrayed*. The present chapter is a mercifully brief
account of the treacherous march toward dictatorship, tyranny and economic
disintegration in post-colonial black Africa.

The Origins Of The African Crisis

Independence did not herald the era of prosperity trumpeted by the
nationalists. Rather, the economic exploitation of the African people
intensified — at the hands of the same elites and nationalists who denounced
the colonial powers for exploiting Africa to develop their European
countries.

Resources were extracted from the rural areas through various legislative
devices and controls for development in imitation of the Soviet model. "A
workers' paradise was to be built." But the elites developed only the urban
areas, built statues and monuments for themselves. During his 1989 New
Year's address, President Houphouet-Boigny of Ivory Coast, for example,
disclosed that "the country's peasant farmers had over the years parted with
four-fifths of the value of what they produced to enable the government to
finance economic development" *(West Africa,* May 1-7, 1989; p. 677). But
over 80 percent of Ivory Coast's development was concentrated in Abidjan
for the benefit of the elites, not the peasants.

As African economies deteriorated, African dictators and their elite
hangers-on furiously developed pot-bellies and chins at a rate commensurate
with the economic decline. Africa's peasants were exhorted to tighten their
belts while the elites were loosening theirs with fat bank balances overseas.
Even the Paris newspaper, *Le Monde*, complained bitterly in March 1990:
"Every franc we give impoverished Africa, comes back to France or is
smuggled into Switzerland and even Japan" (Cited by *The Washington Post*,
March 26, 1990; p.A17).

The manager of the failed *Banque Commerciale de Benin* put it succinctly:

> The basic problem here, beside a lack of competence, is total
> corruption. The top people line their pockets through political
> influence. The president's (Mathieu Kerekou's) adviser, Cisse,
> called *le Marabout* — 'the priest'— stole 5 billion CFA (about $14

million) from this bank. We've traced it to Switzerland, London and Monte Carlo. . .

The chief bandit is the president, along with his associates in the politburo. The chief prosecutor is the next biggest bandit. Another is the minister of justice: all court decisions are determined by bribes. I went to the presidential palace along with a representative of the World Bank. We were asked when the stolen money would be recovered. It was rather difficult to answer, 'Mr. President, *you* have the money'. . .

The top men will have 10 or 15 mistresses who used to run up big debit accounts here, and then go to the *Palais* and say, 'You've got to straighten me out with the bank.'

The rulers now admit that they never understood Marxism, and as a sop to opinion a few people have been jailed. But new *marabouts* have been brought in, and are still at the center of the decision-making' (*The American Spectator*, May 1990; p.31).

By the early 1970s, an economic crisis had emerged. The ruling elites demanded more foreign aid to cure Africa's ills. And foreign aid did pour into Africa — from the West, in part to soothe Western collective guilt over the injustices of slavery and colonialism. But much of the aid was misappropriated by the elite *bazongas* (raiders of the public treasury) and never reached needy peasants. In 1986, for example, the United States General Accounting Office found $16.5 million of food assistance funds embezzled by Liberian authorities. In September 1989, the Nigerian Government discovered to its utter dismay that over $4 billion of its foreign debt was "fraudulent and spurious" (*West Africa,* Sept. 25-Oct. 1, 1989; p.1614). In other words, there was nothing to show for that amount, suggesting embezzlement.

Defective Leadership

The leadership that emerged in post-colonial Africa was given to schizophrenic posturing and arrant sloganeering. "People's Revolution! People's Power!" they chanted. But they never dreamt of giving their own people the *power* to remove an incompetent government they did not want. "Freedom for the blacks in South Africa!" they rightly demanded. But not for their own black people in their own black African countries.

Too many of Africa's post-colonial leaders were afflicted with intellectual astigmatism and displayed a singular lack of cognitive pragmatism and a generally dysfunctional perspicacity of the process of development. They spoke of expanding *external* trade, but not *internal* trade; *external* causes of their economic crises, but not *internal* causes; attracting *foreign* investment, but not *domestic* investment; colonial plunder and exploitation, but not their own Swiss bank accounts.

As Lamb (1983) put it:

> Though Bokassa's regime was as nonsensical as any in Africa, it should not be viewed in isolation. Its absurdity was the tragedy of all Africa, a continent that suffers so much at the hands of misguided leadership. Never has Africa been more in need of men with reasoned voices and clear visions, and never has the honor roll of leadership been so barren (p.54).

It is imperative to draw a clear distinction between the African people (the peasants) and their modern leaders or elites. Elite failure is not synonymous with failure of Africans as a people. The modern leadership, with few exceptions, is a revolting caricature of the traditional leadership Africa has known for centuries under its kings and chiefs. The true African chief is no despot. Even illiterate peasants could see through the transparent hypocrisy of modern African leaders and elites. In fact, in East Africa, they coined an apt Swahili name for them: the *wabenzi* — men of Mercedes Benz.

It is true the Old Guard — the nationalist leaders such as Nkrumah, Kaunda and Nyerere — struggled gallantly to win independence for their people at great personal sacrifices, and their people were profusely grateful. But winning independence for their countries gave none of them an inviolable right to impose themselves on their people and treat their countries as their own personal property. Further, the skills required to wage a struggle for independence should not be confused with those needed to govern a country and run an economy successfully. These two types of skill are not necessarily identical.

Flexibility, tolerance of divergent opinion and the intellectual maturity to accept criticism were indispensable qualities required to govern an African country well. Most of the Old Guard lacked these qualities. They were rigid, intolerant and stubborn. Nkrumah, for example, jailed his critics under the 1958 Preventive Detention Act, while Nyerere for 24 years stuck bull-headedly to a "socialist" path even when things were going so obviously wrong.

As a result, many of the Old Guard led their countries down the road to tyranny and economic ruin and were subsequently booted out or assassinated in military coups. But the soldiers who replaced them were even more egregious. They unleashed savage brutality against their people, ruined one African country after another with brutal efficiency and looted national treasuries with military discipline — Benin, Burkina Faso, Central African

Republic, Congo, Ethiopia, Ghana, Liberia, Mali, Niger, Nigeria, Somalia, Sudan, Uganda, Zaire and others.

Political oppression, civil war, ruinous strife, and chaos have ravaged Africa, leaving the continent littered with human carcasses. Armed with a few bazookas, "useless idiots" blew up their country and people in behalf of foreign ideologies.[3] The most bizarre of Africa's civil wars was Ethiopia's, which raged for more than 28 years and where the combatants were mostly Marxists. Frustrated by his inability to inflict a crushing defeat and in a desperate effort to win public sympathy, a beleagured Comrade Mengistu Haile Mariam pleaded: "If you think my brand of Marxism is bad, wait till you see theirs" (*The New York Times*, Feb. 23, 1990). Black neo-colonialists never questioned the relevance of Marx to indigenous Africa.

Even more unbelievable, the wanton slaughter of Africans was occurring right before the very eyes of the Organization of African Unity (OAU) at its headquarters in Addis Ababa. But this pompously arcane body only recognized oppression when it wore a Western or white face. Each year, the OAU spent millions on glitzy anniversary celebrations, unperturbed by the senseless carnage in Ethiopia. Having had enough of this callous insensitivity, Mundua Yusuf Alai of Khartoum, Sudan, berated:

> The OAU sees itself as striving to unify Africa and one of its responsibilities should be to tackle problems affecting the states and peoples, as in South Africa, the Libya and Chad dispute, and so on. But the OAU has categorically failed in its roundtable work. Even in the country where it was born, Ethiopia, there are several guerrilla groups fighting. But the OAU talks of sending troops to fight the apartheid regime in South Africa.
>
> How will the OAU end the war phenomenon if it purposely forgets the other African internal conflicts — Ethiopia, Sudan, Uganda, Mozambique, and Angola. No African leaders, past or present, have broached this issue for discussion. If they can't address themselves to these issues why bother going to OAU meetings? The failure to solve these problems shows that the OAU will find it even more difficult to tackle South Africa. . .It appears the OAU is bent on condoning the killings of the African people by unacceptable and incompetent leaders, poverty, and disease (*New African*, August, 1988; p.4.)

Africa, often called the cradle of humanity, now has more uprooted persons than any other continent. Though exact numbers are hard to come by, the United Nations estimates that over half of the world's refugees and

---

[3] This terminology is derived from Lenin's use of "useful idiots."

displaced persons today are in Africa. Violence has been the root cause of most dislocation, especially in southern Africa, where 400 children die each day, according to the United Nations. "In every corner of Africa, you will find the refugees," said Godfrey R. Sabati, who was responsible for the refugee program in Zimbabwe in 1987. "It is a terrible sociological problem. These people have not only lost their homes, many have lost hope."

Why did things go so terribly wrong in post-colonial Africa?

B. DEVELOPMENT BY IMITATION: THE "SO-TOO-MUST-WE" SYNDROME

After independence, African nationalists and elites settled down to face the daunting challenge of developing Africa, in a manner consistent with African traditions and necessary to uplift African dignity. At the same time, however, there was a deep-seated hatred of colonialism. Emotions were running high after independence. The elites, euphoric over freedom from the colonial yoke, abhorred reminders of their former subjugated status. Colonialism and imperialism were adjudged to be exploitative and oppressive. Any institution perceived to be "colonial" or associated with colonialism in the slightest way was to be annihilated.

Apart from their hostility toward the "colonial institutions," the elites displayed another inimitable trait: an impatience to develop Africa. They could not be faulted on either proclivity. The colonial regimes were alien and there was clearly the need to develop Africa to suit Africa's own needs, not those of Europeans. The problem, then, was how the elites proceeded to attain their goals. Again, it is important to emphasize that a criticism of the methods and modalities employed does not necessarily mean the goals were unsalutary. As observed earlier, there may be several ways of moving from point A to point B: by walking, running, driving or by using the a rocket-propelled space shuttle. Criticizing one mode as inefficient does not mean one is opposed to getting to Point B. A free debate is vital to determine the most efficient mode. Efficiency is determined by cost and rationality criteria. An "efficient" mode is one which is less expensive and rational. For example, food can be cooked within minutes in micro-wave ovens. But its use in Africa, where there is less premium on time, would be inefficient and impractical.

In most African countries, there were no debates about efficient modalities. One individual, often the head of state, determined the mode. If a poor choice was made, the whole country suffered the consequences. There was little avenue for criticism or agitation for change. Those who were brave enough to express it were brutalized, jailed or driven into exile, as we shall see shortly.

The Denigration Of The Indigenous

Having condemned the colonial system as impoverishing, the nationalists and elites found themselves under tremendous pressure to "prove to the world" that they could develop Africa, and quickly, to shame the colonialists. Nkrumah of Ghana, for example, was determined to "achieve in a decade what it took others a century." He also vowed to "demolish these miserable colonial structures and erect in their place a veritable paradise." Virtually all the nationalists shared similar beliefs.

But there was a pervasive belief among the nationalists and elites that Africa's own indigenous institutions were "too backward," "too primitive" for the rapid development and transformation of Africa. Almost everywhere in Africa, the native institutions were castigated as "inferior." Ashamed of the label of "backwardness," the elites embarked upon a program of development that placed obtrusive emphasis on industry. No longer should Africa be relegated to the "inferior" status of "drawers of water and hewers of wood." Industrialization was synonymous with development. Consequently, agriculture and other primary activities were shunned as too "backward."

The natives were urged to abandon their backward ways and adopt "modern methods." For example, Kenya's Minister of National Guidance and Political Affairs, Mr. James Njiru banned the *True Love* magazine in February 1989, for publishing a cover photograph of naked girls dancing before King Mswati of Swaziland.

> He argued that Kenyans should abandon backward cultures for modern ones that are acceptable to foreigners, but this seems to deny that Africans should be proud of their African culture. There is nothing intrinsically virtuous or respectable in Western modes of dress and behavior (*New African*, March 1989; p.28).

It was widely assumed, not only by African elites but outside experts as well, that the adoption of foreign values was necessary for successful economic development. Development became synonymous with "change." Nkrumah, again, best expressed this attitude. Though agriculture was the main economic activity of indigenous Africa, he felt he could not rely on peasant farmers for a rapid agricultural revolution because they were "too slow to adapt or change their practices to modern, mechanized methods" (Uphoff, 1970; p.602).

Misconstruction Of The Notion Of Development

Development was almost everywhere in Africa misconstrued to mean "change" and the "adoption of modern and scientific methods." In this rote behavior the real meaning was not clear. The approach was akin to what educators call the "refrigerator fallacy." All teachers have refrigerators and therefore if one tried hard enough to acquire a refrigerator, one would become a teacher! The developed countries were industrialized and therefore if one acquired enough industries (and perhaps a nuclear bomb), presto one would become a developed country.

Clearly, this perverted way of looking at things shifted the emphasis away from the rigorous process of training to become a teacher to the rather facile task of acquiring the "symbol" of the occupation to be considered a teacher. Similarly in development, the emphasis was shifted from understanding the *modus operandi* to a preoccupation with its symbols. If an African head to state showed off a brand new shiny piece of imported tractor, it would "prove" that agriculture had been "mechanized." Precisely what that tractor was supposed to do to improve agricultural productivity or whether the support infrastructure existed or not was irrelevant. The mere presence of the tractor was of overriding importance. Such antics and obsession with symbolism betrayed a woeful lack of understanding of the development process.

Economic development does not mean the wholesale and blind acquisition of the symbols and signs of modernity. Nor does it mean everything about indigenous Africa must be rejected in favor of alien systems. In fact, the true challenge for development practitioners is how to *use the existing so-called "primitive, backward and archaic" institutions* to generate economic prosperity. These institutions can never be alienated from Africa's peasants. They are part of their culture. One cannot expect these peasants to suddenly renounce their age-old traditions and ways of doing things. Nor is such abjuration absolutely necessary, as demonstrated by the stupendous success of the Japanese. The Japanese did not have to become "Americanized" or "Sovietized" in order to develop.

Development simply means *improving* existing ways of doing things to make the processes more efficient and productive than before. By productivity is meant producing *more* from the *same or even fewer* resources; or alternatively, producing the *same* amount by using *fewer* inputs. In the African context, development means using the *same* indigenous system to produce *more* output. The principal beneficiaries of economic prosperity ought to be the peasants, not the tiny elite minority which constitutes less than 10 percent in any African country. But one can only improve the efficiency and performance of an automobile, if and only if, one understands how it operates.

In Africa, since the elites did not understand how the indigenous system operated they could not improve its performance and productivity. Figuratively speaking, when the peasants' agricultural machinery needed ordinary firewood to continue operation, African elites, with a little help from Western governments and experts, were pouring in rocket-jet fuel! The "modern" fuel was of course not only useless but destructive as well. It is debatable whether the elites wilfully set out to destroy the indigenous machinery or acted on the basis of innocent ignorance or sheer stupidity. Whatever the case, the result was a stalled machinery. This issue is crucial and perhaps an elaboration would be instructive.

Take the native fishing industry as an example. Africans have been fishing in dug-out canoes for centuries. The object of development here is to land more fish. How that fish is caught is immaterial for a destitute and starving African country. True development in this case would mean improving the indigenous system so that more fish could be landed. The canoes are made of wood. An improvement would mean widening the boats to permit bigger catches of fish. But the elites approached the issue differently. In the development paradigm, they attempted to produce *more* using *more* of inputs they did not have or understand.

The dug-out canoes were too "primitive." "Modern and scientific" methods were better. Accordingly, the elites completely ignored the native fishing industry. When Ghana drew up plans to build modern boats to establish a State Fishing Corporation, it chose pleasure aluminium boats. Worse, "The State Boatyard at Mumford in the Apampam District launched only 6 vessels with a workforce of 40 employees after operating for 9 years" (*Daily Graphic,* Accra, August 14, 1981; p.8).

Meanwhile, the primitive dug-out canoes were faithfully plugging away to deliver the fish, sometimes bumper catches, with little assistance from Ghanaian governments. In 1981, for example, when Ghanaians were starving, bumper catches of fish landed by dug-out canoes were rotting on the beaches. Native fishermen along the coastal areas of the central and western regions were reported "to be refusing to go to sea because there were no prospective buyers following the bumper catches in those areas" (*Ghanaian Times,* July 13, 1981). The Government of Ghana provided no assistance to the native fishermen because "the cold storage facilities of the State Fishing Corporation had broken down and there was no foreign exchange to import spares" (*Daily Graphic,* August 4, 1981).

This wastage also occurred in 1971, 1972, 1975, 1979 and 1980, all because the "educated" officials had never heard of the traditional forms of fish preservation: smoking and salting — practical solutions. Of course to the elites of Africa, dug-out canoes and traditional preservation methods were too "primitive and backward." Only the modern and scientific techniques were acceptable to the elites.

African elites took this peculiar development approach and its concomitant neglect and deprecation of indigenous systems to many other fields as well. In this way, almost every production activity organized by the elites became so dependent on the very inputs Africa did not have or possess the foreign exchange to import. Agriculture, for example, now required chemical fertilizers, tractors and combine harvesters. Without these, the elites were stuck, as "mechanization" was all the rage.

Common sense requires using the resources or inputs Africa has more of: labor and wood. Scientific and capital-intensive techniques are productive and efficient but in a different environment, where the relative costs of inputs are different and where the infrastructure exists to maintain the machinery. In Africa, the more appropriate technology is *labor-intensive*. It is not only *cheaper* but also creates employment as well.

But seduced by modern machines, African elites could not be persuaded that it made no difference to a starving person whether the fish on his plate was caught by a primivite dug-out canoe or by a modern, laser-powered trawler. But the consuming passion for the latter wrought a triple-edged disaster. Not only were the "primitive" native industries neglected but the "modern systems" imported by the elites failed to perform, either due to lack of maintenance or proper operation. Trawlers, tractors, machinery and equipment imported into Africa worked a few months, broke down for want of maintenance and were abandoned. Enormous amounts of foreign exchange were wasted in the process.

C. IMPOSITION OF ALIEN SYSTEMS ON AFRICA

Feeling that they could not rely on Africa's "backward" indigenous institutions, the nationalists and elites searched for some foreign systems to adopt for Africa. But then, they possessed only an imperfect understanding of these foreign systems too — a double jeopardy for Africa. One could not expect African nationalists to be completely conversant with the intricacies and the internal mechanics of the British, French, Russian or Chinese systems. Moreover, each of these foreign systems had evolved through time and reflected the unique cultural and political experiences of their peoples. In every political constitution there is a cultural imprint. The political events experienced by Africans are decisively different from those of Americans and other people. Obviously, implanting an American or Soviet constitution in an African country would be absurd.

African elites were in a fix; their choices were limited. The adoption of Western systems was generally out of the question, as they symbolized a submission to Western notions of "superiority," colonial exploitation and oppression. Since capitalism was synonymous with colonialism, it too was evil and exploitative.[4] The inevitable choice was socialism, the antithesis of capitalism. It was to be the guiding ideology. Only socialism could check

---

[4] This syllogistic error, as was earlier pointed out, risks being repeated in South Africa. There is an ocean of difference between apartheid and capitalism. In fact, the system of apartheid and its horrendous array of controls is not that much different from a Marxist or socialist system.

the evil machinations of neo-colonialism, imperialism and capitalist exploitation, the nationalists argued. Moreover, socialism could be accorded some authenticity by such African concepts as "family pot," "strong sense of community or tribalism" and "sharing." These arguments provided the rationale for the near-universal adoption of one-party socialist state systems under life-presidents in Africa. One convenient argument was that "there was only one African chief and he ruled for life." But these nonsensical arguments for one-party socialist dictatorships could in no way be validated by African tradition. Indigenous African systems were grossly distorted by various African dictators to suit their political purposes.

One-Party State System

As we saw in earlier chapters, indigenous African governments were gerontocracies (government by elders). But the elders were not infallible. Nor was respect for the elders a form of servility. Young adult members of the community could participate in the decision-making process by either attending the council meetings or the village assembly. They could express their opinions openly and freely. The chief or councillors did not jail dissidents or those with different viewpoints. Nor did the chief loot the tribal treasury and deposit the booty in Swiss and foreign banks. More importantly, the African king or chief was chosen; he did not choose himself. Moreover, he could be destooled (removed) at any time.

While it is true that Africans are imbued with a greater sense of community awareness than most Western cultures, it did not mean the concept of the individual was completely absent. Recall the Fanti proverb: "Life is as *you* (the individual) make it." Recall also from Chapter 1 the phrase: "I am because we are." Though the "we" connotes community the "I" (the individual or personhood) was not entirely absent.

An analogous situation is supplied by the phrase: "Man is a social animal." The meaning here is that the human being desires the company of others and abhors living alone. Accordingly, each person yearns for some "togetherness" or "a community." But it cannot be inferred from this disposition that "man is a socialist."

Being a "social animal" (sociable or socialistic) is totally different from being a socialist. Socialism, as an ideology, is rooted in political, economic and intellectual *control by the state.* The ideology of socialism, as understood and practiced, entails government ownership of the means of production; the operation of state enterprises to the exclusion of privately owned businesses; price-fixing by the state and a myriad of state regulations and controls; one-party states and government ownership of the press. In other words, there is an absence of *private ownership, free markets,* political and *intellectual freedom.* Indigenous African systems are *not* characterized by these absences and therefore cannot be classified as "socialism." Economic, political and intellectual repression as well as state *controls*, as we have seen in the previous chapters, were *never* part of indigenous African tradition.

"Freedom from restraint [or controls] is the ruling passion" in Africans, it may be recalled. Terms used to describe indigenous Africa were "enormous political diversity," "cultural pluralism," and "over 2,000 ethnic groups." Certainly, this diversity could never have been produced under rigid economic, political and intellectual controls that are envisaged under socialism. Diversity and socialism, as currently practiced, are antithetical. Indigenous African traditions do not lend any support for the socialist ideology.

It is true the people of Africa pooled their resources together (family pot, working bees, extended family systems, etc.) and helped one another ("communal labor"). But being communalistic or socialistic did not necessarily mean the African peasant was communist or socialist and therefore willing to share his wealth equally with all members of the extended family. Julius Nyerere, ex-president of Tanzania, for example, mistook the peasant's emphasis on kinship and community as readiness for socialism - *Ujaama* (Nyerere, 1962). But even then, the sense of community did not extend beyond one's kinship group. This is important.

As we saw in Chapter 1, there has always been fierce competition among the various ethnic groups in Africa. Nyerere and others focussed on *intra-group* loyalty and cooperation and ignored *inter-group* rivalries. Accordingly, cooperation can be preached and practiced within a group but that between groups is illusionary. Even in traditional African societies, the degree of *intra-group* cooperation was not mandated by the chief. It was determined by each group according to its own demands and circumstances. But modern African leaders delude themselves by believing that they can dictate from above *inter-group* cooperation in their countries composed of various ethnic groups.

It was this fundamental inability on the part of African nationalists to distinguish between "communalism" and "socialism" as well as between *intra-* and *inter-group* cooperation that has caused Africa much ruin. Even if allowances are made for understandable errors and misinterpretations on the part of the nationalists there was a more mundane and grievious transgression.

True socialism was *never* practiced by African leaders. The socialist state, with its coercive powers, became an instrument of oppression and exploitation. Those who expressed views different from the party line saw lives abruptly disrupted and themselves hauled into jail. Under African "socialism," the bourgeoisie riding about in Mercedes Benzes were now the same socialist party hacks and functionaries. A minister in Robert Mugabe's cabinet gave this definition: "In Zimbabwe, socialism means what is mine is mine but what is yours we share!"

'Swiss-Bank" Socialism

The "socialism" instituted in Africa was a peculiar type ("Swiss bank" socialism) that allowed the head of state and phalanx of kleptocrats to rape and plunder their national treasuries for deposit in foreign banks. Julius Nyerere was perhaps the only true practicing socialist, but his Chama Chamapinduzi (CCM) party was hopelessly riddled with corruption. Even Kwame Nkrumah of Ghana, generally regarded as the "father of African socialism," was reputed to have stashed millions away in Swiss and other foreign banks, according to the Azu Crabbe Commission of Enquiry set by the Government of Ghana in 1967 to probe Nkrumah's assets.

Only a few African countries, such as Cameroon, Ivory Coast, Malawi, Kenya, Senegal and Togoland, spurned the "socialist path" and opted to stay with the "Western system." But this system too, like the indigenous African system, was not well understood either. Adopted in these countries were bastardized "Western models" that were characterized by heavy state intervention in the economy, a preponderance of state enterprises, one-party rule, declaration of life-presidents, personal dictatorships — all of which were un-Western. In fact, beyond the diplomatic posturing and ideological rhetoric, there was little real difference between the "socialist" and "capitalist" (or pro-West and pro-East) African regimes.

Strictly from the African point of view, the ideological paradigm was irrelevant. Africans were *not* Americans, Chinese, Cubans, or Russians. In fact, it was probably for this reason that African heads of state declared themselves to be "non-aligned." But then, "non-alignment" turned out to be a strange type of movement that congregated in Havana and Harare to bash only the West. Insidiously, Marxism, Leninism, and all sorts of alien "isms," copied from abroad, were imposed on Africa by the same African nationalists preaching "non-alignment."

The portraits of Marx and Lenin graced the Red Square in Moscow. So too must go Addis Ababa (Ethiopia), Cotonou (Benin), Luanda (Angola) and Maputo (Mozambique). Cuba had People's Defence Committees; so too must Ghana. The colonialists never accepted Africans for what they were and tried to remould them. In the post-colonial period, it was African leaders who were trying to reshape Africans in the image of foreigners.

Back in 1932, Kobina Sekyi, the Ghanaian lawyer and philosopher, wrote:

When each tribe or nation is enabled to develop along its own line, the respective geniuses of the several distinguishable races will harmonise in the establishment of a settled state of peace and prosperity, where development, scientific and social, including moral and political, advance will be steady (*West Africa*, Third Week of July, 1932).

But each tribe or nation can develop along its own lines, *if and only if*, it has the economic, political and intellectual freedom to do so. Incredibly, there are scholars, governments and institutions in the West who still maintain a water-tight separation between economics and politics, adamantly insisting that economic development is feasible under a tyrannical regime. Much Western aid was pumped into African countries laboring under hideous political regimes and wracked by civil wars and political chaos (Ethiopia, Mozambique, Somalia, Sudan, Uganda and Zaire, to name a few).

The route that allows each ethnic group to develop along its own lines is a *loose confederate-type of political association* which grants extensive local autonomy to the constituent groups. This was precisely the system ("indirect rule") adopted in the various indigenous empires of Africa, as we saw in Chapter 5. But after independence this type of rule was anathema to the elites, who insisted on strong, centralized rule and extreme concentration of powers in the hands of one bandit.

The issue here is not cultural nationalism or irredentism but rather a common-sensical observation. Just because California grows apples does not mean Africa too must raise them in order to develop or gain "acceptance" from the West. Even illiterate peasants know that what grows well in one part of the world may wither in another part because soil conditions, topography, drainage systems, temperatures and rainfall may be different. Of course, it is technologically possible to grow apples anywhere, even on the moon, using the latest advances in technology. But the costs would be astronomical, no pun intended.

As noted in the Introduction, economic efficiency, or common sense, dictates that one plants what is suited to one's own environment. In the field of agriculture, the environment consists of the type of soil, the amount of rainfall, the type of pests and diseases, and so on. If this environment is not suitable, implanted seeds will not germinate. The same idea is conveyed by the statement that, a building which is not well-rooted in the surrounding ground culture, will collapse in no time. An application of this reasoning to field of development requires ensuring that a development project, scheme, seed or idea is well rooted in the host environment if the project is to succeed.

Development deals with people. In Africa, the people are the peasants — the majority in every African nation. The environment in the field of development is their socio-economic and political set-up. That is, the whole gamut of their social, economic, cultural and political institutions at the grass-root level. Like a seed, if a development project does not fit into this socio-economic milieu or set-up, it will fail.

Africa's current development crisis emanates from the defective approach adopted by African elites and leaders with considerable support from foreign governments and multilateral agencies. Once again, it is the *approach* which is being criticized, not the *objectives* of development.[5] What occurred in Africa was *development by imitation*. Grandiose projects and schemes were copied abroad and transplanted into Africa.

American farmers use tractors and chemical fertilizers; so too must we in Africa. New York has skyscrapers; so too must Africa in the middle of nowhere. London has doubledeck buses; so too must Accra and Lagos. The Soviet Union has state farms; so too must Africa. In 1964, Nkrumah demanded a bylaw to require all advertisements in Accra to be lit by neon so that the streets of the capital would resemble Piccadilly Circle in London. France once had an emperor. So Bokassa of the Central African Republic spent $20 million in 1976 to crown himself an emperor. Rome has a basilica; so too must Ivory Coast. The United States has two political parties; so too must Nigeria. Accordingly, the military regime of President Ibrahim Babangida created two political parties: the Social Democratic Party and the National Republican Convention.[6] To add more insult, the military regime also wrote their party manifestoes. The list of this type of unimaginative aping ("so-too-must-we" syndrome) in Africa is endless.

It is a shame African elites and leaders lack *original* ideas and cannot use their imagination to craft authentically African solutions to African problems. If all they can do is to imitate, then they might as well bring back the foreigners to come and rule Africa.[7] At the very least, they could copy or improve Africa's own indigenous systems if they were bereft of original ideas.

This issue is important. Before long, most of these foreign imitation projects began collapsing because they had no roots in the indigenous culture. Huge sums of foreign aid were wasted in the process. Africa's enormous $259 billion foreign debt in 1990 was testimony to the numerous "black elephants" littering the continent. Poor African peasants must now pay off a huge foreign debt incurred through elite stupidity.

---

[5] A consensus has now emerged among development experts and practitioners that the old "hand-me-down" approach has failed. The emphasis is now on a "bottom-up" approach.

[6] In the words of the Babangida, one party was "a little to the left and the other a little to the right." But Nigerians promptly dismissed this "Babangida boogie" as "a little to the north and a little to the south." The two parties were dubbed the Northern Republican Convention and the Southern Democratic Party.

[7] The ramifications of this unimaginative aping are too far-reaching to be discussed thoroughly here. They have been explored at length in my forthcoming book, *Africa's Economic Crisis: The Indigenous Solution*.

D. THE ECONOMIC RUINATION OF AFRICA

As we saw in Chapter 8, pre-colonial Africa was characterized by great freedom of movement of people and of trade. A dense web of trade routes criss-crossed the continent, along which the natives moved freely and engaged in trade. Africans have long had an ingrained cultural propensity to trade. Throughout their history, they have been known to travel great distances to purchase goods from "strangers" at cheaper prices to sell at higher prices to make a profit. Much of this activity was free from state controls and regulations. State intervention in trade, commerce and markets by Africa's traditional rulers was the exception rather than the rule. There was no native African law which forbade Africans from entering into businesses if they wished. By nature and tradition, *Africans have always been free enterprisers*. Markets were the nerve-centers of traditional African societies and market activity was dominated by women.

When Africa was colonized, the colonialists sought to control indigenous economic activities to their advantage. Africa's colonial history is replete with successes and failures of these policies. For example, on the Gold Coast (now Ghana), European mining companies sought, without success, legislative curtailment of indigenous mining operations. The two operated side by side throughout the colonial era.

Notably absent during that era were state or colonial government enterprises. A few large European firms and companies dominated the field, but *no indigenous economic activity* was reserved exclusively for the colonial government or European companies. Note the emphasis on indigenous economic activity. Nor would the colonial administrations have been successful had they attempted such repression. That would have entailed an extraordinary expenditure of resources at that time. Africa then had not developed the communications and transportation networks needed for effective control of the natives and their economic activities. Cost was one reason the British adopted the policy of "indirect rule" - administration through the chiefs.

For the most part, the natives were free to go about their economic activities although there were some restrictions on their movements and places of residence in some colonies. The natives could open shops and compete with the European firms. Many did and were successful. There were rich African shopkeepers as well as timber merchants, transport owners, and farmers during the colonial period.

African natives have always welcomed foreigners and foreign firms provided they were willing to play fair. And given the opportunities and access to capital, African natives showed themselves capable of competing with the foreigners.

The Golden Age Of Peasant Prosperity

The period, 1880-1950, may be characterized as the Golden Age of Peasant Prosperity in Africa. Though colonialism was invidious, one of its little known and acknowledged "benefits" was the peace it brought Africa. Tribal wars and rivalries virtually came to halt, although they flared up occasionally. Their amelioration gave Africa a much-needed atmosphere of peace for productive economic activity. In addition, skeletal forms of infrastructure (roads, railways, bridges, schools, post office, etc.,) were laid down during this period, which greatly facilitated the movement of goods and people. This infrastructural development really gave production and economic expansion a tremendous boost. The secret to economic prosperity in Africa is not hard to find. Mere two words unveil this secret: peace and infrastructure.

It is instructive to note that the economic system used by the natives of Africa to engineer their economic prosperity in the 1880-1950 period was their own indigenous system. Except for a few places in Africa, notably in the Portuguese colonies, plantation agriculture was unknown. Cash crops were grown by peasant farmers on their own individual plots, using traditional farming methods and practices. In other words, the natives prospered using their own existing indigenous system with only minor modifications and improvements. For example, the cultivation of cocoa was not mechanized; it was a highly labor-intensive undertaking. Transportation of cocoa in the early 20th century was by human porterage, which gave rise to the pricing of cocoa by the "headload." The building of roads and the introduction of motor vehicles tremendously improved the transportation of cocoa and boosted exports. There were other improvements as well: insecticides, spraying machines, and so on. But the basic system of land tenure and the peasants' discretion over what crops to grow etc. were unchanged. African peasants were generally not forced to cultivate any cash crops. Forced labor in the French, Belgian and Portuguese colonies was mainly for construction purposes.

The fundamental point is that African natives had the *economic freedom* to decide for themselves what crops they could cultivate — cash crops or food crops — and what to do with the proceeds. This economic freedom was a notable feature of their indigenous economic system. Indeed, Kendall and Louw (1986) —two white South Africans — noted: "The freedom that characterized tribal society in part explains why black South Africans responded so positively to the challenges of a free market that, by the 1870s, they were outcompeting whites, especially as farmers" (p.4).

Though this freedom was somewhat circumscribed under colonialism, African peasants prospered during the colonial era. Why then were they unable to continue prospering into the 1980s? The answer is obvious: their economic freedom was somehow snatched from them.

The turnaround came first in South Africa, where according to Kendall and Louw (1986):

> Black success had tragic consequences. White colonists feared black competition and this fear, combined with the whites' desire for cheap labor, resulted in a series of laws that systematically denied blacks access to the marketplace and stripped them of any meaningful form of land ownership (p.4). . .

> The truth is that white farmers felt threatened by blacks. Not only were blacks better farmers but they were also competing with white farmers for land. Moreover, they were self-sufficient and hence not available to work on white farms or in industry, particularly in the Transvaal gold mines where their labor was badly needed. As a result a series of laws was passed that robbed blacks of almost all economic freedom. The purpose of these laws was to prevent blacks from competing with whites and to drive them into the work force (p.12).

In 1869, 1876, and 1884 the Cape Assembly passed a series of Location Acts (the first set of apartheid laws) that sought to protect white farmers from black competition and to force blacks to become wage laborers. Then came the Native Land Act of 1913 and the rest of the story is well known. Now and then, apartheid South Africa grudgingly rediscovered the industriousness of black farmers.

In 1985, the Development Bank, a quasi-government agency, began financing small agricultural credit programs which involved dispensing a package of aid (seed, fertilizer, a few implements and basic advice) to black subsistence farmers at a cost of $150 each.

> According to the Bank's general manager, Johan Kruger, these have been 'quite remarkably successful.' They have significantly upgraded the production of about 25,000 of these smallholders, greatly improved their ability to feed their families.

> 'The perception that blacks can't farm and that people can't make a living on small pieces of land in South Africa is a fallacy,' Kruger said. 'Provided they have the necessary support services and infrastructure, black farmers have shown that they can farm as well as whites' (*The Washington Post*, Dec. 29, 1990; p.A14).

In the rest of Africa, the turning point came after independence. Support services and infrastructure were not provided. Rather, the economic freedom of the peasants was wrenched from them by "Swiss bank socialists," while their economic prosperity was taxed and squandered by vampire elites through a series of edicts, state controls, and decrees.

After independence, many African governments not only nationalized European companies ostensibly to prevent "foreign exploitation" but also debarred the natives from many economic fields. For example, after Ghana gained its independence, the European companies were taken over by the state. Mining operations were monopolized by the state and indigenous gold-mining (*galamsey*) declared illegal. In fact, "Anyone caught indulging in illegal gold prospecting, popularly known as '*galamsey*' (gather them and sell), will be shot, a PNDC representative announced to a workers' rally in the Western Region" (*West Africa*, March 1, 1982; p.618).

In many other African countries, the natives were squeezed out of industry, trade and commerce where the state emerged as the only, if not the domineering, player. Indigenous operators were not tolerated. Indeed, there was a time when the director of the Club du Sahel, Anne de Lattre, would begin her meetings with the frightening remark, "Well, there is one thing we all agree on: that private traders should be shot" (*West Africa*, 26 Jan. 1987; p.154).

Under Sekou Toure of Guinea's nonsensical program of "Marxism in African Clothes,"

> Unauthorized trading became a crime. Police roadblocks were set up around the country to control internal trade. The state set up a monopoly on foreign trade and smuggling became punishable by death. Currency trafficking was punishable by 15 to 20 years in prison. Many farms were collectivized.

> Food prices were fixed at low levels. Private farmers were forced to deliver annual harvest quotas to 'Local Revolutionary Powers.' State Companies monopolized industrial production" (*The New York Times*, Dec. 28, 1987; p.28).

Other African governments also adopted price controls and various legislative instruments for the systematic exploitation of the peasants. Prices of agricultural produce were fixed to render food cheap for the urban elites — the basis of political support for African governments. The prices peasants received for their produce were dictated by governments, not determined by market forces in accordance with African traditions. African chiefs did not fix prices.

But under an oppressive system of price controls administered by the elites, Africa's peasants came to pay the world's most confiscatory taxes. In

1981, the Government of Tanzania, for example, was paying peasant maize farmers only 20 percent of the free market price for their produce. "Studies by the International Labor Organization have indicated that taxation levels in the agricultural sector in Sierra Leone averaged between 30 percent and 60 percent of gross income" (*West Africa*, Feb. 15, 1982; p.446). In 1984 cocoa farmers in Ghana were receiving less than 10 percent of the world market price for their crop. In Ethiopia, Guinea, Tanzania, and many other African countries, peasant farmers were forced to sell their produce or quotas only to state produce-buying agencies. Ghana's experience with price controls was most benighted and disastrous; it is worth recounting a few details.

Ghana's Experience With Price Controls

Nkrumah introduced price controls into Ghana in 1962. Successive governments so expanded their scope that by 1970, nearly 6,000 prices relating to more than 700 product groups were controlled. Between 1980 and 1983, their enforcement reached the height of lunacy:

> In June 1980, a magistrate, Mr. Kwadwo Asumadu-Amoah, jailed a 43-year petty trader, Madam Abena Amponsah, for 3 years at hard labor for making an illegal profit of $1.50 on 6 cakes of 'Guardian' soap. The same magistrate handed down a three-year term at hard labor to an 18-year old boy who made an illegal profit of fifty cents on a packet of matches (*Graphic*, 5 June 1980; p.5).

> In Jan. 1982, Air Force personnel destroyed over 400 tables and chairs belonging to traders at Apampam Store in Takoradi Central Market in a bid to enforce price controls (*West Africa*, Feb. 1, 1982; p.286).

> In Feb. 1982, the PNDC Secretary for the Upper Region, Dr. Awdu Tinorgah, ordered a detachment of the Police Striking Force to enforce price controls, following the refusal of traders at the Bolgatanga Market to sell their items at controlled prices (*West Africa*, April 26, 1982; p.1170).

> Markets were burned down and destroyed at Accra, Kumasi, Koforidua and other cities when traders refused to sell at govern-ment-dictated prices. In February 1982, the Tamale Central Market was set ablaze, causing the destruction of large quantities of foodstuffs, drugs and imported spare parts. Then John Ndeburge, the Northern Regional Secretary, set up a 5-member Committee of

Inquiry to investigate the circumstances leading to the incineration of the market (*West Africa*, March 8, 1982; p.684).

It did not occur to the imbecile "revolutionaries" that they were destroying their own *indigenous* markets, in existence for centuries. Nor did it occur to them that if all the traders, mostly women, were jailed and the markets burned down, food would become scarce, as there would be no place to buy it. Instead, Price Control Tribunals were set up to hand down even more stringent punishment to recalcitrant peasant food producers and traders:

The Brong-Ahafo Tribunal imposed a C12,000 fine on Grace Lamiere, a popular baker in Sunyani, for buying a bag of flour above the controlled price at Gonnorkrom . . . The Tribunal had earlier jailed Dora Mensah, also a baker, for 6 months and fined her C5,000 for exchanging cedis on the black market" (*Ghanaian Times*, June 22, 1982; p.8).

The Ashanti Regional Public Tribunal sitting in Kumasi has jailed Adu-Twum, a farmer, 5 years with hard labour for purchasing 48 cartons of cigarettes above the controlled price. In addition, the Tribunal ordered the bank accounts of one Adjaku, who sold the farmer the cigarettes, his wife and children to be frozen with immediate effect (*Graphic*, March 12, 1983; p.8).

A pregnant woman's defiance to sell her yams cheaply nearly made her lose her 18-month baby yesterday at the Kumasi Central Market. Her baby was flung to the ground and she was slapped and kicked by a policeman who insisted on paying C20 (*cedis*) instead of C100 for two tubers of yam. Yaa Amponsah, who is five months pregnant, refused to sell her yams at that low price.

This happened when a delegation of the Federation of Ghanaian Women went to the market to acquaint itself with the problems facing market women. The delegation intervened and settled the matter. Yaa Amponsah, in tears, said she bought 110 tubers of yam for C5,000 and sold a tuber for C50, thus making a little profit. The onlookers, mostly yam sellers, expressed their disgust at the injustices meted out to them by military and police personnel since price controls were instituted.

The market women cited an instance where a pregnant woman was dragged on the floor by a soldier for allegedly selling above the controlled price. The woman had a premature baby the next day. The women also recounted the hardships they went through trying to buy foodstuffs from the villages (*Graphic*, March 12, 1983; p.5).

It is difficult to suppress the outrage. Even the supposedly "backward and primitive" chiefs and kings of Africa never perpetrated such heinous atrocities against peasant traders. As a result of these inane policies by a "modern and educated" government, prices of locally produced food-stuffs rose by more than 600 percent between January 1982 and April 1983. "The price of a bag of maize, for example, went from C500 in Jan. 1982 to C4,000 in April 1983; and for 9 months, bread disappeared completely from the markets" (*West Africa*, July 11, 1983; p.1597).

The absurdity of the price control measures became apparent when the Government of Ghana could not feed the food traders it had jailed for violating price control laws. "30 prisoners died in Sunyani prison; 39 inmates at another" (*West Africa*, July 15, 1983; p.1634).

For Ghana's economy as a whole, "GNP per capita declined from $483 in 1979 to $447 in 1981, while by 1983, living standards had fallen steadily to some 16 percent of 1972 levels. The Urban Consumer Price Index (1977=100) averaged 363 in 1980, 800 in 1981, 976 in 1982 and by May 1983 was at 2222.6" (*West Africa*, March 19, 1984; p.618). The year 1983 witnessed the lowest nadir Ghana has ever sunk to in its entire history.

It is true that in 1984, Ghana and many other African countries (such as Guinea, Guinea-Bissau, Mozambique, Somalia, Tanzania and Zaire) ended their experiments with price controls at the instigation of the World Bank and the International Monetary Fund (under Structural Adjustment Programs). But the shameful aspect was that it took foreign institutions to tell African governments to remove price controls that do not exist in their own indigenous economy.

E. THE DESTRUCTION OF AFRICAN HERITAGE

So hated was colonial rule that after independence many African leaders purposely set out to destroy anything perceived to be a "colonial institution." The destruction was selective however. For example, the artificial colonial borders were not only retained but also rigidly enforced by African governments. Another negative legacy was the introduction of guns into Africa by the colonialists. Mazrui (1986) noted:

> The guns out in Africa initiated a new culture of violence. The traditional bow and arrow was a very democratic weapon, everybody could make their own bow and arrow. But gunpowder, the gun, that was a revolution in destruction. The era of explosions had arrived (p.232).

As we shall see shortly, African governments did not dispense with guns and means of destruction. But more inimical for the purposes of development was the blind rage directed against every "colonial institution." In setting out to destroy the "colonial institutions," many African leaders did not realize that they were inflicting collateral damage on the indigenous institutions as well — the very institutions which formed an integral part of their own heritage and culture.

The Indigenous Versus The Colonial Institutions

Incredible as it may sound to many, the colonialists did not really introduce any *new* institutions into Africa. What they introduced were merely the more efficient forms of already *existing* institutions — both good and bad. It was probably for this reason that colonialism lasted for nearly a century. Had it introduced institutions which were diametrically antithetical to the existing ones, the demise of colonialism would have come sooner.

The introduction of different forms of the same institutions did not mean the colonialists "invented" those institutions - an extremely important distinction. There were weapons in indigenous Africa: spears, bows and arrows. The Europeans introduced guns, which were more efficient in their kill, although the "primitive" weapons did occasionally triumph in the Ashanti and Zulu wars in the nineteenth century. But it is incorrect to assert that the colonialists "invented" weapons and the institution of war.

Similarly, the institution of slavery also existed in indigenous Africa before the arrival of the Europeans. What the Europeans did was to organize it more efficiently for the extraction of maximum profit with few moral scruples. But here again, they did not "invent" the institution of slavery.

There was also imperialism in indigenous Africa before the arrival of the Europeans. There were various empires (Asante, Mali, Ghana, Songhai, Great Zimbabwe) in which one dominant tribe subjugated other tribes. Further, the colonial policies of "indirect rule" and "assimilation" were copied from existing imperial rule in indigenous Africa, as noted earlier. For example, the Asante Empire in the 18th century was based upon "indirect rule." The conquered tribes merely had to accept a "representative" from Kumasi, the capital of the Asante Empire, and to pay a specified annual tribute in gold and slaves. Recall that the Asante "left the dynasties, the customs, the language, and even the military structure of the conquered provinces intact. All that was expected of them was the regular payment of their annual tributes and the contribution of a military contingent when called upon to do so" (Boahen, 1986; p.61). The only real difference between Asante imperial policy and British colonial policy was the color of the imperialists. Colonial policies, then, were merely a more efficient organization of what already existed.

In pre-colonial Africa, the natives gathered under a tree or at the village market square and debated an issue until they reached a consensus. When the colonialists came, they erected a building and called it "parliament," which means a "place to talk." It did not mean the colonialists "invented" the institution of public debate and free speech.

Another example was the institution of "money." Generally, money serves as a means of exchange and facilitates production and trade. Without money, an economy would grind to a snail's pace. Lenin recognized this when he said, "The best way to wreck the capitalist system is by debauching its currency."[8] Africans were using various commodity monies (cowrie shells, gold dust, salt, iron bars, etc.). It was the colonialists who introduced coins and paper currency, the more efficient forms of "money." They did not *invent* the institution of money.

Africa had bows and arrows; the colonialists brought guns. Africa had periodic rural village markets; the Europeans introduced the urban super-market. Africa was using salt and other commodities as money; the Europeans brought paper money. Africa was moving goods and people by foot (human porterage), caravans, horses and canoes. The colonialists brought more efficient forms of transportation: steamers, roads, automobiles, and railways. The colonialists did not invent these institutions; only the different forms.

Failure on the part of many African leaders to make this distinction led to an indiscriminate assault on many institutions perceived as "colonial." The essence of this destruction of the "colonial institutions" in Zaire was presented by Mazrui (1986):

> The state in Zaire (under Mobutu) is thus privatised not just economically (by appropriating its resources), not just politically (by personalising its power) but also symbolically (by personifying its sacredness). Yet while the glitter of royalty continues in mineral-rich Zaire, both the state and the economy endure the insidious effects of decay.

> *On the more positive side of his policies*, President Mobutu Sese Seko has made the principle of 'authenticity' the central doctrine of his national commitment. By 'authenticity' Mobutu means the pursuit of life-styles and tenets compatible with Zaire's indigenous and ancestral heritage. But Mobutu's most effective realization of authenticity lay not in his explicit cultural policies, or in his rhetoric and eloquence on behalf of African culture, but in his mismanagement of Zaire's economy and his form of privatization of the Zairean state. *By helping to damage and even destroy some of the inherited institutions of the colonial order, Mobutu was inadvertently carrying out patriotic cultural sabotage. By reducing moderniza-*

---

[8] That statement, incidentally, applies with equal force not only to the Soviet economy but to all economic systems that use money as well.

tion and Westernization to a farce, Mobutu helped indigenous culture to reassert itself after the massive cultural onslaught of the colonial era. As the roads decayed, and factories came to a standstill, Africans turned increasingly to older and more traditional ways of earning a living.

Also seriously damaged was the Western invention of paper money. The currency, named after the country, *zaire*, had rather rapidly fallen in value. There were times, for example 1983, when one needed a substantial bag of money in order to pay for a meal in a restaurant in Kinshasa. Mountains of paper money were exchanged for trivia. Faith in the cash economy was being substantially undermined in important sectors of Zairean society. Africans in the countryside are beginning to explore alternative forms of saving as the conflict between the indigenous heritage and the Western heritage deepens (p.18). (Italics mine).

Was Mobutu, under the mantra of "authenticity," really damaging inherited colonial institutions as Mazrui and other African intellectuals claimed?[9]

More importantly, the attack on the "colonial institutions" by African leaders not only impaired their own progress but also arrested the natural evolution of the indigenous institutions as well. Specifically, the rural village market could not develop into an urban market as this form, perceived to be "colonial," was being destroyed. By allowing the "colonial" roads and bridges to deteriorate, they impeded the movement of goods and people. Further, the decay of the colonial schools and universities meant that the indigenous institutions could not evolve into formal educational structures.

The onslaught against the "colonial" institutions, more generally, showed a woeful lack of understanding of the purpose of those institutions. The purpose of "parliament," for example, was to provide a forum to debate national issues. Such a forum existed in indigenous Africa under a tree, never

---

[9] Interestingly, Mobutu did not make his "authenticity" complete by destroying the guns, tanks, and military aircraft the colonialists introduced as well. Further, the eccentricities of Mobutu bear a sharp antinomy to indigenous African culture. African chiefs do not privatize their tribal economies or loot tribal treasuries for deposit in Swiss bank accounts. In a memorandum issued in April 1990 by the Zairean Episcopal Conference,

The Conference accuses the Mobutu regime of creating a 'hybrid' political system, which draws heavily on the 'totalitarianism' of Eastern Bloc, particularly in the methods used to obtain and maintain power. The memorandum further alleges that the move taken by President Mobutu towards 'authenticity' has encouraged the development of a power system which is 'practically monarchical' and which 'neglects traditional philosophy.' The Zairean bishops recommended that the ruling MPR give up its leading role, that freedom of expression should be allowed, and that measures be taken to prevent the flight of capital from the country (*West Africa*, April 23-29, 1990; p.687).

mind how primitive. To expunge all reminders of the hated episode of colonialism was understandable. But it did not require, for example, a destruction of the "Parliament" building. A mere change of name to say "*Indaba*" would have sufficed (just as several African countries adopted African names after independence: Gold Coast to Ghana, Rhodesia to Zimbabwe) and the "parliament" building, whatever it was called afterward, would have continued to serve its purpose.[10] But in "blowing up" the "colonial parliament" without providing an alternative forum, many African leaders denied their people public discourse of national issues and participation in the decision-making process – an African tradition.

The Plight Of The African Chief

The plight of Africa's traditional rulers (chiefs and kings) was perhaps the worst after independence. Although the nationalists and elites also betrayed them along with the rest of the African population, they suffered an additional humiliation before their own people. They were stripped of much of their traditional authority and their powers were severely curtailed.

These actions by the nationalists and elites emanated from two beliefs. The first reason for the assault against the traditional rulers was the general belief among the nationalists that the indigenous institutions, along with chieftaincy, were "too anachronistic" to facilitate the rapid transformation of Africa. The chiefs were regarded as "too conservative" and as stumbling blocks. They were identified with "the old system." After independence, the emphasis was on "the new", "the modern" and industry. The chiefs, tied up with the land and peasantry, did not fit into the grandiose schemes drawn up to modernize Africa.

The second reason was the widespread but unjustified claim that Africa's traditional rulers were "collaborators" of the colonial system, which set the stage for a diminution of their powers and desecration of their authority. According to Dr. S.K.B. Asante,

> In the eyes of Kobina Sekyi, those chiefs who co-operated with the colonial government by supporting the Provincial Council and the 'interventionist' system of indirect rule, were committing triple betrayal. First, they were betraying their old allies, the educated elite, who had now only a minor place as 'attendants' in the Provincial Council system, and who were left out of the machinery of the colonial administration. Second, by accepting new government legislation which sought to strengthen the authority and the

[10] The Japanese call their "parliament" the *Diet* and the Israelis call theirs the *Knesset*. What's the difference?

legal position of the native authorities, the chiefs were betraying the democratic principles of the traditional political system. . .Third, the chiefs were betraying themselves; for in accepting the support of the colonial government they were becoming increasingly dependent upon the British, losing their autonomy and freedom of action and becoming the tools of the colonial administration, mere subordinates in the official hierarchy (*West Africa*, Jan. 10, 1982; p.83).

It is important to see the charges of betrayal against the chiefs as emanating from a power struggle between them and the elites. The intelligentsia was naturally peeved at the perceived reluctance of the chiefs to give them what they regarded as their proper share of influence in the colonial administration. Notice too that the same charges of triple betrayal could also be levelled against the elites who assumed power after independence: they concentrated power in their own hands, betrayed the democratic principles of the traditional political system and became puppets or tools of foreign ideologies.

Traditionally the chiefs had been custodians of land in Africa. But after independence in Francophone Africa, they lost this authority when the administration became much more centralized and customary law lost virtually all standing. Land law was changed in several countries. Guinea, Cameroon, and Zaire and other states nationalized all land. The government of Sekou Toure in Guinea justified the nationalization of land on the need to transfer control from the colonialists and mining companies to the people as a whole.

In British Africa, the policy of "indirect rule" enabled the chiefs to have a substantial role in government. Towards this end, the British established a House of Chiefs in almost all its African colonies. In the early stages of colonialism, the House of Chiefs was mainly responsible for the collection of graduated head tax. But its functions were subsequently expanded to include local government, charged with additional functions such as road maintenance and construction.

The general centralization of administration which occurred in almost all of Africa after independence, except in a few countries such as Nigeria which adopted a federal system of government, left little scope for effective participation of the traditional rulers in government. The nationalists and elites were determined to reduce the powers of the chiefs and exclude them from government.

In most ex-British colonies, the chiefs did not resist the encroachment of their traditional powers. In Ghana, for example, Nkrumah reorganized local government and subordinated the chiefs to elected councillors. The House of Chiefs was subsequently abolished, with muted complaints from the chiefs. In Uganda, however, the Kabaka put up a fierce resistance, which was largely responsible for the rise of Idi Amin and Milton Obote and the subsequent degeneration into political instability and carnage.

Nigeria was the exceptional case, since its federal constitution entailed some devolution of authority toward local authorities. Furthermore, in the struggle for independence, there was little friction between the traditional rulers and the elites. In fact, the position of the National Council of Nigeria and Cameroon in its 1954 manifesto was quite explicit: "Our *Emirs* and *Obas, Obongs* and *Etubons* and *Amayonabos*, are sovereigns in their own rights. This is the verdict of our history. Accordingly, our National Rulers must fit into the position of Constitutional monarchs." But it did not turn out that way.

Beginning under Nigeria's first president, Abubakar Balewa, the Northern Region Government abolished the status of Sole Native Authority. In 1963, the Emir of Kano was capriciously removed by the federal government. After the Nigerian military coup of 1966, the traditional rulers had hoped their fortunes would improve with the new military regime. It was never to be. As the *West Africa* put it:

> They lost their Native Authority police forces under one military head of state; under another they lost more of their role and responsibilities through the Local Government reforms of 1976; they lost their critical authority over land use under a third; and they lost their own forum, the House of Chiefs, under the incoming civilian administration of the Second Republic in 1979. Under the next military government, they were forced for good measure, as it were, to witness the humiliation of two of their senior most colleagues, the *Emir* of Kano and the *Ooni* of Ife, whose passports were withdrawn in 1984 for displeasing the military government; in military idiom, the rulers were further humbled by being ordered not to leave their domain without the prior permission of their Local Government chairmen, the new and sole channel of communication between the traditional rulers and Government. Twenty-five years after the brusque removal of the *Emir* of Kano, the traditional rulers watched the dismissal of the *Emir* of Muri, once again as the outcome of a clash with government, along with central intervention over the appointment of the Sultan of Sokoto himself (20-26 March, 1989; p.431).

The general portrayal of the chiefs as "collaborators" of colonial government was dishonest. It was a calculated campaign by power-hungry elites to exclude the chiefs from power-sharing and governance. As we saw in Chapter 9, many African chiefs put up a gallant struggle against colonialism. But their weak military positions, poor organization and the sporadic nature of the resistance enabled the colonial forces to crush them easily and brutally.

Incredibly after independence, the nationalists and elites suddenly chose to ignore these acts of bravery and cultural patriotism, branding the traditional rulers "collaborators." But even where this was the case, most chiefs took decisions considered appropriate under prevailing circumstances to ensure the survival of their people. Faced with certain death and the routing of their tribes under the heels of the mighty colonial war machine, "cooperation" was perhaps the most expedient method to preserve their realms.

The African chief's foremost prerogative was the survival of his people. As we saw earlier, an African chief generally did not make policy or take decision by himself. He only executed the will of the people. He could not "sell off" his people and expect to remain chief. If a chief "collaborated," it was the collective decision of the people to seek cooperation or an alliance with the colonialists as this offered the best means of survival. Indeed, many African ethnic groups sought alliances with Europeans as protection against belligerent neighboring groups. The Fanti of Ghana, for example, entered into such an alliance with the Dutch in the 16th century, as did many other groups. Within this context, the depiction of chiefs as "collaborators" by the elites was not only unfair but disingenuous as well.

Those "chiefs" who openly collaborated with the colonial government were, in many cases, colonial appointees ("canton chiefs" in French West Africa and ward chiefs in British colonial Africa). Generally, because these "canton chiefs" derived their authority from the colonial government and felt they had the colonial army behind them, many became corrupt and autocratic. The reaction of their people is worth recalling. Some of these "chiefs" were destooled. The Ga people of Ghana destooled their *mantse* and created the post of *mankralo* when the Dutch recognized the *mantse* as the chief or political head. It may also be recalled that the Asante organized *asafo* companies, prior to the outbreak of the first world war, to destool chiefs suspected of collaborating with the colonialists. Some of these quislings were shunned or killed by their people. In the Gold Coast, the British colonialist came to the stunning realization that the Provincial Councils on which the chiefs served were of little use. As A.F.E. Fieldgate, the Acting Secretary for Native Affairs, summed it up in 1937:

> In my opinion, little importance can be attached to the activities of these (Provincial) councils. For the most part the chiefs do not carry their people with them (cited in *West Africa*, Jan. 10, 1982; p.83).

It should be pointed out, however, a few, such as Felix Houphouet-Boigny, managed to serve well in that precarious position and earned the respect of both their people and the colonial administrators.[11]

---

[11] At the age of five he became a chief himself. His uncle, Kourassi N'Go was murdered by a fanatic named Allangba, who had never forgiven the Houphouet-Boigny family for having

In fact, a strong case of collaboration or even cowardice can be levelled at many elites themselves. The struggle for independence was protracted and those elites who lacked the courage to fight colonialism had several options. They could Westernize themselves for defensive purposes. Indeed, many did, aping the trappings of Western culture in the hope that if they acted as Westerners, the colonialists would not destroy them. Other elites exercised the option of joining the colonial administration, an even more blatant case of collaboration.[12]

The final option open to the elites was exit. They could migrate or exile themselves and many did so, choosing to live in Europe for some time. The traditional rulers had no such option. It was they who had to remain, whether they liked it or not, and face the colonialists as well as their people, day in day out. They were in the eye of the struggle, constantly determining how best to deal with the situation. The elites in Europe never had to face this danger. Recall that in Angola, chiefs who failed to secure the required number of slaves demanded by the Portuguese were themselves enslaved. Over a hundred chiefs and notables were sold into slavery in a single year and another hundred murdered by the Portuguese in the 1570s. It was blatantly dishonest for Westernized elites and those who abandoned the struggle, even temporarily, to accuse the traditional rulers of "collaboration."

There are reasons for this vigorous defense of the chiefs. One cannot develop an African economy without the people (the peasants) and their natural leaders (the chiefs). Far from being useless appendages of the "old system", these chiefs are in fact Africa's most important human resource. They are closer to the people, understand their needs as well as local conditions far better than the elites sitting in air-conditioned offices in the capital cities. Furthermore, one cannot reach the African people without the use of chiefs as intermediaries. Even the colonialists recognized this (British colonial policy of "indirect rule").

After Ghana gained its independence, as in Nigeria, the elites made determined efforts to strip the traditonal rulers of their authority. Arhin (1985) charged that:

helped the French to extend their rule to this district in 1909. In 1932, he began his campaign to assist the Abengourou tribe, whose cocoa harvests were being bought at unjustly low price. In 1944, he founded the *Syndicat Agricole Africain* of the Ivory Coast. With this syndicate, the first of its kind in Africa, he prevented 20,000 small planters from being drafted for forced labor.

[12] One example was the case of the Sengalese Blaise Diagne. In 1914, he was elected by the four communes of Senegal to represent them and defend their rights in the French Parliament. But he soon began an active campaign to recruit Africans throughout French West Africa for the French war effort. And worse, he vigorously defended the colonial policy of forced labor. Needless to say, he lost his people's support and in 1928 "won" the elections only with the help of brazen French rigging and falsification of election results.

From 1951 to the present day,... the Governments of Ghana have taken away the authority of traditional rulers by passing laws (or acts) and decrees. In 1951, the Legislative Assembly passed the Local Government Ordinance which substituted Local Councils for the Native Authorities or the Council of traditional rulers. . .The Ordinance intended that elected persons rather than traditional rulers should act as the guardians of the welfare of the community. In 1954, another Ordinance of the Government deprived the traditional rulers of their representation in the Local Councils. In 1958 (a year after Ghana became independent), the Local Courts Act abolished the courts of traditional rulers and took away the authority that the Colonial Government had given them to settle disputes among the people, as they had done in the days before colonial rule itself. Also in 1958, the Legislative Assembly passed the 'House of Chiefs' Act,' which confirmed that traditional councils and the Houses of Chiefs could resolve disputes among traditional rulers (p.110).

There were subsequent laws in 1962, 1969, 1971 and various amendments. But,

The manner in which the Governments of Ghana have applied some of these laws has greatly weakened the position of traditional rulers and made it clear even to those who had no idea of the new laws that the traditional rulers can act only if the central Government wishes them to do so. The Governments have had certain rulers removed from their stools by notifying the public in the *Gazette* that they no longer 'recognize' those rulers. The most famous examples are the removal of the rulers of Akyem Abuakwa and Wenchi by the Government of Kwame Nkrumah, and the rulers of Akyem Kotoku, Wenchi and Yendi by the National Redemption Council under the Chairmanship of the late General I.K. Acheampong (Arhin, 1985; p.113).

More seriously, the humiliation of chiefs and desecration of traditional authority were acts of cultural treachery. From time immemorial, the chiefs had been the custodians and defenders of African culture, traditions, and institutions. An attack against them was synonymous with an assault on indigenous African culture, the very culture the elites vowed to defend with such slogans as Negritude and African personality. And far from being "illiterate" laggards dead set in their old ways, the chiefs have shown themselves capable of transforming themselves. Many of today's African traditional rulers are not "illiterate and backward." In fact many of them are highly educated and have held enviable careers in the civil service, as was pointed out in Chapter 3.

F. THE POLITICAL DESTRUCTION OF AFRICA

The native system of government was misunderstood by many foreign observers who were more obsessed with its "primitive" external manifestations. "Primitive" tontons called the village assembly, not a public announcement over the radio or a published notice in a newspaper. There were no administrative clerks to record the proceedings meticulously. The venue was under a tree or at an open market square, not in an enclosed roofed structure.

Granted, the facilities were "primitive". But there was a tradition of reaching a *consensus*, which is the more important observation. There was a *forum* (village assembly) and *freedom of expression* to reach this consensus. There was a *place* (village market square) to meet and the *means* (talking drums) to call such a meeting, however "primitive." And never mind the fact that no administrative clerk recorded the proceedings in writing. The institution was there, before the colonialists set foot on the continent. More crucial was the existence of the institution, not the outward manisfestations. Although elections were not held in pre-colonial Africa, the councillors and the chiefs were chosen. As Oguah (1984) argued, "If a democratic government is defined, not as one elected by the people but as one which does the will of the people, then the Fanti system of government is democratic."

The Kenya Government concurred. In a Sessional Paper (No.10 of 1963/ 65), it asserted:

In African society a person was born politically free and equal and his voice and counsel were heard and respected regardless of the economic wealth he possessed. Even where traditional leaders appeared to have greater wealth and hold disproportionate political influence over their tribal or clan community, there were traditional checks and balances including sanctions against any possible abuse of power. In fact, traditional leaders were regarded as trustees whose influence was circumscribed both in customary law and religion. In the traditional African society, an individual needed only to be a mature member of it to participate fully and equally in political affairs (paragraph 9).

The Institution Of One-Man Dictatorships

Suddenly after independence, the same African elites and nationalists who railed at the Western misconception about Africa were singing a different tune. Democracy was now a "colonial invention" and therefore alien to Africa. For example, according to Kwame Nkrumah of Ghana, an insidious dogma propagated by the imperialists was that "Western democracy and parliamentary system are the only valid ways of governing; that they constitute the only worth-while model for the training of an indigenous elite by the colonial power" (Nkrumah, 1968; p.8). Democracy an "imperialist dogma?"

Then the Kenyan government, after independence, suddenly decided that, in African society, a person was no longer born free and equal and his voice and counsel were not to be heard unless he belonged to KANU - the sole legal party. Participation in the political decision-making process, regardless of wealth and political affiliation, was not African after all. Claiming that democracy was alien, many other modern African leaders justified the imposition of autocratic rule on Africa. They declared themselves "presidents-for-life", and their countries to be "one-party states." Military dictators pointed to the warrior tradition in tribal societies to provide a justification for their rule, while other African dictators claimed that the people of Africa did not care who ruled them. Most of these claims, of course, betrayed a rather shameful ignorance of indigenous African heritage.

Professor Eme Awa, the former chairman of Nigeria's National Electoral Commission (1987), vigorously challenged these claims:

> I do not agree that the idea of democracy is alien in Africa because we had democracy of the total type - the type we had in the city-states where everybody came out in the market square and expressed their views, either by raising their hands or something like that (*West Africa*, Feb. 22, 1988; p.310).

In a similar blistering rebuttal, Ellen Johnson-Sirleaf, the ex-Finance Minister of Liberia in 1985-86, retorted:

> They tell us that democracy is a luxury in Africa; that a multi-party political system is inappropriate to our traditions; that the electoral process is foreign to our heritage and that participatory politics is potentially exploitative of our masses. Such rubbish is repeated in one form or fashion by even some of our renowned continental leaders. But we know and can see clearly through their attempts to halt the development of political institutions merely to perpetuate themselves in power. This social African legacy which has led to succession only through the barrel of a gun - a legacy which now

threatens us with two political forces - the military and the civilian,
the latter with no means to ensure full political choice or expression.
Add to this a growing disguised military as a political force in the
form of civilianised soldier and we will realise how much behind
Africans are falling in this important aspect of *national development.*
(*Index On Censorship*, May 1987; p.14).

Intellectual Repression

After independence, the nationalists did not only deny their people
political participation but also muzzled them as well. Recall that in Africa's
so-called "backward and primitive" system, the people could express their
views and wishes *freely* without fear of arrest or detention by their chiefs. But
after independence, this freedom of expression insidiously vanished in much
of Africa.

Out of the 52 African countries, including South Africa, only 8 (Algeria,
Botswana, Egypt, Namibia, Senegal, Mauritius, The Gambia and arguably
Nigeria — in 1990) tolerated criticisms of foolish government policies.
Under the colonial system, Africans could not speak out freely against
oppressive policies. Today, after gaining their independence and "freedom",
most are still muzzled by so-called "modern liberators." Currently, the rule
in Africa is to "toe the government line" or engage in a delibilitating
exercise of self-censorship. The least deviation from the "official line" elicits
sanctions, often fatal, against writers, journalists and intellectuals. As a result,
a "culture of silence" grips much of Africa. A national consensus is
impossible to reach since alternative viewpoints are not tolerated. Creativity
is lost and initiative stifled. Sensible, internal solutions elude policy-makers.
Writers, journalists and professors wither on the vine. So low was the level
of intellectual maturity that many nationalists could not distinguish between
constructive criticism and subversion. Any critic was "an enemy" to be
"liquidated." According to Richard Carver, "President Banda is now in his
90s — although in Malawi you would be locked up for suggesting such a
thing" (*Africa Report*, July-August, 1990; p.59).

When newspapers that had lavished praises upon the government carried
an occasional critique of its policies, they were shut down and their editors
arrested. Journalists who for years praised government measures suddenly
found themselves in detention when they "erred" or expressed a single
criticism.

The information media was monopolized by the state and turned into a
party propaganda organ. According to Joao Pokongo, a senior journalist at
the state newspaper, *Jornal de Angola*:

You have to remember that information is a monopoly of the Party.

Every year the MPLA-PT draws up a directive on propaganda to determine editorial policy. On top of that there is day-to-day control. In any case, every journalist knows, and has a duty to know, the essential Party line — he has to know that first so that his writing is in line with it (*Index on Censorship*, May 1990; p.22).

Maria Luiza Fancony, Programmes Director at *Radio Nacional de Angola* admitted: "We learned our trade with help from Cuban, East German and Soviet broadcasters, so naturally we learned their style of making propaganda" (*Index on Censorship*, May, 1990; p.24). Why the censorship?

According to Comrade Roberto de Almeida, Secretary for the Ideological Sphere of Angola's ruling MPLA-PT Party's Central Committee, whose duty it is to oversee the ideological soundness of all the information propagated in Angola,

His fellow Angolans are not yet intellectually mature enough for the news to be reported as it happens. Information has to be prepared in what he calls the 'correct' fashion. This responsibility cannot be left to reporters and editors, hence the need for a properly-prepared statement by the appropriate authorities (*Index on Censorship*, May, 1990; p.22).

Now the insults were coming not from white colonialists but from black neo-colonialists. The same insult was hurled from Zambia's national convention in March 1990. When delegates called for a multi-party democracy, Zambia's socialist Education Minister, Mr. Eli Mwanang'onze, called the Zambian people, "a bunch of illiterates (who) were not mature and educated enough to be pushed into a multi-party system" (*The African Letter*, April 16-30, 1990; p.9).

If a Westerner had made the same statement, the same elites (or better yet, jackasses) would have raised a storm of protests and charges of racism. The despicable irony is that this intellectual repression was now being meted out by the same African nationalists who protested vigorously against the denial of these freedoms during the colonial era.

Back in September, 1958, delegates to the Pan-African Freedom Movement of East and Central Africa met for a conference in Mwanza, Tanzania and adopted a Freedom Charter of which item No. 10 read:

The Conference calls upon the Government of East and Central Africa to remove legal restrictions against the freedom of the press and particularly condemns the unjust prosecutions and convictions which have taken place in some of these Territories against the African Press in particular (Cited in Langley, 1979:780).

Even back then, there was greater freedom of the press, measured crudely by the number of newspapers:

> In the mid-sixties, according to the London-based International Press Institute, there were 299 daily newspapers in Africa. That figure included about 40 papers in the Arab States, mostly Egypt, and about 30 in white-ruled areas of southern Africa. By the early 1980s, only about 150 dailies were left on the continent, and the shrinkage had occurred almost exclusively in black Africa. Nine countries had no newspapers at all.

> The combined daily circulation of the papers in Africa fell during that period from well over 3 million to 2 million. Thus, the circulation on a continent of 455 million people is only about two-thirds of what a single London newspaper, *The Daily Mirror*, sells in a day (Lamb, 1984; p.247).

And there certainly was far more freedom of expression and association during that hated colonial period too. In British West Africa, there was a great measure of freedom to criticize colonial policies. As Boahen and Webster (1970) stated:

> Political associations could be formed without permission from the British and newspapers could operate on the whole free of interference. English law was enforced and lawyers were available to check the worst abuses of colonial rule..

> Because of the longer tradition of Western education in the colonies there was by 1900 a sizeable number of educated people - called the elite - who through their newspapers and associations acted as watchdogs of colonial rule, protesting against its abuses. . .Many moved freely from one colony to the other in the course of their work. Isaac Wallace-Johnson, for example, had been acting editor of the *Nigerian Daily Telegraph* and general secretary of the African Workers Union which he organised in Lagos in 1931. He moved to Ghana where he worked with the Nigerian, Nnamdi Azikiwe, on the *African Morning Post*. . .

> In French West Africa only the four communes - Dakar, St. Louis, Goree, Rufisque - enjoyed a similar position to English-speaking Africans in the colony areas. Those born in the communes enjoyed the status of French citizens and could form political associations and run newspapers. . . The West African press was an important element in keeping the elite united. . . The life of many papers however was short. By 1937, fifty papers at one time or another had

been registered in Nigeria. There were, however, a number of good newspapers which lasted between thirty and forty years and left behind a solid impression on African thinking. Some of the most famous were the *Lagos Weekly Record* begun in 1890, the *Sierra Leone Weekly News* begun in 1884 and the *Gold Coast Independent* founded in 1895. In French West Africa newspaper problems were multiplied, because the readership was small and the censorship was strict. . .

Still, Dahomey's first regular newspaper was *Le Guide du Dahomey* (1920), while *L'Eclaire de la Cote d'Ivoire* (1935) was the first African-owned paper in the Ivory Coast. . .

In British West Africa the press was the most important single element in the birth and development of nationalism. The press kept a constant eye upon British officials, was quick to point out oppression, kept African claims to advancement and dignity alive, stimulated creative writing and never allowed the British to forget that their ultimate aim was to develop self-governing states. The press brought before West Africa the issues of the larger world, especially the black world extending from Africa to America and the West Indies.

The Aborigines Rights Protection Society (1897) was the first important political organization of the elite in West Africa. After its victory over a land issue in 1897 the society, composed of the Fante Chiefs (of Ghana) and their educated advisors, was a watchdog for Ghanaian interests (pp. 275-276).

But after independence, no such watchdogs and independent press were tolerated. Yet, with their characteristic penchant to see evil only in others, but not in themselves, the same African heads of state began railing against the Western media for its distortion and bias in news coverage of Africa. A Pan-African News Agency was established amid much pomp and fanfare. By 1988, even its Congolose director, Auguste Mpassi-Muba, had had enough: "It is high time the official, controlled, censored, muzzled or partisan news gives way in Africa to news based on the diversity of opinions and ideas, with free access to the various sources of official and unofficial informa-tion..The one-party states always want to control information" (*World Development Forum*, Jan. 1988). Africans are angry.

The same tomfoolery and chicanery occurred in Nigeria when the Babangida government boisterously vowed to defend human rights. But when principal officers of the Nigerian Civil Liberties Organization published a report on human rights violations in Nigeria on December 10, 1988, they were arrested and charged with subversion. In an irate editorial, the Nigerian paper, *The Daily Sketch*, scolded:

We claim to be a civilized country but we do not really respect free speech, even when it is responsible. Those who do not hold the same views with government are regarded as traitors, people to be harassed and thrown into jail without trial.

It is in the interest of government that those who hold views different from its own are allowed to air them. Nobody knows best. The person regarded as an enemy may have the better perspective." (Feb. 1, 1989).

But African dictators remained adamantly impervious to reason and appeals. "President Juvenal Habyarimana has ordered that journalists publishing false information or exciting the people against the government should be prosecuted" (*New African*, April 1990; p.17). Following this order, the Rwandan State security head, Augustin Nduwayezu, threatened journalists for writing subversive articles. Journalists like Anastase Seruvumba of *Iwacu*, father Andre Sibomana and Felicien Semusambi, of *Kinyamateka*, have been detained or placed under house arrest.

Hundreds of other editors, journalists, writers, poets, scholars and professors have also mysteriously vanished or been "liquidated" in many parts of Africa. Others still languish in jails. Today, African writers lay their lives on the line for every sentence they write and publish or for every view they espouse in public. As the magazine, *South* (Jan. 1989), deplored:

> Uganda was once one of Africa's most literary countries - Kampala was stocked with bookshops. Makerere University had a well-established drama troupe and Oko p'Bitek's poems were widely read. But economic collapse and political terror silenced the writers and emptied the bookshops. Many of Uganda's best writers are dead: Okot through drink; playwright Byron Nawada on the orders of Idi Amin; playwright and novelist Robert Serumaga, mysteriously while in exile in Kenya in 1980 (p.88).

There used to be many great African writers. During the colonial period! Today, one would have difficulty naming just ten who are not heads of state. Most people would have difficulty going beyond Wole Sonyinka, Chinua Achebe, Ngugi wa Thiongo and Kwesi Armah. Why so few great African writers today? Is Africa incapable of producing intellectual giants and writers?

The basic reason has little to do with genetic inferiority but more to do with the intellectually repressive *environment* instituted in much of Africa by modern governments. According to Lamb (1984):

> President Hastings Banda of Malawi jailed virtually the whole nongovernmental press corps in the mid-seventies. President Ken-

neth Kaunda appoints and fires newspaper editors in Zambia; in Uganda and Zaire, journalists shuttle in and out of jail so regularly that their wives don't even ask where they have been when they reappear after an absence of several days. Equatorial Guinea's president Marcias Nguema Biyogo went one step further: by the time he was overthrown and killed in 1979, *all journalists of note had been executed or were in exile* (p.246). (Italics mine).

In November, 1988, a journalist, Osborne Mkandawire, was tortured to death in Malawi. As *New African* reported:

Osborne was a 37-year old journalist employed by the Malawi Department of Information in the office of the President and Cabinet.

Mkandawire was arrested in early May 1988, reportedly on suspicion of passing information about Malawi to foreign journalists. He was detained without being charged at Mikuyu Prison near Zomba where he is reported to have been severely tortured. He apparently died in November 1988, from injuries sustained under torture. . .

The Malawian authorities have over the years imprisoned journalists and writers whose work was interpreted as critical of the government of Life-President Kamuzu Banda. In 1987, the country's best known poet, Jack Mapanje, was arrested for preparing to publish a volume of poetry that the government apparently suspected would be critical of its policies; he is still in detention, held without charge or trial (April 1989; p.37).

In September 1989, exiled Malawian journalist Mkwapatira Mhango was assassinated in Zambia by agents of the Malawian government. He was one of 9 persons who died after his house was fire-bombed in the Zambian capital of Lusaka on October 13, 1989. Mhango was an official of the exiled Malawi Freedom Movement (MAFREMO). Mhango's crime was to publish an article in the foreign press critical of the Malawi government policies.

Mkwapatira Mhango's brother, Goodluck Mhango is also a political prisoner — apparently in reprisal for Mkwapatira's writings. Goodluck Mhango — a veterinary surgeon, was arrested in Sept. 1987 —shortly after Mkwapatira had published an article which irked someone in the Malawian leadership. The police beat him — causing serious head injuries. He remains in detention without charge at Dzeleka Prison (*The African Letter*, Nov. 16-30, 1989; p.18).

Write or say something which an African government does not like and "Poof!" one is dead or in detention. Africans are angry and fed up with these barbarous acts. It is this intellectual barbarism on the part of "modern and educated" African leaders that has seriously impeded Africa's economic development. No words should be minced here. Twenty-four of the thirty-six poorest nations in the world are in black Africa, despite its tremendous natural resource wealth. Solutions to Africa's intractable problems *cannot* be found in an atmosphere of fear and a "culture of silence" in which people are afraid to propose and debate alternatives. If society's problems are solved by killing people with alternative ideas Africa should be the most developed continent. But it is not. Yet, imbeciles continue to butcher those with different viewpoints. These atrocities have silenced millions in Angola, Ethiopia, Ghana, Liberia, Uganda, Zaire and many other countries. This fear has made it virtually impossible for Africans themselves to come forward with their own solutions to their problems. The inevitable consequence has been a grievous banishment from Africa of a free marketplace of ideas and home-grown solutions. As a result, solutions to African problems must come from abroad, perpetuating the myth that Africans cannot think for themselves and devise solutions to their own problems. Worse, the imported solutions often prove unsuitable for Africa's unique socio-economic topography and circumstances, resulting in wasted foreign exchange expenditures.

Everyone agrees that Africa's problems must be solved by Africans. But how on earth is this possible when they have no *freedom of expression* to propose and debate new ideas and solutions? As Maina wa Kinyatti, former senior lecturer in history at Kenyatta University, bitterly complained:

> Lecturers and intellectuals are arrested because of their ideas. You cannot comfortably teach because the police is planted in the classrooms. Whatever you teach is taped, and if you eventually say something critical against the president, you are detained. Censorship is so tight that even KANU people are scared of what to write because they know that the police can come to their houses and take them away (*Africa Report*, July/August 1989; p.58).

From the University of Ghana, Sahabu Wakilu wrote:

> The political environment prevailing in Ghana today can best be described as 'a culture of terror' and not 'a culture of silence' as the Head of State Flt-Lt. Jerry Rawlings wants us to believe.
>
> If Rawlings is genuinely concerned with the 'culture of silence,' why did his government make attempts on the life of Professor Adu Boahen after the Professor had made his views known on the current political happenings in Ghana?

The clandestine killing of Ghanaians considered to be opponents of the government is now an open secret. Therefore the current indifference of Ghanaians to the government's educational, economic and political reforms is a manifestation of general discontent with the government. If Ghanaians are not talking today, it is because we know it is of no use talking. I know we have enough guts left to ask the government: Why waste 6 billion cedis on an election of district assemblymen who would be responsible to the government alone - when they could have been appointed? Why can't the 6 billion be judiciously used to repair our roads or even build new houses for the suffering workers of Ghana? May I also use this opportunity to appeal to foreign diplomats on visits to Ghana to refrain from making statements hailing the 'success' of the economic recovery program. If it were, why the Program of Action to Mitigate the Social Cost of Adjustment and Development (PAM-SCAD)? (*New African*, January 1989; p.56).

The situation is even more infuriating considering the fact that most African nations have signed or ratified the OAU's African Charter on Human and Peoples' Rights; for example, Cameroon did so in 1987, Ghana in 1989 and Malawi in February 1990.

Article 6 of the Charter states clearly: "*No one may be arbitrarily arrested or detained.*" **Article 7** guarantees "the right to a fair trial in an independent court with a defense lawyer." **Article 8** advocates "religious tolerance" and freedom from religious persecution. More importantly, **Article 9** of the African Charter guarantees "the right to free expression" — freedom which existed in indigenous Africa.[13]

Give Africa back to its traditional chiefs. At least, these so-called "backward and illiterate" chiefs were intellectually mature enough to tolerate criticism and allow *freedom of expression*. African chiefs not only welcomed but also solicited alternative viewpoints as required by custom. In so doing, they availed themselves of options that they might otherwise have overlooked. Take an idea to a chief and he will examine it very carefully, even if it differs radically from his own. If the idea makes sense, the chief will thank you for it. But not many "modern and educated" African leaders.

Bishop Desmond Tutu, a former Nobel Peace Prize-winner, said exactly as much in a speech at Oxford University, London, in June 1990:

I should confess to our shame that on the whole we in modern Africa have not been able to accommodate differences of opinion.

---

[13] African intellectuals, dissidents, lawyers, editors, journalists, opposition leaders and freedom-loving organizations should photostat (xerox) the African Charter on Human and Peoples' Rights and sell or distribute copies to all Africans.

When you differ from someone. . .if you don't agree four-square at every point with him, that is taken to mean that you are his enemy. But that is not traditionally African. . .In traditional Africa, a chief was a good chief because he could work out a consensus, and the consensus arose because people had different points of view. I have to confess, that is a fundamental weakness that we have at the present time (*New African*, August 1990; p.35).

It is this weakness or intolerance of alternative viewpoints that lies at the root of the continent's problems. Without freedom of expression that admits intellectual pluralism, Africa will never solve its problems. Writing in *The Baltimore Sun* (July 22, 1990), S.M. Khalid observed succinctly with admirable prescience: Most traditional rulers (chiefs) arrived at decisions through exhaustive debate involving the entire group and only after a consensus had been reached to satisfy all parties, not through imperious personal decree.

The problem in Africa, as elsewhere, is that without a channel for dissent or public debate, opposition groups that have inevitably emerged will be forced to seek redress through political violence.

The African continent is replete with many such bloody examples, innumerable coups bringing worse military governments to power and civil wars raging in Sudan, Ethiopia, Angola, Mozambique, Somalia and Liberia. Settlements of all these conflicts will hinge on the inclusion of political pluralism by different groups (p.3E).

Military Rule: The Scourge Of Africa

Of all the alien systems imposed on Africa after independence, none has been more heinous and tyrannical than military rule. There is no question that the military plays a vital function in a modern society. It not only defends the territorial integrity of a nation against external aggression but also plays an indispensable role in the maintenance of law and order. Without this, a society can make little progress in its economic development efforts. Unfortunately, this function of the military is not well understood in Africa.

The military has now become the scourge of Africa and the bane of its development. While the roads deteriorated with yawning pot-holes and the universities as well as public services (electricity, sanitation, water) decayed, African dictators found the wherewithal to squander scarce resources on the military. According to Whitaker (1988), "the proportion of African funds going to equip and pay the military has been steadily rising, reaching for example over 40 percent in Ethiopia, and 25 and 20 percent respectively in drought-ravaged Mauritania and Mali"(p.43).

Military expenditures by developing nations have soared over the past two decades. In its 1990 Report on Human Development, the United Nations Development Program deplored the fact that "arms imports in developing countries skyrocketed from only $1 billion in 1960 to nearly $35 billion in 1987. Three-quarters of the global arms trade involves exports to developing countries. Some of the poorest and least developed countries spend far more on their military than on their education and health" (cited by *The Washington Times*, May 25, 1990; p.A9).

Indeed, Sammy Kum Buo, Director of the UN Center for Peace and Disarmament, lamented that "Africa spends about $12 billion a year on the purchase of arms and the maintenance of the arms forces, an amount which is equal to what Africa was requesting in financial aid over the next 5 years" (*West Africa,*May 11, 1987; p.912). Military spending, according to the United States Center For Defense Information, reached $16.9 billion in 1983, up 400 percent from $3.8 billion in 1973. Sixteen African countries spent more on arms than they received in aid. Libya topped the list with $1.9 billion in arms purchases against $52 million in aid. Angola, hard hit by drought, spent $525 million on arms and received $502 million in aid. Nigeria and Mozambique spent $430 million and $260 million respectively on arms and received $48 million and $242 million respectively in aid. Angola even spent more per capita on the military ($892) than on education ($310) and health ($115). Many other African countries similarly spent more on the military than on health: Gabon ($88, $49); Congo ($45, $25); Mauritania ($31, $6); and Zimbabwe ($52, $17). Top arms suppliers to Africa in the 1980s were the Soviet Union (50 percent); France (11 percent); Italy (5 percent); West Germany (5 percent); the United States (3 percent). The Warsaw Pact countries jointly accounted for 58 percent and NATO 31 percent. All these arms purchases brought not an iota of order and stability but instead chaos and carnage to Africa. Most maddening, the arms were used to oppress and slaughter the African people.

In Liberia, the late Samuel Doe's military regime degenerated into savage barbarism that often included grosteque dismemberment and mutilation of dead bodies as well as disgusting cannibalism. In August 1984, students at the University of Liberia went on demonstration to protest the arrest of Professor Amos Sawyer. Troops from President Doe's Executive Guard, stormed the campus to squash the demonstration and fired indiscriminately into the students. After a failed coup attempt in December 1985, this is what Doe's military soldiers did to the coup leader, Quikwonkpa Gbenyon:

At the Barclay Training Ground, before hundreds of spectators, Quiwonkpa's body was chopped up into bits in a macabre cannibal-istic ritual by some of President Doe's soldiers who, astonishingly in these modern times, still believe that by eating bits of a great warrior's body, some of that greatness would come to them. The heart, of course, was the prize delicacy. . .The blood-curdling dismemberment of Quiwonkpa was carried out in the open before hundreds of market women and shoppers. . .I personally saw two soldiers outside the 'Talk of the Town' pub on Macdonald Street dangling what they said was Quiwonkpa's manhood. Other media colleagues reported seeing two fingers, presumably Quiwonkpa's, at Water Street being dangled by jubilant soldiers who indicated they would devour their prize trophy at the end of the day (*West Africa*, Dec. 23/30, 1985. Also quoted in *Index On Censorship*, July, 1988; p.11).

After another abortive coup by Dr. Togba na Tippoteh in December 1989, Doe's soldiers unleashed savage retribution that resulted in the massacre of over 3,000 innocent civilians and sent over 200,000 refugees pouring into Ivory Coast and Guinea. The villages of Kahnplaye and Butuo, for example, were completely destroyed and large parts of the Liberian countryside in Nimba province were virtually depopulated. "A young engineer, Robert Phillips, in no way involved in the uprising (against Doe) was brutally murdered in his bed and his body dismembered" (*New African*, March, 1990; p.17).

According to *The New York Times* (July 9, 1990):

Monrovia, Liberia. July 8 — A young man was stopped last night as he was trying to reach his home. It was dark, and long past Monrovia's dusk-to-dawn curfew.

"The soldiers said, 'Didn't you hear there was a curfew?'" said Dr. Reginald Moreels, a surgeon working at St. Joseph's Catholic Hospital here. 'Didn't you hear about it?' they repeated.

To drive the point home, the soldiers (Doe's) then cut off both his ears and forced him to eat them.

"All night he was bleeding," Dr. Moreels said, "and this morning he was brought to the emergency room here, where all we could do was stitch him up" (p.A3).

The Washington Post (July 10, 1990) also reported that:

In one incident, three soldiers drove a man to Monrovia's Atlantic Ocean shore, ordered him out of the car and shouted: "Go to the beach." The man waved his identity papers.

All three then pumped bullets into his head, back and legs from their US-supplied M-16 automatic rifles just outside the front gate of the home of Dennis Jett, second-in-command at the US Embassy. The soldiers told reporters who watched: "This man is a rebel."

The troops said they believed the man was a rebel because he said he was going to buy rice but had only $1.15 in his pocket. A cup of rice now costs $2 (p.A15).

In Nigeria, on January 25, 1988, the home of Chief Moshood Abiola in Lagos, was invaded by two truck-loads of junior air-force officers led by a Flight Lieutenant. With guns blazing, they overpowered his private security men, disconnected his phone and arrested 15 members of his household, locking them up at Ikeja Airforce barracks. The reason for the attack was a minor traffic accident involving a car driven by Chief Abiola's son, Ayodeji and another driven by an air-force corporal, M.D. Danjuma earlier in the day.

What was alarming about Nigeria was the increasing level of military barbarism. As *New African* reported:

- In Lagos, on January 19, police stormed the chamber of a Senior Magistrate, Mrs. Opeyemi Oke, angry that she acquitted a truck driver whom they claimed had not stopped when challenged by a senior police officer.

- On January 22, soldiers went on rampage at Oshodi, Lagos, burning at least 7 cars of unsuspecting road users when the wife of a soldier was knocked down by another driver. She was trying to cross the Express motorway, instead of using an overhead bridge meant for commuters. Many innocent civilians were also severely beaten up.

- On February 4, Willingie Sagie, 43, the political correspondent of Bendel State Government-owned newspaper, the *Nigerian Observer*, was given 50 strokes of cane by air force men and also forced to drink sewage water, after a minor traffic argument with one of them. A day earlier at Idioroko border, an angry soldier pumped a bullet into the mouth of a Senior Customs Officer, Mr. Tanimowo after an argument over who should seize contraband. Last year, an air-force officer in Lagos sprayed fuel on a detainee and set him ablaze when he refused to confess to a crime.

- On January 22, a group of naval ratings burnt down an office block in protest over the alleged killing of a member of the navy.

Such stories of military vandalism are an almost daily occurrence (April, 1988; p.10).

Elsewhere in West Africa, abductions and brutality by military barbarians were the norm. On December 1, 1988, Mr. Victor Mintah, the past president of the Ghana Institute of Chartered Accounts died in custody. According to *West Africa*:

Mr. Mintah, 55, was taken from his home by agents of the Bureau of National Investigations (BNI) on July 18, 1988. At the time of his death, no charges had been preferred against him, and according to informed sources, he had not even been questioned during his six months of detention. His 78-year old mother has reportedly been in a coma since she heard of the death of her only child. The BNI is reportedly still using his two private cars - a Mercedes Benz and an Opel Kadett - which they allegedly took from his home when they arrested him (Jan. 30 - Feb. 5, 1989; p.164).

On July 17, 1988, elementary school teachers in Ghana decided to stage a 3-day strike.

The teachers' action was triggered by the beating and shaving of six teachers at the Michael Camp military barracks elementary school on July 13. According to the protesting teachers, as part of activities marking the inauguration of the Greater Accra GNT Ladies Society, July 13 was set aside for the cleaning of schools and their grounds. The five teachers together with another teacher arrived at the school slightly late. Major Blake attacked them and had their heads shaved. They were then lined up before the pupils who were ordered to hoot at them. After this treatment, they were locked up in a military guardroom till 6.00 pm that evening (*West Africa*, August 1, 1988; p.1413).

Even this constituted "an improvement in military-civilian relations." Back in 1982, during the heady days of Ghana's "Revolution", common courtesy and decency were constant casualties. Consider:
- Military personnel bundled innocent civilians into articulated trucks and seized 'tro-tro' vehicles at gun-point to load fertilizer at Tema harbor (*Daily Graphic,* Dec. 11, 1982; p.4).
- *The Pioneer* has lamented the fact that certain uniformed men think the revolution has given them a carte blanche to terrorize civilians on the flimsiest excuse.

The newspaper mentioned four recent incidents: the Kumasi Technical Institute student who was shot dead by a soldier at a barrier; the soldier who shot and killed a porter at Ejura, Kumasi; a civilian beaten to death by soldiers for (jumping a queue for soap); and some policemen who attacked the people of Adunku, Ejisu District on their farms, injuring many of them (*West Africa*, Jan. 13, 1983; p.295).

- In Kumasi, a civilian, Mr. Daniel Amoah, was beaten to death for challenging soldiers not to jump a tro-tro (passenger vehicle) queue. After beating Mr. Amoah violently in front of hundreds of timid civilians, the soldiers took him in a taxi to the Two Brigade headquarters, where some soldiers advised them to take him to hospital. On the way, the soldiers dumped Mr. Amoah in the bush and he died soon afterwards (*West Africa*, April 25, 1983; p.1043).

Elsewhere in Africa, military barbarism was running amok. In August 1988, two Belgians, Paul Staes and Jef Ulburghs, tabled a litany of horrifying human rights abuses in Zaire. The report catalogued a series of damning atrocities perpetrated by the Zairean army against the citizens. Over the summer of 1988, the Zairean Green Berets killed several peasants and merchants in the Northern Kivu (Eastern Zaire) region. The army also went on the rampage, plundering and looting in this area and in the Kibali-Ituri region. The Roman Catholic Bishop of Kataliko from Northern Kivu implored Field Marshal Mobutu to keep his troops inside the barracks. According to *New African* (September 1988):

> The two Euro MPs also gave details of rape involving three schoolgirls, Pauline Kavugo (15), Vira Bayira (13) and Rose Kyakimua (10). The three girls were raped by six soldiers in the town of Lumee. There were reports indicating that two other schoolgirls were raped by soldiers in Goma and Bulera-Vuhovi. According to the same sources, 88 women who participated in a women's demonstration on April 19 in Kinshasa suffered the same fate (p.22).

A Zairean exile, Lucien Naki, had this to say:

> The beating and murdering of civilians is declared a security matter. Even murder in Mobutu's cabinet is classified as a state secret. . .Mobutu is a thoroughly unbalancing and destructive force for Africa and for the rest of the world. For too long the world has laughed him off, for too long the world has excused him. Too many exiles have been frightened into silence by the fear that he could wreak terrible revenge on friends and relatives remaining behind in Zaire. I know that by speaking out I risk more lives, but I also know that my silence will guarantee nobody's safety. . .Thousands of Zairean students, on whose training the government had spent millions of dollars don't come back after their studies abroad. More of Zaire's professional talent lives out of the country than inside. Mobutu is worse than Botha and his apartheid (*New African,* May 1989; p.41).

In Burundi in August 1988, the military government, run by the Tutsi minority, massacred an estimated 20,000 Hutus — a number far greater than the official count of 5,000. United Nations officials at refugee camps near the border with Rwanda told of soldiers chasing fleeing Hutus, machine-gunning and bayoneting many. The scale and barbarity of the military carnage shocked and left many Western aid officials exasperated. "Why are we here," asked one European diplomat. "Morally, we should get out and slam the door."

Civil wars and "final offensive" campaigns provided military regimes with the excuse to perpetrate heinous atrocities against innocent peasants. *Africa Watch*, in its Report: *Denying the Honour of Living: Sudan, a Human Rights Disaster 1986-89*, rebuked:

> The Bashir government has embarked on the repression of political opposition in Khartoum on a scale never seen before. In a direct attack on the institutions of civil society, the RCC has purged the judiciary, the army, and civil service, banned trade unions and any form of protest, silenced the press, and detained several hundred political prisoners, including doctors, politicians, journalists and trade unionists. It has set up a new and unofficial security agency which has tortured and humiliated detainees in secret detention centers. . .

> While urging the SPLA to show full respect for human rights, including those of prisoners of war and non-combatants, the Report lays down 8 tough recommendations to the government, from releasing all political prisoners and abolishing the military-run kangaroo courts where defendants are denied lawyers, to disarming the militia and *enforcing the law against slavery* (*Africa Report*, May/June, 1990; p.24).

Next door in Ethiopia, on May 12, 1988, Comrade Mengistu's army entered the town of She'eb, in northeastern Eritrea, and rounded up a large group of about 400 people, men, women and children, including the elderly, the disabled and the blind. Accusing them of collaborating with the Eritrean People's Liberation Front (EPLF), they drove two tanks over the people while simultaneously machine-gunning those who tried to escape.

> Amna, a young woman, six months pregnant, survived because she fell under the trunk of a large tree. Feigning death, she lay until nightfall among the carnage of her fellow townspeople. Five small children, probably covered by their parents for protection, also survived and wandered screaming among the bodies. Amna heard the soldiers arguing whether to kill the children, then agreeing not to waste bullets on them as they would anyhow soon die of thirst.

> At night Amna crept out among the bodies and collected the

children. She hid them under her, and for the next three days and nights they lay pretending death, desperately thirsty, while the soldiers still hung around. When they left she crept away with the children, not knowing where to go until she found a shepherd who gave them water and took them to an EPFL office.

Eighty thousand people escaped from She'eb that day. All the shops were looted and burned by the Ethiopian army, who also slaughtered 10,000 sheep, goats, cattle and camels, putting some of the carcasses down the town's only well, thus polluting it for ever (*New African*, October 1988; p.24).

These savage brutalities drew a protest from Goshu Wolde, Ethiopia's Foreign Minister: "I cannot, in good conscience, continue to serve a government whose shortsightedness and rigidly doctrinaire policies are leading the country and the people into misery and destruction. . .I have watched with helplessness as my country slipped further and further into authoritarianism and absolute dictatorship." In neighboring Somalia, it was the same story of slaughter and carnage. In May 1988, the military government of Somalia had dropped bombs on its own citizens when they demonstrated against President Siyad Barre's 20-year despotic rule. Barre seized power in a military coup on October 21, 1969, and since then the military has sunk deeper from one level of depravity to another. Adam Egeh charged:

Torture, mass detention, execution, human rights violations, confiscation of private properties and the prohibition of all political parties became widespread. In all parts of Somalia, the military regime of Mr. Barre has the ultimate *carte blanche* to either detain or execute any Somali citizen the regime is not satisfied with. In fact, for the past 20 years, hundreds of thousands of innocent people were put to death or imprisoned without going through the legal court procedures. Many politicians, businessmen, religious leaders and young students disappeared and their whereabouts are not known to date. The number of prisoners of conscience is quite enormous in Somalia and international journalists were long banned from reporting on such situation (*The African Letter*, April 16-30, 1990; p.3).

Indeed, one of Barre's own military intelligence officers confessed in an article to the *New African* (July 1989):

I, CALI SELEBAAN SUULEED (HUUBE), am a former Intelligence Officer of the National Security Service of Somalia (NSS), and can confirm the inhuman and oppressive measures instituted in Northern Somalia, in general, and in Northwest Somalia, in particular. In the last few years NSS forces have conducted massive lootings, kidnappings, rapings, killings and the harsh imprisonment of innocent people, without trial. For example, here follows a list of people arbitrarily killed in Burao, subsequent to the May 1988 incident (p.22. He went on to list 68 names).

Church leaders were not spared. Bishop Salvatore Colombo, the Papal Nuncio and a man committed to human rights, was mysteriously murdered. In July 1989, in the early hours of the *Iid Al Adha* day, government forces swooped down and arrested 6 leading Imams after the morning prayers.The *New African* (November 1989) reported that:

Military units, already deployed, showed as little respect for human life as they had in Hargeisa and Burao in the north. Whole sections of the crowd of worshippers were gunned down. Innocent people were rounded up in the hundreds and many were murdered and buried on the Jasira beach.

New African has the names of 144 persons seized from their homes in the Wadajir (Madina) quarter of Mogadishu, on the night of July 16, 1989, who were killed in Danane prison and on the beach.

As the diplomatic corps looked on in horror, arrests continued. . .Even the *Times of London* called for the demise of the unpopular and discredited regime of General Siyad Barre. Research by *New African* has revealed that. . .over 1,000 died (p.11).

In March 1990, *Africa Watch*, a U.S.-based Human Rights group, issued a report entitled: *Somalia: A Government at War with its Own People* (New York). It charged "the regime with responsibility for the deaths of 50,000 to 60,000 civilians since hostilities broke out between the government and rebels from the Somali National Movement (SNM), while half a million have fled to neighboring countries" (*Africa Report*, March-April 1990; p.10).

In hundreds of interviews with refugees, the human rights group described in chilling detail how the government, frustrated in its attempts to defeat the rebels, turned its guns against the civilian population. According to the report, the army engaged in systematic violence toward Isaak clan members in northern Somalia, burning and bombing their villages and detaining hundreds for suspected association with the SNM.

Originally confined to the north, the abuses soon spread to the southern and central parts of the country. "Entire regions have been devastated by a military engaged in combat against its own people, resembling a foreign occupation force that recognizes no constraints on its power to kill, rape or loot" according to the report. Earlier in 1986, an illiterate Isaak peasant farmer was arrested for not informing Siyad Barre's military government of the presence of Somali National Movement (SNM) troops in his area:

> This man lived in a village between Berbera and Hargeisa. He did not know the difference between government troops and SNM soldiers. Yet he was arrested by the National Security Service who cut part of his tongue away with a pair of scissors because he was an Isaak (*New African*, July, 1989; p.6).

Hopping over Kenya into Uganda offered no respite from military barbarism and carnage. Uniformed bandits roamed the Ugandan countryside, pillaging villages and raping women. Even the urban areas were not safe. They relieved car owners of their possessions at gun-point.

> In the last few months, President Museveni's National Resistance Army soldiers have been using their uniforms as cover for armed robbery. They snatch cars at gun-point and drive them around town after changing the registration numbers. In June, two soldiers stopped a prison officer on the Kampala-Jinja road and took away his car. . .Early this year, 20 diplomatic vehicles were snatched in Kampala alone (*New African*, Oct. 1988; p.17).

In northern Uganda, "the army has destroyed grain stores, burned huts — sometimes with villagers inside — shot civilians and taken thousands of prisoners. Lots of people have run away. About 100,000 displaced villagers are encamped in Gulu alone, with 50,000 more in the surrounding area" (*The Economist*, July 8, 1989; p.45).

In November 1989, Major Okello Kolo, a former member of President Museveni's ruling National Resistance Council and the NRA High Command, broke his silence and spoke out to *New African*:

> Incidents of rape, looting, slashing of food crops, razing of homes and food stores, theft of livestock has been going on unabated at the hands of the troops of the NRA. . .Already 150,000 people in the north and east have perished at the hands of the NRA and over 4,000 have been forced into exile (*New African*, November 1989; p.23).

Major Kolo also testified to seeing armored personnel-carriers running over unarmed villagers, killing them. Barely three months after that expose, Major Kolo was found murdered near his village.

In February 1990, the NRA deployed thousands of troops to launch a final offensive against rebel soldiers in the eastern Uganda district of Kumi. As usual, the real victims were innocent peasants caught in the crossfire who had nothing whatsoever to do with the military bandits on either side of

Uganda's senseless civil war. The operation began in earnest when army trucks invaded villages and ordered the people to leave for specified camps.

> The people were simply dumped there and told to fend for themselves by building makeshift huts to live in. It is estimated that over 100,000 people are now cramped into camps where they are without water or latrines. Relief organizations are often denied access and the people are underfed sometimes near to starvation. At Kidongole camp, a Red Cross team was beaten up by the camp commander who refused them access to the starving people. . .

> Apart from the overcrowding, the camps are littered with human faeces as the people have no proper latrines. In some camps soldiers rape little girls. One was reported to be only 9 years old. . .

> At the end of February, health workers at the Church of Uganda hospital, Ngora, the only one in the area, reported that dozens of children had died from diarrhoea related diseases (*New African*, May 1990; p.18).

Back in the early 1970s, it may be recalled that the homes and businesses of the Asian community in Uganda were forcibly seized during Amin's arrant dictatorship. Military vandalism and robberies were rife during Amin's rule.

In the seventies, the military in Africa professed itself to be waging a crusade against corruption and mismanagement in government. But in the 1980s, it became more obsessed with political power itself. The least sign of opposition to military rule was squelched with brutal abandon. Kidnappings and "murders by road accidents" were widely used by Africa's military dictators to frighten their people and maintain themselves in power. One such victim was a Roman Catholic priest, Father Silvio Sindambiwe of Rwanda, who died on November 7, 1989, along with two passengers when his car was in collision with a lorry.

Were these the "professional soldiers" that Africa inherited from the colonial era? Atta Poku of Kumasi, Ghana, did not think so. In a letter, he wrote:

> Africa today has been turned into the world's largest military zone by African soldiers, and one wonders if this is more neo-colonialism. That no military regime has ever succeeded in building any viable economy anywhere in the world, can best explain why Africa is so undeveloped. Under the pretext of revolution, African soldiers turn their countries into fertile grouds for all sorts of unworkable Marxist theories, blinding the people with all sorts of socialist jargons.

The paradox of the African soldier is that they always begin as socialist revolutionaries and end up in the West as one of the bourgeois class they had condemned at the peak of their revolutions. Why these revolutionaries refuse to live their exile in Soviet-bloc countries baffles me. The day African soldiers will realise that a soldier's place is at the barracks and not at state house, mother Africa would begin to write a progressive report (*New African*, August 1989; p.6).

Even the World Bank, which characteristically refrains from political commentaries, is becoming alarmed at the escalating military expenditures:

Military spending has diverted enormous resources from southern Africa's development, and has consumed nearly 50 percent of government expenditures in the countries experiencing the worst destabilization (*Sub-Saharan Africa: From Crisis to Sustainable Growth*, Nov. 1989; p.23).

The *West Africa* magazine, which historically shied away from criticism of African governments, has also begun to complain:

During the 1970s, arms importation by African countries grew faster than any other region in the world, doubling between 1970-77. Since the beginning of the 1980s, this trend has tailed off, due as much to the saturation of military inventories, as the continent-wide economic crisis. But in most African states, defence still consume an excessive share of the national budgets, easily outstripping social spending. One million dollars could provide 1,000 classrooms for 30,000 children, and yet it is the cost of a modern tank. The price of a single helicopter is equivalent to the salary of 12,000 schoolteachers. The policy choice of more tanks, means less classrooms, with inevitable consequences for economic growth and social development. . .

Theoretically, an efficient military institution is an investment. It ensures stability and maintains the stability necessary for economic growth. But all too often in the African setting they are part of the problem. African armies modelled on the Western example, as opposed to Frelimo in Mozambique and the NRA in Uganda, are not productive; they simply consume. There is also a very high probability that the tanks and armoured cars bought for the defence of the country's frontiers', will be used to surround the radio station for the announcement of a military coup, which is statistically likely to be followed by a countercoup (27 March - 2 April, 1989; p.508).

Even military officers themselves are beginning to speak out. Retired General Olusegun Abasanjo, former head of state of Nigeria, has added his voice to the chorus, demanding cuts in soaring military expenditures. He blamed Nigeria's economic problems on the exorbitant amounts of money being spent on defence. "He said Nigeria could not afford to spend 50 percent of its income on defense expenditures and debt servicing and be able to make progress" (*The African Letter*, April 1-15, 1990; p.6).

Former Nigerian Head of State, General Yakubu Gowon, also called for a re-evaluation of the role of the military in African governance. In a lecture at the Oxford and Cambridge Club entitled, "Charting Nigeria's Path to Democracy in this Decade and Beyond," General Gowon observed:

> Nigeria's problems started shortly after independence because the army allowed itself to be polluted and politicised, hence the incessant coups and counter-coups. The military intervention in politics in 1966 started a chain of reaction whose deleterious effects are still relevant in our national life even today, so many years after the ill-advised putsch. . .
>
> The military should not get itself involved in politics. The sooner they leave the stage the better, or else the people may rise up against them (*West Africa*, June 11-17, 1990; p.993).

But these military regimes could not have existed without the support of African intellectuals. Even the egregious Doe regime in Liberia could always find educated oafs willing to sacrifice their principles for a brand new Mercedes Benz. Unbelievably, many African intellectuals, scholars and professionals (lawyers, judges, and even diplomats) still vigorously defend illiterate military regimes, insisting they are uniquely African because of Africa's warrior tradition. The worst of the lot are Africa's "chameleon" diplomats, who boisterously defend brutal policies in their home countries but suddenly change their tune as soon as their governments are overthrown. For example, Zaire's Ambassador to the United States Tatanene Manata wrote:

> With regard to Zaire's protection of human rights, the Department of Citizen's Rights and Liberties was created in 1986 and was the first ministry in Africa dedicated to the protection of human rights. . .This department has begun to fulfill its mandate to inform the citizenry of their rights and to investigate and prosecute violations of those rights in Zaire (*Washington Post*, Oct. 4, 1990; p.A26).

God help Africa when a brutal military regime is the first to set up a department to protect human rights of the oppressed. An exhaustive search and study of indigenous African political systems do not reveal soldiers or men of uniform serving as chiefs or heads of village governments. The heads of these governments were always civilian. The traditional function of soldiers was to defend the village and the tribe against rival tribes or slave raiders. It was in such defensive encounters that the soldiers proved their valor and earned great respect from the people.

It is true that there were warrior tribes and that a warrior could become chief, but such specialization and achievement could scarcely be characterized as forming a "military government" in the sense that all positions of power were occupied by soldiers. In indigenous Africa, the warriors were drawn from the younger age grades. For example, among the Bantu Tiriki of Western Kenya, the warrior age group was called the *mayina*. The age of this group ranged from 26 to 40 years of age. Their formal responsibility was *bali na shibala* ("hold the land" or guarding the country). Warfare was formerly the primary activity of the warriors, but when not engaged in combat, the Swazi warriors "served as labor battalions on public works" (Gibbs, 1965; p.492). In the Zulu kingdom, the warriors in peacetime worked in the *amakhanda* - the military homestead of the royal house. There, the warriors were responsible for "building military kraals, planting, reaping, and making gardens for the king" (Guy, 1979; p.29).

Many ethnic groups did not have standing armies. As Boahen and Webster (1970) put it, "professional military classes were small and standing armies rare" (p.228). In the face of imminent external threat, the chief would summon young men of a certain age grade and present them to the king for war. "In most states, the people *were* the army and the monarchs had no independent full-time forces of their own" (Bates, 1987; p.41). After a war, the army, the young men assembled for that purpose, was disbanded.

The function of the military in indigenous Africa was well understood by the supposedly "primitive peasants." Only in a few African empires and kingdoms, such as Dahomey and Zulu, did the military play an active role in government. But three or four out of over 2,000 chiefdoms, kingdoms and empires in Africa's history hardly constitute "a traditional pattern." Even then, the Dahomean and Zulu military did not turn their guns against their own people, the very ones they were supposed to defend against marauding neighboring tribes. At least, those pre-colonial soldiers knew who their real enemies were.

The historical and cultural evidence does not lend support to military rule as uniquely African. In fact, "historical accounts revealed tension between the military and trading interests in the pre-colonial societies of Africa" (Bates; 1987; p.36). To oppose military adventurism, Wilks (1975) noted the formation of a political party in Asante which advocated "peace, trade and open roads" and opposed the continuation of warfare by the Asante military elite as it threatened commercial interests and development. Elsewhere in Africa, where military forces threatened the commercial interests of subjects within the state, "these interests withdrew their support from that element of centralized polity (the army)" (Bates, 1987; p.32).

Military rule was not a feature of indigenous African political systems. Such rule is as alien to Africa and in much the same way as the colonial rule was. In a speech to the Ghana Academy of Arts and Sciences, Justice F.K. Apaloo cited a policy statement by Kwame Nkrumah on February 1, 1966:

> Normally, the duty of the armed forces is to defend and support the civil government, and not to overthrow it. It is not the duty of the army to rule or govern, because it has no political mandate, and its duty is not to seek a political mandate. . .If the national interest compels the armed forces to intervene, then immediately after the intervention, the army must hand over to a new civil government elected by the people and enjoying the people's mandate under a constitution accepted by them (*West Africa*, Dec. 24 - Jan. 6, 1991; p.3089).

Even some Nigerian military officers themselves expressed the same sentiments. For example, retired Nigerian chief of army staff, General Gibson Jallo, summed it up beautifully: "The army has no moral justification to rule this country (Nigeria)" (cited in *The Africa Report*, July-August 1990; p.52).

How To Rid Africa Of Barbarous Military Regimes

As to what to do with the military, a few Ghanaians had some interesting suggestions:

> Mr. Danso-Boateng suggested: 'The numerical strength of the military must be drastically reduced, the army reduced to one regiment, the air force reduced by half, with all their rockets, bullets and jet fighters confiscated by the civilian-president. The navy could be maintained at present strength because ships cannot come onto the land to be used for coups.' An even more interesting suggestion came from Wilson Blay: 'Lock up all the armories and, let the civilian president keep all the keys.' Kwamena Nyanzu called for the disbanding of the entire armed forces. Mr. Thomas Osei insisted that the armed forces should concern themselves with their traditional role of defense and keep off politics (*West Africa*, Nov. 26 - Dec. 2, 1990; p. 2901).

Costa Rica has no army. Neither did most indigenous African societies. Preaching, however, will accomplish little in Africa. Fortunately, all is not lost. There are peaceful ways of removing a brutal military dictatorship without waging destructive civil wars, as occurred in Liberia (1989-1990) and Somalia (1990). They entail removing *both* the external and internal supports of the military regime.

On the external, perhaps a lesson can be drawn from the experience of Bangladesh:

> Dhaka, Bangladesh — The main opposition parties warned donor countries and agencies yesterday that aid given during the rule of President Hussain Mohammad Ershad would not be paid back.
>
> 'The military junta of President Ershad is plundering public money, and to make that up every year new taxes and levies are being imposed. . .People will not pay the loans back,' Sheik Hasina Wajed, who heads the Awami League, told a rally here. Donors should help a representative government and not 'a government run with the power of the gun,' she said, adding that proper accounts of aid funds are not available.
>
> Begum Khaleda Zia, head of the Bangladesh Nationalist Party, accused Mr. Ershad and his cronies of hoarding aid in foreign bank accounts and said 'people will not bear the pressure of paying back the debt.' (*The Washington Times*, Nov. 7, 1990; p.A2).

Two weeks later, the military government of President Ershad collapsed when aid donors withheld funds.

Internal supports of a military regime are derived from three sources: the military itself, the civil service and the intellectual community. Of the non-military, the civil service is the most critical. Of particular interest and relevance is this passage from a 1979 Report commissioned by a military government in Ghana:

> Finally, the fact should not be overlooked that the Civil Service is, in the final analysis, *the* machinery of Central Government. Without it, the policies and plans of Government will fail, and Government itself will collapse (*Report of the Committee of Enquiry in the Civil Service Strike of November 1978*. Government of Ghana, Accra, April 1979; p.67).

Six months after Ghana's Civil Service strike of March 1978, the military regime of the late General I.K. Acheampong was overthrown in a palace coup. The new military regime of General F.W.K. Akuffo set up the above-mentioned committee of enquiry but failed to resolve the grievances of the civil servants. Another strike was called in November 1978. Exactly six months later, the Akuffo regime was overthrown in a coup by Flt.-Lt. J.J. Rawlings on June 4, 1979.

In Benin, a civil service strike in much of 1989 paralyzed the machinery of government and subsequently led to the removal of the savage military regime of Mathieu Kerekou.

Besides the civil service, a military regime also "uses" the intellectual community to sustain and "civilianize" itself. In a way, one cannot heap all the blame on the soldiers. The opposition in Africa is hopelessly fragmented and endlessly bicker among themselves. Some of the opposition leaders themselves are "closet dictators," exhibiting the same despotic tendencies they denounce in the heads of state they hope to replace. In March 1990 when President Mobutu announced his willingness to permit a multi-party system, Zairean opposition groups met in Brussels. But fighting broke out and before it was over four had been admitted to hospitals with serious injuries. Further, there are always intellectuals willing to sacrifice their integrity and principles to serve under an illiterate soldier. Africa's military dictators survive not so much due to their ingenuity and craftiness but rather due to the crassness of the opposition and the lack of imagination of the intellectual community. As Kwaku Annor observed:

> Liberia's tragedy should be an abject lesson for Africa's academics, who, all too often embrace any coup leader no matter his intelligence or record. Had the MOJA group on the campus of the University of Liberia not provided Doe with 'intellectual' legitimacy, he may not have destroyed Liberia. African universities should be the breeding grounds for democratic interchange and compromise, not hotbeds for rabid radicalism (*West Africa*, Oct. 15-21, 1990; p.2648).

The downfall of President Siad Barre of Somalia (he fled the capital, Mogadishu, in a tank on January 26, 1991) should also be a lesson.[14]

Summary

The post-colonial African story is a tragedy of one betrayal after another. In one country after another, pretentious champions of "liberty" turned out to be crocodile liberators that scattered carnage and human debris in their wake. No sooner had the white colonialists left than a new scourge — black neo-colonialism – emerged. In most places, the new leaders were worse than the colonialists. Independence came to much of Africa but oppression and

---

[14] After 1995, any African intellectual or civilian who serves under a military regime in a capacity above that of Assistant Principal Secretary (for example, principal secretaries, ministers, ambassadors, governors of banks, vice-chancellors, etc.) will be disqualified from serving under any future civilian government, from holding employment in any such government agency or institution and from any contractual dealings with such a government. Collaborating with an alien regime is just as treacherous as collaborating with the colonialists.

exploitation of the African people intensified at the hands of the new leaders. Most of these leaders were booted out in military coups but the "military saviors and redeemers" were the worst.

More painful and unforgivable from the African perspective was the cultural betrayal and the destruction of indigenous African institutions. Suddenly after independence, Africa's own indigenous systems were held up to contempt by the same nationalists. Africans were too "intellectually immature" for multiparty democracy. Native African institutions were too "backward and primitive" for the rapid transformation of the continent. Africans could only develop by adopting alien values and acting like foreigners. Even today, these themes are still being drummed into Africans.

The fundamental problem Africa faces is how to persuade African dictators and the elites to return to their own indigenous roots.

CHAPTER 11

EPILOGUE: CONCLUSIONS AND RECOMMENDATIONS

When, if ever, black people actually organize as a race in their various population centers, they will find that the basic and guiding ideology they now seek and so much need is embedded in their own traditional philosophy and constitutional system, simply waiting to be extracted and set forth.

- Chancellor Williams (1987; p.161).

A. AFRICA BEYOND THE 1990S

The basic thrust of this book has been to provide a description of indigenous African institutions. Of course, this work cannot be regarded as complete but rather as a preliminary work that requires further research and study. There is a certain element of urgency however. Much of Africa's cultural history is of the oral tradition and must be extracted from the elders and recorded before they depart. Nevertheless, it is hoped the contribution made in this book, however incomplete, will provide a useful impetus to further study.

The main difficulty in writing a book such as this originates from grappling with so many extraneous and polemical issues as well as myths about Africa. For example, Africans had no culture and lived on trees. Although these fallacies are extrinsic to the purpose at hand, they make it difficult to separate the chaff from the grain. Whether indigenous African institutions are "backward," "primitive" or "superior" to Western institutions is quite frankly, irrelevant to Africa's present needs. These institutions, regardless of their alleged "inferiority," are an integral part of African culture and constitute the bedrock upon which efforts at development should be based. Many of these structures still exist in modern Africa, although they are battered and tattered. There are still chiefs, kings, tribal councils and even village markets in Africa today.

After independence, it was the responsibility of African nationalists and elites to build upon these indigenous institutions, not only for cultural but pragmatic reasons as well. But as we saw in the previous chapter however, the dismal failure of nationalists and elites to do so in a large part explained Africa's debilitating economic crisis. Clearly, a new Africa must make a quantum leap back to its roots and build upon its own indigenous foundations. This dictum could not have come at a more auspicious time.

The collapse of Marxist systems in Eastern Europe where they were manufactured has proven that these systems will *never* work in Africa, no matter how innovative and determined African leaders are in adapting them to Africa. Nor should African leaders rush off to copy Western or other foreign systems. Africa's salvation does not lie in blindly copying foreign systems but in returning to its own roots and heritage. As Williams (1987) advised: "When, if ever, black people actually organize as a race in their various population centers, they will find that the basic and guiding ideology they now seek and so much need is embedded in their own traditional philosophy and constitutional system, simply waiting to be extracted and set forth" (p.161).

It paid off handsomely for Botswana when it followed this advice — the only black African nation to do so in the post-colonial period. In elegant brevity, *Newsweek* (July 23, 1990) put the issue poignantly:

> Botswana built a working democracy on an aboriginal tradition of local gatherings called *kgotlas* that resemble New England town meetings; it has a record $2.7 billion in foreign exchange reserves (p.28).

B. BOTSWANA: THE SHINING BLACK ECONOMIC STAR

When it gained its independence from Britain in September 1966, doomsayers gave Botswana (formerly Bechuanaland) less than five years to self-destruct and evaporate. Ensconced in the Kgalagadi (Kalahari) basin, Botswana possessed all the ingredients for another post-colonial black African economic disaster. Its society was composed of nine ethnic groups, including the nomadic San who live in the Kgalagadi desert, raising the possibility of interminable ethnic strife.

In addition, about 75 percent of the country's 592,000 sq. km. was desert, bordered by bush and a few fertile areas in the east (in the valley and low watershed of the Limpopo and Shashe rivers) and the swampland of the Okavango basin in the north. The bulk of its largely illiterate population (about 80 percent) lived on only 20 percent of the land area. (Botswana's population in 1990 was 1.2 million).

At independence, Botswana was resource-poor. De Beers had started diamond exploration in 1955 but did not make a find until 1967 (Arapa mine), a year after nationhood. There were some spartan deposits of low-grade coal (in the northeast), platinum, gold, silver, iron, potash, manganese, chromide and uranium. But the country lacked the technical know-how to develop these. There was nothing else by way of industrial activity except a small beef industry. Few prospects were held out for this industry either since it was operating in an African environment where cattle served as a store of wealth and taboos prohibited their slaughter for consumption. To add insult to injury, the cattle were derided as containing more bones than meat.

Drought always posed a serious threat. The most recent was a 7-year stretch from 1981 to 1988. In 1985 alone, this caused a loss of 1,500 jobs in the formal agricultural sector. Ever conscious of the perennial water shortage, Botswana named its new currency the *pula* (which means "rain") in 1976 when it left the South Africa-dominated rand system. But nature was not always so kind.

Landlocked, Botswana was hopelessly dependent on neighboring countries for the transshipment of exports and imports. Nestled between Namibia, South Africa and Zimbabwe, Botswana's development efforts have more often than not been pre-empted and held hostage by extra-territorial occurrences. At independence, Botswana was a little more than a "captive country," flanked by hostile South Africa (which also held Namibia illegally) and Rhodesia, then ruled by Ian Smith. Liberation struggles in these neighboring countries placed Botswana in a precarious geopolitical position. It was sympathetic and supportive of the aspirations for self-determination by black African nationalists. But like Zambia, it was heavily dependent upon South African infrastructure over which some 83 percent of its imports were drawn. Its options in this geopolitical tight-box were further reduced by the bullying tactics of the apartheid regime in South Africa.

After the ignominious Sharpeville massacre (June 1976), thousands of students fled South Africa to seek refuge in Botswana. Soon afterwards, a new wave of refugees from Rhodesia swelled the numbers encamped in Botswana from 3,000 to 21,000 by mid-1979, placing severe strains on budgetary resources and social facilities.

The provision of sanctuary for these refugees made Botswana the target of economic blackmail, intimidation and sabotage by neighboring white supremacist and Marxist regimes. In particular, it earned Botswana the ire of Ian Smith, Botha of South Africa and strained relations with Zimbabwe when it gained its independence in 1980. President Robert Mugabe, the new president of Zimbabwe, accused Botswana of sheltering former ZAPU guerrillas — supporters of Joshua Nkomo who himself temporarily sought refuge in March 1983.

For its part, South Africa accused Botswana of harboring guerrillas of the then bannned African National Congress (ANC). As punishment, South Africa reserved for itself the right of conducting "hot pursuits" of ANC guerrillas based in Botswana. Despite assurances by Foreign Minister Mrs. Gaositwe Chiepe in February 1985 that Botswana was not being used "for planning or executions of acts of sabotage or terrorism," South African security forces launched with a vengeance destructive destabilization campaigns.

In the same month of 1985, a bomb wrecked the house of two South African refugees in Botswana and in May 1985, a bomb exploded, killing Vernon Nkadimeng, the son of the General Secretary of the banned South African Congress of Trade Unions. Subsequently on June 14, 1985, South African commandos staged a 45-minute pre-dawn raid on 10 houses in various parts of Gaborone, the capital. At least 15 people were killed, including a 6-year old child, a social worker and other innocents.

International condemnation did not deter another attack. In February 1986, after two weeks of talks, Botswana reached another accord with South Africa, agreeing to prevent "ANC rebels from using Botswana as a transit territory." But hardly did the ink on that agreement dry before South Africa launched a dawn raid on May 19, 1986, destroying several houses in Gaborone and killing some innocent Batswana. In 1988 came a particularly gruesome raid in which three Batswana women and a South African refugee were killed and their corpses multilated by burning.

At independence, Botswana's prospects of surviving as a viable politico-economic entity were just about equal to those of Mali or Burkina Faso (former Upper Volta): landlocked, plagued by persistent droughts, poor resource wealth, and a small population with a low literacy rate. Cameroon, Nigeria and Zaire were far more blessed with richer mineral wealth endowment, luxuriant vegetation, modestly developed infrastructure and an economically active population. Even Ghana was in a better "take-off" position. Yet, in spite of all its handicaps, Botswana has managed to register an impressive rate of economic advance, astonishing by *any* African standard.

In a little less than two decades (1966 to 1986), Botswana's rate of economic growth averaged an astounding 8 percent per annum while the South African economy was limping along at a miserable 1.5 percent per annum between 1965 and 1985. In 1988, for example, Botswana's Minister of Finance and Development Planning, Vice-President Peter Mmusi, indicated that average real growth rate was running at 14 percent annually and that per capita Gross Domestic Product (GDP) was P2,800 *pulas* ($1,450) — ten times greater than it was in 1978 (*African Business*, Sept. 1988; p.35). Back in 1983, real GPD growth rate was a dizzying 26.3 percent and GDP per capita exploded from P755 in 1982 to P2145 in 1986.

Botswana's foreign debt was about $324 million in 1990 and its reserves, on per capita basis, were the highest in the world.

The first diamond mine to open was Orapa in 1971. By 1988, diamond production had reached 15.2 million carats, earning about 85 percent of Botswana's export earnings of P2205 million. The beef industry too underwent phenomenal expansion, despite the denigration of African cattle and the devastating droughts of 1965/66 and 1982-84 that killed off a third of the national herd. Botswana began to export meat to the EEC, which pays almost 4 times the world price for this meat because of its quality. The Botswana Meat Commission's meat processing plant at Lobatse is the second largest in the world. There are other slaughterhouses in Maun and Francistown to help Botswana meet its 19,000 metric ton EEC quota.

Botswana's economic performance has not been matched anywhere on the African continent in the post-colonial period. Under aging leaders with one-party regimes, Africa's post-colonial economic performance has been unmitigated disaster. Twenty-four of the world's thirty-six poorest nations are in black Africa (or sub-Saharan Africa). Apart from Botswana, exceptions to the general economic atrophy have been pitifully few: Cameroon, Ivory Coast, Kenya and Mauritius — out of the 45 countries that inhabit the sub-Saharan region. Even more disturbingly, by 1990 the paltry number of economic success stories had shrunk to two (Botswana and Mauritius). Across black Africa, Botswana remains a shining star, while black Africa's income per capita fell consistently from $621 in 1981 to $352 in 1987.

Obviously, if Botswana can succeed economically, the rest of the African countries can too. But how? And what were the secrets to Botswana's success?

The Keys To Botswana's Success

Although various analysts have attributed Botswana's success to its mineral wealth of diamonds, a combination of factors have contributed immensely to create the environment vital for economic prosperity. Foremost has been the *absence of civil and political strife*. By contrast, senseless and endless civil wars rage in at least 10 African countries (Angola, Chad, Ethiopia, Liberia, Mozambique, Rwanda, Somalia, Sudan, Uganda and now South Africa).

Second, Botswana enjoys *political stability*. This stability was not engineered by a military dictator or by declaring the country to be a one-party state. Botswana is a parliamentary democracy based upon a *multi-party system*. The main political parties are the Botswana Democratic Party (the ruling), the Botswana National Front, and the Botswana People's Party. Multi-party, contrary to the claims by Presidents Moi of Kenya, Kaunda of Zambia and other African dictators, did not degenerate into "tribal politics" in Botswana.

The excessive number of dictatorships and one-party states is a telling testimony to the political chaos that bedevils black Africa.

Third, the Botswana government has pursued strikingly *prudent economic policies*, allowing pragmatism, rather than emotional rhetoric, to prevail. The Botswana government's commitment to mixed economy has not been directed toward nationalization — no such cases have occurred — but rather toward the provision of good infrastructural support. Recall that in Africa's indigenous economic systems, state enterprises were *not* a regular feature. In Botswana, parastatals were only established to plug the gaps or overcome the deficiencies in the private sector, insteading of competing with or seeking to replace the private sector as was the case in many African countries, especially Tanzania with a "socialist" bent.

Fortunate enough to have an ex-minister of finance as President, (Masire), the government pursued judicious macroeconomic policies of saving windfalls and avoiding excessive government spending during export boom years. These savings provided the cushion to ride out the lean years.

By contrast, when sharply rising oil prices boosted exports from $4 billion in 1975 to $26 billion in 1980, Nigeria went on an import binge. It splurged on prestigious projects, including an $23 billion new capital at Abuja, while vampire politicians transferred as much as $15 million a day illegally out of the country. Nigeria even neglected agriculture, preferring to use cheap oil dollars to import food. Rising public expenditures fueled by oil revenues shifted production from agriculture to services. When the price of oil collapsed, so did Nigeria's export receipts. By 1986, they were down to $6 billion, while external debt rose from $5 billion in 1980 to $25 billion in 1986. The booms in coffee, cocoa, copper prices in the 1970s elicited similar extravagant spending by governments in Ghana, Ivory Coast, Kenya, Uganda and Zaire. Other Third World countries such as Mexico, Brazil, Colombia acted similarly, squandering windfall profits from exports booms only to find themselves in a debt crisis when markets collapsed.

Fourth, Botswana society is multi-racial, composed of ethnic Batswana, Europeans and Asians. These various groups *live peacefully together*. Blatant acts of discrimination are not common in Botswana. Fifth, largely due to its openess and a vibrant press, there is a refreshing absence of corruption — the bane of many African regimes. Botswana has a lively *free press* and *freedom of expression*. Apart from the government newspaper, the *Daily News*, and the government monthly magazine, *Kutlwano*, the country has three weekly private newspapers and four locally produced monthly magazines. The local publications are *not* subject to censorship. In addition, foreign papers and magazines are widely available.

Commenting on the political process in Botswana, Professor Patrick Mulotsi, a lecturer in sociology at the University of Botswana, was pithy:

If you look at the prerequisites of liberal democracy, the rule of law has been highly respected. *A lot of people can say a lot of things with relatively little fear.* There has been a lot of response by the ruling party to debates with the opposition (*The New York Times*, May 16, 1990; p.A6).

Botswana can find solutions to its economic problems because *it permits free debate and freedom of expression.* By contrast, the rest of black Africa is mired in an economic quagmire, for want of ideas and solutions to extricate itself. Intellectual repression prevents those with ideas from coming forward. Only 7 (The Gambia, Mauritius, Namibia, arguably Nigeria, Senegal and now Ivory Coast, and Benin) of the remaining 44 black African countries tolerate freedom of expression and criticism of foolish government policies. As we saw in the previous chapter, these same countries have ratified the Organization of African Unity's Charter of Human and Peoples' Rights whose Article 9 guarantees freedom of expression.

Fifth, Botswana did not ignore its *indigenous roots*. It built upon its native system of *kgotlas*, whereby chiefs and councillors meet "under a tree" to reach a *consensus* on important matters. In fact, cabinet ministers are required to attend weekly *kgotla* meetings. In the rest of black Africa, the indigenous system of participatory democracy and the tradition of reaching a consensus were spurned. In their place, African elites and intellectuals erected one-man dictatorships and *de facto* apartheid regimes. Under these heinous systems, one buffoon dictates policy and imposes it on the rest of the people without public debate or consensus.

Botswana's economic success demonstrates that Africa does not have to renounce its indigenous culture to advance economically. The Japanese did not. Africa's indigenous institutions, almost everywhere castigated as "primitive and backward," can still be used to lift the continent out of its economic miasma. There are other poignant lessons as well: to South Africans that a prosperous, multiracial society can be built and to the rest of Africa that multi-party democracy, prudent government policies and freedom of expression are indispensable to economic development. But the real obstacles to economic progress in Africa are the dictators bent on remaining life-presidents over their own little fiefdoms.

Developing The Rest Of Black Africa

The topic of development is broad and cannot adequately be dealt with in one chapter or in a small section of a chapter. This topic with reference to Africa is treated in great length and detail in my forthcoming books, *Africa's Economic Crisis: The Indigenous Solutions* and *Developing Africa Using Africa's Own Indigenous Institutions.* What follows is a brief outline of the basic principles and steps involved.

Development is a complex process. At the broad level of generality, it may be considered as improving the lot of the people, not just a tiny constituent minority. As such, the process has several dimensions — intellectual, political, economic, legal, social and cultural development. Clearly, it entails more than mere increases in GNP (economic growth). In fact, the latter can occur without development.

This way of looking at the process explains why almost every educated person considers him/herself an "expert," with an opinion or two on how to accelerate the development process. And it is precisely for this reason that a great deal of confusion and frustration characterize development practice. It is probably a case of too many experts spoil the broth.

The development process takes time — decades and even centuries — and it is *never* completed. Like a learning process, it never ceases until death. The highly developed countries are continually "developing." It should be obvious why it is humanly impossible for one person to "develop" an African country.

Several paths may be taken to develop an African economy: capitalism, socialism, Marxism, communism, and indigenism (or indinalism, from Chapter 7). Each route has its own unique advantages and demerits in terms of efficacy, cost, expediency and speed of attaining results. Within each path also, there are various alternatives or variations. But whichever path and form are taken must not be set in stone.

World economic and geo-political conditions are not static but constantly changing. It is imperative to adapt development strategies to these changing circumstances. Obviously, the world Africa faced in the 1950s is definitely not the same world Africa faces today. Consequently, strategies which made sense back then may be woefully inadequate and even counterproductive today. This point is worth belaboring because some African intellectuals, inexorably enthralled by such nationalists as Nkrumah, Nyerere, Kaunda and Kenyatta, are still rigidly wedded to the rhetoric and strategies of the fifties.[1]

Equally important is the fact that "successful economic development" does not mean the resolution of *all* economic problems. There will *always* be unemployment, poverty in the midst of plenty, inflation, deficits, scarcity, and inequitable distribution of wealth. No nation has ever succeeded, or ever will, in the history of the world in solving *all* its economic problems by reducing the aforementioned problems to zero. These problems are never solved or eradicated; they are only minimized. Even when one is fully solved, a new one emerges or an existing one worsens.

This assertive statement is derived from the fact that the "economic problem" which every society faces (discussed in Chapter 7) is never solved.

---

[1] If Nkrumah were alive today, he surely would be disappointed at the fact that the huge sums of money spent to educate Ghanaians went to waste. Post-colonial education in Ghana has produced few, if any, of equal stature and of originality, but only copy-cats of his ideas.

The problem of allocating scarce resources to meet infinite and *changing* wants will *always* exist in every society. New demands (computers, space travel, for example) arise, causing resource shifts and expansions in certain industries (booms, higher prices) and contractions in others (slump, low prices, unemployment). Consequently, there is *always* what economists call "structural unemployment" —unemployment due to changes in the structure of demand. There is also "seasonal unemployment": fishermen when fish is out of season, farmers after harvest, construction workers, etc.

These types of unemployment would not exist if there were no "seasons" and an economy does not have "structural rigidities." Further, the economy must have the capability to instantly train and equip unemployed workers in declining industries and shift them into expanding sectors. But it takes time to retrain unemployed workers and provide them with information about new job opportunities. Even then, workers may not like their new jobs and may resign or be sacked. The labor market does not operate smoothly to match jobs with people possessing the right kind of skills. Because this market operates with what economists call "friction," there is always "frictional unemployment." This type of unemployment cannot be eliminated.

For this reason, economists define full-employment as occurring when the total number of job seekers is equal to the total number of job vacancies. Note that full-employment does not require zero unemployment. It may sound like a contradiction in terms to have unemployment when the economy is operating at full-employment. But that unemployment is frictional. For the U.S. economy, this was estimated at 4 percent of the labor force in the 1980s. Thus, full-employment occurred in the United States when the rate of unemployment was 4 percent.

It is necessary to expatiate on economic problems because various African leaders (for example, Kenneth Kaunda of Zambia and Flt.-Lt. Jerry Rawlings of Ghana) often made statements to the effect that they would only hand over power when their country's economic problems had been solved. Since economic problems are never solved, such statements meant they had no intention of relinquishing political power.

The refusal on the part of African dictators to step down should be viewed with grave concern, as it often has resulted in unnecessary destruction, and brought untold misery and suffering to millions of innocent Africans. In Liberia, the refusal of the late Samuel Doe precipitated a civil war (December 1989 - December 1990) which caused the slaughter of over 2,000 civilians, much destruction, and famine and wiped out any development progress the country had made. This same refusal produced similar results in Ethiopia, Somalia, Sudan, Uganda and Zaire. As we have had the occasion to remark, the excessive number of dictators in Africa who refuse to step down constitutes a real obstacle to the continent's progress.

To reduce the complex development process to a manageable proportion, it would be useful to think of it in terms of a building. Assume for the sake of simplicity that "development" means making a transition from a "thatched-roof hut" to some elegant building. Several questions may be asked: What *type* of building, *where* to build it, *who* will build it and *how* (the state or the people), what type of building *materials* to use (cement, wood, glass, slate, adobe, bamboo), who will *pay* for it and who will *live* in it? Note that an elegant building does not necessarily have to be made of cement, just as an edible fish does not necessarily have to be caught by a trawler.

But before these preliminary questions are addressed, Africa's current dictators, civilian or military, must be removed, since development now means repairing the devastation and neglect wrought by these same dictators. It makes no sense whatsoever to ask the *same* African dictators who ruined their economies to repair them. Westerners should know this, since when a company goes bankrupt, it is not reorganized under Chapter 11 and placed, together with a massive infusion of new capital, in the hands of the *same* incompetent management which ruined it in the first place. It makes one then wonder why Western governments, institutions and aid agencies would provide millions of dollars in economic rescue or restructuring package to the *same* incompetent African dictators who have destroyed their economies.

As we saw in the previous chapter, these dictators have a peculiar way of defining elegance or development. Their vision of "development" empha-sizes grandeur (prestigious projects, basilicas, etc.), blind imitation of foreign systems, a buildup of their political power, and a development of a personality cult and a Swiss bank account. Ninety percent of the time, these dictators are preoccupied with clinging to power; forty percent of the time they are nursing their foreign bank accounts; thirty percent of the time they are thinking of "control." They have "negative" time to attend to their countries' economic ills, which explains Africa's economic decline.

These dictators treat their countries as their own personal property. An African country does not belong to any one particular cabbage-head, any more than the Philippines to Ferdinand Marcos. Even "backward" chiefs never acted as if the whole tribe belonged to them. It is the African people themselves who must determine what type of building is best suited for them, not what one individual copies from abroad to impose on them. This determination must be the collective will of the people, arrived at by *consensus*.

With the type of building determined, the next question is where to put it; that is, in what type of *environment*. Obviously, one would choose a quiet and peaceful neighborhood, not a war zone or a crime-infested area and risk being dispossessed of it. Next, a decision must be made on the *materials* to be used. Common sense and cost considerations require the use of materials that are in plentiful local supply, rather than expensive imported materials. To start, a *foundation* must be laid and as the building takes shape an *infrastructure* (steel beams, plumbing pipes, electrical wiring) installed. Note that a building is put up in *sequential* stages. Walls are erected *before* windows are installed in them. Similarly, the "shell" must be complete *before* a roof is placed on the building. After completion, the building must be *maintained*. Note also that with the entire process, there is no such thing as "the key constraint or stage." The *type* of building, the *environment*, the *foundation*, the *infrastructure*, the *sequence* and *maintenance* are all important. None can be ignored if the building is to last. The words underlined have significant correspondence and duality with the process of development.

Development does not occur in a vacuum but in an *environment*. Obviously, an environment characterized by violence, civil wars, anarchy, repression, military barbarism and lawlessness, arbitrary arrests and seizures of private property can only operate to impede development. There must be cessation of Africa's inane civil wars and political strife.[2] There must also be a restoration of the rule of law, respect for human rights, fair trials and order. As we saw in earlier chapters, most of these requisites were met in the so-called "primitive" African societies. There was the rule of customary law; the African chief or king had to obey the law or risk destoolment (Chapters 3 and 4). There were courts, not tribunals, and court decisions could be appealed (Chapter 2).

The development process must also have a *foundation* or an ideology. As argued throughout this book, Africa's development must be rooted in its own indigenous institutions (indinalism or indigenism - Chapter 7). The supporting *infrastructure* are roads, transportation and communications networks, financial institutions, law enforcement, judicial system and defense. Note that the functions of the tribal government were mainly confined to the provision of infrastructural services (Chapter 6). It was the chief's duty to maintain the road and bush paths. The chief was also the judge and was responsible for the defense of the tribe. It was also the chief's duty to provide a peaceful atmosphere for his people to engage in trade.

Before discussing the *sequence*, it should be pointed out that, like a building, the development process or projects require periodic maintenance. Just as roads and bridges can deteriorate for want of maintenance, so too can the political leadership decay for want of renewal. In most of Africa's traditional system, kings and chiefs who failed to bring prosperity were removed. Similarly, African leaders who ruin their economies must be thrown out.

The development *sequence* has been deferred to this point, not only because

---

[2] In fact, foreign aid or economic development assistance to *any* African country where there is a civil war, should be withheld and placed in escrow until the combatants come to their senses and sit at the negotiating table — the same solution they prescribe for South Africa. It makes absolutely no sense whatsoever to supply aid to build roads, bridges and railways only to have them blown up by insurgents.

of its importance but also because, for decades, it was spurned by many —
including Western scholars, aid donors and bilateral institutions — as
irrelevant. Since one does not place a roof over a building when the
foundation has not been laid, neither does one initiate a development step
before its time is due.

The development process, as noted earlier, has many dimensions:
economic, political, social, cultural, intellectual and legal development. But
in what *sequence* should these occur and which should come first?

For decades, many scholars and experts — in both Africa and the West —
ignored this issue. And when recognized, it was vehemently argued that the
sequence was not relevant, with the insistence that economic development
was feasible under authoritarian regimes. The examples often adduced were
Hong Kong, Malaysia, Singapore, South Korea, and Taiwan. But it did not
occur to these scholars that they were citing the *exceptions*. If over 120
dictatorships in the Third World tried this "strategy" and a few succeeded,
that hardly recommended this strategy as viable and worthy of emulation.
Exceptions do not make the rule or provide the basis for policy. If anything,
the same evidence rather pointed to the overwhelming failure of development under dictatorial regimes.

Even the World Bank and the IMF miscalculated, believing that
economic reform was possible under tyrannical African regimes. In the latter
part of the 1980s, 37 African countries embarked upon the task of
structurally reforming their inefficient and corruption-ridden economies
with financial assistance and tutelage from these institutions. But it quickly
became apparent that dishing out huge sums of money to African dictators to
reform their economies was futile. Economic *perestroika* was not possible
without a political *glasnost*. Only two (Ghana and Tanzania) were adjudged
"successful reformers." In March 1990, a disappointed World Bank
concluded that, overall, "adjustment lending appeared to have been
relatively less successful in the highly-indebted countries and in *sub-Saharan
Africa*."

C. THE SEQUENCE OF REFORM

A consensus has now emerged that economic reform alone in Africa,
much as elsewhere, is meaningless unless coupled with political pluralism,
respect for freedom of expression embracing human rights, press freedoms,
independent judicial systems and the rule of law. Even some of Africa's
leaders agreed on the need for political pluralism. Flt.Lt. Rawlings, Head of
State of Ghana, noted that: "There can be no economic development in an
undemocratic atmosphere" (*West Africa*, May 28-June 3, 1990; p.913).
Similarly, President Yoweri Museveni of Uganda, in a speech before the
OAU in Addis Ababa, observed: "There is no way you can develop the

economy without democracy" (*The New York Times*, July 10, 1990; p.A3). So which should come first: democracy, economic reform, or human rights?

This author believes the ideal *sequence* should run from the *intellectual* to *political* to *economic* and finally to *social* development. An African country which embarks on "reform" or "development" must first start at the intellectual level. By intellectual reform or development is meant restoring the *freedom of expression* that existed in traditional Africa (Chapter 6), *freeing the press* and removing it from state ownership and control. Freedom of expression is the *sine qua non* of all human rights. Recall the Yoruba proverb: "Only an organism knows what is best for itself." But how can the welfare of the organism be determined if it cannot express itself? Congruently, only Africans know what type of "building," political and economic systems, are best for themselves. But how can this determination be made by Africans *without* freedom of expression?

Without this freedom it is impossible for Africans to participate in the decision-making process and reach a *consensus* on development issues. Recall that participation in the decision-making process and consensus were indigenous African traditions. Further, denial of freedom of expression banishes from Africa the free marketplace of *ideas* needed to solve the continent's problems. Solutions to Africa's problems cannot be found in a "culture of repression, terror or silence."

Sequentially, Africans must have intellectual freedom first, then political reform, then economic reform and lastly social reform. In pushing for economic reform, as was the case under Structural Adjustment programs, many were putting the cart before the horse. Before we examine in more detail the intellectual, political and economic reform in the *sequence* enunciated, perhaps it would be useful to explain in lay-person terms the notion of "development" under various ideologies and "isms," using the "building" paradigm:

APARTHEID:

Black and white people put up the building. The government takes it over, throws out the blacks and reserves it for whites. Blacks then must pay the rent for the upkeep of the building.

CAPITALISM:

A private individual or company puts up the building, with the infrastructure provided by the government. The private owner or the landlord rents it out to the people and charges $5,000 a suite. Those who can afford the rent secure living quarters. Those who cannot or fall back on rent payments are thrown out into the streets (homelessness).

COMMUNISM:

The people put up the building. It is seized (nationalized) by the government and occupied by communist *apparatchiks*. The people are driven out and crowded into the dilapidated wooden shacks that serve as servants' quarters where they pay a rent of $1 to the government.

FOREIGN AID DEVELOPMENT:

The people put up the building, using funds (on credit) and imported materials (cement, fiberglass, asbestos, stained glass, marble, self-cleaning, thermostatically-controlled microwave ovens, and high-tech snow ploughs) supplied by the aid donors. The environment in which the building is placed or who takes it over is of no concern to the donors.

INDIGENISM:

The people put up the building (thatched-roof hut), using primitive materials (adobe, cow dung, bamboo and stones) and own it themselves. Infrastructure is supplied by the chief. But the chief or king cannot take over the building *without* a full tribal court hearing or evict people from the land, as it belongs to the ancestors.

MARXISM:

The people put up the building and it is taken over by a workers' dictatorship. The bourgeoisie class is driven out to live in the squalid servants' quarters where they must pay a rent of $10,000 for each unit to subsidize the comfortable living of the Marxists. The people, the peasants, have no place in this system as they are not "workers" — wage-earning factory workers:

"Angolans who own cars can fill their tanks for less than a dollar, and international telephone calls cost only pennies. One local boasts of getting a round-trip ticket to Paris on Air France for the equivalent of two cases of beer. Luanda does not even pick up its own garbage; the job is contracted out to a foreign company using Filipino workers lured to Angola with fat paychecks, special housing and First World garbage trucks.

Of course, the chief beneficiaries of all this are the city's westernized elite and their foreign business bedfellows. Many of life's necessities, on the other hand are not available at subsidized prices. For the poorest residents, survival is impossible without resort to *candonga*, or illegal trading" (*Insight*, Oct. 1, 1990; p.13).

MILITARISM:

The people put up the building. A fufu-head wielding a bazooka seizes it and shoots the people:

"In February 1988, when drought victims refused to participate in the government resettlement program in the northern town of Korem, Ethiopian troops opened fire on thousands, killing at least 20" (*The Wall Street Journal*, Feb. 12, 1988; p.1).

ONE-PARTY AFRICAN SOCIALISM:

The people put up the building and it is taken over by the state. The top floor, complete with imported luxury commodities, air-conditioning, swimming pools and garages for Mercedes Benzes, is reserved for top party officials. Lower-ranking officials occupy the lower floor while the people are crowded into the servants' quarters where they pay a rent of $1,000 for the maintenance of the building:

"The enduring symbol of this social stratum is the Mercedes Benz. Zaire reputedly imports more Mercedes than anywhere in Africa and Kinshasa's Mercedes dealers prosper while all around them crumbles (*New Internationalist*, June 1990; p.19).

"The governor of the Dakar-based African central bank can reach his 13th floor office without having to step out of his car. One of the many perks that go with the region's highest-paying job is a private lift (elevator) to hoist him and his Mercedes to work (*South*, May 1988; p.34).

SWISS BANK SOCIALIST DEVELOPMENT:

The people put up the building and it is taken over by the state. The top floor, complete with imported luxury commodities, air-conditioning, swimming pools and garages for Mercedes Benzes, is reserved for top party officials. Lower-ranking officials occupy the lower floor while the people are crowded into the servants' quarters where they pay a rent of $1,000 for the maintenance of the building. Part of the rent money is deposited in Switzerland:

"Algeria's former prime minister, Mr. Abdelhamid Brahimi, said recently that officials of the ruling *Front de Liberation National* (FLN) had pocketed $26 billion in bribes and commissions on foreign contracts. The present prime minister, Mr. Mouloud Hamrouche, called the charge 'grossly exaggerated' but did not deny its gist" (*The Economist*, April 14, 1990; p.51).

"In April, 1989, the Christian Association of Nigeria revealed that more than 3,000 Nigerians operated Swiss bank accounts and that Nigerians were near the top of the list of Third World patrons of Swiss banks" (*West Africa*, April 10-16, 1989; p.570).

"The Zambian President, Kenneth Kaunda (the architect of Zambia's socialist ideology of 'humanism'), dismissed as 'a big lie' recent allegations that he had transferred $6 billion in state funds to personal bank accounts abroad" (*The New York Times*, August 15, 1990; p.A6).

"If you steal, do not steal too much at a time. You may be arrested. Steal cleverly (*yiba na mayele*), little by little" - President Mobutu Sese Seko of Zaire in an address to party regulars.

"Every franc we give impoverished Africa, comes back to France, or is smuggled into Switzerland and even Japan" (*Le Monde*, Paris newspaper, March 1990).

SCIENTIFIC ISLAMIC SOCIALISM (Mauritania, Sudan):

Arabs and black Africans put up the building. It is taken over by the government and declared the property of Allah. It is reserved exclusively for the followers of Islam (Arabs) and blacks are thrown out to live in the servants' quarters as slaves. Those who complain have their limbs hacked off scientifically (amputation).

WORLD BANK/IMF STRUCTURAL ADJUSTMENT:

The people put up the building. It is taken over and ruined by the state. The World Bank and IMF enter and try to wrest ownership out of the hands of the state into private hands by asking the *same* incompetent government to find the buyer. The people have no say in these transactions.

We now examine the *sequence* of reform: intellectual, political, and economic.

Intellectual Reform (Freedom Of Expression)

Freedom of expression is not the product of any political system or ideology. It is a universal human right, defined and guaranteed in international law. . .Everyone has the right to freedom of opinion and expression; this right includes freedom to hold opinions without interference and to seek, receive and impart information and ideas through any media regardless of boundaries.

— Article 19 of the 1948 Universal Declaration of Human Rights by the United Nations.

———————

As we saw in the previous chapter, freedom of expression, rather shamefully, does not exist in the majority of African nations. Even the blacks in South Africa now have greater freedom of expression than their counterparts in independent Africa who want to free them. In most of "free and independent" Africa, the norm is defined by proscriptions, banning of books and hauling editors, writers and journalists into jail and murdering dissidents. As Samuel F. Luwero bitterly complained:

We must not forget that Uganda has a bad name for imprisoning people, especially ministers, who cross paths with the President. Grace Ibingira, Mathias Ngobi, Dr. Lumu, George Magezi, Balaki Kirya, Evaristo Nyanzi, Dr. Lwanga, Professor Y. Kyesimira, Professor Lule, Godfrey Binaisa, and most recently Paul Muwanga and Moses Ali, are some of the many Ugandans victimized in the past just for *expressing a different opinion* from the President's. Others who were not so lucky, had been murdered (*New African*, Jan. 1991; p.4).

Quite frankly, the African people are fed up with these barbarous acts on the part of "educated" leaders — the same leaders who complain about a "book famine" in Africa. How in perdition can Africans write books and articles when they are persecuted, jailed and murdered for expressing viewpoints different from their governments'? There is no *cultural* justification whatsoever for this intellectual barbarism. African chiefs never did this; most were intellectually mature. Said one Ghanaian chief, the *Okyehene* Osagyefo Kuntukununku:

> Future governments would do well *to encourage a dialogue between themselves and the populace, confront contrary views with well reasoned arguments rather than intimidation and detention.* Suppression of dissent and the denial of the right to express contrary views can only encourage sycophancy and opportunism. (The chief) called for a free press to enhance dialogue, efficiency and accountability and to champion the cause of victims of governmental vindictiveness and arbitrariness (*West Africa*, August 27 - September 2, 1990; p.2372).

But preaching is not enough. This author will fight any attempt by intellectual barbarians to ban his works. And so too should other African writers. If this present book has nothing to offer, the African people themselves would reject it. It is not the business of an incompetent African government to ban it. The list of African countries where this book is banned will be published in future editions on this page and the list sent to the United Nations, the OAU, the World Bank and the IMF.

To Westerners, this may sound "naive" and "emotional." But of all the professions in Africa, none has suffered a worse fate than writers and journalists. Other professionals can ignore injustices, remain silent and continue to make their living. But writers and journalists cannot survive in an environment where they are hounded, detained or "liquidated" and their books banned. These acts, if you come to think of them, do not only constitute intellectual backwardness but are also counterproductive and achieve precisely the opposite results.

The Futility Of Banning Books — A Digression

In an editorial, the *West Africa* magazine noted that: "In general, those countries which allow some freedom of expression find that it serves as a safety valve, a vehicle whereby rulers may better know the ruled. Likewise, where this openness is suppressed for whatever reason, these factors of stability are removed" (Nov. 20-26, 1989; p.1919).

The irony is that, banning an organization and arresting or harassing its leaders does *not* achieve the intended purpose of extermination. In fact, it rather achieves precisely the contrary results. Too many governments worldwide refuse to learn from this simple fact. For years, the Polish government banned *Solidarity*, harassed and arrested its leader, Lech Walesa. But the organization did not die. Rather, it thrived and Walesa was awarded a Nobel peace prize. Subsequently, *Solidarity* came to form the new Polish government in September 1989. In other Eastern European countries, poets and teachers, hounded by communist dictators in the past, later emerged to become their countries' presidents. In Nigeria, Wole Soyinka was hounded and jailed for two years in 1967. But he too later gained international recognition, receiving the Nobel prize for literature.

If a government bans a book or a newspaper, that would confer a "scarcity and curiosity value" on the publication and it would be precisely the very book or newspaper which the public would want to buy and read because they would suspect it contains some truth the government does not want them to know and that the government is trying "to hide something."[3] Their curiosity would be piqued. In addition, the ban would sanctify and draw more attention to the victim or the author. In fact, the persecution of an author or journalist by a hated and oppressive regime rather transforms him into a martyr or a hero. Because what is "evil" in the eyes of the "devil" must be "good." As the Nigerian writer, Peter Ezeh, put it:

> There is one basic truth governments which stifle the press need to know, and that is that only good work on the part of the government, inspired by the sincere desire to satisfy the great majority of the governed, can effectively frustrate a bad press where such actually exists. People are intelligent enough to be a good judge. To paraphrase de Rivarol, 'In the long run, one always loses when one attacks ideas with bullets. Only ideas can successfully attack ideas.' Censorship leaves the impression that the censor has something to hide (*Index on Censorship*, Aug. 1988; p.18).

When Mrs. Margaret Thatcher banned Peter Wright's book *Spycatcher* in 1988, it moved up to the top on *The New York Times* worldwide best-seller list. In fact, the greatest favor a government can ever do for an author is to ban his or her books and writings.

Nor is the business of governments to ban organizations. These organizations have various viewpoints to propagate in the marketplace of

---

[3] Banning a book can at times be embarrassing. Once on a visit to Meharry Medical College in Tennessee, where he studied, Life-President Hastings Banda of Malawi was presented with a book which he recommended to his cabinet as an indispensable reading material. It was later discovered to the general embarrassment that it was already on the Malawi Censorship Board's banned list. This list even included the Simon and Garfunkel song, "Cecilia." The reason was that Banda's hated "Official Hostess" was called Cecilia Kadzamira (*Africa Report*, July-August 1990; p.58).

ideas. If their viewpoints have no merits, again the public will reject them. By banning them, the government leads the public to think that their ideas or agenda are sacrosant, which may not always be the case. The ANC of South Africa, UNITA of Angola, Mwakenya of Kenya and many other groups and newspapers were all banned. But they were not destroyed.

The Soviet Union also learned a similar lesson the hard way. For years, it spent considerable resources to jam the broadcasts of Radio Free Europe. But curious and determined Soviet citizens went to extraordinary lengths to acquire sophisticated radio equipment to listen in. Suddenly, the jamming stopped under *glasnost*. One Soviet student, Falina Sologubova, complained to *Pravda*, the official newspaper: "Now that the jamming of Radio Free Europe has stopped, it is not worth wasting time to listen to it."

But governments in Cameroon, Ethiopia, Ghana, Kenya, Malawi, Somalia and many African countries refuse to learn similar lessons. Alternative viewpoints are not tolerated and governments cannot distinguish between *constructive criticism* and *subversion*. Any critic of a government policy is "an enemy" to be "liquidated." Mysterious disappearances and detention have silenced many, producing "a culture of silence" in much of Africa. Consider for example:

Ghana:

> There are said to be up to 500 political prisoners in Ghana, most of them held under the Preventive Custody Law of 1982, which empowers the government to hold, indefinitely, anyone suspected of threatening state security. In recent months, suspected political opponents have "disappeared," and mutilated bodies have washed up on the beaches of Accra (*The Independent*, U.K., August 13, 1990).

Zaire:

> A report released by the Lawyers Committee for Human Rights asserts that the Government of Zaire has engaged in a "systematic pattern of abuses" that includes arbitrary arrests and beatings, banishment of political opponents and severe restrictions on *freedoms of speech and the press*.

> The report, "Zaire: Repression as Policy," comes at a time when when President Mobutu Sese Seko has stated his intention to liberalize his country's political system and move toward free elections.

> In April Mr. Mobutu announced an end to his one-party state and the sanctioning of three opposition parties. But the report asserts that only a month later Zairean security forces attacked students at

the University of Lubumbashi, killing at least 12 students, in response to a series of protests. . .

The Lawyers Committee for Human Rights, based in New York, is an independent watchdog group that reports on human rights conditions around the world. Its chairman is Marvin E. Frankel, a former United States Federal judge (*New York Times*, August 28, 1990; p.A7).

African writers are irate. This uncivilized detention and murder of people the government does not agree with were *never* part of indigenous African culture. Recall that one of the fundamental rights of the African people was "The right to criticise and condemn any acts by the authorities or proposed new laws" (Williams, 1987; p.174).

African governments need to be reminded that Article 9 of the Organization of African Unity (OAU) Charter of Peoples' and Human Rights, which many of them have signed, guarantees freedom of expression. For example, Cameroon signed it in 1987, Malawi in 1988 and Ghana in 1989. Furthermore, Article 19 of the 1948 Universal Declaration of Human Rights by the United Nations, of which *all* African nations are members, emphatically stated:

Freedom of expression is not the product of any political system or ideology. It is a universal human right, defined and guaranteed in international law. . .Everyone has the right to freedom of opinion and expression; this right includes freedom to hold opinions without interference and to seek, receive and impart information and ideas through any media regardless of boundaries.

African nations which do not respect their citizens' right to freedom of opinion and expression ought to be expelled from this world body. *Every* African intellectual, regardless of ideological predilections, must vigorously defend the right of other Africans to express their views freely without fear even if he/she disagrees with those viewpoints just as the Ga and the Igbo fiercely defend each tribesman's right to free expression. If this freedom of expression did not exist in indigenous Africa, there hardly would have been any cultural, artistic and political diversity. Western governments and aid donors persuading African governments to sell off inefficient state enterprises must insist that the media, a state-owned enterprise in Africa, be the first to be placed on the auction block before any loans can be made.

Political Development

Having restored *freedom of expression* and of the press, the next issue to tackle is what type of government would be best suitable for a present day African nation? Should an African country today be considered as one huge tribe or an empire composed of several tribes under one rule?

At one level, an African country may be considered as an amalgram of diverse lineages, as in a typical village. If the chiefs were able to keep the different lineages together in a village, then obviously an "educated" African head of state ought to be able to keep his country together. The chiefs succeeded by instituting a type of government that permitted a high degree of autonomy and independence. Council meetings over which the chiefs presided were open and free. Any adult could participate in the decision-making process. For this reason, the people were not alienated from the village government. They felt they were part of it.

At the other level of generality, Africa may be considered as an "empire," comprising several different tribes under one rule. At the empire level, we saw that almost everywhere in indigenous Africa, there were *state councils*. Councils, councils, and councils were there at the village, provincial and the national levels. Council positions were *hereditary*, meaning that the ruler could not appoint and remove the councillors. Thus, they were an *independent* body which served as an important check against despotism. We may not like accession to political positions based upon inheritance. But as we argued in Chapter 6, abolishing "hereditary positions" only serves to pave the way to autocracy.

If an African country is considered as "an empire," several vistas can be gained by drawing upon Africa's own indigenous history. The empires that lasted in Africa were the Islamic ones. The Ghana empire lasted the longest, 800 years, from A.D. 300 to 1276. Next were the Mali and Songhai empires: from 1238 to 1488 and 1488 to 1591 respectively (de Graft-Johnson, 1986; p.109). The strictly indigenous Lunda empire that lasted three centuries and enjoyed considerable expansion may also be mentioned.

Two factors explain why these various empires lasted for so long. One was religion and the other was confederation or "indirect rule." At the local level, kinship ties and genealogical links with ancestry were sufficient to provide a cohesive force and serve as the basis for government. But more was needed to build an empire composed of several different tribes and with different ancestral allegiances. For the Islamic empires, religion supplied this unifying force. The Lunda accomplished this by investing the office, rather than the individual, with the privileges of kinship.

The second reason for the durability of the Islamic and Lunda empires was the adoption of a confederacy-type (indirect rule type) of government. Under this type of government, the constituent tribes enjoyed a considerable degree of autonomy. For example, seven dynasties of the Kingdom of Cayor, a province in the Ghana Empire, never accepted Islam. Yet, they were tolerated and allowed to remain in the empire until it was sacked by the Almarovids in the 13th century. These dynasties included the Akans of modern-day Ghana (the Asante, the Akim, the Akwapim and the Fanti). The Wolof, the Tulucor and the Serer of Senegal also refused to embrace Islam in the beginning but still remained part of the Ghana Empire.

The high degree of tolerance of non-Muslims was demonstrated by the fact that, in the Ghana empire, imperial succession was matrilineal - an old African tradition. That is, in the event of the death of the emperor, only his sister's son would succeed him. It may be noted that matrilineage was the custom of the Akans, but a practice which was diametrically opposed to the Islamic code under which women play little role.

Furthermore, Islam was not forcibly imposed on the subjects. Conversion was gradual and generally peaceful. Diop (1987) emphasized:

> While the Arabs did conquer North Africa by force of arms, they quite peacefully entered Black Africa: the desert always served as a protective shield. From the time of the initial Umayyad setbacks in the eighth century, no Arab army ever crossed the Sahara in an attempt to conquer Africa, except for the Moroccan War of the 16th century. From the third to the seventeenth centuries, not one conquest was ever launched by way of the Nile: that of Sudan, accomplished with the help of England, came only in the nineteenth century. Nor was there ever any Arab conquest of Mozambique or any other East African territory. The Arabs in these areas, who became great religious leaders, arrived as everywhere else individually and settled in peacefully; they owe their influence and later acceptance to spiritual and religious virtues (p.102).

Attempts by a few Islamic rulers to impose their religion by force merely accelerated the destruction of their empires; for example the Oyo and Bornu empires in the nineteenth century.[4]

In sharp contrast to Islam, military force proved to be an ineffective welding tool. The Asante kept their empire glued together by military force. The empire would have lasted much less than a century were it not for the limited autonomy granted the vassal states. In the Zulu empire, however, the centralization of power and militarization of the society under Shaka proved unworkable. Several vassal tribes broke away from Zulu domination and Shaka's reign lasted only ten years.

Above all, the basic lesson from African empire-building is that tolerance, accommodation, peaceful coexistence and autonomy work best with a collection of different ethnic societies. Davidson (1970) observed tersely:

> If Anglo-Saxon England accepted conquest by 400 Norman

---

[4] The current events in Sudan where Islam is being forced on all, including the Christian South, are uncomfortably portentous.

knights, it was less for their military strength than for their careful accommodation with the Anglo-Saxon socio-moral order. African conquerors behaved no differently in the kingdoms they took or founded. . .What they actually imposed was not *their* rule, but a rule modified by accommodation with the customs of the peoples among whom they settled. . .Superior military power at a crucial point had always to be reinforced by ritual acts of compromise. Out of these accommodations came systems differing from the Luba kingdom as much as Plantagenet England differed from France of the House of Valois; but the differences, in Africa, as in Europe, remained of form, not of content (p.194).

When the Europeans employed this "accommodative" approach, they enjoyed fruitful relationship with Africans for over 400 years (1456 - 1880). But when they carved up Africa into pieces at the infamous Berlin Conference and imposed their rule on Africa, they were expelled in less than a century (1880 - 1960).

How A Modern African Nation Should Be Governed

If an African nation today is considered as a conglomeration of diverse tribes, what type of government would be most suitable for such a nation? A black African drew up a constitution for such a system:

There should be elected a king-president, two ministers - viz., one superintends internal and external affairs, and the other industry and education - and a chief justice. For the purpose of deliberating on the mutual affairs of the Confederate states, a Confederate Diet should be established at Mankessim, having two divisions - the Royal, in which all the kings, with the principal chiefs or grandees, should have seats; the other, the Representative Assembly, to which each province should send a certain number of representatives (one chief and one educated person), obtained by the votes of all citizens. The fundamental law of the country should guarantee to every citizen equal rights and protection, and direct and indirect participation in the Government. The King-President is to be elected from the body of kings. He should be made an ex officio member of the Legislative Council, where his presence should be only required when subjects affecting or relating to the interests of the Confederation are about to be discussed; and should hold that appointment as a Government nominee.

That was written back in 1868 by Dr. James Africanus Horton, in his book, *West African Countries and People,* (London: W.J. Johnson, 1868). That book was a plan for self-government for West Africa which included the Fanti Confederation, part of whose constitution is reprinted above, and a Republic for Accra - both in Ghana. Notice that, after decades of independence and vast sums of money spent on "education," very, very few African leaders and elites could boast of having drawn up a constitution which even approaches the well-defined democracy drawn up in 1868.

At the very least, a modern-day government structured along Africa's own indigenous political tradition should have the following:

1. A head of state,

2. A Cabinet chosen by the head of state,

3. A Council, where positions are *'hereditary'*.

"Hereditary" here means that the councillors *cannot* be removed by the head of state. It does not necessarily mean "father-to-son" principle of succession. How the councillors are chosen is for the African people to decide. Furthermore, how the council is called — *ndaba, mbuza* or National Assembly — is immaterial. But council there should be; not a military junta or a politburo. We now know that the indigenous system of government was one of participatory democracy under chieftaincy based on *consensus*.

Council members should be representatives of every *identifiable* group in the society — farmers, fishermen, soldiers, students, teachers, lawyers, etc. Indigenous African political systems did not lock anyone out of the decision-making process. Recall that in 19th century Sengalese society, slaves, *djam*, sent their representative to the king's court. Even European merchants also sent their representative to King Alfonso's court in Angola. In this scheme, political parties may be considered as "groups" of individuals sharing common ideological beliefs and they too should send their representatives to the council. The emphasis on multi-partyism in the manner of Western systems excludes non-political groups, which is *un-African*.

There is no reason why the head of state should necessarily be the head of a political party. In the indigenous system, even a slave could be king (Jaja of Bonny of the Niger Delta in the 19th century). The head of state should be elected from the councillors or the representatives. In this way, the leader of *any* group, even the army, can become president. There are other important advantages as well.

First, it is far easier to count and recount the votes of the councillors than those of the electorate at large. This scheme eradicates election rigging. Second, it would save a tremendous amount of resources that could be better spent elsewhere. The fact that the United States elects its president in a national election at considerable expense does not mean African countries must do exactly the same for their political systems to be called "democratic." It is the use of the imagination and intelligence which is important, not the ability to copy. And if elections are abhorred, the presidency may be *rotated* among the leaders of the various groups. Recall the rotational system among the Gikuyu and the Yoruba.

This is a rather rough sketch of a political system for a modern African country. The details need not detain us here. Of couse, better systems can be devised by the experts. But then again, freedom of expression is needed to air them, as Africans are dissatisfied with their current regimes.

Growing Demands For Democratic Pluralism

In the latter part of the 1980s, there were demands for greater democracy and political pluralism. But these demands were met with stiff resistance (Sierra Leone, Tanzania, Uganda, Zimbabwe); curfews, arrests and detentions (Cameroon, Central African Republic, Congo, Gabon, Ghana); truncheons, tear gas, stun grenades (Ivory Coast, Senegal); and bullets (Benin, Ethiopia, Guinea, Kenya, Liberia, Niger, Somalia, Zaire). The following is a sample of reasons offered by African dictators for their resistance:

President Obiang Mbasogo (Equatorial Guinea):

"Political pluralism would send convulsions through the population" (*West Africa*, July 24-30, 1989; p.1230).

President Mobutu Sese Seko (Zaire):

"Zaire has no need for *perestroika*. Its one party-state system is the most elaborate form of democracy" (*South*, Feb. 1990).

Blaise Compaore, Head of State of Burkina Faso:

In my opinion, multi-partyism is not the ultimate solution for resolving Africa's problems. Creating a multi-party system in Africa will only encourage those on the outside to descend upon those who serve their interests. Political freedom must be developed, but not at the expense of the sovereignty which protects a country against capitalist exploitation (*West Africa*, March 26 - April 1, 1990; p.481).

President Momoh of Sierra Leone:

> As your President, I have to say it loud and clear — multi-partyism at this point of our social and economic development will only spell doom for us and take us right back to those old dangerous days of divisiveness, conflict, victimisation and vindictiveness that we have happily left behind for well over a decade. . .The principle and practice of the system of popular participation under the one-party democracy over the years has proved to be very useful." (*West Africa*, July 9-15, 1990; p.2078).

President Robert Mugabe of Zimbabwe:

> "A one-pary state system that includes people of different shades of opinion is far superior to anything in the West" (*Insight*, Nov. 5, 1990; p.31).

In Cameroon, President Paul Biya reacted strongly to demands for multi-partyism calling them "maneuvers for diversion, intoxication and destabilization." Commenting on events in Eastern Europe, Rawlings of Ghana said he hoped "reforms in the East will be reciprocated by similar changes in the West." What about Ghana? "NO!" said the state-owned *Ghanaian Times*. In a two-part editorial, it condemned the change in Romania and elsewhere as the "work of imperialism." Meanwhile in Kenya, President Daniel arap Moi was furiously dismissing a multi-party system as "garbage" and to those preaching it, he vowed to "hunt them down like rats." In Zambian president Kenneth Kaunda's estimation, "reintroduction would be a national disaster" (*The Economist*, June 2, 1990; p.48). Earlier in March 1990, when delegates called for a multi-party democracy, Zambia's socialist Education Minister, Mr. Eli Mwanang'onze, called the Zambian people, "a bunch of illiterates (who) were not mature and educated enough to be pushed into a multi-party system" (*The African Letter*, April 16-30, 1990; p.9).

Kenya's Vice-President Professor George Saitoti insisted that the one-party systems in Africa were derived from African traditions. Recall that this was the same Kenya Government which asserted in a Sessional Paper (No.10 of 1963/65), that:

> In African society a person was born politically free and equal and his voice and counsel were heard and respected regardless of the economic wealth he possessed. Even where traditional leaders appeared to have greater wealth and hold disproportionate political influence over their tribal or clan community, there were traditional checks and balances including sanctions against any possible abuse

of power. In fact, traditional leaders were regarded as trustees whose influence was circumscribed both in customary law and religion. In the traditional African society, an individual needed only to be a mature member of it to participate fully and equally in political affairs (paragraph 9).

As S.B. Tejan-Sie, a Sierra Leonian lawyer, put it: "If anything, a system which confines political power to only one political group is alien to our culture and traditions and has failed politically and economically for over a decade and half" (*West Africa*, April 23-29, 1990; p.663). Here is the view of another African, B. Honu:

> The self-righteous claims which continue to be made by some African leaders and their advisers that democracy is foreign to the continent and that unfavorable international economic order is the source of Africa's current problems are unconvincing.

> To claim that democracy is un-African is nonsense. Before the white man came to Africa, each tribe or kingdom was practising a unique (participatory) form of democracy. Traces of this can still be seen in Ghana and many other places on the continent (*New African*, Jan. 1991; p.42).

Other angry Africans spoke out. Fed up with all the nonsensical arguments by African leaders for a one-party state, Ghanaian Professor A.B. Assensoh wrote:

> Frankly, if there were no *insane* and *illiterate* dictators, no crippling nepotism or tribalism in political, diplomatic and even civil service appointments, and no transparent economic-cum-political backwardness among many of Africa's political leaders, then a one-party state could mean much in the governance of African countries (*West Africa*, March 12-18, 1990; p.424).

Under pressure from their people, aid donors and international agencies, African leaders attempted some grudging "democratic reform." But the actual "democratic steps" taken were rousing performances of the "Bongo boogie," the "Babangida twist," the "Moi massamba," and the "Rawlings shuffle" — a little to the left, a little to the right, one step forward, two steps back, a sidekick and a flip to land at the same place. Much ado about voodoo democracy.

In 1988, Kenya's only legal party, the Kenya African National Union (KANU) suddenly adopted a peculiar system of voting by which voters queued behind the portraits of their chosen candidates. For their "votes" to be valid, they had to stay in line from 12.00 noon till 6.00 p.m. when the polls closed. Professionals and businesspersons were effectively disenfranchised.

In Nigeria, preparations feverishly began in 1987 to return the country to civilian rule in 1992. A constitution was drafted under the watchful eyes of omniscient soldiers and by a 1989 military decree only two parties -the Social Democratic Party (SDP) and the National Republican Convention (NRC) - would be allowed to exist. To give more substance to this form of democracy by fiat, the military government went further and drew up the constitutions and manifestoes of the two parties it had created. The government claimed politics in the past had been divisive in Nigeria (pitching the Muslim north against the Christian south). It was this friction that contributed to the onset of the Biafran War (1967-70) in which over one milion lives were lost.

The military government imposed two political parties on Nigeria, apparently in an effort to avert political and religious partition or divisiveness. But Nigerians were not impressed. They called the SDP the *Southern* Democratic Party and the NRC the *Northern* Republican Convention.[5]

In addition, much effort and emphasis were placed on "educating" civilians on how to rule themselves. A Centre for Democratic Studies (CDS) was established for this purpose and its director, Professor Omo Omoruyi, disclosed that aspiring politicians will have to pass two examinations for certificates leading to "competence in the Nigerian Constitution" before they can hold public offices. "They must be a way of ascertaining whether they know how Nigeria is governed," he explained. Naturally, there was to be no such certificates for aspiring military heads of state, despite the fact that the military has held power for 20 out of 30 years of Nigerian independence. (In Benin, Congo, Ghana, Somalia, Togo, Uganda and Zaire, the military has also ruled for much longer than civilians).

One would think that black African leaders who pontificated to the world about "freedom for blacks," "majority rule," and "one man, one vote" themselves understood these concepts. If a Kenyan or Nigerian had challenged these puerile "democratic" exercises, he would have been rewarded with a jail term or death. But had Pretoria declared South Africa a one-party state and insisted that blacks vote by queueing behind portraits of candidates; or had decreed that only two black political parties, of its own choice and manufacture, would be allowed to exist in the post-apartheid era;

---

[5] A better way of achieving the same objective was to stipulate that *any* group could form a political party if they wanted to but they can win an office *if and only if* they manage to poll *at least* 5 percent or 10 percent of their votes in *all* regions of the country (north, south, east and west). This way, a party that wins 98 percent of its votes in one region is "tribally-based" and therefore unqualified to hold office. This is better than forcing everybody into two political parties.

or that blacks must be "educated" and must pass two examinations to ascertain whether they know how South Africa is governed before holding public offices, the governments of Ghana, Kenya, Nigeria and Zambia would have denounced these vehemently as racist arrogance and a palpable effontery to black people.

Ghana's District Assemblies: A Closer Look

Quite often African governments make phonetic sounds ("returning to our roots") and draw up lofty ideas and then turn them into a farce. Ghana's district assembly concept was one typical example and it is necessary to discuss this in some detail.

In 1988, the military government of Ghana decided, commendably it should be noted, to implement its much-vaunted "participatory democracy" model. The government-controlled press was full of praises for this concept, dubbing it "Returning to Our Past." Finally, there was a credible attempt to build upon Africa's own indigenous tradition of *participatory democracy*. The country was demarcated into 110 districts and district elections were held from October 1988 to February 1989. But the whole exercise itself, quite apart from the fact that it never utilized the existing indigenous system, was severely flawed.

First, the military government employed the services of a Bulgarian expert (note: of the pre-1989 revolutionay stripe), and spent 8 billion *cedis* (or $32 million) for this exercise. The implication was that a Bulgarian knew more about indigenous African political institutions than Ghanaians.

Second, this "grass-roots" democratic model made no provisions for national, or even regional, elections. Nor were such issues publicly entertained. Ghanaians, by implication, were not yet ready to choose their heads of state in national elections. Third, over 2 million Ghanaians living outside the country were disqualified from voting. It defeated the very purpose of "participatory democracy" to lock out Ghanaian expatriates from the process. Fourth, the Ghana Government reserved for itself the right to nominate a full third of the representatives of the district assemblies. If modern equivalents of true collaborators of military regimes were needed, they were none other than those district appointees.

Soon after the district elections, the government profusely congratulated itself and patted itself on the back over the immense success of the program. "Justice D. F. Annan, PNDC member, said the government is satisfied with the outcome of its political and economic programmes and is particularly pleased with the turn-out for the district level elections" (*West Africa*, March 27 - April 2, 1989; p.496). The turn-out was a deplorable 60 percent, far lower than anticipated. Nonetheless, when the District Assemblies (DAs) got down to work, it soon became apparent that the planners had done little homework.

Conflicts of authority, power struggles between nominated, presiding and elected members, abuse of power, corruption and indiscipline emerged which drew a condemnation from the same government that created them:

> Mr. Kwamena Ahwoi, Secretary for Local Government, has expressed anger at the activities of some Assembly members who, he said, were using their offices to intimidate public officers and to claim undeserved favors.

> He said some had claimed the power to destool chiefs, and others had actually gone ahead to do this. Mr. Ahwoi cited the case of an Assemblyman who purchased his own gong-gong to rival that of a chief, while another member had employed a bodyguard.

> Mr. Ahwoi denounced these "negative attitudes," but said they should be seen as teething problems (*West Africa*, May 1-7, 1989; p.704).

Unfortunately, the "teething problems" did not go away. They multiplied when even government agencies refused to pay property rates to the DAs. The government itself reneged on its promises of partial payment of the salaries of DA employees. These problems necessitated a review of PNDC Law 207, under which the DAs operated. The Secretary admitted the problems were serious enough to require urgent solutions. These problems were:

> How to share assets and liabilities between old and new districts; transfer of assembly members; refusal of parastatals and state agencies to pay property rates to district councils; the non-payment of 50 percent of the salaries of employees of district councils; and confusion over the roles of district secretaries and assembly members.

> Mr. Ahwoi said one of the disturbing features of the new local government is the gradual transformation of electoral areas into development units, splitting hitherto cohesive societies because some Assembly members made promises to the electorate which they want to fulfil to ensure re-election (*West Africa*, Oct. 2-8, 1989; p.1664).

Still, the problems festered. Some DAs became overzealous in the imposition of levies and taxes. This again prompted another outburst from the government:

Mr. Ahwoi, Secretary for Local Government, has urged the DAs to effectively manage the revenue they collect instead of devising unauthorised ways of generating more revenue. . .He said audit reports on District administration were not encouraging in spite of the checks put in place. . .

Speaking to the Abura-Asebu-Kwamankese DA, Mr. Ahwoi said that under a 1987 law, the Assemblies are prohibited from levying general or specific rates on agricultural produce. . .Some levies and tolls are clearly illegal and citing as an example the decision of the Hohoe DA to impose bridge tolls at Kame" (*West Africa*, Oct. 23-29, 1989; p.1780).

But all these fell on deaf ears. Arbitrariness, corruption, indiscipline and lapses continued:

The Sekyere East DA has banned under 18s from attending concerts, dances, film and video shows. Defaulters will receive between 6-12 lashes of the cane and their parents reprimanded or fined C500. Organizers of shows attended by such youth face fines of C1,000 - 3,000 (*West Africa*, Dec. 18-24, 1989; p.2125).

The Northern Regional Secretary has been directed by the chairman of the PNDC to take administrative responsibility for the East Gonja district following the removal of the district secretary (government appointed), Mr. B.A. Alidu for persistent drunkeness (*West Africa*, Nov. 20-26, 1989; p.1949).

The Upper East Regional Secretary, Mr. L.K. Molbila, has expressed concern over poor attendance at assembly meetings among members of the Bolgatanga DA. . .Seven members of the Ho DA are to forfeit a day's seating allowance for failing to turn up for a meeting. . .According to the district secretary, Mr. Frank Gyamwodie, the 27 meetings of the Assembly last year had an attendance of between 56 and 65 members out of 81. . .The Adansi East DA has ordered the arrest of Dompoasehene, Nana Kwasi Buabeng and Nana Yaw Frimpong, assembly member for the Aboabo electoral area, for obstructing the work of the assembly. Nana Buabeng is alleged to have constantly prevented the assembly's surveyor from surveying and measuring land owned by tenant farmers in the district. Frimpong is said to have flouted the assembly's authority by urging people not to agree to the assembly's decision to register tenant farmers (*West Africa*, April 16-22, 1990; p.643).

The appointments of three dictrict secretaries have been terminated. They are Messrs William A. Adinkra, Amos Yamoah and John Bediako of Techiman, Assin Foso and Berekum dictricts respectively. . .The financial administration of the Techiman district since 1988 is to be investigated.

The government has also announced the setting up of a three member committee under the National Investigation Committee to investigate allegations of maladministration and impropriety against the former Tema District Secretary, Mr. George Yankson. Among others the committee will investigate the award of some construction contracts by the Tema district administration, the allocation of market stalls, the alleged diversion of some District property to the Secretary's home town and possible cover by district officials of the real culprits in a case of embezzlement of money belonging to the Tema Cooperative Bakers Union (*West Africa*, July 9-15, 1990; p.2076).

A year after the implementation of the "participatory democracy" program, the problems had become so serious as to make "most people skeptical about the ability of the DAs to perform their democratic and developmental roles" (*West Africa*, May 7-13, 1990; p.757). Again, this prompted the government to prepare a 5-chapter monograph: *Making the District Assembly Work*. Of particular interest were the last three chapters.

Chapter 3, "Integrity and Knowledge" deals with some ethical concerns which include the declaration of assets by assemblymen and the fact that an assemblyman or woman should act in accordance with public rather than private interest. The fourth chapter proceeds to examine those "Qualities and Values" which an assemblyman or woman should possess, including empathy, maturity, dedication, competence and patriotism.

The final chapter, "The People and the Assembly," is concerned with the role of the people in the working of the DA. The process of recall, which is the termination of an assemblyman's term of office before its natural expiry date, is portrayed by the author as "recognising the existence of the people" (p.43) (*West Africa*, May 7-13, 1990; p.757).

That monograph should have been thrown at the military government itself. Having wasted $32 million, it was exhorting the District Assemblymen to be "competent" and to act "in accordance with public rather than private interest." It directed that the people should have the right to recall an assemblyman when the people did not have the right to recall members of the ruling PNDC. In other words, the military government was preaching *accountability* when it held itself accountable to no one.

Time and time again, one encountered this intellectual astigmatism in post-colonial Africa. African governments never judged themselves by the *same* standards they preached to others. The most grotesque instance of this occurred in June 1990 when five West African nations (Ghana, Guinea, Nigeria, Sierra Leone, and The Gambia) pompously marched off to Liberia under the flag of ECOWAS (Economic Community of West African States) to oust military dictator, the late Samuel Doe, install an interim government and hold "free and fair" elections. Of the five, only The Gambia had what could be considered periodic "free and fair" elections. What about Ghana for example?

At a Sunyani Conference, Ghana's head of state, Flt.Lt. Rawlings, said:

> For Ghanaians democracy cannot simply mean holding elections periodically whilst people continue to suffer poverty, misery, illiteracy, poor health and unemployment. After noting the turn-out in the district assembly elections, he said no objective observer can doubt the PNDC commitment to a free and fair electoral approach (*West Africa*, July 16-22, 1990; p.2124).

Was the District Assembly concept "democratic?" On August 1, 1990, the Movement for Freedom and Justice (MFJ) chaired by Professor Adu Boahen issued this statement:

> We consider the suggestion that the district assemblies be used to constitute structures of government at the national level a fraud and an imposition. For though the principle of local and district level structures of government is laudable, the current district assembly structures are vitiated by a number of undemocratic characteristics they possess. First, the district assemblies were imposed on the people of his country without any real discussion and the consent of the people. Nor can the composition of the assemblies be said to be democratic considering the fact that one-third of their members are appointed by the PNDC. Further, the head of the district executive, the most powerful office in the system, is the District Secretary who is a PNDC appointee. The district assemblies themselves are severely restricted in their deliberations by PNDC Law 207 and have no legally recognized means of contributing to national policy formulation. On the contrary, they simply implement national policies and decrees dictated by the PNDC. For all these reasons, we can safely say the district assemblies are not a true expression of the democratic will of Ghanaians and therefore cannot be used as the

basis for the development of the future national political system of our country.

Economic Development

Economic reform should come *after* intellectual and political reform. Economic development means an improvement in the lot of the people — the peasants, the majority in *every* African nation. The bulk of their activities are in the primary sector (agriculture, fishing, pastoralism, hunting, lumber, etc.).[6] Furthermore, these peasants are imbued with entrepreneurial skills and are willing to take risks. They produce and sell their goods on open, free markets. Common sense suggests that a viable and sustainable development strategy must focus on the primary sector with a special eye on developing markets. The marketplace has always been the nerve center of traditional Africa, as we saw in Chapter 8. The market performed important economic, political, social and religious functions. Perhaps it would be useful to take an African country and show how it should be developed as a test case.

Benin: A Test Case

Benin is a typical West African country, rich in cultural traditions but poor in mineral resources. Fortunately, its indigenous sector still exists:

> Sixty years ago Cotonou was a cluster of villages surrounded by lagoons. Today, it is the economic capital of Benin with a population of 170,000. Its nerve centre is the Dantokpa Market. Animated from early morning to late at night, scores of small retailers line its *voms*, or streets. Mobylette repair shops, dressmakers, millers preparing corn flour and cabinet-makers carving red wood ply their trades next to traditional healers patiently waiting for clients. Vendors of pimento, peppers, spices and vegetables with piquant odors stand behind their stalls, while itinerant peddlers are everywhere selling dried fish, potato-fritters and corn flour.
>
> Near the old port are the stands selling textiles, the domain of the "Mama Benz." These vigorous business women usually ride in shining Mercedes cars, hence their name. Impressive by their girth and the sumptuous cloth they wear, their spectacular success has

---

[6] The secondary sector is industry or manufacturing, while services constitute the tertiary sector.

been built on the sale of colorful textiles, most of which they import
from the Netherlands.

In the port, the fishmongers selling whole fish are doing a brisk
business. . . The fishermen get to the open sea in their dugout
canoes that are decorated with brightly painted or intricately carved
designs (*West Africa*, 3-9 April 1989; p.514).

Real development of Benin should begin with *improvements* to Dantokpa
Market to make it prosper. This is what is meant by "returning to the roots"
(vigorous business women, dressmakers, millers, small retailers, fishermen)
and also "using the *existing* institutions" (indigenous markets and traditional
chiefs) to generate economic prosperity.

An *improvement* to Dantokpa Market would be *any* undertaking that
increases the volume of trade and enhances the *freedom*, convenience as well
as the safety of transacting business at the market. Recall from the previous
chapter the successful agricultural support program provided by South
Africa's Development Bank from 1985. "Provided they have the necessary
support services and infrastructure, black farmers have shown that they can farm
as well as whites," said Johan Kruger, the Bank's general manager (*The
Washington Post*, Dec. 29, 1990; p.A14). The support provided to South
Africa's "subsistence" farmers was a small package of seed, fertilizer, a few
implements and basic advice at a cost of $150.

Applying this lesson to the Dantokpa Market, the neccessary *support
services and infrastructure* would entail providing the following:

1. Roads and transportation networks to facilitate the shipment of goods
    and people to and from the market; improved buildings that provide
    better protection from the weather (rain and sun).
2. Electricity or lighting to enable the Market to extend opening hours;
    places of convenience; and security or secure areas where traders can
    leave their wares.
3. A general atmosphere of peace, security, order and *freedom* for traders
    to conduct their business.

Recall that the period 1880 to 1950 was one of unparalleled peasant
economic prosperity in Africa. The colonialists did not undertake much by
way of development. But at least there was peace and a fair degree of
economic freedom for Africans to produce, sell what they wanted and at what
prices. In addition, the colonialists, in some cases at least in West Africa,
built a few markets for African natives.

After independence, African nationalists and elites could not initiate *real*
development as we saw in the previous chapter. First, they were too obsessed
with "the modern and scientific" and in particular with industry. "Dantokpa" markets and dugout canoes were too "primitive and backward." Second,
most of Africa's intellectuals displayed an ideological hostility to the market

as an economic institution. It was regarded as an instrument of capitalism that was synonymous with colonialism despite the fact that the market had existed in pre-colonial Africa for centuries.

Consequently, an unrelenting assault was launched on African markets in the post-colonial period as we saw in the previous chapter. The economic *freedom* of Africa's traders was snatched from them through various devices as price controls and trade restrictions. Traders who violated them were jailed and threatened with death by firing squad. For example, in much of the 1982-1983 period, the military government of Ghana was actually blowing up and burning down indigenous markets because traders refused to sell their wares at government-dictated prices.

Since independence in the sixties, none of the modern black African governments, with the possible exception of Botswana, has built a market for its peasants or improved upon an *existing* indigenous market. Rather and as was to be expected, they built "modern, air-conditioned supermarkets" whose shelves, more often than not, were bare. Nor did the nationalists and elites establish *peace* for the indigenous markets to prosper. Rather, civil wars, political strife and chaos disrupted the lives of the peasants and produced carnage and an enormous number of refugees across Africa. It never occurred to African elites that Africa's peasants could not produce food or trade when they were fleeing from wars and political strife.

Recall that one of the traditional functions of the African chief was to provide a peaceful atmosphere for his people to engage in trade. These "primitive" African chiefs did not fix prices and blow up markets when traders refused to comply. The African chief may be "backward" but he is Africa's most important human resource. The elites and nationalists never regarded him that way. The African chief, despite all the condemnations and negative imputations, commands far more respect and authority from the people than corrupt and inept government officials seated hundreds of miles away at the capital. He understands the people better and has a far superior understanding of local conditions than central governments. Obviously, the chief ought to be the fulcrum in *every* rural development project. In particular, chiefs should play a pivotal role in agricultural development and rural schemes generally. As American journalist, Neil Henry, noted:

> While the power of Ghana's governing political authorities has proved ephemeral during the nation's first three decades of independence, the popular influence of village chiefs has never waned. They remain virtually indispensable to the fabric of Ghanaian culture and society. . .

> 'The people know their chief better than any government official,' said T.K. Boakene, clerk of the Central House of Chiefs. 'That is why the government cannot do away with the system. The chief is

everything in the community. He is judge, economist, planner; he is the link between the ancestors and the future' (*The Washington Post,* July 27, 1990; p.A34).

The "backward and illiterate" chief can also play an instrumental role even in wildlfe conservation as this story from Zambia indicates:

LESSON UNDER A MANGO TREE

"Mr. Lewis," queried Chief Malama, "when you enter someone's house, do you knock before you enter?"

"Yes," replied Dale Lewis, an advisor on management of wildlife resources in Zambia and now the uncomfortable center of attention at a *village meeting.*

"Then why have you created a national park in my area without asking permission? Why do you need to study elephants on our side (of the river)? What is more important. . . : people or wildlife?" Perhaps, Chief Malama continued, outsiders didn't understand the attitudes toward wildlife held by the local people. Animals had contributed little to the improvement of the area. Only wealthy safari hunters from foreign countries were permitted to shoot, and even as local villagers were deprived of meat, the hunters would hang the carcass of an animal on a tree as bait. "We are honest people," said the Chief. "We do not like poaching, and we have been keeping the animals here for a very long time. If I beg help for building a clinic or grading our road, the government refuses. Yet, this is the area where both government and (foreign) individuals benefit from our wildlife. We are forgotten. . .Teach us how to manage wildlife by ourselves and we will protect and keep the animals here always."

Thus began a village meeting that Lewis describes in *International Wildlife* and that, he says, changed the course of conservation in Zambia. The message was clear: The elephants he was seeking to conserve were animals dependent on the forage found on Chief Malama's terrain, which was outside the game park across the river. Whatever he wished to accomplish had to be done with the cooperation of the chief's people.

"The first step," writes Lewis, "was to host a workshop (to) bring together experts from around the country." After "an incredible amount of work and frenetic planning," more than 40 delegates arrived from Zambia's capital. Chief Malama spoke to them, they listened and a new era began.

Among the many and far-reaching results: The National Parks and Wildlife Service "recruited young men from surrounding villages to serve as village scouts, or law enforcement officers, in the Malama Chiefdom. *In less than three years, poaching of elephants and rhino declined by more than 90 percent.* . .By 1988, thirty-one people were being paid from the sales of hides, meat and teeth from a sustained-yield harvest of hippos, impalas and buffalo. . .Affordable meat was made available to residents and a net profit was banked after each year's harvest *to reinvest in the area's development.* Safari hunting. . .became an important asset to the community. . .Forty percent went to community projects and 60 percent was spent on wildlife management costs. . .(Eighty) percent of the employees on the safari hunting staff had to be local residents."

Writes Lewis: "The flood-plain grasslands on the east bank, which my studies had shown were so crucial to foraging elephants, were kept unburned, and gun-shot disturbances were low since poaching had been all but eliminated." The elephants began to return to the east bank of the Luangwa River, as they had before. The model program has spread to other areas of Zambia and has become part of a national program, replicated in 32 separate game management areas.

"What those years were all about, I've come to see," concludes Lewis, "were *not scientific hypotheses or research papers in the name of science.* And they were not about wildlife management techniques. . .*The lesson under the mango tree is that in Africa conservationists need a different calling, one that is sensitive to the needs of the local people* (*World Development Forum*, Washington, D.C., Vol. 8, No. 15, August 31, 1990; p.1).

Now note the following. First, they *reinvested* the net profit in local banks, *not Swiss banks*, for the area's development. Second, they sat under a *mango* tree with their chief. Where they sat was irrelevant as long as the outcome of the discussion was productive. Similarly, it is immaterial whether native fishermen use dug-out canoes so long as they are able to land more fish. But African leaders and elites were more interested in laser-powered fishing trawlers than dugout canoes.

It was this educated class which failed Africa. It was not the "backward" peasants who were the obstacles to Africa's progress but rather the intellectual backwardness of elite mentality which was the stumbling block. The elites failed to build upon Africa's own indigenous institutions. They humiliated and stripped African chiefs of their traditional authority. More unforgivably, they copied alien systems to impose on Africa. Quite frankly, the African people are fed up being molded in the image of foreigners. Americans have their culture, which we in Africa respect. The Russians and Chinese also have theirs, which we respect. But we also have our own indigenous culture, which we expect African leaders to respect. Most of these leaders were not *true* Africans. Lest we forget, the African chief does not impose himself or foreign ideologies on his people. As one incensed Ethiopian put it:

> We Ethiopians are fed up of Marxism of any kind. We do not want to be a litmus paper for testing all sorts of Marxist denominations. We have gained nothing out of Marxism but famine and poverty. Disregarding the current changes in Eastern Europe now, the Tigrean People's Liberation Front (TPLF) and their allies are advocating for Albanian type of communism. We plead you to stop helping this anti-democracy movement. They are the true enemies of all democratic forces in the world. They use your pounds (sterling) to fight democracy on the pretext of fighting the notorious Mengistu Marxist government. This is the right time to say enough is enough (*Focus on Africa*, BBC magazine, July 1990; p.64).

Enough use of Africa as a laboratory for foreign systems and its people as guinea pigs for foreign experiments. **THE ANCESTORS ARE ANGRY AND AFRICANS ARE ANGRY — AT THEIR LEADERS AND ELITES.** Even the animals are too: "Angry elephants trampled a Namibian to death and buried him in sand, leaving a branch to mark the spot where he died" (*The Washington Times*, Dec. 25, 1990; p.A2). Next time perhaps, the elephants would make a better pick from among Africa's numerous black neo-colonialists.

MAP 1: PRINCIPAL LANGUAGES AND PEOPLES OF AFRICA

1. Anyi
2. Akan
3. Arusha
4. Asante
5. Bambara
6. Bantu
7. Basoga
8. Baule
9. Bulom
10. Bushong
11. Copts
12. Dinka
13. Dogon
14. Dyola
15. Fanti
16. Fon
17. Fulani
18. Ga
19. Gikuyu
20. Hausa
21. Igbo
22. Junkun
23. Kanuri
24. Khosa
25. Kru
26. !Kung
27. Luba
28. Lunda
29. Luvale
30. Mande
31. Mandingo
32. Mende
33. Mossi
34. Mutapa
35. Nuer
36. Nyoro
37. Pakot
38. Rwanda
39. Serer
40. Shona
41. Sidamo
42. Songhai
43. Soninke
44. Susu
45. Swahili
46. Temne
47. Tiv
48. Tonga
49. Tsimiherty
50. Tswana
51. Tukulor
52. Vai
53. Wolof
54. Yoruba
55. Zande
56. Zulu

MAP 2: TRANS-SAHARAN TRADE ROUTES

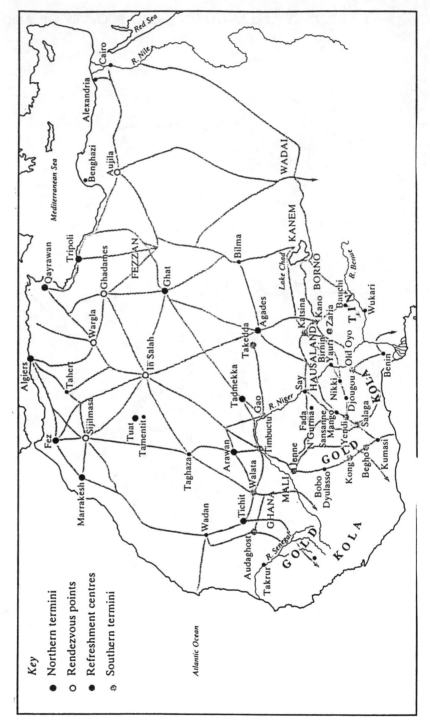

Courtesy: Boahan (1986)

MAP 3: PRE-COLONIAL AFRICAN STATES AND KINGDOMS, 10TH - 16TH CENTURY

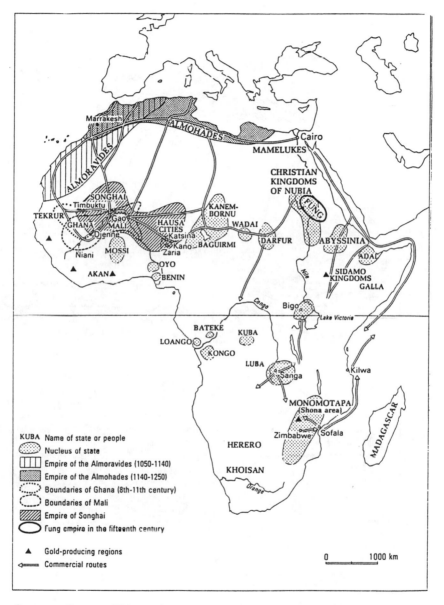

Courtesy: Coquery-Vidrovitch (1985)

MAP 4: PRE-COLONIAL AFRICAN STATES AND KINGDOMS, 18TH - 19TH CENTURY

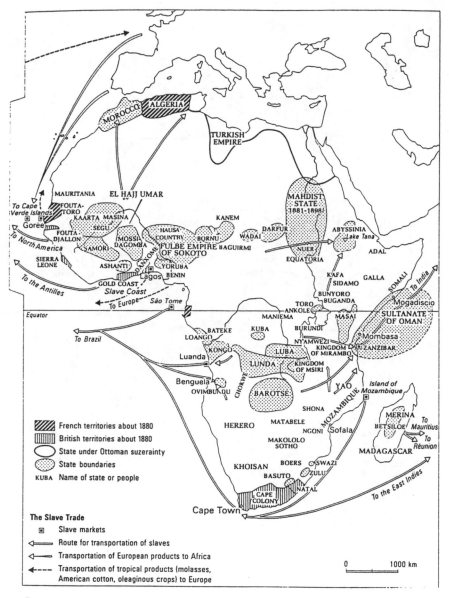

Courtesy: Coquery-Vidrovitch (1985)

MAP 5: COLONIAL AFRICA—1913

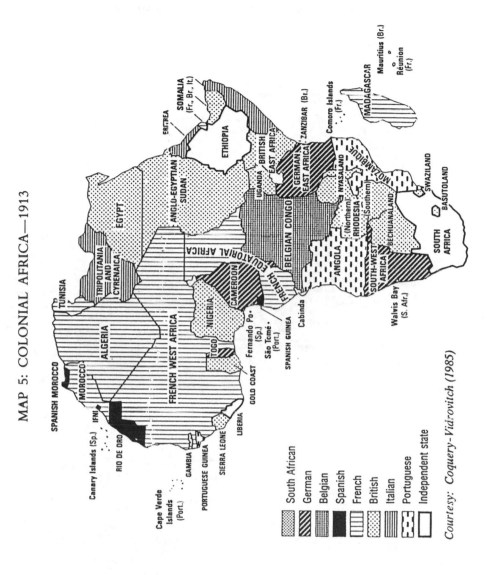

South African

German

Belgian

Spanish

French

British

Italian

Portuguese

Independent state

Courtesy: Coquery-Vidrovitch (1985)

MAP 6: POLITICAL MAP OF AFRICA—1990

* DEMOCRACIES: Algeria, Egypt, Botswana, The Gambia, Mauritius, Senegal

* MONACHIES: Morocco, Swaziland

Courtesy: African-American Institute, Inc.

BIBLIOGRAPHY

Africa Review. Lincolnwood: National Textbook Company, 1988.

Amoah, G.Y. *Groundwork of Government For West Africa.* Illorin (Nigeria): Gbenle Press, Ltd., 1988.

Andreski, Stanislav. *The African Predicament: A Study in the Pathology of Modernization.* New York: Atherton Press, 1969.

Appiah, Peggy. *Tales of An Ashanti Father.* Boston: Beacon Press, 1967.

Apter, David. *The Politics of Modernization.* Chicago University Press, 1967.

_____. *Ghana in Transition.* Princeton University Press, 1972.

Arhin, Kwame. *Traditional Rule in Ghana: Past and Present.* Accra: Sedco Publishing Limited, 1985.

Austen, Ralph. *African Economic History.* Portsmouth: Heinemann, 1987.

Bandow, Doug. "The First World's Misbegotten Economic Legacy to the Third World", *Journal of Economic Growth*, Vol. 1, No. 4: 17, 1986.

Bankole, Timothy. *From Cradle to Grave.* London: Garvin Press, 1981.

Baran, P.A. "The Political Economy of Backwardness." *Manchester School of Economics*, January 1952.

Barker, Jonathan S. "The Paradox of Development: Reflections on a Study of Local-Central Political Relations in Senegal." *In The State of the Nations; Constraints on Development in Independent Africa* edited by M. F. Lofchie, 1971.

Barnes, Leonard. *Africa in Eclipse.* New York: St. Martin's Press, 1971.

Bascom, William. *The Yoruba Of Southwestern Nigeria.* Prospect Heights: Waveland Press, Inc., 1984.

Bates, Robert H. *Markets and States in Tropical Africa.* Berkeley: University of California Press, 1981.

_____. *Essays on the Political Economy of Rural Africa.* Berkeley: University of California Press, 1983.

Bauer, Ludwig. *Leopold the Unloved.* London: European Books, Ltd., 1934.

Beidelman, T.O."Swazi Royal Ritual," *Africa* 36: 373-405, 1966.

Bekker, J.C. *Customary Law in Southern Africa.* Cape Town: Juta & Co. Ltd., 1989.

Bell, Morag. *Contemporary Africa.* New York: John Wiley & Sons, Inc., 1987.

Berglund, Axel-Ivar. *Zulu Thought-Patterns and Symbolism.* Bloomington: Indiana University Press, 1989.

Berman, B. "Structure And Process In The Bureaucratic States Of Colonial Africa," *Development And Change*: Vol. 15; pp.161-202, 1984.

Bing, Geoffrey. *Reap the Whirlwind.* London: MacGibbon and Kee, 1968.

Birmingham, David. *Central African to 1870*. London: Cambridge University Press, 1981.

Boahen, A.A. *Topics in West African History*. New York: Longman, 1986.

Boahen, A.A. and J.B. Webster. *History of West Africa*. New York: Praeger, 1970.

Bohannan, Paul. *Africa and Africans*. New York: The Natural History Press, 1964.

Bohannan, Paul and George Dalton eds. *Markets In Africa*. Evanston: Northwestern University Press, 1962.

Bohannan, Paul and Laura. *Tiv Economy*. London: Longmans, 1968.

Bourdillon, Michael. *The Shona Peoples*. Gwelo (Zimbabwe): Mambo Press, 1976.

Bundy, Colin. *The Rise and Fall of the South African Peasantry*. Cape Town: Lackshaws (Pty) Ltd., 1988.

Busia, Kofi Abrefa. *The Position of The Chief - In the Modern Political System of Ashanti*. London: Oxford University Press, 1951.

——————. *Africa in Search of Democracy*. New York: Praeger, 1967.

Carlston, Kenneth S. *Social Theory and African Tribal Organization*. Urbana: University of Illinois Press, 1968.

Casely Hayford, J.E. *Gold Coast Native Institutions,* 1897. Excerpted in Langley (1979).

Chisiza Dunduzi K. *Africa: What Lies Ahead*. New York: The African-American Institute, 1962.

Christensen, James Boyd. "The Role of Proverbs in Fante Culture." *Africa*, July; Vol. 28, No. 3, pp. 232-43, 1952.

Cohen, Ronald. "The Kingship in Bornu" in Crowder and Ikime, 1970.

Colson, Elizabeth. "Social Control And Vengeance In Plateau Tonga Society," *Africa,* Vol. 23, No.3: 199-211, 1953.

Colson, Elizabeth and M. Gluckman eds. *Seven Tribes of British Central Africa*. London: Oxford University Press. 1951.

Coquery-Vidrovitch, C. "The Political Economy Of The African Peasantry And Modes Of Production," in Gutkind and Wallerstein, 1976.

Crowder, Michael and Ikime Obaro, eds. *West African Chiefs*. New York: Africana, 1970.

Curtin, Philip *et al. African History*. New York: Longman, 1988.

Daaku, Kwame Y. "Trade and Trading Patterns of the Akan in 17th and 18th Centuries," in Meillassoux, 1971.

Davidson, Basil. *African Kingdoms*. Chicago: Time/Life Books, Inc., 1967.

——————. *The African Genius: An Introduction To African Cultural And Social History*. Boston: Atlantic Monthly Press, 1969.

_____. *The Lost Cities of Africa.* Boston: Little, Brown and Company, 1987.

deGraft-Johnson, J.C. *African Glory.* Baltimore: Black Classic Press, 1986.

Dickson, Kwamina B. *A Historical Geography of Ghana.* Cambridge: Cambridge University Press, 1969.

Diop Cheikh Anta. *Pre-colonial Black Africa.* Westport: Lawrence Hill & Company, 1987.

Douglas, Mary. "Lele Economy Compared with the Bushong: A Study in Economic Backwardness," in Bohannan and Dalton, eds., 1962.

Dupire, Marguerite. "Trade and Markets in the Economy of the Nomadic Fulani of Niger (Bororo)," in Bohannan and Dalton, eds., 1962.

Ellis, George W. *Negro Culture in West Africa.* New York: The Neale Publishing Company, 1914.

Evans-Pritchard, E. E. "The Zande State." *The Journal of the Royal Anthropological Institute,* Vol. 93, Part 1, pp.134-54, 1963.

Fallers, L. "Equality, Modernity and Democracy" in *New States: The Quest for Modernity in Asia and Africa.* New York: Free Press of Glencoe, 1963.

_____. *Bantu Bureaucracy: A Century of Political Evolution Among the Basoga of Uganda.* Chicago: Chicago University Press, 1967.

Falola, Toyin. "Nigeria's indigenous economy." in *Nigerian History and Culture.* ed. Olaniyan, 1985.

Feierman, Steven. *The Shaamba Kingdom.* Madison: University of Wisconsin Press, 1974.

Field, M. J. *Social Organization of the Ga People.* Accra: Government of the Gold Coast Printing Press, 1940.

Forde, Daryll and G.I. Jones. *The Igbo and Ibibio-Speaking Peoples of South-Eastern Nigeria.*London: International African Institute, 1950.

Garlick, Peter. *African Traders and Economic Development.* Oxford: Clarendon, 1971.

Gellar, Sheldon. "The Colonial State," in Martin and O'Meara; pp.122-140, 1986.

Gibbs, James L. Jr. ed. *Peoples of Africa.* New York: Holt, Rinehart and Winston, Inc., 1965.

Glazier, Jack. *Land and the Uses of Tradition Among the Mbeere of Kenya.* Lanham: University Press of America, 1985.

Gluckman, Max. *Custom and Conflict in Africa.* Oxford: Basil Blackwell, 1959.

_____. *Politics, Law and Ritual in Tribal Society.* Oxford: Basil Blackwell, 1965.

Gray, Robert F. "Economic Exchange in a Sonjo Village," in Bohannan and Dalton, eds., 1962.

Gulliver, P. H. "The Evolution of Arusha Trade," in Bohannan and Dalton, eds., 1962.

Gutkind, Peter. "Editor's Introduction" in *The Political Economy of Contemporary Africa.* Sage, pp. 7-29, 1976.

Gutkind, Peter and Peter Waterman. *African Social Studies: A Radical Reader.* New York: Monthly Review Press, 1977.

Gutteridge, W. F. *Military Regimes in Africa.* London: Methuen & Co. Ltd., 1975.

Guy, Jeff. *The Destruction of the Zulu Kingdom.* London: Longman Group Limited, 1975.

Hamer, John H. "Sidamo Generational Class Cycles: A Political Gerontocracy." *Africa,* January; Vol. 40, No.1, pp.50-70, 1970.

Harris, Joseph E. *Africans And Their History.* New York: Penguin, 1987.

Herskovits, M.J. and Harwitz, M. eds. *Economic Transition In Africa.* Evanston: Northwestern University Press, 1964.

Hill, Polly. "The Pledging of Cocoa Farms." Unpublished Research Paper, Achimota, Ghana, 1958.

_____. *Rural Capitalism in West Africa.* Cambridge: Cambridge University Press, 1971.

_____. *Development Economics on Trial.* Cambridge: Cambridge University Press, 1987.

Hirshman, Albert O. *The Strategy of Development.* New Haven: Yale University Press, 1958.

Hodder, B. W. "The Yoruba Rural Market," in Bohannan and Dalton, eds., 1962.

Hull, Richard. W. *African Cities and Towns Before The European Conquest.* New York: W.W. Norton & Company, 1976.

Iliffe, John. *The African Poor.* New York: Cambridge University Press, 1987.

Isichei, Elizabeth. *History of West Africa Since 1800.* New York: Africana Publishing Company, 1977.

Jackson, Michael. *Allegories of the Wilderness.* Bloomington: Indiana University Press, 1982. Karp, Ivan. "African Systems of Thought," in Martin and O'Meara, 1986.

Kenyatta, Jomo. *Facing Mount Kenya.* London: Secker and Warburg, 1938.

Kluckhorn, Richard. "The Konso Economy of Southern Ethiopia," in Bohannan and Dalton, eds., 1962.

Kopytoff, Igor, ed. *The African Frontier.* Bloomington: Indiana University Press, 1989.

Kotecha Ken C. with Robert W. Adams. *The Corruption of Power: African Politics.* Washington, D.C.: University Press of America, 1981.

Koyana, Digby Sqhelo. *Customary Law in a Changing Society.* Cape Town: Juta & Co. Ltd., 1980.

Lamb, David. *The Africans.* New York: Vintage Press, 1983.

Lamphear, John. "Aspects of Early African History," in Martin and O'Meara, 1986.

Langley, J. Ayo, ed. *Ideologies of Liberation in Black Africa, 1856-1970.* London: Rex Collins, 1979.

LeVine, R.A. "Wealth and Power in Gusiiland," in Bohannan and Dalton, eds., 1962.

_____. *Dreams and Deeds; Achievement Motivation in Nigeria.* Chicago University Press, 1966.

Lewis, I.M. "Lineage Continuity and Modern Commerce in Northern Somaliland" in Bohannan and Dalton, 1962.

Makec, John Wuol. *The Customary Law of the Dinka People of Sudan.* London: Afroworld Publishing, 1988.

Mandela, Winnie. *Part Of My Soul Went With Him.* New York: W.W. Norton & Company, 1985.

Manning, Patrick. *Francophone Sub-Saharan Africa 1880-1985.* New York: Cambridge University Press, 1988.

Martin, Phyllis M and Partrick O'Meara eds. *Africa.* Bloomington: Indiana University Press, 1986.

Marx, Karl. *Capital: A Critique of Political Economy.* Chicago: Kerr, 1915.

Maylam, Paul. *A History of the African People of South Africa: From the Early Iron Age to the 1970s.* Cape Town: David Philip, 1986.

Mazrui, Ali. *The Africans.* London: BBC Publications, 1986.

Mbiti, John S. *African Religions and Philosophies.* New York: Doubleday & Co., 1970.

McCall, Daniel F. "The Koforidua Market," in Bohannan and Dalton, eds., 1962.

_____ed. *Western African History.* New York: Praeger Publishers, 1969.

Meillassoux, Claude. "Social and Economic Factors Affecting Markets in Guro Land," in Bohannan and Dalton, eds., 1962.

_____ed. *The Development of Indigenous Trade and Markets in West Africa.* Oxford: Oxford University Press, 1971.

Menkiti, Ifeanyi "Person and Community in African Traditional Thought: in Wright, 1984.

Mensah Sarbah, John. *Fanti Customary Laws*, 1897. Excerpted in Langley, 1979.

Merton, R. *Social Theory and Social Structure*. Glencoe, Ill.: Free Press, 1957.

Messing, Simon D. "The Konso Economy of Southern Ethiopia," in Bohannan and Dalton, eds., 1962.

Miracle, Marvin P. "African Markets and Trade in the Copperbelt," in Bohannan and Dalton, eds., 1962.

_____. "Capitalism, Capital Markets, and Competition in West African Trade," in Meillassoux, 1971.

Myburgh, A.C. ed. *Indigenous Criminal Law in Bophuthatswana*. Pretoria: Sigma Press, 1980.

Nicol, Davidson, ed. *Black Nationalism in Africa, 1867*. London: Africana Publishing Corporation, 1969.

Nkrumah, Kwame. *Ghana; An Autobiography*. London: Nelson, 1957.

_____. *A Handbook on Revolutionary Warfare*. London: Panaf Books, 1968.

_____. *Revolutionary Path*. New York: International Publishers, 1973.

Northrup David. *Trade Without Rulers: Pre-Colonial Economic Development in South-Eastern Nigeria*. Oxford: The Clarendon Press, 1978.

Nyerere, Julius K. *Ujaama: The Basis Of African Socialism*. Dar es Salaam: Government Printer, 1962.

Nzongola-Ntalaja, ed. *The Crisis in Zaire: Myths and Realities*. Trenton: Africa World Press, Inc., 1986.

Obichere, Boniface I. "Change and Innovation in the Administration of the Kingdom of Dahomey," *Journal of African Studies*, Vol.1, No.3:325, 1974.

Ogot, B.A. *History of the Southern Luo*. Nairobi: East African Publishing House, 1967.

Oguah, Benjamin Ewuku. "African and Western Philosophy: A Study", in Wright, 1984.

Olaniyan, Richard ed. *Nigerian History and Culture*. London: Longman Group Limited, 1985.

Olivier, N.J.J. "The Governmental Institutions of the Bantu Peoples of Southern Africa", in *Recueils de la Societies Jean Bodin XII*. Bruxelles: Fondation Universitaire de Belgique, 1969.

Onwuanibe, Richard C. "The Human Person and Immortality in Igbo Metaphysics", in Wright, 1984.

Packard, Randall M. *Chiefship and Cosmology*. Bloomington: Indiana University Press, 1981.

Rappaport, Roy A. *Pigs for the Ancestors*. New Haven: Yale University Press, 1969.

Roberts, Brian. *The Zulu Kings*. New York: Charles Scribner & Sons, 1974.

Sertima, Ivan. *They Came Before Columbus: The African Presence in Ancient America*. New York: Random House, 1977.

_____ed. *Blacks In Science: Ancient and Modern*. New Brunswick: Transaction Books. 1987.

Seymour, S.M. *Bantu Law in South Africa*. Cape Town: Juta & Co. Ltd., 1970.

Schapera, I. *The Tswana*. London: International African Institute, 1953.

_____. *A Handbook of Tswana Law and Custom*. London: Oxford University Press, 1955.

_____. "The Sources Of Law In Tswana Tribal Courts: Legislation And Precedent," *Journal of African Law*, Vol.1 No.3:150-162, 1957.

Schneider, Harold K. "Traditional African Economies," in Martin and O'Meara, 1986.

Sithole, Ndabaningi. Extracts from *African Nationalism*, in Langley ed. 1979.

Skinner, Elliott P. "Intergenerational Conflict Among The Mossi: Father And Son," *Journal of Conflict Resolution,* Vol. 5. No.1: 55-60, 1961.

_____. "Trade and Markets among the Mossi People," in Bohannan and Dalton, eds., 1962.

_____. "West African Economic Systems," in Herskovits and Harwitz eds., 1964.

_____. *Peoples And Cultures Of Africa*. New York: Doubleday/ Natural History Press, 1973.

Smith, Michael G. "Exchange and Marketing among the Hausa," in Bohannan and Dalton, eds., 1962.

Smith, Robert S. *Kingdoms of The Yoruba*. London: Methuen & Co. Ltd., 1969.

Stride G.T. and Caroline Ifeka. *Peoples and Empires of West Africa*. Lagos: Thomas Nelson, 1971.

Tardits, Claudine and Claude. "Traditional Market Economy in South Dahomey", in Bohannan and Dalton, 1962.

United Nations. *Human Development*. Report By United Nations Development Program, New York, 1990.

Vansina, Jan. "Trade and Markets Among the Kuba," in Bohannan and Dalton, eds., 1962.

_____. *Kingdoms of the Savannah*. Madison: University of Wisconsin Press, 1975.

_____. *The Children of Woot: A History of the Kuba.* Madison: University of Wisconsin Press, 1978.

Vaughan, James H. "Population and Social Organization," in Martin and O'Meara, 1986.

Whitaker, Jennifer S. *How Can Africa Survive?.* New York: Harper & Row, 1988.

White, C.M.N. "The Role Of Hunting And Fishing In Luvale Society," *African Studies,* Vol. 15 No.2: 75-86, 1956.

White, E. Frances. *Sierra Leone's Settler Women Traders.* Ann Arbor: University of Michigan Press, 1987.

Wickins, Peter. *An Economic History of Africa.* Oxford: Oxford University Press, 1981.

Wilks, Ivor. *Asante in the Nineteenth Century: The Structure and Evolution of a Political Order.* Cambridge: Cambridge University Press, 1975.

Williams, Chancellor. *The Destruction of Black Civilization.* Chicago: Third World Press, 1987.

Wilson, Peter J. "Tsimihety Kinship And Descent," *Africa,* Vol. XXXVII, No.2 pp.133-153, 1967.

World Bank. *Toward Sustained Development in Sub-Saharan Africa.* Washington, D.C., 1984.

_____. *Sub-Saharan Africa: From Crisis to Self-Sustainable Growth.* Washington, D.C., 1989.

_____. *World Development Report.* New York: Oxford University Press, annually.

Wrigley, Christopher. "Speculations On The Economic Prehistory Of Africa," *Journal of African History,* Vol. 1, No.2:189-203, 1960.

Wright, Richard A. ed. *African Philosophy: An Introduction.* Lanham: University Press of America, 1984.

Yelpaala, Kojo. "Circular Arguments and Self-Fulfilling Definitions: 'Statelessness' and the Dagaaba", *History in Africa,* 10:349-385, 1983.

PERIODICALS

Christian Messenger, Presbyterian Church monthly. Private, Accra, Ghana.

Daily Graphic, owned by the Government of Ghana. A daily newspaper, Accra, Ghana.

Daily Sketch, a private daily in Nigeria.

Insight, private monthly magazine published in Washington, D.C.

Ghanaian Times, owned by the Government of Ghana. A daily newspaper, Accra, Ghana.

Index on Censorship, a privately owned monthly published in London and
    dedicated to the defense
of freedom of expression.
National Concord, private daily published in Lagos, Nigeria.
New African, a privately owned monthly published in London.
Newsweek, private American magazine.
Punch, a privately owned weekly, Kumasi, Ghana.
South, a privately published monthly from London.
The African Letter, a private newspaper published by black Africans in
    Toronto, Canada.
The Continent, a private newspaper published by black Africans in Washing-
    ton, D.C.
The New York Times, a private daily published in New York.
The Nigerian Tribune, a private daily published in Lagos.
The Wall Street Journal, private daily published in New York.
The Washington Post, private daily published in Washington, D.C.
The Washington Times, private daily published in Washington, D.C.
Time, private monthly magazine; published in Chicago.
West Africa, a privately owned weekly, London, England.
World Development Forum, news bulletin by Hunger Project, non-profit,
    based in San Fransisco.

APPENDIX A: OTHER PUBLICATIONS BY THE AUTHOR

1990 "African Dictators," *Emerge*, April, 1990:26-32. (Published in New York by African Americans)

b. "Africa Muzzled: The Erosion of Freedom in Africa," *International Health and Development*, Winter:30-31.

c. "Zimbabwe: Another Ghana," *Journal of Defense and Diplomacy*, Jan./Feb. 1990:43-59.

1989 "Human Rights and Economic Development: The Case of Africa." In *Human Rights, Development and Foreign Policy: Canadian Perspectives*. Halifax: Institute for Research on Public Policy.

b. "Africa's Survival." Review of *How Can Africa Survive* by Jennifer Whitaker (New York: Harper & Row, 1988) in *World & I*, January, 1989.

c. "Africa's Culpability," *Journal of Defense and Diplomacy*, May 1989, Vol. 7, No.5: 58-61.

d. "The Political Economy Of Reform In Africa," *Journal of Economic Growth*, Spring 1989, Vol. 3, No.3: 4-17.

e. "Why Can't Africa Feed Itself," *International Health and Development*, Summer: 18-21.

1988 "Restoring Africa's Free Market Tradition," *Backgrounder*, July No. 661 (Heritage Foundation).

b. "Assessing Oliver Tambo." Review of *Oliver Tambo Speaks* (New York: George Braziller, 1988) in *World & I*, August, 1988: p.410.

c. "African Peasants And The Market Economy," *Human Studies Review*, Vol. 5, No.3, Spring 1988.

1987 "African Freedom of Speech," *Index of Censorship*, Vol. 16, No. 1, Jan.

b. "Africa's Economic Disaster: Some Unorthodox Solutions," Paper presented at the invitation of the U.S. State Department (Feb. 17) and published in *Open Forum Quarterly*.

c. "Economic Solutions For Africa." A Review of *The Africans* by Ali Mazrui for *The World & I*, March, 1987.

d. "Africa. Myths and Realities," *Salisbury Review*, Vol. 6, No.2, Dec.

e. "Crocodile Tears." Review of *Tears Of The White Man* by Pascal Bruckner (New York: Free Press, 1986) in *Policy Review*, Winter, 1987.

f. A Review of *Development Economics On Trial*, by Polly Hill (New York: Cambridge University Press, 1986) in *Journal of Economic Growth*, Vol. 2, No. 2, Second Quarter.

g. "South Africa: The Ultimate Solution." Review of *After Apartheid: The Solution*, by F. Kendall and L. Louw (San Francisco: Institute of Contemporary Studies, 1986) in *World & I*, Vol. 2, November.

h."African Intellectuals and the Neglect of Economic Reality." Review of *The Africans,* by Ali Mazrui (London: BBC Publications, 1986) in *Journal of Economic Affairs,* April/May.

i."A Blueprint For Africa's Economic Reform," *Journal of Economic Growth,* Vol. 2, No.3, Fourth Quarter: p.3.

j."Indigenism: An Alternative Approach To Development," in *Proceedings: Pennsylvania Conference of Economists, May.*

k."Economic Atrophy In Black Africa," *The Cato Journal,* Vol. 7, No.1, Spring/Summer, 1987: pp. 195-222.

1986"Lessons of African Market Tradition," *Journal of Economic Affairs,* Vol. 7, No.1, Oct/Nov: p.33.

b."Zaire: The Epitome of an African Kleptocracy," *Journal of Defense and Diplomacy,* Vol. 4, No.10; October.

c."Africa's Agricultural Disaster: Governments Are To Blame," *Journal of Economic Growth,* Vol. 1, No.3; Third Quarter.

d."Capital Flight From The Third World," Testimony before Congressional Sub-Committee on Telecommunications, Consumer Protection, and Finance, in *Congressional Records,* May 8; Serial No. 99-125.

e."The Real Foreign Debt Problem," *The Wall Street Journal,* April 6; p.30. Reprinted in two Economics texts: *Economics in America,* and *Macro-Economics,* 1987/88.

f."Famine In Africa: The Real Cause," *Journal of Economic Affairs,* Vol. 6, No. 2; January: p.17.

1985"African Rights," *Policy Review,* No. 35; Winter 1985: p.8.

b."The Laffer Curve: An Alternative Derivation From The Demand Side," *Proceedings of the Pennsylvania Conference of Economists,* May.

c."The Namibian Paradox And US Policy In The Third World," *Carver,* Vol. 3, No.1.

1984"The Foreign Exchange Crisis: Real, Artificial Or Imaginary," *Foreign Trade Review,* Vol. XIX, July.

1974"The Demand For Money In Nigeria," *Economic Bulletin of Ghana,* Vol. 4, No.1.

1973"The Teaching of Economics in Africa," *Economic Bulletin of Ghana,* Vol. 4, No.1.

EDITORIAL PAGE AND OP-ED ARTICLES:

"Not By Aid Alone," *The Washington Post,* April 2, 1990: A11. Reprinted by *International Herald-Tribune* (Paris).

"In Africa, Independence Is Far Cry From Freedom," *The Wall Street Journal.* March 28, 1990. Reprinted by *Jeune Afrique Economie* (Paris).

"Black Tyranny: A Deafening Silence," *The New York Times,* March 28, 1989; page A15. Reprinted by (*Reader's Digest* Canadian Edition in August 1989 and International Edition in April 1990).

"Africa's Injustices Aren't All To The South," *The Christian Science Monitor,* Jan. 26, 1989;p.19.

"Holding Black Africa To Democracy's Account," *The San Francisco Chronicle,* Jan. 18, 1989.

"Blacks Are Really Free In Only 2 African Nations," *The San Francisco Examiner,* Dec. 21, 1988.

"Tyranny Reigns Throughout Africa," *San Jose Mercury News,* Dec. 11, 88.

"Who Ruined Africa? Don't Blame The Colonialists" *The Los Angeles Herald Examiner,* Sept. 23, 1988.

"Africa Doesn't Need More Aid; It Needs Less," *The Hartford Courant,* August 4, 1988; page B12.

"Blame Africa's Own Leaders For 'Black Elephant' Aid," *The Globe & Mail (Canadian),* August 4, 1988; page A7.

"Democracy African Style," *The Globe & Mail,* Oct. 6, 1987; page A7.

"Muzzled Media Is The Norm In Black Africa," *The Globe & Mail,* March 30 1987; A7.

"Truth's Fight For Freedom," *The Times of London,* Jan. 17, 1987: p.20. Reprinted in *The Crusader.*

"Deja Vu In South Africa: Another Rhodesia?" *The Hartford Courant,* December 5, 1986.

"To Help South Africa, Study Rhodesia's Fall," *The Press-Enterprise,* Sept. 26, 1986; p.14.

"In An Economic War, Everybody Is a Loser," *USA TODAY,* Sept. 9, 1986. This article won a Silver Merit of Award Certificate (City News Syndicate, Dickson, Tennessee).

"African Suffering: Elites and Folly Caused the Crisis," *The Globe And Mail,* May 30, 1986; Reprinted by *The Daily Mail* and by the United Nations in *UN EMERGENCY NOTEBOOK ON AFRICA,* 1986.

"To End Hunger, Set The African Peasants Free," *The Times of London,* May 27, 1986. Reprinted by *The Australian.*

"Third World Kleptocrats Play US For A Dummy," *The Press-Enterprise,* March 12, 1986.

"The Other Apartheid Regimes - In Black Africa," *The Reading Eagle,* August 20, 1985.

"By Any Color It Is Tyranny," *USA TODAY,* Aug. 8, 1985.

"Apartheid-Like Systems Exist In Black Africa," *The Atlanta Journal,* July 28, 1985.

"Why Single Out South Africa," *The Times of London,* August 1, 1985.

"A Double Standard In Black And White," *The Wall Street Journal,* July 22, 1985. Reprinted in several newspapers:

- *The Providence Journal* (Rhode Island). *The Royal Gazette* Bermuda).
- Paraphrased in *McClean's,* a Canadian weekly magazine,
- Was the subject of discussion on a PBS TV program, Pittsburgh, April, 1986.

"The Truth In Lending To Third World Governments," *The Wall Street Journal,* Oct. 11, 1984; p.32.

SYNDICATED ARTICLES

"Assessing Africa's Crisis," Syndicated by Heritage Foundation Syndicate Features, August, 1988.

"The Tyranny of Anti-Apartheid Militancy," Syndicated by Heritage Foundation Syndicate Features, Nov. 1987.

"What Next After Sanctions," Syndicated by City News Syndicate, Dickson, Tennessee, Dec. 1986.

"Not Just South Africa But the Whole African Continent," Syndicated for world-wide distribution by Singer Communications, Anaheim, Oct., 1985.

SPANISH

"Africa no necesita mas ayuda," *La Prensa,* Buenos Aires, Argentina, June 26, 1989.

"Quien tiene la culpa de la ruina Africana?," *Catahuya Internacional,* Barcelona, Spain: March 15, 1989; page 76.

"El Reinado de la Opresion en Africa," *Ultimas 10Noticias,* Caracas, Venezuela, March 4, 1989.

INDEX